ROUTLEDGE LIBRARY EDITIONS:
HISTORY OF EDUCATION

ABBOTSHOLME

ABBOTSHOLME

By
CECIL REDDIE

Volume 28

LONDON AND NEW YORK

First published in 1900
This edition first published in 2007 by
Routledge
2 Park Square, Milton Park, Abingdon, Oxfordshire OX14 4RN

Simultaneously published in the USA and Canada
by Routledge
711 Third Avenue, New York, NY 10017
First issued in paperback 2014

Routledge is an imprint of the Taylor & Francis Group, an informa business

Transferred to Digital Printing 2007

© 2007 Routledge

All rights reserved. No part of this book may be reprinted or reproduced or utilised in any form or by any electronic, mechanical, or other means, now known or hereafter invented, including photocopying and recording, or in any information storage or retrieval system, without permission in writing from the publishers.

British Library Cataloguing in Publication Data
A catalogue record for this book is available from the British Library

Library of Congress Cataloging in Publication Data
A catalog record for this book has been requested

ISBN 978-0-415-43274-0 (hbk)
ISBN 978-0-415-76177-2 (pbk)
ISBN 978-0-415-41978-9 (Set)

Publisher's Note
The publisher has gone to great lengths to ensure the quality of this reprint but points out that some imperfections in the original copies may be apparent.

Frontispiece.

Yours sincerely
Cecil Reddie

Copyright.

[CONTRIBUTIONS TOWARDS THE ORGANISATION OF A NORMAL TERTIARY (HIGHER SECONDARY) SCHOOL FOR ENGLISH BOYS OF ELEVEN TO EIGHTEEN BELONGING TO THE DIRECTING CLASSES]

No. 2.

Abbotsholme

BY

CECIL REDDIE

WITH TWO PORTRAITS
AND THIRTY ILLUSTRATIONS

LONDON
GEORGE ALLEN, 156, CHARING CROSS ROAD
1900

[All rights reserved]

Dedication.

IN EVER GRATEFUL RECOGNITION
OF THOSE
TEACHERS
YOUNG AND OLD, HERE AND BEYOND,
WHO TAUGHT ME TO SEE, TO FEEL, TO THINK AND TO ACT;
OF
OUR ABBOTSHOLME PARENTS,
WHOSE FAITH IN OUR WORK, WHILE YET INVISIBLE,
ENABLED US TO ATTEMPT IT;
OF
MY COLLEAGUES, PAST AND PRESENT,
WHOSE LOYALTY TO THEIR CHOSEN LEADER
AND UNSELFISH DEVOTION TO THEIR CHOSEN TASK,
AMID MANY DOUBTS AND DIFFICULTIES,
RENDERED POSSIBLE THE MEASURE OF SUCCESS WE HAVE ACHIEVED;
OF THE MANY
FAITHFUL HELPERS AND GENEROUS FRIENDS,
WHO LIGHTENED OUR LABOURS AND SMOOTHED OUR PATH;
AND OF THE
SONS OF ABBOTSHOLME,
WHOSE NEVER-FAILING SYMPATHY AND AFFECTION
HAS BEEN A FULL RECOMPENCE FOR ALL ANXIETY AND WEARINESS;
AND WHOSE LOYALTY TO THE IDEALS OF THEIR SCHOOL
HAS MADE EVIDENT THE NOBLE POSSIBILITIES OF ENGLISH BOYHOOD,
WHEN FREED FROM DISTORTING SYSTEMS AND
SUFFERED TO GROW NATURALLY AND HARMONIOUSLY.

Preface

IN an age submerged with books, ample apology is due for inflicting on it yet another; the more so when the author (as in the present case) has neither talent, time, nor taste for literary composition; but, on the contrary, feels a growing conviction that words and books, less by quality than quantity, exert an exaggerated influence in our lives, producing new perils to body, mind, and character. Reading means sitting. Reading Words is not seeing Things. And the inordinate flood of printed matter that pours through, or at least over, the average brain, disorganises steady thinking more seriously than even our modern chaotic life.

In the field of Education, moreover, we need not a new Theory or another Book, but an actual Pedagogic Laboratory. More would be learned by living in such a place one day than could be gleaned by perusing a dozen learned works on Pedagogics—if, at least, we had learned to observe Things and Deeds, instead of merely devouring Descriptions of them.

But mankind has so long been fed on an Education

Preface

through words, that men, naturally, reward the Phrase-monger more highly than the Doer.

The present Book has been published for two reasons.

The School with which it deals has, without seeking any such publicity, attracted much attention in many portions of the world. And this has led to such innumerable inquiries, criticisms, and misapprehensions that we have been embarrassed, and our work hindered, if not harmed.

It was impossible to answer all inquirers, to criticise all critics, or to correct all errors. Consequently, inquirers thought us indolent or unwilling, little guessing the strain publicity entails. Critics believed their wildest accounts of us correct, because we made no sign; and their errors have been repeated, and even magnified. Our actual work has been ignored by some, belittled or belauded by others, and carefully estimated by only the few.

We have been constrained, therefore, to steal, from the scant leisure an Educator can possess, a moment here and there, to put together these disjoined fragments, in order, if possible, by one effort now, to answer friends and foes alike in a single little Book.

The book, we hope, will save us from all charge of lack of courtesy, of lack of gratitude and modesty. We believe many will care to know how we launched our tiny Craft, what was our Quest, and how we fared on the Voyage. We trust our friends, who have given us such unstinted sympathy, will under-

Preface

stand our earlier silence was unwilling. We hope our adversaries will admit, that if misguided, we have been honest. We think all will acquit us of imagining that we have spun our schemes clean out of our own head, or fancying that we have deserved all the praise that has been lavished upon us.

We wish our work to be understood and fairly judged: not, however, by suburban drawing-room gossip, but by facts.

That, breaking new ground, we should have been faultless, is to expect too much. That, amid such praise, we should be wholly worthless, is to concede too little. Without wishing to claim too much, we yet do not desire in insincere, mock-modest fashion, to pretend that so much able criticism was lavished merely on a phantom. We have indeed been praised and scolded for many things we never did. We have not been praised nor scolded for many things we have done. We write this book, to save our time, to help on, we hope, our work, and to press upon others the ideals and methods which we have found, from ten years' trial, so good. But we dare assert this: that the best of our work has never been described, nor ever will, we hope. For the really vital elements in education defy description, partly because of their subtlety, and partly because of the natural, and very proper, reticence we ought to maintain in matters so intimate to individuals.

As regards the Plan of the Book. The main part is almost purely History: reprints of articles by

Preface

ourselves or others, or extracts from the public press. Some of these, written in haste, or under difficulties, required some revision; and this, wherever necessary, we have not scrupled to make: but we have, in every case, made the modifications suit the actual facts of the time in question, and have, in no case, essayed to rewrite the paper from our more mature standpoint of to-day. Few were written for the present purpose; but, for this very reason, they will, we think, best reflect the facts.

The other part concerns less this particular School than the general question of our national education. Quotations from the Press are purposely made full; scraps are apt to mislead. We trust the inevitable repetition, inseparable from a work so put together, will be forgiven by our readers. And we hope the English public will not refuse a hearing to the warning of calamities in store, accusing us of want of patriotic spirit. We believe that England has been great and may be great again. But we believe her life is to-day full of the seeds of dissolution, and that self-examination alone will bring that self-knowledge which will lead to repentance and redemption.

To help, in a humble corner, the creation of a nobler Englishman, to organise a nobler English-speaking Empire, to aid the Ascent of Man—this has been our sole aim.

C. R.

ABBOTSHOLME, *December*, 1899.

Table of Contents

CHAP.		PAGE
I.	INTRODUCTION	1
	"A New School." The 1st Foundation, 1889. Press Notices, 1889–1890.	
II.	A PIONEER SCHOOL AT WORK, 1890. Press Notices to the End of 1893.	57
III.	A DUTCH PROFESSOR'S VISIT AND VERDICT, DECEMBER, 1892.	93
IV.	FOUNDING THE "OLD BOYS' CLUB," EASTER, 1893	105
V.	A BRIEF HISTORY OF ABBOTSHOLME DURING 1893–4.	111
	(*a*) First Visit to Jena, April, 1893.	
	(*b*) Reorganisation of the Instruction, May, 1893.	
	(*c*) Purchase and Organisation of the School State (the 2nd Foundation of the School, March, 1894).	

Contents

CHAP.		PAGE
	(*d*) Visit to the Teachers' Congress and Education Exhibition at Stuttgart, June, 1894.	
	(*e*) Visit to Oxford and Edinburgh Summer Meetings, August, 1894.	
VI.	OXFORD AND EDINBURGH CONTRASTED	119
VII.	THE REVISED PROSPECTUS, SEPTEMBER, 1894	131
VIII.	ANSWERS TO THE ROYAL COMMISSION ON "SECONDARY" EDUCATION, OCTOBER, 1894	151
IX.	A FRENCH VERDICT IN "LA SCIENCE SOCIALE," OCTOBER, 1894	193
	Critique on this in *La République Française*, November, 1894.	
X.	A BRIEF HISTORY OF ABBOTSHOLME DURING 1894–5	213
	(*a*) Plans for Rebuilding the School-House.	
	(*b*) Plans for Planting School-Colonies.	
	(*c*) Pestilence at Home and War Abroad.	
	(*d*) The Founding of "The Abbotsholmian."	
	(*e*) The "Old Boys' Gathering," Easter, 1895.	
	(*f*) Inspection of the School by a Veteran Educator, June, 1895.	
	(*g*) The First "Parents' Gathering," July, 1895.	
XI.	ENGLISH VERDICTS, DECEMBER, 1895, TO OCTOBER, 1896	243

Contents

CHAP.		PAGE
XII.	German Verdicts . . .	. 251

    (*a*) Visit of Professor Rein, of Jena, September, 1896.
    (*b*) Arrival of Dr. Lietz, October, 1896.
    (*c*) Emlohstobba.
    Press Notices.

XIII. An English Exposition of the System in Process of Development at Abbotsholme   409
    Press Notices.

XIV. A French Savant's Verdict . . 425
    Press Notices.

XV. Some Weighty Criticisms upon the Three Books 549

XVI. "Educational Ideals and Methods," 1897   575
    "Les Aphorismes d'Abbotsholme" (From *La Suisse Universitaire*).

XVII. Schools and Projected Schools on Abbotsholme Lines . . . 585
    In England, Germany, France, Russia, Switzerland.

XVIII. The New Buildings, 1899 . . 605
    The 3rd Foundation of the School.

Appendices 623

Illustrations

[*We have to express here our deep gratitude to Herr Karl Neumann, one of our colleagues since Spring 1890, for the beautiful collection of nearly 300 photographs illustrating the Place and Life, which he has generously made for the School. Of these we reproduce here 30. The "River Dove" we owe to the kindness of our former colleague Mr. W. Clifford Pilsbury.*]

NO.		TO FACE PAGE
1.	The New School Abbotsholme, as it was in 1889. (Taken Easter, 1894)	2
2.	The Kitchen Garden (Summer, 1890)	20
3.	The Master's Common Room (Summer, 1892)	34
4.	The Old Dining Hall (Summer, 1892)	56
5.	Big School (Summer, 1892)	78
6.	The School Group (Winter Term, 1892)	92
7.	A School Excursion (Summer, 1893)	104
8.	Characters in the Play (Christmas, 1893)	110
9.	Cæsar Gladiators—the Easter Tournament (1893)	118
10.	Bee-farming—Hiving a Swarm (Summer, 1893)	130
11.	Felling Trees: removing the branches (Winter, 1894)	150
12.	The Old Workshop (Summer, 1892)	192
13.	Building a Pigeon House (Winter, 1892)	212
14.	Putting up the Pavilion (Summer, 1892)	242
15.	The Cricket Pavilion Finished (Summer, 1892)	250
16.	The River Dove (Summer, 1892)	268

Illustrations

NO.		TO FACE PAGE
17.	Our Home-made Boats (Summer, 1892)	380
18.	Helping Build the Brick-Dam (Summer, 1894)	396
19.	Potato Harvest (Winter, 1893)	408
20.	In the Hay Field (Summer, 1891)	414
21.	Unloading and Stacking Hay (Summer, 1893)	424
22.	The Last Load (Summer, 1892)	444
23.	View from the Big Chimney, looking North (Summer, 1899)	534
24.	View from Toboggan Hill, looking North-West (Summer, 1893)	538
25.	View from the Big Chimney, looking South (Summer, 1899)	548
26.	Gardening and Geometry (Spring, 1896)	574
27.	The New Buildings, from the North (Winter 1899)	584
28.	The School Buildings, from the South (Winter, 1899)	604
29.	The Abbotsholme School-e-State in 1899	622
30.	Plan of the New Buildings	638

PORTRAITS.

1. Dr. Cecil Reddie, Headmaster of Abbotsholme
   By Midwinter & Co., Clifton, Bristol.   *Frontispiece*
2. Dr. Hermann Lietz, Headmaster of Ilsenburg   To face 259
   By Herr Karl Neumann, Abbotsholme.

1. THE SCHOOL HOUSE. (*Easter, 1894*).

Copyright

CHAPTER I.

Introduction.

CHAPTER I.

INTRODUCTION.

> " Beginnings are alike, it is Ends which differ.
> One drop falls, rests, and dries up, but a drop;
> Another begins a mighty river : so one Thought
> May settle a Life, an Immortality."
> BAILEY: *Festus.*

IN the Preface we have stated the motives which induced us to publish this book.

The Introduction to the Story of Abbotsholme, its Ideals, Foundation, Organisation, and Development ought to be an answer to the question—often addressed to us: "What led you to become an educator, and why did you desire to found a new type of school?"

In order to give a satisfactory answer to this question, careful consideration was necessary; and though at first hesitating to open before the Public that intimate part of one's life which belongs entirely to oneself, yet, at the same time, in appealing to the Public to support an Educational Reform so radical as that we have attempted, we felt that the Public had a claim to know, in some measure, how such an idea germinated in our mind, and through what processes it went before it took the decided form under which we present it.

The saying that the formation of a man depends upon the circumstances amid which he grows up is only true partially.

The same circumstances have different effects upon men of different dispositions.

Every one, who has travelled step by step along the road of his past life, must have observed that his actions in later life frequently find their explanation in elements of character scarcely realised at the time and subsequently completely forgotten. Indeed, of most of our thoughts and actions in our maturity, we should doubtless, if we examined carefully, find the germ present unconsciously in the days of our earliest childhood.

We ourselves could mention many incidents to prove this were it not that they belong rather to the intimacy of a confidential talk between friends than to the open court of publicity.

As we force our memory to look back again upon the youngster who puzzled so often his companions and himself, and who seemed, sometimes, to live a life quite different from theirs, we realise that the boy indeed explains the man.

For us life became early a reality. At the age of eleven the death of both parents had broken up that which nothing can ever fully replace—home and

Introduction

home-ties, which, with soft, silken meshes, cast a web of infinite subtlety around the heart.

We went to school, and found ourselves a stranger amid some two hundred boys. The situation for them was, for the most part, different from what it was for us. They could look on school from the fixed and secure vantage-ground of home : to them school was, at most, a second interest. To us, on the contrary, school was home. Transplanted, in a moment, from the atmosphere of family life, to the more or less rough and selfish atmosphere of school, we were forced to try and find some new object with which to allay the hunger of the heart, increased as it was by a not unnatural idealisation of the scenes and persons which had vanished. We had, indeed, as early as we can recall, a bias towards idealising not only the absent but the present. And amid our new surroundings this tendency grew apace, and unceasingly we kept constructing in our imagination an olympus of heroes, built out of the most perfect types we found around us, as objects of reverence and worship.

Well we remember studying their every action, and drinking in every word they uttered. We arrayed them in all the glory of boyish fancy, and wearied ourselves in trying to discover why each spoke and acted as he did. For, to our inexperience, every act and word expressed a conscious motive, and we blamed our ignorance severely when we failed to divine what the motive was.

Thus we grew up until about our seventeenth year.

We had passed the time, so dear to boys, when the muscles are felt growing and hardening daily. We had come to the time when, after a period of mental stagnation, brain and intellect again become alert. We grew more critical, nor did our heroes escape our scrutiny. Somehow, as, one by one, they had grown older, each had in turn seemed less satisfying. And one by one they had fallen from the pedestals upon which youthful enthusiasm had placed them, leaving, however, undimmed the memory of moments of earlier heart-whole worship, never to be forgotten.

It was a time of heart-sickness, for we had not yet acquired the philosophic mind which perceives that only the Idea is real, the substance merely shadow. We craved for a living God which should be visible, a human being in whom some plenitude of heavenly fire burned. For the Divine Figure placed before us by Religion, amid its remote and foreign surroundings, seemed to have little connection with England in the nineteenth century, or with the life of Boyhood; and the life and doctrines which spoke from the pages of the Gospel, obscured by antique phraseology and oriental hyberbola, seemed little in harmony with the practical ideals which were urged upon us by our teachers, or with the ideals forced upon us by the Greek and Roman classics which formed our chief intellectual food; in fact, our education, instead of leading to unity and harmony, was producing day by day a feeling of hopeless division and discordance. The mass of conflicting principles which kept entering our

Introduction

mind, these we were left to co-ordinate as we might find it possible, and therefrom to construct a rule of conduct suited to our actual life.

It is possible that all are not conscious, even dimly, of such lack of harmony as we describe. But we cannot believe that our experience was exceptional, or that, even where half unconscious, the effect can be otherwise than destructive to the evolution of a harmonious human being.

The result to ourselves was that we kept the Ideal presented by Religion in a kind of secret chamber of the mind, while we selected, as said above, a number of heroes from our surroundings and idealised them to serve as living examples for daily use.

Our hopes with regard to these, which originally had soared too high, now as they and we grew older began to sink too low. And our disenchantment threatened to bring cynicism or indifference.

At this critical moment we chanced to meet a lady-relative, somewhat our senior. She was full of quiet sympathy, and gifted with strong character and quick intelligence. Womanly intuition discerned our case, and womanly tact dispersed the gathering gloom and prevented, what so often happens, the growth of a cold, hard scepticism.

When we returned to school, our elder heroes had left, and the empty temple was ready to receive a new Pantheon.

Thus far the bias of our intellectual tastes had been towards logic and mathematics, relieved by natural science, all, however, sharply separated from our daily life. But from this time forward we discovered an increasing interest in the actual present and in all subjects which touched, however remotely, on human life and character. We found ourselves, we knew not why, reading works on art, philosophy, religion, and history, yet never venturing to talk much about our vague desires and aspirations to companions or teachers. The latter, we thought, would suppose we should rest content with the orthodox program and the official faith.

Having failed to find among elders or equals in age the perfect ideal we sought, yet longing to meet it in corporeal form, after a period of inactivity and indecision, we turned to the younger generation, resolved, if it were possible to find favourable material, to strive and create in more plastic boyhood the ideal we had failed to see incarnate in grown youth.

This led to a careful self-examination. Lack of home and family support had taught us early self-reliance. To lean on Authority had become impossible to us, and we were amazed that our teachers so often quoted, with such devotion, Greek and Roman oracles, as if their voices were final. We wanted, not statements, but reasons; and if reasons were not forthcoming, we preferred to rest in honest doubt until we could discover reasons for ourselves.

In class, while others attended more or less to the work in hand, we watched the living Play and Picture before our eyes, striving to divine the motives which moved the actors in the Drama.

At dinner, while the boy in front of us ate, we speculated on his character. The daily conversation was to us mainly tedious as regards the subject-matter, and what we wished to discuss ourselves was as tedious, no doubt, to our companions. They and we inhabited different worlds, though in the same room.

Our own problems were of this kind : What *is* this world ? What is our real duty ? Why do we learn this, and not that ? And we wondered that neither boys nor masters seemed interested in such problems.

In every normal human being there are two elements —the mental and the emotional—and nearly always one or other is dominant, even when both are firmly joined together. In our own case, at this time, these two elements were of perhaps nearly equal force, but absolutely separate. To ourselves we appeared to live in two distinct compartments, and of this we had become more and more conscious. By degrees we had found natural science, though interesting, too purely intellectual and cold. On the other hand, while we cherished the beautiful stories of Roman and Hellenic heroes, which we had read in English years before, we did not find our blood stirred by the stammered reading and semi-English translation of Greek and Latin literature in class ; and the mind was wearied by the attempt to realise the meaning of the subject-matter and distracted by the unending excursions after dull grammatical rules. The atmosphere of such work was so unnatural and conventional that one was glad to look out of the window and see the real trees and hills still there.

The solution of our difficulties came suddenly and unexpectedly. A friendship with a youngster supplied the needed link. Our wish to educate him produced in us a passion for knowledge unfelt before, that we might have the pleasure of imparting it. And this incident really decided the future, although for many years we were not wholly conscious of it. For it was this youngster who, years after, persuaded us to attempt to be an educator.

Our school days ended, and we entered the University. We had chosen Medicine, for we hoped it would connect science and human life. But we were disappointed when we found its aim less to keep people healthy than to cure them when they were ill. And after our first medical examination was passed we gave it up, reasoning that physicians would be less needed if people were taught the laws of life.

We felt vaguely about our medical studies, that medicine, as Göthe says in *Faust*, labours

> "Um es am Ende geh'n zu lassen
> Wie's Gott gefällt."

The science did not seem certain enough to please our desire for certitude. It was too coarse to suit our feelings, both physical and moral. It was too material and mechanical to satisfy a nature which was travelling fast towards poetry and metaphysics. Desiring, therefore, something fixed and basal, and forced to speedy decision by the need to do something, we turned to Natural Science, notwithstanding its remoteness from human life ; and, as compensation, we pursued our study of medicine and other more human sciences privately and in our own way. The University curriculum was indeed by no means our main concern. We devoured books innumerable, especially during the first year, striving at one bound to gain a complete grasp of our contemporary national life. For in leaving school we had felt, like a child, curious to see the real world, let out of a nursery. Nothing learnt at school seemed to give a clue to the actual life of the city and the big world.

Of the books which interested us most, might be named those on philosophy and religion, and more particularly the writings of Beaconsfield, Carlyle, and Ruskin, from which we obtained our first clear ideas of a remodelled national life, and of a reformed education as one of the means for creating it.

But our educators were not limited to official Teachers at the University and to Books. There were also our friends, and in particular one, who at this time touched with a master-hand the part of our nature which had been most starved or crushed at school. He was a man of extraordinary gifts, mainly, perhaps, in the direction of Art and Poetry, but touching also on Philosophy and Religious Mysticism.

He started us more or less upon a new tack. But at this moment circumstances led us to Germany, and, until our return two years later, we were unable to follow up the new line of investigation he had suggested to us.

In Germany, notwithstanding our English prejudices, we at once observed strong evidence of superior intellectual life and social order.

First of all the instruction in the University was enormously better than it had been at home. It was more comprehensive, yet more exact; the language was clearer and the reasoning more cogent.

Their Body of Science seemed organised under their Professors, as their huge national Army under their veteran Generals. In the vast Library the same method reigned under the same supreme administrative talent. Even the Booksellers, all of whom appeared men of culture, several being University graduates, reigned over their Book-stores like a Quartermaster-General over his department.

Wherever one turned there was method, clearness, organisation, and withal general contentment and *gemüthlichkeit*, which powerfully contrasted with the squalid disorder and discontented unrest of England. And one contrasted the intellectual freedom and definite knowledge of the German with the amateurish vagueness and conventionalism of the Briton; and the German loyal recognition of the ascertained conclusions of Science with the tendency towards sectarian private judgment produced by the Briton's narrow horizon, ignorance, and insularity. Every day in Germany one felt the mind expanding and the fog melting away.

As our studies came to an end, the vital question again arose : How earn an honest living (that is, a living by work really needed) ? We were already weary of abstract science ; to be a mere chemist, we had no wish. Pure Science was too remote from human life, and we abhorred the notion of a Factory in which our whole life would be wasted in elaborating some patent soap, or another hideous dye. We looked round for something more congenial that would be also really needed by mankind. We had vague thoughts of teaching, but to teach for money was repugnant. However, the early friend to whom we have referred, by this time an officer in a distant province of the empire, decided us, and we returned to England with our mind made up.

Here we met again our artist friend. He had been acquainted with Ruskin and was deeply imbued with his ideas. He introduced us also to some of the best thought of France, which afterwards became invaluable for our educational work, which we now commenced.

We had at Göttingen followed some lectures at the university on Socialism, in which the facts quoted were largely drawn from British Blue Books. This had kept alive our interest in Sociology.

On our return home, through some of our friends, we were introduced to a Society interested in social questions, which brought us into contact with several persons who exercised an immense influence upon our mind. In particular there were two. One, who had had a distinguished career at the university, had developed original but very sane and wholesome views on social questions. If they were tinged, perhaps, with some elements of democratic enthusiasm, they were quite free from anything approaching public theft or violent prescriptions of any kind. They owed their origin, doubtless, to a profound knowledge of our social chaos, and a powerful sympathy arising from strong affections. The other was a man of most remarkable capacities, whose object appeared to us nothing less than the creation of a Synthesis of universal Thought and Action. While the former aimed mainly at a reorganisation of the social Environment, in order to achieve emancipation of the unit; the latter aimed mainly at a reorganisation of Knowledge which would enable the human unit to reconstruct society.

We must ever regard these two men, together with that other, to whom we referred above, as having exercised, perhaps, the most decisive influence upon our educational ideas. We will not attempt to go into details, which could not interest the public; but, briefly, we received from one a strong desire to assist in social reconstruction, from the second the idea of an intellectual synthesis, and from the third the suggestion of a harmonious union between ethics, æsthetics, philosophy, and religion.

The influence of these three men upon us was not

Introduction

due only to the intrinsic excellence of their characters or to the mere fascination of their ideas, but also to the important fact, that their influence reached us at the psychological moment. We were prepared to receive it, and were able to put it to some use, before the fresh vitality of the ideas, as too often happens, had time to evaporate. While these three were the most potent individual forces acting on us, there were others, either before or afterwards, which, if not so intense, yet exercised nearly as great an influence owing to close intimacy during many years.

Such, then, were the stages so far, through which the forces round our life had impelled us on our voyage of educational discovery.

On becoming a schoolmaster, the first thing we found was, that the mere fact of being a teacher by profession raised an immense wall, unknown before, between us and our pupils; indeed, it is hardly too much to say that we learned, probably, as much of Boy Nature, its doubts and difficulties, before we commenced our professional duties, as, perhaps, we have been able to discover since. This showed us at once the chief reason why all educational systems and teachers must fail, more or less, to achieve the highest results. It appears as if from the moment a thing is done consciously, of set purpose, and for a living—in short, as soon as the left hand knows what the right hand is doing—that moment one ceases to wield the magic wand.

During our school and university days, from a

rather accentuated leaning to mathematics and natural science, we had passed, as related above, to a more accentuated interest in human life. In the former period, the intellect, in the latter period, the affections, had had more play. At the time now reached, we found these two sides of our nature coming together, for the first time, into a very happy harmony.

Amongst other influences which led to this, may be put the society of a few friends — artists and musicians—whose company was vastly more congenial to us than that of the hard-headed, and somewhat cold-blooded, scientists among whom our special studies lay, although we recall with pleasure a few marked exceptions.

On the whole the votaries of Art for Art's sake would have been more agreeable to us at this time than the votaries of Science for Science's sake. But those we knew best belonged to neither of these extremes, having instead more or less a foot in each world. Stimulated by these many harmonising influences, we commenced our scholastic work, earnestly desiring to help create a *higher type of human being*, able to cope with the increasing extent and complexity of modern knowledge and modern life, and able by a better development of the affections to seek to develop a more wholesome type of human society. But, on account of the vast field which we beheld, we were filled with misgiving when we considered how wretchedly inadequate for such a work our own training had been. Not knowing anything scarcely of the history or literature of education, we had little idea what an immense movement was already going on throughout the world, endeavouring to grapple with the very questions more or less which had dimly arisen in our own mind.

Unfortunately circumstances forced us to commence our work without the needful preliminary studies; and we began our isolated attempts at what would now be termed "Child-study," almost completely ignorant of all the classical works on education, and not even aware to what a large extent other minds were working at the same problems.

Had we been able to study, even for a few years, the experiments of others, our own future work would have been easier, and the outcome more valuable. But, on the other hand, such study and experience might have chilled, as is so often the case, the wish to innovate, or might have fettered the freedom with which our mind approached its task.

Be that as it may, the fact remains that the causes of our attempting this work were those described. It was not due, in the remotest degree, to any special book, nor to any special institution, dealing with education. We had taken as our model the "public school," with whose life and work we were very intimately acquainted, and whose faults we had studied and suffered from, in our own, and in our friends', experiences. And by our own observations and experiments, through many years, we had discovered that many boys had, like ourselves, been starved where they should have been fed, and that they had nevertheless found none who seemed willing (or perhaps able) to teach what they vaguely yearned after, wants which they could not, then, even express.

While most heartily and sincerely acquitting our own teachers of all blame, seeing they were only working in a traditional machine, and undoubtedly did honestly what they supposed, or had been taught, should be done; we must, nevertheless, assert that, while we wanted bread, we received too often mere stones.

In trying to estimate the influences which were most active in our school life, and produced the most lasting impressions on our nature, we must place first and foremost the magnificent position of the school amid unparalleled scenery—mountains and sea, woods and fields, and gorgeous skies, with the spectacle spread out before us of one of the loveliest cities in the world. Next we must place the spacious grounds and stately buildings, an atmosphere of dignity and culture, and a free and open life. Such was the place.

If the plan of studies was too restricted and too artificial, at any rate there was some provision for the needs of one who, careless of words and phrases, loved to roam through woods and over fields and by the salt waves, to see with his own eyes the real world; or who loved, on occasion, to visit the big city, not to "grub," but to watch the curious types of people in that immense menagerie.

Introduction

In the school, moreover, there was some provision at any rate—especially in the earlier days—for natural science, and many a spare hour in the laboratory one spent trying to discover Nature's secrets for oneself. Whether through design or carelessness we know not, but luckily our hours in those days were not—as is now, alas! too often the case—assigned all day and every day to unalterable tasks of work or games. We had indeed much free time, bad for the idle boy, but most valuable to the diligent who thus could make up, in some degree at least, for the serious limitations of the school curriculum.

Music was fairly strongly cultivated in the school, and this most refining of influences, as well as most social of arts, was alone a power of enormous benefit.

While, therefore, we recall the intellectual studies in the class-rooms with but little pleasure, because we got little satisfaction from "classics," "mathematics," or "modern languages," we, none the less, recall with gratitude the general life of the place, as well as our personal intercourse with the masters.

Our hope, at first, had been to institute reforms within the bosom of the "public school." It had great merits. Unlike the nation at large, it recognised, at least in theory, the obligations of corporate life—obligations which the ghastly selfishness and *laissez faire* of our towns and trade seemed to deny. But our schools, though slowly, have had reluctantly to follow the general downward course of our national life. Under the demoralising influence of an unnaturally inflated trade with its deadly concomitants, swollen towns, overworked or idle crowds of undisciplined units struggling they know not for what, yet never content, the very notions of Community and Commonwealth have well-nigh perished. The "public schools" have yielded to the same force. No longer places of leisure—without which true education is impossible—they have become steam-driven factories for turning out by the dozen hastily crammed candidates for examinations. Their chief value to-day is that they still keep alive, in some faint degree, the legacy of earlier and wholesomer days, which every true educator in them knows he cherishes with all his heart and mind and strength.

After some years' experience, we felt that reform within the old type of school would be difficult if not impossible. And at this juncture an event took place which had a decisive influence on our future. A new school on modern lines was to be opened in London, and our commanding officer suggested our application.[1] We did not get the post, but his cordial recommendation first put the thought into our head, that we might venture ourself to undertake a responsibility so grave. We resolved, therefore, to open a school in which our dreams and aspirations might, perchance, find fulfilment.

[1] See Appendix A.

2. THE OLD KITCHEN GARDEN FROM THE NEAR COTTAGE. (*Summer, 1870*).

Introduction

A NEW SCHOOL[1]

The following is a short account of the educational aims and methods of the school to be opened in the Peak District of Derbyshire on October 1, 1889, by the undersigned :—

>CECIL REDDIE, B.Sc., Ph.D.
>R. F. MUIRHEAD, M.A., B.Sc.[2]
>WM. CASSELS.[2]
>EDWARD CARPENTER, M.A.[3]

There has been in recent times a growing conviction that the educational processes in our secondary schools have become stereotyped on artificial and unsatisfactory lines, which in many ways narrow and distort the physical, intellectual, and moral nature which they profess to educate. It is therefore proposed by the undersigned to start a New School on somewhat different lines.

In this school an attempt will be made to develop harmoniously all the powers of the boy—to train him in fact how to *live*, and become a rational member of society. Whatever his destined life may be—whether that of a practical man or that of a student, whether in the Colonies or at home—he will be able to fulfil his part all the better, and will be himself a more complete man for having at an early age had all the different sides of his nature well developed. At a later time he may have to specialise considerably, and for this the school will make provision.

Now it has long been recognised by many of our leading

[1] Reprinted from the *Pioneer*, April, 1889.
[2] Retired December, 1889, at the close of the first School-Term.
[3] Retired April, 1889, before the scheme was put into execution.

educationists that great changes in our present methods are urgently needed. Yet the general advantages, secured to English boys by the life and culture of the "Public Schools," are not only patent to ourselves, but have aroused the admiration and envy of leading men abroad. Almost alone of all schools in the world, the great "Public Schools" of England have aimed at cultivating, not merely the intellectual powers, but the physical, social, and moral nature of the youth as well. At their best they have created at once a wider home and a miniature world, and combining thus the larger Family with the smaller State, have given English boys the manly bearing and independent habits which fit them peculiarly for life, and make them not merely students, but men. Any improvement therefore in education should be based upon the ground-idea of the "Public School" system. But with the best in this should be incorporated all those influences which modern culture and the present needs of society have shown to be desirable.

Admitting, then, the many excellent features of the Public Schools, it is nevertheless very widely felt that they fail to meet adequately the needs of our present life. In spite of all that has been said and written on school reform, the majority of our youth still waste a large part of their school career in studying subjects, such as the dead languages, which only a few really require in after life. They merely touch upon modern languages and natural science. They remain ignorant on nearly all points touching their personal life and their relations to society. And the history of their own country, with the life and thought of the modern world is left almost a blank.

School games, moreover, which hitherto have supplied

the only means of physical education, need reform quite as much as school work. There is considerable analogy between the cram of athletics and the cram of "classics." The boys are tied down, with little regard to individual tastes, to playing the same few games. And these—mainly Cricket and Football—are highly elaborate and artificial. All this has been chiefly due to the initial difficulties which surrounded first efforts at the organisation of physical exercises. But now that they form an essential element in school life everywhere, such restriction is no longer required, as before, by considerations of school discipline. It is further unwise that boys should be constantly herded together, as, for instance, on the cricket or football field, to watch gladiatorial shows till their conversation is narrowed down to mere athletic "shop." They should have a wider horizon than the walls of the playing-fields. The want simply of more ideas is one of the chief sources of the corrupt imagination and conversation found in schools.

If we are to wait until the present schools adopt reforms, which well-informed persons see to be urgent, we may have to wait long. The reason is not hard to find. The schools are hampered by numberless traditions, by the exigencies of their position in relation to the universities, and by the keen competition which prevents one of them from introducing any vital change before the rest. Large and old corporations are no longer masters of themselves. A spectre or ghost, intangible, invisible, which is above "Governors," Headmaster, the Staff, and all combinations of these, really presides over almost every school. It is more conservative than any or all of the ruling powers.

Nor yet is reform easy from the outside. Who is to

initiate it? The parents have little time to study the question; nor are they well able to combine so as to secure for their sons the training most desired, and the State can do little, for these schools, although called, somewhat inaccurately, "Public Schools," are practically independent kingdoms.

That immense reforms will ultimately have to be made in these schools is undoubted; but must parents live half a century to see improvements introduced which they would wish their children to enjoy now? We believe that a large and ever-growing number of parents is dissatisfied with the education now available, and will strongly support a school, founded on better lines, which will secure all the real advantages offered by the best existing schools together with those which flow from a careful study and application of the methods of the modern Science and Art of Education.

In true education two objects must be kept in view; first, the general growth of the entire nature, and second, the fitting for some special work in the community. Therefore in The New School the education will be arranged in two stages: first, *general;* secondly, *special.*

I. GENERAL EDUCATION.

The harmonious development of the whole nature of the boy will be the foundation of the entire system of The New School. The training will, therefore, be (1) physical and manual, (2) artistic and imaginative, (3) literary and intellectual, and (4) moral and religious.

The boys will receive training in some of the manual arts, in drawing, painting, and music; in the different departments of mental activity which will comprise mathematics, including logic, natural science, language, literature, and history ; and all these will be handled from the ethical stand-point.

1. PHYSICAL AND MANUAL.—The physical training will not be derived wholly from mere games, but in a certain reasonable proportion from useful manual labour.

A healthier circulation of life-energy will thus be promoted, which will banish many of the well-known physiological troubles incident to those who have no steady work employing body and brain together, but whose school-life alternates between mere sports and mere books.

A more wholesome feeling will be aroused towards manual labour, also a sounder conception acquired of the conditions of labour and of the quantity of work involved in the execution of any given manual undertaking. This is impossible to those who merely talk or read about labour but have never handled the tools.

A more healthy social feeling will be developed. The boys will not only acquire certain capabilities of permanent value, but will learn to do for themselves and for each other much which they are usually allowed to expect from servants.

The training in manual work produces a manipulative dexterity, a steadiness and concentration of mind and will, and a habit of exactness in practical matters which mere book scholarship seldom supplies.

The experience so gained would also develop powers of resource and of self-reliance, and afford a valuable practical preparation for the work of later life, in whatever sphere, whether at home, in the colonies, or elsewhere.

The training of the body will be secured partly by the

muscular work involved in industrial occupations. But physical work alone does not suffice for perfecting the human body. For this exhilarating exercises are indispensable. They stimulate the healthy growth of the body in supple grace and compact symmetry, and promote that frank, hearty, and instinctive appreciation of its beauty, which is essential to true education. Moreover, to render the body strong, clean, and lovely is a religious duty. Therefore the claims of Athletics will in no respect be ignored, but rather extended and rendered less artificial and mechanical. The Athletic training will be compulsory to a reasonable extent, but varied and adapted to suit different capacities and dispositions.

It is also intended that instruction in outline be given in those occupations which have very close relation to the personal needs of the boys. Thus they will be shown the processes of boot-making and tailoring,[1] not to make them expert workmen in these departments, but to rouse interest in the subject of clothing generally, and to teach its proper relation to the human body. Similarly they will be taught cookery,[1] and other branches of domestic economy. In these ways the boys will have opportunities of acquiring a sound knowledge in all matters which more directly affect their personal health and life, subjects which are at present almost completely ignored in our schools.

[1] I have not yet seen my way to carrying out this item in my original program, though some cookery and butter-making has been tried from time to time. First, there is the general incompetence of servants and their class prejudice to bar the way; and, secondly, there is the fact that cultivated women are fast forgetting the right field for womanly talents and influence in their foolish attempt to turn themselves into second-rate men, and study subjects from which even boys and men are now becoming mercifully delivered.—C. R.

Opportunity will be given the boys to learn on the farm lands the rudiments of agriculture and gardening, and so to become acquainted with some of the processes of food-production. They will also be taught riding and driving, and the care of the ordinary farm animals. Some useful activities of this sort will be compulsory for all, but each will be allowed to choose his line. The garden produce required will, as far as possible, be grown on the school grounds, and be partly managed and tended by the pupils themselves, under suitable direction. Farming operations will be actually carried on, in order that a fair acquaintance with the theory and practice of farm-work may be obtained. This is a real, though little regarded, necessity of true culture, and also forms a sound preparation for colonial life. Such operations are, moreover, those in which boys would take a special delight. It is felt also that mutual services of this kind for one another and the school cannot fail to develop in the boys habits and sentiments of special value.

2. ARTISTIC AND IMAGINATIVE.—Care will be taken to develop the eyes, ears, and other senses and all the powers of the body thoroughly; to train the reasoning powers; and to stimulate the imagination by Poetry, especially through the stirring incidents of history immortalised in songs and ballads, the learning and singing of which will be made a special feature. Efforts will be made to render, moreover, the whole atmosphere stimulating to the dormant æsthetic sensibilities. Their school home will be made beautiful and that, as far as possible, by themselves. Too often the school surroundings are bare and uninteresting. In this we shall follow Ruskin and Thring.

In the conviction that the imaginative faculty is best

developed by the education of the innate creative instinct, it is proposed to train the boys as far as possible through the creation of the objects of their daily lives, especially where these can be made beautiful. With this object they will be taught carpentry, carving, metal working, modelling, &c., and other branches of the handicrafts in connection with drawing and decoration.

3. LITERARY AND INTELLECTUAL.—The English tongue should form the foundation of the mental education of English youths. But the study of English should not be limited to the dilettante work so common in this subject. At The New School it will mean as careful a training in grammar and composition as that usually obtained in the study of the ancient classics; but it will be on those very different lines developed in some recent valuable publications. The scholars will be trained to have complete command of the mother tongue, both for speaking and for writing; and to understand and appreciate its literary treasures.

A thorough knowledge of at least one other of the chief cognate languages is of the greatest value, not only in itself, but as an aid to the complete mastery of the mother tongue. Moreover it is now recognised that French and German can be made fully equal to Latin and Greek as a mental discipline. They are besides, as spoken languages easier to master, and of far more immediate use. Both are of increasing value at the present day in connection with political, scientific, and commercial pursuits; and the literatures of France and Germany have a much more direct bearing on modern life than have those of Greece and Rome. Every boy will therefore learn French or German; indeed, unless there be special reason to the contrary, he will learn both these tongues. Latin and, if possible, Greek will be taught to all, in, however, only their very simplest elements, to aid the full comprehension of English and also of Modern Latin—French, the key to all the Romance tongues. In those cases where the ancient tongues are required for some definite object, they will be more fully taught, in special classes, at a later stage.

All these languages will be taught by what most allow to be the natural method. Grammatical analysis, instead of preceding, will follow facility in the practical use of the tongue.

In History and Geography, as in all other studies, the progress will be from the modern, concrete, and particular, to the older, more abstract, and general. The history of the world, particularly of the Hebrews, the Greeks, and the Romans, and in later times, of the British Empire, and of Europe during this century, will be taught in close connection with Geography. The boys will study translations of the best ancient authors, and be made acquainted with the art creations and other remains of the famous nations of antiquity, as illustrating their social and mental life; and the conditions of modern English life will be studied by visiting fields of British industry.

The teaching of Natural Science will proceed similarly from the observation of external and obvious facts to the more hidden and abstruse generalisations; moving, on the one hand, from the direct knowledge of the human body and the laws of its health, onwards to Sociology and Economics; and, on the other hand, from the knowledge of common things to the separate Sciences of Botany, Zoology, Chemistry, and Physics. The young and tender brain should not be fatigued by the painful effort to master abstract laws and cumbrous terminology, before it is stored with simple concrete examples by which to interpret them. Thus the life, habits, and external parts of animals will be studied before their internal organs and skeletons, the forms and structure of plants before their classification, and the names and appearance of the stars and planets before the laws of their movements.

At the same time it is recognised that to some extent all Natural Sciences must be taught together. The curriculum of these studies will be planned not so as to give the boy (as is now so usual) different and unconnected branches in successive Terms, but rather so as to lead him successively through continually deepening analyses of life and the world. And, as far as possible, the whole will be taught in the most natural way—namely, as it has grown in the human mind historically, which is the way it tends to grow in each child.

In connection with the Natural Science department there will be Laboratories for Chemistry and for Physics, a Museum, and a type Botanic Garden.

Excursions will be made to places of interest in the country round, and the boys will be encouraged to study the Geology, Botany, and Zoology of the district, and to do practical work in Geography and Surveying.

The training of the memory and the careful teaching and storing up of systematised knowledge is, of course, in its place, indispensable, and will receive due attention, but will not be made, as is often the case, the only or chief object of the curriculum.

The mathematical discipline will begin with Arithmetic and Practical Geometry, in which theory will go hand in hand with practice, and for which illustrations will be found dealing with the actual experiences of the boys. The higher branches of Analysis and Geometry will follow, and special attention will be paid to graphic methods of representation. Throughout these studies the comprehension of abstract ideas will be facilitated by constant reference to illustrations and applications; while care will be taken to train the logical faculties by tracing the evolution of mathematical science from the two fundamental operations of counting discrete, and measuring continuous, magnitudes.

As a means of Education, Music is very important, having its practical, artistic, scientific, and social sides; and it is intended that all these shall be dwelt upon in proper degree. Unison, and part, singing especially will be taught to every boy.

4. MORAL AND RELIGIOUS.—As regards the moral training at The New School, the following principles will be kept in view. Morality cannot be taught by lessons and sermons, as if it were merely one among various branches of study. It is rather the outcome of the whole influence of the school, as this is expressed in every act of the school life. Nor yet can morality be taught merely by example, without the aid of Ideas, and it is also necessary that the ideas and example be accompanied by Sympathy. For love, like the sun, draws forth a bright healthy life in all around. The moral influence of a school is, moreover, the joint product of all its members, and to be lifegiving, requires that a hearty affection bind them all in one harmonious fraternity. As the moral influence of the school will be mainly through sympathy in this indirect way, every effort will be made to develop

between boys and masters and all members of the school a fearless frankness and cordial trust which is the best way to communicate a more developed moral feeling from one person to another. The school should be a Home, moreover, as well as a training-place, but not a mere barrack or monastery; and, as a home, it should be beautiful and harmonious.

It is the general sentiment that Morality, or the doctrine of right and wrong, must be taught in connection with some general conception of the Universe and Man's destiny in it, that is, in connection with Religion. But the religious instruction given here will be suited to the young, and therefore as undogmatic and unsectarian as possible. The fundamental principle that by Love alone Man is redeemed from his baser self, as taught by Jesus Christ, will form the centre of this teaching. The history of the Christian Church, and some account of the great World-religions will form part of the general curriculum. The religious services will be beautiful but simple, the influences of Music and Art being combined with practical instruction in the laws of right conduct.

II. Special Education.

It remains to indicate what practical pursuits the boys at the proposed school will be fitted for. In the first place, the school is not intended to "cram" boys for the capture of prizes and scholarships. This is at present a serious evil in our schools. It involves the neglect of the less gifted, for the unfair and unhealthy over-driving of the more brilliant; an injustice to the majority, and an injury even to the more fortunate for whom the others are neglected. Besides, the false and artificial stimulus of competition for prizes not only develops unduly the selfish instincts, but is apt to supplant the right motive for exertion, and to lead to the short-sighted and pernicious notion that prize-winning is the chief object of education. The boys should be made to feel that life is not a mere lottery, but that every earnest and wisely directed effort inevitably brings its own reward.

Up to the age of fifteen the education will be the same for all. After that age, the destined career of each boy will decide in some measure the nature of his further studies. Boys will be prepared for entering the Universities of Britain and Germany; or will be specially prepared for public examinations. There will also be a special training for commerce, for manufacturing pursuits, and for agriculture at home and abroad. An endeavour will be made to secure practical advice from architects, engineers, manufacturers, and business men, as to the course of study required for these various occupations, and the school will offer to supply them with boys trained specially to suit the needs of given posts. In this way it is hoped the school will become a medium of communication between parents and employers and thus assist parents in the difficult quest after openings for their sons.

The school will be opened on October 1, 1889, and probably in the Peak district of Derbyshire.[1] This locality is very central, and within easy reach of London and the populous towns of Yorkshire, Lancashire, the Midlands, and Scotland. The bracing upland climate and the varied scenery of this beautiful country, and the comparative remoteness of the nearest towns, will

---

[1] No suitable house exactly in the Peak district was heard of, and then Abbotsholme was found, which solved the difficulty.

guarantee to the scholars the health and freedom of a country life, which are so necessary to the young but which are now becoming daily harder to secure.

Finally, we hope that all interested in education in general, and in this scheme in particular, will aid us with advice and criticism, and by making the project widely known among those to whom it is likely to be of advantage.

ENGLISH AND SCOTTISH CRITICISMS UPON THE NEW SCHOOL.

In order to estimate the worth of any new creation, we need to know how it was greeted by Public Opinion at its birth. That is the moment, when the substantial yet unsatisfying Old can best be contrasted with the attractive but untried New—the Wilderness, in this case, of unwholesome instruction, with the Promised Land of sane education; competitive "cram," with educative co-operation.

The following Notices are those which happened to fall into our hands. Other criticisms may have been written which did not reach us; if so, we regret it. These, however, are enough, perhaps, to indicate the public verdict. They were written (with, I think, two exceptions) without my knowledge, and by persons unknown to me. The opinions are, in all cases, those of men uninfluenced, certainly, by any personal consideration.

From the numerous private letters, received from all parts of the British Isles, I do not quote. They might, by some, be thought to voice merely the views of individuals, and not the deliberate convictions of unprejudiced critics.

3. THE MASTERS' COMMON ROOM. (*Summer, 1892*).

Copyright

Introduction

THE LANCASHIRE EVENING POST, *May* 27, 1889.

A NEW SCHOOL.

Readers of *Wilhelm Meister's Wanderings*, the sequel or continuation to *Wilhelm Meister's Apprenticeship*, which, next to *Faust*, is the most remarkable of Goethe's writings, will remember the description which the author gives of a unique educational province. This province is presided over by educationists, whose ideas are of the very highest, and whose methods are of the very best, though withal different from those commonly adopted in many scholastic establishments, from the special and peculiar regard which is paid to the cultivation of the moral nature of the pupils in general, and from the manner in which, in the matter of intellectual training, the special aptitudes of each pupil are studied, so that each may have the best education which a capable human judgment, acting in co-operation with nature, may give. The picture which Goethe draws represents the high-water mark, so to speak, of educational aims and methods. So much is this so, that Goethe's views, as a whole, are ordinarily pronounced as utopian. Knowing how little encouragement there is in this very materialist age for the carrying out of such high ideals, we were not a little surprised to receive a few days ago a sort of prospectus or pamphlet, entitled, "A New School," setting forth a scheme of education which it is actually intended to put in practice, and which more nearly resembles in its proposed aims and methods the scheme which Goethe pictured than anything else to our knowledge now existing.

The New School, which is to be opened in Derbyshire in October next, is promoted in the belief that to bring about a true system of education it is necessary to break away from many of the conservative and conventional traditions and practices of the Universities and existing Public Schools. The harmonious development of all the faculties will be the foundation of the entire system of The New School. To particularise a few of the points in which The New School will differ from the old schools, we may note the following. The physical training will not be derived wholly from games, but in a certain proportion from useful manual labour. In the artistic training care will be taken to stimulate the imaginative faculties by poetry, especially through the stirring incidents of history immortalised in songs and ballads, the reciting and singing of which will be a special feature. In the moral and intellectual training the English tongue must of course form the foundation of the mental education of English youths. The boys will be trained to have complete command of their mother tongue, both for speaking and for reading, and to understand and appreciate its literary treasures. As regards foreign languages, the promoters believe that French and German can be made equal to Latin and Greek as a mental discipline. For this reason, and because of their more immediate use, they will be taught in preference to Latin and Greek. Latin and Greek will only be taught in their simplest elements to aid to the full comprehension of English. In cases where the ancient tongues are required for some definite object, they will be taught more fully in special classes. History, geography, the natural sciences, and mathematics are next alluded to as subjects of instruction. Then comes music. At no period will it be sought to "cram" the pupil for the capture of prizes and scholarships. The promoters of The New School well remark that it is an evil which involves the neglect of the less gifted for the unfair and unhealthy over-driving of the more brilliant. Furthermore, the false and artificial stimulus of competition for prizes not only develops unduly the selfish instincts, but is apt to supplant the right motive for exertion, and lead to the short-sighted and pernicious notion that prize-winning is in itself the end of education. "The scholars should be made to feel that life is not a mere lottery, but that every earnest and wisely-directed effort brings its own reward."

When the all-important subject of moral and religious training comes to be spoken of, the promoters take very high ground indeed. As to moral training, they well remark that morality cannot be taught by sermons, as if it were simply one among the various branches of study. It is rather the outcome of the whole influence of the school. As to religious training, the promoters take up a broad position. They quite recognise the sentiment that morality, or the doctrine of right and wrong, must be taught in connection with some general conception of the Universe and Man's destiny, that is, in connection with Religion. But the religious instruction they will give will be suited to the young, and therefore as undogmatic and unsectarian as possible.

Such is in very brief outline the nature of the aims and methods of the New School. But for the high reputation which the promoters possess already as educationists, and our belief that they are men of sterling worth and honest purpose, and also men of means sufficient to start a scheme such as this with the prospect of giving it a fair trial, we should fear that they were much too ambitious. They possess, however, all the qualifications necessary. We shall look, therefore, with hope at the progress of their undertaking.

Introduction

THE RUSKIN READING GUILD JOURNAL, *June*, 1889.

A NEW SCHOOL.

PREFATORY NOTE.

The Editor has much pleasure in drawing the attention of readers of the Journal to the Prospectus of A New School just issued, and in recommending the School itself to all who are dissatisfied with the education now available, and who are willing to support a school, "which will secure all the real advantages offered by the best existing schools, together with those which flow from a careful application of modern improvements in the Art of Education."

No. I.

The pamphlet deserves the attention of all who see the imperfections and vices of the education in vogue, or have ever thought of a perfect system of training for boys, and is especially interesting to disciples of Ruskin. One does not need to go very far in the study of Ruskin to be aware that his main distress is that in all directions effort is determined by a false ideal of life; and not only is a considerable section of the community coming to be at one with him, but many rising men in various departments of work are pressing forward to make beginnings with a social reformation. In education there is perhaps a more immediate chance for a body of Pioneers than in any other province. Here a start may hopefully be made—given men of the requisite capability, wisdom, and courage. And such, emphatically, are the men who have put their hands to this project of A New School. Setting out with a clear conception of the true end of education, they are marked off from school-projectors in general, who are content with stating a curriculum (and that mainly traditional), assuming that it must be good for the boy somehow, or who aim at fitting the boy for a spectral "success in life," measurable by what he secures in the scramble for fortune's prizes. Education, as understood by the founder of The New School, means the training which leads to life—nay, which is life itself. The pamphlet has this sentence, among others, respecting the great public schools of England—"they have, at their best, created at once a wider home and a miniature world." Never have those institutions been more nobly lauded in a phrase. The New School will imitate them so far, but it will be in advance of them, alike in the subjects to be studied, in the methods of teaching, and above all, in the means to be provided for developing the whole nature of the boy. In the literary and intellectual department the main stress is laid, as it ought to be, on *Modern Languages* (English first and foremost, then French and German) and *Natural Science*. Latin and Greek are assigned a place, but not the chief place. "Classical" literature is most precious, but surely the privileged position held by the dead languages in the great public schools and in the universities is at this date a scandal. The idea that there is nothing to compare with them as instruments of mental discipline is certainly superstition. As to natural science, history, and geography, mathematics, &c., the account given in the pamphlet of the methods which will be used in the teaching of these things shows that Dr. Reddie and his colleagues have thoroughly studied the philosophy of instruction. There are two fine paragraphs on the moral and religious training, which ought to satisfy reasonable Christians of every sect.

The aim of The New School is education "unto the perfect man." Consequently their system embraces elements of culture which have hitherto been neglected in schools, but which, whatever be the fate of the present undertaking, must enter into the education of the future. Useful manual labour is to form part of the physical training, and there is to be instruction in agriculture, gardening, as well as in handicrafts that are fitted to develope the sense of beauty and the creature instinct. This is the most striking feature of The New School, and the justification of it is written in pithy sentences. Most noteworthy also is the place given to poetry, which has never been properly understood in schools as a means of education, but is now to be raised to its due rank. Care is to be taken "to stimulate the imaginative faculties by poetry, especially through the stirring incidents of history, immortalised in songs and ballads, the learning and singing of which will be made a special feature."

The style and spirit of the prospectus are admirable, and every sentence conveys the impression of thorough mastery of the whole subject in hand. May The New School prosper !

JOHN WELLWOOD.

No. II.

Education is the happy hunting-ground of theorists, the quagmire of experimentalists. One would think that with all that has been written, and said, and thought—earnestly thought too—on the subject, that there was little left for any one to add. And yet only the other day the parent of a growing boy lamented to me, in well-grounded despair, that he really did not know what to do with Harold. He could not think of exposing him to a public school to undergo the tyrannies and temptations that he had undergone himself. I could only reply that a day school, however good, has disadvantages which more than counterbalance all the drawbacks of public school life: especially that the day boy has to divide his allegiance between his master and his father in a way that makes all definiteness of discipline and directness of purpose impossible.

"I shall have to teach Harold myself," said he. "So you ought," said I, "if you can."

But how many parents can? Ruskin's mother, in an age when ladies were not supposed to be learned, could ground him in Latin until he was ten, and then was forced, with a sigh, to turn him over to the minister. When he went to Oxford he was a fish out of water—a salmon out of water—but out of his element for all that. Universities, and life in general, are not as they should be, and set no premium on the holiness of home training; and any scheme of schooling must take things as they are, and make the best of a bad job.

The best is certainly not made when you try to cram a mixed batch of boys with abstract "classics and mathematics," cricket and football, and nothing else. The system is simply a survival of the Renaissance, based on the assumption that all these boys are born gentlemen and scholars; that they will never have to work for their living except as lawyers and clergymen; and upon the hope that, in the large majority of cases, silk purses can be made out of sow's ears.

Meanwhile, if not scholars and gentlemen, could we not make men of our lads; beings with hands and eyes, and—is it too much to hope—with hearts? Men are made continually, but not by the present educational systems. There are few schools which are so unfortunate as not to possess one or more masters whose personal aims and influence, like those of a good priest in a corrupt church, reach beyond and counteract the influence and aims of the institution they work under. But their hands are tied: their aims are bounded by the necessities of competitive examinations, and their influence too often ends just when it should be beginning to exert itself.

I have no personal acquaintance with the authors of a prospectus just put forth proposing the foundation of *A New School*, on a new system. I do not know if they are born teachers with a genius like Miss Allcott's Professor Bhaer (by the way, was there ever a German with a name written like that, or is it just a bit of lady-like mis-spelling?) but the men who could evolve the Ideal are not unlikely to be the men who can carry it out. If they can carry out what their prospectus promises, or half as much, they will do what many lawgivers and philosophers have desired to see, but were not able. They propose a country school in Derbyshire, where boys shall be taught to use their hands and eyes all in manner of practical ways ; and their brains, not in the empty accomplishments of gerund grinding, but in useful acquisition of thorough English, sound science, and the modern tongues. "Classics" and mathematics to be kept strictly to the rudiments, except for those boys who show an aptitude, at the age of fifteen, for abstract scholarship. They are to ride, and to groom their ponies ; to carve, and, I hope under strict supervision, to decorate their chapel ; to garden, and to eat their vegetables, supplementary of course to a liberal diet ; to cook, but not to eat their messes ; to make boots and coats, but not necessarily to wear them. Most boys do all these things in their holidays, more or less, with the help of some old fisherman or gardener, to whom they often look back in later days as their real and true pastor and master ; but surely it must be a great advantage to any lad to have these practical details and experiences brought within the range of his serious attention as part of his education ; not only because it makes him manly, but also because it gives him sympathy and insight into labour and the labouring classes, without which the employer is a tyrant, and the customer a fool.

And another thing,—and still more important with regard to school life. The temptations to which boys are especially subject are chiefly those of comparative idleness in the intervals of violent exercise and violent study. This industrial system provides exactly that resource of moderate exertion occupying, but not fatiguing, body and mind, which all the wisest thinkers prescribe both for young and old. The pupils of Dr. Reddie and his colleagues are not to neglect study or athletics, but both are to be tempered with varied industrial occupation. All the best work in the world has been done under circumstances like these ; all the highest refinement of heroic Greek, chivalric, mediæval, and cultured modern life has co-existed in its finest examples with a certain amount of manual labour, in some cases, no doubt, only as play ; but where it has been absent the result has been disastrous either to body or to mind. The value of The New School is in its recognition of this principle. If a man of intellect is caught carpentering, his friends call it a hobby, and laugh at him ; if he is found gardening he is a little ashamed ; but the boys of The New School are to be taught the dignity of labour, and if there are any born gentlemen among them they will be none the less gentlemen for it, and the others will have no false standards put before them.

The religious teaching of The New School is, perhaps, not sufficiently defined in this preliminary prospectus to win the confidence of a good many intending parents. Its morality is defined enough ; though after all the government of a school is in this respect like other governments, and "that which is best administered is best." But if a well-planned constitution offers any safeguards, the best are offered by The New School.

My son is only a baby yet in long clothes. By the time he is old enough to be a schoolboy, I am very much afraid The New School will be too full to take him in.

W. G. COLLINGWOOD.

EDINBURGH EVENING DISPATCH, *July*, 1889.

THE LEADING ARTICLE.

A remarkable experiment in scholastic education is about to have a trial. Certainly unique in the history of education in Great Britain, it is probably also without parallel even in the Transatlantic country which has invented Toppolobampo. Dissatisfied with our modern system of juvenile training, a few enthusiastic educationists—themselves all brilliant scholars—from the English and Scottish Universities have joined forces for the establishment of a secondary school to run on new and untried lines. The English public school system they deem the most advanced type of existing disciplinary institutions. The fundamental principles that regulate, or are supposed to regulate, public school training will form the basis or ground-plan of the new school. Agreeing in their elemental foundations, the two superstructures afterwards part company at a very divergent angle. The new school, if anything, is to be catholic, cosmopolitan, universalist, in its aims and methods. Up to fifteen all the boys will receive the same general training in matters physical and manual, artistic and imaginative, literary and intellectual, moral and religious. After this age some decidedly novel suggestions are made as to training in special subjects. But before the time for specialisation arrives, all the energies of the new school are apparently to be directed to developing an "all-roundedness" in their boys. Their minds are to be impressed with a panoramic reflex of nature. Nothing could better illustrate the scope of these experimental educationists than the mention of the fact that they intend to make all the boys acquainted with domestic economy, gardening, and agriculture, not with any idea of making them expert workmen in these subjects, but in order to rouse interest in those matters which have so close a relation to one's own personal needs.

The science of education is at least as old as Socrates. The great principles that have animated the educational writers of all ages are very much the same. From Plato to Milton, and from Rousseau to Spencer, the fundamental propositions of educational treatises all exhibit a remarkable similarity. It would seem that the Science and Theory of Education were in a tolerably advanced stage a couple of thousand years ago even in Europe. That the Art and Practice of Education have made little or no progress during these ages of time is probably due conjointly to the want of imagination in the man of practice and the want of practicality in the man of theory. In other words, the antediluvian character of our modern schools is due to absence of experiment in scholastic art. It cannot be disputed that the educational processes in our schools run in lines antiquated, artificial, and eminently unsatisfactory in results. The Latin language, it has been truly said, was killed by the analytic method of teaching the Latin grammar, and all other discipline, of course, followed the same analytic method. The consequence is that were the human being not such a splendid animal as in essence he really is, our system of education must have driven him into the back woods and polished him off long ago. From mere observation of methods and partial results it is difficult to avoid coming to the conclusion that our Primary Schools have for their chief aim the dissemination of penny-dreadful reading, and the use of chalks upon the walls of public buildings. Secondary schools in the same way appear to be institutions for the wholesale manufacture of imbecile athletes, pedantic prigs, and molluscous "mashers"; while the Universities find their great function in demonstrating the futility of Board Schools, and in stereotyping the absurdities and distractions of the "Public Schools." Fortunately, the success of these institutions in their self-appointed task is very moderate. Luckily for humanity, a good many men are able to pass through the machine without appearing at the other end as beautifully-turned sausages, indistinguishable from all the other sausages. At this juncture the experiment of Dr. Reddie, in founding The New School, marks at any rate an exceedingly meritorious desire to advance the Art of education, to bring it up more on a level with the congenital Science, so far behind which at present it lags. Educationists all over the country will watch their experiment with much interest.

THE STUDENT, *July* 12, 1889.

Students' Representative Council, University of Edinburgh.

"A NEW SCHOOL."

This is the appropriate heading of a prospectus which we have just seen, and to which we would draw the attention of our readers.

Feeling that we are bound, as far as possible, to keep the men of this University in touch with past students and their doings—anxious also to do justice in our own small way to enterprise and originality, especially where education in the widest sense is concerned, we feel that we should be very remiss did we not devote a portion of our space to describing what is a real advance in education, initiated by Dr. Cecil Reddie, a distinguished graduate of this University, who, in conjunction with two Cambridge graduates, is about to start a new school in Derbyshire. These men have felt the growing popular conviction, that the educational methods in our "public" and other schools are no longer adapted to meet the requirements of modern life, and accordingly in their program they aim at more fully realising the true Ideal of education, to develop harmoniously all the faculties of the boy—to train him how to live, in fact, and become a rational member of society.

Our pioneers, in their prospectus, then proceed to discuss school life and school training as they are.

They speak of the many acknowledged good points in the present methods, and of the manly and independent tone resulting therefrom, but they also argue, and argue we feel conclusively, that these schools are fettered by methods which are traditional and obsolete. We must all agree with them here. Almost every one of us is too young yet to have got into that groove in which so many so continually find themselves in later life, when "laissez aller" is their only motto, and they look back on the golden haze of their distant schooldays, and speak of them as "the happiest days of my life, my boy—only wish I were going back with you," and of the school itself as "the best school in the United Kingdom, sir—made me what I am!"

From such a state of mind and soul, the saints deliver the boys of this generation! It is probably that of a man who knows how to make money, but who, in the act of acquiring that knowledge, has lost far more than he has gained.

We all remember hours devoted to sheer cramming of subjects which were so taught as to be absolutely nauseous, and so learned as to have been long since practically forgotten. Most of us are, alas! cramming other subjects now, which in their turn will go, leaving us with not much knowledge, and less healthy brain.

The promoters of "The New School" start with the assumption that their boys should be taught only what will be of service to them later, either by its bearing on their proposed after-careers, or by equipping them better, whatever those careers may be, for a sane and healthy life.

Briefly, then, the training will be as follows :—

Up to the age of fifteen, all will have practically the same education, which is discussed at great length in the prospectus, far more fully than we can discuss it here. We are glad to see that physical and manual training take such a prominent position on the program, and that Cram and Competitive Examination, those two great bloodsuckers which frighten the average man and kill many of his most brilliant fellows, those two bars against honest work and originality, are declared against distinctly and in set terms by the promoters, who believe that a greater and more permanent success than is now seen, will be attained by a wiser arrangement of subjects, and by their new methods of teaching.

While the general education is going on, there will be special efforts made, and special opportunities given, for discovering each boy's particular aptitude, and after fifteen each will have his work arranged to fit him for his proposed after-career, whatever that may be. In the meantime, we are happy to believe that the general tendency of each boy's surroundings and life will have been to make him a true man and an honest gentleman, and we hope to live long enough to meet some of these lucky fellows, and to judge for ourselves of the success of an enterprise which has our best wishes, and which we may be able to report upon again, when it has fairly started.

THE SOWER, *July*, 1889.

A FELLOWSHIP SCHOOL.

Some time ago the New Fellowship issued a proposal for the establishment of a school on lines consistent with the principles which it advocates. Up to the present, circumstances have not admitted of the practical realisation of this scheme under the direct auspices of the Fellowship; but the members hail with great satisfaction a separate effort which some friends and associates are about to make, to establish just such a school as was contemplated in the circular which the Fellowship issued. An attempt will be made to develop harmoniously all the faculties of the boy—to train him how to *live*, in fact, and become a rational member of society. This harmonious development of all the faculties will be the foundation of the entire system of the school.

Negotiations are almost completed for the lease of a commodious house called Abbotsholme, with adjoining land, on the banks of the Dove, near Rocester, Derbyshire, a picturesque yet accessible region. The school will be opened in October next.

R. E.

BEDFORDSHIRE TIMES AND INDEPENDENT, *August* 17, 1889.

A NEW DEPARTURE IN BOYS' SCHOOLS.

We have before us the prospectus of what is called "The New School," which is to be opened for boys at Abbotsholme, Derbyshire, in October, and which presents so many novel features that we think our readers will be interested in learning something about it, as a sample of what will probably be the School of the Future. Those who work and are otherwise interested in the Bedford Schools will therefore do well to make themselves acquainted with the character of this new departure, that they may see what is likely to be the nature of the competition which the Bedford Schools will have to meet. Something may, moreover, be learnt by our Governors and Masters from "The New School." The new institution has received the approval of a great number of the most eminent educationists and other prominent men and women of the day.

The prospectus says:—The object of this School is to provide, for boys between the ages of ten and eighteen, an education of a thoroughly modern and practical character, keeping steadily in view the purpose of all right education—to teach the boy "the laws of health and the exercises enjoined by them, and habits of gentleness and justice, and to prepare him for the calling by which he is to live." The whole life at the School is planned to develop harmoniously all the faculties, physical, artistic, intellectual, and moral ; and for this purpose the mornings will be devoted to study, the afternoons to athletics and manual work, and the evenings to art and social recreation. Since so many collapses in after-life are due to an enfeebled physique, every boy at the School will be required to join, to a reasonable extent, in some of the athletic exercises, and to take up also some regular manual work. This last, it is felt—besides its more obvious and practical uses—ensures an even and steady distribution of energy over the whole body, and so reduces the liability to disturbances of health which comes from much mental and sedentary work. It also enables more time to be given to physical development than is possible merely through the agency of games ; and the results being tangible can be estimated by the boys themselves. Further, since manual work trains the creative instinct, it will form a natural introduction to the Art Studies. These will consist of modelling as well as working in wood and metal, and every boy will be taught drawing and singing. The boys will assemble in the evenings for music, recitations, and other social entertainment. The curriculum will be divided into two stages.

I. General Training (Lower School).

In accordance with the aims indicated above, the earlier education— up to about fifteen years of age—will be of a general character, all the boys receiving the same training. They will be carefully taught the laws which rule their personal life, and the physical, mental, and moral habits necessary to produce and maintain sound health. With the same end in view, they will pass through a general course of natural science, having particular reference to their daily surrounding and needs, and serving as a solid foundation of useful knowledge upon which their later, more specialised, studies may rest.

At this period they will also be taught to use the instruments of knowledge, in particular, language and elementary mathematics. The basis of training in language will be English. French will follow, and later German. But only one language will receive a large share of attention at a time, fewer hours being devoted to French, for instance, when German has been commenced. In studying languages, composition, grammar, and analysis will be learnt together, alike to ensure correct speaking and writing, and to form part of the mental discipline ; while literature and history, especially English literature and history, will be brought in to expand and enrich the mind. After some progress has been made with French, Latin will be commenced, to render intelligible the important Latin element in French and English. In the case of certain boys Greek will be taken up in a similar way towards the end of the general education; but the actual time given to Latin and Greek up to fifteen will be small. Considerable latitude will be permitted to the boy in his choice of the artistic and manual work which he takes up. On account of the wide range of studies, every boy's bent and ability should be readily discovered, and the parent and master guided in deciding his subsequent course of work.

II. Special Training (Upper School).

About the age of fifteen the boy will not only have begun to show where his tastes and abilities lie, but will have to consider what his ultimate work in life is to be. At this age, therefore, his studies may become more specialised. They will naturally vary according to the line he selects. The main lines at present contemplated in the school curriculum are the following: Preparation—For the Universities and Technical Colleges of Britain and Germany. For Public Examinations. For Commercial Life. For Art, Engineering, and Agriculture.

It will be noted that while "classical" studies do not occupy so large a place in the general scheme of education as is usual, those boys who have special faculties in this direction will receive special training; but as this is not the case with the majority of boys, particular attention will be paid to giving these a sound scientific education to fit them for practical work in various lines. It is not proposed in the above to teach a trade or profession, but to direct the boy's attention to work of practical value in the line he has selected, that he may afterwards get the utmost available benefit from the technical college, the office, or the farm.

LEADERETTE ON THE ABOVE, August 24, 1889.

In publishing, last week, long extracts from the prospectus of "The New School" in Derbyshire, we hoped to do two things; to excite some degree of admiration for the new departure which appeared to us a very wise one, and to stimulate the Governors and Masters of our Bedford Schools to imitation and emulation. Of course, in bringing before Bedford parents such an admirable prospectus, we ran the risk of enticing boys from the Bedford Schools. To tell the truth, we should not be sorry if this risk were sufficiently realised to compel the attention of the leaders of educational opinion in Bedford to the subject. It is a safe prediction to say that no public school will be successful a generation hence if it is still worked upon the lines on which our Schools here and most schools elsewhere are now worked. The sooner this is practically acknowledged the better. School teaching must become the training of the man rather than the cramming of the examinee, and that training must proceed on sound psychological principles.

PALL MALL GAZETTE, *August* 26, 1889.

"THE NEW SCHOOL."

I. AN INTERVIEW WITH DR. REDDIE, THE HEADMASTER.

Let not the gentle reader be alarmed. It is not of a new school of philosophy that we are speaking, but of a new school in the common usage of the term—a new departure, that is to say, in those necessary institutions which are designated in the old Bidding Prayers as "places of sound and religious learning."

The New School has a very attractive exterior, being a large country house in the Elizabethan-Victorian style, situated in spacious grounds on a hill overlooking the Derbyshire Dove. But there are many schools nowadays which have these advantages; and what is new in The New School must be sought elsewhere. Dr. Cecil Reddie, the Headmaster, called upon us the other day to appeal for a sympathetic hearing, and the appeal was backed from so many quarters that it could not be refused. The New School, we had been told, was Ruskinian to the backbone; its object was to fulfil "the master's" idea of education—to teach the young Englishman "the laws of health and the exercises enjoined by them, and habits of gentleness and justice, and to prepare him for the calling by which he was to live." And besides, the New School is at any rate new, and it is the function of the *Pall Mall Gazette* to keep its readers abreast of the newest ideas. This argument, at least, was irresistible, and we had much pleasure therefore in receiving Dr. Reddie, to learn at first hand the essential outlines of the scheme:—

WHAT IS THE SCHOOL OF THE FUTURE?

"Of course," said our representative, "your school is to be a day school?" (For the *Pall Mall* has often urged that the School of the Future will be founded on the Home, and will not take boys away from the influence of home and family life just when they need it most.)

Introduction

Dr. Reddie, however, strongly demurred to this view of the matter. "I do not agree with you," he said, "that the School of the Future will be the Day School; the tendency is quite the other way. The level of morality is not any higher in day schools than in boarding schools. Indeed, I believe the very contrary to be the case. No, The New School is a boarding school."

THE GOSPEL OF MANUAL LABOUR.

"And what is the next 'feature'?"—"Well, our whole idea is to follow natural, instead of conventional, lines, and to develop harmoniously all the faculties of the boys. For instance—it is a little difficult to pick out particular 'novelties' for you; but one chief innovation is the stress we lay on manual training." "Carpentering, and so on, I suppose? But have not these been introduced into most 'Public' Schools by this time?"—"No doubt they have," replied Dr. Reddie, "but not as an essential and compulsory part of the curriculum, as we propose. In our view the education of the physical faculties is as important as that of the intellectual. Hitherto physical education has been restricted to athletic games. This is a great mistake. Violent physical exercise following on sedentary mental work is very bad for boys. The scheme of The New School is to combine athletic exercises with manual training. Since so many collapses in after-life are due to an enfeebled physique, every boy at the school will be required to join, to a reasonable extent, in some of the athletic exercises, and to take up also some regular manual work.

HALF WORK AND HALF PLAY.

That the new school "means business" in the importance it attaches to manual training is clear from the Time-table which Dr. Reddie showed us, and which, as somewhat of a curiosity in the educational line, we subjoin:—

Morning.		Afternoon.	
6.10 A.M.	Rise (in winter at 7)	1.0 P.M.	Dinner
6.30 ,,	Drill	1.30 ,,	Organ or Piano Recital
6.45 ,,	First School	2.0 ,,	Games, Gardening, Workshops, &c.
7.30 ,,	Chapel		
7.40 ,,	Breakfast	6.0 ,,	Tea
8.30 ,,	Second School	6.30 ,,	Singing, Recitations, Music, &c.
10.15 ,,	Break for Lunch		
10.30 ,,	Third School	8.30 ,,	Supper and Chapel
12.15 P.M.	Bathing	9.0 ,,	Lights out.

It will be seen that only the mornings are to be devoted to what is usually called "study"—the afternoons and evenings been given up to athletics, manual work, art—in the shape of wood-carving, brass-beating, painting, and glee-singing—and "social recreation." It should be added that no lesson, except writing, drawing, practical chemistry, &c., which involve comparatively little mental effort, will exceed three-quarters of an hour; and, with regard to the long interval before breakfast, that "every boy will have a light meal immediately after rising." Oh! that one had been born in the days of The New School, instead of in those of the Old!

ENGLISH AND FRENCH VERSUS LATIN AND GREEK.

The last distinguishing feature to which attention was drawn by Dr. Reddie was that the ordinary method in the teaching of languages would be reversed. Ordinarily, "as every schoolboy knows," the grounding is in Latin and Greek, and French and German are only thrown in—too often as a mere farce—at the end. Dr. Reddie's views on the matter are very different. "The basis of training in language," he thinks, "should be English, French should follow, and later German. But only one language should receive a large share of attention at a time. After some progress has been made with French, Latin should be commenced, to render intelligible the important Latin element in French and in English. In the case of some boys, Greek should be taken up in a similar way towards the end of the general education.

All this is a New School, certainly; but will not its masters have to begin by educating the parents up to it? On this point, however, Dr. Reddie seemed well satisfied. The school is to start in a month, and he had already promises of sixteen scholars. "Mostly, I suppose," said our representative, "from Scotland. All good causes," I was assured the other day, "find their best support in Scotland."—"The New School," said Dr. Reddie, "must be an exception. All our promises are from England. The Scotch are, I suppose, too cautious; they will come in in time, but are waiting to see the experiment tried." "On the *corpus vile*," suggested our representative, "of the English schoolboy."

II. AN INTERVIEW WITH MR. EDWARD CARPENTER.

It may be well to supplement the explanations of the Headmaster with a few words from Mr. Edward Carpenter, with whom another member of our staff had some conversation the other day:—

Introduction

THE GOSPEL OF POTATO-DIGGING.

The place given to it in the regular curriculum is not the only difference between the gospel of manual labour, as it will be understood at Abbotsholme, and the same thing as already introduced at many of our public schools. Mr. Carpenter is an exponent of what may be called the Gospel of Potato-digging; and something of that sort is implied in the physical training to which the afternoon school-hours are to be devoted. For skill of eye and strength of limb, for handiness and hardiness of body, the simple outdoor life of farming and gardening is as necessary, in Mr. Carpenter's view, as the joinery and metal-work which are more customary. Soil, to his mind, is no more contaminating than shavings; education may condescend to plough and spade as well as to plane and chisel. Field-craft and handicraft may go hand in hand Chips are not everything. If a man is the better man all round for making a good mortice he will be none the worse for driving a straight furrow; and he will certainly be more in touch with Nature—with that large part of his fellow-men who get their living from the soil, and with those knottiest problems of the present day which spring from the same source. The captains of our elevens generally leave school on terms of perfect familiarity with twenty-two yards of cricket-pitch. With the exception of that strip of ground, they know as much of the earth they walk on as a fly does of its window-pane. At Abbotsholme they will mark out the year by seedtime and harvest, the county calendar, as much as by the date when cricket begins and football ends, when cricket ends and football begins. As good old Andrew Marvell sang:—

> "How could such sweet and wholesome hours
> Be reckon'd but with herbs and flowers?"

Adjoining farm lands have been chartered and the best of teaching has been engaged. "Don't think we have absurd or impracticable notions," said Mr. Carpenter; "we don't cry that salvation comes from the soil, or make a fetish of the thing in any way. Throughout this undertaking we have been bent on making practical a few admittedly good ideas which the public schools, in the whirl of competition, cannot readily adopt. This farming experience, which is only one item in the choice of manual labour which we offer, will be most useful to the increasing number of boys who are destined for the colonies. In everything we keep in touch with the practical. To take another instance: Our daily program obviously disqualifies us for taking places in the cramming competition, but we shall be all the better able to prepare boys for the less exacting examinations, for ordinary honours at the universities, for business, and for everyday life."

Much more Mr. Carpenter said as to the spirit which guides the new educational enterprise, and especially as to the pains that will be taken (in all unaffected ways) to encourage such a frank and friendly intercourse as may make it possible for masters to be of some practical help to boys in the everyday battle of life. But these are the things which belong to no system, and in which the man is everything, his system nothing. If The New School fulfils its promise, if it succeeds in giving its boys a life which does not alternate between mere books and mere sports, but pays at least equal heed to everything that *emollit mores nec sinit esse feros*, it will justify all the enthusiasm of its promoters. After all (thought our representative), if it is an experiment to send a boy here, is it less so to chuck him into the *laisser faire* world of the ordinary Public School?

THE "PALL MALL GAZETTE" ON THE NEW SCHOOL.

The *Pall Mall Gazette* of Monday last contains a very interesting account of an interview between one of its representatives and Dr. Cecil Reddie, Headmaster of The New School, which is to be opened on October 1st. This school, situated at Abbotsholme, on the Dove, in Derbyshire, probably marks an epoch in the history of secondary education in Britain. We should have been glad to have given the *Pall Mall's* account of the enterprise in full had our space allowed, and shall but indicate the general tendency of the school, referring all inquirers to the Headmaster, Dr. Cecil Reddie, The New School, Abbotsholme, on the Dove, Derbyshire. The new school will, of course, be a boarding school. The great aim of the school will be to train up the boys to be *men* in the noblest sense of the word, develop all their faculties not on conventional but natural lines, and great attention will be given to the physical development which comes not from games alone, but from compulsory and essential manual labour also. Parallel with development of the intellectual powers will run the growth and fostering of the physical and manual (football, cricket, &c., gardening, farming, &c.), the artistic and imaginative (wood carving, brass beating, painting, glee singing, &c., &c.), and the moral and religious faculties. Another distinguishing feature will be that English will be the fundamental language taught; then will come French, then German, Latin and Greek following to show the part they played in the formation of modern languages. The best available English translations of the great Latin and Greek classics will be studied. All the boys will receive a similar general education, and prepare for university, for business, or every-day life. Such is the very barest outline of the main features of the latest attempt to put in practical form the ideas of modern educational reformers ; and bearing such a stamp of practicability we foresee in it the dawn of a glad day for teachers and scholars alike.—*Dunfermline Journal*, August 31, 1889.

MANCHESTER EXAMINER AND TIMES, *September* 9, 1889.

A very interesting educational experiment is being tried in Derbyshire. Dr. Reddie, lately an assistant master at Fettes College, has opened a boarding school at Abbotsholme, near Rocester, on highly original lines. The new features are almost bewilderingly numerous. Dr. Reddie breaks away from conventional lines as completely as Plato did when he set about founding his "Republic." But Plato's Republic could afford to be unconventional, because it only existed on paper, and its founder admitted, even while he was engaged in drawing up the scheme of it, that it was never likely to be realised on earth. Dr. Reddie, on the other hand, is not merely writing an educational and political novel ; he is preparing to show us his ideal school as a working reality. One of the points on which he lays great stress is manual training. Carpentering, as a healthy recreation, has been introduced already in many schools ; but The New School proposes to make it an essential and compulsory part of the curriculum. Games are to be encouraged, but hardly to the extent reached of late in the great public schools ; regular manual work, supplying even and steady exercise directed to a useful end, will in some measure take their place. Secondly, only the mornings will be devoted to "study" in the narrow sense of the word ; the afternoons and evenings will be given up to athletics, manual work, art (which will include woodcarving, painting, and singing), and "social recreation." No lesson which involves serious mental effort will exceed three-quarters of an hour. Another feature of The New School is the prominence given to music ; after dinner every day there is to be an organ or piano recital. Lastly, Dr. Reddie joins the revolt against Latin and Greek. He intends to make English the basis of training, and to follow that up with French, and afterwards with German. It is sufficiently obvious from this sketch that any adequate criticism of the program of this " School of the Future " would involve a discussion of most of the educational problems of the day. Here it is only possible to offer one or two remarks. Perhaps the first reflection that will occur to a student of the history of education will be the thought that these same educational problems of to-day are wonderfully like those of two thousand years ago. Our problems are complicated by the battle of ancient and modern languages. The fortunate Greek had the best of ancient languages for his native speech, and could afford to despise other tongues as barbarian. But otherwise his questions were very much our questions. The reference already made to Plato's immortal treatise was not an arbitrary one. Dr. Reddie's scheme is full of reminders of Plato, especially in its insistence on the harmonious and equable development of mind and body, and in the stress that it lays on Music. Perhaps this is the most interesting of all the new departures; for a new departure it may fairly be called, though the great day schools, as well as the boarding schools, are now learning how to brighten an occasional hour with singing in unison. The influence of music on mind and character seems as great a mystery now as it was in the days of Plato. That it may have a great power for good or for evil is undoubted; but the precise connection between music and morals is very far from being understood. Hence an experiment on a large scale with music is something like an experiment on a large scale with electricity. It is playing with a power that is too vast for control, and the end no one can foresee. Probably most of the season-ticket holders at Sir Charles Hallé's concerts would be surprised to hear that they were trying a considerable experiment on their emotional nature. Yet, if they are auditors in any real sense, such is the truth, and the experiment in the case of a boy's unformed nature is vastly greater. The three-quarters of an hour limit for lessons is worth considering. This is the duration fixed for lectures at a German University, and, though Oxford lectures are supposed to last an hour, there is at least one distinguished lecturer who, by invariably arriving ten minutes late and occupying five minutes with a roll-call, ingeniously reduces the hour by a fourth part of its length. Boys are often expected to fix their attention on one subject for an impossibly long time, though the difficulty which even grown-up people find in continuously attending to a speech or a sermon for so much as half an hour ought to teach parents and schoolmasters the unreasonableness of their expectation. Of course, the success of Dr. Reddie's daring experiment remains to be seen. His boys, if he fulfils all the promises of his prospectus, ought to have a bright and happy time. Will they be able, on the completion of their school career, to compete with boys educated on more conventional lines? Probably Dr. Reddie would reply, and with great justice, that the real test of education comes at thirty, not at sixteen. There is a sham education that produces plentiful blossoms in boyhood, but no fruit afterwards, whereas a healthy and vigorous maturity should be the aim of all youthful training. At the same time, in an age of keen competition, it is not always easy to make up for a lost start; and Dr. Reddie will have to prove that boys educated on his system are not too severely handicapped at the outset of the race. For the sake of educational progress it is to be hoped that he will get a fair field for his experiment, and good material to work upon. His schemes have more than a limited interest, and may set other schoolmasters thinking of ways and means for making school life the harmonious development of mind and body that it ought to be.

4. THE DINING HALL. (*Summer, 1892*).

Copyright

CHAPTER II.

A Pioneer School at Work. 1890.

CHAPTER II.

A PIONEER SCHOOL AT WORK, 1890.

THE following paper gives a brief sketch of the School during its first year of existence. It was written under great difficulties as to leisure, which will, I trust, excuse its shortcomings.

I have to express my obligations to Mr. J. H. Badley, one of my former colleagues, for assistance in writing several of the sections.

A PIONEER SCHOOL AT WORK.

(REPRINTED FROM "THE PIONEER" OF JANUARY, 1891, WITH A FEW CORRECTIONS AND ALTERATIONS.)

The New School Abbotsholme, in Derbyshire, opened on October 1, 1889, and has thus just completed its first year. This is then the proper moment to offer to the friends of the school some account of what has been done.

First we would return our grateful thanks to the editor of *The Pioneer* and the many kind friends who encouraged us at the start and aided us with counsel and support. That we have not, since the opening, told them of our doings until now, may have seemed ungracious. Our reasons were weighty. First of all, we had neither time nor energy even for the first of duties—the returning of thanks. Every moment was needed by our work here. Then, too, we wished to have something definite to report —some story of things done, as evidence that the confidence bestowed on us so generously had not been wholly misplaced.

Offering as we do our hearty thanks to all those whose kindness helped us to attempt this work, without which it might have remained unessayed, and must have been still harder to fulfil, we feel that we have less to show after all than we would wish. The office of criticism, however, does not belong to us.

We have done what we could, with the materials which came to hand, to overcome the difficulties in our path, and the prejudices which a new project encounters.

Not only had we undertaken a new kind of training without buildings made for the purpose, without being able to select a special group of boys for the experiment, but we had even to train ourselves for the work.

To have made the experiment under the best conditions we ought to have designed and built our own school-house, laid out our school estate, and planned every detail ourselves; we ought to have started our work, not with a group of boys such as might chance to turn up, all at different stages of growth, and trained under different influences, but with a select band picked for our purpose. And we ourselves ought to have been trained in the very same type of school as that which we wished to create.

We stumbled on the house we wanted almost without

looking for it. It was the first we saw, and though many more were visited, they were not so suitable. We were lucky, moreover, most lucky, with our boys. Almost all entered into our plans with enthusiasm, especially the seniors who had been at other schools. This was an agreeable surprise, for boys are apt to appreciate a school better when they have left. To the *sixteen*, with whom we started work a year ago, we owe much. Again, to find masters fit for the work was difficult; we needed exceptional men, men who could work on new lines, with originality and enthusiasm, but who would at the same time be willing to sacrifice many of their own wishes, and abate somewhat of their own ideals, for the general good. In this, too, we have been fortunate.

But our good fortune did not end here. Every one knows the saying, "The parent is the schoolmaster's enemy." We, of all people, might have expected to find this true. "A new broom sweeps clean," no doubt, but it is often expected to do more than sweep. "A new school on ideal lines" would be expected to do everything, and that at once. It would be expected to make bad boys good, lazy boys keen, delicate boys sturdy; and this in one year or term. Some letters indeed reached us asking if we did not prepare a boy to be a bishop or an admiral of the fleet. Other parents, again, wrote asking if we would guarantee that the school was absolutely perfect, that there would be no wicked boys, no ill-mannered ones, no stupid ones, to corrupt theirs. Curious it is how our own boys never can do wrong. Most of those, however, who inquired did seem to know what the real purpose of education was; and we have much cause to be grateful for the cordial kindness shown the school and ourselves by almost every parent of boys here. They have indeed recognised most warmly the good work done, and that has been our main encouragement to go on.

In giving some account of our year's work, it will be convenient to sum it up under the different heads of Physical and Manual, Intellectual, Artistic, Social, and Moral and Religious Development, for if it be admitted that education should not deal with only one of these, any educational system should be judged by its aims, methods, and results along all these lines.

I. Physical and Manual.

The aims kept in view, as stated in the circular issued last year,[1] have been these : to bring about a more wholesome physical development among the boys than is practicable merely through games ; to develop a knowledge of, and interest in, industrial occupations, and an appreciation of work done for all and necessary for the Commonwealth ; and, in particular, to promote a steady flow of nervous energy over the whole body during a larger portion of the day than is possible under the usual conditions of life at school.

With this in view, every boy is obliged, unless prevented by ill-health, to join in out-door pursuits, and to take part for several hours every day in some kind of drill, games, such as football and cricket, in carpentry, gardening, or the like. In carrying this out, the nature of the place, the farm, stables, and large gardens have been of the greatest assistance. How the day's work is arranged will be best understood from the following time-table. This varies with the different seasons ; we give that of last season.

[1] " A New School " (see p. 21).

TIME TABLE.

6.55 Rise [in Summer—Rise, 6.10 ; Drill, 6.30 ; School, 6.45–7.30].
7.15 Military Drill, Dumb Bells, or Run (according to the weather).
7.30 Chapel.
7.40 Breakfast—after which Dormitory Parade (bed-making and teeth-cleaning), and Violin Practice.
8.30 to 10.45 School (during the first Period, 8.30–9.15, the boys visit, in batches under captains, the earth cabinets in the garden).
10.45 to 11.15 Lunch, and, if *fine*, Lung drill in the open air, stripped to the waist (to teach breathing).
11.15 School.
[In Summer, if fine and warm enough, 12, Singing ; 12.20, Bathing in the River.]
1.0 Dinner.
1.30–1.45 Music Recital in Big School.
2 to 6 Drawing, Workshop, Gardening, Games, or Excursions on Foot or Bicycle, &c., &c.
6.0 Tea—after which Violin Practice.
6.45–7.30 Singing [in Summer the work omitted at 12].
7.30 Shakespeare Reading, Lecture, Rehearsal of Play, Concert, &c., each upon the appointed day.
8.30 Supper.
8.40 Chapel.

But how has this worked ? The best way to answer the question will be to enumerate some of the things done.

The first term (Winter, 1889) there was everything to put in order, a garden overgrown with weeds, a farmyard buried beneath accumulations of rubbish, dingles to clear, and so on. The first gardening operation was trenching and manuring, the first engineering work making and draining a road. Gates to tar, buildings to paint, the results of six years' neglect to repair—all this afforded abundant occupation. A football ground was enclosed, and, despite our scanty numbers, many a good game was played on it. In the workshop most had to learn the very elements of carpentry; but before long many were making simple things for use in the house.

The next term (Spring, 1890) there was still much left to do; forcing-frames to repair or remake, glass-houses to set in order, painting (including the proper mixing of paint), glass-cutting and fixing, and plenty of such jobs as the laying of a pig-sty and making of a duck-pond. Our farm man being laid up three days with influenza, three boys volunteered to fill his place in attending to the animals. Riding and also driving was taught by three of the elder boys, who also went to a fair and bought a horse. There was some bathing and fishing, and term ended with athletic sports.

Then came the Summer term with extended garden and farm operations, culminating in the making and carrying of hay; cricket and tennis took the place of football; bicycling and photographic expeditions became a favourite way of using the free afternoons; and one of the happiest hours of the day was that spent bathing in the river and in the sunlight on the banks. An excellent swimming place was found and furnished with a diving-board; a shelving beach opposite served for the learners; and under the teaching of the best swimmers all made good progress.

Meanwhile the boys had not been idle in the workshop.

From simple shelves and the like the majority had got on to picture-frames. A table, cupboard, diving-board, steps, duck-house, and wood-house—these were some of the things made. The list will show the principle observed, to set thoroughness, usefulness, and the service of the community above merely ornamental and selfish work. Lately, two boats have been built, and a third is on the stocks. The boys also saw some good cabinet work, for much of the oak furniture of the school was made by the resident craftsman in the workshop. On the farm the live stock had been steadily increasing. Horses, cows, fowls, pigs, ducks, and bees, but especially the horses and poultry, had been partially tended by the boys. It should be added that in the organisation and superintendence of all out-door work, games, &c., the elder boys were given a large share.

Some results of the varied routine of work are visible in the things made in the past year, and in the material improvements everywhere effected; but still more important, if less visible, results remain to be recorded now. There has been a steady growth of interest in the manual work itself. To the majority it was at first new and strange. But we have not been mistaken in supposing that in this direction the interests and aptitudes of some boys would find fullest scope. Even for the rest it is of high educational value. As already said, the organisation of the various departments was by degrees largely taken over by the boys themselves acting under direction. This principle has been carried, as far as possible, into everything. Our plan is to work the boys in three stages. The Juniors we train to trust fully and obey cheerfully the Seniors. The Middies are made to understand the

Why of everything. The Seniors are trained to *direct* the Juniors.

The influence of the life on the physique of the boys seems to be excellent. Some of the figures we have obtained are appended; but as yet the time has been too short for plotting out curves of development. The first measurements of mass, height, and chest girth were taken in March, 1890, one week before the end of the term, and, since then, they have been taken a few days after each term begins and a few days before each term ends (in order to avoid the error arising from disturbed appetite at these exciting seasons).[1]

Our object was to discover the rate of growth, in order to see the physical effect upon a boy of the altered conditions of his life, to see if each was being properly nourished, and if the place and life suited him. As the feeding of the boys was very carefully studied and was in many ways peculiar, we wished to be sure that it was answering our expectations. Some boys, moreover, were vegetarians from birth. We wished to satisfy ourselves that the vegetarian diet arranged for them here was sufficient.

Our educational work may of course be greatly aided by

---

[1] In many schools distinct allowance has to be made in the kitchen for the boys' probable loss of appetite during a week after beginning and end of term, due to a variety of causes, such as home sickness, excitement from novelty, change of air (climate), and of habits; nervousness at the unknown, after-effects of a journey, or excitement before it. I cannot, however, say that I ever observed this loss of appetite in boys here, except on the last morning at breakfast just before they start, and on the first night of term, at tea, just after their arrival. I have aimed at eliminating excitement by keeping everything moving on like a chronometer, steadily and quietly, up to the last possible moment, instead of having a sort of slow running down of the clock.—C.R.

A Pioneer School at Work

the comparison we can thus make between each boy's rate of growth at home during vacation and at school during term. If a boy loses weight, or gains weight more slowly at school than at home, then probably either the diet or the climate, or the school life is unsuitable for him. If many boys were to lose in this way, then it would be clear that there was something seriously at fault in our method and our life. To the other question—the quality of the added mass, its texture and its form—whether the boy is being *refined* while he is growing—to this, of course the Balance furnishes no clear answer. But it is important that the refining should, at any rate, not be at the expense of the gross mass. Well, our results so far are very interesting.

MASS (without clothes)—

During the Easter Vacation (4 weeks' interval).

Boys.			lbs.		each. lbs.		each per week. oz.
11	at Home	lose	15·25	—	1·37	—	4·4
7	,,	gain	11·87	+	1·62	+	5·4
3	{at School during Vacation}	,,	5·5	+	1·75	+	6 nearly

During the Summer Term (11 weeks interval).

			lbs.		lbs.		oz.
27	..	gain	101·87	+	3·75	+	5·5
3	..	lose	4·75	—	1·62	—	2·4

During the Summer Vacation (10 weeks' interval [nearly]).

			lbs.		lbs.		oz.
15	..	gain	44·12	+	2·87	+	4·7
6	..	lose	5·25	—	0·87	—	2·3

HEIGHT (with feet bare)—

During the Summer Term (11 weeks).

	ins.		each.
25 Boys gain	17·75	= nearly	0·75
5 ,, lose	2·12	= under	0·5

During the Summer Vacation (10 weeks).

	ins.		each.
18 Boys gain	8·5	= nearly	0·5
3 ,, lose	1·12	= nearly	0·5

If now, in the case of the *Masses*, we take the algebraic sum for each period, we obtain the following—

In the Easter Vacation each Boy at Home made — 0·6 oz. per week
In the Summer Term ,, ,, School ,, + 4·7 oz. ,,
,, ,, Vacation ,, Home ,, + 3·0 oz. ,,

It would be absurd to make too much of these figures, resulting as they do from such a short experience. But the general result, so far ascertained, is certainly good, and makes us believe that not only are we right in collecting these details as a check on our work, but that our system of feeding and clothing, and the general life here is building up big and strong men. It might be mentioned here that we have had a marvellous freedom, not merely from illness of a serious kind but even from trifling headaches and colds. The only illness we have had, was the influenza, which, being clearly infectious, was, notwithstanding every precaution, brought back by some after the Christmas vacation. But, though about a dozen took it, they had it in the mildest form, and all got over it in three or four days without any outside help whatever. This healthiness, in connection with the figures above, point to the conclusion that the conditions of life here are very favourable.

A Pioneer School at Work

These results may be due largely to climate, but must be due, in a high degree also, to the habits, the routine, the ideas, and the cheerfulness of the place. The boys are taught to see that every one ought to be healthy; that disease is the result of error, ignorance, overwork, misapplied work, or vice. They are taught to be careful in their personal habits, and made to understand the principles of personal and social hygiene; so that they co-operate themselves in the effort to keep the school wholesome throughout. Without this conscious co-operation, little can be done.

Those whom illness has threatened now and then are the staff. Living as we are the whole day with the boys, the nervous tension has been exhausting, and we had to learn to regulate our enthusiasm more skilfully. But after all, the strain of a first year is exceptional and should not be taken as typical of what is normal at a school of this kind.

II. INTELLECTUAL.

In all brain work our Aims have been the following: to train the boy to deal with *things* as well as with *words;* to pass upward from the *concrete* to the *abstract;* to show the *practical bearings* of the various items in the school work; and to arouse in the boys a feeling of the *use* of what is taught, and the desire to *learn for learning's sake,* without stimulus of marks and prizes. Our determination to dispense with the latter, so far from diminishing the scholars' interest in their work, has tended rather to intensify it, for they are thinking only of the subject, and not of accidental rewards. The staff too, having no elaborate calculations to make, have the *whole time for teaching*. During the past year we have begun teaching the following subjects :—

1. *Language*.—As a means of expression of observation and thought ; and in the first place our own. Speaking, reading, and writing, all means of education which have been too much neglected, receive here special attention, as well as grammar and simple composition as essential to the intelligent comprehension and expression of thought and feeling. After English we have taken French and German as supplying the means of comparison and contrast necessary to the understanding of language. So far, these have been used, instead of the usual Latin grammar, to furnish part of the necessary mental discipline. It is not, however, our intention to dispense with Latin altogether. In our scheme it comes in at a later stage, when some advance has been made in French and German. As for *method*, we speak the language as much as possible and keep grammatical intricacies in the background.

2. *Mathematics*.—In the lower school arithmetic and algebra are taught as far as possible together. The relation between arithmetic and logic is shown, as also the growth of the higher rules out of simple addition. Every effort is used to make the work concrete and to render the knowledge of the simplest operations intelligent and conscious. Algebra has been taught as a means of expressing and verifying the truths of other branches of mathematics in an abstract form ; for this purpose a general knowledge without the laboured learning of formulæ has been thought sufficient, except for those boys who show special aptitude or who will require special knowledge of the subject. Geometry has been taught mainly by the graphic method, and Practical Geometry, taught by the help of models and

the blackboard, has been preferred to Euclid's method. The work has been intimately connected with drawing, surveying, mechanics and engineering in general. Here again the importance of logical accuracy of expression has been insisted on. Particular attention has been paid to geometrical drawing. Working-drawings of picture frames, lockers, tables, &c., have been made for the workshop, and maps have been prepared from actual surveys of the gardens and outbuildings. Another practical branch of mathematics, Book-keeping, has been taught to every boy, and in connection with this, the accounts of different portions of the expenditure of the school have been given to certain of the boys to keep ; thus the accounts of the farm, garden, workshop, out-of-door-work, games, stationery, and books, chemical laboratory, drawing department, food, and fuel, are in their hands.

3. *Natural Science.*—That Nature-knowledge is as necessary for the education of the mind, as daily food for the growth of the body, is the obvious axiom with which we have started. Every boy therefore studies it. This does not, however, mean a particular branch, to the exclusion of the rest. The science is taught in cycles, starting from the ordinary facts and objects of daily life, and widening and growing in complexity with advancing experience and perception. In teaching it we approach it at the same time from the opposite sides of objective and subjective knowledge. Elementary facts of physics on the one side, the laws of personal life and of social health on the other. Elementary physics leading to dynamics and chemistry ; hygiene and the boys' relation to the school and to each other, developing into economics, have been the subjects taught. The simplest experiments,

made when possible with the commonest objects and without special instruments furnish our starting-points, and the aim throughout is to make the teaching thoroughly concrete by constantly referring to these fundamental experiments. Accurate descriptions and drawings have been made an essential part of the boys' work.

4. *Geography and History.*—The former as a link between Natural Science and Human Science has occupied a larger place in the program of all the boys than usual. The main work in history has been to show that human life is largely moulded by physical conditions, and that the geography of a country furnishes the chief key to its national, commercial, and spiritual development. English history has been made of course the groundwork. In both geography and history the aim has been throughout to awake intelligent interest in the observation of cause and effect and in the characters and movements of the drama rather than to load the memory with mere facts and dates.

As in class no marks are assigned, and there is no changing of places, it has not been necessary to arrange the various sets with reference solely to the boys' intellectual development. The latter may be the best arrangement for economising teaching, but it unwisely neglects other factors of progress recognised by a more complete conception of education. It is distinctly preferable to take into account all factors, physical, mental, and moral, and to organise the school upon a physiological basis. Our school order is one of age only ; and while in each department we let the best take the lead, we do not allow, still less force, a boy to specialise in one branch and neglect the rest, but by making his necessary work wide and varied and showing the relation and intimate connection of all its parts: we promote in him an "all-round" development. In the case of boys possessing obviously special gifts, or intended for special professions, the usual program of work has been largely altered; but in no case has any one of the four main divisions above enumerated been entirely omitted. An examination in all book work has been held every term, to test the knowledge, progress, and intelligence of each boy. The examinations have taken place two complete weeks before end of term so as to give time for correcting errors, and for bringing the term's work to a clear and distinct finish. The reports sent home at the end of each term attempt to sum up the term's results in every branch, and to indicate as clearly as possible each boy's absolute position in evolution compared with the normal or ideal youth. The parent's criticisms are invited and their co-operation forms an essential part of the scheme. The term's report is, so to speak, our invoice of goods sent home each vacation.

III. ARTISTIC.

1. *Drawing.*—The aim here has been first to develop in every boy a general useful power: to train hand and eye to steady accuracy, neatness, and quickness, enabling him to sketch apparatus seen or to illustrate ideas imagined; secondly, to discover latent talent among the boys, which is only possible where the subject is compulsory for all, and is taught for many hours in the week; lastly, to train the eye to see the harmonies of form and colour, and the aesthetic feelings to discern false taste. To realise this, drawing is taught to every boy.

Those who show talent for either aesthetic or mathematical work, or who need to gain proficiency in some branch for their special career later, work an hour daily. In the Geometry and Natural Science Classes drawing is insisted on, and on the other hand in the Drawing Class working drawings are got ready for the workshop. These have been chiefly for picture frames, and for such things as sets of lockers, tables, &c.

2. *Music.*—One of the chief features of the school is the music. Every boy is taught singing; more than two-thirds of the whole number learn instrumental music, and of these several learn violin as well as piano. There is an orchestra of eight boys. All have a fixed time and place for practice, which for so large a number is not very easy to arrange. Most of the boys are taught individually the right use of the voice. This is generally neglected in schools, yet it is as important for reading and speaking as for singing. In connection with this elocution, and occasionally on fine days lung drill is practised in the open air with the body stripped to the waist. Every week there is a musical evening, and every day a piano or organ recital after dinner.

There can be no doubt that this wide use of music has had a valuable influence upon the boys; their interest in practice is keen and sustained, and their appreciation of classical work is a growing factor in the school life.

3. *Literature.*—A considerable amount of reading aloud is done, in the belief that more is learnt from good reading than from mere class work in literature; and in this way the best Literature of the world and in particular that of this country and this century has been brought before the boys. One evening a week is specially set apart for reading Shakespere, and every day the chapel services are used not only to intensify the moral and religious life but to

train the aesthetic powers by associating the noblest ideas of human duty with the loveliest flowers of poetic genius.

IV. Social.

A great feature in the School is the substitution of social recreation in the evening for the customary preparation of work for the following day. Our object has been to accustom the boys to quiet, healthy, and rational amusement, in the society of persons older than themselves, and thus to teach them self-restraint without frigidity or awkwardness, and to train them to read aloud, or play the violin without a nervous shyness, or the nervous self-assertion which comes mainly from self-consciousness. The room in which the evenings are passed is only used for Chapel and for these social gatherings, lectures, and concerts. All noise is forbidden. The idea of the place being happy harmony, pictures, furniture, and statuary are chosen with this in view, and the room, its contents and the use made of it are intended to present together the idea of complete and harmonious life.

One evening in each week has usually been devoted to a lecture ; these have been given on subjects as varied as Greek Mythology, Trade Unions, Bee Culture, History of Music, &c. The last has been a course of lectures, extending over the greater part of a term, and copiously illustrated with selections from the works of the composers treated of. The lecture on bees was given in connection with the making of new hives in the workshop, to show the whole process of scientific bee-culture. For these hives a bee-house has just been built by the boys.

From the first there has been a large number of dramatic entertainments of different kinds, varied with recitations, songs, and the like, for which the boys fitted up a theatre. We have regarded performances of this kind as an integral part of education rather than a mere annual display. Some have been got up entirely by the boys, from impromptu charades to short comedy; and one term the story of Shakspere's Merchant of Venice was given by them on a larger scale, with scenery painted in the school.

There has been a Debating Society; and of late a School Magazine called *Strays*.[1] This is not a mere chronicle of passing events. They occupy but a page or two, the rest being devoted to literary work. It is largely illustrated, and appears but once in the term. The time and trouble spent on it make it of real use in developing literary and artistic power; and further it helps to bring before the boys the ideals of which the school as a whole is the embodiment.

Of special pursuits taken up by the boys, photography has been the chief. There are as many cameras as violins, and in the summer a good deal was done with them with excellent results. There is much in the immediate neighbourhood to repay the labour of carrying a camera; and Dovedale is easily reached by train or bicycle. A Museum is the next thing to establish; but our aim will not be so much to put away a collection of specimens in cases, as to make the whole house into a home for interesting and beautiful objects. For this, time is necessary, but at least a beginning has been made. Copies of

---

[1] The School owed the excellent conception of *Strays* to two of the masters, Mr. J. H. Badley and Mr. W. Clifford Pilsbury, who jointly organised and edited the boys' contributions, and themselves generously contributed literary matter, as well as drawings in line and in colour which served as charming models for the boys.

pictures by the great masters, casts of the best sculpture, furniture of the simplest and best make, these are no little in themselves, for without doubt the surroundings of our daily life exert an educational influence too often underrated.

V. Moral and Religious.

It is difficult to speak about such a subtle matter as the religious atmosphere of a school ; nor is it wise to speak about it at length. But it would not be right to pass over the matter altogether, the more so that, as we understand religion, every part of the life here is intended to be saturated with it. In other words, our wish is to present life to the boys, not as if divided into religious and secular fragments, but as one organic and harmonious whole. We wish them to realise that the day's routine from beginning to end is, after all, one long yet varied religious service, planned to perfect to the utmost every person here in body, soul, and spirit ; in senses, emotions, and thought. While the athletics, manual work, and physical culture perfect and refine his outer range of faculties, while the book-work and lectures develop and equip his mental powers, while the objects of beauty and variety of pursuits keep his heart glad and his eye bright, we do not forget that some portion of the day should be devoted to the highest duty of all. For one fourth of an hour, as the day begins, and again before it ends, the whole household gathers to express its community of hopes, of faith, and of endeavour, by an outward sign ; and with such resources as a young settlement can command, of lovely things, and harmonies, and thoughts, to direct the mind to the best and most exalted Ideals known to us. Children should not be vexed with dogmas which puzzle even learned men. They will hear of these when they are older. For our purpose it is enough and best to turn their minds towards those ideals which no one refuses to reverence, rather than to the doctrines which divide humanity. We wish them to bathe in the beautiful sunlight, rather than frighten each other with each other's shadows.

This, then, is what we have done in the year past. It is a beginning, yet no more than a beginning. Every step in advance makes another step at once possible and necessary. Already we are compelled to extend our borders: we have overflowed our present house, and annexed a cottage. We are planning more additions. We wish to dam the river and make it more suitable for boating. We have a bridge to build — the first of many engineering works in contemplation. We must add to our workshops and laboratory. All this needs time and effort, and encouragement from all who appreciate what we have done. We do not rest content with the past, but after taking stock of what we have actually accomplished, we remain firm in the convictions that inspired us, and strong in hope for the future.

October, 1890.   C. R.

PRESS NOTICES.

The Press notices of the School reprinted above criticised of course only our Aims and Methods, not our Practice. The First Year's Report: "A Pioneer School at Work," which describes our practice, is here appropriately followed by some Press notices, &c., which reflect public criticism upon the actual life of the School during

5. BIG SCHOOL. (*Summer, 1892*).

Copyright

its early years—in so far, that is, as its various customs attracted the attention of Parents or the Public.

Engineering, *August* 8, 1890.
THE EDUCATION OF ENGINEERS.
To the Editor of *Engineering*.

Sir,—As you endorse " P.'s " appeal by publishing it, and thus absolve correspondents beforehand from the charge of advertising, the following particulars may be offered to your readers respecting a school, the methods of which, in many respects novel, seem to be peculiarly well suited to the mental and physical training of lads destined for engineering. This is "The New School," opened last autumn by Dr. Cecil Reddie, at Abbotsholme, Rocester, on the Derbyshire side of the Dove. A newspaper article brought it to my notice, and a careful visit of inspection led to my placing there a boy of twelve. Two later visits, and the boy's return after one term's work, have led to the decision to send two of his brothers as well. Latin is not taught to the younger boys, and only to the seniors sufficiently to assist them in the study of their own and other modern languages : it is not followed as a means of mental discipline. Science, as " P." recommends, takes its place for that purpose, coupled with practical hand work, systematically carried out in the workshop, in the garden, and on the farm. The house is a fair-sized mansion of modern build, well found with conservatories and orchard houses, &c., and with a considerable estate attached, through which winds nearly a mile of the river Dove, providing good bathing, and some day, it is hoped, boating, when the boys have themselves carried out certain projected works in the way of dams and cuts. Bookwork begins early, and is over before the dinner-hour ; the rest of the day is divided between the workshops, cricket, and other games, field or garden work, and, in the evening, music, and a social gathering in—actually—a " drawing-room," where also ladies are to be found. Good engravings and other objects of beauty are everywhere. In all the school subjects the blackboard, and models and specimens, are used where possible, and it is clear that my boy has come back after one term with a better foundation for scientific training than I have been accustomed to find as the result of years of the ordinary perfunctory miscalled science-teaching of schools. Another unnatural thing about him (seeing that he is not a gushing youth by nature) is his liking for the masters. "They take so much trouble with us; they explain everything to us." Indeed, his first letter from school, more gracious than graceful, said, "It is like all holidays, they teach us in such an interesting way," and this is the key to what I think is going to be a great success. Hygiene is one of the subjects of study, and physiology as affecting health, and in matters of dress, diet, discipline, and exercise the school reflects the opinions certainly unconventional and possibly peculiar, but as I think mostly very wise, of the energetic man who has founded it, and who has collected round him a staff of masters apparently as earnest as himself. Companionship between masters and boys, without espionage; hardiness and manliness without roughness and brutality; earnestness without priggishness; and reasonable gentleness without namby-pambyism, seem to have been attained. Absent from home, I am not able to refer to the really interesting Prospectus of the school, but it sets forth (quoting from Ruskin, I think, but I do not remember the exact words) that its object is to teach habits of gentleness and justice, and the laws of bodily and mental health and their application, and to fit boys to earn their own living in after life. These objects seem to me in fair way of fulfilment, and after years of fruitless search I believe I have found a satisfactory school at last. It is not a cheap school, of course, but it is less costly than any of the "public" schools, even including many to which the title scarcely applies. If there are any other schools at all similar in principles or practice they are unknown to me, and certainly not from want of inquiry, for I share "P.'s" views completely, except that while abandoning classical study as a system of mental training, I would retain Latin as an aid to the understanding of modern tongues. When I last saw the school, some underground culvert or drain had burst in the orchard, and great works of engineering were in progress. The boys, in flannels, and not much of them, wallowed joyfully waist-deep in water and mud. A dam arose and the floods were curbed, and I thought I had never seen Kindergarten principles better applied in practice. The boys had something to talk over that evening.

Yours faithfully,

WEYMOUTH, *August* 5, 1890.   M. R.

A Pioneer School at Work

PALL MALL GAZETTE, *April* 18, 1891.

THE NEWEST "NEW SCHOOL" IN PRACTICE.

A TESTIMONIAL BY A PARENT TO "ABBOTSHOLME."

On the 26th of August, 1889, the *Pall Mall Gazette*, in an appreciative article, set forth the novel Program of " The New School" at Abbotsholme (Derbyshire), near Rocester, with the result that the writer paid it a visit early last year, when it was in the second term of its existence. What he saw so pleased him that he placed one of his sons there at Easter, and the result of two other visits to the school, with observation of the progress made by the boy on his return home for the summer holidays, led to two of his brothers being sent back with him. The father of three New Scholars—with more " coming on "—has a right to an opinion about The New School, and he offers it for what it is worth, though he has not the skill of a "special commissioner," and is entrusted with the expression of no one's views but his own.

The New School has apparently been designed by anticipation to meet the views of that vigorous scholastic reformer, the Emperor William II.—or, rather, so much of the Imperial views as may be found reasonably consistent with those of that very different authority, Mr. Ruskin. The school is to be a preparation for *life*, not for scholarships and exhibitions. Greek is scarcely in its program, and Latin is valued mainly for the help it gives in learning other languages and in understanding other literatures. Languages, science, art, and *handicraft* are the means of mental discipline ; and the importance attached to hand-work, as a means of training the mind as well as the body, is one of the most striking features of the educational system of Dr. Cecil Reddie, the Head-master. Scholarship, as a distinct aim in life, is not discouraged ; but "classical" studies (including Greek) will be regarded as special for certain boys only, just as military studies might be carried on, but only for boys who intended to enter the army.

Like Dr. Reddie (as quoted in your article mentioned above) the writer believes in the boarding-school as "the School of the Future." In these days of specialising, the art of making boys into men is a trade by itself, like other manufactures. The average parent is an expert in something else—not in this ; and, since the processes of manufacture should in this case be at work almost day and night, it is well that the raw material should be uninterruptedly in the hands of the skilled workman. " Home influences " are, or ought to be, good, but among us lazy and luxurious moderns they tend neither to steady work and discipline, nor to simplicity of life. It is easier, in fact, to import the humanising influences of home into the school than the discipline and simplicity of school into the home. It is apparently upon this line that Dr. Reddie is working : he regards the hours out of school as educationally the most precious, and endeavours to treat the boys as though they were in a Home ruled by a parent with nothing else to think about than the intellectual, moral, and physical improvement of his sons. There is interesting and healthful work, and play, for the boys from morning to night, and masters ready at all times to help in either ; yet there is no more espionage than at any public school. There are compulsory games, but these are alternated with gardening, and even farming, work—for a good deal of land is attached to the mansion which forms the school-house, and it has good gardens and glass-houses. As much as two hours daily are spent in the workshops, or in such building operations as are involved in the maintenance or improvement of the farm buildings ; in fact, the writer's first view of his son as a New Scholar revealed him at the top of a ladder in company with a pail of whitewash, of which he had transferred a little to the roof of a shed, and more to his own person. Perhaps he did not look pretty, but he had rarely looked so useful.

It is part of this very practical system of training that the spelling of h-o-r-s-e is a prelude not so much to rubbing down the noble animal (as in another famous but very different school) as to riding him ; they also who work in the peach-house eat of the fruit thereof. Hence the boys seem to enjoy the life thoroughly. He of the whitewash, not previously a demonstrative person, commenced his first letter home—"I am enjoying myself very much here. It seems more like holidays than schooltime. We are taught in such an interesting way." And when he returned after his first term, he was so full of praises of the masters (without any exception) and of the trouble they took to "explain things," that, as stated before, two of his brothers were sent to share in these unusual joys. And the only thing which caused misgiving to their fond parent was the outrageous and unnatural state of happiness in which he found all three when visited during the term. Surely these urchins have *nothing* to do but to enjoy themselves, was the parental doubt. But there was evidence to the contrary. No longer are our "little Adams fed at learning's woful tree" : it is a joyful tree now, thanks to new and better methods, probably as well known elsewhere as at The New School. But it is easy to imagine that where the chief studies are Natural Science, Art, Mathematics, and History, learning may wear a pleasanter face than where Latin and Greek push all other subjects into the background.

That Dr. Reddie's system can lead to great results of the class which the *Pall Mall Gazette* is so diligent in tabulating can scarcely be supposed. Perhaps such successes may be bought too dearly, and Dr. Reddie holds that a large section of the public agrees with him in thinking so, and hates the whole system of competitive cramming. The writer, himself a competition man, certainly does so; and he would rather see his boys grow up manly, healthy, sensible young fellows, with high ideals and the love of their neighbours in their hearts, and then send them forth to win such success as in the long run these qualities mostly bring, than have them crammed with knowledge, doubtless good for the winning of pecuniary prizes in early life, but good for little else.

Physiology and hygiene and "the laws of health" are systematically taught. This alone is a new departure of enormous value. Most things a man can learn better after he is grown up than while he is at school; but knowledge of the laws of health has, perhaps, its greatest use in youth. No doubt a boy who won't eat sweets because his grandfather died of gout, and who has been taught the possible connection at school, may be derided as a prig; but he is likely to make older bones than his less instructed brother. The family was not pleased when the before-mentioned youth (aged thirteen) made the seaside lodgings unbearable last summer if his cold bath was not always ready in the morning. But his father remembered his own schooldays, and recognised an improvement. And "the laws of health" cover even more important matters than diet and hygiene.

A high scholastic authority, lately quoted in the *Pall Mall Gazette*, says he cannot give up fagging: upon it depends the prestige of the magic "sixth." Yet at Abbotsholme this time-honoured institution is absolutely wanting,[1] notwithstanding that the system of making the older boys largely responsible for the younger ones is in force. The gentleness of the older boys in their dealings with their juniors is, in fact, very striking. Here, it is evident, people can be gentle without being namby-pamby, manly without being brutal, earnest without being prigs. The

---

[1] I did not divide the School definitely into Fags, Mids, and Prefects till 1892, so that the above is quite true. The hierarchic organisation, however, is in my view essential in school-life as well as in all communities. But I do not believe in having Prefects of 14 to look after boys of 10, nor Prefects of even 17 and 18 unless trained and supervised.—
March, 1898.   C. R.

teaching of Ruskin is avowedly over it all, and if there be some of us elders who think his counsels too perfect for this generation, we may at least be content to see them given a fair chance with the next one. The furniture, if plain, as becomes a school, is artistic ; good engravings are on the walls ; all the physical surroundings of the boys are pleasant, and even beautiful, and no trouble is spared to make the moral environment the same. How shall all this affect the future honours list ? The writer cannot say, but he thinks he knows how it ought to affect the lives of men.

BRADFORD OBSERVER, *March* 9, 1892.

An enterprise undertaken with a view of contributing towards the desired changes in society, which formed the subject of a lecture in Bradford last week, is the foundation of "The New School Abbotsholme," near Uttoxeter. While Mr. Edward Carpenter was in Bradford we gathered from him somewhat of the ideal which this novel departure in the training of boys sets before it. The main object is to give to the boys a more all-round education than is usual in ordinary schools—to educate, that is to say, not only the head, but also the hand and the heart. It is aimed, in the life of the boys, to cultivate their intellectual capacity, but in addition to give a much larger place to manual work, and also to social intercourse and moral influences. With this object the plan of work devotes the mornings only to book-learning or "lessons," the afternoon entirely to manual and physical exercises, and the evening to social enjoyment. The manual work includes practical joinering, gardening associated with botanical observation, a little road-making, haymaking, and attending to poultry and other live stock. A certain amount of housework is also done by the boys. There is, for instance, a dormitory drill, when all the beds in the room are turned and made with the simultaneity of a regiment of soldiers. The evening occupations, which include recitations, music, and simple dramatic performances, are intended to have the effect of promoting a cordial and sociable feeling between boys and masters. Such abnormal studies as cramming for scholarships, and particularly for scholarships at an early age, are entirely discouraged. The general theory of the school is to develop the boy's nature up to the age of about sixteen, so as to lay the foundation of a good man, and after that age to begin to specialise his education in accordance with his probable avocation in life. The school is entirely in the hands of the Headmaster (Dr. Reddie), who is full of enthusiasm and impregnated with the social and educational ideas described above.

PALL MALL GAZETTE, *August* 22, 1892.

"AN OFFSHOOT OF ABBOTSHOLME."

"The New School Abbotsholme," in Derbyshire, which was described in the *Pall Mall Gazette*, now three years ago, has already prospered sufficiently to put forth an offshoot. This is a new "new school," to be opened shortly by Mr. J. H. Badley, M.A., at Bedales, Hayward's Heath. In the main, "Bedales" will be conducted on the lines of Abbotsholme. There is no royal road to knowledge; but "what is wanted," says the prospectus, is "a substitution of the mountain-path for the treadmill"—a happy phrase. But probably the newest thing about these "new schools" is the prominence given to manual labour. Everybody at Bedales is to learn not only practical carpentering, but market-gardening. "It is visibly productive for the common good; it is healthy outdoor work; and it helps the design of touching life at as many points as possible by giving boys a practical idea of what is, after all, the staple work of the world." Of course there will be the usual school games also; but undoubtedly the modern "athletic mania" will stand some tempering with potato-digging.

PALL MALL GAZETTE, *October* 5, 1892.

SCHOOLING WITHOUT TEARS.

A CHAT ABOUT "BEDALES."

"It's pretty; but will it work?" was probably the comment of a good many readers on the outline which appeared in these columns three or four years ago, of "The New School Abbotsholme." It has worked so well that Dr. Reddie's lieutenant, Mr. J. H. Badley, is now starting yet another New School on his own account on lines in the main the same, and with views on the Greek Particles and potato-digging, short hours indoors and long out, to say nothing of that enticing "light meal before early school," all only confirmed and defined by the experience gained at the pioneer institution. Determined to be educationally up to date, therefore, we asked Mr. Badley in his turn to take up his parable.

WHAT IS WRONG WITH THE PUBLIC SCHOOLS?

"The points in which we faddists want reforms," he explained, "are—in a couple of sentences—the early specialisation, which exerts its narrowing influence just as much on 'modern sides' as ever it did under the monopoly of the Latin grammar and the all-pervading atmosphere of individual competition, with its machinery of marks and prizes and scholarships, subordinating the higher ideals of education to what will 'pay,' and the interests of the majority to those of the few who are to swell the school honour lists. Involved in all this is the inevitable neglect of character-training, general culture, the humanising side of life. These are roughly the things which we think it may be easier to reform in new schools free from the outset to work by new educational lights."

"'I see Bedales is described as '*A school for boys of about nine to fifteen.*' Do you contemplate a boy going on to a public school afterwards?"

"Certainly, if the public school and university course is what he is destined for. All I ask is that the years up to fifteen should be rescued from competitive specialising in a narrow groove, either 'classical' or 'modern,' and devoted to laying a sound foundation and developing the various faculties harmoniously."

"And the means? Could you pick out a few main features?"

"FEATURES" OF THE NEW SCHOOL.

"The broad range of studies, calculated to find out every boy's particular bent; the organised training of body equally as of mind; the introduction of manual arts and crafts into the regular course; the reform of teaching methods in 'bookishness' and other respects; the short hours of pure brain-work, and the time spent in the open air; the attention paid to health, food, personal habits; the training of character by substituting appeals to public spirit for appeals to individual rivalry, by developing the social side, and by a strong element of womanly influence in the school."

"As to hours?"

"Only four hours of brain-work; four hours of physical or quasi-physical work—hand, eye, and ear; ten hours for sleep, and the remaining six for meals, games, &c. Brain-work in the morning; bodily work and play in the afternoon ; in the evening, not 'preparation,' but music, reading, and the 'humanities.' "

"Is not your range of study rather too large for your short hours ? "

"No ; experience proves that children can absorb much more in a morning's work if there is variety in it. Then, too, a course of science and language teaching, which would be wide indeed if one took, say, first optics and then astronomy, 'did' French before beginning Latin, and so on, becomes quite practicable, without either muddle or cramming, when one carries forward science as a whole and language as a whole and aims only at laying a sound elementary foundation. And there is a tremendous gain in time and energy when one does not lavish several hours a day on Latin grammar and memory-work."

"Ah ! that brings us to a knotty point. How do you decide the battle of the 'classics' at Bedales ? "

THE "CLASSICAL" CONTROVERSY : LATIN, BUT ENGLISH FIRST.

"In a way which will please the zealots on neither side, I fear. We abandon frankly the idea that the " classics " are studied at school for the sake of the literature. The literary value we try to bring home in readings, stories, translations. Latin will have its place for all, if only as the best training in the laws of language, which are also the laws of thought. But these the boy will have got some understanding of from English teaching before he does a word of Latin, and grammar will have lost half its terrors and all its mystery by the discovery that it can be deduced from the unconscious methods of his own everyday talk. Latin, by all means, but English first. The time is gone by for 'a scholar and a gentleman' to grow up knowing next to nothing of his own country so long as for a few years of his life he can put together a passable verse in Latin."

THE "GOSPEL OF POTATO-DIGGING."

"Does not the 'Gospel of Potato-digging' savour a little—if I may say so—of 'fad' ? "

"No doubt, if you christen it so, and take it out of its place in the system as only one of many means to an end. Surely most people feel a tendency at schools to overdo cricket and football—over-specialisation in games as well as work—and to regard athletic prowess as the main end of school life. And some games tend to become a class distinction and to suggest a contempt for 'work.' This, as well as the use and pleasurableness of the various handicrafts, has given rise to the idea of manual labour as an element in a liberal education. Already a workshop forms part of the equipment of a school. In getting a step further putting carpentry as well as drawing and music into the regular curriculum, and adding gardening as well, we regard the alternation of these various arts and crafts with pure brain-work and pure games as preventing over-pressure in either."

No Marks, no Prizes.

"I gather that marks and prizes will not exist at Bedales? Would you eliminate the spirit of emulation altogether?"

"Oh, no! Where it takes the form of common effort, of public spirit, of *esprit de corps*, it is as good a force to work with as man need wish. I don't care for telling each boy that if he beats the others he will get a copy of Dr. Somebody's 'Self-Made Men' in treed calf. But I have no objection at all to telling a class of boys that if they all do their best they will get an extra half-holiday. Marks and prizes after all, only act as a stimulus to a few boys near the top, and one can well dispense with that stimulus when it is done as part of a general reform of teaching methods: an attempt to put in practice the ideas formulated by modern scientific educationists. To awake the faculties about any new piece of knowledge before appealing to mere memory; to proceed to the unknown organically from the familiar; to aim at developing a subject in the order natural to a child's mind hearing of it for the first time, not in the order which seems natural to a text-book writer rearranging knowledge which is to him a commonplace: these are some of the principles I mean."

All Work—but Half Play.

"And in practice? Could you give a few illustrations?"

"Well, in language teaching (for modern languages, that is) I have decided to adopt M. Gouin's system, lately described in the *Pall Mall Gazette*. A member of my staff is now studying the system with M. Gouin himself. In carpentry I hope to avail myself of the Sloyd system, and in class-singing—like the Board Schools—of the tonic sol-fa. But there are scores of small ways in which a teacher can apply the great maxim that *doing* and *making* should go hand-in-hand with learning.

Barracks and Home: Woman's Influence.

In the course of some remarks on character training and the *laisser aller* policy of many schoolmasters, Mr. Badley said:—

A Pioneer School at Work

"It is not caution so much as moral cowardice which is silent on the difficulties of boys at a critical period of their development. The science course of every boy should include some elementary physiology. But since mere head-knowledge, though better than mere ignorance, is not enough to keep a boy or man from going wrong, more can be done by establishing a frank and friendly footing with the boys individually, and securing a healthy and open atmosphere for happy comradeships among the boys themselves. Above all, I place the abolition of that curious relic of the monastic habit of thought which deprives boys, when herded together at school, of that which is one of the best and most effective forces of home life—the presence and direct influence of women. The School of the Future is probably the mixed day-school. But as things are, there are immense advantages attaching to the common life of a boarding-school when it is not divorced too hopelessly from the home and allied too much to the barracks."

Two Sorts of Human Beings.

"One word more, Mr. Badley. Say what we will of cramming, there are boys for whom a liberal education and a start in life are dependent on their paying their way by prowess in the examination-field. Would not such a boy be handicapped in the race by starting at Bedales?"

"Undoubtedly, up to the period of 'minor' or 'junior scholarships,' perhaps even later; it depends how far a given examination takes into account organic power of using faculties as compared with concrete acquirement. If the parent's wish or necessity is that the boy should carry off these prizes at all hazards, I would rather not have him. But, of course, I believe that the reformed system of education is bound to tell in the end, even in the pure 'scholar,' much more in the man, the citizen, the cultivated human being. Even the boy who wishes to take university honours may not be ready to sacrifice everything else. And we are—or we ought to be, 'for let not him that putteth on his armour boast as he that putteth it off'—proportionately better equipped for turning out the man of affairs, action, business, everyday life, to say nothing of the colonist. A lad who can handle an axe as well as a bat, splice a broken trace, mend his own clothes like a sailor, swim a swollen ford, level a road, knock together a box or a table, graft an apple-tree: a lad who has learnt that these and other things which are useful to men are not unworthy a gentleman—such a lad is obviously the ideal colonist. In a London office or chambers the things themselves are not so obviously indispensable; but the sort of resourceful and self-reliant character which they imply is nowhere a drug in the market, and the open-air feeling which they suggest is perhaps all the more valuable in a boy's experience if his after-life is destined to be spent in the hum of a town. A boy who does not 'know a hawk from a hernshaw,' who cannot give a name to the simplest flower he meets on a country walk, nor tell a single star in the sky of a clear night, to whom a field of barley is as a field of wheat, and the rotation of crops as much a mystery as the precession of the equinoxes ; a boy who knows fish as they appear at table ; and to whom the lie of the strata in a quarry-cliff says no more than the combed graining on a deal door ; a boy who would be non-plussed by half the small contretemps of life if he happened not to be at one end of a bell-pull with a servant at the other—such a boy may get along through the world in a good enough black coat, but . . . . well, he's a poor product, surely, of this world of ours ! "

SEED-TIME, *January*, 1893.

The latest news from The New School Abbotsholme, Derbyshire, is that Dr. Reddie and his assistants are going ahead very well with forty boys in the school. The organisation has been improved, the material to work on is good, and the results have been in every way very satisfactory. Their work has been tough, but the fruit of their labours is now beginning to be seen.

REVIEW OF REVIEWS, *November* 15, 1893.

TWO EXPERIMENTS:
"ABBOTSHOLME" AND "BEDALES."

Along with other signs which are now visible of a stirring among the dry bones of education, two schools have lately been founded on somewhat novel lines, embodying in several respects what may be called *Review of Reviews* principles. One of these, Abbotsholme, was founded five or six years ago, and, under the vigorous and enthusiastic care of Dr. Cecil Reddie, the Headmaster and Founder, is now an assured success. Bedales, which was founded only last year by Mr J. H. Badley, formerly Dr. Reddie's Assistant-master, and like him an educational enthusiast of strong practical bent, promises apparently no less well. The two schools are quite independent, and to some extent each has its own lines ; but they both set in the forefront the principles to which I referred. Among these is the recognition that half our old Teaching Methods are as obsolete as the stage coach. In our days, educationists have begun to learn their business afresh, studying from the point of view not of the teacher merely but of the taught.

The result of this is the development of systems like the Kindergarten, Sloyd, Tonic Sol-fa, and M. Gouin's, and the free use of models, games, and the magic lantern for the purposes of work as well as play. Dr. Reddie and Mr. Badley are strong on Reform of Educational Methods, on the plan of enrolling eye and hand along with ear as the schoolmaster's Triple Alliance, and calling nothing common or childish which may help to interest a child and make him catch some notion of what his teacher is driving at. Allied with these reforms in method is the doing away with the system of narrow competitive cram under which Latin Grammar and other things, excellent in themselves (science, for instance, in many so-called modern schools or "modern sides" of classical ones), are to monopolise an English boy's best learning years, to the practical exclusion of all knowledge or interest about the great facts of his own country, past and present, here and over seas. This blunder is doomed. National patriotism is worthy of a place among the school subjects of the new era. Another impulse of the times, equally healthy, is the instinct of escaping from the eternal round of factories, machines, and machine-made education, with its competitive individualism, to the atmosphere of manual crafts and outdoor industries. Dr. Reddie and Mr. Badley maintain that, at most schools, the alternative is between book competition and games competition, and that even our good British sports, with their possibilities for bringing out the spirit of co-operative comradeship, tend to become a sort of specialised class-amusement, as if cricket were the only kind of work a gentleman could properly do with his hands. Mr. Ruskin with his road-making and weaving, Edward Carpenter with his market-gardening, Mr. Gladstone with his tree-felling, should highly approve the way in which at these schools gardening and carpentry and the like are put into the regular day's program.

In some photographs which have been sent me, Abbotsholme boys are seen building a cricket pavilion, a boat, a dovecot; Bedales boys bridging a lake, draining a football field, digging a garden bed. One breezy photograph shows the Abbotsholme boys bringing the hay harvest home, in fine old style, with harp, sackbut, psaltery and all kinds of music. The idea is that the varied day with its alternations of manual and brain work and games, and social recreations in the evening, is so interesting that the youngsters need less driving during the brief hours at the desk. Very brief these seem, compared to the usual time-table ; but then both Abbotsholme and Bedales disavow any wish to be a wheel in the great "Competition Mill," the pivots of which are scholarships and money prizes. Marks and prizes, by the way, are dispensed with at both schools, and I am assured that their presence is not at all missed.

But of those points which deserve special mention in these pages perhaps the chief is what I may call the Anti-obscurantism of both these schools on the great character question.

Both assert strongly the schoolmaster's duty to look after Character equally with mind or body. No school on earth can make up for the want of a good home in this respect. But it is something to have the importance of the thing practically recognised. How the special dangers and difficulties to which growing boys are open are slurred over at the average public school is a commonplace. Things may not be quite so bad as they were made out by a recent writer in the *New Review*; but from Dr. Welldon's reply, equally with the article itself, it was clear that in the hushing-up policy, as in other things, Headmasters are apt to follow instead of leading the average British worshipper at the shrine of Ydgrun. How absurd it is to herd boys together on the barrack system, away from all home and womanly influences, and then to affect to be shocked at some of the worst features of barrack life reproducing themselves ! Not a word is said frankly recognising the boy's difficulties and temptations : Björnson's bold advocacy of simple lessons in physiology would be scouted out of court, and then, when a scandal comes out, a scapegoat or so is made—often some wretched youth more sinned against than sinning, who is ruined for life to bolster up the great conspiracy of silence—and everything goes on as before.

At the present day happily the braver and more earnest schoolmasters are beginning to rebel against old superstitions in this matter, and there is a refreshingly healthy tone about the pronouncements of Abbotsholme and Bedales on the subject.

6. THE INMATES. (*Winter, 1892*).

Copyright

CHAPTER III.

A Dutch Professor's Visit and Verdict.
December, 1892.

CHAPTER III.

A DUTCH PROFESSOR'S VISIT AND VERDICT, DECEMBER, 1892.

A VISIT TO AN ENGLISH BOARDING SCHOOL.

(Translated from the Dutch with the Author's permission.)

From VRAGEN VAN DEN DAG.—*H. Gerlings, Amsterdam* ; *January*, 1893.

ONE need not be a very sharp observer to see, even in a very short visit to England, the immense difference which exists between the education there and that in Holland. One fact, which shows itself instantly, is this : in Holland it is an exception to send boys to Boarding Schools ; in England it is the rule.

The crusade preached in Holland against such institutions has had this consequence, that they are only used for boys who have to be prepared for an early examination (as, for example, that for the Navy or Army), or for boys who are unruly at home, for whom therefore the Boarding School is necessary, as a kind of reformatory.

In Holland boys of all classes have the same *primary* education. From the completion of the 6th to the completion of the 12th year, they attend the public Primary Schools. Subsequently, boys of the artizan clsss, &c., become apprentices, while, of the rest, those who desire a Secondary Education separate, going either to the Hoogere Burgerschool (Realschule), or to the "Gymnasium" ("Classical" School).

The former group are intended to become Engineers, Manufacturers, Indian Civil Servants, Merchants, Agriculturists. They finish their education either at the Polytechnicum of the Colonial Institute at Delft, or at one of the Commercial Schools, or at the Agricultural School of Wageningen.

The latter group go—after their course at the "Classical" School—to one of the four Universities, Leiden, Utrecht, Groningen, or Amsterdam, in order to study Law, Medicine, Natural Science, Philology, Philosophy, Theology, &c.

In Holland, therefore, the boy is sent to a Boarding School only when it is absolutely inevitable, while in England every father sends his son there, if he can possibly afford it.

But in England also the Boarding School has been attacked. Who does not remember the philippics of Dickens' "Nicholas Nickleby," &c.? These attacks, however, did not destroy, but improved, them.

Involuntarily the question presents itself: why has England preserved an institution which Holland has condemned? Are the Englishmen more conservative and more attached to old customs than the Dutch? I do not believe it, and I am delighted to find Professor Pierson of Amsterdam University supports this view. What he says, in the October number of *De Gids*,[1] both about the detestable and stultifying examination mania in Holland and about the conservatism of our professional scholars must be approved by every thoughtful man. To repeat his own words :—

"The Dutch system of education, with its ignorance of pedagogics, has produced a young generation devoid of life, energy, and self-reliance."

In England it is different. One finds there possibly less theoretical knowledge, but certainly a more healthy and vigorous race, able to go through the world on its own legs. Both countries are rivals in sticking to deep-rooted old customs; therefore there must be another reason why the English retain schools which we Dutch have nearly abandoned.

The reason, in my opinion, is this: In Holland our ideas about education are quite different from those of the English. I remember reading, some months ago, an article in one of the leading English papers, *The Daily Telegraph*,[1] a extract from which will make the difference clear to every Dutchman.

"Our whole system of modern education may be open to the reproach that the bulk of the boys can go through school creditably without acquiring any great amount of book-learning, at least to an extent commensurate with the cost of their education. At French, and still more at German Gymnasia (and we may add, even more at the Dutch), boys undoubtedly learn more at less cost. On the other hand, *if the object of*

[1] October, 1892.

education is not so much to impart knowledge as to train the pupils for the business of life, our English school system may fairly claim to be successful."

Here lies, in my opinion, the difference between the English and, if I may so call it, the Continental education.

The former strives to train pupils for the business of life, the latter strives to impart knowledge.

As we gradually realise what *The Daily Telegraph* means by "Education for the business of life," the difference between the English and the Dutch ideas becomes still clearer.

It is, of course, the aim in Holland also to prepare boys for the business of life. But we expect to attain this by cramming them for the innumerable prescribed examinations which must be passed before a boy, or man, is handed over to the public.

What, on the contrary, is the aim which the Englishman has in view? Listen to the same article: "Learn to be clean morally as well as physically, to speak the truth, and to be just and honourable in all your dealings; . . . to be manly, brave, and upright." While with us the cardinal point is the development of the mind (so, at least, it is called), with them the main thing is the formation of character. And with what results? Though every Dutchman may be surprised at the inferior knowledge of his social equals in England, it is an undeniable fact that when we are competitors in the struggle for life, the Englishman gets the better of us.

In my opinion this is mainly due to the fact, that the English boy is sent away—as a rule in his tenth year—to a school where he learns to shift for himself, to work his own way up and to fight his own battles.

But any one who might conclude, that people in England are satisfied with the present organisation of education there, would make a great mistake. On the contrary, Primary and Secondary Education are both constant subjects of discussion.

In Holland the education of the boy is divided up, much to the detriment of harmonious development. The school exists only to instruct. The master does not, and cannot, attempt to study, and form, the boy's character. The latter is *supposed* to be done at home. But is this done, and can it be, in reality? In most cases I think we must say, No. The majority of fathers see their sons only during meal-times, for the boys are either at school or busy with their "home tasks." Besides, most of the fathers are absorbed in business which gives them no leisure as a rule till the boys are in bed.

8

I will not deny that the plan of keeping children as long as possible at home has the great advantage of making the family tie, especially between brothers and sisters, much stronger ; but there is a great disadvantage. Our boys remain awkward much longer. It is not necessary to compare Dutch boys with English boys of the same age to prove this. It is sufficient to compare a Dutch Naval or Military cadet of sixteen, after his one year's training, with a boy who has remained at home. At once one sees the difference : the former has learnt to act for himself, *i.e.*, to shift for himself and go his own way.

English parents confess openly and honestly that they are not able to educate their own children properly themselves, and that therefore rather than do it improperly, they hand them over to persons who make education their exclusive study.

At the beginning I myself, I must confess, disapproved of the English system, and was a warm defender of the idea that " the child ought to be educated to manhood by, and in the bosom of, his whole family. I was the champion of the opinion that it was the beautiful task of the parents to guide and form the characters of their children."

I discussed this point frequently with English parents, accusing them of employing the boarding-school system to cloak their own love of ease and comfort. But the following events ultimately obliged me to change my mind. My brother-in-law, who was unable to look after his son's education on account of his being resident in Mexico, handed the boy over to me with the express directions to place him in a particular English school. In carrying out his instructions, I had the opportunity of visiting this school and becoming acquainted with some of those persons who devote themselves entirely to the education of boys. I think it will be interesting to give an account of my impressions of this school, especially as it differs in several ways from most of the so-called " Public " Schools of England, such as Eton, Rugby, and Harrow.

Many complaints had been made in England about the antiquated methods of instruction, and especially about the insufficient harmony in the curriculum and the inadequate provision for physical (not to mention intellectual and moral) education.

Amongst these critics was the man who founded in 1889, " The New School Abbotsholme." Not content with mere complaints, he proceeded to realise his ideas of physical, mental, and moral education, by creating a practical scheme.

In the centre of England, and in the county of Derbyshire, know for its beautiful scenery and healthy climate, near the romantic Dovedale

A Dutch Professor's Visit and Verdict

and the busy potteries, close to the village of Rocester, this pioneer discovered a large country house with extensive grounds and gardens. Though the place looked like a wilderness, as it had been unoccupied for six years, nevertheless, its size made it suitable, and the healthy, beautiful country decided him to make it his base of operations.

On the 1st of October, 1889, The New School Abbotsholme was opened. The aims and methods of the new enterprise were described in a short pamphlet, and a brief Prospectus issued. I extract some passages stating the objects of the school :—

"1st. To bring about a more thorough physical development among the boys than is practicable merely through games.

"2nd. To develop knowledge of, and interest in, industrial occupations and an appreciation of work done for all and necessary for the common good ; and—

"3rd. To promote a steady flow of nervous energy over the whole body during a larger portion of the day than is customary under ordinary conditions."

The main principle on which this system seems based is : Make the boys, before all things, into strong and healthy *men*. The old adage, "Mens sana in corpore sano," peeps through everything. Especially on a personal visit one can see how this principle has been logically carried through. The most careful mother cannot show a greater anxiety for the health of her darling than that which is brought into practice here. "You will remember, Madam, how you used to weigh your first-born during the first months, in order to see if the growth of the baby was normal." Here the same thing is done ; every boy is weighed and measured at the beginning and at the end of every term. Accurate accounts are kept in order to see if height and weight are normal. The results show if the adopted system of feeding, clothing, &c., is satisfactory. Do not be afraid that your boy will become a "Malade imaginaire ;" nothing of the kind. "The boys are taught " (I quote again) "to see that every one ought to be healthy ; that disease is the result of error, ignorance, overwork, misapplied work or vice. They are taught to be careful in their personal habits, and are made to understand the principles of personal and social hygiene so that they coöperate themselves in the effort to keep the school wholesome throughout."

One sees immediately that at the head of this school is an intelligent person penetrated with the teachings of modern hygiene. And the results ? Splendid ! At my first visit to the place, I was struck by the fact that all the thirty-five boys were fresh and healthy-looking.

When my nephew, after four months, came to spend his holidays with me, I hardly recognised him.

The greatest care is taken to secure cleanliness and fresh air. Every boy takes a cold bath on getting up. Every soiled article is immediately removed from the bedroom. The windows are only closed when it is exceptionally windy. In case of illness (unless merely of a trifling kind) the patient sleeps in a separate room. There has not yet been, however, during the three years' existence of the school, a single case of serious illness.

The boys get up in summer time at 6.10, in winter time at 6.55. They are allowed twenty minutes for bath and dressing and for stripping beds. On coming downstairs they get biscuits and milk, after which comes drill. Next follows class for three-quarters of an hour, chapel, and then a substantial breakfast. Half an hour follows, in which they make their beds, clean their teeth, and visit the earth cabinets. From 8.30 till 12 come classes, usually with a quarter of an hour between each for running about outside. Between twelve and one singing, or in summer swimming in the river which runs through the estate. At one dinner. I was very much impressed by the substantial nature of the banquet and the conviviality of the boys. Imagine a large room, simply furnished, a buffet and dresser in natural oak, the walls painted in harmonious colours, with two large windows giving a delightful panorama; in the centre of the room a large table, occupied by Dr. Reddie and his staff of assistant-masters, the ladies, and any guests who happen to be visiting the school. I found some on all my visits, thanks to Dr. Reddie's hospitality. Round this main table were four or five others occupied by the boys divided into groups; those of the same age, and those that are chums as much as possible together.

What drew my special attention was the fact that everywhere, on buffet, mantelpiece, and on each table were flowers, though all my visits were in the winter (November or February). The flowers which I noticed everywhere were grown in the conservatory, and are looked after partly by the boys. The etchings, photographs of celebrated masterpieces, and engravings, are also nearly all framed by them.

The boys are not in any way hindered from full liberty to converse and they help themselves. There is no constraint, and the whole impression is decidedly agreeable. Dinner is opened and closed by chanting a Latin grace. As soon as dinner is finished Dr. Reddie gives out any orders for the rest of the day. He divides the boys into dif-

A Dutch Professor's Visit and Verdict

ferent groups, and gives each of them their task. After that, all of them, boys and master, go to the large hall—a plain, but artistically-furnished room, with a splendid outlook. Here some music is performed, generally something of Beethoven, Chopin, Schumann, or Bach (the Maestro particularly beloved in England). After music is over, the boys disperse. One group goes to the drawing-class, another goes to the workshop, another works in glass-house or garden, or they all go an excursion or play football.

At six o'clock all meet again in the dining-hall for tea, a meal composed of bread, butter, meat, jam, and tea; after which singing lessons are given to some, while others occupy themselves with reading and studying their parts for the theatre.

Once a week—on Wednesday evening—the day when the violin professor comes from Derby, all meet together in the drawing-room, where all kinds of performances are given. Everybody contributes what he can. I assisted once at such an evening, and not only amused myself greatly but enjoyed hearing a very good performance of Beethoven's "Moonlight Sonata." I remember still a very nice youngster of about twelve who recited a very funny monologue, to the great delight of us all, visitors as well as schoolfellows.

I think that these weekly gatherings afford an excellent training, because—as the Founder well describes it—" it accustoms the boys to quiet, healthy, and rational amusement in the society of persons older than themselves, thus teaching them self-restraint without timidity or awkwardness, and training them to read aloud or play the violin without the nervous shyness or the nervous self-assertion which comes mainly from self-consciousness."

It is to be wished that every educational institution would imitate this excellent and useful example.

The development of the boys' artistic powers is also a matter of great solicitude. The room where the boys spend their free time and amuse themselves suggests the idea of complete and harmonious life. One finds there the photographs or copies of some of the most celebrated masterpieces of pictorial and plastic art. Neither the dining-hall nor the big school suggested any idea of one being at a school. The boys are made comfortable, and the result is satisfactory, because, notwithstanding strict rules and a strict application of them, Abbotsholme never suggests the idea of a barrack or a prison.

Involuntarily one gets the impression that the boys are contented and happy. It is hardly credible, but nevertheless true, that the school is their pride. Every one exerts himself to contribute something to make it as perfect and beautiful as possible. When one remembers that everything, which now looks so exceedingly well kept, was three years ago a mere wilderness, and keeps in mind that this change has been mainly done by the boys, one recognises how splendidly this system works.

Everything is made on the spot, tables, chairs, picture-frames, and even two boats, by the boys, under the guidance of a skilful workman; while gardening is done under the supervision of a trained gardener The hay is cut and the crop harvested by the boys.

They have a regular bee farm under the supervision of one of the masters, Mr. Neumann, a German. They have put up a telephone which connects the main buildings with the cottages, where some of the masters live.

On the excursions made per foot or per bicycle, photographs are taken of the best views, and these are placed in an album with short descriptions by those boys who feel inclined. It looks as if everything was done by free-will and nothing by compulsion. And so indeed it is.

The end at which the Founder has aimed, that everything should be done for the common weal, or commonwealth, this is, in every respect, obtained.

Those who would like to know more about the work done by the boys should read the report published in the *Pioneer* of January, 1891, in which is paid the following homage to the boys :—"We were lucky, most lucky, with our boys. Almost every one entered into our plans with enthusiasm, especially the seniors, who had been at other schools."

At Abbotsholme the antagonism which usually exists in a school between boys and masters has been avoided by the same means which will end the struggle between capital and labour, *i.e.*, by coöperation and participation." Masters and pupils coöperate together and share in the result—an expanded life for all. "My learning is playing and my playing is learning," as the old Dutch song says, finds here its practical realisation, for in this school even the recreation has to some extent a utilitarian aspect.

I am sorry that I can only dwell briefly on the system of instruction. But one thing I know, namely, that special attention is given to reading, writing, and elocution, details of education, which, as the Headmaster of this school remarks, are too often neglected—the truth of which remark we know only too well in Holland. Further, they have abandoned the old English method of teaching first Latin and then modern languages.

Here they begin with French, then teach German, and finally Latin, and in some cases Greek.

An important place in the curriculum is given to Geography and History. From their own mouth you can hear on what lines these subjects are taught.

"In both Geography and History the aim has been throughout to awaken intelligent interest in the observation of cause and effect, and in the characters and movements of the drama rather than to load the memory with mere facts and dates."

There is no cramming for examinations.

Great value is laid on the reading of good books, and the school possesses already a valuable library.

A school of an existence so short cannot, of course, exhibit the results of its instruction yet. The concrete case which lies within the limits of my own personal observation give me every reason to believe that Dr. Reddie and his staff will succeed in the mental instruction quite as well as they have in the physical and moral training.

I should like to describe the interior organisation of the school and other points, in order to show with what pedagogic tact and knowledge everything—even small details—have been considered.

Everything bears the stamp of earnest reflection, from the Rules for the Dormitories to the Boys' Term-Reports, and the Hints to Parents.

The impression which every visit to Abbotsholme makes one feel more and more, is this: that the education of the boys is in the hands of a man endowed with a rare pedagogic instinct, and animated with the firm resolve to go steadily on along the road which he has, after mature consideration, traced out.

J. C. VAN EYK, LL.D. Utrecht.
Member of the Royal Institute of Ethnography
and Geography, and formerly Professor of
Public Law.

Amsterdam, December, 1892.

7. A SCHOOL EXCURSION. (*Summer, 1893*).

Copyright

CHAPTER IV.

Founding the Old Boys' Club. Easter, 1893.

CHAPTER IV

FOUNDING THE OLD BOYS' CLUB, EASTER, 1893

[Reprinted from the *A.O.B.C. Magazine*.]

WHEN, at our first "Old Boys' Gathering," on Easter Monday, 1893, it was proposed to form an Old Boys' Club, many of those interested felt this difficulty—something to keep old comrades, once crew of the same bark, but now scattered over literally the whole world, from losing sight and rumour of each other; something to aid cement the sacred bonds of Boyhood Friendships, which must snap if chance tear us too far or too long from one another; something to help to bring those Loves to noble social fruition: this we all desired. For had we not heard how the bright Son of Hope had stepped forth to tread the thorny track of Real Life, and perished, not because faithless or craven-hearted, but because, through long struggle and manful endeavour, he had stood alone. After the warm and joyous life of school, the world's cold blasts were all too stern, and he perished because of comrades he had none near.

It was easy to feel this need, and to desire a remedy. It was easy to propose an Old Boys' Club, something to help to bridge the river of difficulty, which every lad must cross the moment he leaves the shelter of school. It was easy to suggest the wisdom of having some organic body, outgrowth of the school itself, which should take the traveller by the hand and initiate him into Life's mysteries, and warn him and guide him among the manifold temptations of the world. For when the Youth leaves his second home to enter the great world, does he need guides less than the boy does who first leaves home for school? And what better or more natural guides could he have than the elder comrades of his happy boyhood? Did he not already know their characters and their care for him? Would he not rather follow them than strangers? And could they not describe the road well, since they had but newly passed along? Moreover, had not they and he all lived the same life, loved the same laws, learnt the same lessons, looked forward to the same wise liberty? All this was evident. It was easy to suggest the Club, but many must have felt the question arise; and if so, if we make a Club, what next? What will it do? Here was the difficulty; nor can I remove it now. All things begin with a Thought. If the thought is vital, it will soon shape to itself a body. If it is sterile, lifeless, no resolutions, no regulations, no mere machinery, however elaborate, can make it, or keep it, living. But if the Idea has life, a body and outward machinery can make that life effective, and bring it to full fruition.

When therefore the Old Boys made themselves a Club, and decided to have a Multiple Voice, they gave these ideas wings. Now we can talk to one another, and already we feel the wilderness shrink, and we seem, although so far apart from them, to touch and commune with the absent.

Some of us never doubted the Club would become real.

Founding the Old Boys' Club

The central thought, the centralising feeling, even the habit of continual correspondence, were all already in existence. The only need was to give what already existed a name. Now we have our Wings we shall do more.

So much for the "Club Mag." Another means of uniting us, less easy, unhappily, of attainment, is the Yearly Gathering. This thought will also, in due course, take body and become reality. Let us not hurry. All good things grow.

In conclusion, let us briefly record our Aims. Members of a Common Home, we shall strive to be loyal to it and to each other, remembering that love, to be fervent, must be concentrated; but also that love must be ever expanding, if it is not to become selfish. The Love for all men is not the beginning, but the end. If we do not love our brother, who is, or was, at our side, we shall never really love a stranger. But if we love faithfully and fervently the comrade, who is visible, whose life we also live, whose temptations we understand, whose thoughts and ideas we share, we may learn perhaps some day to love Humanity and the Divine Spirit of the universe. Some people to-day want to begin the other way. Like men of long ago, they fancy they can love the abstract before they have learnt to love the concrete case. They are ready, they believe, to die for the Universe, but cannot give up one little whim for the sake of the friend beside them. In religion, and in love, as in all our works and ways, we have been taught to begin with that which is near, concrete, real to us. Then we shall gain strength and knowledge which will lead us to greater conquests, as we mount the Golden Stair. We must, then, love first those around us; at home, our parents, our brothers and sisters ; then, at school, our comrades, in that miniature world. But we must not let our love end here. The love of all is not the beginning, but it *is* the end. Do we never see family love become only an enlarged selfishness ? Do we never see the love of school perpetuating and stereotyping the most ludicrous or dangerous traditions ? Do we not see—even in England, which we justly deem the noblest country on earth —customs, like the fossil remains of defunct monsters, worshipped in place of the true ideals, thus paralysing all progress. Honouring the good in past days, but ever reaching after the greater good the future has in store, let us aim at that *Liberty, which is obedience to the Law*, not merely the fragment of divine law we now possess, but the whole law which pervades the vast abysses of the Universe and the fathomless depths of Man's soul.

How are we to attain this real Liberty ? By love, imagination, and will. For " love is the realisation of the impossible ; the imagination realises all that it invents ; the will accomplishes everything which it does *not* desire." In particular we must train the affections, that highest, but most neglected, part of education. For " to love is to live, to love is to know, to love is to be able, to love is to pray, to love is to be the Man-God."

When we have learnt to love, we shall strive to hand on to others all we have ourselves attained. And in giving away our life, we shall discover the greatest mystery of all, that mathematically as we give away our life, our life grows wider and more intense.

To sum up these, our Aims, in one phrase : we shall strive to be Lords of our Life, and Givers of our Life, but especially Givers.

C. R.

8. A GROUP OF ACTORS. (*Christmas, 1893*).

Copyright

CHAPTER V.

A Brief History of Abbotsholme during
1893=4.

CHAPTER V.

A BRIEF HISTORY OF ABBOTSHOLME DURING 1893-1894.

On the opening of the School, we had been warned by several friendly veterans that all would be well for the first three years, but that then our troubles would begin. The parents and public would then demand Results. This, however, was fortunately not our experience. We had, indeed, from the very first encountered many hitches, troubles, and disappointments, but we were spared, mercifully, this additional trial. Our parents were not as others. The results they looked for were not examination lists, but health, intelligence, interest in work, growth of character, and devotion to the school. And every day our aims became clearer to them and us, and our faith and theirs more firm.

Our first tasks had been the organisation of the general life, the discipline of the servants and household, the creating, in boys and masters, of the right spirit. The last problem to attack had been the elaboration of the class-instruction, for this we knew would be the hardest.

We had already, from the first, an excellent Work-Plan and Time-Table. The range of subjects, and the order of subjects, all this was fairly satisfactory, and has remained almost unaltered to the present time. We had, moreover, from the first, aimed definitely at making work indoors and out of doors a unity, interrelated and interlocked, as far as the abilities of each master could carry it. In particular, in all that concerned Mathematics and Natural Science, Hygiene and Economics, we had freely used the school surroundings and the school community as our fundamental object lessons.

But none the less we were suffering from precisely that which hampers English enterprise in every field of work—the want of clear, systematic, philosophic theory, to render our concrete, practical, instinctive work a really intellectual power. We all knew vaguely that all correct instruction begins with simple, concrete facts, and proceeds inductively to abstract principles, and that from these one passes deductively to apply the doctrines reached to the fresh problems of practical life.

The whole staff had been engaged for some time endeavouring to elaborate a more definite sequence of studies, and to simplify the teaching by a more distinct coöperative interlocking of the work.

But the magnitude of the task was enormous, and we could not neglect the actual teaching in order to construct a detailed scheme.

(*a*) First Visit to Jena, April, 1893.

At this moment we were fortunate in getting the precise help we needed most. Dr. J. J. Findlay, who had twice visited the school and given us many friendly criticisms and much valuable advice, had, in the selfsame quest, discovered "Jena and Professor Rein." He

A Brief History of Abbotsholme

wrote and urged us to go there, and in April, 1893, we arrived in Jena, intending to stay two nights.

Next morning we visited the *Uebungsschule*, and listened to *Oberlehrer Schotz*. The impression of that morning can never be effaced from our memory. We saw for the first time what teaching was, and for a full fortnight we sat five mortal hours, one after the other, and drank in that which is creating modern Germany.

But we did not rest content with seeing the practice, we read diligently the Herbartian theory in the excellent "Pädagogik im Grundriss," by Professor Rein. And, as if by magic, the fog lifted, and we saw a new instructional heaven and earth. The impression wrought upon us by the book was deep; it was confirmed by intercourse with the distinguished author. We found, indeed, at Jena, in an eminent degree, that cordial welcome which seems to flow from the German heart to all who search for knowledge, and are willing to work. Thanks to the freedom of their intercourse, their easy social customs, and the total absence of reserve, in a few days we had lived years. There was a real communion of spirits, which in England would have required a decade of time, and a special miracle from Heaven, to develop. It is quite clear that one cause of British intellectual inferiority is our foolish social standoffishness.

In Jena were all nationalities, all brought together by one force, the wish to learn. Among others we met, we mention with pleasure Mr. Van Liew, who was translating into English Professor Rein's book to which we have referred, and Dr. Hermann Lietz, whom we were afterwards to know so well.

(*b*) Reorganisation of the Instruction, May, 1893

We returned to England and to Abbotsholme feeling we had behind our aims the arguments of an entire philosophy. We could now say to our staff, not merely we think this, let us do that; but this is what an entire army of thinkers in Germany, America, and all enlightened countries are doing. In England, at that time Herbart and Rein were, alas! names almost unknown.

Our staff caught the enthusiasm, and we set to work to reorganise our curriculum, and above all our method of class-instruction, for that rather than the work-plan was our weak spot. We do not mean to say that in all respects we regarded the Jena plan as superior to our own. We did not adopt their theory of concentration as then developed in Jena, whereby all the work centred round the history. But we remodelled our Humanistics, in which region we had been least well educated ourselves, leaving our Naturalistics, in which branches Jena had appeared to us less strong, in somewhat the same state as before. We adopted the scheme of two circles of thought, one connected with Space centering in the school, the common home of all; the other connected with Time, and travelling from the school as starting point, to England, France and Europe, Germany and the World of To-day, and finally to Rome and the Origins of Culture.

For we felt that after all it is impossible to control all that passes into the boy's mind. He must therefore learn to co-ordinate the impressions which enter according to a double scheme. On the one hand is the eternal *Now*, on the other the unending *Becoming*. Place and Time, Geography and History, Natural or Divine Law (which-

A Brief History of Abbotsholme

ever name be preferred), on the one hand, and the Evolution of Human Consciousness on the other. And even if in school we could follow always a logical or historical sequence, out of school the impressions will come without order of any sort, especially in our modern life, and the boy must learn to connect his impressions and pigeon-hole them for himself.

(*c*) PURCHASE AND ORGANISATION OF THE SCHOOL-STATE (THE SECOND FOUNDATION OF THE SCHOOL, MARCH, 1894.)

Our pedagogic labours were, however, now interrupted by a new danger. Our lease would soon be up, and we had either to leave, or, if we could, buy the school estate. Through the generous assistance of a friend, we bought the place, and on the 14th of March, 1894, consummated the second foundation of the school. It was like the removal of a nightmare. It had been impossible to work our best when we knew not if we might not have to give up everything. We were now free, we could organise our little kingdom from end to end to serve our educational needs. We could also, in due time, rebuild our School House, and at once we commenced building our castles in the air and sketching out plans on paper.

(*d*) VISIT TO THE TEACHERS' CONGRESS AND EDUCATION EXHIBITION AT STUTTGART, JUNE, 1894.

Our more immediate need was, however, school furniture and teaching apparatus, and for this we went in June, 1894, to Stuttgart. Here we attended a *Lehrerver-*

sammlung, at which 3,000 German teachers were present, and spent a week in the exhibition of school material, examining all that German ingenuity could produce for the assistance of the teacher. We brought back, or bought soon after, a complete set of the best maps in existence, as well as the best existing school-desks, and many books and diagrams, &c. During our visit we were most hospitably entertained by the family of one of our old boys, Hans Müller, who resided there.

(*e*) VISITS TO OXFORD AND EDINBURGH SUMMER MEETINGS, AUGUST, 1894.

The summer vacation of 1894 brought us new opportunities for pedagogic study. We despatched three of our staff, one to Jena, another to Edinburgh, and a third to Oxford, subsidised from the school exchequer, to study under Professor Rein, Professor Geddes, and Mr. Courthope Bowen and others. We ourselves went to Oxford and afterwards to Edinburgh, where we met, for the first time, M. Demolins, little dreaming, as he pertinaceously catechised us about our school, that he meditated incorporating our chance conversation in a book.

In the following chapter we reprint an account of the impression made on us by the summer meetings at Edinburgh and Oxford, though they had nothing directly to do with Abbotsholme, for we are of opinion that it is essential that schools should from time to time study what Universities are really doing, in order to keep in touch with any advances they make,

9. CÆSAR'S GLADIATORS. (*Easter, 1893*).

Copyright

CHAPTER VI.
Oxford and Edinburgh Contrasted.

CHAPTER VI.

OXFORD AND EDINBURGH CONTRASTED.

IMPRESSIONS OF THE SUMMER MEETINGS AT OXFORD AND EDINBURGH.

By CECIL REDDIE, B.Sc., Ph.D.
Headmaster of The New School Abbotsholme.

(Reprinted from *The University Extension Journal*, Nov. 15, 1894.)

I HAVE been asked to give, in a short space, my impressions of this Meeting and my opinion as to its general character and utility. This then is the aim of the present article. Having visited a Summer Meeting this year for the first time, first at Oxford, then at Edinburgh, I am, if not learned in the subject, at least not *blasé* with it. What follows I offer not as a critic claiming to decide dogmatically for or against what he has seen, but as an educational enthusiast keen to study, and learn from, all efforts after larger living.

To the English reader, Oxford is more familiar than Edinburgh. Therefore comparison—which is always useful—will be doubly valuable here.

Will the reader place before him photographs of each city and the program of each Meeting, and call up before his mind's eye all he has ever heard of Oxford and of Edinburgh. For the character of each Meeting must be decided already largely by the place. This, throughout the centuries, has moulded University and City, and through them the Men who to-day would form the ideals and guide the destinies of an Empire.

Oxford is an epitome of England, a museum of the creations of every century. All is full of interest. Most is beautiful, but it is a beautiful unorder. The air is heavy, almost solid; and only what is substantial seems able to breathe and live there.

All this is reflected in the Oxford man. Half his heart is in the past, even when he is striving most to create a future for University and Fatherland. He is a mine of culture, but, like the town, he reveals no planned order. His vision of the whole seems broken by attention to the medley of parts. He is a fine product of England's ideal of education, a wholesome, human, all-round man. He is not nimble-witted; but brain and body are close-knit together. His words are real, solid, and beautiful in form, like his own Colleges and the woods and winding streams of his magic home. In him we find morals, manners, knowledge, and physique, in fine harmony. The monastic traditions, which still make him eat in the dark, sit on backless benches, study by candle-light, and hold aloof from the "outsider," gives him a slight austerity of manner; but underneath will be found a generous heart, glad to yield its pearls of culture if sure no swine are near.

What a different vision is called up by the word Edinburgh! Here it is City, rather than University, which dominates. Perched upon the Burg of Edwin we look round upon a scene without rival—the loveliest city of the

Empire, perhaps even of the world. Close by, upon this height, Professor Patrick Geddes has set University Hall, which to me seems likely to become the model of the University of the Future—University no longer for a class, the rich, the scholar, but for men and women, married or single, student or teacher, worker or thinker, artist or artizan, lawyer, doctor, merchant, or what you will, all in one community, all in some measure fellow-workers, all in touch with one great central purpose—to help on the Ascent of Man.

In Edinburgh, as in Oxford, are memorials of the past. But the Castle, which takes us back to a time when the Oxen ford was only a ford, is now but a barrack, High Street, with its historic mansions, is a mere slum, Holyrood below is a combination of ruin and hotel. Across the gardens, once the North Loch, lies below us the New Town, clean, respectable, and common-place—product of the nineteenth century. There, separated from old Edinburgh by a great gulf, moral, intellectual, and social, as well as topographical, live Professors, Judges, and the Cultured, of all professions or of none, while University and College of Justice are surrounded by vendors of fish, old clothes, and all that is common and unclean. The University indeed is here a building rather than a body, sending forth her sons each night to bivouac throughout the town wherever they please. It is a bundle of lecture-rooms and laboratories, not a home.

Where the old town first grew at the Castle gates, on this wooded height commanding the whole city and marvellous panorama beyond—to south over spires and domes and spreading suburbs, towering Arthur Seat and massive Pentlands; to north over New Town and sea dotted with ships and islands, far away the purple Grampians—upon this unique spot a stroke of genius has created University Hall. Mansions long grown foul with base use have, under the architect's touch, become suddenly ornaments of the city. Instead of filthy " close " we find charming court, which transports us to Nüremberg and the Middle Ages. Rising phœnix-like from the decaying past, the Hall inaugurates a new life, in which all classes may find common ground and common work, realising the true meaning of the word University—which signifies Universal. For it, like Catholic Church, should include all, not merely men of one pattern, but all sorts and all conditions, excluding only the lazy and the vile.

These surroundings also are reflected in the Edinburgh man. When he looks back at the past, it is to find argument for fresh aggression in the future. To him reverence for the old is not master but slave. The air, bold scenery, and cruel winds give him a certain hardness, bony strength, grasp, and agility, which colour his morals, manners, and physique, but above all his intellect. For indeed it was intellect rather than whole man that Scottish education had mainly cultivated, till England and the railway imported athletics and manners and more of Saxon breadth and geniality.

While therefore at Oxford the air and antiquities induce worship of the magic of tradition and lull to dreams of the past, the gusty heights and limpid aether of the "northern Athens" inspire to new conquests of the mind, and her sordid relics of the past impel to create more lasting monuments of human genius for the ages to come.

But what has all this to do with the Summer Meeting? Surely it were folly to discuss lectures and lecturers and omit what dominates the whole ? Is not Environment, or what of old was called the Tutelary Goddess of the City after all the main fact ? Can we doubt that over Oxford and over Edinburgh hovers the *Genius loci*, attended by all the mighty dead whom he inspired ? Shall we deny an influence because it is intangible ? Do we not see these influences incarnate in the men and manifest in each Meeting ? At Oxford the program is colossal but ill-coordinated. The teaching body is an army of distinguished, but independent, generals. The lectures are highly-finished, admirably delivered; but lack connection with each other. The whole works to no final issue. No master-spirit controls the whole. The printed program is a chaos. Neither it nor University recognise enough the obligation to advise. The student is supposed to know his wants, and where his wants can be satisfied. He is like the artizan turned loose into a Museum or Art Gallery—without guide. Delightful freedom to wander at will as a freeborn elector, but sad waste of precious time. In short, the University knows how to lecture, but not how to teach. The student is amazed at the erudition and charmed with the easy grace of the lecturer, rather than fed with the knowledge or stimulated to self-activity by being admitted to see his Teacher at work. He goes to be fed at the monastery gate rather than to be initiated into the mystery of a craft. He returns feeling how far above him are the happy dwellers in this enchanted city, and how hopeless for him to aspire to enter there as fellow-worker. He is willing to adore the Gods of this Olympus, but not as Gods who will descend to redeem. He feels also, however, be it said honestly, that much that he sees is unnatural, like the discoloured light that streams through a painted window, and that much which is there prized would look foolish in the presence of the eternal hills. In this do we not see trace of the ecclesiastical influences of the past, which ever tend to divide Priest from People, and to shut out daylight in order better to fascinate the worshippers' imagination with the rush-lights of dead dogma?

When one sees in the flesh the power and glory of Oxford, one marvels, not that she has done so much, but that her influence in England is so small. How different were England to-day, had Oxford been in vital contact with her through all these centuries! Even now her force is mainly escaping through a dozen safety-valves, not doing effective national work. For instance, what better explains the collapse of the House of Commons than a debate at the Union? While the Union plays at Parliament, and Parliament plays the fool, the Empire slips from our grasp. If Oxford did her duty, artizans would not want " labour members," nor to substitute for " cultured selfishness" the still worse selfishness of the ignorant. In answer it will be said that we feel all this, and are honestly trying to open our Halls and our hearts to all England. May it be said without offence that Oxford has much to learn and much to unlearn, if she would sit on the intellectual throne of England? Her sole chance lies in this Extension work, and above all in the Summer Meetings. In both she is learning to know her future subjects, but while her itinerant preachers are arming her subjects, the Summer Meeting alone will teach her subjects to reverence and love her. But she must not aim at merely fascinating them with her beauty; she must lay aside much of her finery, and must admit her new subjects to real citizenship.

Oxford and Edinburgh Contrasted

In many ways the Edinburgh Meeting is the opposite of that of Oxford. Although of older date, and held more regularly, it is far smaller. But it is compact and organic. The teachers, if young, are Generals of Division, under a great Field Marshal, who directs the whole campaign. The Edinburgh Meeting is, in fact, mainly the creation of one man, who with many and various gifts and sympathies in all directions, must be pronounced an intellectual genius of the highest order, whose colossal plans should not be measured by the embryo which as yet is visible. The work at Edinburgh is as yet not large, but it has in it the germ of something immense and significant. If the execution falls short of the design, let us remember that excellence of execution often cripples progress. More too can be learnt and expected from the bold but crude touches of genius than from the polished completeness of highly-trained mediocrity. One would like to see the daring and brilliant program of the north wedded to the fine finish and solid strength of Oxford. Then there would be a work!

While in every way Oxford holds us to the solid ground and ripe experience until we almost forget the vast universe beyond, Edinburgh seems to sweep us up into unsubstantial cities in the clouds, and sets our brains ablaze with vast projects, till the solid earth seems to melt away. The vastness of scope and consequent incompleteness of detail, while inspiring new mental life, yet suggests some unreality. There is often a lack of reverence for men and ideas of the past; but then Teachers of a new Cult must always singe, if not quite burn, the Gods of a dying civilisation. There is some lack of the feeling of responsibility—the fault of intellectual giants, who forget, or do not realise, that children require blinking dolls, and that daring speculations unsettle the immature. But these dangers are removed by the close contact of Teachers and Taught in seminar and salon, amid the social enthusiasm which is so unique a feature of this gathering.

In fact, judged as an instrument of education, the Edinburgh Meeting must take rank above that of Oxford. For here the student is not regarded as a barrel to be filled at the University vat, nor plagued with delusive examinations to see how much he has taken in. He is welcomed as collaborator, and is initiated into the mysteries of the cult. The Syllabus gives him a key to the whole meaning of the work, and at the same time a lesson of remarkable educational value. It is one thing to see the finished product of a factory exposed for sale in a handsome shop; quite another to see the raw stuff take shape as it incarnates the thoughts of the worker. In Oxford we see the statue finished, lovely. In Edinburgh we sit with the sculptor and see the marble begin to breathe. To see the Seminar at work condensing all that is known to date, criticising it, propounding new hypotheses, setting to work to test their worth, and summarising the whole in lucid diagram—this is indeed to see a University at work.

In Edinburgh we find women teaching, and teaching admirably, Science and Music and Painting. We find Science and Art hand-in-hand. We find lecturers attending each other's lectures, so that the teaching staff grows every year more an organic unity. Chief merit of all, the course awakes, without satisfying, our interest in every realm. It forces us to set to work ourselves, and it gives us a chart of the unknown, which, if not final, is enough to give us courage for fresh explorations.

Oxford and Edinburgh Contrasted

At Oxford and Edinburgh many Americans and foreigners were among lecturers and students, giving an international character to the Meetings which cannot be too much commended. One wishes that more could be done to attract our kin from over seas to the premier University of the English-speaking race. But, if Oxford does not seize her opportunity, she will have to yield the proud title of Imperial University to her young rival in the North. Already for years Edinburgh, whose *alumni* in numbers equal, if not exceed, those of Oxford, has been the favourite resort of students from the Colonies. Why should not Oxford open her doors to them, and also to Americans, who now pass by in hundreds to the Universities of Germany?

At both Meetings many students were school-teachers, and the majority women. (Truly in education women are leaving men behind.) Nothing better surely can be wished than that teachers of all grades should have their opportunities of refreshment and inspiration. Perhaps these Meetings would attain their highest usefulness if they were organised definitely for teaching teachers. Some such definite aim would solve many difficulties of organisation. The value of a Summer Meeting is not to be gauged by its mere size, but by its organic complexity, harmony, and completeness. Such a scheme as this might bring redemption to the secondary schoolmaster—the most incompetent, but least ill-satisfied, teacher in the country. For if English *education* is the best on earth, English *instruction* is probably the worst. It would be a boon if Oxford and Edinburgh next year organised a Teachers' Course, with model lessons, given by model Teachers, to real children. It is admittedly absurd to teach Chemistry without experiments. Why should we have educational theory without the concrete example? Similarly the Extension Lecture system might be made to reanimate the Schools throughout the country, by bringing new life and fresh ideas to relieve the dull routine for boy and master.

These are my impressions of the Oxford and Edinburgh Meetings, and my opinion as to their general character and utility. If anything appears exaggerated, obscure, or biassed, let it be remembered they are but impressions, and time and space were short.

10. BEE FARMING. (*June 21st, 1893*).

Copyright

CHAPTER VII.

The Revised Prospectus, September, 1894.

CHAPTER VII.

THE REVISED PROSPECTUS.[1]

The New School Abbotsholme,

ON THE DOVE,
DERBYSHIRE.

(*Opened 1st October*, 1889.)

AN EDUCATIVE SCHOOL FOR BOYS.
PROSPECTUS.

(*Revised 1st October*, 1894.)

Five years' experience has led to several alterations, which are now incorporated in the Scheme, but experience has also shown that the main lines on which the School started are not only good ideally, but are easy to work practically.

Postal Address—ABBOTSHOLME, NEAR ROCESTER, DERBYSHIRE.
Telegrams—ABBOTSHOLME, ROCESTER. (No Charge for Porterage.)

GENERAL AIM.

THE School, which was opened in 1889, is intended to provide for boys, between the ages of about 11 and 18, an all-round *Education* of an entirely modern and rational

[1] The prospectus of 1889 attempted to divide the School curriculum into two parts : from 11 to 15 General Education, and from 15 to 18 Special Education. Very early this had to be abandoned as I found it impossible to complete the General Education in 4 years and undesirable to specialise before 18. The Prospectus was therefore modified, and in the summer of 1894 put in this final form.—C. R.

character based upon the principles of Educational Science,[1] and adapted to the needs of the English cultured classes.

"A short account of the Aims and Methods of The New School" was published in the Spring of 1889, and the lines indicated have been, in almost every particular, adhered to.

In the year 1890 a "Report of the First Year's Work" was published, showing how the original program was being carried out. These papers are now out of print, but at an early date will be published the first number of the School *Year-Book*, entitled, *Abbotsholme*,[2] which will give a full account, with illustrations, of the life and work of the School in its present more developed and better organised condition.

The Abbotsholme Estate contains within its bounds a great variety of features—hill, plain, dingle, wood, river—and so constitutes an *ideal miniature kingdom*, the citizens of which are furnished by the School. It thus serves admirably for the purpose of a fundamental, ever-present *Object Lesson* (whether for Geographical and Realistic, or for Historical and Humanistic Studies), from which the

---

[1] It is not possible to give Parents, within the limits of a Prospectus, a treatise upon Education. Those interested in the subject are recommended to read carefully the following books, with whose views the Aims and Methods of this School are in close sympathy, and they will get a very clear notion of the meaning of the Curriculum, &c., adopted at Abbotsholme.

"Outlines of Pedagogics," by Professor Rein of Jena. Sonnenschein, 1893, 3s. 6d.

"Student's Fröbel," by Herford. Isbister, 2s. 6d.

"Educational Reformers," by Quick. Longmans, 3s. 6d.

"Occasional Addresses," by Professor Laurie of Edinburgh. Clay, 5s.

[2] George Allen, Ruskin House, Charing Cross Road, London, W.C.

whole Teaching can start, by which all new ideas can be measured, and round which the entire work can be concentrated.

The *whole Life* at the School is planned so as to develop narmoniously all the powers of the boy—physical, intellectual, artistic, moral, and spiritual—to *train* him, in fact, *how* to *live*, and become a wholesome, reasonable, and useful member of Human Society.

As the worth of a community is not to be measured by its mere size, but rather by its cultural complexity, the aim at Abbotsholme is to build up not a huge and unwieldy, but a compact and highly organised *Educational Laboratory*.

The School is planned to hold ultimately only one hundred boys; and as it contains, though on a small scale, all the main factors which produce a civilised community, its central purpose is to bring the boy into conscious harmonious relation with this miniature world, as the surest way of making him into a *Man* and a *Citizen*.

While the School surroundings provide a complex Geographical Object Lesson, the School community itself, including Teachers, Pupils, and Attendants, &c., constitute the requisite Object Lesson for the measuring of History and the understanding of Social Life.

Digging in the Garden, damming streams in the Dingle, felling or planting trees, &c., the boy is learning the ways of Nature, at first hand, in the oldest and best of all Laboratories.

Coöperating outside and indoors with other people, he is learning, likewise, the fundamental laws upon which rests all Human Society, by seeing for himself how all parts of this little Social Organism fit together.

At Abbotsholme, then, as the Naturalistic studies spring

out of the actual features of the place, and are employed to interpret to the boy this Environment, so the Humanistic studies are illustrated by analogies drawn from the School community itself, and the evident interdependence of all members of the same is used at the starting-point in the study of Sociology, Morals, and Religion.

As regards the *Teaching Body*, the aim has been to make the Staff an Organic Unity. Accordingly the Masters share fully in the complex life of the place, in order that all may be, as far as possible, of one heart and one mind.

Nothing is more fatal for a boy than to be tossed about from one influence to another ; to receive one set of ideas from one Master, and another, and perhaps antagonistic, set from another, and be left, unaided, to harmonise the two for himself, if he can. It would be like the presence of two fathers in one family.

But where the Masters are much together they catch the same spirit, and learn to use the same methods. The result is greater coöperation in the teaching, and greater harmony in the boy's development.

The constant companionship of the boys with their Teachers is good for both. Both are humanised ; the boy is brought in touch with Manhood, and the Master gets a fuller view of the responsibilities of Fatherhood.

The working of the boys with the Workmen on the Estate is also good for both, and the likeliest way of obviating class prejudice and social strife, and promoting a feeling of social duty.

CURRICULUM.

The higher the organism, the longer should be the *period of growth*. For boys this period is the School life. In the case of boys of the cultured classes this period should last until the completion of the 18th year. Up to that age the boy should not be allowed to specialise, but should enjoy the widest possible education, so that his whole nature may develop to its utmost harmonious extent. All specialisation at School, whether in Athletics, in Latin, in Mathematics, in Chemistry, or in anything else, is a mistake, and in the long run leads to premature stoppage of growth, physical, mental, or moral, and produces narrowness even in the direction specialised.

Education cannot be both broad and special at the same time. The attempt to combine these opposites leads to an overburdened curriculum, overstrained brains, and ultimate collapse. School education should be of the broadest possible character, not only because it develops a bigger personality, able subsequently to do everything better, but because, till they are 18, few boys show what they are best fit for, and it is impossible to have satisfactory schools or satisfactory education unless a large number remain at school until the feeling of responsibility is well awake. For it should not be forgotten that if the elder boys in a school while untrained and ignorant are the worst guides for youngsters, they become when trained and instructed in many ways the best.

At Abbotsholme this natural relation of boys to one another is recognised and carefully organised.

The education provided at the School is in every

respect of an all-round, non-specialistic, liberal character, and is continued as late as is practicable.

But in order to meet practical difficulties, due to the present unorganised state of the educational machinery of the country, the School allows the elder boys to specialise to some extent, in order to prepare them for distinct work, such as Entrance Examinations to Universities, Technical Colleges, &c.

The School does not undertake to cram boys for Scholarships, or for *Competitive* Examination.

The experience of five years has shown that this all-round education not only does *not un*fit a boy for ordinary pursuits, but, indeed, renders him more able to specialise in any direction with profit when the right time for it comes.

SITE AND BUILDINGS.

Abbotsholme stands 320 feet above sea-level, on the western slope of Dove Ridge, overlooking the Dove, which is a quarter of a mile from the house. The country round is remarkably fine and open, and, being nearly all permanent pasture, is like a vast park. There are no towns near, the air is bracing, and the district one of the healthiest in England.

The situation is very central. There is easy railway communication with all parts of the Britains.

The School is within easy reach of Dove Dale and other beautiful spots, and also within reach, by rail, of the Potteries, of iron, coal, and copper mines, and of silk, cotton, and other factories. Occasional visits to these places form part of the educational scheme.

The Revised Prospectus

The house is one mile from Rocester village, once a Roman camp, and later the seat of the Abbey from which Abbotsholme derives its name.

The Schoolhouse, which is surrounded by gardens and orchards, stands in the middle of the Abbotsholme Estate of 133 acres, the whole of which is the property of the School.

There are extensive glass houses and farm buildings, also a Workshop and Chemical Laboratory outside the house, heated by hot water.

About a mile and a half of the Dove winds through the estate, affording good fishing and bathing. Every boy learns swimming, unless forbidden to bathe by his physician. Boys who can swim are allowed to boat.

The river surrounds on three sides the Holme, or island meadow, used for the Playing Fields, which on the near side is bounded by the brook dividing the counties of Derby and Stafford.

There are grounds for Tennis, Cricket, and Football, and on the hill a good Tobogganing place.

The boys may keep Bicycles (not Tricycles), and a few can be taught Riding and Driving.

The sanitary arrangements are all excellent. The water is obtained from a private reservoir, upon the hill behind the house, fed by deep springs.

For slight ailments there are sick-rooms in the back wing; and in case of infectious illness, one of the four cottages on the estate can be used as a hospital.

Abbotsholme

ABBOTSHOLME SCHOOL and Estate are the property of the Headmaster, whose intention is to place the whole eventually under a Trust, to ensure that the Aims and Methods of the School be maintained.

TRUSTEES.

C. KEGAN PAUL, M.A., formerly Assistant Master in College, Eton.
ROBERT OSWALD MOON, M.A., New College, Oxford.
One Trustee elected by the Abbotsholme Old Boys' Club.
Two more to be hereafter appointed.

HEADMASTER.

CECIL REDDIE, B.Sc. Edin., 1882, Ph.D. (magna cum laude), Göttingen, 1884 ; Fettes Exhibitioner, 1878, Hope Prize Scholar, 1880, Vans Dunlop Scholar, 1882, Edinburgh ; Lecturer on Chemistry at Fettes College, 1885–7 ; Assistant Master at Clifton College, 1887–8 ; Lecturer on the Scottish University Extension, 1888.
[*English, German, Latin, History, Geography, Natural Science, Mathematics.*]

ASSISTANT MASTERS.
(October, 1894.)

Date of Appointment.

Feb., 1890. KARL NEUMANN, Certificated Teacher, Grand Ducal Training College, Neukloster, Mecklenburg Schwerin.
[*Organ, Piano, Theory of Music, Workshop, Biology, German, Bee-Culture.*]

Feb., 1890. WILMOT CLIFFORD PILSBURY, Art Master, South Kensington ; holding Engineering and Science Certificates, Mason College, Birmingham.
>[*Drawing, Painting, Workshop, Surveying, Mathematics, and Natural Science.*]

Dec., 1892. ARTHUR JOHN HOMER HAWKINS.
>[*Riding, Farm and Garden, Military Drill, Dumb-bells, Boxing, Bookkeeping.*]

Jan., 1893. R. L. LANCELOT, Cert. Assoc. Board, Royal Acad. Music and Royal College of Music, London ; Directorial-Zeugniss, Conservatorium, Leipzig.
>[*Piano, Singing, English, French, German.*]

July, 1894. STANLEY DE BRATH, M.I.C.E., late Assistant-Secretary in the Public Works Department of India.
>[*English, French, Physics, Mathematics, Engineering.*]

Sept., 1894. W. J. MORRELL, M.A. and Scholar of Balliol College, Oxford.
>[*English, Latin, Greek, Mathematics, History.*]

N.B.—The present Staff will be found in *An Educational Atlas* (see Appendix B).

LADY SUPERINTENDENT.

MISS FLORENCE REDDIE.

Matron—MRS. KEYS,

Non-Resident.
HERBERT NEWBOULD, ESQ., Professor of Violin, School of Music, Derby.
Physician—B. HEYWOOD HERBERT, Esq., Medical Officer of Health, Uttoxeter.
Solicitors—NICHOLL, MANISTY, & Co., 1, Howard Street, Strand, W.C.
Auditor—J. H. RICHARDSON, C.A., Derby.

PLAN OF EDUCATION.

The whole Education is conceived and organised so as to develop in the boy a strong, self-reliant, disciplined, and moral *Character*.

To produce this, the two means which are available, *Guidance* and *Instruction*, are made to coöperate.

I. GUIDANCE.

The boy is guided (1) by forces moulding him from outside ; (2) by influences acting upon his heart; in other words, by *Force*, mild or vigorous, and by *Affection*, strong or gentle, conscious or almost imperceptible.

(1) The *external* forces—Government—comprise :—

- (*a*) The direct control by the School authorities.
- (*b*) The Rules and Customs of the place.
- (*c*) The daily Program of Work, &c.
- (*a*) The general moral atmosphere (tone) of the School community.

> [It will be observed that these four influences are arranged in their proper *historic* order. The reverse order is, however, the order of effective value. For while the general tone is the result of long-continued direct personal control, and so the last in order of time, it is the first in order of merit. For the less direct the government, the more subtle, deep, and lasting in effect.]

The Revised Prospectus

(2) The *internal* influences—Training—are :—
  (*a*) The life and example of the Teacher, as object lesson.
   [This includes the example of the boys, especially the elder ones.]
  (*b*) The direct influence and affection between Teacher and Pupil.
   [This includes the influence and affection between the boys themselves.]
  (*c*) The various social Festivals, Commemorations, &c.
   [*E.g.*, The Queen's Birthday, the National Fête; Foundation Day, the School Fête; the Concerts, Expeditions, &c., &c.]
  (*d*) The Chapel Services.

II. Instruction.

The aim of the instruction is :—
1. To cultivate an all-round, healthy *interest* in nature and in human life ;
2. To develop *power* (faculty) ;
3. To build up well-selected and well-arranged *knowledge ;*
  the whole being directed to the development of a circle of ideas which will fortify the character.
   [It may be said, that while the *Instruction* develops in the boy interest in all directions which will preserve him from idleness, and the knowledge and power which will enable him to judge and act rightly, the *Guidance* will accustom him to wholesome habits, and place before him the pattern of a well-arranged community and life, and will dispose him to *wish* and to *will*, to judge and act rightly.]

It is only possible to give here the briefest outline of the work done at the School. Further particulars will be given in the *Year-Book* already referred to.

Abbotsholme

TIME-TABLE.

	SUMMER.		WINTER.	
	WEEK-DAYS.	SUNDAYS.	WEEK-DAYS.	
6	6.10 Rise. 6.30 Early meal; Drill. 6.45 First School.			6
7	7.30 **Chapel**. 7.40 **Breakfast**.	7.30 Rise.	6.55 Rise. 7.15 Drill. 7.30 **Chapel**. 7.40 **Breakfast**.	7
8	8.0 Dorm. Parade. 8.30 Second School.	8.0 **Chapel**. 8.20 **Breakfast**. 8.45 Dorm. Parade.	8.0 Dorm. Parade. 8.30 Second School.	8
9		9.0 Letters Home.		9
10	10.15 Break; Lunch. 10.30 Third School.	10.15 Church Parade—**Church**.	10.0 Break; Lunch. 10.15 Third School.	10
11				11
12	12.15 Bathing.	12.15 [Mid-day Chapel when wet.]	12.0 Drawing, Workshop, Garden.	12
1	————————	————Dinner.————	————————	1
2	Piano Recital.	1.30 Organ Recital.	Piano Recital.	2
3	2–6 ⎰ Drawing. Workshop. Garden & Odd Jobs Games. Laboratory.	3.0 **Free Time**.	2–4.30 ⎰ Drawing. Workshop. Garden & Odd Jobs. Games. Laboratory.	3
4				4
5		5.0 Lock-up. 5.15 Choir Practice.	4.30 Afternoon School. 6.0	5
6	————————	————Tea.————	————————	6
7	6.30 Evening School.	6.30 Reading with Tutors.	6.30 **Free**. 7.0 Singing. 7.30 ⎰ Lectures, Debates, 8.30 ⎱ Concerts, Reading, Theatre.	7
8	7.15 Singing, Recitations. 8.30 ————————	7.30 **Chapel**. ————Supper.————	————8.30————	8
	8.40 **Chapel**. 8.50 Bed.	8.40 Bed.	8.40 **Chapel**. 8.50 Bed.	
9				9

No lesson exceeds three-quarters of an hour, except Writing, Drawing, Practical Chemistry, &c., which does not so much tax the attention.

Boys in the Upper School, who are preparing for definite examinations, &c., have extra work and tuition not shown in the Time-Table, which refers mainly to the Lower School. Piano and Violin hours are also not shown, but in no case are they taken out of the usual play time.

There is a FREE HALF on Thursdays, and extra half or whole holidays are given occasionally for expeditions, &c.

The Revised Prospectus

As shown in the annexed Time-Table, the day is divided into three parts. The Morning is devoted to class-work indoors; the Afternoon, to physical and manual work out of doors; the Evening, to Music, Poetry, Art, and Social Recreation.

Although it may thus be said that the morning is devoted to the intellect, the afternoon to the body, and the evening to social intercourse, yet there is no attempt made to divide up either the boy or his work into distinct parts unrelated to one another. On the contrary, the interlocking of the work and life is one of the most important principles recognised and carried out at Abbotsholme; for the more the entire work is connected and made to react as a unity upon the whole personality of the boy, the more satisfactory and lasting is the influence exerted, and the result achieved.

PHYSICAL AND MANUAL PURSUITS.

1. Gardening, odd jobs, work on the Farm, Bee-Culture, &c. Some work of this kind is compulsory for all.
2. Carpentry [for Juniors, Sloyd; for Seniors, useful or artistic work (making tables, cupboards, &c.)]; compulsory for all.
3. Drill, including Dumb-bells, &c., Military Drill, &c.; compulsory for all.
4. Games, &c., Football (Rugby Union), Cricket, &c. (Bathing, Tobogganing, &c., in the season); compulsory for all, to obviate loafing, &c.
5. Engineering, Surveying, &c. Work of this kind is given to picked boys.
6. Basket-making and similar finger work, Clay-model-

ling, &c., are given from time to time, more especially to the juniors.

7. Boating, Fishing, Bicycling, Excursions, Photographing, Boxing, Fencing, &c., are encouraged, and times arranged.

The above pursuits come chiefly in the afternoons. The facts and experiences thereby acquired are used for illustration in the class work; and the boy is encouraged to apply the knowledge obtained in class when thus engaged outside.

INTELLECTUAL INSTRUCTION.

The basis of the intellectual instruction is the observation of *Things* (and People) and their *Movements* (and Actions), in connection with which the boy has to use *Language*—his own (English)—in order to register and communicate his *Thoughts*.

He is best taught to speak and write his own tongue in connection with his own observations of Nature and Man.

By analysing his English speech, he learns the fundamental construction of all language, and is then led on to study French, German, Latin, and in some cases Greek, in this order, following modern methods of instruction, and a carefully planned sequence of studies.

Side by side with the study of the languages, and in close relation with them, he studies the corresponding geography and history, and, to some extent, literature and art. He also passes through a course of the general

The Revised Prospectus

geography and history of the world in especial relation with the Hebrews and the Christian Church.

The study of *Things* (*Natural Science*) begins with the most common events of ordinary daily life, and carries the boy through a well-considered series of typical phenomena, such as will give him possession of the main facts and laws manifested in the universe. He thus learns that all Natural Science is essentially *one*, and learns to apply the ideas suggested by each to the study of the rest. He is in particular taught carefully the laws which govern his own life, and the habits, physical, mental, and moral, necessary to produce and maintain sound health.

Mathematics are taught as far as possible by concrete examples and in close connection with Natural Science.

Morals and Religion are taught similarly in connection with History, illustrated by concrete examples of human action.

POETRY, ART, MUSIC, SOCIAL RECREATION.

The boys hear much good *Literature* read, and learn short extracts from the poets by heart.

Drawing in all its branches is compulsory for all, and to it much time is given.

The Drawings and Designs required for Carpentry and Clay Modelling are made in the Drawing School, and graphic methods are widely used in the Natural Science work.

The School possesses many excellent photographs of pictures by the great masters, and several good casts; and an effort is made to interest the boys in all such work.

Singing is compulsory for all with any ability. All learn to copy music, and are taught the elements of musical theory. Both the Tonic Sol-Fa and the Staff notations are used, and much time is devoted to voice-production.

The boys hear some good music every day; a large number learn Piano or Violin, or both; there is an Orchestra; frequent musical entertainments are given, and occasional lectures, with illustrations, upon the great composers.

The boys assemble every evening in Big School, to meet the ladies, masters, and any visitors who may be at the School, and learn to behave and to amuse themselves in a sensible fashion.

ETHICS AND RELIGION.

It has been already pointed out that the training of the will or character is the fundamental aim of the Education given, and accordingly this aim pervades and influences the whole life and work of the place.

In addition to the influences and instruction already described, the following means are specially directed to this end.

1. *The Chapel Services* are intended to condense and focus all the highest influences and ideas of the place, by setting before the boy definite maxims of conduct associated with the actions of ideal persons, the whole series of pictures being grouped round the Person and Life of Jesus Christ.

2. The boys *learn by heart* portions of the *Gospels* and and selections from the *Psalms*.

3. The *religious instruction* given is adapted to the young, and is therefore as undogmatic and unsectarian as possible.

The Revised Prospectus

4. The boys are divided into Fags, Mids, and Prefects, and are *trained* to understand their relation to one another, and their responsibility for each other. A special effort is made to educate their affections.

5. No prizes or marks are given. The boys are made to feel that virtue is its own reward, and that every bit of wisely planned and well-executed work must bring ultimately a good result.

SPECIALISATION.

As has been already said, special studies do not belong to school life.

In practice, however, under present educational conditions, some sacrifice of principle is advisable, in order to enable boys to fit in with institutions elsewhere. Accordingly the elder boys are allowed in some measure to do special work, fitting them to enter Universities or other places for professional study.

In the near future it is to be expected that Specialisation will be recognised as belonging not to School but to subsequent education. At present we have Schools trying to do the work of Universities and Technical Colleges, &c., and in consequence Universities, &c., obliged to do the work of Schools.

The curriculum at Abbotsholme is designed to give the boy a solid foundation upon which subsequent Specialisation can rest. Without such firm foundation, Specialisation will be impossible or delusive.

At the same time the wide range of studies provided gives every boy an equal chance of showing his peculiar bent and ability, and so the work in life for which he is peculiarly fit.

Among the pursuits already entered upon by boys educated at Abbotsholme are the following : Theology, Medicine, Engineering, Chemistry, Merchant Service, Land Surveying, Banking, Manufacturing, Commerce, Printing, Agriculture, Music, &c.

REFERENCES.

When the School was being founded in 1889, it was felt desirable to obtain the public support of a considerable number of persons, known in the educational world, as a guarantee to parents that the aims and methods of the School were based on sound principles.

A large number of influential people kindly allowed their names to appear on the Prospectus to mark their approval of its objects, and, thanks to their support, the School made an excellent start.

But the School having now had some years of prosperous life, it is felt that the time has come when Parents should be referred not only to those who approved of the Aims, but to those who have also had experience of the Results—that is, to the Parents and Guardians of Boys educated at Abbotsholme.

The names of these will, on application, be given to those intending to send boys.

11. WOOD CUTTING. (*Winter, 1894*).

Copyright

CHAPTER VIII.

Answers to the Royal Commission on Secondary Education, Oct. 1894.

CHAPTER VIII.

ANSWERS TO THE ROYAL COMMISSION.

ROYAL COMMISSION ON SECONDARY EDUCATION.

6, OLD PALACE YARD, LONDON, S.W.,
April, 1894.

SIR,—I am directed by Mr. Bryce to express the hope that this Commission may be favoured with an expression of your opinion upon some of the more important topics which come within the scope of their reference, a copy of which is sent herewith.

I have accordingly the honour to ask you to consider the enclosed paper of queries, which have been proposed in order to elicit the views of persons interested in, and specially qualified to express opinions upon, questions of Secondary Education as regarded from various points of view.

You will perceive from the note at the end of the paper that your opinion is requested not upon all the topics mentioned in the Queries, *but upon those only which you may be disposed to deal with;* and I may add that it is requested primarily, for the information and guidance of the Commissioners, that anything you may say will be deemed *confidential if you so wish,* and that *none of your answers will be published without your express permission.*

Should any point included in these Queries be, in your opinion, of sufficient importance to require a *separate treatment,* or should there be *any point not included,* on *which you wish to express an opinion,* the Commissioners will be glad to receive from you a statement of your views in the manner most convenient to yourself.

I am,
Your obedient Servant,
WILLIAM N. BRUCE,
Secretary.

To C. REDDIE, Esq.

REFERENCE.

To consider what are the best methods of establishing a well-organised system of Secondary Education in England, taking into account existing deficiencies, and having regard to such local sources of revenue from endowment or otherwise as are available or may be made available for this purpose, and to make recommendations accordingly.

ANSWERS TO QUESTIONS PUT BY THE ROYAL COMMISSION ON SECONDARY EDUCATION (SENT IN DECEMBER 24, 1894) BY CECIL REDDIE, B.Sc., PH.D.[1]

Being interested not so much in merely one school or one class of schools, as in Education in its widest sense and widest application, I take the liberty of replying to

[1] I have to express my thanks to Mr. Stanley De Brath, M.I.C.E., who was at the date in question one of my Assistant Masters here, for kindly typewriting these answers from my MS.

Answers to the Royal Commission 155

all the questions about which I have come to definite conclusions.

I write as a specialist in Education, not as a Statesman. To me it seems more important that our education should be sound than that our machinery should be symmetrical, and in any case I can write with knowledge about practical teaching, whereas I have no command of the facts which would justify my advancing fixed conclusions regarding the State machinery for controlling the national education.

I have aimed at brevity and clearness, and that has made it necessary to speak in bold metaphor and to draw rough outlines which I hope will not seem dictated by over-confidence in my own conclusions, nor by underestimation of the difficulties to be met.

It is the Teacher's duty and privilege to sketch the "Impossible"; it is the business of the Statesman to find out how that Impossible can be realised.

Let me in a few words preface my replies to the questions set with a short statement of what I consider the main defects of our present arrangements.

1. "Secondary" education cannot be finally dealt with apart from "Primary" and "University" education.

2. We require *simplification* all round, and to have a distinct line drawn between the work to be undertaken by each type of educational institution. At present the mere lack of clearness regarding the work to be done by each school, muddles all minds from the cabinet minister to the dunce of a country school. We have all kinds of schools, many trying to usurp each other's place. All this needs mending.

3. It is necessary that education become once more

saturated with religion, and that the moral training of the nation be made the first and final aim. Secular education does not exist: education is either moral or immoral, is either religious or irreligious. By "moral and religious" I mean, not what some adults understand by these words, but what the phrase means to a schoolboy or school-girl. Most "moral" and "religious" teaching as now practised is simply nothing more than waste of time. Whatever the superstitions, or aspirations, of parents, they are not educating but miseducating when they thrust metaphysics, abstract doctrines, and hard sayings down their children's throats. Mothers are punished if they poison the child's body; perhaps it should be more clearly taught that it is criminal for them to poison the child's mind. It is poisoning the mind if they introduce indigestible dogmas which the child's mind cannot receive.

If this pedagogic fact were known, many School Board fights would not have taken place.

But while excluding hard sayings we have no right to leave children uninstructed as to their duty to their neighbour. When they know more about their duty to their neighbour, they will know more of their duty to God.

4. While education must once more put morals and religion (*i.e.*, character training) in the forefront, it must next reform its entire curriculum as regards both studies and amusements.

First, as regards studies. Too much attention has been given to *book work*, *words* apart from *things*, *analytic* studies, and *memory* work. A few powers have been developed and the rest neglected. In particular the fetish worship of Latin and Greek must be renounced. It means no real nsight into Roman and Hellenic life, but a weary in-

Answers to the Royal Commission

digestion over Latin and Greek phraseology. "Modern side" studies have been pursued in a similarly wrong way. They are often mere cram for so-called "practical life." No true aim has been kept in view, and accordingly the curriculum is without plan or order. Moreover method in teaching is conspicuous by its absurdity or its absence. Exact training of the eye, ear, voice, hand, &c., has in no big school obtained proper recognition.

Amid the confused whirl of examinations, teaching is impossible ; and amid the struggles to cram, teachers have forgotten education, whose real work is development of power and the building up of character. A reform of secondary education means, then, a reform of the curriculum as well as of the aim. It is more important that English merchants should be honest than that they should be technically instructed. Moral training is the first thing, and the next is a reformed curriculum throughout all stages, not the mere clapping on of "technical" subjects in a haphazard fashion, in hopes of rescuing our commerce from disaster. English life throughout is in a bad way, because the children of the well-to-do are so hopelessly ill-instructed in all that concerns real life. A mere spoonful of technical instruction is not going to help us, but an entirely reformed curriculum will.

5. Hardly less absurd, however, is the modern athletic curriculum. Once—long ago—boys *played* games. Now they are in training for the *business* of football *war*, where the combatants contend, with one eye upon the *Athletic News* and the other upon the gate-money. Once exercises were invented by the boys, and each school made its own game. Now a committee of gladiators try to settle the football rules for every school and schoolboy in

the world, without considering in the least the needs of boyhood or of school life. The moral purpose of games has been forgotten, and even the mental and physical purpose of the game is fast getting lost sight of. Football tours suggest—not the revelling of young blood in the delights of Nature—but the pothouse, and crowds of betting adorers of brute strength.

The athletic mania, at first both necessary and excellent, has done its work and is now degrading us. In fact, it would be a national benefit if this superfluous energy were drilled and disciplined by compulsory military service. The latter is not a mere war game, but a magnificent training in patriotism, discipline, and duty, all which characteristics appear noticeably absent from the masses of Englishmen to-day. There is, for the moment, a great cry for technical instruction, Sloyd, &c., but no one seems to consider that mere accretion of subjects in a curriculum will never produce organic unity in the plan, nor as the result, orderly growth in the boy. To most Englishmen these technical subjects are so many fads, which are to be tried to-day and dropped to-morrow. Money is being lavished, buildings are springing up, prizes, scholarships, certificates are being instituted, to induce some interest among our restless and unsatisfied populace. Bad national habits are thus being formed which will only be extirpated generations hence. Few seem to aim at taking a glance at the Nation as a whole, and at the National Estate as a whole. No one seems to ask how can this Nation's Property be best managed, not in the interests of the classes, nor of the masses merely, nor even in the interests of the whole Nation of to-day, with its petty selfishnesses and its mean ambitions; but in the interests of the immortal English People which has been offered the Empire of the World.

I. Universities.

Every educational institution which instructs people after their school days should form *part* of a corporation called The University, granting Diplomas certifying in simple English what a man can do, whether plumbing or carving, or writing Latin Verse.

All Universities, Technical Colleges, Industrial Colleges, &c., &c., of the British Empire should be federated, that is, should allow complete freedom to their students to go from one to another. All should form part of the British Imperial University.

The work of the University is *specialisation*. The work of the School is *general culture*. If all Schools gave only all-round education, every University could be organised for entire specialisation. Half the inefficiency of schools and of universities arises from this fact, that schools specialise, and hence universities have to teach the A B C of every subject, the moment the beaten track, for which the schools prepare, is left.

The "public" schools specialise, on the "classical" side, Latin and Greek; on the "modern" side, French and Physics. In one class they specialise for engineering; in another, for the army.

Then we have every imaginable degree of degeneration of the "classical" ideal of education down to the ghost of the ghost of the ghost of it, as in the higher grade Elementary Board School which teaches baby Latin to boys who are going to forge steel, when they have not been taught to clean their teeth, which is nationally of far greater importance. There is no reason, apart from tradition, custom, vested interests, and stupidity, why Latin and Greek, Grammar and Philology, should be treated differently from Chemistry, Engineering, Carpentry, or any other kind of study. All can be used for mental discipline if the Teacher can *teach*.

It is contrary to physiological and psychological law to plunge a boy into the difficulties of Latin before he has got used to the idea of a foreign country and has learnt to speak some foreign tongue. We might as well throw a boy into the Atlantic to make him swim, before he has learned in a pond or bath.

Moreover the type of mind which excels at "classics" is by no means of necessity the highest; in some cases it is the least original, least vigorous, least complex. Hence the docility of the pupil and the abnormal development of the mere memory. This is borne out by more than one instance in our national history; many who have shed lustre upon the English name did not undergo the sterilising influences of a "classical" curriculum. Tested by other means, the petty heroes of our present examination system would find their places often strangely reversed. Many a last would be first, and first last.

If we consider the enormous bribes offered to boys to induce them to study Latin and Greek, and the number of clever boys thereby caught, we may comprehend that the real worth of these studies has never yet been estimated aright. If these picked boys had from the first studied Natural Science, their ability would have been, with as much sense, attributed to "Science." A reorganised system of "secondary" education means then, primarily, the relegating of Latin and Greek studies to their proper

Answers to the Royal Commission

place, which is a place in the background. This is all the less to be deplored because the world no longer wants such an army of specialists in those languages, and the few retained by society to annotate texts could be used with advantage to put back into those literatures the divine *soul* which since the hunt after scholarships commenced, has suffered desecration, if not destruction, at the hands of pedants, who have mistaken the learning of phrases and the study of grammatical analysis for the appreciation of philosophic thought and poetic feeling, and the worship of Ideals.

1. *What should be the age (a) of entrance, (b) of competition for College Scholarships?*

(*a*) Eighteen for *normal* boys; none should remain at school later, none enter the University earlier, unless for very special reasons.

(*b*) Scholarships are an utter absurdity. They should be abolished and the funds thus set free be taken to increase the means of national education in all its grades, and to lower the education fees for all. No one should be bribed to study. If education were cheap, all could study who really wished to. The energy consumed in examining candidates for these bribes would be set free. The examiners would have time to discover merit by observation, and to teach and guide the promising pupils. The candidates would escape the demoralising cramming which places the school nearly on a level with the gambling house.

2. *How has the examination of Schools by the Universities worked?*

How many University examiners know anything at all about education? They have been in a groove all their lives, and can only see how well the youngsters fit the old groove. Of course the examining of Schools by the University is better than sheer chaos in saving the energies of teachers and in offering some standard. But the system of examination, as practised, is out of date, and was never based on a knowledge of pedagogics.

The examiner ought to see :—

(1) The *life* the boy leads, and his *environment*.

(2) The *curriculum* he goes through.

(3) The *way he is taught*, and the *way he responds to the teaching in class and out of class*.

Examinations are largely based upon the idea that teachers cannot be trusted to give honest opinions of their pupils. If a teacher is not honest let him be removed from office and trained till he be honest.

Every school, in place of the mark-book with its complicated system of averages and bonuses, should keep a record of :—

(1) The Work done, shown by the Work-plan, and Time-table.

(2) The Method of Instruction dominating the Teaching.

(3) The Results achieved, shown by the way the Boys live, behave, and converse.

3. *Could the Universities attract a larger number of "Science" and other students by a better provision of instruction, or by any other and what means ?*

The University would attract plenty of students for every conceivable subject if all could study what they wished, at small expense.

Only those should be allowed, however, to enter the University (in the normal manner) who had the *School leaving certificate*, of which more below.

Answers to the Royal Commission 163

(N.B. All candidates, who had not been to School, &c., would require special consideration.)

The Government should carefully avoid the mistake of instituting any more bribes in the shape of prizes and scholarships. Let all work be done for the work's sake. In the end this will attract the best material of all.

The moral deterioration, produced by marketing the treasures of wisdom, is daily getting more visible. We see it in the loss of that fine sense of honour which was so marked in "public" schools twenty years ago. It is shown by the remarks boys make about their future career, in which money largely bulks: what will bring in coin; not what will be worth doing for its own sake and for honourable renown to follow.

II. Secondary Schools and their Arrangements.

1. *Is it desirable that public provision should be made for Preparatory Schools, either Day or Boarding?*

No public money should be spent until all respectable schools at present existing are under public inspection, and the rest abolished.

When all schools are registered and brought into some state less chaotic than that they are now in, then the question of more schools can be faced; otherwise we may expect a vast waste of national money and energy. The Englishman has a great notion that he can do anything, at once, without long training, and without careful coöperation with others. The result is confusion tenfold worse than before.

2. *Where an Upper (or so-called "First Grade") Secondary School exists, is a separate Lower (so called " Second Grade"*

or "*Third Grade*") Secondary School needed, and, if so, whether under the same management?

There should be only *three* kinds of schools, each with three divisions (see *diagram* of this in the Atlas [1]).

A. The school for the Briton who will be one of the *muscle-workers*. He leaves school at fourteen *at the earliest*. As in this class puberty is reached at fourteen or before, a great effort should be made to keep the lad till fifteen at school and under guidance. [If the nation could screw up the courage to find the money, *it would pay to keep all boys till eighteen.*]

B. The school for the Briton whose work requires knowledge of the modern world, particularly about his own Empire, and about the two chief nations of Europe, the French and the Germans, and about our relatives, the Americans. He leaves at sixteen.

C. The school for the Briton who is to be a *leader*, whether in Politics, Law, Teaching, the Church, Army, Navy, or Commerce, &c., &c. He requires *an all-round education up till eighteen*, when he leaves school.

Each kind of school should have three divisions.

The "*Primary*" school (A) should have :—

(*a*) Kindergarten for children, mixed boys and girls, aged ... ... 3 to 7

(*a*) Fore-school for mixed boys and girls, aged 7 to 11

(*a*) School (1) for boys
       (2) for girls } ... ... 11 to 14

The *separation* ought to be made at *eleven* (not later),

---

[1] "An Educational Atlas." (Allen, London, 1900.)

Answers to the Royal Commission

at which time the girls of the class in question approach puberty, and become dangerous to the boys, who develop later.

The "*Secondary*" school (B) should have likewise :—
(*b*) Kindergarten for children, mixed boys and girls, aged ... ... 3 to 7
(*b*) Fore-school for mixed boys and girls ... 7 to 11
(*b*) School (1) for boys }
   (2) for girls } ... ... 11 to 16

The "*Tertiary*"[1] (C) should have likewise :—
(*c*) Kindergarten for children, mixed boys and girls, aged ... ... 3 to 7
(*c*) Fore-school for mixed boys and girls ... 7 to 11
(*c*) School (1) for boys }
   (2) for girls } ... ... 11 to 18

No girl or boy should stay later than eighteen. (We are considering at present only the *average normal type*. Cripples, Imbeciles, Moral Idiots, &c., must be considered apart.)

The *reasons* for the *three* sets of schools are as follows :—
(1) The children to be educated
  (i.) start with different inherited powers ;
  (ii.) belong to different physical, mental, and moral atmospheres ;
  (iii.) will grow at different rates.
Therefore
  (i.) must be handled differently at the start ;

---

[1] I suggest the names "*Primary*," "*Secondary*," "*Tertiary*," for simplicity ; but, as those words are already in use, we might instead call them : schools A, B, and C. The names are not unimportant by any means. The clear Nomenclature of German Art and Science is one enormous advantage in their schools, as our ridiculous absence of system is a fatal drawback in ours.

(ii.) must have different degrees of culture in their environment;

   (iii.) must have different mental meals, and feed at different speeds.

(2) If we mix children in different states of culture, we degrade the better, by the contact, more than we elevate the worse. For it is always easier to go down than to go up. A good boy may perhaps save one companion. A bad boy will corrupt a dozen. And this is more true the larger the numbers.

(3) We must not forget that the democratic dream of equality is a delusion. If we try to use education to *keep* people equal who are born equal; or worse still, to *make* people equal who are born unequal; we commit an outrage on nature and are false to the very meaning of the word Education.

We have to *draw out of* each *all* we can; but every water-spring has not the same *flow*, nor the same *quality*, of water. Let those who still hanker after equality become schoolmasters for a week. They will then abjure that amiable but misleading doctrine, and aim, instead, at making every child as good as *it* can be made. Our schools must be of three kinds complete throughout with three divisions, because, as a matter of fact, children can be so classed and probably always will be.

But we can easily transfer children from one school to another, if all schools be arranged as is here suggested. To make this possible, the work in each up to the age of eleven will be, as far as possible, the same. Any child who is fit for pro-

Answers to the Royal Commission 167

motion physically, mentally, and morally should be promoted.

The fees for all schools should be, if not the same, at any rate not so different that riches would confer a great advantage.

The three divisions of each kind of school need not be under the same management, because all schools would be mainly on the same lines, and hence children could pass easily from one to another without risk of not fitting in.

3. *Is the system of competitive entrance scholarships satisfactory?*

Competitive entrance scholarships are an evidence of absolute ignorance of true education. It is a horrible crime to make children compete at all. There should be a standard to pass, in order to ensure that the school suited the child; but no competitive test. The *whole* child (physical, mental, and moral) should be tested.

4. *What measures, if any, are required to facilitate the passing of scholars from one class of school to another?*

All schools should be very cheap, and then passage would be easy; and no schoolmaster ought to wish to keep back a boy if fit for a better school. Indeed the boy would either go on to a higher school or else to some branch of the Imperial University (see below). He would not remain longer in the school when he had got from it all it could do for him.

5. *Should Secondary Schools include a distinctly technical department, or should distinctly technical instruction be given in separate schools?*

Technical instruction is specialisation, and *is out of place in the school.* Every school should teach the great foundation principles of natural science as well as of human science, but without specialising. Technical studies should begin only when the boy, or girl, leaves school. School is the place for developing general powers of thought, feeling, and action ; in short, for *education*. It is not the place for teaching any trade, craft, or profession.

When the program of school studies is adequately drawn up, it will be seen that there can be no time for any specialisation. The boy requires to be taught all about *his own life*, and *what his body, his thoughts and feelings can do for him*.

Premature technical (*i.e.*, specialising) instruction, whether literary, scientific, or manual, always means a neglect of the *moral* education.

The children of the " A " school might specialise at 14, not before.

The children of the " B " school might specialise at 16, not before.

The children of the " C " school might specialise at 18, not before.

This subsequent specialisation should be carried out in *Colleges*, each of which should form part of the *Imperial University*, which should typify the National Unity of all classes in their several spheres of labour.

It is necessary for the production of National Unity and for the avoidance of strikes and squabbles and class hatred, that the interdependence of all specialising institutions should be made unmistakable. This requires a proper nomenclature, and a close alliance under one supreme head and one supreme rule.

The Imperial University would then have its local "Universities" of Oxford, London, Manchester, Melbourne, &c.; its University Colleges, its Polytechnics, Technical Schools, Naval and Military Academies and Industrial Institutes, divided thus—

Primary *Schools* (A) send children at 14 into Industrial *Colleges*.

Secondary *Schools* (B) send children at 16 into Technical *Colleges*.

Tertiary *Schools* (C) send children at 18 into Professional *Colleges*.

The Industrial Colleges being for boys from 14 onwards, should very carefully take account of the fact of puberty.

The Technical Colleges being for lads from 16 onwards would similarly have to take account of their age. At present the nation only provides protectors to guard the costly products of the highest seminaries of learning—the "public" schools. Surely these should require the nurse least. No *school* should have any technical (that is, specialistic) department whatever.

These three classes of Colleges would all form part of the University. It should be a *compulsory* part of the studies in each class of College to visit others and learn their relation to each other, to emphasise the fact that handwork does not constitute the only title to the name worker, and that the professional man's first duty is to understand the work and lives of the men in the more elementary departments, whose labours he ultimately directs.

As regards the *Tertiary* schools, our boys need to be made *men* before we make them experts in philology, chemistry, or engineering. To be men, and fit to govern workmen, they must have all their faculties awake and this will be impossible if they specialise before 18.

6. *When should technical instruction begin?*

Technical instruction ought to mean instruction in the application of natural science to distinctly bread-earning arts, not to mean instruction in the great general truths of nature, which in the "Tertiary" schools should be taught very fully to all. Technical instruction then, as defined above, belongs only to the next stage—namely, University education—and begins at 14, or 16, or 18, as already shown.

7. *What is the best method of proviaing Secondary Education in rural districts?*

This can only be answered when we have a map showing the distribution of schools over the kingdom.

Why should not children go by train? Special carriages for school-children should be reserved, and the railway companies be made responsible.

It is to be noted that mere local schools should not exclude boys from a distance. Change of scene, change of climate, change of companionship; all these are vital factors in true education.

III. Leaving (Abiturienten) Examination.

1. *Should it exist?*

Leaving Examination: Yes, undoubtedly.

2. *Who should conduct it?*

The school itself. The staff of a school should give its certificate, and take the consequences if its certificates lose value through being granted for poor work.

Why should not a school staff be as fit to grant a School diploma as university teachers are to grant a University diploma?

Is it not evident that a school staff must know better

Answers to the Royal Commission

the worth of a boy than a visiting university teacher, who never teaches boys, but only youths above 18?

Let each set of teachers be made to do the work it can.

3. *What advantages should it carry?*

The *school diploma* should state exactly what the boy had studied year by year, during the whole of his school curriculum. It should also state how the subject matter was treated. The report of the Government inspector for each year should be appended. If, as is probable, a written and oral examination was held each year to test the year's work, the boy's attainments for his age should be mentioned.

The school diploma should cover the entire life of the boy, and rigorously state his attainments, physical, mental, and moral. It should be regarded as given on oath, and mis-statements should be punished as perjury. The school diploma should possess the same advantages that a university diploma possesses; if from a good school, much and *vice versâ*.

4. *How far ought it to be uniform?*

Until the general system of secondary education is educative, entire freedom should be granted to Experimental Schools. Any forced uniformity at the present time would mean the extinction of all progress.

5. *What is your opinion of the working of present examinations conducted by the Universities?*

The Universities ought to be obliged to open their doors to any well-educated boy or girl who is likely to profit by the wider opportunities the University gives.

The present stereotyped entrance examinations exclude much excellent material, and in particular most boys with special *originality*. My own observations at school and since convince me that exceedingly dull boys are frequently admitted, and many really able boys excluded.

Oxford and Cambridge are to be pitied for still making Latin and Greek compulsory. One does not know which is most astonishing : the state of ignorance which does not see this, or the state of prejudice which will not see it. Such is the mental bias due to bad education.

IV. INSPECTION AND EXAMINATION.

Are they, or is either of them, desirable? Who should conduct them? and should the same authority conduct both?

For (a) *Endowed or Public;* (b) *Proprietary and Private Schools?*

Inspection is the best way, if not the only way, of really telling the worth of a school.

Inspection should cover the entire life, and not merely a part, least of all the mere intellectual part, of the life.

The Government ought to inspect.

Examinations should be arranged for by the school upon its own responsibility.

All schools should be treated alike.

The Inspector should know his work. Otherwise the whole thing is worse than useless.

The Inspector's report should be published compulsorily by the State.

V. ENDOWMENTS; WHETHER OR NOT NOW APPLIED TO EDUCATION.

1. *What additional power (if any) is desirable for changing* (a) *their application;* (b) *their situation?*

Answers to the Royal Commission

Full power should be granted, both as regards *object* and *place*.

2. *What authority should exercise that power?*

All endowments should be under State control.

3. *What should be done with endowments now applied to (a) elementary education; (b) apprenticing?*

All endowments should be applied to cheapening and improving education; never wasted on scholarships or prizes. The *reward for excellence* should be *increased opportunity; never money*.

VI. Relation of Elementary and Secondary Schools.

1. *Should Higher Grade Elementary Schools (a) remain; (b) be established where now wanting?*

This has been practically answered under II. The names Elementary and Secondary should be abolished. They mean, as now used, nothing exact. What is a "secondary" school? English carelessness about names and general ignorance of the meanings of words should be fought with in the schools and in education, if nowhere else. After the introduction of all the new titles which have been proposed, a still larger dictionary and guide to the intricacies of English educational nomenclature will be requisite, than is needed now. Our "system" is already the most insanely chaotic and complicated in the world, as pointed out recently at Oxford by the Principal of Vermont University. Let us not make it worse.

Some desire to run one class of schools against another. This is as wise as was the building of the

Manchester Ship Canal. Of what use nationally was it to benefit Manchester at the expense of Liverpool? and of what use is it to build elementary schools to run into the work of, and compete with, "secondary" schools of one kind or another?

Therefore—

(*a*) Leave whatever exists, till it be seen how all fits together.

(*b*) Establish nothing till the map and plan of campaign is worked out.

2. *Is the effect on them of Science and Art grants satisfactory? and if not, why not?*

The Science and Art grants have had some influence, as discipline; and have in a feeble way made the insular Britons understand that there is such a thing as method, uniformity, coöperation.

But if we ask about the progress of artistic education or scientific education under that department, it must be admitted that here, as in all we do, we are mainly *shopkeepers* (as we are called abroad), and in our anxiety to turn the school into a factory and shop, we are destroying all possibility of *education*.

As long as we look not at the work, but at the "results," *i.e.*, the amount of coin we can get, whether for hats, ships, cotton shirts, or Latin Grammar—so long we shall have no education, no increase of intelligence, but a woful increase of the dullest stupidity. Cram of Art and cram of Science are not perhaps the invention of the Science and Art Department, but the latter has certainly fostered cramming and injured real education. Nevertheless, the organisation has drilled people, and the English require plenty of drill.

3. *At what age should children leave Elementary for Secondary Schools?*

This has been answered above. (See II.)

When the schools are organised and the work adequately arranged, then a child could and should be removed from one school to another at the end of any year or term, if found fit physically, mentally, and *morally*. But do not let promotion depend on mere wits, any more than on mere muscle, or mere morals; and give some weight to *manners*.

There is visible a fatal tendency to imagine that mental education improves the morals. The exact reverse is the fact. Mental power is merely a sword, and a sword is neither moral nor immoral. To give a child a sword and teach it sword exercise won't prevent, but render more likely, its stabbing its mother. *The more the wits are developed, the more the affections need to be trained* to keep the character balanced. This is the chief blot on our national education now. It has given more attention to wits than to morals.

The same argument applies to all the talk about *Technical Instruction*. This may make a mechanic or a merchant clever, but never honourable and honest.

VII. TEACHERS.

1. *Training:*

(*a*) *What do you consider the best system?*

I do not understand the meaning of this question. Are there different *systems* of learning medicine?

Once the medical student went and was articled to a practitioner, and picked up under his personal guidance the mere rudiments of his art. This is in some measure the way our "Secondary" Teachers pick up the mere rudiments of their art; only, the necessary personal guidance is, in the "public" schools, scarcely ever forthcoming, and so the rudiments are very rudimentary.

The "system," as hitherto practised, is no proper system, though it might be made to grow into a workable one if the schools were overhauled from top to bottom.

The other course followed is to have *training colleges*, like Medical Schools. Here expert teachers should teach the art, not by lecturing from books, but by teaching from the living concrete; not from a few stray cases, but from regularly organised bodies of children, in dealing with whom educational art and science could be studied in all its branches.

(*b*) *How far is the same system applicable for the teachers of Secondary and for those of Elementary Schools?*

All children are a great deal more alike when young than when older. Moreover, there can be only one way of getting a sound scientific grasp of any art.

Therefore, evidently, *teachers of "Secondary" or any other schools, clergymen*, and *university teachers*, should all pass through the same training as Elementary teachers receive.

All education must begin in the same way, in the Kindergarten and the Fore-school, and no teacher, however able, can teach any one—however clever—unless the former knows *the way in which the latter's circle of ideas has developed, and is developing*.

There is another reason. It is highly desirable that all Teachers—in all grades of the profession—should be highly honoured and closely *bound together in the bonds of brotherhood.* The present water-tight compartment system is a source of national weakness. There is too much worldliness in place of devotion to quiet duty. There should be promotion possible all the way up and all the way down. It would not be a bad thing if some of the cultured, but quite untrained and unskilful, "University" men would teach in the elementary schools, where there would be a splendid moral harvest —if no intellectual one—to reward careful husbandry.

On the contrary, it would be no bad move to have the junior forms of "Secondary" schools taught by trained Elementary Teachers. Elementary Teachers are thorough, but too mechanical and wooden. "Secondary" teachers, as a rule, don't teach. The majority harangue the boys and write or talk elegantly. They often show an appetite for absorbing knowledge themselves, but they don't instruct. They can't, because they have probably never seen good teaching, and have learned only to *get*, and not to *give*.

After seeing the marvellous work in the Elementary schools of Germany one is appalled at the waste of time, energy, and money in our English "Secondary" schools. One can only liken the difference between the two kinds of teacher to the difference between a surgeon and a butcher. The surgeon removes the leg without staining his cuffs; the butcher hacks and hews, and bespatters with gore himself as well as his victim.

(c) *Should the Universities take any, and what, part in the work?*

If the "Universities" wish to avoid being left behind, they will take up this most pressing work.

But if the Government, as is to be hoped, means

to govern all subordinate people and institutions in the land, it will make the Universities move, and tell them what to do.

The Universities should institute Education Departments and organise training colleges at every school where opportunities for such work could be provided. Training apart from a school is like lecturing on medicine without a hospital or patients. On the other hand, we have to beware of the narrowing traditions of Schools, and the early ossification of Teachers.

Training means a total reform of the "Public" Schools. It is not, perhaps, too much to say that the upper and middle classes are being far worse educated than the lower. It is principally our false views as to what education means that blinds us to this. The common notion among the masses, that they are excluded from a sort of educational paradise hidden away in the adyta of the Public Schools, is due to their ignorance. Some day they will wake up and discover that the upper-class education is largely a fraud; that it does not produce intelligence, but a baneful dependence on memory, a puny circle of ideas, and a trust in mere conventional phrases.

Men trained in the world of real life, in contact with real nature, seeing the sun, not through drawing-room curtains, but in his naked splendour, will find that they have got hold of the real principles of nature and human life. They will make better governors, better lawyers, better teachers, better parsons, than the race of those reared on words, phrases, conventions, and superstitions.

The new education is due to a democratic and intellectual revolt against conventions.

Answers to the Royal Commission 179

What is chiefly needed is to provide as good education for the higher kind of worker as is in some slight degree already provided for the lower. Then, but not till then, will a reformed nation have adequate Leaders to guide it amid the ever-increasing complications and difficulties of advancing civilisation.

2. *Registration. Under what conditions should it be allowed? What privileges should it carry? Who should direct it? Should it be compulsory? and, if so, whether for all teachers, ana on the same lines for all teachers?*

Registration should be bound up with licensing, and should involve a small annual fee. No man should be suffered to teach unless registered and licensed.

The registration and licensing should be entirely in the hands of the Imperial Ministry, acting upon the advice of Imperial Council of Education. (See IX.)

Only those who have graduated in Pedagogics at a Training College (whether attached to a school or to a university) should be eligible for registration.

All teachers should be required to graduate in Education. The degree should be Bachelor of Education (Primary, Secondary, or Tertiary), *i.e.*, B. 1st Ed., B. 2nd Ed., &c., according as the teacher was destined for the A, B, or C school. (See II.)

These degrees should be granted only by a registered Training College.

Promotion from the Primary to Secondary, and from Secondary to Tertiary Bachelorship, should be granted by the Imperial Ministry alone, and only upon the recommendation of the Imperial Council of Education, instructed or not by the Local Authority. (See IX.)

The Central Ministry should also have the power of

promoting Bachelors to be Masters, and Masters to be Doctors of Education, upon the same recommendation, for distinct merit in the discharge of pedagogic work. The Doctor's degree should be reserved exclusively for the Headmasters of schools, seeing that their duties in importance, complexity, and difficulty, far transcend the duties of any subordinate master.

Only registered teachers, thus properly trained, should be allowed to hold pedagogic appointments, except in the following cases :

(1) In the case of temporary emergency, due to illness or such other sufficient reason, a non-registered (and unlicensed) teacher should be allowed, for not longer than one calendar month to fill the gap. If required for a longer period than one month, but not for more than the current term of three months, a temporary license should be requisite. To obtain the license the Headmaster as well as the Teacher should be bound to apply to the Ministry of Education, stating the circumstances, and the qualifications of the latter, and paying a small fee.

Infringements of this rule should be punished by fining both the Headmaster and the Teacher, and by publishing the fact.

(2) Each registered school should be allowed to apply for a license authorising it to have a certain number of students of Pedagogics seeking training qualifying them to become teachers. Only such schools should be allowed to have such students as were properly equipped for training purposes, and only under regulations approved by the Imperial Ministry.

It would be desirable to encourage progressive schools

Answers to the Royal Commission

to train students, because nothing is more difficult to get, yet nothing more important to have, than a constant and steady supply of good Teachers, *trained in the atmosphere of a thoroughly good school, and able to use its anatomy and physiology as object lessons.* This would produce more effective teachers than a Training College or system of mere books and talk. Perhaps one year at the University Training College and two at the Training College of a School, would, if combined, yield the best results, avoiding the superficiality of the College, and the superstitious worship of tradition of the School. All teachers should be required to join a corporation or guild (Teachers' Guild), which should in turn elect a committee to appoint representatives to sit in the Imperial Council.

VIII. DISTRICT AUTHORITIES FOR SECONDARY EDUCATION.

1. *What should be the area of a District Authority (e.g., a county or a group of counties)?*

2. *Should this authority be an existing one (e.g., the County Council) or one created* ad hoc, *by legislation or otherwise? and if so, how chosen?*

3. *What should be the Borough Authority (a) in county boroughs, (b) in smaller boroughs? Should it be an existing one (e.g., the Town Council or School Board) or created* ad hoc *? and if so, how chosen?*

4. *How should the respective jurisdictions of the District and Borough Authorities be adjusted (e.g., should the District Authority have any and what powers over (a) county boroughs, (b) other boroughs)?*

5. *What elements ought to be represented on District or*

other authorities for Secondary Education (e.g., Universities, Local University Colleges, Teachers)?

6. *Should a District or Borough Authority have any and what powers in respect of—*
    Elementary Education;
    Control over Governing bodies of Secondary Schools;
    The creation of new Seconaary Schools;
    Rating;
    The re-arrangement of endowments;
    Examination or inspection?

I do not feel that I have information sufficient to deal with the questions in this section. They belong moreover more to the Statesman than to the Teacher.

It is to be hoped, however, that the first need of English Education will not be forgotten—namely, the need of a uniform organic system, based on sense and not on custom. Such a system should be imposed from above in the first instance. No educator can wish to see local authorities elaborating schemes out of their own heads, and setting up a fresh collection of local schools, soon likely to become, like the present so-called "Public" Schools, beyond effective national control. Local control is excellent, and so is local interest, but until Secondary Education is fairly organised, let the power be at headquarters. Nor should we wish to prevent boys going to any part of the country which they might prefer, in search of the climate, scenery, and other peculiarities, as well as school atmosphere, most suited to their needs.

On the other hand, if enterprising County Councils desire to attract boys from a distance, as Town Councils try to draw visitors to their Winter Gardens or sea-bathing, &c., we may have a fresh outbreak of the competitive fever which already does so much to demoralise the schoolmasters, as it has nearly quite demoralised the merchant.

IX. CENTRAL EDUCATIONAL BOARD.

(*a*) *Is any and what Central Board needed?*

These questions are questions for the Statesman. To the schoolmaster who takes a glance round at the general national ends to be secured by all schools, all teaching, all education, in Church and State (for it should be understood that the parson is a teacher too, and each church an educational institution), it seems absolutely necessary that the entire educational machinery should be placed under national control.

No millionaire, and no company, and no sect, should have the power of instituting a huge seminary which may exert sooner or later a gigantic influence on English life, and on the national development, without the sanction and control of the Nation.

(*b*) *What should be its functions ?*

The Central Educational Board, which might with advantage bear a more agreeable title, such as Imperial Ministry of Education, should have the following duties.

(1) To issue all the *compulsory* regulations prescribed for any State (*i.e.*, Endowed) Institution undertaking the education of the young, whether physical, manual, mental, or moral. As improvements are instituted by this or that school, these should be added by degrees to the minimum program of all schools so as to bring all schools into line again. All schools endowed, or assisted, by public money should be called *State* Schools.

(2) To license private Experimental Schools, where pedagogic research could be carried on, with a view to discovering improved methods, which could afterwards be made compulsory items in the national seminaries. No private school should receive help from public money, but every private school should be inspected at the public charge and the report be published at the public charge, compulsorily.

(3) To be supreme educational judge of methods, which had been tested by individual teachers, or carried on in individual private schools or elsewhere. In fact, the Central Board would act largely as the Royal Society does, or should, towards individual scientists.

(4) To arbitrate in all disputes between the Heads of schools and the Governors, or local Authorities, having rights of supervision with regard to certain matters, *e.g.*, sanitation, &c.

(5) To instruct all local authorities, or governors, as to their functions and duties towards the school, which duties should be, roughly, (i.) to see to the carrying out of the prescribed structural sanitary arrangements ; and (ii.) to punish all neglect on the part of subordinate authorities by fine, *e.g.*, architects, builders, plumbers, &c. No school board, for instance, should be able to waste the ratepayers' money, without incurring the risk of a reprimand and a fine imposed by the Imperial Ministry for neglect or incapability. In fact, the Imperial Ministry (Central Board) should be to the Local Boards what Parliament is to the County Councils, or the Head of a firm to the Heads of departments. The Imperial Minister would have his subordinates constituting the Education Department of the Civil Service, and the Imperial

Ministry (Central Board) would be to him as the Indian Council is to the Viceroy.

(*c*) *Should they be exercised alone or in conjunction with a minister?*

The Imperial Ministry (Central Board) should be composed of educational experts, controlled, but not coerced, by the Cabinet Minister of Education.

The Board should not be muzzled, but should be allowed to state and publish its policy in cases where the Cabinet Minister either refused to adopt that policy, or initiated changes opposed to that policy.

(*d*) *How should such a Board be composed?*

It should contain members elected to represent such great bodies as the Teachers' Guild, The National Teachers Union, &c., &c., which understand school work. The colonies should be represented; for part of our duty is to provide teachers for colonial churches, universities and schools of all sorts, which they cannot do so well for themselves.

A German, a French, and an American expert should be on the Board in order to give the criticism from outside, which is so indispensable.

Lastly, all pedagogic bodies should have free access to the Board.

The Board should be elected for a fixed number of years and be well paid out of some of the funds at present wasted on scholarships. Its duty should be to propose measures to the Minister, and to criticise any measures proposed by him, before they are taken into Parliament. The Board would thus act as a sort of Grand Committee on Education.

(*e*) *What restriction should be imposed on its powers, so as to leave sufficient independence in the local authorities, and sufficient variety in the schools?*

The Central Government should only have power to regulate State (Endowed) schools. Private schools would need a license certifying the possession of proper premises and a properly qualified Head. The aim, work-plan, and time-table of every school should be made public, and also the scale of fees charged. It should be illegal to alter fees without notifying the fact and having it published and endorsed on the license. The aim here is to prohibit underselling.

With the substitution of inspection for examination, it will be possible to get more variety in the schools and more initiative and independence in the teachers without the necessity of fundamentally different programs.

The majority of schools will have to follow definite and well-approved lines. But a certain proportion of schools will always be needed to act as *Educational Laboratories* where pedagogic experiments can be carefully executed, and the results annually published for the enlightenment of the Imperial Ministry of Education (the Central Board). The results, which are approved, would gradually become a compulsory addition to the national educational program.

X. MISCELLANEOUS.

1. *Should there be a registration of schools, as distinct from teachers? And if so, under what conditions and with what privileges?*

All schools, whether public or private, should be registered and licensed. No school should be allowed to exist unless thus registered and licensed.

Every school should be required to prepare a yearly

Answers to the Royal Commission 187

report, stating exactly what has been accomplished during the school year. A copy of this should be sent to the Imperial Ministry.

Each school would have to be registered, as undertaking distinct work (see II.) and as of class A, B, or C.

No School or Headmaster should be able to recover fees in a court of justice unless duly registered.

The purpose of the license is to compel each school annually to announce its continued existence, and to contribute a small sum to the cost of national educational management.

Each Registered School should have the right to grant a Diploma, stating exactly the worth of the boy physically, mentally, and morally, when he leaves.

Fees paid to any registered school should be deducted in estimating income tax.

2. *University extension classes: what should be their relation to Secondary Education?*

University Extension lectures could be made very useful to schools in introducing short courses of lectures during term, in order to open out new vistas and increase the wealth of facts and ideas.

They cannot be made part of the ordinary systematic curriculum. Extension lecturing is one thing, skilled school teaching is another, and quite different, thing.

The extension lectures would do two things. They would give the boys a new current of thought, and a new world to explore in imagination; and they would bring a fresh whiff of air from the Universal life outside, to keep the somewhat jaded schoolmaster from premature ossification. No examinations whatever should be associated with this work.

3. *Continuation and evening schools: ought they to be deemed agencies for Secondary Education?*

I do not understand this question. In (II.) I have endeavoured to show the place for evening schools. It is a pity the English nomenclature is so entirely lacking in sense. What is a "continuation school"? It is really necessary that not merely Institutions should be devised, but that they should obtain appropriate titles. Our slipshod names are a sign that our institutions are devised by those who are not taking a comprehensive view of the ends to be secured by each part of the pedagogic machine. The "evening" or continuation schools for class A would not interfere with schools for B or for C. (See Atlas.[1])

4. *How far should regard be had to existing schools Proprietary or Private, or Higher Grade Elementary, in considering the question of founding new public schools?*

It would be prudent before spending money on new schools, to find out exactly what schools already exist. We want to know geographically where the schools are, the number of boys in each, their program of studies, their general life and aims. This, with maps and diagrams, should be published to insure that the circumstances are clearly and completely understood, without which we might be trying to carry coals to Newcastle. Before making any new schools let us use to the utmost all the resources we have. This is not only prudent, but simple justice to all concerned. Let every existing school get the chance of recognition as part of the National Educational system. If any school refuse to accept a place, let it please itself, and take the consequences.

[1] See footnote, page 164.

5. *What is your experience of the teaching of boys and girls in the same day school, or the same day classes?*

I have had very little experience myself of teaching boys and girls together, but I have frequently discussed this matter and kindred subjects with both young and old, and give shortly the conclusion come to. The prevalent belief, that boys and girls are meant by Providence to grow up together and to be much together in early life, and that many evils arise from boys and girls being educated apart; this belief I consider to be based upon too slender a foundation. I have above (see II.) suggested that children should be educated together until 11 years of age, but not longer, for these reasons:

(1) It is not natural but quite unnatural, to make boys and girls after that age work together, study together, play together. They do not naturally wish to do so, but naturally tend to have separate work, separate interests, separate games. (At least, healthy boys do. Girls, after some struggle to become boys, do indeed seem to resign themselves, as it were, finally to the inevitable.) This education together becomes still more unnatural if they are made to compete with one another.

Men and women do not respect one another more, but less, when obliged to compete with one another. Boys feel the same towards girls. We may anticipate less affection, less chivalry, and less respect even, where boys and girls are made to compete. But, however good our educational plans, some competition must arise between scholars in one class, and hence there will be a tendency towards hostility rather than towards affection. All that weakens real affection—I do not mean sentimentality—between the sexes, degrades their relation to one another.

(2) Familiarity breeds contempt. Boys idealise girls when not too much with them, and *vice versâ*. Put them side by side every day for years, and the relationship will probably not be refined or exalted, but perhaps vulgarised and degraded.

(3) The isolation of the male and the female is essential, if each is to have the peculiar electrical potential, which constitutes the essential sex factor, and from which flows not only all the possible vices, but all the possible virtues.

Put your boys and girls together, or your men and women together, overmuch, and, if you do not, by such close contact, increase the electrical polarity, and hence the danger of disruptive electrical discharge, you will by slow electric leakage reduce the danger of explosions at the expense of the very electric potential, out of which all virtue has to come.

To break a boy's spirit is not the way to obtain a powerful character, and to tame the savage male is not the way to produce men of valour, ability, and goodness. Virtue consists in the control of the positive energy of the man, not in its removal.

(4) The vices of boys and girls—often attributed to their not being trained together—would only be increased if without long centuries of education in these matters, they were thrown more into each other's company.

The cause of vice is mainly lack of knowledge and of training. All children should be taught the laws of life, and above all should have the affections carefully cultivated and educated. When this is done, it will be found that boys are just as modest and clean-minded as girls, and that men can be as clean as women.

(5) It should not be forgotten that, while in the

male puberty slowly developes, the girl, according to medical authorities, becomes a woman in a few months. Therefore I think that it would be wise to separate boys and girls between 11 and 18, as much for the boys' sakes as for the girls'. We should aim at retarding puberty in the male, for it is generally found to be later in the higher types. But it is to be feared that the co-education of boys and girls would accelerate the masculine development, and this would be disastrous, both for the individual and for the nation.

CECIL REDDIE.

ADDED NOTE.

The above questions, put by the Royal Commission, indicate the problems at present demanding solution, according to the views of responsible public men. I trust this is sufficient apology for inserting my answers here. It is not enough to organise a school. If the latter is to endure, it must be designed to fit into a system of national education. The Tertiary School I am endeavouring to organise is not intended to suit the whims of a few faddists, but the normal wants of the Directing Classes of a Reorganised English Nation.

C. R.

March, 1898.

12. THE WORKSHOP. (*Summer, 1892*).

Copyright

CHAPTER IX.

A French Verdict
in "La Science Sociale." Oct. 1894.

CHAPTER IX.

A FRENCH VERDICT IN "LA SCIENCE SOCIALE," OCTOBER, 1894.

QUESTIONS DU JOUR.

LA RÉFORME DE L'ÉDUCATION.[1]

UN NOUVEAU TYPE D'ÉCOLE.

Si l'on pouvait jamais prétendre résumer la question sociale en une formule, on paraîtrait autorisé à dire qu'elle est surtout une question d'éducation. En somme, il s'agit actuellement de s'adapter aux nouvelles conditions du monde, qui exigent qu'on se rende capable de se tirer d'affaire par soi même. J'ai montré ailleurs comment les vieux cadres, sur lesquels on avait l'habitude et l'on se croyait même le devoir de s'appuyer, sont, aujourd'hui, brisés ou insuffisants.[2] .

Nous avons la bonne, ou la mauvaise chance, comme on le voudra, d'arriver au moment où s'accomplit cette évolution fatale. Tout le malaise que nous éprouvons vient du contraste qui se révèle entre notre système d'éducation, conçu d'après des méthodes vieillies, et les nécessités nouvelles de la vie : nous continuons encore, tranquillement, à former des hommes pour une société qui est définitivement morte. Il est excessivement difficile de réagir contre une pareille éducation : je ne sais pas si mes lecteurs s'en rendent compte pour eux-mêmes, mais je ne constate que trop bien le phénomène en ce qui me concerne. Je sens

---

[1] *La Science Sociale, suivant la méthode d'observation.* Directeur : M. Edmond Demolins. 9e année, tome xviii., 10e livraison. Livraison d'Octobre, 1894. Paris ; Firmin-Didot.
[2] *Comment élever et établir nos enfants ?* 1 broch. in-16. Firmin-Didot.

parfaitement qu'il y a deux hommes en moi : l'un, par l'étude scientifique des phénomènes sociaux, voit ce qu'il faut faire et peut en disserter plus ou moins doctement ; l'autre, emprisonné dans sa formation première, écrasé en quelque sorte sous le poids du passé, ne peut pas faire ce que voit le premier, ou ne peut le faire que difficilement et partiellement. . .

Mais ce qui est difficile pour nous et à notre âge, ne l'est pas pour nos enfants ; eux, du moins, sont encore comme une cire molle qui peut recevoir des impressions nouvelles et les garder. Si nous sommes condamnés à rester sur la rive, aidons-les à franchir ce Rubicon. Voilà, oui, voilà la grande œuvre actuelle des pères de famille : ceux qui ne la font pas manquent au premier de leurs devoirs et ils en seront cruellement punis dans leurs fils.

Je voudrais, en ce qui me concerne, remplir ce devoir vis-à-vis de mes enfants ; aussi ai-je mis à profit, cette année, un nouveau séjour en Angleterre, pour examiner de plus près et à un point de vue pratique cette question de l'éducation. Je souhaite que cette enquête apporte autant de lumière à mes "confrères," les pères de famille français, qu'elle m'en a apporté à moi-même.

I.

Quoique l'éducation anglaise soit beaucoup mieux appropriée que la nôtre aux nouvelles conditions de vie, quoiqu'elle réussisse mieux à former des hommes d'initiative, habitués à ne compter que sur eux-mêmes, cependant les Anglais se préoccupent plus que nous des réformes à apporter à la formation des jeunes gens. . . .

Pour bien comprendre la difficulté en présence de laquelle ils se trouvent, il ne faut pas oublier que l'Angleterre ne forme pas un type social homogène : trois éléments ont concouru à sa formation : le Celte, le Normand, le Saxon. Les deux premiers se rattachent, comme nous, à la formation communautaire ; le troisième, seul, appartient à la formation particulariste. Dans un article publié récemment dans cette Revue,[1] M. Paul de Rousiers a fort bien exposé, et je n'ai pas à y revenir, comment cette double formation crée, dans les écoles de la Grande-Bretagne, deux tendances très opposées. A vrai dire, ces écoles sont le produit de l'influence celtique et normande combinées, mais constamment et insensiblement modifiées par l'influence saxonne grandissante. . . . En d'autres termes, les méthodes sont restées anciennes, tandis que l'esprit s'est renouvelé. C'est cette opposition qui crée tout le malaise scolaire dont l'Angleterre souffre actuellement et qui explique les efforts que

[1] Voir la livraison d'août, p. 101.

font nos voisins pour en sortir. L'esprit saxon, grandissant depuis un siècle, cherche la formule de la nouvelle école, de celle qui répondra pleinement à ses besoins et à sa formation sociale.

Ce besoin, c'est, essentiellement, de faire des hommes pratiques et énergiques, et non des fonctionnaires ou de purs lettrés.

M. de Rousiers cite, comme expression la plus complète de ce progrès scolaire, les huit *Grammar schools* et les deux *High schools* de Birmingham.

Ces écoles sont, en effet, une curieuse manifestation de l'évolution qui est en voie de s'accomplir en Angleterre, mais elles n'en sont pas la dernière expression. Cette évolution a déjà dépassé ce point, ainsi qu'il m'a été donné de le constater lors de mon dernier voyage.

Un jour que je causais avec M. Geddes sur l'enseignement en Angleterre, il me dit : "Nous attendons demain, au *Summer Meeting*, un homme qui pourra vous intéresser, car il est le fondateur et le directeur d'une école établie dans le centre de l'Angleterre et conçue d'après un type nouveau ; c'est le docteur Cecil Reddie." Je fus bien étonné, le lendemain, quand on nous présenta l'un à l'autre.

Il y a, chez nous, un type classique du directeur de collège, du professeur : tenue correcte, vêtement sombre, longue redingote noire, air plus ou moins solennel et compassé d'un homme convaincu qu'il exerce un sacerdoce et qui le laisse voir ; la démarche lente, l'attitude réservée, la conversation remplie de sentences propres à former l'esprit et le cœur de la jeunesse. Surtout de la dignité, extraordinairement de dignité.

L'homme qui me serrait vigoureusement la main était tout différent. Avez-vous quelquefois essayé de vous représenter un pionnier, un squatter, dans le Far West ? Quant à moi, je ne me le figure pas autrement que le docteur Cecil Reddie. Grand, mince, solidement musclé, remarquablement taillé pour tous les sports qui exigent de l'agilité, de la souplesse, de l'énergie, et avec tout cela, un costume qui complète bien la physionomie, le costume du touriste anglais : blouse en drap gris avec ceinture dessinant la taille, culottes courtes, gros bas de laine repliés au-dessous des genoux, solide paire de chaussures, enfin, sur la tête, un béret. Je donne ces détails, parce que ce type de directeur me semble être l'image vivante du type d'école que je vais vous décrire : l'homme est bien la représentation exacte de l'œuvre.

Le lendemain, qui était un samedi, jour où les cours sont suspendus, nous étions perchés, le docteur Reddie et moi, sur le siège d'un des immenses omnibus anglais qui emmenaient en excursion les membres du

Summer Meeting. Pendant tout le trajet, et pendant la plus grande partie de la journée, M. Reddie m'exposa l'idée et le plan de son école, répondant à mes questions et m'en posant à son tour.

" L'enseignement actuel, me dit-il en substance, ne répond plus aux conditions de la vie moderne ; il forme des hommes pour le passé et non pour le présent. La majorité de notre jeunesse gaspille une grande partie de son temps à étudier les langues mortes, dont très peu ont l'occasion de se servir dans la vie. Ils effleurent les langues modernes et les sciences naturelles et restent ignorants de tout ce qui concerne la vie réelle, la pratique des choses et leurs rapports avec la société. Notre système de jeux a également besoin d'une réforme, autant que nos méthodes de travail. Le surmenage (*cram*) athlétique est aussi réel que le surmenage classique. Ce qui rend la réforme difficile, c'est que nos écoles subissent l'influence des Universités, pour lesquelles elles préparent un certain nombre de leurs élèves. Or, ces Universités, comme toutes les vieilles corporations, ne sont pas maîtresses d'elles-mêmes ; un spectre invisible et intangible plane au-dessus du directeur et des maîtres : c'est l'esprit de tradition et de routine, qui a plus de force que l'autorité elle-même.

"Fort bien, mais comment votre école parvient-elle à modifier ce système d'enseignement ?

"Notre but est d'arriver à un développement harmonieux de toutes les facultés humaines. L'enfant doit devenir un homme complet, afin qu'il soit en état de remplir tous les buts de la vie. Pour cela, l'école ne doit pas être un milieu artificiel dans lequel on n'est en contact avec la vie que par les livres ; elle doit être un petit monde réel, pratique, qui mette l'enfant aussi près que possible de la nature et de la réalité des choses. On ne doit pas apprendre seulement la théorie des phénomènes, mais aussi leur pratique, et ces deux éléments doivent être joints intimement à l'école, comme ils le sont autour de nous, afin qu'en entrant dans la vie, le jeune homme n'entre pas dans un monde nouveau auquel il n'a pas été préparé, et où il est comme désorienté. L'homme n'est pas une pure intelligence, mais une intelligence unie à un corps et on doit aussi former l'énergie, la volonté, la force physique, l'habileté manuelle, l'agilité. . . ."

A mesure que le docteur Reddie me parle, je vois peu à peu se dégager l'idée qui domine et inspire son œuvre, mais elle est encore quelque peu confuse et voilée. Je lui demande alors de m'indiquer, heure par heure, l'emploi d'une journée. Ce tableau et les détails qu'il me donne,—et sur lesquels je vais revenir,—jettent plus de lumière dans mon esprit, et je commence à apercevoir assez nettement le mécanisme de l'institution.

M. Beveridge, qui, depuis trois ans, suit mes conférences au *Summer Meeting*, et qui est un lecteur de la *Science sociale*, avait bien voulu m'inviter à rester chez lui jusqu'à la reprise de mes conférences, le lundi matin. Je lui demandai s'il avait entendu parler de l'Ecole du docteur Reddie. Il me répondit qu'il était allé la visiter et que son fils aîné, âgé de treize ans, devait y entrer dans un mois. Il ne s'était pas contenté d'aller la visiter, il avait encore écrit à plusieurs pères de famille pour savoir s'ils étaient satisfaits de l'enseignement donné à leurs fils. Les réponses qu'il me communiqua me frappèrent par la concordance des appréciations et par l'indication des résultats obtenus : on en jugera par le texte que je donne intégralement :

"Cher Monsieur,

"... Mon fils est resté un an et demi à l'Ecole d'Abbotsholme : il était âgé de quinze ans ; il y a acquis plus d'intelligence qu'il ne l'avait fait dans les écoles qu'il avait suivies auparavant. Il a grandi physiquement et moralement et j'ai été plus que content des résultats obtenus. Le docteur Reddie est un homme d'une individualité très forte et né professeur ; j'estime que la méthode et les principes de l'Ecole sont excellents. Mon fils aimait extrêmement l'Ecole et le genre de travail qui s'y fait, et je crois que c'est un sentiment général parmi les élèves. L'allure morale est parfaite et je suis sûre que vous ne pouvez rien fair de mieux que d'y envoyer votre fils."

"Cher Monsieur,

"En réponse à votre lettre au sujet d'Abbotsholme, je suis très heureux de satisfaire à vos questions.

Nous avons à Abbotsholme deux garçons, et ils s'y sont, tous deux, perfectionnés sous le rapport de la santé. Ils nous écrivent que le dernier terme s'est passé très paisiblement et qu'ils se trouvent très heureux. La vie y est très saine. On apprend aux enfants à se suffire à eux-mêmes et à être très indépendants. Je trouve le ton moral de l'École élevé et, autant que j'en puis juger, les élèves sont recrutés dans un milieu choisi.

"Il existe une grande franchise entre les maîtres et les élèves. Un des professeurs est venu fêter le Christmas avec nous et nous avons été frappés de voir dans quels termes fraternels il était avec nos garçons. Ces derniers affectionnent tous leurs maîtres.

"Notre fils aîné a fait de rapides progrès dans ses études. Le second est plus en retard, mais bien plus éveillé, et tous deux sont devenus plus actifs. Il y a là un champ très ouvert à la personnalité.

"Il n'y a pas d'enseignement dogmatique particulier : on fait seulement les prières du matin et du soir ; en dehors de cela, les élèves vont à l'église paroissiale. Nous sommes congréganistes et nos garçons sont toujours heureux de retrouver leur chapelle.

"Nous espérons envoyer bientôt un autre de nos fils à cette Ecole, mais il est encore trop jeune : il n'a que huit ans et demi. . . ."

" CHER MONSIEUR,

"Je peux répondre, avec le plus grand plaisir, a vos questions sur l'Ecole d'Abbotsholme, car mon fils y est depuis quatre termes. Il s'y trouve très heureux et en retire un grand bien. Vous avez pu vous rendre compte, par le prospectus, du but de l'Ecole. L'enseignement classique n'est pas très développé, mais on enseigne les langues modernes et tout ce qui est utile et nécessaire aux garçons dans la vie. Le caractère moral et la santé sont particulièrement étudiés.

"La nourriture est excellente et variée, très différente de celle qui est donnée ordinairement dans les écoles.

"Les principes professés dans le prospectus sont rigoureusement et soigneusement suivis par un homme d'un esprit et d'un caractère très décidés, et en même temps plein de sympathie pour la jeunesse.

"Cette Ecole ne comprenant qu'une cinquantaine d'élèves, chaque enfant peut être plus étudié et suivi avec plus de soin. Je n'y suis resté qu'un jour ou deux et j'ai été grandement impressionné par le charme de la vie.

"A mon avis, ce système d'éducation n'a pas de défaut, excepté (et vous pouvez trouver que ce n'est pas un défaut) le besoin d'un enseignement particulier de l'Ecriture sainte.

"La maison est très saine et très confortable. J'ajoute que les maîtres sont des hommes très agréables et très cultivés. Evidemment, le Dr Reddie cherche, dans ses professeurs, des caractères élevés et affinés, afin d'influencer les garçons dans le bien. Plusieurs d'entre eux sont très bons musiciens."

L'opinion que m'exprimait M. Beveridge et les jugements que l'on vient de lire m'engagèrent à pousser plus loin mon enquête : j'en consigne ici les résultats.

II.

L'Ecole fondée par le docteur Reddie a été ouverte, au mois d'octobre 1889, à Abbotsholme, dans le Derbyshire : elle est située en pleine campagne, au milieu d'un domaine rural, qui est, ainsi qu'on va le voir, un des facteurs importants de ce nouveau système d'éducation. . . .

Elle procure la sensation de la vie réelle et non d'une vie artificielle ; elle reproduise l'aspect de la maison paternelle et non celui d'une caserne, ou d'une prison.

Tout autour, l'air, la lumière, l'espace, la verdure, au lieu de cours étroites et enfermées entre de hautes murailles. Cette première vue extérieure donne l'impression d'une résidence agréable : il n'a pas encore été démontré qu'un collège doive nécessairement avoir une apparence rébarbative.

Cette impression persiste, quand on pénètre à l'intérieur. . . Comparez cela avec nos odieux réfectoires de collège, et ce premier aspect des choses vous donnera déjà une idée très différente du système d'éducation que l'on doit suivre ici. . . .

C'est la vie de famille : l'enfant n'est pas arraché violemment de la vie réelle ; il n'est pas transporté dans un monde à part et complètement artificiel ; il a seulement passé d'un *home* dans un autre, qui en reproduit fidèlement l'image. . . .

Tel est le cadre ; voyons maintenant le tableau.

Je crois que le plus simple est de reproduire d'abord l'horaire de chaque jour, et d'en suivre ensuite les grandes divisions :

6 h. 15 : lever (en hiver 7 h.), suivi d'un léger repas ;
6 h. 30 : exercice d'assouplissement et du maniement d'armes ;
6 h. 45 : première classe ;
7 h. 30 : chapelle ;
7 h. 45 : déjeuner (*breakfast*). C'est un sérieux déjeuner à l'anglaise avec œufs, jambon, etc. ; ensuite arrangement des chambres : chaque élève fait son lit lui-même ;
8 h. 30 : seconde classe ;
10 h. 45 : lunch léger ; s'il fait beau, exercice des poumons en plein air, déshabillé jusqu'à la taille ;
11 h. 15 : troisième classe ;
12 h. 45 : chant, ou natation dans la rivière, suivant la saison ;
1 h. : dîner ;
1 h. 30 : exercices à l'orgue, ou au piano ;
1 h. 45 : jeux et travaux de jardin et de culture, ou excursions à pied, ou à bicyclette ;
4 h. : travail à l'atelier ;
6 h. : thé ;
6 h. 30 : chant, répétition de comédies, musique, concerts, etc. ;
8 h. 30 : souper et chapelle ;
9 h. : coucher.

La première impression qui se dégage à la lecture de cet horaire, c'est la variété d'exercices qui composent la journée. On sent la préoccupation d'éviter le surmenage et de développer de front toutes les aptitudes naturelles : instruction classique, instruction manuelle, instruction artistique.

La durée se décompose ainsi, entre les diverses catégories de travaux :

Travail intellectuel	5 heures.
Exercices physiques et travaux manuels	4 h. 1/2
Occupations artistiques et récréations de société	2 h. 1/2
Sommeil	9 h.
Repas et temps libre	3 h.
Total	24

Ajoutons, que le dimanche, il n'y a pas de classe ; les élèves sont maîtres de l'emploi de leur temps.

En somme, chaque jour de la semaine est divisé en trois parties bien distinctes : la matinée est surtout consacrée au travail intellectuel, aux études scolaires ; l'après-midi, aux travaux manuels sur le domaine, ou dans l'atelier ; la soirée, à l'art, à la musique, aux récréations de société.

Essayons, en suivant cette triple division, de nous rendre compte du fonctionnement de la nouvelle Ecole et des résultats qu'elle produit.

La méthode suivie, pour les études scolaires, est dominée par les principes suivants : " Mettre les élèves en rapport autant avec les choses qu'avec les mots qui les expriment, de manière à procéder constamment du concret à l'abstrait. Elever les jeunes gens dans l'idée de faire usage de ce qui leur a été enseigné et avec le désir d'apprendre pour eux-mêmes, sans le stimulant des récompenses et des prix."

D'après une opinion très répandue en Angleterre et aux Etats-Unis, la méthode qui consiste à pousser au travail par l'émulation entres les élèves est défectueuse : elle fonde le progrès sur la jalousie mutuelle et non sur le sentiment du devoir ; par là, elle développe un mauvais penchant de la nature humaine. Pour transformer les enfants en hommes, il faut les traiter comme des hommes, en faisant appel le plus possible à leur conscience. " Cette méthode, me dit le docteur Reddie, loin de diminuer l'intérêt des enfants pour le travail, tend, au contraire, à l'augmenter, parce que cet intérêt a pour objet non une récompense, mais le travail lui-même. Il ne faut pas que les enfants puissent croire que le prix, la récompense honorifique, soit le but et la fin de l'éducation. Les écoliers doivent apprendre que la vie n'est pas une loterie, ni la satisfaction de la vanité."

Je crains que cette manière de voir ne paraisse bien surprenante à un lecteur français, car tout notre système d'enseignement est fondé sur une méthode opposée. . . .

L'enseignement des langues, particulièrement des langues modernes, tient une grande place, dans la nouvelle école et il se distingue nettement de la méthode qui est généralement suivie. Je n'étonnerai certainement personne en affirmant que nous étudions les langues, mais que nous ne les apprenons pas. Manifestement, notre méthode est mauvaise.

Celle de M. Reddie me paraît plus efficace. Pendant les deux premières années, c'est-à-dire pour les enfants de dix et onze ans, l'enseignement est donné en anglais. Pendant les deux années suivantes, on parle le plus possible en français ; puis, également pendant deux années, en allemand. Le latin, et, pour certains élèves qui le désirent, le grec, ne sont enseignés qu'ensuite.

On comprend, sans qu'il soit besoin d'insister, que cet enseignement polyglotte n'est possible qu'à la condition de suivre une méthode pratique, qui consiste, du moins pour les langues vivantes, á apprendre d'abord à parler et à laisser au second plan la grammaire, dont l'étude ne vient que plus tard et dans la mesure strictement nécessaire à la connaissance usuelle de la langue. Cette méthode, généralement inconnue des professeurs de langues, est celle de la nature elle-même. . . .

L'enseignement des mathématiques est concu avec le même caractère pratique : on fait faire aux élèves des applications des calculs qui leur ont été enseignés : par exemple, ils confectionnent certains ouvrages dont il leur faut combiner les mesures ; ils se livrent à des travaux d'arpentage. On leur a distribué les comptes de dépense de la ferme, du jardin, de l'atelier, des jeux, des fournitures de bureaux, du laboratoire de chimie, de la classe du dessin, de la nourriture, du chauffage ; ils doivent les mettre en état et faire, pour cela, tous les calculs nécessaires. On conviendra que cette manière de procéder donne à ces études abstraites un intérêt particulier ; chacun en voit l'utilité pratique. Les chiffres s'animent, ils deviennent vivants, ils instruisent à conduire une maison, une exploitation industrielle ou commerciale, ils préparent, en un mot, des hommes pratiques, ils prennent vraiment un caractère social.

L'étude des sciences naturelles a pour point de départ l'observation directe : cela est d'autant plus facile que l'Ecole est établie à la campagne, et que les enfants peuvent recueillir aisément de nombreux spécimens du règne minéral, végétal et animal. En outre, la vie, les habitudes, les parties externes d'un animal sont étudiées avant les organes internes et le squelette ; les formes et la structure des plantes, avant leur classification ; les noms et les apparences des astres et des planètes, avant les lois de leur mouvement. Les excursions, que nous avons vues figurer sur l'horaire, sont une excellente occasion pour faire ces diverses observations. La science devient ainsi plus naturelle, plus intelligible, plus attrayante ; elle pénètre plus facilement dans l'esprit et s'y grave plus profondément. L'étude laisse après elle, non pas le dégoût, comme il arrive trop souvent avec nos méthodes, mais le désir de pousser ses connaissances plus loin, même après la sortie du collège, grâce à l'intérêt qui a été une fois éveillé.

L'histoire est enseignée d'après une méthode qui tend à se rapprocher de celle que nous suivons dans la Science sociale. On se préoccupe surtout d'exciter l'intérêt " par l'*observation de la cause et de l'effet*, dans les caractères et les mouvements du drame, plutôt qu'en promenant la mémoire à travers les faits et les dates." On cherche à déterminer les relations entre les caractères physiques et politiques du pays et leur développement commercial. On commence par l'étude de l'histoire d'Angleterre, puis on étudie des périodes caractéristiques de l'histoire du monde. Avec l'histoire romaine, un type de société à grands pouvoirs publics, qui a contribué plus largement à l'expansion de la race au dehors. . . .

En somme, l'idée qui domine toute la partie scolaire du programme, est de ne jamais séparer la théorie de la pratique et d'aboutir, autant que possible, à des connaissances utilisables pour se conduire dans la vie.

III.

L'après-midi est presque exclusivement consacré aux travaux manuels et aux exercices physiques : c'est l'éducation du corps après celle de l'intelligence. Etant donné le souverain mépris, que notre système d'enseignement témoigne pour le corps, c'est certainement cette partie du programme qui doit étonner le plus un père de famille français. . . .

L'après-midi (de 1 h. 45 à 6 heures) est consacré aux travaux de jardinage et de culture, aux travaux à l'atelier, ou à des excursions à pied et à bicyclette.

" Notre but, dit le Programme que j'ai entre les mains, est de développer l'éducation physique, le savoir et l'intérêt dans les occupations industrielles, l'énergie dans les entreprises et une appréciation exacte du travail accompli, soit qu'on ait plus tard à le faire soi-même, soit qu'on ait à le diriger. Beaucoup de défaillances dans la vie sont causées par la faiblesse physique : aussi les enfants doivent-ils faire, chaque jour, des exercices physiques et un travail manuel. On en sent le besoin pour donner de l'énergie à tout le corps et pour diminuer sa sensibilité, qui provient du surmenage intellectuel et de la vie trop sédentaire."

Ici encore, la préoccupation a été de faire accomplir des travaux qui aient un objet et une utilité pratiques, afin de se rapprocher toujours le plus possible de la réalité de la vie. On peut dire que les élèves ont presque bâti eux-mêmes et aménagé leur Ecole : comme Robinson dans son île déserte, ils ont créé une grande partie des objets qui les entourent et dont ils jouissent.

Au moment de la fondation de l'Ecole, le jardin était plein de mauvaises herbes, la ferme remplie de décombres : le tout fut approprié par les élèves. Ils ont fait ensuite des chemins et établi tout un système de drainage. Ils ont goudronné les barrières, mis en peinture les boiseries et les bâtiments, créé un jeu de football avec ses clôtures. Dans l'atelier, ils apprennent les éléments de la menuiserie et de la charpenterie et ont fabriqué eux-mêmes un grand nombre de meubles à l'usage de la maison. . . .

Pendant l'été, les travaux dans le jardin et dans la ferme prennent naturellement plus d'importance ; le cricket et le tennis remplacent le foot-ball. . . .

Dans le temps même où j'écris cet article, je reçois une lettre de M. Beveridge, qui vient de conduire son fils à l'Ecole d'Abbotsholme et qui veut bien me faire part de ce qu'il a vu :

"Au moment de mon arrivée, m'écrit-il, plusieurs enfants étaient occupés à peindre un jeu de cricket, qu'ils avaient fabriqué eux-mêmes l'année précédente.

"Il est question, en ce moment, de jeter un nouveau pont sur la rivière, qui a trente à quarante mètres de large ; les piles seront en maçonnerie, afin d'avoir une résistance plus forte. Tout cela sera fait par les élèves. . . .

"On a aussi formé le projet d'augmenter les bâtiments de l'Ecole jusqu'à ce qu'ils puissent contenir cent élèves, nombre extrême que le Dr. Reddie pense pouvoir diriger d'une façon complète. Comme travail préparatoire, les élèves sont chargés d'arpenter le terrain et de dresser le plan exact de l'établissement.

"Près de la maison, il y a un laboratoire temporaire de chimie, et un atelier de charpentier où les élèves, sous la direction de Herr Neumann, que vous avez vu à Eimbourg, font des travaux variés, soit pour leur usage personnel, soit pour l'Ecole. On a l'intention, au terme prochain, d'entreprendre des travaux sur bois, d'après la méthode progressive du *Sloyd*, que vous avez vue fonctionner au *Summer Meeting*.[1]

"Dans l'intérieur de la maison, je constate l'absence de tout luxe futile,

[1] Nous publierons prochainement, dans le Bulletin, un article sur le *Sloyd*, par M. V. Muller, qui nous accompagnait à Edimbourg.

tandis qu'au contraire le mobilier des pièces est des plus confortables. Au lunch, j'ai été frappé de l'apparence heureuse et exempte de contrainte des enfants. Ils étaient assemblés autour d'une demi-douzaine de petites tables, chacune présidée par un professeur. Les prières des repas étaient chantées avec élan et enthousiasme.

" La franchise et la confiance des enfants vis-à-vis de leurs maîtres est très remarquable. Ces derniers ont l'habitude de se promener au milieu de leurs élèves et de se comporter avec eux plutôt comme leurs aînés que comme des personnages d'une caste différente. Ils font constamment usage des expressions de langage des élèves et parfois même emploient certains mots de leur jargon. La seule distinction est une sorte de manteau académique porté par les maîtres.

". . . Le Dr Reddie regarde comme un point important d'initier les élèves à la connaissance des affaires du dehors ; ainsi, il leur confie des messages très sérieux, les envoie retirer son argent de la banque, etc. . . ."

Ces diverses occupations usuelles, ces divers travaux manuels ne sont pas seulement un élément d'éducation, un moyen d'acquérir une foule de connaissances pratiques que la théorie ne peut donner ; ils ont, en outre, pour but de développer le corps, de le mettre en bon état et de faire ainsi des hommes capables d'affronter avec succès les difficultés de la vie. On comprend dès lors que M. Reddie ait tenu à se rendre compte, d'une façon très exacte, en quelque sorte mathématique, du résultat obtenu, à ce point de vue.

" Nous avons voulu, dit-il, constater le degré de croissance des enfants, afin de voir s'ils étaient bien nourris et si cette vie était convenable pour leur santé. Pour cela, nous avons établi comparativement la croissance de chaque garçon pendant le temps passé à l'Ecole et pendant les vacances. Si le développement corporel avait été moindre pendant le séjour passé à l'Ecole, il est clair que nous aurions dû considérer notre régime comme défectueux. Il est vrai que nos balances ne nous renseignaient pas sur le degré d'agilité et de souplesse acquis par nos jeunes gens, mais il était important de constater que ces qualités n'avaient pas été acquises au dépens du poids *mass*. Les résultats que nous avons constatés sont intéressants."

Suivent deux tableaux comparatifs, le premier, relatif au poids, le second relatif à la taille, où l'on distingue, pour chacun de ces deux cas, ce que les jeunes gens ont gagné pendant la période d'Ecole et ce qu'ils ont gagné pendant la periode des vacances. D'après cette constatation établie, c'est pendant la période d'Ecole que le développement corporel a été le plus grand.

A vrai dire, cette conclusion ne saurait étonner, car le genre de vie que nous venons de décrire est éminemment favorable au développement physique. "Sans faire trop de fond sur ces chiffres, poursuit M. Reddie, ils prouvent du moins, qu'avec son système de nourriture, d'habillement et de vie, notre Ecole est une fabrique d'hommes forts et solides.[1] Nous avons eu à constater peu d'indispositions ; même les maux de tête et les rhumes sont rares.

Le régime que nous suivons apprend aux jeunes gens que l'homme doit avoir une bonne santé et que les maladies sont le résultat de l'erreur, de l'ignorance, du surmenage, d'une mauvaise entente du travail, ou bien du vice. Nous attachons beaucoup d'importance à enseigner à nos élèves à être très soigneux dans leurs habitudes de propreté et d'hygiène personnelle. . . .

IV.

Avec les travaux scolaires, qui occupent la matinée, avec les travaux manuels et les exercices physiques, qui occupent l'après-midi, nous sommes arrivés à six heures du soir, qui est l'heure du thé. Il reste encore trois heures jusqu'au moment du coucher. Comment va-t-on les employer ?

Suivant la définition de M. de Bonald, "l'homme est une intelligence servie par des organes" ; nous venons de voir comment la matinée était consacrée à développer la première et l'après-midi à développer les seconds. Mais l'homme est encore autre chose : il est un être, je ne dis plus seulement social mais sociable. Pour développer tout l'homme, il faut donc le former en vue de cette sociabilité, il faut en faire un homme bien élevé, qui puisse à la fois trouver et apporter de l'agrément dans la société de ses semblables.

C'est à façonner cet "homme du monde" que sont employées les trois dernières heures de la journée. Le procédé est intéressant à examiner.

"Notre but, dit M. Reddie, est d'habituer nos jeunes gens à n'être ni gauches ni timides, et à se plaire dans la société des personnes plus âgées. Aussi, chaque soir, se réunissent-ils au salon, où ils se rencontrent avec les dames de l'Ecole et les étrangers qui viennent nous visiter. La pièce dans laquelle se passent ainsi les soirées a été arrangée pour donner l'impression du bonheur et de l'harmonie : les meubles, les dessins, les statues ont été choisies dans ce but."

De six à neuf heures, l'Ecole est donc transformée en un salon de famille ; mais on ne se contente pas d'y causer : ce temps est consacré à

[1] Cette appréciation me rappelle un mot bien typique du directeur d'une Ecole anglaise, que m'a cité M. Geddes : pour affirmer la supériorité de sa maison, il se vantait de donner à ses jeunes gens un pouce de largeur de poitrine, de plus qu'aux jeunes gens de toute autre école.

faire de la musique et des chants, à répéter des comédies, à donner des concerts.

La musique, en effet, joue un rôle important à l'Ecole. " C'est une de nos principales préoccupations, dit le Programme. Chaque semaine, nous donnons des soirées musicales et, chaque soir, des exécutions de piano. Cela a une grande influence sur les enfants. Les élèves possèdent autant de violons que d'appareils photographiques."

Pour les représentations dramatiques, les jeunes gens ont construit eux-mêmes un théâtre. Ces exercices, d'ailleurs, ne sont pas considérés comme un pur divertissement, mais encore comme un moyen sérieux d'éducation. Enfin, chaque semaine, une soirée est consacrée à la lecture des œuvres de Shakespeare.

Nous aurons donné une idée assez complète de cette partie de la vie de l'Ecole, en ajoutant qu'il y a deux Sociétés pour les controverses sur divers sujets et que les élèves publient un journal (*School Magazine*), qui est une sorte de chronique des événements de l'Ecole, avec illustrations et partie littéraire. " Cette publication développe les aptitudes littéraires et l'habileté artistique ; elle donne aux élèves l'idée que leur Ecole est un petit monde complet."

Un autre élément, qui concourt également au développement du sentiment artistique, est la constitution d'un Musée, en voie de formation et qui comprend déjà des copies de tableaux de grands maîtres, des sculptures, de beaux meubles, etc.

La journée, qui a été commencée par une visite à la chapelle, se termine de même. Cependant l'Ecole ne se rattache à aucune des sectes du protestantisme ; les pratiques religieuses n'ont donc aucun caractère dogmatique ou confessionnel (*undogmatic and unsectarian*). A la chapelle, comme dans la prière qui est faite avant les repas, on se borne à des lectures tirées de la Bible, à des hymnes ou à des invocations d'un caractère moral et religieux général. Mais, comme la journée du dimanche est libre, les enfants peuvent suivre leur culte particulier dans les paroisses voisines.

Au point de vue religieux, le Programme s'exprime ainsi : " La religion tient la grande place dans la vie, et la vie doit en être saturée. Nous ne présentons pas la religion aux enfants comme si elle était une partie de la vie, mais comme un tout organique et harmonieux, qui doit pénétrer l'individu tout entier, malgré la variété des sectes religieuses. Pendant un quart d'heure, le matin et le soir, on se réunit pour exprimer la foi et l'espérance par des signes extérieurs."

Telle est cette Ecole et tel est son programme. Cette expérience est extrêmement intéressante en ce qu'elle me paraît marquer une évolution nettement accentuée vers un système d'éducation plus approprié aux conditions nouvelles de la vie sociale. Par son caractère pratique, par sa préoccupation dominante de former l'homme et tout l'homme, de développer en lui, au plus haut degré, toutes ses facultés, toute sa puissance d'énergie et d'initiative, cette Ecole tranche résolument, avec les divers systèmes d'enseignement. . . .

Edmond Demolins.

UN NOUVEAU TYPE DE COLLÉGE.[1]

Lorsqu'on a, comme nous, le bonheur ou le malheur de vivre dans une époque de transition, on ne peut pas souscrire sans réserves à l'affirmation de l'Ecclésiaste "qu'il n'y a rien de nouveau sous le soleil." Les nouveautés ne se comptent plus dans l'industrie, le commerce, l'agriculture, les sciences physiques et naturelles : elles ont transformé de fond en comble l'ordre économique, et nous condamnent à nous adapter à des conditions d'existence que nos pères n'ont pas connues. La vapeur, les chemins de fer, les téléphones ont rapproché matériellement les peuples et les individus, et les ont divisés moralement en mettant en présence et en conflit leurs prétentions et leurs intérêts ; ils ont créé les Etats désunis d'Europe et d'Amerique qui, sur tous les points du globe, se disputent la clientèle pour leurs blés, leur coton, leur laine et leurs métaux. La guerre de tous contre tous est un fait indéniable ; il peut attrister le philanthrope, mais il ne saurait être traité par le penseur comme une quantité négligeable.

Toutes les hypothèses de Darwin, la lutte pour la vie, l'élimination des faibles et la domination des forts semblent devenues, sinon pour toujours, du moins pour longtemps, la loi des sociétés modernes. Si l'on est excusable de trouver cette loi bien dure, il serait puéril de l'ignorer systématiquement et de la méconnaître. En passant de l'état semi-patriarcal à l'état instable, la famille a perdu le pouvoir de protéger ses membres incapables, et les tentatives des gouvernements pour la suppléer n'ont abouti qu'à multiplier, d'un côté les fonctionnaires et de l'autre les socialistes. Les débouchés ne manquent pas seulement aux marchandises, ils manquent aux hommes, qui n'ont pas été habitués à compter sur eux-mêmes et qui reprochent à la société leur propre impuissance, due, il faut bien le recon-

---

[1] *La République Française, Journal du Soir :* Jules Méline, Directeur Politique. Léon Gambetta, Fondateur, Mardi 6 Nov., 1894.

naître, aux lacunes de l'éducation traditionnelle. L'ancien mode de formation a dressé d'incomparables générations d'aristocrates et de lettrés ; mais, s'il peut rester le luxe des riches, il refuse toute satisfaction aux besoins de la majorité des hommes, qui cherchent le nécessaire plutôt que le superflu.

Les Anglais, gens pratiques et avisés, ont compris depuis longtemps déjà qu'à une situation nouvelle doit correspondre une éducation nouvelle : à tous les genres de sport qu'ils affectionnent, ils préfèrent encore celui de l'initiative et de la volonté et s'efforcent par tous les moyens d'en inculquer le goût et l'habitude à l'enfance et à la jeunesse. Ils aiment à commander autant que nous aimons à briller, et voient dans le développement de la volonté chez les enfants la condition *sine quâ non* de la suprématie commerciale, industrielle et politique de la Grande-Bretagne.

Un Anglais, le docteur Reddie, a cependant accusé ses compatriotes de trop sacrifier encore à des traditions surannées à Eton, à Rugby et dans les universités, et, pour bien préciser le sens de ses accusations, il a fondé en 1889, à Abbotsholme, dans le comté de Derby, une école qui, d'après M. Demolins, le clairvoyant directeur de la *Science sociale*, serait en harmonie parfaite avec les exigences des temps nouveaux. Le cadre de cette école est celui de tous les collèges d'outre-Manche : la verdure, les arbres, les eaux vives, la pleine campagne où se dressent des cottages à l'usage des professeurs et des élèves, une ferme, des ateliers et des laboratoires. Dans ce milieu souriant et coquet, l'enfant pourrait s'écrier, comme la jeune captive d'André Chénier :

"Ma bienvenue au jour me rit dans tous les yeux."

Il reste une personne et ne disparaît pas sous un numéro d'ordre.

Il y a temps pour tout dans l'école d'Abbotsholme : pour l'intelligence, pour le corps et même pour la vie mondaine. La matinée est réservée à la culture intellectuelle, l'après-midi aux travaux manuels et la soirée aux arts d agrément, à la musique et à la poèsie. Le collège se façonne ainsi à l'image de la vie, il en a la souplesse et la variété et ne se laisse pas emprisonner dans la rigidité des formes artificielles. Dans sa méthode d'enseignement, M. Reddie se propose " de mettre les élèves en arpport autant avec les choses qu'avec les mots qui les expriment, de manière à procéder constamment du concret à l'abstrait et d'élever les jeunes gens dans l'idée de faire usage de ce qui leur a été enseigné et avec le désir d'apprendre pour eux-mêmes, sans le stimulant des récompenses et des prix." Il ne confond pas l'inutile avec l'idéal et considère la devise ;

Primo vivere, deinde philosophari, comme la plus impérieuse des règles de conduite pour ses contemporains.

Or, pour vivre, pour gagner sa vie, la connaissance *réelle* de plusieurs langues modernes est le premier et peut-être le plus précieux des outils. Ses élèves consacrent deux ans à l'étude de l'anglais, leur idiome maternel, deux autres années au français et autant à l'allemand, mais ils n'apprennent pas les langues étrangères à la façon des muets qui lisent et ne parlent pas. Pendant les deux années réglementaires qui leur sont respectivement attribuées, le français et l'allemand constituent le langage courant et usuel dans les classes et les travaux pratiques, à l'étude, à l'atelier et au salon ; ils s'incrustent ainsi dans la mémoire et dans les habitudes et ne s'en laissent plus détacher. L'analyse grammaticale suit l'usage des mots et ne le précède pas. En nous écartant, dans nos lycées, de cet ordre naturel et logique, nous n'arrivons qu'à être muets en plusieurs langues. S'il est excessif de tout ramener à l'utile, n'est-il pas insensé de mettre dans son bagage intellectuel des notions de linguistique qui, jamais, ne serviront à rien ?

Même en mathématiques, M. Reddie se méfie des abstractions, ces ombres qui cachent des vides, suivant l'expression de Joubert, et se plaît à élairer les théorèmes par leurs applications. Des opérations, d'arpentage rendent en quelque sorte tangibles les formules de la géométrie, et la comptabilité quotidienne de la ferme, de l'atelier, du jardin et du laboratoire forme un vivant commentaire de tous les calculs et de tous les chiffres qui se sont déroulées dans les leçons du matin. Les fractions, les proportions, les règles de l'intérêt, grâce à ces procédés, se dépouillent de leur caractère mystérieux et pénètrent de gré ou de force dans les esprits les plus fermés

Quant aux sciences naturelles, elles ne sont pas transformées en nomenclatures aussi stériles que repoussantes ; on observe la fleur sur sa tige, le bétail dans l'étable et la nature du sol dans les champs. L'atelier fournit l'explication des leçons de mécanique, et les manipulations du laboratoire révèlent les secrets de la chimie. Ainsi comprise, la science n'est pas une chose morte, elle vit et s'adapte aux besoins intellectuels des vivants. La théorie et la pratique ne sont jamais séparées et se prêtent un mutuel appui.

Figurer dans le monde avec agrément est aussi une arme et un moyen relatif de supériorité ; M. Reddie s'en est souvenu. Tous les soirs, de six à huit heures, ses élèves remplacent le rabot et l'équerre par le piano ou le violon, et font alterner les interprétations musicales avec la représentation des drames de Shakespeare. La musique n'est pas plus mauvaise que celle des amateurs en France, et charme tout à la fois les exécutants et leurs auditeurs.

Prise dans son ensemble, la réforme de M. Reddie, qui inspire des pages enthousiastes à M. Demolins, ne ressemble pas à ce que nos voisins appellent un saut dans la nuit et paraît seulement constituer un nouveau pas vers cette éducation plus utilitaire que littéraire qui est le vœu secret du présent et sera peut-être une grande ressource pour l'avenir.

A. B.

13 BUILDING A PIGEON HOUSE. (*Winter, 1892*).

Copyright

CHAPTER X.

A Brief History of Abbotsholme during 1894=5.

CHAPTER X.

A BRIEF HISTORY OF ABBOTSHOLME DURING 1894-5.

(*a*) PLANS FOR REBUILDING THE SCHOOL HOUSE.

It was on March the 14th, 1894, as related above in Chapter V., that we had bought the School Estate.

The day following we commenced to consider the rebuilding of the School House. But we little dreamed that four years would pass before we could begin to execute our plans. There were, however, many difficulties to surmount.

First of all, our schemes were far-reaching, for we did not wish to follow the time-honoured English plan of living from hand to mouth, changing a bit to-day, and a bit to-morrow, until the School Buildings should become a veritable chaos.

To us, personally, the English towns, the English houses, railway stations, &c., seemed most inadequate. All were the outcome of the English fog and insularity, want of ideas and lack of social coöperation. All bore the stamp of selfish individualism, and all preached mental and social chaos to the wearied beholder. In a School designed to develop Harmonious Growth this would, we knew, be fatal. For a School like this it was essential to have a Kosmos. The buildings, we felt, moreover, ought to symbolise the whole Theory of the School, as the human body summarises and foretells the history of the soul. Accordingly, we commenced betimes to excogitate our plans. In their main features they were settled before the summer of 1894 was past. During the autumn the architects commenced their work, and in January, 1895, submitted the first draft of the drawings. A second batch, more in accordance with our instructions, were ready by March; but these also we had to discard; so difficult was it for one mind to grasp what another mind required. We had of course from the first insisted that only an educator could *plan* an ideal school house, even if only an architect could carry his plan to successful realisation. What we really needed all this time was the power to *draw*, and thus express our thoughts; and we realised, as never before, how absurd it was to teach the writing of mere words in preference to the universal written language of Nature and Mankind.

(*b*) Plans for Reorganising the School Staff and for Planting School Colonies, etc.

While we were planning the rebuilding of our city, or, to change the metaphor, the planning of a more daring cruise, we wished to test our ship's company to see if all had stomach for the enterprise. For we did not wish, in the middle of the ocean, to have to change our crew.

We fully realised that our lieutenants could not remain with us for ever, and we desired, as time went on, to plant our colonies, as already said above. But we did not

A Brief History of Abbotsholme

wish to lose our crew in the midst of the dangerous crisis in our history, which we dimly felt would come, when we were shifting cargoes from our old three-decker to our new armoured battleship. With this in view we drew up a frank declaration of our policy, in which we aimed at securing ourselves against the dangers indicated above. We print this paper, although we should, if writing it now, express our aims in a somewhat different way.

THE NEW SCHOOL ABBOTSHOLME.

Memorandum, showing why each master at Abbotsholme School is requested to sign an agreement on appointment.

In requesting each of my lieutenants to sign an agreement upon accepting office under me at Abbotsholme, I wish my aims to be clearly understood. I desire to build up a highly skilled permanent staff at Abbotsholme, such as will form an organic unity, without which the School can never realise the aims I set before me to carry out.

This organic unity requires that the Life and Work of the School should be planned and carried out in a far more scientific manner than has hitherto been usual at schools. It requires that the Head Master should in reality, and not merely in name, direct the whole work of the School; that each of his lieutenants should be admitted thoroughly into his confidence, and should be made to apprehend and to comprehend, the aim of the entire program.

To accomplish this, it is requisite that the Head Master should, as far as is practicable, live with his lieutenants, that he should know thoroughly, by means of personal observation and inspection, what each man is doing, should criticise each man's work, and place at his staff's disposal, as far as possible, his own experience and skill.

If, however, this is done, it would not be fair, that, notwithstanding such supervision and assistance, his lieutenants should be free of all obligations and should be at liberty to use the resources placed at their disposal, not for the School, but for their own private advancement. For this would mean the weakening of the position of the School as regards other educational institutions. On the contrary, they should be so bound as to enable the Head Master to give this detailed assistance with the complete assurance that his action would not prejudice his own and the School's interests.

The experimental results achieved at Abbotsholme are the property of the School, and not of any individual who is assisting in carrying them out; and therefore no individual has any legal or moral right to make those results, or the methods of obtaining these results, known to outsiders, nor to allow outsiders, whether visiting the School or not, to get to know about these results except as sanctioned expressly by the Head Master in writing.

If any master should prefer not to agree to be bound in this manner, he will of course be regarded as merely a temporary master, and will not be admitted into the confidence of those who have signed this agreement, and will not be allowed to participate in the advantages which the agreement renders possible.

On the other hand, if any master decides to sign this agreement, it will be the duty as well as the desire of the Head Master to give the master the fullest assistance in his work that is possible under the given circumstances.

The purpose hereby in view is, first of all, to strengthen

the School by having complete harmony and unity among all members of the permanent staff, and in the entire working of the School. This could not fail so to raise the reputation of the School for sound and vigorous work as to lead to an increase in the number of applications and to the possibility of establishing colonies in suitable localities elsewhere. In founding colonies the interests both of the parent School, and of the colonies, and of the public should be kept in mind.

The second purpose in view is to start and establish such colonies. These children of Abbotsholme would spread over the whole land most effectively the principles and practices which are peculiar to Abbotsholme. For it must be remembered that nothing is easier than to imitate a program on paper, but nothing is harder than to work out such a program in reality. We should desire real children and not bastards to arise from our labours here. Such colonies moreover would furnish the legitimate outlet to masters of ability who had perfected themselves in the methods of Abbotsholme. They would also be able to look forward, after having served the parent school long and well, to a wider field in which to develop the same rational and scientific education, and perhaps to bring it to fuller perfection.

Time alone can show which men are fitted by nature for responsible work of this kind, but all would be the better for aiming at some such work in the future. Who knows if the call will come to him, or when it may come? The opposite policy of jealousy and competition leads to endless evils, which are not compensated for by the fascinating but spurious liberty to do just what one likes without thought of ultimate national educational disorder.

The aim in view here is to organise the School so that it may reproduce itself, when it has reached maturity and reproduction is at once reasonable, advisable, and necessary.

We do not want to keep our knowledge, ideas, experimental results to ourselves. But we do not want either that they should be given to others by unauthorised individuals in a disorderly and imperfect manner, or that they should be handed over to strangers who have not likewise had the training in the life.

We wish the skill and knowledge derived from living this life to be the natural birthright, so to speak, of all duly admitted citizens of Abbotsholme. We do not want ambitious strangers to adopt our program when they are not animated with our spirit. For it is not merely our work which is the important and vital matter, but the spirit in which all is done. We should like to see all similar schools federated with ourselves, resolved to avoid all competition, and, on the contrary, resolved to strengthen one another by cordial coöperation.

This is the Ideal, sketched out, of a rational and natural development of Abbotsholme into an alliance of similar schools. One step in this direction will be taken if each master enters into this agreement, which alone will render the Ideal practicable.

The above paragraphs, for the most part, do but formulate the obligations, which, whether explicitly stated or not, are implied when any one is admitted into the inner working of any undertaking of this kind. It has seemed better, however, to state these obligations thus clearly, in order to prevent all misunderstanding.

October, 1894.   C. R.

This declaration of our policy was, after a little natural hesitation, accepted by the members of our staff who had been invited to do so, and we proceeded forthwith to carry out our plans.

(c) Pestilence at Home and War Abroad.

But the Spring of 1895 brought us a spell of evil luck. It was the year of Influenza, and after some thirty of the boys and masters had been attacked, the strain of nursing them, without doctor or outside help of any kind—which indeed, it was almost impossible to get, for all the world was ill and doctors and nurses worked to death—the matron and we ourselves collapsed. Although every one recovered without a single complication, our own health was for a long time nearly broken.

A worse trouble was to follow. We were plunged into a series of foreign wars. It seemed suddenly as if our little kingdom was the most important spot in Derbyshire.

The Parish Council Act had but newly come into force, and our local statesmen were all upon the war-path.

More than half a dozen rights-of-way were claimed, and we were in imminent danger of finding our privacy destroyed. However, by patience and diplomacy, these claims were all disposed of. The majority of claims were definitely rejected, one was left undecided, as of little moment, and one was settled by a decent compromise. The war fever subsided as suddenly and as inexplicably as it had arisen. But hardly had we warded off these dangers, when another more serious one arose. This was a claim by a powerful neighbour to a right of road along our private carriage drive. The negotiations dragged on for eighteen months. We were face to face with a serious legal war in the High

Court, when by a small concession, allowing a partial user for a limited period, we finally secured ourselves against all risk of this aggression in the future.

In the March of 1897, and shortly after the legal settlement was signed, we recommenced the elaboration of our building scheme.

The excavations commenced in the autumn of that year, and in the summer of 1898 the foundations of the new buildings were duly laid.

(*d*) THE SCHOOL MAGAZINE—INTRODUCTORY.
[Reprinted from *The Abbotsholmian*.]

A word is perhaps needed to explain why the first number of the school chronicle appears in the friendly embrace or the Old Boys' "Mag."

As all Abbotsholmians know, the original school magazine, entitled *Strays*, was a very ambitious work, full of charming illustrations in black and white or colour, all which, together with the text, was done by hand. The first number appeared in the Summer of 1890, and the enthusiasm of its contributors then promised at least one a term. Even this, however, was found impossible, unless the ordinary work of the school was to be pushed aside.

Other numbers appeared—in all, eight. The earlier numbers were mainly due to Mr. Badley and Mr. Pilsbury, the later to Mr. Pilsbury, aided largely by Old Boys. But it was troublesome to send the manuscript backwards and forwards to those at a distance, to get their contributions written, or painted, in. Moreover, when the number was finished, the illustrations, at any rate could not be reproduced and circulated. Few, therefore, got benefit from the work.

A Brief History of Abbotsholme

Another chronicle of our life and doings we have in the *Photographic Album*, which we owe mainly to Herr Neumann. This gives us, almost from the opening of the school, a record of most of the events in our history. It contains already over two hundred photographs, including a group of the whole school taken each term. But here again only a small circle benefits.

In the autumn of 1893 some materials were got together for making the first number of a school chronicle. We then discovered that an energetic member of the Old Boys' Club had also planned a magazine. This eventually saw the light last Christmas.

As there seemed, however, hardly room or use for two separate papers, some one suggested that the two might appear as parts of one, to be called *The Abbotsholmian*. This would prevent overlapping of news, and would be a link between the school and the Old Boys' Club.

It remains to state briefly the aims of *The Abbotsholmian*.

It is the duty of every community to keep some record of its work, if not for the edification or amusement of outsiders, at least for the education of its own citizens. Only when a man begins to reflect does he emerge from childhood ; and if a school is to understand its own organic life, it must keep some record of its growth.

The Abbotsholmian, then, in the portion contributed by the school, will be primarily a simple record, made by the boys themselves, of their school-life. It will strive to reflect faithfully, not merely the athletic, or any other particular side of that life, but the whole. It will not in any way trespass upon the ground occupied by *Strays*, which will, we trust, continue from time to time to encourage and guide literary and artistic efforts among us.

Indeed, if *Strays* permit it, we should wish to select occasionally from its pages, in order that our record of the boys may not be without some samples of their art. Again, *The Abbotsholmian* will not attempt to record the results of the more serious scientific experiments of the school. These must be reserved for the occasional appearance of our Year-book, which will attempt to record our work as it appears to the philosopher.

What the Old Fellows will do with their portion of the chronicle, it is for them to say. But I trust that it will not merely relate to their gladiatorial prowess, or university distinctions, but reflect their whole life, and that of the soul as well as that of the soul's husk.

And now what will our chronicle do for us? If we want to understand history—that is, the story of that strange compound-animal, Humanity—we must study the portion of it that comes within our reach. Our life here is simply the life of the whole in miniature. All the passions, interests, grovellings, and aspirations that have ever moved mankind are in our midst. By quiet scrutiny we shall learn something of this human monster, or giant man, and that must be our key to history. Term by term we shall thus have our "annals"—or simple truthful record of events as they appear day by day to us. To get such candid reflection of the daily life is not so very easy or usual as to be deemed superfluous. One of the most urgent needs of the day is to train people to see straight, and to describe accurately what they do see.

From our jottings, again, we may hope to put together, from time to time, successive chapters of a real history, no longer mere chronicles of isolated actions, but connected

A Brief History of Abbotsholme

story, showing how the *Zeitgeist* and the ebb and flow of the social ocean mingle their influences with the aspirations and puny efforts of the unit man or boy.

C. R.

(*e*) The "Old Boys' Gathering," Easter, 1895.

[Reprinted from *The Abbotsholmian*.]

As all Abbotsholmians know, after many former meetings of Old Fellows at Christmas Concerts, on Foundation Days, or at Hay-makings, and other festive seasons, we gradually settled upon Easter as the best time for the Annual "Old Boys' Gathering." The first meeting was held in 1893, when the club was started, as all may read in the Old Boys' "Mag." of last Christmas. A second and still more successful gathering took place at Easter, 1894, when we celebrated the purchase of Abbotsholme, unfurling the school banner to the sound of heavy artillery from the roof!

Not the least among the charms of these two meetings had been the presence of the new generation living the old life, and so bringing back to us, as only they could, the daily routine of auld lang syne. One chief use of such gatherings seems to be this calling up of the old life, this reviving of the old aspirations, which sometimes look rather visionary in the work-a-day world with its matter-of-fact details and mean ideas. Very interesting it is to see our quondam fag, now decked out as a prefect, marching his squad about with appropriate solemnity; and some, I think, like the opportunity thus given us of dropping a friendly hint "from the Old Boys' point of view," when, as will happen, I suppose, in the "best regulated schools," the youngsters think themselves shockingly ill-used, because they don't always get things quite their own way little knowing how they will look back with wistful regret when once they are in the iron grasp of real life.

Few of us realised last February, when the well-known invitation card arrived, that the gathering this time would be in vacation. And as on Thursday, April 11th, we walked across the fields towards Abbotsholme, with the thoughts of those former meetings in our minds, we were, many of us at least, sadly disappointed on hearing that the boys were gone. We soon changed our minds, however, when we realised that the happy chance that brought Easter this year in the vacation, alone had made it possible for so many of us to be asked, and for all to sleep at Abbotsholme. Since September 1894, the school had been quite full, and guest-chambers at a premium.

We find on our arrival a goodly array of old fellows, and several ladies, and other friends of the "Head," already assembled. On the notice board we see a complete list of invited guests with notes and explanations from those who cannot come. Soon everybody feels at home; but that is somehow in the air, we think. A time-table more lenient than that of yore tells us the hour of breakfast, of dormitory parade, and so on. Another list indicates our dormitories, and duly announces who presides as captain. Gradually it dawns upon us that we shall feel more "at school again" this time than ever was possible at gatherings during term, when we slept in spare rooms, or in hammocks in the "Lab."

Next day was spent in wandering round to see all the old haunts, and note improvements. There was a splendid show of "hyacinths," planted, we learned, the year before by Mrs. Drugman, whom, by the way, every one was glad to see at the meeting. She had come all the way from Cannes. Others had come from places hardly less remote. One was from Darmstadt, another from Bonn.

In the evening we had the old service for Good Friday from the school prayer-book.

The following day we invaded the river and the punt, under a cloudless sky and blazing sun, weather which, with our usual luck, lasted the whole six days.

Towards midday we had a flying visit from Chaplin to attend the meeting of the Club Committee, at which the business for the General Meeting was settled. Directly after tea, was held in big school the annual General Meeting of the club. The President, in an introductory address, sketched out some of the uses for which the club existed. He did not wish it, he said, to be a mere athletic society, nor a mere literary, philosophical, or musical society, but all of these together, and more. He hoped the club would be as many-sided as the school, and be a means of keeping the old fellows in touch with all aspects of our complex life. By help of the magazine and of gatherings such as the present, he thought that the old ideals, which it was the chief aim of the education pursued at Abbotsholme to awake in every boy, could be best kept alive during the stormy and critical years which come between the quiet days of school and the quiet days of mature life. He did not regret the absence of the boys on the present occasion. During term he never could see much of visitors, not even when they were "old boys." The life at Abbotsholme was for him one of ceaseless exertion. Therefore he was glad that the accident of a late Easter had brought them together during the quiet of vacation. He thought, too, the old fellows would all see more of each other now than they had been able to do during the previous gatherings in term. Both kinds of meetings had their uses, and he did not wish it to be supposed that no future gathering would come in term.

Reports followed from the secretary, the treasurer, and the editor, and then came the election of new members. The subscriptions for the bridge at the bathing-place were announced, and the secretary was instructed to thank Piercy minor, the head boy, for the £20 contributed by the school.

In the afternoon we practised for an "impromptu concert" which came off in the evening. Minstrels were luckily present in force, so we managed a very fair program, and realised more than ever the advantage of music being so strong a feature at the school. The ancient charms of big school were, on this occasion, enhanced by the unaccustomed acquisition of the conservatory as smoking-room. We patriarchs beheld with some disdain, however, the latest additions to the club vainly endeavouring to look happy behind immense cigars. We must not mention particulars, but we think one "very young gentleman" went rather early to bed. Our delightful smoke-room, with its lovely background of flowers, was not however sufficient for some ardent votaries of the weed. They attempted—in vain, be it said, for the honour and reputation of the school, and of the acting commandants in the upper regions—to profane the sacred shrines of Morpheus with the worship of nicotine, but were ignominiously worsted.

Easter Sunday was spent much as Good Friday had been —church in the morning and walks in the afternoon. In the evening we had the usual school service for the day with a sermon from the Head.

A Brief History of Abbotsholme

On Easter Monday most of us went an excursion to Dovedale. In the evening there was another impromptu entertainment in big school, at which some excellent recitations were given by A. Riden, S. Unwin, and Mr. Edward Reddie, the headmaster's brother, whom O.A.'s will remember as "Sir Anthony Absolute" in the "Rivals" at Christmas, 1892. Next morning the guests began to melt away, and there was brought to an end not the least interesting of our many festivities at Abbotsholme.

FLOREAT ABBOTSHOLME !

S. U.

(*f*) REPORT OF THE INSPECTION AND EXAMINATION OF THE NEW SCHOOL ABBOTSHOLME, JUNE 24–28, 1895. BY H. COURTHOPE BOWEN, M.A., LATE LECTURER ON THE THEORY OF EDUCATION AT THE UNIVERSITY OF CAMBRIDGE.

I resided in The New School Abbotsholme, from June 24th–28th. I inspected the buildings and grounds; looked with great care into the Educational Plan and the Time-tables of the school; repeatedly listened to the teaching in the various classes and put questions to the boys about their work; and was present at the drill and the out-of-door occupations of many different kinds.

Speaking in quite general terms, I may say at once that the School seems to me to be in a satisfactory state, and to be making steady and most encouraging progress towards the accomplishment of the very high aim which it has set before it.

Taken as a whole the Educational Plan is, in my opinion, excellent, and its details are arranged with great skill and thoughtfulness. I know of no other school in which the predominant aim is so markedly the development of the boy's *whole* nature, moral, physical, and intellectual, and none in which the effort to bring his knowledge, power, and skill into harmonious inter-relation is so carefully maintained. No doubt much remains to be done, before this aim can be fully accomplished; for instance, more accommodation is needed for dormitories, class-rooms, and workshops, and some of the school subjects have to be brought into closer connectedness with others, but very much has already been done, and the school is working well.

The feature of the school which is the first to attract attention—and which is also one of the best—is the time given to out-of-door occupations in garden, field, and dingle, and to manual work in the workshops.

The occupations and manual work need perhaps a more thorough organisation; but they are healthy, suitable to boys, and afford not only a good training in practical skill, but also, by being so contrived as to be of real use to the school community, provide a most valuable experience in public service and public duty, and cultivate a feeling that honest work of all kinds is worthy of honour. The same good influence, I think, is exercised by the dormitory drill.

The grounds of the School are beautiful in themselves and well suited to the above purposes, and the bathing-place is a real boon.

The School has to some extent outgrown its buildings; but otherwise the latter are satisfactory.

The drill, both with apparatus and in the open, was fairly good. But in both cases it seemed to me to lack something in smartness, briskness, and exactness—faults which further perseverance will no doubt speedily correct.

I have spoken of the Educational Plan and the Time-table with praise—and they richly deserve it. But I should like to make one or two suggestions which from my experience I think might prove useful. In my opinion English Literature—studied as literature—should have a definite and honourable place in the curriculum, and should be taught in close connection with the Nature Study, Drawing and Painting, and English Composition. It is the true centre and inspirer of æsthetic training, and a most valuable help to moral teaching.

If English Grammar is taught properly—and it seems to be so taught at Abbotsholme, though it might be more inductive—it might be discontinued in Set A, and probably also in Set B.

The following is a list of the lessons which I heard given, and the subjects on which I asked questions in the various sets :—

SET D.

Set Master : Mr. R. L. Lancelot.

Lessons : English Composition, Geometry, Drawing, French, Chemistry. I asked questions on Geography, and English History.

I thought that both the English Composition and the French were well taught; but the lessons in the other subjects, though careful, were somewhat devoid of interest.

In the Geography the mental-picturing was good, and a satisfactory amount of knowledge (right in kind) was shown. The English History also showed plenty of interest and a satisfactory amount of information. A bright form.

Set C.

Set Master: Herr Karl Neumann.

Lessons: Arithmetic, German, Physics, Geography, English History, Reading, Economics, and Biology.

I asked questions on Arithmetic and Geometry.

The lessons on German, Physics, and English History all seemed to me good average lessons; and the lesson on Geography, closely connected as it was with History, evidently stirred the boys' interest and made them think. The Reading lesson was very satisfactory on the whole; but I thought that the master should read aloud himself much more—it is hard to expect the class to listen to poor reading, and it does them no good—and that every lesson should begin with five minutes' exercise in clear voice production. The lesson on Economics was careful and real, but lacked something in liveliness. The lesson on Biology—for which sets B and C were joined—seemed to me a good one. The way in which my questions on Arithmetic and Geometry were answered showed very plainly that these subjects were skilfully and clearly taught, and that the boys were gaining an intelligent grasp of them. Indeed, the impression on me was that the class was under firm and kindly government. A bright, intelligent set of boys.

Set B.

Set Master: Mr. W. Clifford Pilsbury.

Lessons: Book-keeping, Algebra, German, Reading, History of England, Biology, Physics, Economics.

I asked questions on Analysis, Arithmetic, and the History of England. The lesson on Book-keeping I thought needlessly elaborate in detail and not sufficiently clear and convincing. The lessons on Algebra, German, and Reading do not call for any particular remark. The lesson on the History of England was good in substance, but rather too much a matter of dry details, to my mind. The lesson on Physics was careful, but too much an exercise in taking down notes neatly, and too little an exercise in the use of scientific method. The Economics was taken in conjunction with Set A.

The boys answered intelligently and accurately the questions which I put on Analysis; and they acquitted themselves very fairly in Arithmetic, though my impression was that they would do still better were there a little less working out of exercises and a little more oral and mental work. Still they did very fairly. They seemed to have a fairly intelligent grasp of the History of England in the seventeenth century. The class was somewhat uneven in ability.

SET A.

Set Master : The Head Master.

Lessons : English Composition, Economics, Latin, German Geography, Physics.

I asked questions on Algebra and talked a good deal with some of the boys.

The Essays I looked at showed that most of the boys had something to say and could say it decently. The plan of connecting the Economics closely with the actual facts of the neighbourhood seemed to me an excellent one; making the subject real, rousing the interest of the boys, and practising them in using the results of their own observation. The lesson on Latin seemed to me a good one, but lacking somewhat in vivacity. I heard but very little of the teaching of Geography in German, but it struck me that perhaps some of the boys were not quite versed enough in the language to allow of their thoroughly grasping the subject-matter.

The answers on Algebra were fair, but showed that the class was very uneven, and not very far advanced for their age, except in two cases. Nevertheless, both in school and in the playground it was impossible not to be very favourably impressed by the tone and manners of Set A.

It remains for me to remark on the Drawing, and the Singing and Music. I inspected a great number of drawings and was present at two lessons in Drawing. The work seemed to me to be mainly connected with Geometry and Mechanics. To my mind Drawing should be mainly connected with Nature Study and Literature, and should be much bolder and freer than anything I saw.

I am not an expert in Singing and Instrumental Music, but am very fond of both, and a firm believer in their great educational value. They are rightly made prominent at Abbotsholme, and I thoroughly enjoyed the examples of both which were offered me.

I trust that, in what I have said, I have made it quite clear, that I think the School is doing good work; and that I am convinced it will do still better, as the initial difficulties of organisation gradually disappear. The aim it has set before itself, though difficult to accomplish, is a high and a valuable one, and all who are interested in sound education must wish The New School Abbotsholme continued and increased success.

> (*Signed*)
> H. Courthope Bowen, M.A.
> Formerly Headmaster of the Grocers' Company's Schools, Hackney Downs, lately Cambridge University Lecturer on the Theory of Education, &c., &c.

June 29, 1895.

In his "Odd and End Notes, Supplementary to the Report," Mr. Courthope Bowen added: "Eventually, I think you will have to raise your fees to £90, £100, and £110. What you provide is worth even higher fees.

> "(Signed) H. C. B."

(*g*) The First "Parents' Gathering," July 20, 1895.

[*Reprinted from The Abbotsholmian.*]

Several days before the 20th, great preparations were made in order that the house and grounds might be seen at their best. The whole of the 19th was devoted to practising. On the eventful morning the weather was, in spite of all hopes, miserable. There was a drizzling rain, which developed into a steady downpour. Breakfast over, everything was made ready for the reception of the guests, most of whom had arrived in the neighbourhood the evening before. About 10.15 a.m. Big School was full. The sisters were present in strong force, all very curious to see how their "little brothers" were getting on! The concert went off without a hitch, the program being as follows :—

PROGRAM.

Introduction	"Morning Prayer"	Neumann.
	The Orchestra and Choir.	
Solo Piano	"Impromptu"	Schubert.
	Smith.	
Quartette	"Barcarolle"	Wagner.
	Ebbs, Denton ii., Denton i., Mr. Lancelot.	
Motet	"118th Psalm"	Neumann.
	The Choir.	
Recitation	"Andreas Hofer"	Körner.
	Robinson iv.	
Orchestra	"Largo"	Händel.
Part Song	"Hark, hark the Lark"	Cooke.
Solo Piano	"Tarantelle"	Macfarren.
Solo Violin	"Menuet"	Boccherini.
	Ebbs.	
Part Song	"Ye Spotted Snakes"	Stevens.
String Quartette	"Adagio and Finale"	Haydn.
	Mr. Newbould, Ebbs, Denton ii., Denton i.	
Recitation	"Changed"	Calverly.
	Piercy ii.	
Orchestra	"Au Bord de la Mer"	Dunkler.
Vocal Quartette	"Sleep, my Sweet"	Hatton.
	Messrs. Hawkins, Newbould, Neumann, and Couper.	
Solo Violoncello	"L'Elisire d'amore"	Alard.
	Denton i.	
Orchestra and Choir	"The Pilgrim's Chorus"	Wagner.
Orchestra	"Off to the Cricket Match by North Stafford Express"	Neumann.

The final numbers, Wagner's "Pilgrim's Chorus" and "Off to the Cricket Match by the North Stafford Express," Herr Neumann's latest musical sketch, were received with enthusiastic applause. Immediately the concert was over, the guests adjourned to the dining-hall to see the specimen lessons. Herr Neumann led off with "die Badestunde." The boys were transported forthwith to the "Fatherland," and made as though they would disrobe and bathe, regarding the floor in the light of German water, and the chair as a German diving-board, the whole lesson being of course in German. Next came a French lesson for the juniors by Mr. Lancelot. It illustrated teaching from a picture, and went off very well. The "Unknown" class, composed of boys selected from the whole school, to be taken by Dr. Reddie, had to be abandoned, as bathing-time had now come. Happily the rain had ceased, and boys and fathers rushed off to the river to bathe, and see the duck-hunts, which were very amusing. While this was going on Dr. Reddie piloted the ladies through the dormitories and class-rooms in which were exhibited the school furniture, maps, engravings, and photographs, not forgetting the admirable Charts of History copied from the originals of Mr. Branford and Professor Geddes of Edinburgh. In class-room B some drawings and paintings of the past five years were exhibited.

At two o'clock lunch was ready in the tent, which had been set up on the tennis court. The honour of taking in the young ladies fell to the prefects. Lunch was preceded and followed as usual by the Abbotsholme Grace, chanted by the whole school, the organ being rather faintly heard in the huge space.

Dr. Reddie then rose and proposed "Our Queen, our Country, our Empire," remarking that it was easy to be patriotic about a monarch who was one of the ablest and wisest of crowned heads, the mother of her country in the highest sense, and one who promised to be instrumental in promoting the reorganisation of the Empire, which was one of the most important needs of the day.

The toast was drunk with great enthusiasm, being immediately followed by "God save the Queen."

Next came the toast of the day: "The Abbotsholme Parents and Guardians, past and present, coupled with the name of Mr. Joseph Simpson, a very old friend of the School." Dr. Reddie remarked that the Abbotsholme Parents were a most important body, seeing that, but for them, we should not have been there at that time. The toast, which was received with loud cheers, was followed by "Long may they live."

Mr. Simpson in reply said that he had always been a warm supporter of the school, that he had had a cousin, and now had a nephew in it, and, being a neighbour, had heard a good deal about it. Although at first strange rumours had been afloat about the New School, the whole neighbourhood had now come to respect and appreciate it. He proposed "Long life and success to Abbotsholme and to the Headmaster and Miss Reddie."

In his reply the headmaster related some stories which reached him soon after the school was opened. According to one account it was a lunatic asylum; according to another it was a Chinese temple.

Dr. Reddie then proceeded to read the Inspector's Report in all its unsoftened severity. He remarked that he had aimed at being inspected as the Board Schools were under the new code. Accordingly, he had told nobody when the inspection was to be, lest any one should prepare expressly for it. He had wished the school to be seen not arrayed in "company manners" for the occasion, but in its ordinary condition, at its worst rather than at its best. He had carried this policy so far, however, as himself to forget the day of the Inspector's arrival, so that Mr. Courthope Bowen was actually in the house before he remembered the day had come.

Mr. Bowen had stayed four or five days in the school, going here and there just as he pleased, seeing all there was to see. He had inspected the place and the inhabitants, masters as well as boys, so that he was in a position to report upon the whole life and work. As they all knew, Mr. Bowen was a veteran in the cause of education, so that his opinion (Dr. Reddie felt) would carry great weight. The Head then proceeded to read the Report in full. From it we quote, by permission, the following extract :—

"I resided in The New School Abbotsholme, from June 24th to June 28th. I inspected the buildings and grounds; looked with great care into the educational plan and the time-tables of the school; repeatedly listened to the teaching in the various classes, and put questions to the boys about their work, and was present at the drill and the out-of-door occupations of many different kinds.

"Speaking in quite general terms, I may say, at once, that the school seems to me to be in a satisfactory state, and to be making steady and most encouraging progress towards the accomplishment of the very high aim which it has set before it. Taken as a whole the educational plan is, in my opinion, excellent, and its details are arranged with great skill and thoughtfulness. I know of no other school in which the predominant aim is so markedly the development of the boy's whole nature, moral, physical, and intellectual, and none in which the effort to bring his knowledge, power, and skill into harmonious inter-relation is so carefully maintained."

The Report was listened to with profound interest, and at its conclusion was loudly applauded. The parents appeared especially to appreciate the fact that it had evidently in no way been " cooked " before being " served up."

After reciting some of the improvements effected during the year, Dr. Reddie concluded by proposing the last toast: " The New Education, the New Generation, and the long-expected Regeneration."

We drank this of course with enthusiasm. The company now moved to the terrace, whilst we rushed off to put on war-paint for the next item in the program—drill. The war-paint for the occasion included " whites," blue socks and red sashes, singlesticks and shields, the last being decorated with the " crest " of each, concocted and painted by himself. First came a " march past in companies." This was followed by dumb-bells, bar-bells, clubs, and a general salute. Then came the climax. The regiment was divided into two parts, and each advancing from opposite ends of the field at the charge, dashed into the enemy. In the furious *mêlée* which ensued, a great many shields were broken. When the bugles sounded " cease firing," the companies quickly re-formed, and a " march past in line " concluded the drill, which was very creditably performed.

A match on the cricket field was the next attraction— Fathers *v*. Sons." The Fathers lost the toss, but were put in by the Sons " to give them a chance " (!) All the same, our side were not over-confident, and were immensely delighted when the last wicket fell for only 32. Mr. Tom

Bolton made "cock-score" with 16 not out. The "Sons" then went in and made 38 for 5 wickets, Robinson ma. getting 17 not out—not by the most classical cricket. The match was stopped by a terrific thunderstorm at this moment.

The ladies had early left the field after seeing the discomfiture of the elder team, to solace themselves with tea in the tent, and to be shown all round the place by the "kids." The cricketers came up for a later tea at 7. At 7.30 the big bell announced chapel, with which the long day was to conclude. Once more we were reminded, as we had been at the concert, of our limited space, owing to which the invitations had been confined almost entirely to the parents of Abbotsholmians past or present, only one of the old boys even being present, and he by mere accident. But they had had a gathering all to themselves at Easter.

The service was the shortened form for Sunday evening out of the Abbotsholme Prayer Book, commencing with the 42nd and 43rd Psalms, taken as one, and sung to Fussell's chant. After the introductory prayers came the 62nd and 91st Psalms, sung respectively to the 7th and 3rd Gregorian tones.

Then followed a lesson (from Carlyle's "Past and Present," bk. iii., chaps. xi. and xii.), followed by the magnificent 118th Psalm to the 3rd tone, and the "School" Psalm (144th) to the 3rd tone, 2nd ending, both of which were sung with fine effect.

For the second lesson, was taken the noble passage (from Mazzini's "Europe") commencing with the well-known words: "Man is not changed by whitewashing or gilding his habitation." The hymn "Sun of my Soul" followed, and then the concluding prayers, among which was included the *Paternoster*, chanted in Latin to the original Gregorian music.

Directly after chapel, was sung The School Song, and then all said good-night.

The gathering had been arranged for a Saturday in order that the parents might have their boys, if they wished, on Sunday for the whole day.

The holiday, asked for by Mr. Bowen, came on the Monday, so we had plenty of time to recover from our exertions before work recommenced on Tuesday. Thus passed off the memorable first "Parents' Gathering."

G. L. C.

14. PUTTING UP THE CRICKET PAVILION. (*Summer, 1892*).

Copyright

CHAPTER XI.

English Verdicts.
December, 1895, to October, 1896.

CHAPTER XI.

ENGLISH VERDICTS,
DECEMBER, 1895, TO OCTOBER, 1896.

St. James's Budget, *December* 20, 1895.
THE NEW SCHOOL ABBOTSHOLME.

Imagine a country in which the Cabinet Minister is not theorist and amateur, but trained practical statesman : in which the employer does not "make business," but organises labour : in which the directing classes neither cringe nor frown, but direct.

England might be that country if the secondary school fulfilled the function which some educational reformers believe it could fulfil. There are embryos which, under natural conditions, become frogs ; but which, if placed in a peculiar medium, remain tadpoles all their lives. This on the word of the experimental biologist.

Educators are, to be sure, usually wanting in experiment. But whether or no they see that the school, and not the boy, is father to the man, they must admit that the social and political condition of England to-day is not all it should be. For this, the experimental educators (where they exist), or at least some of them, blame the Secondary School, in that it (they allege) tends to fix the boy at the tadpole stage. The men of the upper and middle classes thus arrested in development, are (so the argument runs) deprived of the exercise of those functions, which would naturally fall to them as the Directing Class ot the community. Result : Social disorganisation.

Among the experimental educators who cannot be accused of either slackness or deficiency in experiment must be counted the founder and headmaster of The New School Abbotsholme. Some six years ago Dr.

Cecil Reddie set up and organised an Educational Laboratory on the estate of an old monastery in one of the most charming spots of rural England. The "Abbot's Home" became "The New School," and an old-world Derbyshire valley, scarce awake from its mediæval slumber, was roused to the needs of the future by the inroad of half a hundred boys in picturesque attire, who may be expected to play no ordinary part in the twentieth century. Statesmen, landlords, captains of industry, naval and military officers, judicial and ecclesiastical leaders—in a word, the temporal and spiritual guides of the next generation—this was the species into which the embryos were to be transformed. But "The New School" is an educational laboratory with machinery devised to forward the development only a single stage—that between the ages of eleven and eighteen. The earlier part must perforce be left to the Home, the Kindergarten, and the Fore-school; the later stages to the Universities and years of professional Apprenticeship. The nation awaits a complete and harmonious system of education for the men and women of its directing classes. For the men and women of the industrial classes it has already got a system—of a kind.

Meanwhile the problem which confronts the secondary schoolmaster is this—given a boy whose efforts and labours in life, whether of thought or of action, will lie, for the most part, in the field of guidance and control, of organisation and leadership; what agencies, forces, influences may be most advantageously brought to bear upon him between the ages of, say, eleven and eighteen, so as to perfect all his powers as a man and prepare him for his life's work? Truly, a stupendous problem!

The solution offered at Abbotsholme can only be adequately studied on the spot. It can only be hinted, certainly not described, by the casual visitor.

The round of a boy's day at Abbotsholme begins (in winter) with drill and a short run before morning chapel (7.30 a.m.). Breakfast, over by 8, is followed immediately by "Dormitory Parade." No one who has not seen soldiers at work can picture dormitory parade. A boy "prefect," as non-commissioned officer, presides over each dormitory. The office is no sinecure. The prefect is responsible for many and various things, from the airing of the beds up to the tone of the room. "He is not to rest satisfied with a mere mechanical observance of the rules, but aim at developing a manly bearing in all his fellows, and discourage both effeminacy and roughness. He is to encourage all wholesome fun, but to put down any attempt at foul talk or tedious jest."

Whatever becomes of the rest, the prefect is not likely to remain a tadpole. He is already well on the road to maturity. His evolution is effected through administrative devolution. And this method of education through responsibility is one of the main principles of the Abbotsholme Laboratory, and pervades the whole school life.

But to return to Dormitory Parade. The boys sleep in wool and oxygen. The latter is secured by rural surroundings and open windows; the former by substituting blankets for sheets. On going to bed the boys clean their teeth and wash all over—not forgetting their feet—that they may sleep their nine hours with clean bodies and clean mouths. This for their own sakes. The morning tub is less a cleansing than a tonic or sheer delight. The Head of the school, moreover, believes that a clean body exerts a subtle purifying influence upon the mental and moral nature.

Breakfast done, the boys file off to their respective dormitories. The spectator who accompanies them is bewildered by a sense of incipient earthquake. The air darkens with flying blankets and revolving mattresses. The scene rapidly changes: order comes out of chaos. The boys have made their beds. And this, under the command of the prefect, they have done with skill, precision, neatness, and celerity, the result of drill under capable leadership. Such is Dormitory Parade, and it may be taken as a sample both of the ideals and of the methods ir vogue at Abbotsholme.

Among the many points in which this school differs from the conventional type one is conspicuous. It is the conscious and systematised effort made to train and evolve to highest perfection the moral nature. The typical day school, with its brilliant achievements in mental gymnastics, treats the boy mainly as an intellectual novice. The typical boarding school, with its brilliant achievements in bodily gymnastics, treats him mainly as a physical novice. Abbotsholme does both, but also regards him and chiefly as an ethical novice. Its plan of education is organised upon the assumption that the soul, as well as the mind and the body, responds to surroundings. The man, beautiful as Apollo and clever as Ulysses, but morally at the tadpole stage—or lower—is not unknown in England. Morality was not "one of the subjects" at his school. To be sure you cannot make silk purses out of sows' ears. But what they are trying to do at Abbotsholme is to bring to bear upon the moral nature a set of disciplined forces, parallel to those intended to educate the boy mentally and physically. Now the most cogent moral force known is that which springs from a sense of affection and responsibility combined. At Abbotsholme the whole place breathes at once kindliness and duty. Every boy seems to be entrusted with some responsible office for the benefit of the community. It may be the care of a flower or an animal, the inspection of water supply or drains, of woods and forests, or of river, or boats. Yet all is done carefully, promptly, and cheerily. And here may be noted an important feature in method. It is the correlation and concentration of school forces. The "prefect" is no mere aristocrat who stands and magnificently watches the "fag" at work, but an organiser and co-worker; and his moral control is inextricably bound up with definite labour in the garden, farm, or workshop, for which he is responsible. The aim throughout is thus to combine and correlate physical, intellectual, and moral training, so that the three act and react upon each other, providing an object-lesson for a sermon, which, however, is already rendered superfluous, for love and duty soon blend into a habit of body as organic, fixed, and unconscious as the smile of a genial hostess.

Let it not be thought that on the side of physical evolution the idea of beauty in form is forgotten at Abbotsholme. Athletic exercises are cultivated, but are restrained and controlled. For "athletic cram" is too frequently practised in natural reaction against "intellectual cram." At Abbotsholme drill and gymnastics hold an important place in the day's program, and football, cricket, and other amusements alternate with gardening, farm-work, bee-culture, carpentry, and engineering jobs. An admirable piece of bridge construction, over a tributary of the river Dove, deserves incidental record, especially as it was built for the Parish Council, and made an object-lesson in civic duty.

The endeavour in the general plan of education is to regard the school property itself as a permanent primary object-lesson—a miniature of the big world into which the boy is soon to pass. The school community and estate is essentially a microcosm, with its manifold activities, agricultural, industrial, administrative, and spiritual. This view of the school permits of an effective parallelism in the physical, mental, and moral training of the boys. In the all-round development aimed at, the various subjects of instruction and means of discipline thus reinforce, instead of cancelling, one another, which they tend to do if you exhort to temperance on Sunday and enforce ten hours of study on Monday.

One of the chief subjects of intellectual discipline for the elder boys is political economy. The school community, with its manifold demands and supplies, is the type-concrete case out of which the principles of economics can be educed and abstracted. Political economy thus treated concretely and inductively, and at the same time with a mathematical precision in its deductive reasoning, can be made a mental discipline of the highest order. And it has this advantage over purely abstract studies, such as algebra and logic, that the pupil is at the same time developing his reasoning powers, storing his mind with useful facts, and learning to take an interest in, and comprehensive view of, life. It was the writer's privilege to be present at a lesson in economics given to the top form by the Headmaster. The lesson was based upon some gardening operations the boys had just been doing, and the answers from the lips of boys of sixteen and seventeen showed that they had acquired such a grasp of economic principles as would have enabled them to make a fair show at a university examination, and that, moreover, in a subject usually reserved for post-graduate study.

The all-round training imparted to the boys at Abbotsholme is found, as tested by results, to afford an admirable foundation for university studies. At the outset, perhaps, an Abbotsholme boy suffers in competition with lads specially trained and prepared in the subjects of competitive examinations; but, when it comes to the higher university examinations, the all-round developed boy more than holds his own with those who have specialised prematurely. This is a valuable educational result to the credit side of Dr. Reddie's Pedagogic Laboratory. For it is a result which might have been predicted, but could only be verified by experiment.

As on the moral and physical sides, so the curriculum of intellectual studies at Abbotsholme departs in many ways from the orthodox school course. Space does not admit of details here. It must suffice to say that, in reorganising the scheme of intellectual instruction, the endeavour has been to incorporate and utilise the advances in knowledge and progress in method secured by the great educational reformers of the past and the present. In other words, the curriculum is based, not on use and wont, but on a recognition of the realities of contemporary life and thought.

V. V. B.

NAVY LEAGUE JOURNAL, *March*, 1896.

Dr. Cecil Reddie, the Headmaster of Abbotsholme School, has joined the League, and with him four of his staff and forty-six of his boys. We could not have more welcome recruits; and we hope that the boys of other public and private schools will follow this example. Not long ago a very excellent letter from a public schoolboy appeared in the *Daily Graphic*, suggesting that we should lecture at the public schools. Now our chief want is want of money, and till we have this indispensable requisite we cannot do what we wish. Dr. Reddie and his boys will help us forward, they have not criticised but acted. Those who would know more of Abbotsholme and the most interesting experiment in education which Dr. Reddie is trying, are recommended to look up a back number of *St. James's Budget*, where a full account of the school appeared. Mr. Ruskin would be delighted with it.

SEED-TIME, *October* 1, 1896.

A NURSERY FOR CITIZENS, AND A PARADISE FOR BOYS.

Having spent lately, with my wife, a fortnight of summer weather in a place of the above description, it occurs to me that some readers of *Seed-Time* may be pleased to hear of our experience.

Southward, in Sussex, for the last three or four years has been dedicated to boys of the upper-middle class, a boarding school of an unusual sort, Bedales.

In that sort it had only one predecessor. I refer to Abbotsholme, in Derbyshire, which was founded in 1889 by Dr. Cecil Reddie. One of his assistants, Mr. J. H. Badley, a Cambridge first-class classic, fired by his experience there, resolved to found a school on somewhat similar lines. The whole school curriculum and methods of management, instead of aiming, by an appeal to selfish motives, to excite each pupil to do *the* best—*i.e.*, by outdoing all the rest, try to develop impartially the powers of all the boys, and to get each to do *his* best, in the spirit of coöperation and good-fellowship.

Bedales, the later of these two experiments, already numbers some forty boarders, most of them at present drawn from London.

Looking back to my visit, and comparing Bedales with schools in general, I cannot but feel that, not to speak of boys, English society owes a debt to Mr. and Mrs. Badley for boldly, and not without grave financial risk, undertaking this experiment in education. Parents have now the chance, here or at Abbotsholme, of securing for their children an all-round education of real value for the purposes of life, at the same time that the teacher makes his appeal to the boys' higher rather than their lower motives, to the social rather than the egoistic ones.

E. D. GIRDLESTONE.

15. THE PAVILION FINISHED. (*Summer, 1892*).

Copyright

CHAPTER XII.

German Verdicts.

CHAPTER XII.

GERMAN VERDICTS.

(*a*) VISIT OF PROFESSOR REIN OF JENA, SEPTEMBER, 1896.

IN the autumn of 1896, Professor Rein, who had been lecturing at Cambridge and Edinburgh, paid the school a short visit. The weather behaved ill, for it poured almost every day, and the School was not seen to the best advantage. Our guest, however, after his exertions, was glad of the enforced repose, and was not sorry to find that, owing also to the weather, our party was small, the only guest besides himself and Mrs. Rein being Madame Michaelis, of the Fröbel Institute. It was during this visit that we heard again of Dr. Lietz. In explaining to Professor Rein our plans for the development of the School, we had deplored the fact that it was impossible to find in England adequate teachers. High salaries might attract the merely clever man, but we knew the type. Such men arrive in meek disguise, but, once installed, are apt to impair the harmony of the place. And in a school of this character, which is also a home, it was far more important to have a simple, honest man, even if not deeply erudite, than an intriguing *marchand de soupe*, who might be clever at getting himself on, but who would do no real service for the boys or for the School, even if he failed to turn it upside down. We wanted, moreover, what Germany can produce, a trained teacher, and so we pressed our guest to help us.

(*b*) ARRIVAL OF DR. LIETZ, OCTOBER, 1896.

The consequence was that, a few weeks later, we saw once more our old acquaintance of 1893, Dr. Lietz, who meanwhile had been *oberlehrer* in the Jena *Uebungsschule*, under Professor Rein's direction. He came, therefore, thoroughly trained in the methods so admirably developed there, to aid us in the work of organising the instruction. We had found this task immensely difficult. The absolute dearth of Englishmen equipped for the Abbotsholme type of school was more and more evident as our curriculum became more definite. Moreover, a master at Abbotsholme required to have, apart altogether from his character, his knowledge, and ability to teach, the social instincts and intellectual culture indispensable in a man who is to live, also, in one's house, at close quarters and in a confidential relation.

In asking for a German teacher, the thought had crossed our mind, What if he is a mere instructor, and not a *man?* We had been reassured upon this point. Boys and masters alike were amazed when they found how entirely the newcomer entered into our complex life, and in this seemed more English than the English. Dr. Lietz was a prodigious worker, and as his class hours were less than half a dozen, he had before two months were over mastered most of the details of our life, and had thrown it into the form of a charming story. In it he has unconsciously idealised the place, and all the inmates. But though we recognise this, we are none the less grateful to have our faults left out of sight and our virtues magnified, for new and struggling communities need the encouragement which comes from praise, as certainly as old and decaying institutions require the stimulation of the scourge.

We had already, in 1894, begun to write a history of our work, and for it had prepared some twenty illustrations. Illness and other troubles had stopped our labours, the plates lay idle, and we gladly lent them to Dr. Lietz to make his book more interesting to the Germans. For having, out of regard for us, concealed to some extent the identity of Abbotsholme by the simple devise of reversing all the names, he was afraid his readers would be sceptical unless he showed these pictures of the actual life described.

In return he allowed us to reproduce the book in English, and the translation of *Emlohstobba*, which was made in 1897, comes now, for the first time, before the English public, although portions of the book have already appeared in French, in M. Demolins' second book, *L'école Nouvelle*. The German original was very well received in Germany, and has been read in most countries of continental Europe. Its marked success enabled Dr. Lietz already in April, 1898, to open a German Abbotsholme at Ilsenburg in the Harz.

The translation has, with Dr. Lietz's entire approval, been amended as regards some small matters of fact in which he was in error. We have not, however, allowed ourselves the same liberty with regard to the matters of opinion which, in his story, are put into the mouths of various speakers. The reader who peruses our own book will have little difficulty, we think, in judging how far these opinions coincide with the actual life and thoughts of Abbotsholme.

I have to express my very special thanks, in this place, to my friend Dr. R. O. Moon, for his valuable aid in making the translation, and for the willing help of many of the boys in the same enterprise, and finally to Professor Rein for kindly writing, so long ago as 1897, a Preface to the English Edition.

As Germany is, undoubtedly, the most powerful, best organised, and most progressive country in the world at the present time, German Criticism is, we feel, of especial value, particularly in all that concerns Instruction. And our deliberate opinion is that England will yet have to learn many lessons from Germany, if our Educational System, our National Organisation, our Philosophy and our Religion, not to speak of our Army (and, we fear too, our Navy) are not to remain very largely the "wonder and astonishment of the world for antiquated absurdity." Their willingness to learn from abroad is the secret of their success, as our British ignorance and prejudice are the cause of our backwardness and will be the probable cause of the Decay and Dissolution of our Anglo-Keltic World-Dominion.

EMLOHSTOBBA.

November, 1896.

DR. LIETZ.

Copyright.

Emlohstobba:

Fiction or Fact?

PICTURES OF THE SCHOOL LIFE
OF THE PAST, PRESENT, OR FUTURE

BY

HERMANN LIETZ

*Licentiate of Theology and Doctor of Philosophy, University of Jena;
Formerly Oberlehrer in the University Practising School at Jena;
Sometime Director of the Progymnasium and Höhere Töchterschule,
Kötzenbroda, near Dresden; late Assistant Master at Abbotsholme*

TRANSLATED FROM THE GERMAN WITH THE AUTHOR'S SANCTION

WITH A PREFACE BY

WILHELM REIN

*Professor of Philosophy and Education, and Director of the
Pedagogic Seminary, at the University of Jena*

AUTHOR'S DEDICATION.

DER NEUEN SCHULE

EMLOHSTOBBA

UND DER

ÜBUNGSSCHULE DES PÄDAGOGISCHEN

UNIVERSITÄTS SEMINARS

ZU JENA

IN DANKBARER TREUE

PREFACE TO THE ENGLISH EDITION.

I HAVE great pleasure in writing a Preface to Dr. Lietz's charming and instructive book, "Emlohstobba!" For its description of the scenery, house and gardens, the life of the place, and the work and play of the boys, carries me back to my visit to Abbotsholme last year.

The spirit which reigns in that Home of Education speaks to us audibly in these pages, and brings before our eyes an institution on English soil, which is carrying into practice the high aims so long familiar to us Germans in the works of our great teachers, Pestalozzi, Herbart, Fröbel, &c. How happy the boy must be who lives at Abbotsholme, in that pedagogic kingdom, where no disturbing influences upset the educational aims and work of the place; where full freedom is enjoyed in carrying out the ideals which the Director of the School has rightly apprehended to be the true ones; where the culture of the intellect is balanced by the culture of the heart and of the body, and instruction in workshop and garden is balanced by the refining influences of art, morals, and religion.

In a very satisfactory way the life and instruction are intertwined, and made to coöperate in the perfecting of each, the life of yesterday furnishing examples to the teacher to-day, and his instruction finding its application in the life of to-morrow.

In Abbotsholme School the Educator lays claim to the entire personality of the boy—body, mind, and spirit—in order to produce men of vigorous will and stable character.

As regards the means for getting this, the religious and moral education admirably coöperates with the culture of body and brain, to strengthen the whole nature, so as to produce in reality that harmonious personality which is, alas, too often only a phrase.

I heartily congratulate, therefore, *The New School Abbotsholme* upon its work, which is so ably described by Dr. Lietz in his book. I see a school community organised throughout according to the best educational principles, striving to develop to the utmost all the powers of the growing boy. Nothing appears to be neglected in this school, which an Educative School should undertake. Care is taken to secure the freshness and grace, strength and beauty, natural to the healthy body; to train hand and eye in the fields and workshops, as well as in the house and class-room; to train the young to find interest in all the life around them; to teach them to reason as well as to remember, and to love their companions as well as to strive to outstrip them. All this is done without suggesting prizes, or any reward other than the natural result which follows all work well done.

This school is able to open men's eyes to the folly of the excessive attention and recognition usually bestowed on the memory of mere words and phrases; to the folly of the so-called "classical" education, namely, the doctrine that the training of the mind is best attained through "formal" studies, such as Latin grammar and Greek verses. These in reality employ precisely the same powers as are used in the study of French or physics, but the latter subjects have in addition an intrinsic value not possessed by Latin or Greek. This school shows the folly of allowing a boy to grow up ignorant of the body which he carries about with him all his days, in all his enterprises, and through which alone he can come in contact with the world and his fellow-men; ignorant of the fundamental laws of the universe—the house in which he and all men live—and ignorant of the best thoughts and feelings of the greatest men of his own country and epoch, and of the problems to be solved by himself and the age he lives in. In this fresh and touching, striking and convincing book, which betrays the enthusiasm of a true Educator in every page, we learn the needs of boys and nations at the present time.

I trust that Abbotsholme School will attract the attention of all who care about education—parents, teachers, and Cabinet Ministers. From schools like this will come forth vigorous men fit to create and to direct a nobler social life in the future.

WM. REIN.

JENA, *July* 19, 1897.

INTRODUCTION.

GENTLE READER, have you ever felt that the school you used to attend as a child really gave you the education which you now see would have been the best? Are your own youngsters, at this very minute, being educated so as to turn out quite healthy, and capable of doing some real good in the world? Do you find them content with their life at school? Or do they make constant complaints about the "awfully hard Latin and Greek prose," about the "endless work," "the dreary lessons"; tasks that compel them to "crib" from their neighbours. In spite of his aching head—brought on by too much book-work this morning—must your youngest boy, perhaps this very moment, stop behind for yet another hour of the same dreary grind? Or will he presently bring home, as a particularly agreeable gift from his master, an evening task, crammed with mistakes, to be done over again? Or do his dull, watery eyes betray evidence of a pedagogic flogging?

With such experiences in mind, did you ever put to yourself this question? Is there anywhere in the world to be found a School for Boys, which is free from these numberless proofs of Boy Martyrdom—a School where, in place of a mere one-sided training of the understanding, or mere stuffing of the memory, one might find an education and harmonious culture of the whole being: Body, Arms, Legs, Eyes, Ears, Muscles, and Sinews, as well as Intellectual, Æsthetic, and Moral powers ? Or is this thought of a harmonious development of the whole man only the pretty, but impracticable, dream of a Pestalozzi ? Can it be that such a dream as this has anywhere in this world been translated into fact ?

To all these questions you will find an answer, if you will visit with me a School in a land, which for the present I will not name. Be assured, however, that if this country is neither Germany nor France, it is, nevertheless, not in the Moon.

16. THE RIVER DOVE. (*Summer, 1892*).
Copyright

A DAY IN THE NEW SCHOOL-STATE EMLOHSTOBBA.

CHAPTER I.

THE SCHOOL-STATE, EMLOHSTOBBA, IN THE GREY DAWN.

LET me transport you with me into the midst of a pleasant land.

It is early morning. Towards the east the sky is growing bright. In the grey twilight we pass through meadows, which here are still green, and on which, although it is already November, shaggy sheep, beautiful red cows, and horses, in large numbers, are grazing peacefully. The fields are divided from each other by hedges of hawthorn. Upon the greensward, thus protected, the animals are feeding without whip, or dog, or shepherd to worry them.[1] We are not in the sunny South, and yet, even here, winter seems loth to take up his abode. So the herds remain outside, night and day, without fear of frost or hunger. If the grass gets too short, some hay, fetched from the barn in yonder corner of the pasture, is thrown down for food. Plough-land for corn is scarce

---

[1] In Germany hedges are almost unknown, and hence the shepherd and his dog are necessities. (TRANSLATOR.)

seen anywhere; for the rich corn treasures of foreign lands provide a cheap abundance of wheat, oats, barley, and maize.

We have just passed through a small village, whose name, Orcastra, takes us back to the days when the Romans had a camp there, and find ourselves at once in the open country. We go across some meadows beside a small, clear river, whose rapid current winds hither and thither through the wide valley, and at length enter the precincts of our little School-state.

For here, in fact, we find a small *imperium in imperio*. A score or so of great grass fields, broken by wooded hills and miniature valleys, make up the small estate which is the school domain. Through these territories winds for a mile the above-mentioned river Evod. Beautiful, lofty trees, some of them rare and valuable, rise picturesquely out of the rich herbage. Small labels here and there state the name and country of the more interesting. For a moment the visitor believes himself in some vast botanic garden.

The outlook is not over a town, where a thousand conflicting forces trouble the scholar, and draw him away from the influences of the School. It is over fair, open country. The teacher in such a scholastic principality can live completely with his boys, and devote to them all his strength and thought. They can all breathe the pure air of heaven, without fear of drawing in with every breath a thousand poisonous microbes.

Such is the spot where our Educator carries on his arduous and responsible work. Aided by scenes like this, and in many other ways, his love of Nature and of Natural Life is nourished, strengthened, and satisfied.

This landscape, with hills and vales, flat meadow lands, woods and brooks, and winding river, lies spread out like a scroll before the boys, forming an ever-open first and final text-book of Geography. But we must tear ourselves away from this charming picture, which contains, we note, all the most important geographical types—Hill, Valley, Plain, River, &c., &c.; and now ascending a slope, we enter the beautiful and well-designed school-house, with its large, airy, and well-lighted rooms. Already from outside we have noticed that at least one window in every room is either half or fully open. The opening and shutting is accomplished by pushing half the window from below upwards, or *vice versâ*.[1] In the open fireplace, built in the old German style, a brightly blazing fire provides that, amid all this fresh air, the room shall not lack geniality and warmth. Indeed, everything invites one, gentle reader and guest, to rest awhile in this wholesome and home-like dwelling, and to pass a Day at School with our young friends, the pupils. I will allow myself the pleasure of conducting you round.

CHAPTER II.

HOW WE SPENT A MORNING IN THE NEW SCHOOL-STATE.

LOUD peals the bell. To us visitors it seems a trifle early. It is not yet seven o'clock. Nevertheless, in a few minutes, we tumble out of our woollen bed-clothes—

[1] Nearly all windows in Germany are casements opening laterally. (TRANSLATOR.)

for in this land they have, it seems, already abandoned, and almost forgotten, the unwholesome feather-bed.[1] We hasten to go betimes into the boys' sleeping rooms; for we want, of course, to see the entire life of the place. We notice that during the night nearly all the windows have been wide open, and are still. No dearth of water is to be observed here. The whole body goes into a big flat bath, about a metre wide; is washed in cold water, and then rubbed with a rough towel. All the boys, big and small—the ages run from eleven to eighteen years—do the same. Although it is November, no one shirks this wholesome practice, which custom has made, indeed, a daily necessity, and which, all know, confirms and strengthens body, mind, and character. Nor, although there are no partitions or curtains, and all are naked, is there the faintest sign of shrinking or self-consciousness, nor, on the other hand, any lack of proper modesty; but all show that happy blending of instinctive reserve and manly self-respect, which furnishes one of the deepest lessons in practical morals, more eloquent than a hundred sermons, and more wholesome than a hundred pious pamphlets.

Like lightning the boys slip on their clothes, and we are able to admire the eminently practical, wholesome, and picturesque School Uniform. In this, as in so much else, we recognise that the Educator in this School-state excludes no part of human life from his survey, but accepts responsibility for studying and organising all.

[1] The typical German bed contains a sloping wedge-shaped bolster, on which the body lies aslant; and in place of bedclothes there is a huge feather-bed, or eider-down quilt, which has a habit of falling off in the night. (TRANSLATOR.)

German Verdicts

Young and old, big and small, all wear the same costume—a woollen shirt, with woollen collar ; knicks and coat with waistband, all of wool (without linings or stuffy padding), and therefore porous and easily washed.[1] Such a uniform allows and even invites one, to run and jump at ease, instead of compelling one, to sit and walk sedately. The slavery to clothes, or at least to fashions, is here abandoned.

Once more the bell sounds. In a few minutes we see a crowd of sturdy, merry youngsters hurry downstairs. None can be home-sick, none can appear with hanging head in a place where reigns such joy and enthusiasm. They form in line in front of the entrance-door. A few commands from the Master, or Prefect in charge, and off rush teacher and pupils for a "run" along the carriage drive, to the boundary of the School territory and back, 1,200 yards in all. Of course each wishes to be first, and perhaps it will be a master who, by these morning runs, has retained his youthful freshness.

After a brief interval we pass into the School Chapel. From the walls all round gaze down upon us a number of the great moral and religious Heroes of Mankind. Each picture, or statue, preaches its silent sermon of duty and high ideal, alike to master and boy.

The series, as a whole, incarnates, as it were, the entire Duty of Man, to himself and fellows and country, as well to the Universe and God. These silent presences, with their steadfast gaze, set the imagination on fire, and inspire us to "Love and Duty," the motto of the School.

[1] In Germany (and, it is to be feared, elsewhere too), clothes are fearfully and wonderfully made, and, not daring to approach the wash-tub, are soon saturated with germs and all uncleanness. (TRANSLATOR.

The boys came in and sat quiet and earnest. They are used, moreover, to do this in the absence of the masters, and thus learn self-government and self-control through self-respect. Presently the masters file in. They wear a toga-like mantle, not unlike the robe of the German Professor or Divine. And, indeed, the Teacher is not only school Master, but also Priest. We kneel with the School community: with them we sing one of the simple but lovely hymns belonging to this people. The melody reminds us strikingly of the most beautiful German Folk-songs. Next we listen to a few pregnant sayings from the lips of Jesus Christ and His Disciples, or from the lips of their predecessors or followers, the Prophets and Teachers of all ages, ancient, middle, and modern. Some time in the School-year is devoted to each of the great Leaders of Humanity, and occasionally especial notice is taken of the pictures on the walls. But, running through the whole year, comes the Story in sections, not merely of the sufferings and death, but of the daily life, and in particular the words and deeds of the great Master of all. We now sing one of the most beautiful of the Psalms to the old Gregorian music—to-day it is the 91st—and finish with a few short prayers from the beautiful, but simple School Liturgy, ending usually with the Lord's Prayer, that masterpiece of simple, terse, and pregnant religious aspiration.

We leave the Chapel not without a certain feeling of solemnity and calm. Precisely this simple, childlike, undogmatic, religious worship seems to fascinate and satisfy us. Moreover, this union of noble and profound ideas with artistic, lovely, and solemn ceremony and surroundings, this harmonious blending of form and substance this it is which so deeply touches us. Nevertheless, our appetite now demands our attention, and to assuage it there is more than enough in the Dining Hall.

In every one's place—for Teacher and Pupil alike—is set a soup-plate, full of grey, steaming brew. The guest, wont to see only his "morning coffee,"[1] looks rather askance at it. But scarce has he tried shyly a mouthful or two, when this wholesome and nourishing mess of oat-meal porridge, with sugar and thick cream, seems as good to him as it does to the boys around him. We do them but justice, when we admit that they would a thousand times rather have it than coffee, and would not go without it for any consideration in the world. We rejoice to see how the piles of brown whole-wheat-meal bread, the mountains of white bread, the great dishes of fried fish, and of scrambled, poached, or boiled eggs disappear : for such are the substantial viands which people in this country like for breakfast. In particular we notice the preference for cocoa. Marmalade, too, and jams of every sort are provided. Nevertheless, one notices no trace of intemperate eating, which is, however, after all, largely the natural result of insufficient, unwholesome, or uneven provision. The numerous glass houses in the gardens ensure also to-day, as indeed always, that there shall be no dearth of fresh flowers on every table. Over the fireplace, the " Last Supper," by Leonardo da Vinci, reminds us in what spirit such meals should be taken. Other pictures all round this room, symbolising the

[1] The German on rising, takes a cup of coffee, with perhaps a roll and butter, nothing more. Perhaps this philosophic meal, in the course of years, has produced his superior brain power. The English might try the experiment, to quicken their slower wits. (TRANSLATOR.)

dangers, duties, or victories of our daily life, together impress upon us, that also our physical life must be used for moral and divine ends. As everything else throughout the School, so Art herself is made the handmaid of education. Her silent influence is, indeed, more eloquent than all our tongues. She saves us many a word and many a frown, or lends our fleeting arguments the power of her unchanging presence.

As a matter of course, every meal is, as the picture of Da Vinci has already suggested to us, shared by the entire school community. Boys and masters all share the same food (save where different age, health, or temperament renders some small difference advisable or necessary). For the common meal, like the common prayer, is a great unifier. Nor is a boy taught moderation by seeing his elders consuming, at a separate board, dainties denied to him, but deemed necessary for less hungry, though perhaps more fastidious, maturity.[1]

Meanwhile it has struck eight. We now see the boys at a new sort of work, at which, may be, our German mothers would shake their heads, but which even they could not do quicker or better than these lads. It is a work which will make them handy at home, tidy and useful, and will initiate them into some of the mysteries and worries of domestic life. It is "Dormitory Parade." The windows are still wide open, for during chapel and breakfast the

---

[1] On reaching middle life, when the digestive organs enter naturally a less active period, no one should eat so much as hitherto. Unfortunately the slight decline of digestive strength then observable leads most people to eat still more, or, worse still, to commence stimulating the jaded appetite by means of alcohol, the fruitful source, not only of drunkenness, but of most diseases, physical, mental, and moral. (TRANSLATOR.)

rooms and beds are being aired. Now the blankets are tossed from hand to hand and well shaken, pillows are beaten, and quickly the bed is made, as it only can be made by those who are to sleep in it. The bed consists of nothing more than a wooden bedstead, with spring mattress, a wool mattress and blankets. No soft fusty featherbed, nor eider-down quilt is allowed here, to enervate and make effeminate. Everything moreover is done rapidly and methodically; and an excellent spirit reigns in the room the whole time. In case of need there is the Prefect to see that all goes well. He is the eldest, or rather foremost, in the room, and through his office is trained to feel and bear responsibility. He has to see also that the fellows clean their teeth, for this they must do every night, and every morning after breakfast.

Thus pass ten or fifteen minutes in the main building or in the cottages (for some of the boys sleep in four smaller houses, each under command of a special master). At the same time the boys pass out in squads, each under its captain, to perform, in the garden, the necessary offices of nature. They are carefully taught (for in this school no part of the body is forgotten or neglected) the necessity of regularity in all the functions of the body, and the importance of understanding all these details of daily life. They see moreover that even the lowliest functions of our nature can subserve great ends, for all rejected by the body is employed to nourish the garden crops; and what is too often a source of disease, becomes here a source of wealth.

Presently from all parts of the building we hear music. The boys are at "violin practice." We observe that they have devoted their twenty minutes to it conscientiously, although apparently not forced to do so by any very obvious supervision.[1]

CHAPTER III.

SOME HOURS SPENT IN FRANCE, GERMANY, AND ROME, WHILE STILL IN EMLOHSTOBBA.

At half-past eight we are sitting with the lower division of the "German Class," called here, sensibly enough, the "Thirteens," to indicate the average age. (It corresponds to our German Tertia B.) Is it an hour of instruction? Are we really in a foreign land? At a signal from the teacher the boys come forward, one after the other. Each has, as his part in the work, to imitate some particular action; to take off his shoes, or put them on, or greet his neighbour, &c., &c., the whole series of movements being closely related and following naturally. This boy or that explains these operations by means of the corresponding German sentences. Sometimes the Teacher gets help from the boy's imagination (see below, where we discuss the use of pictures) and transforms the class-room into a Swimming Bath, or Dormitory, a Dining Hall, Shop, Hotel, Workshop, or Railway Station, a Post Office, Railway Carriage, or Burning House, &c. In all cases,

---

[1] The German practice, in most things, appears to be to leave as little as possible to the initiative of the boys. This saves them from some mistakes, avoids some waste of time and enables more of organised instruction to be given; but the boys lose the opportunity of learning how to repair disaster and how to discover by themselves new facts and new methods. (Translator.)

the boys connect the actions and objects with the corresponding German words. For example, they are making a cupboard, and the following is the conversation : "I take a board, fetch a saw, measure the angle and length. I place my model before me. I measure the length of the cupboard, and from the working-drawing, I calculate the length of the wood, &c., &c., &c." We see that even the youngest is seldom in a fix as to the meaning of a word, or as to the order of events, whatever be the subject. The *content* of the words *interests* them. They learn thus a wealth of words which, if they should ever go into a foreign land, are precisely those they would at once have to use every day.

In this school all instruction in language starts from the Principle—that as the mother-tongue is learnt, so, as far as possible, must other tongues be learnt, namely, first of all, by speaking. In the French, German and Latin Classes—for this is the order in which the languages are studied here [1]—hardly a word of the mother-tongue is used, but all is done respectively in French, German, and, as far as possible, even Latin. Commencing always with actual observations of the School Environment, they connect the words, to the utmost extent possible, immediately with tangible objects or visible actions. Next they deal with Pictures of things and actions; and so on. Curiously enough one never sees, during such lessons, a youngster dreaming or ill-tempered. In this lesson, as in all other language lessons, the boys showed a lively interest

[1] Quite recently (1896) one celebrated German Gymnasium has tried the experiment, which has been practised in Abbotsholme since 1889, of taking French, before the time-honoured Latin. The great advantage of the innovation makes it probable that soon the plan will be followed in all German Secondary Schools. (TRANSLATOR.)

in the work. They did not seem in the least to deplore that here no one insisted on prancing round upon that favourite Hobby Horse of " Extemporalia." [1]

Indeed such grand public events are quite unknown here. Nor is any trace to be found here of "drumming it in," "pouring it in," "cramming it in," nor of learning by heart the most elaborate grammatical exceptions possible, before one can understand or speak a single sentence of the language of every day.

Or are we to call by the name *grammar*, the system used here, whereby the boys first describe events in the present, then as having happened yesterday, and then as about to happen next week? If so, at any rate, during their "grammatical exercises" no sign was to be observed of discomfort or dislike. Every word or phrase that had been learnt was employed whenever an opportunity arose. The Teachers of French and German here either were foreigners, or at least had been a long time in foreign lands, and they spoke almost entirely in the foreign tongue.[2] Occasionally the boys write letters home in the foreign tongue, and even Divine Service in Chapel, as we

---

[1] For this magnificently-sounding but terribly-feared German-made pedagogic torment there is in English no adequate word. The German pedagogue sits and reads aloud, from some dull and dry book, sentences containing the greatest possible number of grammatical pitfalls, and the luckless youths have to write down at once the Latin or Greek equivalent. Their work is then elaborately corrected with red ink; marks are assigned, and sometimes an unhappy youngster for his blunders gets (like Agag) "hewn in pieces" (*durchgehauen*). (TRANSLATOR.)

[2] English and French are, in Germany, pretty usually taught by Germans. The reasons are obvious. The French would not be very comfortable in Germany, and the English seldom know their own language, and are never trained to teach it or anything else. (TRANSLATOR.)

shall see hereafter, sometimes aids the foreign language lessons.

None of the Periods of instruction lasts longer than three-quarters of an hour, and the minutes go only too quickly in a class where all join in the work so heartily. A quarter of an hour's interval follows. This comes as far as possible after every lesson, to enable the backward to get extra help, the lazy extra work, and the bright and eager complete relaxation.

After a sufficient dose of fresh air in the Break, we enter the French Class, called here the "Elevens," because the average age is about eleven (corresponding to the German IV and IIIb).

Near the Blackboard—which, we see, is of ground glass, and delightful to write on—hangs a picture. It represents the daily life of a French village in winter.

The boys relate to us in French what they see in this picture, write the difficult words first on the glass board and afterwards in their note-books. Next they exchange the picture for a map of France. This, of course, has been got from France (as that of Germany from Germany, and those of other lands each from its own country), and has been made therefore by Frenchmen and reflects their latest scientific knowledge or political ambition.[1] By the help of this map of France the class travels in thought from Paris to Toulon. On the road only French, of course, is spoken. We have, however, not only spoken French, we have at the same moment learnt French

[1] English Statesmen would find it useful, sometimes, to supply the English Foreign Office with the last French Atlas, wherein youthful France is taught, thus early, what slices of territory are next to be "reunited" to the French Dominions. It might spare them some surprises. (TRANSLATOR.)

geography and French manners and customs; all this, moreover, without missing our beloved "Plotz's celebrated Grammar," in which not a single "*Exception*" can, by any miracle, be found to have been omitted.

In this school they pass on to grammar only after they have to some extent learnt to speak the language. What they know they analyse, and thus construct gradually their own grammar, and learn to enter methodically, in a special book, all new words under appropriate headings. Their grammar, thus constructed, curiously enough contains chiefly the universal rules required to be used every day, and avoids as far as possible all exceptions which occur perhaps once a year, or, may be, not even once in a life-time. In the syntax we draw attention mainly to those cases where the foreign idiom differs from that of our own tongue. For we make, of course, the mother-tongue the foundation for all language studies, and the grammar of our own tongue the key to universal grammar.[1]

Marvellous were the results of the three principles employed here in teaching foreign languages. The association of the language—

1. With some particular *Occupation* taken out of the boys' ordinary school-life; or

2. With Observation Pictures of life, at home or abroad; or,

3. With scenes and events taken from the Geography,

---

[1] In Germany they explain, it would seem, the known by the unknown, the familiar German idiom by comparing it with the unfamiliar Latin equivalent, as if the construction of the Latin sentence was necessarily always a key to the construction of the German. This method is not unknown in England, too. (TRANSLATOR.)

History, or Literature of the corresponding country, and *imagined* without the aid of pictures.

To see the last-named method more fully developed, we will go on to the "Fifteens," not however until we have refreshed ourselves by joining the boys at their "lunch" of milk and biscuits in the "Second Break," playing afterwards in the courtyard to clear our heads, stretch our limbs, and drive the blood all over the body to prevent it collecting and congesting where not needed, thus causing fidgets and inattention in the next period of work.

On entering the class-room we see on the walls various charts, showing the political condition of Europe in successive centuries, and in the middle a picture representing the "Battle of the Goths at Vesuvius." Here, in this foreign land, we are going to see a German History lesson given by a trained German Teacher, in his own German tongue. And, indeed, he could not have given the lesson in the language of this country, even had he wanted to, for he had only recently begun to study it. Latin and Greek he could speak, and, as Orientalist and Germanist, some Hebrew, Gothic, and Anglo-Saxon as well, but not a hundred words of this language. For, although it was not Hottentot, but on the contrary the tongue of one of the most important cultured nations of modern times, our German Teacher had, strange to say, never been taught it, neither at the Gymnasium, nor at the University. Nevertheless, a few days after his arrival, the Headmaster said to him, "Will you come and give a lesson to Set X in German History?"

Well, it went better than could have been expected. By the help of gestures and pictures even the deaf and dumb can talk. How much easier still must communication be between those who after all speak only different languages. We had, moreover, our German maps, pictures and books to help the eye, as we listened to the German words and phrases. The charts and pictures of the History of Civilisation principally aroused the delight of the boys, and they are indeed well designed to awaken interest, arouse observation, and teach to think. The same applies to the "Historical Picture Atlas," as well as to the book of Historical Sources and the " German History from Pytheas to Wilhelm II." [1] related in poems by German poets. We listen to the boys talking German. With the help of the other boys and of the Master they speak it very fairly. We observe that our German class knows about Alaric, Theodoric, Teja, Karl Martell, Karl the Great, &c., as well, or perhaps better, than German boys would know about the heroes of this country.

After the boys have described these pictures in humble prose, they recite the glorious deeds, there depicted, in the soul-stirring stanzas of poets like Dahn, Lingg, Möser, and von Platen. We see with delight how enthusiastic the class becomes, while reciting historical poems such as "Thusnelda in Captivity," "Velleda," "The Grave in the Busento," "Gothic fidelity," "The Last of the Goths," &c. The historical Primer is neither in much request, nor in much honour. It is the mere ghost of history.

---

[1] Some spasmodic efforts have been made in England to do for English Geography and History what Germany has done for German Geography and History. The English work is unfortunately handicapped by the usual drawback of English scientific and social work—ignorance of the work of others and dislike of coöperation. (TRANSLATOR, 1898.)

The boys honestly confess that they do not care for these lifeless skeletons, but much prefer the original authorities and the historical poem. Both make memorable scenes, events, and characters, living realities, depicted in words which will live; and therefore we are well able to dispense with the skeleton Primer, and leave it to the crammers and the crammed.

From the blackboard we copy into our note-books, in distinct, systematic order, the successive topics of the historical matter, as it was developed by the combined exertions of boys and master. In studying the history of the neighbouring nations, we start from the corresponding events and institutions in this country. Thus the National History which is studied for two years before beginning that of France and Germany, serves as a standard with which foreign history can be compared. The historical matter was so attractive to both master and scholars, that they could easily overcome any difficulties in the language used, through the interest thus aroused. By thus combining languages with other instruction there is, moreover, always a double advantage; first, the acquisition of the language in question, and second, the knowledge of the corresponding Geography, History, &c. This method was also applied occasionally to Natural Science and Mathematics. Throughout the period the scholars seemed to have forgotten that they were also having a language lesson. The sensation of *ennui*, which is sure to be present whenever a master feels that he is dealing merely with a "Class," though the usual accompaniment of a language lesson was not present here. The boys did not want to think about the French or German sounds and rules, but to hear about Alaric, Karl the Great, Theodoric,

Napoleon, and Teja ; and it had become evident to them all, that this could only be done in the French, or German, language.

Time does not admit of our staying so long with the "Romans" as we did with our young "Frenchmen" and "Germans."

On entering we notice at once that our "Romans" are older than both the "Germans" and the "French"; and we are pleased, for it is certainly harder for boys to realise the life of Rome ages ago than life in France or Germany at the present day. Consequently Latin should be studied last. Every one in this school has become firmly convinced, from his experiments, that a boy ought first to master his mother-tongue thoroughly, and then learn to speak and write, up to a definite standard, the tongues of the two most important living foreign nations, before he begins to study the so-called "classical" Latin and Greek, even when he means to make eventually a special study of them. He will make much more progress, and get a more real grasp, both of the form and the content, both of the grammar and the living thought, if he has first obtained an adequate hold of his own tongue, and also learnt to think in two foreign languages. The classical scholars pretend that Latin is an *Elixir Linguæ*, a sort of wondrous mental Sloyd, invented by philanthropic Romulus for the benefit of German (and other) boys for ever after. Once learnt, all other languages become mere child's play ; all other studies—Mathematics, NatureKnowledge, Geography, and History—superfluous. The Latin scholar, in short, as we daily see, is able to do everything, upon this world, better than anybody else ! If this wonderful language had not been invented by the prophetic philanthropy of

Rome, we should have had to invent it now ourselves! If we wish to teach a boy to swim, we take him out, far into the deep Atlantic, and throw him in, being well persuaded that, if he can swim there, he can swim in any pond in Europe. This is at least the method of our "classical" philologists. If a boy can master Latin, he can master all our foolish little modern languages. If he knows Latin Grammar, he will not need to know the grammar of his mother-tongue. If he knows all about Roman civilisation, it is unnecessary that he should study that of his own country at the present day. Is not the "classical education" of our directing classes perhaps the cause of the deplorable state of Europe now? But, it is said, can we regard a man as educated and cultured, when he cannot read the literatures of Rome and Greece in the original? Are we to deprive our ablest boys of the privilege of reading Homer in the omnibus, or reciting Sophocles as he drinks his morning coffee? What will happen if our Soldiers, Judges, Doctors, Clergy, Statesmen never learn to read Thucydides or Plato, or Cicero or Cæsar? Would you have them read "mere translations"? To all such questions the teachers in this school reply: "Do we need to read Isaiah in Hebrew, or the Gospel of St. John in Greek, in order to gain inspiration from those authors?" All are not meant to be experts in Hebrew Grammar, any more than to be specialists in Arabic, Persian, or Sanskrit. It is enough that a few become students of Greek or of Latin; the vast majority will be content to leave the minute study of dead tongues to "classical" scholars, in order themselves to have leisure to give their strength to the more serious study of living Humanity.

It is believed here that special studies of every kind

should be the work, not of the School, but of the University.[1]

In this Latin class our guest notices with surprise the absence, even here, of the Reading Book, with its thousand disconnected sentences thrown together anyhow: one about Balbus's wall or Caius's garden; a second about Scipio's grave; a third about Miltiades' Victory, and so on; thus taking the boy, within five minutes, over Europe, Asia, and Africa; from the year 1000 B.C. to 100, 1000, or 1870 A.D. Instead of wasting our energy on disconnected, and therefore useless, knowledge, we practise the language here on a subject-matter, which has intrinsic value of its own, and which is, moreover, interesting to the boy. In the elementary Latin class the daily life of the school is once more, we see, made use of as a material for the Latin lesson. We hear the following conversation :—

> Prima luce tintinnabulum sonat. E cubiculis eximus.
> Omnes ordine ante portam stant.
> Luna etiam nunc lucet.
> Sed sol jam oritur.
> Lunæ solisque radios spectamus.
> Tota cohors numeratur.

---

[1] The votaries of "classics" have already unwittingly abandoned their best and proper stronghold. They have dropped compulsory Greek, which was worthy to be retained, and have clung to Latin, a poor substitute for the tongue of Homer, Aischylos, and Plato. A distinguished German professor, speaking on this matter, told the writer that, as far as its educational value was concerned, the whole Latin literature might be burned without mankind suffering, in his view, one atom of injury; whereas (he went on to say) the Greek literature, whose continued study in our schools is imperilled, has an absolutely inestimable worth and imperishable vitality. (TRANSLATOR.)

> Tres ex pueris tardi sunt.
> Hi igitur poenam dant.
> Tum signo dato iter facimus.
> Sexcentos passus celeriter currimus.
> Deinde eodem revertimur.
> Nonne currere amas?
> Currere amo.
> Quid tu census?
> Equidem dormire malo.
> At hic cursus corpus sanum facit.
> Nonne corpus sanum habere vis?
> Hoc maxime volo.
> Itaque quotidie curras, sic enim mentem sanam in corpore sano habebis.

As our young " Frenchmen " learn French, in learning French Geography and History, so the elder " Romans," besides Latin, study Roman History and Civilisation. But our aim in Latin is a considerably lower one than our aim in French and German. The main facts of Roman civilisation are studied by reading chiefly those Roman authors whose writings are especially connected with this country, *e.g.*, Cæsar and Tacitus. Advanced specialisation we leave entirely to the University. Of Cicero's speeches and " Latin Prose at Sight" (in the style of Sallust or Livy) our guest saw no trace. Our study of Rome starts with the cultural remains of Roman occupation in this land. The boys do not wade through every detail of Cæsar's descriptions of the endless Gallic wars, but study rather the descriptions by him and Tacitus of the life and manners of the Kelts in Gaul and Britain, and the customs of the different tribes of Germany—and this with real pleasure.

But it is already high time that our guest should tear himself away from the language instruction. It had received his entire approval, all the more because it seemed to him to be an excellent means for bringing the different nations of the world nearer together, which he saw was one of the objects of the school. He noticed as a natural result of this kind of language-teaching, an appreciation by the boys of the peculiarities of other nations, and at the same time a comprehension of the faults and virtues of their own country.

But he saw with satisfaction also, that these youths did not lose in the least degree their feelings of Patriotism,[1] although they had come to recognise in the citizen of another land a brother to be at least respected, rather than an enemy to be slandered or shot.

During the rest of the morning and again in the afternoon, our guest was able to see that instruction in Things, Natural Science, and Mathematics, was not in the least neglected to give preference to the study of Words, Language, and History. He expected no less from the highly developed modern culture of this people, and from the vast success it had achieved in industry and commerce.

He noticed, meanwhile, that indoor class instruction did not recommence directly after dinner, but, for obvious reasons of health, not till digestion would be nearly over. From 2 till 4.30, while their blood was still full of fresh food and energy, the boys had outdoor active work, enabling them to disperse the nourishment over the whole frame. They did not return to indoor work until 4.30, when, in Winter, it was nearly dark outside; while in

---

[1] The Patriotism which consists in shutting out foreign manufactures, ideas or people, however excellent, and in glorifying all home products, however bad, is not Patriotism, but treason and national suicide. (TRANSLATOR.)

Summer they continued, he was told, in the open air till tea, at six o'clock.

He observes that the Naturalistic studies are, as much as, or even more than, the Humanistic studies, based, perfectly rightly, upon the occupations and life of the School-state. The chief text-book for Geometry is not, strange to relate, Kambly or any other similar book, but the workshop with its beams, boards, sheets of cardboard, &c., of all sizes and shapes. After this it is the landscape, river, fields, hills, and trees, &c. From these concrete cases the fundamental geometrical figures are learnt, and with these "Geometry" is practised, for Geometry means, of course, as all know, "Earth Measurement." The very name tells young and old alike that, without these practical measurements, there can be no real Geometry, just as without botanical excursions there can be no real Botany. While, therefore, the boy works outside, in garden, farm, or workshop (of which you will hear more directly), he learns at every step Mathematics and Natural Science. Our guest noticed thus with pleasure, that all the instruction started from these practical experiences and observations, and upon them built both foundation and superstructure. This alliance of Manual Training and Drawing (for this art comes mainly in here), with the teaching of Mathematics and Natural Science, reminded our guest strongly of the alliance of instruction in Language with the literary, historical, and geographical studies, which we have described above. He saw here also that no dead, abstract theory, or mere mathematico-physical "Grammar" was learnt, but that everywhere the instruction was based on practice and living experience, on what the boy had seen, attempted, or done. He saw that facts were collected, sifted, and classified, and finally summarised and expressed as Laws and Principles in the most simple phrases or formulæ, and explained, wherever possible, by Hypotheses. The mere learning by heart of dead, useless statements ; the mere babbling over of crowds of mathematical formulæ and abstract propositions ; in short, all empty and mechanical, all purely theoretical academic phrases and abstractions are banished from the Nature Studies, as in the Humanistic Studies the thought-stifling historical Primer, and the soul-destroying Grammar Book.

Nothing is taught which the Scholar will not be able, in after life, to use, for we desire not mental fat but intellectual muscle.

The first part of the Geometry lesson was held, not in the class-room, but in the Lower Far Dingle. Here the boys measured the dimensions of two of the 170 trees which had been lately felled. The whole class then returned, at the double, with the master and our guest to the class-room, where they calculated on the blackboard the cubic contents and the value of the timber, learning, by the way, "the squaring of the circle," both according to Mr. Euclid's[1] method, and also according to that of the practical Land Agent.

When our guest examined the Time-table and Work-plan, he discovered to his delight that instruction was given in personal and social Hygiene and in Political Economy, which included the study of organised Government, as well as that of unorganised Trade. It seemed, indeed, obvious that the boys should learn about their bodies and the body politic at least as much as about Latin

[1] Many boys who have studied "Euclid" for years suppose it is, like "Kinematics," the name of a branch of Mathematics. (TRANSLATOR.)

Grammar. He afterwards, at half-past four, discovered that these lessons were not mere names on the Time-table, and observed that no boy's thoughts during these studies wandered to the approaching Christmas, or Easter, vacation. In the Hygiene period the boys and teacher were discussing together why they wore their particular school uniform, and not the fashionable "Notë" or any other. They learnt how, and why, one of their comrades was, for the moment, ill, and the simple remedies, &c., which would soon make him well. In the Economics period they learnt, not merely how money is earned (or at least "made"), but above all how it can best be used. For this they employed, not a wearisome "Primer of Economics," but the actual transactions of the citizens of the school. Moreover, the experiences of two of the boys, who the day before had visited the nearest town, to fetch money from the Bank and do other business for the school, were utilised in this lesson.

In the period devoted to the study of Government and Law, the attention of the elder boys was turned to a certain cause, pending at that moment in the High Court of Justice, about a disputed right of way over the private carriage drive leading to the school. The class-room was converted into a Court House, the matter was treated according to the legal forms, and the rival claims stated with as much fairness as possible. Subsequently Laws were cited, in answer to a question raised by one of the Prefects, who was anxious to execute more satisfactorily the duties of his office. The guest observed that here too the teaching started always from the actual life of the School-world in order to lead the scholars ultimately to comprehend the customs and institutions of their Fatherland.

Nature Science and History, these two, formed the organic centres round which were grouped the two great departments of instruction[1]—the study of the external world (Realistics) and the study of the world within (Humanistics). These two spheres touched in Historical Geography, exactly as the common life of the school-community touched Nature in the School-estate. In order not to obscure the Unity of Nature, the commonest phænomena of every day were examined, now from the physical, now from the chemical, and anon from the physiological point of view, and not merely as disconnected facts, but in connection with the vast generalisations which the facts naturally and inevitably suggest, and by which they are easily bound together in our minds.

CHAPTER IV.

THE MIDDAY DINNER AND MIDDAY REST IN THE SCHOOL-STATE EMLOHSTOBBA.

FOLLOWING our unfortunate German habit, we have already spent too much time over the details of the Instruction

---

[1] In 1893, on my first visit to the Jena Practising School, I found their plan was to concentrate all the work round the history-instruction—as that most nearly connected in their view with the formation of *character*. This led to some straining. I did not therefore adopt that plan here, but continued to interlock all the work as I found it convenient. Moreover I do not consider that the study of Nature is less moral than the study of Humanity; and so while I fully concur with the Herbartian doctrine that all the instruction should aim at fortifying the character, this can be attained in the Natural Science periods as well as in the Humanistic periods. Our plan is to focus all the work round two centres; but this has been explained further elsewhere. (TRANSLATOR.)

given here. To be sure, we have not yet seen any instruction in the Mother Tongue, but this we can perhaps witness another time. We cannot see all in one day.

It is getting close on dinner, and, after that, we shall follow the boys to various parts of the School-state and discover then, perhaps, the main advantage of the education given here. For while the morning is devoted to instruction of the Mind, the afternoon is given, almost exclusively, to culture of the Body by physical work and games, and the evening to the enjoyment of Art, Music, and Social intercourse.

After the morning's work, we all meet at one o'clock for an excellent, but simple, dinner. As the last youngster hurries in and the clock strikes one, a Prefect closes the door, one of the musical boys touches the organ, and immediately the whole assembly chants the stately Gregorian grace (borrowed from Old England's eldest school, Winchester) :—

"Benedic nobis, Domine Deus, atque iis donis tuis quæ de tua largitate sumus sumpturi, per Jesum Christum, Dominum nostrum. Amen."

We get here a touch of true education, for the new should be always wedded to the old. At the same time we observe a pedagogic influence of great value, whether we regard it from the Historical, the Artistic, or the Moral point of view. For if grace be said at all, let it be said with dignity and as if we meant it. Let us not mumble it half apologetically, half pompously, as if we were excusing the superstition or the banquet. Grace over, two Masters, and later two Prefects, take command at the carving-tables and dexterously divide the mighty steaming joints, not forgetting to suit the platefuls to each boy's wants. This office falls, each week, on the Prefects in rotation. No boy, therefore, need leave the school without having learnt this useful art.

At this, the chief meal of the day, one does not see two, three, perhaps four dishes come in with meat alone, followed by a little salad and a few pears on tiny plates. Here all believe firmly that meat in large doses is bad for every one, and particularly for the young, the cultured, and the chaste. A good pudding, therefore, nearly always appears on the table to the great delight of everybody. To-day, indeed, we have "Emlohstobba pudding," an invention of the Monarch of this School-state, and it does the inventor every honour. But, if any one is an adversary of vegetarian diet, he had better not come to us on Mondays, for then the school kitchen proves that we can live very well on vegetables alone. On two other days in the week our chief dishes at dinner consist of vegetables and fish. Lovers of alcohol, too, would not find much in their line. We recognise the medical fact that alcohol, in every form and quantity, is bad, particularly for the youthful organism, and we are aware of the social fact, that nearly all crimes and many diseases are caused by its consumption. None of the boys, therefore, as you see, take any, and we Masters try and set them a good example. The good milk of our cows, and cocoa and tea from the colonies, take the place of alcohol, which Nansen, even amid the anxieties and perils of Arctic exploration, entirely dispensed with. And you can see that beer and wine are not necessary for boys if you look at the healthy and robust appearance of all the citizens of the school.

After the tones of the final grace—" Benedictus sit Deus in donis suis. Amen."—have died away, we file out into Big School, where one of the music masters, and after him one of the boys, plays the piano, organ, or violin. The visitor agrees with the Choir Master that these pieces of classical music, interspersed with well-known national airs and ballads, all carefully selected to be suitable to the boys' ages, refine and exalt the artistic taste and consequently the moral feelings of the youngsters, just as much as the statues and pictures round the room. Without, therefore, wearisome moral sermons, contempt for all vulgarity and baseness, in Art or in conduct, slowly but surely takes possession of their minds. Thus Art is invoked once more to aid in building up the character. This rest between dinner and afternoon work, thus sweetened by music, is invaluable for the boys' physical health.

In going out of Big School, our guest overheard Nospmis, a youngster of thirteen, saying to the Choir-master, "Oh, Herr Namuen, the other day, when I was in Nodnol, I was taken by my people to hear Wagner's *Lohengrin*. I enjoyed myself so much, and should have liked to have joined in the singing, as I knew many parts of the Opera quite well through your playing them after dinner."

CHAPTER V.

AFTERNOON WORK AND PLAY IN EMLOHSTOBBA.

"As I already like your boys," said our guest, "I should like to spend the afternoon also with them." "To do that you will have to change your clothes," said the Director of Outside Work. They go together to the dressing-room, where they put on a blue or white jersey, blue socks, and white flannel knicks, called "cuts" (which come down only to the knees). This costume at first feels too chilly, but quickly proves itself to be just the right thing for the work to be done. "You don't get a chance here of catching cold," cries an urchin, laughing, as he sees our guest hesitate at the scanty outfit. "If you had come a few weeks ago you might have helped the fellows dig up our potatoes, or you could have helped us cut and cart away the grass-sods and earth in the Lower Meadow, where we are making a skating-pond. If you are inclined and not too stiff in the joints, you can come and climb this tree and help us cut off the side branches. We are taking them off before the tree is felled, to prevent the trunk splitting as it falls; but if you think it may be dangerous up aloft, stay down here and help fell the tree when we have done."

Every kind of garden and farm work is done here by the fellows and masters. One thing, however—you must not remain an idle spectator; if you did, you would soon see looks of surprise, or receive friendly hints or invitations to join in the work. If all these efforts seemed useless, you would most likely be politely turned out, and after you had gone, you would be utilised by the boys as a living object-lesson of sloth, unhandiness, or funk. You must do your work here in all weathers, good or bad, and you must not remain indoors on account of wind, or rain, or cold, but hurry off promptly to wood or field, garden or glasshouses.

There is always plenty of work to be done on this extensive farm, and no work is despised, not even the dirtiest or the least pleasant. The gentle reader may, perhaps, think that these boys are the children of poor people, forced by urgent need to do this sort of work. Not in the least. The boys to be seen, here wheeling barrows full of earth, and over there tarring gates, are the children of parents who wish their sons to become sturdy men, not learned invalids; who do not mind giving a good many hundred pounds for a good purpose: for such they feel this sort of real education is. They pay the £100 a year, moreover, without wasting two words, and consider the money well spent, for they leave their boys four, five, six, or even seven years in the school.

You will, no doubt, agree with me that as the teaching of modern languages is used here for cultivating friendly feelings between different nations, so the manual labour of these boys of the directing classes will form a firm bridge over the yawning gulf between different sections of the community. You would be quite mistaken if you fancied that our fellows did not like this work, or at least the doing of it, in bad weather; or if you thought that we had occasionally a general strike of boys, or of masters, or of both together. Not a bit of it. A general stoppage of work has never taken place yet in this little State of ours. It is far too well organised for that. Duties and rights are too closely connected, and too justly apportioned, for disputes to arise. Not long ago you might have seen the fellows digging out the fish-pond—and, to be sure, for that sort of work they do not wear too many garments. As old Horace says, "Non semper imbres nubibus hispidos manant in agros." "Sunshine follows rain." If, as in that case it was, the work is, for once in a way, really very hard or disagreeable, or horribly dirty, the boys are comforted by the thought of a jolly bath after; or they reflect how much better tea will taste after this bit of hard work ; or they remember how wholesome such work is and how valuable for after life ; or they look forward to the Summer term, when they have the most splendid fun of all—haymaking ; for then one sees, not only contented, but radiant, faces. Nobody, then, not even the laziest, stays indoors willingly. Even the unlucky youth who was yesterday in the sick-room (which usually is empty) with a headache or cut foot, turns out and takes up a rake or pitchfork and joins his applauding comrades in the hay-field. His "speedy recovery" is, no doubt, caused by the thought of the approaching Harvest Home, and perhaps by a fear lest he should be unable to take part in the procession, the songs, and the supper. The harvest festival properly begins when the boys bring up the last load from the Lower Meadow, with full orchestral honours, and stack it in the Barn. This is considered here perhaps the chief event of the year, instead of, as in most countries, and in most schools, the Latin Disputation a few years ago, and the Latin or Greek "*Viva Voce*," or the Summer Examinations nowadays. Perhaps, after all, this Harvest Home, with the thoughts and feelings it arouses, does more for the ultimate and permanent welfare of these boys and of Humanity at large, than all the above-named solemn "disgorgings" of words, phrases, and mere book-learning, at which the chief item, perhaps, is a description of the Harvest, in Greek Iambics, by a youth who has never once in all his life seen the Harvest gathered in.

After Teachers and Pupils, Prefects and Fags, have been doing this useful work out-of-doors for an hour or so in the afternoon, in Dame Nature's own realm, learning to understand better, and use more surely, that great laboratory of wisdom and endless transformation, they go into the different Workshops with their guest, to train their eyes and muscles, and all other physical powers, whilst incarnating thought, will, and feeling, in wood. The Workshops are large and roomy, and contain all the chief tools of the joiner, carpenter, and turner. Each boy has his private box in which he keeps his own tools; for even "Socialists" will find (if they try the experiment), that communism in a workshop is disastrous—at least to the tools.

If you like, you can now visit a division of boys in the joiner's shop. Some are busy at the benches, under direction of Mr. Sille, making some more cases to hold our ever-increasing mass of charts, diagrams, pictures, and other *Anschauungs* material. But perhaps you would prefer to work with these fellows at some useful agricultural implement, a post, railing, wedge, broomstick, beehouse, or ladder; or with those at some simple piece of furniture—a shelf, music-stand, footstool, table, or whatever it be the division has on hand.

Mind, however, you do not get laughed at by our youngsters. Or are you, perhaps, an exception to the rule, and, having been brought up in the country, have been tutored by some old village wheelwright (or as Reuter calls him, "cart-maker")?

You do not succeed in planing very well! Well, see how easily our lads use plane, saw, hatchet, hammer, and drill. The masters here are not like that mother who, fearing danger to thumbs and toes, can scarce find a place in the house where her urchin of eleven will not get at those "shockingly dangerous instruments." We see, to our surprise, that even the "Fags" here do not chop or cut their fingers so often as we do ourselves, and as most professors and Cabinet Ministers would unless they were of the stamp of old Professor Rückert of Jena, or of old Mr. Gladstone, each of whom chopped his own firewood, and yet never lost his character as learned professor or doughty political warrior. The former, I am sorry to say, is long since dead; the latter, a fine sample of vigorous old age, is still in right good health, and will, we hope, long continue to enjoy it.

"But what is that curious spectacle down at the river?" cries Herr Namreh. "Let us hasten down." As we approach, sounds of axes, hammers, and saws, strike upon our ears. Piles are being cut, driven in and fixed, boards are being sawn into lengths by the "Seventeens" and "Eighteens." It is the Top Set, most of whom are Prefects. Some, it appears, do not mind, even in this cold weather, standing in the river up to their waists to steady the piles as they are driven in. "Why are they so keen and energetic at their work? What is this for?" "They are making a boathouse. Some of the parents have lately had sent from Canada several splendid canoes. The rest the boys have built themselves, and you may be sure they will celebrate the opening of the Boathouse before many weeks are over." Looking at their earlier buildings, the Fowlhouse, Cricket Pavilion, Beehouse with its twenty hives, and other erections of various shapes and sizes, mostly built of rafters and boards, our guest feels satisfied that the Boathouse runs no risk either of ridicule from visitors or of damage from floods.

All these houses, &c., are constructed by the senior boys, and they have come to think, by now, that they ought to build at least one house every third term.

We notice with pleasure that our young friends have a certain pride in their handiwork, and are persistent in finishing, to the last nail, any work they have once commenced. This is as it should be. For thus strength of character, we confidently hope, will slowly, but surely, be developed in them.

On the way home from this work, the boys and masters passed near a newly constructed bridge, and the following characteristic story of its origin was related to the visitor: "You see that little branch of the river. The bridge over it had from age become quite unsafe. One day a request to repair it was received from the neighbouring Parish Council. It was, of course, the duty of the Parish Council to do these repairs itself, but the School wished to do something for that newly instituted Body in token of friendly welcome. The matter was referred to the School Parliament by the Government of the School. The boys unanimously agreed instead of repairing the bridge to reconstruct it, and their proposal was accepted by the Government. The first company of the School Engineer corps asked for the commission, and received it. At the usual hours fixed by the time-table for such outside undertakings, they commenced work, and with such enthusiasm that in a few days the bridge was finished. On a scorching July afternoon, a solemn Inauguration was held by the School Community. The Parish Council was asked to open the bridge and to declare it fit for traffic. The 'Burgomaster' made an excellent speech, in which he expressed his delight that boys of gentle birth should learn, in this practical way, to value the work done by the great industrial army of the nation, and thus to respect and care for the individual soldiers of that vast host. The Monarch of the School-state replied to the effect that the industrial army required leaders, and the only leaders of any use were those who knew what work the industrial army had to perform, and who could properly direct them in the doing of it. The School Band thereupon played 'Rule Britannia,' and the regiment presented arms. The old bridge was in a few minutes broken up by the engineers, and the new bridge opened to the public. The Pioneer troop on such an occasion of course put forth its full strength, and a sub-lieutenant, called Nosnibor, so overexerted himself under the sun's broiling rays, that he fainted, and had to be carried to the school. The others meanwhile quietly completed their work. In the School Magazine for that year his comrades wrote: 'He was carried home like a warrior after a battle, who had been wounded while doing his duty.'" At the conclusion of this story our guest remarked, "Your School has performed an act of civic duty, and that day's work will not be forgotten by your scholars so easily as were the long pieces of poetry, or bits of natural history, which we at school in Germany had to learn off by heart. It seems to me probable that if your fellows had been placed in Crusoe's famous island, they would have known far better what to do than that marvellous person himself, for the ruler of this School seems to think it even more important for his pupils to live the life of Robinson Crusoe than to study merely the famous book."

"What is this curious building?" presently asked Herr Namreh, as they suddenly came upon a tarred wooden erection in an idyllic situation, sheltered by a plantation behind and by sprouting hedges in front. "It is the Bee-house," answered one of the boys. "I was one of the bee-

German Verdicts

masters who helped to build it. Come inside and see the hives. We made all these ourselves, and as all the hives are now full, we can supply the School with lots of honey. One of the masters is head Bee-master, and knows all about making queens and stopping swarms. We began in 1890 with two old straw hives, and have now made twenty of wood and glass" (*vide* picture).

But we must leave this quaint methodic bee-world with its busy hum of work, which seems to symbolise very fitly the School itself. It is now time for football, and we are asked: "Would you not like to see one of our School-battles? The School is divided into four different sections, and the two pairs play—yes fight if you like—twice a week. You are just in time to see to-day's game." Down below in the level meadows by the river, we see groups of fifteen players in characteristic dress, on one side Whites, on the other Blues. Herr Namreh hurries to the battlefield, and arrives just as a vigorous scrimmage is taking place. The two sides are trying, with all their might, to push one another back. Heads and shoulders disappear in the mass; but we see here and there faces dripping with sweat, and hear half-stifled gasps. Now the Blues are giving way, but all the same no one thinks of relaxing his efforts, till suddenly the ball comes flying out of the scrimmage. Like lightning it is seized by a boy standing close behind, and in a second he is off to the opponent's goal. The defenders try to stop him or overtake him, to get the ball themselves; but he succeeds in carrying it behind the goal-line, and obtains a "touch-down."

As our guest, after the game was over, walked up with some of the players to the house, the captain said, "If you had been here a few days ago you would have seen a foreign match, played against the school across the valley." Foreign matches are, of course, the most exciting. Each school selects fifteen of its best players to uphold its honour in the battlefield. The non-combatants of either school assemble to see the battle, and encourage by loud shouts their own side, and not infrequently cheer the other side too for some specially fine piece of play, or for every bit of plucky defence if they are losing. At the end, three cheers are raised by the conquerors for the beaten side, so that the spectators know at once who has won, and this is followed by three cheers for the conquerors given by the vanquished side.

The home team then invite their opponents to tea, and neither the winners nor the vanquished, by word or look, give the faintest sign of elation or dejection at the result. It would in this land be considered unworthy of a gentleman to fail in any way in self-restraint and good manners, especially at such a moment. In quiet, modest delight at their victory the winners guard against wounding their guests, and prove their magnanimity by praising every bit of their play which showed pluck and skill.

The same day at 7.30 our guest was able to watch another kind of fight. It was the usual evening set apart for wrestling and boxing. Part of the school has assembled in the fencing-room. A chalk ring is on the floor. Two young fighters come forward carrying huge stuffed gloves. The challenger throws one glove upon the floor, and the other picks it up and returns it, in token that he accepts the challenge. Before beginning the contest they shake hands cordially. Then the blows begin. Both are careful not to show any pain by wincing, and not, during the whole contest, to act like a coward. This fine exercise gives boys coolness, presence of mind, a keen eye, and pluck. The time fixed for the round is up. Presently others come forward to have a wrestle. They are two of the elder boys. This time the fight is long and even. They move hither and thither. First one, then the other, is uppermost. Then a signal is sounded. Their time is up. Both have done well. They shake hands and step back into the audience. The guest notices that this salutation before and after the boxing match is just as little a mere formality as the cheering in the case of the football match, and, like all good customs and manners, tends to keep alive the good sentiment it was originally intended to express. Good fellowship is in no wise disturbed by these fights, however energetically and pluckily they are fought. Our guest is surprised and delighted to see that no quarrels or disputes arise here from these games and fights. No one takes offence easily. If any one breaks a rule he is immediately pulled up by the whole body of players, or, in doubtful cases, by the captain. Every one subjects himself to this general authority without ado and without grumbling. "I cannot think," our guest remarks, "of a better way for teaching boys cheerful obedience and hearty coöperation than that furnished by these contests. Our youngsters in Germany are, with a few exceptions, still well-nigh unable either to work or to play together. Every moment they take something amiss: some one gets sulky and 'won't play any more.'" "No one would think of such a thing here," was the reply. "But," rejoined Herr Namreh, turning to another point, "are not many arms and legs broken in these rough games?" On the Continent he had heard and read the most fearful stories about them, but now he was able to convince himself, from the various examples witnessed, that in these contests dangerous wounds were seldom inflicted. True, he once or twice saw blood flowing from a leg or arm or face, and perceived occasionally a boy wince at a bad fall or hard knock. But it was over in a moment. As to football, all the boys assured him that they preferred playing Rugby to Association, and our guest convinced himself that Rugby was far the better game for boys, as it exercised all the muscles of the body much more thoroughly than Association, which was the only football he had seen thus far played in his own country. To be sure, the Monarch of the School, Dr. Eidder, had fourteen years before, while studying at Göttingen, taught the scholars of the Gymnasium there the Rugby game, and they had learnt to like it and play it well, but somehow in other places the Association game had been the one introduced.

The boys of this School are not everlastingly wrapped up carefully in cotton-wool and silk, as in some places they are. They are trained to be hardy and venturesome, for only thus, according to the general sentiment here, will they be capable in after life of doing anything worth doing. All this our guest could see from an incident which had happened a few days before, and which was at this opportunity related to him.

On the day in question the sky was veiled in grey, the wind whistled, and it rained in torrents. Football could not be played: what was to be done? Suddenly the bugle sounds the command, "Run to Notsram!" Five minutes later the whole school stands ready equipped for the run. White knickerbockers, jerseys, socks, and football boots form the entire dress. All are bare-headed and bare-legged. "Off!" sounds the signal, and they start. The head-boy is in front, near him the slimmest and longest-legged. Through puddles and brooks, over ditches and fields, over sticks and stones, they go. No one lags behind. On, on to the finish! Not a step of the course does one of the little band shirk. And now back again. The run has lasted about half an hour, and the lads, big and small, have run nearly as much as a German mile. If a boy is really lazy, he is quickly made to exert himself by the shout of the Prefects at the end of the train, who function as Whippers-in. But as they pass steaming along one sees only merry faces. Not a stitch of their uniform is left dry. Sweat from inside, rain from above, and mud and water from below, have soaked their clothes through and through. Some clean warm water will soon remove all dirt and damage and stiffness. First there is a warm, but gradually cooled, bath for the body. In due course there will be a bath too for the uniform.

"They must have escaped from a lunatic asylum. Hold them!" cry some astonished strangers who happen to meet the running troop.

"All right, run away!" shout the lads in merry chaff. "None of you can overtake us."

"Oh, how dreadful! this won't do for my poor dear, delicate child!" cries a lamenting mother, wringing her hands as she watches from her door the lads tearing by. She would rather let her dear little boy melt out the marrow of his spine beside the stove, or get consumption from sitting in stuffy rooms, than let him 'catch his death of cold' (or rather, get strong) in the fresh air. "Take your overcoat and 'comforter,' and do not forget your umbrella," or else, "Now stay indoors, boys, and keep out of the mud and wet," says the father, "or your clothes will get wet and your boots dirty!" Perhaps he has not got a washing-tub or a clothes-brush in the house, or else he prefers that his son should be made into an effeminate doll, a lounger in public-houses, or loafer and good-for-nothing, rather than be made to run the risk of a trifling cold. Those who talk and act so are certainly not citizens of this land. They must be foreigners—perhaps from the kingdom of Ynoxas—for here every father and mother want their boys to grow into men. The bell sounds four o'clock in the afternoon. Our small workmen, football players, or runners hurry into the house from workshop, run, or battlefield. A bath all round soon puts everything right, and after slipping into their clothes they are ready for Afternoon School, which comes from 4.30 to six o'clock.

CHAPTER VI.

A QUIET EVENING AFTER A HARD DAY'S WORK AMONG THE BURGHERS OF EMLOHSTOBBA.

It strikes six o'clock. "Pray, Herr Namreh, come in and have some tea." This is here the chief evening meal. On every table there is some really well-made tea, which no one drinks without cream or milk, and hardly any without sugar. Fruit, fresh and stewed, and bread, brown and white, are in plenty on the tables, besides butter from the farm and honey from the school-hives. We look round to see if there is any alcohol, but "tea with a little rum in it" is absolutely unknown here, and would indeed be considered ridiculous.[1] Notwithstanding the simplicity of the meal, neither old nor young would exchange it for all the most *recherché* dainties and drinks of Dressel in Nilreb.

We note that the boys sit, not, as in many schools at long tables holding perhaps fifty each, but at a great many small tables containing only seven to ten, reminding us of our restaurants in Germany. But while at breakfast a Prefect and at dinner a Master presides over each, at tea the boys sit alone, grouped mainly according to age, but also so that their mutual influence may be salutary.

At breakfast the Prefects obtain some training as future fathers, in watching after the good manners of their tables. They see that all have fair play, and put down piggish eating, waste, and all selfishness.

At dinner the Masters, at their several tables, help the dishes, and see that every boy eats a proper amount or salt and vegetables, and whatever his peculiar constitution requires, and that he has neither too much nor too little.

At tea the boys sit alone, in order to be free to carry out (or neglect) of their own accord, the hints or exhortations they have received at the earlier meals. They are not allowed to stoop over their plates; but to make this precept practicable they sit on chairs and not on flat boards, the cheap and unwholesome relic of penurious barbarism, still, however, to be found in Educational Palaces, which they disgrace. As the boys in the Classrooms here use those skilfully constructed benches which only our German pedagogic enthusiasm seems able to

---

[1] Tea in Germany is expensive, and is therefore usually drunk very weak. This may perhaps account for the widely prevalent custom of taking rum in it. (TRANSLATOR.

produce, which render curved spines, squinting eyes, and hollow chests impossible, so in the Dining-hall they are able, and are required, to sit upright, and the necessary means for this purpose—a chair—is duly provided. The boys are not allowed to read at meals—an unwholesome practice allowed at some schools ; on the contrary, it is recognised that the best aid to digestion is friendly and interesting conversation, and that no time is better suited for such intercourse than the meal-hour. But if the same people are always sitting together for a dozen weeks their mutual society becomes tedious and indeed intolerable. Quarrels arise for no real reason, but simply because all need fresh society and change of company as we need fresh air and change of scene. All men become asphyxiated if they live too long amid their own exhalations, even when these are not merely physical or intellectual, but of the highest spiritual quality. Nansen tells us how his devoted band, even in the constant presence of great hardship and never very far from mortal peril, had fits of loathing for each other, which only temporary isolation could allay. This universal tendency, which explains so well some of the quarrels between friends, many of the bickerings between neighbours, and most of the unhappy misunderstandings of married life—a tendency which should be understood by all—is here recognised and provided with a remedy. The boys are broken up into these groups of seven and ten, and sit in different companies and at different tables, so that thrice in the day they shall have change of companionship. At breakfast they have the Prefect to criticise, and at dinner the Master, so that only at tea do they need to criticise each other and quarrel thereover if they wish to. The Prefects and others are not herded all day long with others of exactly the same capacity or age, so that their usual condition is one of mutual competition. It is well understood here that every one requires alternately periods for outgiving and periods for in-taking. For Prefects to be always with juniors would be disastrous alike to both, but not less so for Prefects to be herded with Prefects, Middies with Middies, or Fags with Fags, all day.

In schools where boys are all of one age, or where (as in the French Lycée) they only mix with (and even only see) boys of the same age, such restrictions, instead of obviating the well-known moral, mental, or physical explosive tension, produce the very evil they are intended to eliminate.

What is more spiritually barren than the moral life of so many upright persons and small religious cliques; what more dull than the intellectual atmosphere of many gatherings of learned men; what more useless to others (and even to himself) than the physical vitality of the professional athlete?

Life is given us, not to hoard up, but to pass on to those who need it. The goody-goody, armchair Saint, like the rich epicure of old, is doomed to spiritual impotence, because he hoards up his superabundant spiritual dainties as an offering to Heaven, while the world of sinners around him dies for want of the tiniest crumbs which daily fall unheeded from his religious banquets. He has ceased to minister of his spiritual riches to the erring and the outcast, and the condemnation is his own spiritual death. At a vast annual cost he keeps up a gorgeous temple and ample ceremony, but will not suffer the poor and needy even to approach the doors, still less to share the luxury of seductive perfumes, enchanting melodies, and lustrous decorations. Yet these, selfishly employed, slowly but surely undermine the moral life.

In the rich university and the palatial school do we not see something similar? The proud self-satisfaction and rapacious selfishness of the intellectual Specialist dooms him to mental impotence. Regarding his mental gifts as given for private gain or pleasant home consumption, he ceases to apply his intellect or to use his intellectual stores in the pure, unselfish service of humanity. Slowly but inevitably his "science for science' sake," "art for art's sake," and "culture for culture's sake," languish and die, or form malignant excrescences.

Similarly, the mere Sportsman, who chooses a yet lower type of existence, whose only idea from morning to night is self-indulgence, eating, drinking, sleeping, unlimited muscular exercise (which to be really perfect must, he thinks, be void of all productive value), followed by unbounded satisfaction of all other animal propensities: this sort of pampered animal, although rapidly becoming the most fashionable type, is doomed to physical impotence. Instead of being fit to impart life to others, he cannot even pass it on without disease to his own offspring. For the physical life always degenerates where the wholesome necessity to work for daily bread is removed. Of course such a sportsman's life is possible only to the poacher and the monied man, who, although without any duties, are both, alas! allowed to be social parasites with comparative impunity.

All such isolation is fatal to harmonious evolution. In Emlohstobba, therefore, all isolation of this sort is discouraged. The masters are not herded in a Common

Room with nothing to discuss but "Sport" and "Shop," relieved at intervals by fits of mutual esteem as they fraternise over the unfathomable deficiencies of all Headmasters and especially of one. The object of every school, it is recognised here, should be not only to educate the pupils, but to train also with scrupulous care the pupils' Educators. To train Masters, Teachers, Educators, to be hereafter fit and worthy Heads of schools, this is never allowed here to pass out of sight. Therefore to awaken in every master a proper sense of his responsibilities, all have ample opportunities of seeing the boys frequently and of joining fully in their enterprises, instead of being jealously excluded from all society but their own. The result is that they enjoy their work thoroughly, and become, not only better teachers and masters, but better Men. They are not, therefore, driven by depressing conditions, as in many of the ordinary schools, to take to drink or gambling or worse vices. On the contrary, the close intercourse with their pupils keeps their hearts young and satisfies their natural and wholesome desire to impart their ideas and influence, and they learn daily as much as they teach, or perhaps more.

The masters live, also, on the most intimate terms with the Monarch of the School-state. He visits their classes and hears them teach, and offers criticism and advice to each one; while he also listens with sympathy to their suggestions and criticisms on the life and administration of the place, and carries out as soon as possible all that are sensible and practicable.

On all sides our guest observed unswerving devotion to the School-state, and to the high ideals which it was endeavouring to realise, and he was glad, for he knew how useless for real education even this life would be, unless all teachers were bound together in loyal and hearty coöperation.

After tea follows a brief interval, and then music practice; for Music is pursued here daily with real enthusiasm. The guest notices that all the boys (unless their voices are breaking or some other physical cause exempts them) are carefully taught, not only to sing, but to speak and to breathe. They are not allowed to shout and ruin their voices, but are taught to sing softly and with expression, generally without the help of any instrument. In this school, music is not regarded as a mere accomplishment, something apart from the rest of the educational work. On the contrary, it is known to be a means of physical and intellectual, but above all of moral and æsthetic, education, of the very highest order. It is considered far more important here that every boy should be able to sing than that he should know how to write or to spell. Most of the boys play some instrument as well. To-day they are preparing for the Concert, which is given every year at the "Christmas Gathering of Neighbours," for which the Choir Master usually composes an original Musical Sketch. This year it is entitled, "A Merry Christmas," and is accompanied by a huge Christmas-tree and an Interlude, during which a group of merry youngsters comes in and performs a Toy-symphony—a concert within a concert. The most important orchestral instruments are to be seen at this practice. Besides violin and 'cello, organ and flute, there are drums, bugles, cornets, and trumpets. After our guest left the room, he heard the sound of nightingales, syrens, and other weird noises which belonged, he fancied, to the Hobgoblins which would attend upon "Father Christmas." He thought, as he went upstairs, how the children from the village, and even their fathers and mothers, would enjoy the Festival, which, in another month, would have come.

He was glad to think that in this land people had not forgotten that cosy and happy Season which so completely idealises domestic love and Family Life—the root of all Religion as it is of all human existence. He thought how wise it was of the Monarch of this School that he did not seek to teach morality as a mere Code of Duties, but connected it with those beautiful and touching allegories which, true to the method of all great teachers, conceal profound philosophy under the charming disguise of a fairy tale.

"But where are the two or three hours indispensable for the preparation of class-work?" inquires Herr Namreh. He was soon to discover. The music had ceased. All had again become quiet. What are our friends doing now? Towards 7.45 p.m. we wander through the class-rooms to see. There we found the boys quietly working, the juniors under the superintendence of the Prefects. They are busy revising the day's work or writing notes upon it. Revisal time lasts only forty-five minutes, for the principal part of the work is done in class. The view taken here is that the master who imposes on a boy much extra work after four or six periods in class, either takes it too easy himself or employs faulty methods, or else wishes to absorb the boy's interest entirely in his own branch of study. As we go from one room to another, we meet a boy with flushed face who has just come in with the letter-bag. "Where have you been?" "I have been to the post at Retsecor, to fetch the school letters;" and the boy passes on with them to the Headmaster's study. "Why do you let a boy go such a distance in the dark?" asks the visitor. "Can't you manage without sending the pupils on such errands?" The master who accompanied him answered, "This going to post is another means of education; it strengthens the feeling of responsibility and trustworthiness, and, in winter, develops courage and hardiness. Seven boys are privileged to undertake this duty each term. Whether they walk, or ride, or bicycle, they have to face darkness, fogs, floods, and all weathers, and have to take care not to fall into river or brook. The fellows take some pride in performing this service conscientiously, not buying grub for themselves, or bringing it home for others; and amongst other things they learn to appreciate the feelings of the country postman, who brings them their letters in a snowstorm.

"A few days ago, towards night, a boy suddenly fell ill. The Headmaster (who is himself the chief physician of the school, having made at the University some study also of medicine) recognised the disease and the medicine required. This was, unluckily, not to be found in the usually well-stocked school dispensary, and it was nearly five miles to the nearest druggist. Outside the night was pitch dark, with howling wind and rain. We were going to send the coachman and dog-cart, but several boys volunteered to go. . . . Presently one of them whizzed off on his iron-horse, and disappeared in the darkness. He was back long before the trap could have returned. When this boy, Ekoorb major, in a few years is managing his father's tea plantation in distant India, he will be doubly thankful that we have given him the opportunity and means of becoming a man; and that, instead of merely repeating to him one of our chief maxims, 'The duty of an Emlohstobba boy is to become a man,' we have arranged the whole life here so that each can, nay must, become one."

Towards half-past eight, Herr Namreh went with his companion to the Dining-hall, to have a light supper of cocoa and biscuits with the boys. After supper the entire household—masters, boys, and ladies, menservants, maid-servants, and guest—assembled once more in the Chapel. The day's work was closed, as it had been begun, with a beautiful service. To-day our guest heard, in this foreign country, the hymn *Nun danket alle Gott*, which being sung in German, transported him back to his home in the Fatherland.

"Herr Namreh," said one of the Masters after Chapel, "will you come up to my study for a little."

Several boys came in for advice or friendly counsel, encouragement or warning. As during the day, so here now, there was no loud or angry scolding of the boys. It seemed here that those who wished to develop self-control in the boys considered it beneath them, as well as detrimental to their influence, to fail in self-control themselves.

Again the door of the study was opened, and a boy of about seventeen years came in. He had already during the day impressed us favourably by his quiet, serious manner. We heard him ask advice about some of his work, and were glad to hear his modest but definite reply, when asked what he was going to be, "I should like to be a school-master."

Such words, from such a boy, filled our guest with peculiar pleasure; and he found, afterwards, that the

Headmaster also had been more pleased by those few words than he would have been, had he been a German, by getting, say, the order of the Red Eagle of the fourth or third class, or an increased salary of several hundred pounds. Why so? Was it simply because this would be, one might suppose, the school in which the youth, after finishing his studies, would begin to follow his chosen profession? Not at all; but because it was no bad sign of the influence of a school that one of its scholars had come to regard the profession of a Teacher as the highest. Do we usually find in schools this enthusiasm for teaching, or is it in this instance (our guest asked himself) simply the result of the way in which the work of education was here actually carried out?

Meanwhile the Masters and Prefects had severally gathered, each to discuss briefly the events of the day. Once every week more lengthy meetings of these bodies take place. At the Masters' Meetings, questions about the organisation, government, and administration of the school are those chiefly considered; and at the Perfects' Meeting, some question about the Fags, the games, the Magazine, fishing or rabbiting, a concert or an expedition.

Every four weeks comes a Debate, and three days ago the following question stood among the Agenda, "Should a son follow the profession of his father?" At these debates the boys are taught to follow the forms that should be observed at all public meetings. They learn to speak freely and fearlessly before strangers, to keep to the point and to aim at definite results. Oratorical talent also is recognised, encouraged, and guided. Dr. Eidder, however, remarked to the guest, "We do not want to encourage mere talking, which is often greatly overdone, especially now-a-days. Many fundamental questions, on the other hand, sure to arise in a boy's future life, are here discussed in this miniature parliament; and when he enters the big world he will be able to look after himself all the better if he has had to consider problems here, and been accustomed to discuss questions now, which some day must be faced and answered by all. He will thus gain some measure of strength, and will not be liable to change his convictions at the very first breath of criticism. Too often boys at school have nothing to think of but games and sports, or their particular narrow range of examination subjects; and when they go out into the world and into the modern town, with its scramble, its vice, its chicanery, they are too easily swept away into the stream of custom. We must not forget that the dissolute are more enthusiastic to propagate evil than the righteous to sow good seed. The former have, moreover, more leisure as a rule to lay traps."

Meanwhile our youngsters have gone to the dormitories; and the Prefects soon join them. Again all wash in cold water, not forgetting the feet and the teeth, so that they may quietly sleep their eight or nine hours, clean inside and out. A quarter of an hour later, we softly open the door of one of the rooms and hear only the regular breathing of quiet slumber. The peaceful serenity on the face of each boy tells us that he sleeps with the feeling of having done an honest day's work—his duty to his Home and his School—and so earned the right to enjoy such repose now, and such opportunities for healthy growth again on the morrow. To us the sight of this placid, child-like innocence is an inducement to work more vigorously still for their harmonious development, and to aim at this supreme result that, when they are grown up, they may retain that imperishable treasure, the true innocence, right instinct and intuition of childhood which miseducation destroys or neglects, united with the tried strength and ordered wisdom of maturity.

The boys are sleeping peacefully, but the hearts and brains of their educators remain awake far into the still night to keep watch over them, and to devise fresh plans for their development. Others also are lying awake and thinking, those, namely, who have come back from the troubled life of the big world to visit their old school-home and to breathe again the clean atmosphere of their childhood.

CHAPTER VII.

A QUIET CHAT IN THE COMMON ROOM, AFTER A LONG AND EVENTFUL DAY IN EMLOHSTOBBA.

FROM the dormitories, our guest goes with us to the "Common Room," which corresponds to a German *Konferenz-zimmer*. On his way there he notices, in a corner, an oddly-constructed sledge, which has just arrived. To his inquiry as to its use, Mr. Snikwah replies: "Our chief amusement in snowy weather is tobogganing down the hill behind the school. The fellows are now anxiously awaiting ice and snow, which this year is later than usual. You ought to be here when it comes, and see the whole school flying down Toboggan Hill. Big and little, young and old, scholars and masters, and even the Head, all take part. The sledges are well made and do not upset too easily. Tobogganing is splendid fun for every one, and is one of the best cures

German Verdicts

for fellows afflicted with a fit of slackness, and for all muffs, prigs, and dandies. If any one comes here like a fop with tall hat, cane, and kid gloves, he soon drops his mincing ways."

"But are not the masters looked down on by the boys for joining in such frivolity?"

"By no means," was the reply; "on the contrary, they rise in the estimation and affection of the fellows, who are always keen to have them join in the fun. The masters here are Companions, not Policemen."

"Then clearly," thought the visitor to himself, "the schoolmaster I once saw in Nedserd, who was terrified at the mere thought of travelling on the electric tram, would here have been despised."

"This sledge," continued Mr. Snikwah, "comes from the icy land of our forefathers; do you see the label 'Stockholm'? From it the fellows learn a bit of Geography and History by the way. It and this beautiful map of Scandinavia, both sent us by his father, will be agreeable mementoes of the young Swede, Nosnedron, when he leaves. He is only fourteen, and is now spending his second term with us. He learns, to be sure, more from intercourse with the boys, than from the work he does in class. On the other hand, his mere presence here makes Sweden better known to us, and more appreciated by the boys, than any text-book could make it. The same result has been produced, as far as the German language and civilisation are concerned, by several boys from Germany, who are here now, and by some we have had before, who were either Germans or had lived some time in Germany. We have also had boys from France, Holland, Belgium, the United States, Mexico, Canada,

South Africa, Australia, New Zealand and India. This intercourse with companions from foreign or distant lands, influences the morals of the boys even more powerfully than their minds. It puts our English boys on their mettle to mix with brilliant boys from abroad. It also plants firmly in their hearts the great truth, which the language lessons lead up to, namely, that all nations are appointed, not to fight with each other, but to work together for the great ends of Humanity. Our foreigners remain, even here, good Patriots ; nor do they denationalise us. On the contrary, the intercourse and friendly rivalry set up, not only teaches the fellows of different races mutually to esteem and appreciate one another, but also to discover their own national peculiarities and shortcomings." And they passed on into the Common Room.

"Do you hear that loud noise outside?" exclaimed Herr Namreh suddenly.

Again there was a shrill whistle.

"Where does it come from at this late hour? Can it possibly be some more of your boys?"

"Suppose we go out and see what it is," said Mr. Snikwah.

Accordingly master and guest went out into the clear night. Countless stars shone in the heavens, and below the river was glistening in the moonlight.

"What is that going on on the farther bank?" asked the guest.

Both listened and the master smiled. To him, no doubt, the sound was familiar from earliest youth. Presently the stranger also perceived the cause. Across the water in a meadow, under the moon and the stars, some youths were playing football.

"Who are they? Not your boys?"

"Oh no," was the answer; "they are working men and boys out of Retsecor village. After work all day indoors, instead of drinking in the village taverns, they are playing their favourite game in the fresh air."

"Ah, now I see the connection here between the life of your schools and the life of your common people," exclaimed Herr Namreh, "and can see how the schools might do away with bad national habits, by setting the example of a healthier life."

And as they turned back to the house he said to himself: "Play on and take your fun, stout-hearted workers, soldiers of the great industrial army of the nation, and receive at least my thanks, for your hard day's toil, whose fruits millions enjoy daily, without a thought of you and your scanty pleasures."

He was pleased when Mr. Snikwah said, as they entered the house, "There is not much wholesome fun for them down in the village. Some day we hope to do something for them. All we have done so far is to have a yearly Gathering of Neighbours at Christmas, to which some of them come."

It was just about ten, as they returned to the Common Room. There our German guest met two visitors, to whom he had already been introduced at tea. One of them was an "Old Boy" called Sinkram. He had come, as many more come, back to his old school-home. Every term there are some, who come not only from homes near at hand, but from America, India, or, it may be, Africa. They call to mind the good old times spent here.

"Why do you come back?" Herr Namreh asks the former scholar,

"Oh, we want to see again the old places where we worked and played. We want to see if the houses, bridges, boats, and furniture still exist, which we helped to make; we stop to meditate before a tree we perhaps planted years ago. We try and find out if the school regulations still exist, which we once helped to draw up, and whether the laws are still as justly enforced as they were in our time. The prefects, and especially their mouthpiece, the Head Boy of the school, pay a good deal of attention to our advice, and particularly to the advice of those who are favourably mentioned in the School Magazine, and who have shown, by their after career, the good stuff they are made of. The fellows would be mightily ashamed if, on any point, they got from us an unfavourable criticism, or if they were told by us they were abandoning the good customs of the school."

A master, Mr. Niwnu, who had himself been educated in the school, here addded, "Would the old boys come back here in such numbers, if they did not feel grateful for the kind of education which was given them, or if they had not found it useful and helpful in their various experiences, at home and abroad?"

On these visits the old boys subject themselves, of course, entirely to the ways of the school, and do not go away without having grown young again, nor without having received the help and friendly counsel they needed.

"Every year," so Sinkram told our guest, "there is an Old Boys' Gathering, to which as many come as can possibly get away from their studies or professional duties, to spend the five days' holiday at the old place. Every one then relates his adventures, exchanges notes, revives old friendships, gets news for the Old Boys' Magazine,

All day we fish, bathe, boat, play games or wander round and in the evening entertain the ladies and other guest with concerts, plays, and other amusements. In short, we live once more just the old life and, as far as we can become, for a brief space, boys again."

The other guest in the Common Room is a mother, Mrs. Newruc. She has come to see again her most cherished treasures—her rosy-cheeked, fair-haired " Benjamin " and his two slim elder brothers—and, for once in a way, to take part in one of the lessons with them. Nor do we wonder at this, though she assures us that she is so happy and quite satisfied about the well-being of her boys here. She knows how devotedly they are attached to the school. Her motherly heart gratefully acknowledges the love and care shown them. She knows that she could not, at home in the town, educate them so well as they are educated here. It was not love of ease or want of affection for them, she assures us, that prompted her to remove them from the unhealthy atmosphere of the huge world-city with its five or six millions of inhabitants, but her parental conscientiousness and care. She ends with the words : " In the holidays my boys talk to me and their young sister about nothing but the school. They think of nothing else. They wonder that all the children in the country do not come to their school ; for a better one, they are certain, cannot exist."

What this mother told him, our guest heard from many others. Some of the parents told him laughingly, or half complainingly, how they had to be doubly careful in the holidays to manage everything at home as well as possible. For the youngsters were always imagining themselves at school, and saying : " At Emlohstobba things are done like this, and we ought to do them here in the same way." Thus Emlohstobba exerts its educative influence far beyond its mere physical boundaries, and makes its theories and its life felt in the streets of distant cities and in the hearts and minds of thousands who have never seen it, or never, perhaps, even heard its name. This gratitude from mothers and fathers is a recognition that our work is not in vain, and induces and encourages us to labour on quietly and steadily at our responsible and anxious task, without ceasing to advance, and without losing heart at our imperfections.

CHAPTER VIII.

"THE PARENTS' GATHERING."

ONCE in the year, our guest is now informed, generally in summer, the parents come to the school *en masse* to join in "The Parents' Gathering." It is, of course, the greatest event in the whole year for every one. Our young citizens exert themselves for weeks before, to put their dominions into faultless order. They exert themselves now more than ever, in order to be able to show their parents, on the great day, what they can do in the class-room and in the concert-hall, in the fields and in the garden, whether at work or at play. They are not indifferent about even the smallest details, for everything concerns ultimately the honour and glory, not merely of themselves and their School, but of their Country and world-wide Empire. They rightly consider all the guests of the school as their personal guests too, and receive every one, if possible, with full musical honours. Picture to yourselves the three days of this delightful gathering.

The parents have not come here to listen to pompous orations from blind or deaf old Privy Councillors from the Ministry of Culture, about a school which they see, or hear of, perhaps once a year, and about boys whom they have never seen, or heard of, at all. Neither have they come to hear the Director of the school read out a list of prizes and honours, which the half dozen boys with the best memories have, after careful cramming, managed easily and ingloriously to secure, but which the rest, including perhaps the really ablest and most original, have, after careful neglect, necessarily failed to secure. It is not believed here that good characters can be formed amid perpetual competition, in class and in the field, for selfish preëminence, any more than that a State can grow strong amid the internecine struggles of towns, railway companies, directors of industry, or armies of operatives; whether these struggles amount to open physical war, or are limited to veiled physical, mental, or moral intimidation; whether the struggles are about provinces, markets, ideals, or daily bread.

It is believed in Emlohstobba, that boys who all day long are trying to overreach their intimate companions, during this most generous and most impressionable period of youth; who are urged day after day by their masters, to look out only for marks and prizes, and other such material and personal gain, and to avoid the culture of the affections as something childish, dangerous, or even unnatural: such boys, it is believed here, when they grow up, become the incapable directors, unscrupulous merchants, selfish profligates, and dishonest or ignorant statesmen and prelates, who are the cause of the overwhelming disasters now threatening all European civilisation.

Nor is it believed here, that such lists of personal gains furnish any just criterion of the real worth of a school; of the educational system, the skill of the teaching, or the excellence of the whole life. It is believed that this commercial grasping after pay turns the hearts and minds of teachers, parents, and pupils, away from the fundamental aim of education and of life, and blinds them to the ruin of the character which this training in selfishness produces.

It is believed at Emlohstobba, that the fundamental aim of education is nothing else than the aim of Christianity: that the school should be a church; the teacher a prophet and initiate; the pupil a neophyte and catechumen: that the place and life should produce citizens, with the hearts and ideals of soldiers or sailors, willing to work for the Commonwealth or Fleet, and for it ready to die; not that seven or more years of expensive instruction should end in producing a regiment of lads with dull intellects, selfish hearts, frigid manners, and with the ambitions and aspirations of shopkeepers.

Those who desire to separate the study of the Divine in Nature from the study of the Divine in Man, who would have for week days secular schools, and for Sundays sunday schools, must not be surprised if they should find the result of their scheme the production of a nation with one code of morality for Sunday, and another code of immorality for the week. And those who see what sacrilege it is to divide the human unity, body and soul and spirit, into secular and religious fragments, must beware how they render such division inevitable, by mistaking their own religious phraseology for the eternal essence of Divine Truth. Both parties should remember that the educator must obey the laws of psychology; that he must give the child child's food, and reserve the abstruse generalisations of theology for philosophers. The young child must have fairy tales, or else, when he is old, he will feel something missing in his life. He may live on, half conscious of this want in his nature, but, when adult, he will have a serious relapse into childishness. Do we not meet worthy people, who having been deprived of wholesome imaginative tales when they were young, so suffer from the unfulfilled craving, that they lose their common sense, and grow absurdly credulous, just as others fed on too much philosophy or "morals" or "religion," feel, when grown older, no delight save in scepticism? And so it is with religious education. If we give children the wrong religious food, they are either poisoned or starved. The Educator is more fortunate than the Physician. The patient can be forced to drink poison; but the pupil's mind as a rule quietly rejects what is not its proper nourishment, and dies, not of poison, but of mere hunger.

At Emlohstobba, the unity of the teaching is preserved throughout, and when the parents come to this gathering, they obtain a glimpse of the entire school life. They do not hear of "results," but see for themselves the processes which produce results. They see the boys, not only at the concert, or the cricket match; but see them taught in class or workshop or garden, learning in Hall, and Chapel, and all day long, to be *men*.

As they watch, or listen to, the performances of the

youngsters, they are filled with pride, not perhaps unalloyed with anxiety, lest their own son should fail to do his best. The boy is full of quiet confidence, with perhaps just a touch of secret pride, at now having a chance of showing his elder sister what he can do; for she returns each holiday well crammed from the High School, and twits him about his ignorance. The fathers grow young again as they play cricket against their boys—and are visibly pleased to be beaten. They hurry down to the river and race them in the water, while the mothers and sisters go round, and inspect where Tommy sleeps and Harry keeps his rabbits. Thus do parents and sons exchange experiences and learn something fresh about each other; and the Parents' Gathering cements the alliance between School and Home, without which harmonious education is impossible. At the close of the usual banquet, all enthusiastically join in the parting toast—"Good luck to the New Education, the New Generation, and the long awaited Regeneration." Most of this our guest learnt in the Common Room as he turned over the pages of *Naimlohstobba*, the school Magazine which appears once every year at Christmas. It is, he notices, written jointly by all the Citizens, past and present, of the school. In it he found some introductory remarks by the Monarch of the School-state, the annual Chronicle by one of the boys, the annual Budget of the youthful Chancellor of the Exchequer with the revenue and expenditure of the school treasury. He saw that a sum of some five or six hundred marks had been voluntarily subscribed, and had been admirably laid out, by the youthful administrators. Among other things this Magazine related how friends of the school had subscribed 1,300 marks for the building of

German Verdicts

a bridge across the river. It gave accounts of excursions into the neighbouring mountains, and of visits to factories in surrounding towns. It gave a charming picture of the wide ramifications of the complex school-life; and, best of all, nearly everything was written by the boys themselves. "This is a hundred times more interesting to read," remarked our guest, "than the multitude of official school programs of some countries [whose names he would rather not, in this foreign land, betray] taken all together. I get more education out of this, than from hundreds of our annual school reports on the Continent. He was assured that our boys would gladly send it to any school on the face of the earth which cared to have it, for a small contribution towards the postage and printing. Our guest thought that certainly no one would repent, after reading it, of having spent a few pence to get it. Looking through the Magazine, Herr Namreh was delighted to find how frankly, honestly, and naturally, it reflected the sentiments and opinions of the scholars, about their school-life. What is the best proof of the good character of an educative school? Surely it is the love of youths who have not been miseducated. Not, therefore, without emotion did Herr Namreh read, at the end of the last year's report, the following touching words of a scholar who was then leaving :—

"This made an excellent end to an excellent term. After the Chapel Service for the Last Day of Term, came the School-song, and then the Good-byes which all were heartily sorry to have to say. At the mystic hour of five next morning we were all awake, and by 6.30 were all crossing the fields in the early morning light, leaving Emlohstobba behind, with a feeling in the throat never to be forgotten."

CHAPTER IX.

HEALTH, PUNISHMENTS, ETHICS AND ÆSTHETICS AT EMLOHSTOBBA.

OUR visitor had, after the numerous impressions of the day, still all sorts of questions on his mind. He was pleased, therefore, that in spite of the lateness of the hour there happened to be some of the masters left in the Common Room, who could answer him. Among many other questions, he put the following :—

"What sort of health do your scholars have? I noticed to-day that they all looked fresh. But perhaps my observations deceived me. Can the boys really stand this sort of life?" One of the masters, Mr. Sille, who like the rest was the picture of health, and who had, he learnt, already made a tour round the world, got out a book entitled "Health Statistics."

"In this book," said Mr. Sille, "every case of illness during the past year has been carefully recorded. We have, moreover, excellent hygienic sick-rooms, but, as you saw to-day, they are usually empty. In this Report you will find that there have been three surgical cases (which were luckily nearly all of a trifling character) to each medical one."

"What is the reason for the good hygienic condition of the boys?" asked Herr Namreh.

"First of all, simple, wholesome food. This, as far as possible, is made up of vegetables, eggs, milk, and butter; but includes, in addition, our own mutton, veal, and pork, fed on the place.

"The object we have in view is to produce, on the School Estate, as far as we can, all the food we require;

and for this every part is laid under contribution—wells, gardens, fields, ponds, and streams. The estate thus provides us with a great variety, not only invaluable for the table, but equally so for the class-room.

"We prohibit all importation of harmful things, such as alcohol in every form, hot spices, dainties from home, and sweets from the village. Nearly all rich people overeat, and most diseases in them come from excesses at the table. We are healthy, moreover, because of the kind of life we lead, the frequent change from mental to physical work, and the hardening process we put ourselves through to increase our strength and vitality. You would find that there are few colds, coughs, and catarrhs here, because the fellows are not muffled up in too many clothes and don't sit in stifling rooms; because rain, cold, storm, or the dirtying and wetting of boots and clothes, is not here considered a reason for confining the boys indoors, or for interrupting their runs and games and out-door work; because great-coats are seldom used and seldom needed, for the fellows do not sit doubled up over their books for three, four, or five hours on end, but follow, in this and in everything, the greatest of all teachers, mother 'Nature'; because they are not coddled and petted, but are made tough and hardy; because they are not made merely to repeat by heart, but, as far as possible, to imitate in their lives 'The Hardy Norseman' and 'Hearts of Oak.' They are trained to be clean in all their personal habits, and are taught to recognise Sunlight, Fresh Air, and Clean Water as the three best and greatest Physicians.

"Their historical ideals are, of course, the same as those of all other schoolboys: the Athenians at Marathon, the Spartans at Thermopylæ, the Anglo-Saxons under

Alfred, the Goths under Alaric, the Germans under Hermann, and the English under Harold; who showed their courage, strength, simplicity, reverence for woman and generous ways, throughout all their wanderings and struggles. Their heroes are Jonathan, Perikles, Cæsar, Beowulf, King Arthur, Siegfried, Alfred the Great, Harry the Fifth, Bayard, Raleigh, Cromwell, Washington, Nelson, Wellington, Bismarck, Livingstone, Gordon, and Nansen. But to impress these heroic characters deeply upon their hearts, we do not merely use pictures and poems, or dramatical and plastic representations; still less do we discomfort, or rather, profane their memories by cramming in Text-book paragraphs. We let our boys, here and now, live over again the boyhood days of humanity. We do not merely talk about the heroes of antiquity; we make our boys become in imagination Athenians, Spartans, Romans, Goths, and Anglo-Saxons; we fight beside them like the Athenians at Marathon, and bathe with them like the Spartans in the Eurotas; we wrestle, run, and leap, like the ancient Olympic combatants; we let them take part in the business of the State, as it was done in the Agora at Athens in the good old times, and try to make our Stage into an exponent of morals like the ancient Theatron. We let them see beautiful things, and make them study and practise Art, as was done in the days of Pheidias. Although Greek is not drummed into them for seven years—nay, just because we do not place that triple wall of brass between them and the glorious old Hellenic culture—they become better Neo-Hellenes, and cull more of the living essence of Homer, Aischulos, and Plato than those who regard it as their main object to stammer out a smattering of that language without ever being able to really speak, read, or understand it. Though we do not attempt, in such a school as this, to make our boys learn Anglo-Saxon, or write innumerable notes about Middle-High German, yet the rising generation here, like their old German and Norse forefathers, daily develop their strength and youthful powers by felling trees and building boats, by working in the garden and field, by wandering in the woods far and near, and, when occasion comes, riding and hunting ; at all times, and in all places, revelling in, and thus worshipping, the beauties of nature created so perfect by the finger of God—in short by trying to be simple, straightforward, natural, honest, true, and good.

"The ancient Hebrews, the Hellenes of old, and our brave Teutonic ancestors, did not live in order that our youth to-day might be oppressed with the weight of thousands of Text-book paragraphs and historical dates, or that they might be made to stutter out fragments of old languages, which, notwithstanding their merits, have now, none the less, become dead. This burden still rests, however, on some schools and schoolboys, like a nightmare. The old Hellenes, the Romans, the Hebrews, and Anglo-Saxons, as indeed all other men, lived their lives in the hope that everything, which was wholesome, noble, and good in them, might live on after them in all men, for all ages. They knew how to live themselves, and they taught their children how to live. To us they preach also this sovran truth : 'First, and above everything, teach your boys to feel and to think, to will and to speak, to be silent and to act—in a word, to *live* : then, and not till then, teach them to read, to write, and to calculate. Do not forget, amid this book wisdom, with which you so over-abundantly equip them, that you should give them also, and above all, the wisdom of life. ' Primo vivere, deinde philosophari ' should be the motto of all schools and all universities.' "

" And what is the condition of morals in your school ? " Herr Namreh next asked. " I have certainly been most favourably impressed by your boys in this respect. They are well-mannered, frank, and friendly. Is their character satisfactory in all other ways ? "

" The moral statistics," replied another master, Mr. Repooh, who, distinguished for his prowess at football, was also remarkable for his absence of self and presence of mind in other things as well, " show that serious cases occur but seldom. We are all out and about, mingling with each other in all kinds of ways, at odd moments and at all sorts of jobs not usually done at schools, so that, without special design, we come upon the fellows unexpectedly, hear their familiar conversation, and so get to know their real sentiments and dispositions. We therefore can advise and help them before it is too late. We are also saved from much evil by the circumstance that the school is remote from towns and far from public-houses and—that curse of schools—the tuck-shop. Our boys see and hear nothing low, and have no opportunities either to drink or to ' guzzle.'

" To be candid, we do not find it possible to dispense entirely with punishment. But we do not confine the lazy or disobedient boy to a class-room, and leave him there alone to injure, perhaps, both mind and body ; nor do we make him ' stay in ' with others of the same sort, to concoct, perhaps, evil, or to corrupt each other. On the contrary, we bring the dull, weak, or wicked boy in contact with the healthiest, most moral, and most industrious. They become his companions by day and night, at work and play; in class and at gardening; in Chapel, in the Dining-hall, and in the Dormitory. The boy of character can thus show his virtue in the best of all ways, by reclaiming the feeble and erring, instead of holding himself aloof, like a Pharisee or moral prig, and leaving the others to become incurable. If better companionship, example, and sympathy are of no avail, we do not keep the bad boy *in*, but keep him *out;* instead of *sitting*, we keep him *running;* instead of games he gets more gardening, or instead of workshop he gets more football; at length he learns to do whatever he has to do with all his might, and at the proper time."

"That was the reason the boy was running up and down in front this morning," here interposed another master, Mr. Yetsnat.

"And do you never use the cane save to beat carpets: or do you only beat the boys' clothes and never have to beat their backs?" says our guest.

"Sometimes we must, but not often. Some boys need licking—others would be injured by it; others, again, require no more than a word or a look. But it would be great folly to renounce corporal punishment under all circumstances. It is, after all, only another language expressing the will. Masters who bind themselves never to cane are like fathers and mothers who spoil their children at home. All goes well for a time, and then somebody else has to make up for their omissions.

"In giving punishments we act according to the following principles. We gradually increase the penalties, always, however, associating them with the offence; we change the kind of punishment, and alternate strict discipline with acts of kindness, which show the offender that, in punishing his offence, we have not lost faith in him.

"But we do not allow kindness to degenerate into favouritism, petting, or weakness. A boy will always despise a master who lacks strength of will or of purpose. As a rule the lad simply ridicules and detests him. In his master he should find strength, wisdom, and justice, united always with kindness, gentleness, and affection. To his pupil the teacher should strive to be father and mother in one.

"If all our efforts fail, we are, at last, forced to expel the boy from the school, thus frankly admitting that we are unable (or unfit) to educate him, or he is unable (or unfit) to become educated by us. And if so, let some one else be free to try. This punishment is, we believe, the worst we can inflict, yet the most just. To exclude from a life so rational, so rich, and so delightful, is, like the exclusion of Adam and Eve from Paradise, reserved for those only who are unworthy. For them, indeed, expulsion is inevitable, and in reality they exclude themselves—we do but register the judgment they have themselves pronounced.

"But we hardly ever have to proceed to such extreme courses. The good example of the big fellows, the friendly intimacy of the masters, the natural and happy mode of life—all these influences conspire to save us from such painful necessity.

"The main thing, of course, is to treat the boy with entire frankness and confidence. We show him that we do not believe that he would willingly deceive, or disobey, us. We try to arouse, or increase, in him the feeling that all such conduct is both foolish and degrading. We endeavour, as far as we can, to remove any inducements to error, by keeping, as far from our State as possible, everything that would make it a government by police, espionage, or trickery. We do not make the boy write 'Extemporalia' in which we have laid a hundred traps to trip him up, and then punish him for falling into the traps thus cunningly prepared. We do not give him a problem which, however hard he tries, he cannot solve, and then for punishment give him it to write out a hundred times. We do not forbid him to do that which he naturally wants, and ought to want, to do. We give him wide scope for independent initiative, and leave him unhampered by petty capricious rules. We allow him to use unconditionally, and to defend freely, all the rights which we have granted him, and allow him to use his own discretion as to how he will carry out the duties assigned to him and those under his command. For this reason he obeys us willingly and cheerfully, because he sees that it is not our private whims but the essential laws of the school, which require his obedience. We inspect and judge his work, and praise or blame him frankly, as is just, and he listens without sulking or expostulations. For he sees us daily working hard, and hourly following the same strict laws; he knows that for our mistakes, not only others, but we ourselves must suffer; he therefore respects us, hears us patiently, and silently resolves to do his next work perfectly. He knows the school regulations, and the punishment following on their transgression. He knows that our personal will cannot, and ought not to, dispense with law. For without law no community can exist. Therefore he takes his punishment, when it comes, without grumbling, and does not afterwards appear unduly sensitive or hurt.

"Sometimes a boy will voluntarily come, admit his fault, make amends, as far as he can, and even beg for punishment as a right. When he welcomes the just penalty thus, we feel that the fault is already purged, and forgive the doer at once, and do our best to obviate the fatal consequences of his error. Both masters and boys respect him, perhaps more than before he went wrong, for nothing is harder and rarer than to admit a fault and be willing to atone or suffer for it.

"All such open repentance, therefore, ought to be held in especial honour. Usually people try and pretend they are faultless; and this is natural, for society punishes error with such absurd and unthinking severity, that men are made liars and hypocrites. In nothing is mankind to-day so far from healthy conditions as in this. There is no proper hierarchy of virtues, no proper graduation of iniquities, and there is no longer any forgiveness of sins. The 'traditional laws of men' also, which stand in place of Divine law, are obscure or uncertain. Every day we see the solemn decisions of judges as solemnly upset by other judges, only to be solemnly upset once more by a Higher Court; until the effect left on the public mind is this: that law is a mysterious ogre, irrational and irreligious, which, like Pilate washing his hands, while pretending a love of justice, condemns the innocent and frees the guilty, solicitous alone for its own comfort and worldly aggrandisement.

"Mankind no longer respects the law, for it sees no real logical or religious sanction underlying it. To win votes, unjust laws are made; to win lucre, these laws (such as they are) are twisted and perverted, till the nation believes finally that it is useless to be honest, but very useful to be rich, cunning, and unscrupulous.

"In the school it is essential that the boy should be able to respect the law. Here he helps to make the laws, and practises voluntary obedience to them, in his daily work and play. Thus he learns self-control, and the necessity of public order.

"Will he not, in this way, learn to govern himself ultimately in greater things? As Fag he daily shows, or as Prefect he daily exacts, obedience. Will these habits, ingrained from long use, bear no fruit? The quantity of good stuff which has quietly developed in the school, and which never fails to show its worth when wanted, is one of the best aids we have in the moral education of newcomers. The boys' own good traditions will tolerate no laziness or vice. The springing up of unhealthy growths is thus prevented. Evil tendencies do not easily manifest themselves, but, if they should, are easily nipped in the bud. The quiet example of the majority does more than much talk or many blows. Obviously the excellence of the educative system, and of the methods employed, combines with the features of the place and the personality of the teachers, to create the ethical standard reached.

"As the boys are taught above all things to rule themselves, we require this quality in the highest degree from ourselves. To pass a sentence of punishment, not to speak of carrying it out, in anger or passion, seems to us most dangerous and disgraceful. No citizen of our State, small or great, can be doubtful of our inward displeasure and contempt for what is wrong. A mere look, or even silence rightly used, has more effect than many words or blows. Words may only affect the ear and not the heart; and blows may only reach the skin and not the understanding, and may kill the sense of honour instead of vivifying it.

"The horse that has become accustomed to the lash, heeds no longer word or whistle. It is only a bad rider or driver who cannot get on without the whip. A good one effects more with a decided word or a slight movement of the knees or reins, than another can with innumerable lashes.

"So it is with a teacher. He who has trained his pupil to notice the fall of a needle, will not need to fire off a cannon to make himself heard and obeyed."

Herr Namreh agreed and observed, "I was very much astonished at dinner to-day, when I saw the boys suddenly rise to sing grace. Although I was sitting close beside it, I had not heard the gentle sound of the bell, which even the boys farthest off had noticed."

"Just so," continued Mr. Repooh, "that almost inaudible sound preached us a whole sermon on the right teaching of attentiveness, and on the refining of the powers of hearing, seeing, thinking, and feeling. The mere look of the Monarch or his Ministers says more to a citizen in this State than hours of exhortation amid inattention or uproar would elsewhere. Disorder here is unknown and is rendered impossible both by our ethic and æsthetic teaching. We hardly ever need to reprimand or punish, because our whole school-life is organised according to accurate observation of child nature, and responds to the desires and aspirations of the boy. It provides for the feelings and thoughts which are stirring in his soul, as well as for the needs of his muscles and his bodily appetites. The opportunities for healthy activity in every direction, free from restraint, invite the vigorous energies of boy-nature to find wholesome outlet. The youngsters have little inclination to break rules, because they are treated like rational beings. We do not first force them to be unhealthy or wicked, and then punish them without sympathy or discrimination."

CHAPTER X.

RELIGION AT EMLOHSTOBBA.

"I SEE you take every care here to develop moral strength, but how stands the matter with regard to religion? I noticed, for instance, on questioning the boys, that one youngster did not know his catechism by heart, and seemed ignorant of several stories in the Old Testament, which, in German schools, have to be read and learned. I confess that I was not displeased, for I am not a Consistorial Councillor, and cannot agree with everything they exact from our schools."

Another master of the school, Dr. Steil, answered the guest.

"We wish to elevate religion from being a matter of words, and of mere intellect, to being a matter of instinct, affection, and practical life. Every just and competent judge, who has spent a few days here, has acknowledged that the whole atmosphere of the school is at once moral and religious. Well, religion and morals are, of course, inseparable. Whether we are in the chapel, offering prayers and thanksgiving, or in class or in the fields, studying the marvellous works of God in history or natural science; or are wandering by the river, in the wood or on the hills; or are standing under the starry heavens and gazing into the dark abyss; always, and in all places, we are offering up Divine service. Religion is too sacred and subtle a matter, too much an affair of the feelings and affections, of the inward life and will, to be adequately handled in class or taught like an ordinary subject, say, mathematics. To keep a fellow in for an hour, to give him marks, to put his name in the Punishment Book, because he does not 'know' such and such a 'piece' of religion, makes one pause overwhelmed with disgust. In religion's own name, and in the name of conscience, let us guard against everything which may desecrate religion and conscience; against everything which might cause the most sacred ideas to be regarded with levity or loathing. Is not the latter often the inevitable result of our traditional religious teaching? Have not, all of us, felt that strange physiological sickness, or psychological repulsion, at what our teachers were pleased sometimes to tell us was a part of 'religion,' we knowing in our souls it was not?"

As the master spoke, the following thoughts passed through Herr Namreh's mind.

On religious grounds they will avoid holding up to their boys, as an example of virtue, Abraham, who, by dint of prevarication, turned his wife into a means of profitable trade with Pharaoh, and yet remains (according to the traditional view) the pious and blessed patriarch.[1] They

[1] It is impossible to give, within the limits of a footnote, the reasons for the particular instruction in religion given here. But it may be useful to inform the reader briefly what the practice at Abbotsholme during our eight years' existence has been. It is this: to avoid as far as possible reading any passage in the Bible which is unfit for the young mind, either on account of difficulties due to obscure meaning or grammatical construction, or on account of allusion to things and actions unsuited to a boy's stage of growth. On the other hand, it has seemed to me impracticable to omit all mention of such personages as Abraham, Jacob, and David, seeing that they are everywhere household names. To exclude all mention of them would probably arouse a boy's curiosity, when for instance he heard such expressions as "the God of Abraham, Isaac, and Jacob," or "the Son of David." Besides, portions of the history of each of these men are very beautiful, and have become deservedly part of the circle of thought of all cultured persons. Otherwise, doubtless, it would have been simpler to have omitted all mention of them. But it does not follow that even if we must read parts, we need read the whole, of the biographies of these men. And my own practice has been to read only the passages least open to objection, pointing out, of course, when necessary, the faults and blemishes in each character in so far as that was required by the passage read. I have not attempted to make a real character sketch of any of them, feeling that this, if needed, would be best done by our Bishops and Professors of Divinity, when they become more aware of the necessity of a revision of religious instruction, to bring it into harmony with the ascertained facts of modern pedagogic research. Before very long the world will certainly be forced, in the interest of improved education, to revise the Bible, if it is to remain the textbook of religious instruction. This is too serious a task for a hard-worked schoolmaster. But it is none the less his duty, as the duty of all teachers, not to continue to use methods or books, however hallowed by ancient custom or tradition, when he perceives that, from the point of view of educational science and his own experience, their use is harmful and thus indefensible.

With many of Dr. Lietz's arguments for a revised Bible few thoughtful and unprejudiced persons will probably disagree. It is certainly refreshing to find a graduate in theology, and one recognised as fully qualified to enter the State Church of a country like Prussia, attempting to remove what has long been a stumbling-block to the young and a will preserve them from hearing too much of Jacob, who, at one and the same time, was arch-father, and, guided by his mother, arch-deceiver to brother, father, and family. They will omit much of the story of King David, who was the Lord's Anointed and sweet singer of Israel, and yet at the same time and in the same person, was (if it can be credited) a usurper, adulterer, traitor to his country, and at heart murderer even at the very moment of his death. They will not make them learn, in the First Book of Moses, or in the Books of Samuel and Kings, about Oriental morality. The Bible, used only, as in any school it should be, in the form of re-edited selections, in which incomprehensible grammar and wearisome repetitions are carefully excluded; such a school Bible as this, and the entire World-literature, provides them with a rich treasury of appropriate and typical religious characters. They will prefer to show their boys those persons mainly, who are marked out as the best, personalities with which the deepest and noblest thoughts of mankind are inextricably bound up, but not such as are connected at the same time with crimes and vices. What would the boys think of Beowulf, Alfred, or Nelson; what of Hermann, Alaric, or Barbarossa; what of Frederick the Great or William the Victorious;

hindrance to the cause of true religion. It has been a source of real gratification to me to find that our instinctive practice here is in harmony with the views of an influential, and steadily increasing, number of earnest professors, teachers, and clergymen in Germany and elsewhere. For Dr. Lietz is by no means the only educator who wishes to see removed the greatest hindrance to a real religious culture for Europe—namely, the present system of instruction which, instead of edifying the understanding, really perverts the healthy instincts of the young. More upon this important subject appears elsewhere. (TRANSLATOR.)

where would their sympathy for all these be, if they were told in the same hour and breath, not only of their conquests, their courage, and their patriotism, but of murders, treachery, lying, and theft, as having been ascribed to them? Will not the effect be the same in the case of Abraham, Jacob, and David? Moreover, do not Pharaoh, Esau, and Saul, judged by the boy's or girl's instinct of right and wrong, appear the better men, however much we try to persuade them of the reverse? I should, indeed, be anxious about the moral judgment of any child who did not feel so. A boy with any sense of justice will turn away from such figures with contempt, to a Scharnhorst, a Nelson, or an Arminius. He will indeed, if he has Teuton blood in his veins, turn his back upon us, if we suggest anything bad about them. Let us direct the religious and moral judgment of youth, and not misdirect it. No one with a right discernment will belittle or despise the piety of the old Benedictine monks, or underrate their knowledge of mankind or the excellence of their national educational system. Would the regulations of their Order have forbidden, without good cause, the reading of the first seven Books of the Bible? Would Wulfila, the real apostle of the Germans, have left, without good reason, the Book of Kings untranslated? The Bible in its entirety is a book for mature age. Those alone will love it in later life who have had presented to them in their youth that only which suited their age and attracted their uncorrupted instincts then.

"In our Chapel services, history lessons, and lessons in natural science," pursued the master; "in our quiet talks during chance rambles by the river, in the woods, or under the starry skies, we relate or read to our young friends about the religious geniuses of mankind, the great prophets of every age and nation, and especially about the greatest of them all. The teacher then ceases to be a mere instructor or drill-master—which indeed here he is not at any time—he becomes a disciple of the prophets and, in the true sense of the term, a priest of Humanity and of God. If he does not feel overshadowing him the very breath of the prophetic and Divine spirit, if he does not feel within him a passionate yearning for perfection, let him abstain entirely from undertaking any teaching of this kind. If he has not a touch of the sacred fire, he can only profane such work by meddling with it. He will be at best a mere 'Educational Official,' and at worst a *marchand de soupe*. His school will be for a time a factory to manufacture profits, and then a sink of rottenness.

"We do not try to lecture on religion to our pupils, but to live religion before them and with them. Our pupils must never see or hear us scoff about sacred things, nor find us indifferent or indulgent about what is wrong. They must observe in us reverence for what is holy, indignation at wrong-doing, pitying gentleness for weakness, and boundless readiness at all times to help every one. They ought to see each of the masters doing that which Jesus did to his disciples and to all men, forgiving, helping, reproving, healing, consoling, encouraging; in a word—loving.

"We notice how Jesus gradually conquered the hearts of his disciples, without dogmatic teaching about his office and title, and without theological lectures as to the metaphysical nature of his existence. We notice how men strove to become his disciples, to behave themselves towards God and their comrades and the rest of mankind as he wished them to, and to feel towards all men the boundless love which he felt for them. Just because Jesus did not put himself at an infinite distance from them as 'Second Person of the Trinity,' as 'God,' they were able to receive him into themselves.[1] It was thus that his influence penetrated their lives, and that he became their friend, brother, leader, and model—their Ideal. No points of dogmatic controversy have any place in our community, because they have no place in educative instruction or in an Educative School. By means of a strong and high wall, so to speak, we keep them from entering here. We have no occasion or time for disputing on these matters. We leave that to the theologians and metaphysicians. Such things should be discussed at the universities among adults; they have no place in schools or among the young. The main thing in religious education at school is to select such examples of religious life as are suitable to the successive stages of the boy's development and the successive stages of civilisation. Then we must present them in such a way that they may act powerfully upon the feelings, thoughts, and aspirations of the boy at the particular age to which he has come. This instinct, or principle, caused the Heliand poet, for example, to represent his Jesus as a kind of Saxon Duke. Let us imitate the methods of these great National or World

[1] The question is not: Was he God? The question is: What is the right way to give religious instruction? I think that in our anxiety to pay honour to Jesus Christ with our lips we have forgotten to imitate his methods of teaching. "I have still many things to tell you," he says, "but you cannot bear them now." (TRANSLATOR.)

teachers. What our boys want to learn about is mainly courage, sincerity, self-control, fair play, modesty, generosity to foes, and fidelity to friends. What they do not want to hear about is cowardice, base self-indulgence, conceit, double-dealing, envy of foes, and treachery to neighbours and intimates.

"Let them hear about Alfred the Great, Oliver Cromwell, and Victoria the Good; about Frederick the Great, Scharnhorst, and Von Stein; about Queen Louise and 'Unser Fritz'; let them hear of Confucius, Buddha, Solon, Socrates, Plato, Seneca, and Marcus Aurelius; let them hear of Moses, Joseph, Jonathan, Elijah, Amos, Isaiah, Jeremiah, Judas Maccabeus, John the Baptist, John, Paul, Wulfila, Arnold of Brescia, Petrus Waldus, Wycliffe, Huss, Hieronymus, Savonarola, Martin Luther, Zwingli, Calvin, Knox, Cranmer, Hans Denck, Fénélon, Heinrich Francke, Paul Gerhardt, Wesley, Gordon, Carlyle, Ruskin, and others like these. This 'Celestial Bodyguard of the Immortals' helps us to realise not only the immense elevation of that one Personality unapproachable in the presence of death, but, above all, to feel dimly the greatness of that unique life —divine in its heroic deeds, in its strong, calm love and in its silent fortitude. As the successive spurs and endless peaks on peaks of the gigantic Himalayas help us to realise vaguely the stupendous height and unsurpassed majesty of Everest, so all these heroes help us to grasp in some far-off faint degree the unique splendour of that one supreme Presence.

"You will never make sound, healthy youths enthusiastic for merely passive heroism. At their age they crave for heroism that acts. But in the life of Jesus Christ and in the stories of the old prophets we can find material enough from which to pick out for our boys classic examples of heroism, human and divine. Why do you not use these lives fully, instead of dwelling on tales about Jacob's treachery or the twelve plagues of Egypt or other 'miracles'? Should we not find subjects more worthy in our old Norse Sagas and in the religious myths of the old Germans and ancient Greeks than in these stories from the Old Testament, which to a boy seem either immoral, incomprehensible, or merely marvellous; stories which cannot be said to exercise any really strong moral or religious influence on the character.

"To strengthen still further the impression made by our daily religious life and by these types of supreme religious excellence we use also, as far as we can, the influence of Art. During Divine service there ever gazes down upon us from the Chapel wall that glorious symbol of Maternal love—Mary with the infant Jesus—expressing, too, the divinity which should shine in and around every child born into the world. Around the room we see the great Teachers who, in all times and among all nations, have led mankind onwards and upwards to God. We sing the most touching songs and melodies, in which divinely inspired composers have essayed to express their inmost religious yearnings. Such are the surroundings, amid which our boys, led gently to filial reverence by the subtle magic of painting, music, poetry, and sculpture, hear the great prophets of all time discourse about God and things Divine. Aided by such surroundings, their minds open to the everlasting truths enshrined in the classic literatures of the world, truths which become slowly, but indelibly, engraven on their hearts."

"Is Chapel, then, your hour for religious instruction?" asked the guest.

"Yes and no," replied the master.

"They are not obliged to hear overmuch of the Israelitish law of three thousand years ago, about murder, adultery, theft, slander, Sabbath-breaking, and idolatry—laws better suited for adults than for children—but are led rather to study in the Sermon on the Mount the far nobler Decalogue of Jesus. Thus it is that we are striving, in happy fellowship with our boys, to construct out of the entire subject-matter of our teaching, after the example of the great and pious Amos Komensky and others, a Boy's Code of Duties. In this Code will be found enumerated not merely negative and passive virtues, but, above all, positive and active morals and religion. In it, besides gentleness, mildness, pity, humility, and love of others, our boys will not have to seek in vain for Ideals essential to wholesome boyhood, nor for Virtues requisite in our modern life—friendship, courage, patriotism, generosity, magnanimity, self-sacrifice, fidelity to one's calling and one's friends, to one's rulers and all mankind.

"We do not separate religion from the rest of life. In the two most magnificent Cathedrals of the capital of this country you see, beside statues and pictures of prophets and apostles, memorials of the best and noblest generals, statesmen, scholars, and poets. We know that many a time, in the political and social life of this country, religious beliefs have been decisive, and perhaps are now. Well, as is done in our mighty Fatherland, so we would do in our small State. We do not separate religion from History, Language, and Natural Science. We are occupied with it, directly or indirectly, in all the subjects which we study. The separation of secular and profane from religious and ecclesiastical history and literature we condemn as being absurd, unnatural, and dangerous—a relic of scholasticism. For our educative work we should find an anti-religious literature or history as little valuable as we should a religion which at any time did not make itself felt as a living reality in the words and works of heroes, artists, thinkers, poets, and statesmen. A natural philosophy which should pretend to stand in direct opposition to the religious conception of the world could have as little value in education as any so-called religious view of the world's creation and evolution which stood in opposition to the ascertained facts of natural science. We cannot tolerate any schism between the head and the heart of our pupils, between their instinctive intuitions and their educated understanding. Such religious matter as we introduce into our teaching comes, with absolute impartiality, in all the studies, whether they be language or history or natural science.

"Did the boys of ancient times or of the Middle Ages receive such complex intellectual 'religious instruction' as we find imparted to-day in most of the schools on the Continent? Surely not. Was, then, humanity on that account less pious formerly than now? In our hours for meditation, in our Chapel services, and in our whole moral and religious life we strive to proceed exactly in accordance with the nature of the child. Our service in Chapel is not dull and lifeless, leaving boys or masters, servants or guests untouched or perhaps bored. It is not like the Oriental praying-mill, which works the same whether priest and people are absent or not; nor is it accompanied by elaborate ceremonial, which fatigues the senses it satiates and narcotises the mind it neglects. On the contrary, it is for all the most important opportunity in the daily life for reflection. Every guest who comes to us, no matter to what religious body he belongs, feels himself, as you did to-day, deeply affected by our Chapel service. Certainly I have never noticed so marked an influence in the school services I attended elsewhere. They were too formal and dry, or conventional and cold; they appealed too much to mere intellect, and were often too dogmatic. Nor could I detect that they produced any deep and lasting effect upon the boys. I admit that it would be the same here if our hymns, melodies, Liturgy, and Lessons were not so chosen as to touch the boys and become cherished memories. They are not derived from the old prayers of Hieronymus, Augustine, or other ancient fathers of the Church that I have found in school Liturgies elsewhere, but spring chiefly from the religious life of our own nation. With immense care they are chosen so as to be in harmony with the most exact pedagogic principles; and, as the old Liturgies suited the epochs in which they were compiled, so we wish ours to suit the religious and moral needs of our own day.

"We have therefore endeavoured to discover and employ all the experience and treasures that others on similar quests have gathered. In this attempt we feel thankful and proud that, as members of this nation, we are in a special position of advantage. In this country religion is not, as in some, a thing apart. On the contrary, it permeates the National and Social life. We find, for instance, special services for the beginning and end of term; for days of School or National rejoicing and mourning ; for good fortune ; for calamities at sea ; for Harvest and all other great events in the School or National life. Religion is not regarded as something strange, unscientific, or ridiculous (acknowledged merely as a harmless and decent conventionality). It has become something that is believed, revered, and actually practised. A religious spirit has developed here, which we seek to cherish and intensify and with which we strive to link all new ideas. Thus we would cultivate freedom of thought without losing piety.

"As to the attitude of this Nation to dogma. Dogma is not exactly rejected, but it is not immoderately emphasised. Relatively, it has lost in significance. It contributes little now, that can be called essential, to our religious sentiments or life. In the School, therefore, we are careful to avoid introducing it forcibly or artificially. But we are also careful not to attract attention to it by childish and anxious efforts to keep it out. Precisely because our boys know and care little about dogma, for that reason the Hebrew Scriptures and the Gospel, prayer, and all religious acts and habits are more effective living forces here than in places where religion is associated with an ecclesiastical machine and regarded as a social convention, or in places where it is associated with phrases and doctrines beyond the mental grasp of the young and out of real touch with the physical, mental, and moral problems of the present day. We choose what is noblest and most beautiful and touching in the Bible or other Literatures, and read such passages continually, until they become familiar, but not tedious ; and we apply the teachings to our own life here.

"It is impossible to choose Psalms, or Prayers, or

Lessons which shall be quite free from dogma. Each must convey some doctrine, as each must have been written by a mind which took some definite glance at the great world. If we exclude from our Liturgy all that fails to express our feelings or thoughts of to-day, we shall but write an ephemeral 'theology' after all, which to-morrow will seem to our children antiquated. The only solution of our problem is to present to them, like the successive pictures of a panorama, all the great epoch-making religious conceptions of the world, embalmed in the priceless and immortal words of the greatest thinkers of all nations. Such a Liturgy at once suits every age and every stage of growth; such a Liturgy alone can render possible Common Worship and Common Prayer; such a Liturgy alone is all-embracing—Catholic. To exclude dogma entirely is impossible; but, were it possible, it would express only the dogma of 'no dogma.' Each Psalm and Hymn, each Poem and Prayer, every Sermon, Chant, or utterance of any sort—each and all must express the more or less clear beliefs or aspirations of its author, or of the epoch which gave it birth. Are we to exclude all the charming stories of our childhood? What could be more ridiculous than a Liturgy which, written for a child, should ignore the Babe of Bethlehem; or a Liturgy which, written for philosophers, insisted that the Ideal Man was at the same time miraculously a Vine?

"But the Bible has no meaning for us, except in so far as it tells us of something definite to do. Thus used, it becomes far better known and more appreciated, than long commentaries and interpretations could make it. Such exegesis has often as little effect in discovering the vital truths enshrined in the Gospel, as a physican's dissecting knife would have had in giving life to the corpse of Lazarus.

"What elsewhere remains unattained, and is, in fact, made unattainable, because false methods are employed, that we accomplish here unconsciously. Others make their boys learn by heart, Psalms, Hymns, Maxims, and explanations of the Catechism. Consequently all is learnt with loathing and forgotten without regret.

"We do not need to 'set' such 'lessons,' and so are not obliged to 'hear them'—repeated by rote. We trust simply to the daily singing of chosen psalms and hymns, and to the frequent enunciation of heavenly precepts in our beautiful Liturgy. Consequently these precepts become imprinted on their minds without effort, and work imperceptibly but unceasingly upon their hearts. One of my friends on the Continent, once told me how, as a child, he had wept the whole evening through because he had not been able to remember some dull and difficult hymn, or some long, incomprehensible piece of Catechism; things which, although beyond his powers, had still to be studied in spite of hours of overwork. He told me how next day he returned to class in anxiety and terror; how in spite of all his efforts he only received in Divinity a 'moderate' or 'not quite satisfactory,' and how he was, therefore, made to feel himself an irreligious scoundrel. He told me how, in the Sixth and Fifth Forms, the treatment of Paul's Letter to the Romans, and of St. John's Gospel, utterly spoiled his interest in those writings for years subsequently. Well, no one has anything of that sort to fear here.

"Although—nay, because—we do not enter here into elaborate analyses of, say, the uses and varieties of Prayer, and do not learn off by rote maxims about it, Prayer becomes something not only dear to us, but indispensable. We do not wish ever to have it omitted in the school; the place could never last without it. In our prayers we are daily reminded of what we know in our heart of heart are our Duties and our Ideals. They help us to exalt the powers of the soul towards its completeness. At prayer we look, so to speak, into a bright mirror and behold afar off the ideal type we would imitate, and should, in fact, be like. It is then that we are seized with passionate yearning, with sorrow or joy, with courage or despair. It is then we feel remorse—the true judgment and penalty, and first step towards redemption. It is then we make new resolutions. These moments are our real 'religious lessons.' Pray do not imagine that these contain denunciations or exhortations merely about Sins, Godlessness, and Unbelief. If any one should preach much to children about sins, and bring before them the dogma of the atoning death of Christ (based upon observations of the general sinfulness of mankind and their supposed incapacity for good), we should say his educational wisdom appeared to us doubtful and even dangerous. For he discourages, when he should encourage; he produces a sort of moral sloth and spiritual easy-goingness, when he should spur on to moral effort. Our religious education is not an imitation of the conventional and traditional system of many clergymen. But have the majority of these been taught how to get hold of, and to care for, the souls of the young? Our 'Divinity lesson,' we believe, possesses this peculiarity, that it inculcates, not theory, but practice. At such moments we do not trouble about the folded hands of the boys, or the peculiar garments of the Teacher. The difference between teacher and taught has vanished, or been forgotten. As we stand, boys and masters, facing one another, we strive to think of ourselves as at the most, Prophets and Disciples, Novices and Initiates. And do you not think that such 'Divinity Lessons' are better and easier to give, and to apply, than yours, or those of other Schoolmasters and Clergymen? Here it is, that our highest duties and ideals as educators are to be found. Do not imagine we fancy by any means we have reached perfection. No, but that at least we are striving to attain unceasingly, and with all our might. The problem of religious instruction adapted for the present epoch is, in fact, by no means yet solved. It has, in many ways, not even yet been adequately stated. In nothing, throughout the great realm of education on the Continent of Europe and far beyond its limits, will there be greater changes than in this. That is our conviction."

It was already very late and time to separate for the night. "We will say 'good night,' for to-morrow we must be up betimes and be again at our posts fresh and alert," remarked the masters, as they left the guest with a friendly hand-shake.

CHAPTER XI.

HERR NAMREH'S REFLECTIONS.

HERR NAMREH was now left alone in the Common Room. Deep in thought he sat down before the open fireplace. It seemed as if a new world had opened to him. He was forced to smile at the beliefs of some people he had met in earlier days who fancied they had reached perfection in their educational knowledge and practice. It seemed to him as though some brightly shining stars had indeed long since risen above the horizon, but that mankind had been too blind to behold them, too void of feeling to observe them, or to draw from them consolation and help. For how infinitely little of the ideals of the great Educators of all peoples and all times had he seen realised upon earth.

For most people, they appeared never indeed to have lived. But in this school, it seemed to him, there were some illumined by their light. Would it were so everywhere! What if only the sun could break through, victoriously driving away the mists and darkness which still dominated the wide field of education! What if only the educative wisdom of the Great Masters of the past were to be translated from books into facts! Like a heavy burden there weighed down upon him the consciousness of the magnitude and multitude of problems imperiously demanding solution. Then gathering himself together once more, with an effort, he cried, "Here at least a beginning has been made by the work of brave pioneers."

After all that he had seen and done that day, Namreh felt very tired ; but he could not, nevertheless, omit, before retiring to rest, to write, as he sat before the fire, the following memoranda in his diary. Afterwards, on longer acquaintance with the school, he found them to be absolutely true.

It appears to me to-night as though I had spent a day in a small Ideal State. How I wish that everything in the great world were arranged as it is in this small community!

How healthy are the citizens, and how excellently is their work adapted to the age of each! How well they organise their little world! How courageously they fought for it in the football battle! How keen they were in practising for the match beforehand! What a fine thing it is for them that they are warriors, artists, labourers, craftsmen, government officials, teachers, judges, and merchants, all in one!

In all they did, they were, moreover, by no means mere bunglers. Considering their age, they showed quite decent proficiency. Of course some were better than others, say, as organisers. But thus they showed precisely which profession in the big world would some day best suit them, What splendid comradeship reigned in this State! To me that appeared to be the prevailing idea in it. How kindly the older boys helped the youngsters at their work! I felt in this little State as though I had joined a large family. A common love for worth, ability, and thoroughness seemed to bind all its members together. How admirably did the union of merriment and courage, shown in their games, contrast and harmonise with the energy and practical skill shown in their manual labour, and the quiet cheerfulness displayed in their artistic work, with their attentive eagerness in class, and their proud, but modest, self-control in everything. I was relieved to find here, at last, none of that selfish irritability which always forebodes some evil intention against itself; none of that slavish feeling, which does not dare, with steady gaze and voice, to express its own inclinations; none of that childish hypocrisy which, void of will, void of ideas, and void of decent pluck, stands abject before authority, only to make a senseless boast of independence behind its back;

none of that lack of responsiveness and freshness (sure sign of unhealthy precocity or premature collapse) which I had so often, to my great sorrow, met with among boys in other places. Instead of that I found in them alertness, elasticity, and fertility of mind—good augury that they will have the courage, and the strength, to carve their way through life with success, be that way rough or smooth, be it at home, or among strangers across the ocean.

What a blessing it was that here the scholars were spared the spectacle of masters "kneiping" in the taverns and playing "Skat;" that here temperance was not looked at with contempt, but with respect—in fact was taken as a matter of course. Excellent too it was, that sickly, broken-down, nervous, pale-faced creatures, only half able to see and hear, were not put here as educators, to live before the gaze of unbroken and uncorrupted youth; but, on the contrary, powerful and manly figures. Good it is, too, that these masters not only read and tell of the ancient Athenians, Romans, and Germans, their games at Olympia, and their exercises in the Campus Martius; but, above all things, can themselves join the boys in fencing, wrestling, running, and swimming. That they do not merely talk about health in the Hygiene lesson, but are themselves healthy. Would that all teachers would prefer intercourse with their pupils, and the practical application of their noble art and science, Pedagogics, to the dead bookishness they delight in and the frequenting of the public-house![1]

---

[1] In one of the most famous schools of Germany, recently visited by myself with one of my colleagues, we were shown by the boys a magnificent building which had been built and fitted up by the masters for Kegelbahn (skittles) for their own exclusive use. The boys pointed out

It is a good thing too that the master here does not excuse himself from the teacher's proper work by saying: "I have no time for intercourse and play with boys; I have enough to occupy me with my own family." Here—with the exception of one—the masters are unmarried. Like the brothers of the good old order of Monks, they devote themselves entirely to the work of education, and do not suffer themselves to be diverted from it by anything. But they do not lack a family; the boys are their children, their colleagues are their brothers; and there is no lack of the softening and refining influence of women. The Monarch and his Ministers, moreover, know and feel that a tremendous responsibility rests upon them, that they must set the highest example. They know that their noble calling is at once that of Prophet and of King: that each must hold to this ideal, live up to it, and make it, as far as in him lies, incarnate before his boys: that each must strive to be to them father and brother, physician and priest.

All take part, therefore, as comrades, in the pleasures, griefs, and struggles, the work and the play, of those entrusted to them. At the same time they seek to make themselves unnecessary, and their pupils, as far as possible, independent and fit to become their own guides.

From their young friends they expect no tasks, whether

---

with glee at one end the "tap-room," adding: "That is where the masters retire, between the games, to drink and rest after their exertions." Not far from this building we were shown the sacred spot where the Primaner (Sixth Form Boys) were lying under the trees smoking long German pipes. This privilege they jealously guard; but occasionally they allow a Secondaner (Fifth Form Boy) to smoke as a special reward for having backed up their authority. Premature smoking, with all its consequences, is thus pretty well ensured. (TRANSLATOR.)

mental or moral, which they do not, could not, or would not, undertake themselves.

How is this good result achieved at Emlohstobba? Football and other Games alone would do it just as little as excessive cramming of mere knowledge. A few hours a week of Slöyd and Handicraft, three more pictures for each class, a statuette or two, a magic lantern, or four more music lessons all round : all this will not, by a long way, lead to the regeneration of mankind.

The pedagogic talent, which is revealed here in every part of the Educational plan ; the proper sequence of studies and the intimate interlocking of all parallel sections of the work ; the consistent organisation of even the smallest details, in order to realise the highest Educational Ideal ; the courageous abandonment of every custom and convention, of every subject and method, which does not work for this Ideal ; the acceptance—often inspired solely by Faith and Hope—of the proper materials for study and of the true methods for teaching, and their skilful employment ; the entire daily life of the School-state, the spirit pervading the whole Community, and the complete devotion of everybody to their great task—to all these the success of Emlohstobba is due.

To me it appears, that we have here the fundamental requisites of a satisfactory school. Its burghers would assuredly not wish to pose as faultless models of virtue. But it is evident that they are following the best course, the boys to become, and the masters to remain, really capable men and useful citizens.

Do they, then, at Emlohstobba, want to put back civilisation ten centuries or more, and return to the days of rude Barbarism ? Certainly not. But they despise—or rather deeply regret—the present unnatural division of men into two great classes—the slaves of manual toil, and the slaves of learning (both the big and little Heroes of the Arm-chair), who are ever poring over books. Here they are absolutely convinced that the great social questions of to-day will never be solved, nor the social gulf between classes and masses bridged over, until the student of words can use plane and hatchet, spade and football, as well as pen, and paper, and books. Nor that it will be solved until the mill-hand knows how to overcome the mental and moral paralysis which threatens to destroy him, without possibility of escape, unless he ceases to work day after day, like a mere machine, polishing, it may be, all the year round, nothing but points of pins, and unless he can acquire the leisure and the taste to enjoy intellectual and artistic recreation. Nor yet will it be solved until we study the social condition of Modern nations with that ardour and exactness, which we have until now squandered almost exclusively upon merely two *languages* of the ancient world.

Dull machine-slaves and arm-chair philosophers will never understand, nor like, each other. Both are slowly but surely approaching their doom. The latter will not escape it by becoming Mill-hands themselves for three months—though that, of course, would be an excellent experience for all our learned friends—nor by making everlasting speeches, or lengthy books, about the social question. We must have the courage to introduce the health and strength of earlier times into our modern world of science and industry, of steam and electricity; we must bring back into our modern life all the noble ideals of the past, of our German and Scandinavian forefathers and of the Romans, Athenians, and Hebrews.

And we must make working models of the new civilisation we would create, by founding small Communities, such as Schools, in which the fusion of ancient and modern virtues may be accomplished, and the results made manifest to all.

By this means our modern Civilisation may be preserved from decay. Otherwise, like that of the highly-cultured Roman world, it will perish.

Do we not already hear from East and furthest West, the dull, distant rumblings of the gathering storm? (I do not refer to France.) Are we still so blind that we cannot see the signs which announce the opening of a new Epoch —like that when the Migrations of the Barbarians overwhelmed the Roman Empire? A civilisation, under which people are daily getting weaker and less sensible, more unhealthy, more unnatural and effeminate, must go to perdition—even though it possess the highest possible degree of material wealth.

Let it be, therefore, our Ideal to combine mental and moral with physical excellence, *Mens sana in corpore sano!*

Germany cannot be too happy, too proud, or too thankful, that he, who some day may have to lead, not Germany alone, but perhaps Northern and Western Europe too, as Generalissimo in war against the hordes of Asia, has already, years before, pointed out the aim and means which must be adopted, to save Europe from the Modern Huns.

This is why we should follow him. He demands a vigorous youth.

He has painted a picture and interpreted it with the legend, " Peoples of Europe, unite ! "

Do you, Heads of Schools, suppose you are following him, while you still prefer to study, just the same as before, the ancient culture, which our German forefathers hated as they hated nought else upon this world, and a race which a thousand times they found untrue and faithless; rather than the life and character of our neighbours and blood relations, the English?

Do you suppose that this absolutely necessary Pan-European alliance,—announced with a prophetic instinct as if by some German sage of yore,—between the Nations which safeguard the Culture of Europe, can take place so long as our youth, who have to stand in the first ranks of our people, cannot speak the language of our neighbours and cousins, the English, and have not the remotest conception of their Culture or their Character?

One must lament that such a reminder of danger was necessary from without. For our first duty as Teachers is to form our plans solely with regard to the peaceful development of our Country internally. But in the future, even more than in the past, there is a foe within to conquer, who is harder to beat than any foreign enemy. (I do not speak of any party. Political questions do not concern Educational Science). There is that terrible state of misery to remove by peaceful, moral, civilising work; and those vices to destroy which arise out of the ever-increasing struggle for existence: Materialism, Slavishness, Unmercifulness, Hypocrisy, and Theft.

Our duty is to help the innumerable weaklings who, in this murderous internal struggle, are threatened with death both of Body and Soul.

Our duty is, first and foremost, to save our own bodies and souls from the ever-increasing Might of Evil.

All this needs a sturdy Youth, and, therefore, needs a New System of Education.

Turn back, then, while there is yet time! Or the cry may be heard, "It is too late!"

CHAPTER XII.

NAMREH'S DREAM IN EMLOHSTOBBA, AT DEAD OF NIGHT.

At this point Namreh's pen falls from his hand. Slowly he sinks back in his chair before the fire, and after the unusual exertions of the day falls placidly asleep.

Then he has an extraordinary dream.

He sees a mighty funeral pile, and upon it blazing a vast accumulation of books. Here and there he can still snatch one from the conflagration, and would fain save a few. He looks at one. It is a Latin Prose exercise-book belonging to a Third Form boy of twelve. It contains far more red than black ink. He flings it instantly back into the flames.

"Ah!" he thinks as he picks up another, "here is a treasure worth saving!" But the book, whose countless rules and endless annotations disgust him is Parry's "Greek Grammar." "Not another second shall you plague boys," he cries, and throws it into the very middle of the fire.

"Here is a third, and so beautifully bound; what a pity to burn it!" But it is an "Historical Primer," and Namreh recalls the long and weary hours in which it once quenched his love of history. With delight he hurls it into the blaze, for he remembers that day on which he began a new existence, the day when he took his first draught from the living Sources of history, and when for the first time his astonished mind grasped the great fundamental ideas of Historical Philosophy.

After failing thus to find anything worth keeping, he had well-nigh lost the wish to try any more. But from where he was, he could still read the titles on the covers; nothing but "Grammars," "Sets of Exercises," "Primers"—nothing whatever but books for cramming the memory and making the mind mechanical and dull. Namreh turned in his sleep and smiled, for he thought in his dream how splendidly they blazed.

"What," he cries again, "is this enormous heap, not yet fully alight?" With some trouble and danger to himself, he extricates with an iron rod a few fat Blue Books. He reads. They are "Regulations for Schools and Colleges," from the Ministry of Education. With a shudder he gazes at the mass of confused rubbish and bewildering names collected there; long-winded, obscure directions for "Elementary Schools," "National Schools," "Continuation Schools," "Technical Schools," "Public Schools," "Great Public Schools," "Endowed Grammar Schools," "Third Grade Schools," "Public Day Schools," "Intermediate Schools," "Preparatory Schools," "Board Schools," "Higher Board Schools," "Higher Grade Board Schools," "Polytechnic Schools," "Technological Schools," "Art Schools," "Handicraft Schools," "Schools of Technical Art," "Commercial Schools," "Higher Commercial Schools," "Voluntary Schools," "Church Schools," "Upper Grade Secondary Schools," "Lower Grade Secondary Schools," "High Schools," "Higher Schools," "High-Class Schools," "First-class Schools," "Seventh Standard Schools," "Proprietary Schools," and "Private Schools"; directions for "Artizans' Institutes,"

"Mechanics' Institutes," "Central Institutions," "Colleges of Science," "Agricultural Colleges," "Provincial Colleges," "Colonial Colleges," "Staff Colleges," "Training Colleges," "Higher Training Colleges," "Affiliated Colleges," "University Colleges," "Naval Colleges," "Universities," and "Teaching Universities"; directions for "Assistant Masters' Associations," "Headmasters' Associations," "Preparatory Schoolmasters' Associations," "Private Schoolmasters' Associations," "Public Schools Assistant Masters' Associations," "National Associations," "Technical Education Associations," "Headmasters' Conferences," "Science and Art Departments," "Education Departments," and for "Committees of the Secret Council on Education"; regulations for entrance examinations for the Army, Navy, Civil Service, Colonial Service and Woods and Forests; regulations for examinations for Scholarships, Sizarships, Postmasterships, Demiships, Studentships, Fellowships, Lectureships, Exhibitions, Bursaries, and Prizes.

A still greater disgust, however, overwhelms him when he fails to find anywhere among these regulations what to him is the most indispensable thing of all. With a cry of horror he flings the whole pile into the centre of the burning mass.

One book alone he keeps, for it seems worth having. It was the Report of the Great Conference of the Teachers' Guild in the Capital of the Empire. In it he found at least some sensible educational ideas. And then he picked up the "New Scheme of Work for Secondary Schools," which, in consequence of that Report, had been elaborated at a recent Headmasters' Conference.

Alas! in many ways it failed to put into practice the

better ideas contained in the Report. Still, compared with earlier schemes, it showed signs of some improvement.

Both of these books, therefore, he kept, anxiously regarding them as a pledge and earnest of that better education which his sanguine spirit anticipated would come some day.

In his dreams Namreh sees millions of children dancing, delirious with joy, around this mighty bonfire. A crowd of persons, most wearing spectacles and all an angry frown, essay to quell these deafening shouts. Are they the teachers of bygone centuries, or of this?

But what are these men whose silvery hair and venerable looks are so conspicuous among the curly-headed ruddy youths? They are looking on with smiles. Nay, can it be believed, they are helping in the work. Is not that Komensky? Is not this Pestalozzi? And this Herbart? Are not those there Rousseau, Fröbel, Old Jahn, and Arndt; these here Locke, Milton, Thomas Arnold, and these Spencer, Carlyle, and Ruskin? On the far side, stand colossal forms of Cranmer, Knox, and Luther. They are hurling their own Catechisms and Prayer Books into the flames as vigorously and joyfully as did Luther, in days gone by, the Papal Bull. Namreh hears them, he fancies, crying derisively, " Burn away fast, your day is done : had we guessed how fools would misuse you, and children suffer from you, we would have perished ere we wrote you."

Yet once more he descries a group—it seems like a sickly crowd of " classical philologists "—for he hears a wail of anguish as they bemoan this deed of Vandalism, this obscurantic fiery holocaust, amid which *their* world of culture, art, and science, crumbles in final dissolution.

But, on a sudden, there is silence. For, like a Phœnix, rising aloft out of the quivering flames, appears a majestic youthful Form, his body sheathed in glistening armour, and on his dazzling helm a golden crown. Announced by clash of arms and trumpet blast Heralds spring swiftly forth, and amid deafening acclamations proclaim the accession of a new Monarch—destined to give to a dying world an *Education which shall teach men to Live*.

CHAPTER XIII.

NAMREH WAKES UP AT SUNRISE.

A LOUD bell rings. The sleeper starts up, full of alarm after his weird dream. That awful fire and those shouts, mingling in his dream with the noise of the bell, have terrified him.

Wherever is he? Namreh glances towards the window. In the far east the sun is climbing the heavens slowly and majestically. The mists in the valley which had shrouded the meadows are melting away, and now the entire stretch of beautiful landscape shimmers and sparkles before his eyes in the morning splendour. All round he sees and hears new awakening life.

Hark! he hears clear voices of boys, singing joyfully their morning hymn. Birds add their notes to the concert of praise, and the sounds reverberate back from the wooded hills, in honour of the Most High.

Presently, below his window, he sees the crowd of cheery lads rush by for their morning run. In a moment he is below, to greet them on their return.

He gazes keenly and searchingly into their eyes. In their midst, he feels once more alive. His mind recalls those venerable countenances and that majestic youthful Form of his dream. They too would look down, he thinks, smiling and well-pleased, upon these youths. He cries aloud, "Let the Old perish, if only the New is like this! Instead of Stones, let our youth at last have Bread!"

The fire of his dreams now seems to him like the morning brightness of a new day—the Beacon-signal announcing the Palingenesis of true Education.

CHAPTER XIV.

DREAM OR FACT?

"AND is all this book only a dream too?"

Probably the Gentle Reader now asks: "Where can I go to find such an Educational Kingdom? Must I make a balloon, or must I seek for this spot with Nansen in the Far North, or wait until the year Two Thousand?"

"Not so. What I have written is neither mere phantasy, nor yet Prophet Vision. The School-state, described above, has real existence."

"Where, then, in all the world is this Emlohstobba?"

I answer: "Everywhere under God's sky, on God's fair earth, where a band of men and boys, with healthy bodies and healthy minds, are dedicating, with enthusiasm, the full strength and virgin energies of body, soul, and spirit to the glorious work of Education: where a band of teachers following nought in all the wide world but this one aim, without thought of selfish ease or selfish enjoyment, without thought of their own deserts or their own fame; but led solely by love and sympathy for the young, are knit together by the unalterable resolve to help in the development of a higher and healthier generation; where a band of teachers, trained for this work from their boyhood by an all-round, sane, and wholesome life, have grown up in a free country among free men; where this noble Fellowship, sustained by the common worship of Ideals like these, is allowed to follow its high calling, unvexed by the cramping fussiness and meddling authority of those who do not understand.

"Go, then, each one of you, and seek each his own Emlohstobba. I trust you will find many."

But you reply: "I have neither time nor opportunity for a further search. Nor am I quite convinced I should find what I seek. So tell me, at least, of one Emlohstobba. When I have seen one, I will believe there may be more. If you cannot name one, I shall have to suppose you have deceived me, and that all this time you have been relating a mere pedagogic 'Two thousand years hence!'"

I must, therefore, do what you ask.

"I should have been better pleased, however, not to have named the place. You in Germany are too far away, and, besides, the main thing is, not the Name of the school, but the Ideal it represents and symbolises. Mere personal or local interests do not concern us: not the name of the school, but only the pedagogic Principle.

"People, however, have got so used to the old traditions of the Middle Ages, that they can scarce believe in the new ideas, which the changed conditions of modern life demand. They require to see with bodily eyes, and to hear with bodily ears, before they can bring themselves to believe that the Ideals and Principles described above are practicable.

"Any such may read the names mentioned in this book from right to left. They will then discover the Place where I have found these Ideals realised in comparative perfection.

"I trust you have not, like inquisitive Novel-reading young ladies, already turned over the last few pages. But even if not, you have doubtless long since guessed that the country wherein our School-state lies is the British Isles. If you would see The New School Abbotsholme, you must travel north-west from London, viâ Derby, for four hours by rail, to the little town of Rocester. Your visit will be right welcome in this Kingdom on the river Dove. For also in their hospitality the English are true descendants of the old Anglo-Saxons.

"Other Emlohstobbas, in other lands, you can now seek out and name.

"For me it is enough to have shown that *one* exists. Its existence proves that such Schools are possible. That is the main thing.

"One is enough for my proof. It may be that there are more elsewhere, which realise these ideals even better. If so, Abbotsholme will feel no greater joy than in learning from them, and the World at large will be all the more interested to hear that this New Type of School is finding recognition.

"I have not, in the least, attempted to give in this book an outline of the main features of English Education. On that subject you can read the excellent *Letters* [1] by Wiese—particularly the first part. You may study also with advantage the 'Zeitschrift of Foreign Educational Conditions.'

"If you do, you will find that this School possesses many of the peculiarities characteristic of the English 'Public School'; but you will also find much more which is totally different.

"It has not been my intention, however, to attempt a complete scientific exposition of the Ideals even of this School.

"In England they love to start with *deeds*, and to develop their Theories inductively from their Facts. The Ideals of Abbotsholme have already stood the test of seven years, and we have been for many months busy putting the results into systematic order.

"The present book only attempts to paint a few pictures to illustrate the life and ideals of this type of school.

"It is very incomplete. The Guest must not pass merely one day here; he must live many days in our midst, and in summer as well as in winter.

"Then he will get a complete picture."

---

[1] "Deutsche Briefe über Englische Erziehung." Von Dr. Wiese, Wiegard und Grieben, Berlin, 1877.

CHAPTER XV.

IS THIS A TYPICAL SCHOOL OF THE FUTURE.

THE question now arises : Is Abbotsholme to be regarded as one of the best types of Secondary Schools of the future?

That it possesses pedagogic completeness it by no means supposes, for it knows that no such thing as perfection exists upon this earth. But it is conscious of being animated by an inconquerable determination to attain the highest degree of efficiency possible. For seven and more years it has steadily and silently pursued the great aims above described, and is still pressing onward with the unexhausted energy of youth. It tests its work constantly, and, as soon as better methods are found, adopts them. For it believes that the worst blunder a school can commit is to fall behind the age, or to share in its faults. The aim of Secondary Education it conceives to be this : to train the new generation of well-born boys to avoid the evils of false or excessive culture, so that by pressing on, like true pioneers, before the march of civilisation they may render themselves fit Leaders of the Nation in the ever-increasing struggle for existence.

Abbotsholme is not concerned to claim the doubtful advantage of complete originality. Its feeling is rather that of filial gratitude to all the great Masters of Educational Art and Science—and not merely those of its own land, such as Wyckham, Ascham, Mulcaster, Milton, Locke, Arnold, Ellis, Carlyle, Spencer, and Ruskin, but at least equally those of other countries, such as Rabelais, Montaigne, and Rousseau ; Ratke, Komensky,

Pestalozzi, and Mazzini ; Fröbel, Ziller, Stoy, Dörpfeld, Rein, and Willmann.

Its practical aim is to combine the best educational results achieved by the German, French, and Anglo-Saxon nationalities. It wishes to bring to their fullest development body and soul, intellect and heart, practical craft and creative imagination, without losing the harmony and unity of the character.

The boy who at eighteen has tasted some of the best thoughts of Hebrew, Hellenic, and Christian Antiquity, and has drunk of the choicest vintage of Italian, French, and Spanish, German, Norse, and Anglo-Saxon Literature ; who besides telescope and microscope, can use pencil and violin ; who is at home not only in Library, Museum, or Laboratory, but also in Workshop or Garden, Farmyard or Forest ; the boy who can run and jump, dance and sing ; who is at ease in river or boat ; who can cast a line and bring down a bird on the wing ; the boy to whom the Geography and History and Institutions of his Fatherland are not unexplored continents ; the boy who knows how to live healthily, and how to defy, not only wind and weather, but the demoralising influences of modern life—this boy does not belong in the least to the regions of fable ; he is the realisable Ideal of our School.

FINIS.

17. OUR BOATS. (*Summer, 1892*).

Copyright

FOREWORD, AS AFTERWORD,

TO THE GERMAN EDITION.

WHEN studying at the University of Göttingen, I was struck with the able teaching I observed in many German Educational Institutions, and with the admirable organisation of public affairs throughout Germany. This was by no means confined to military matters, but was equally noticeable, or even more so, in what I may call the organisation of peace, that is to say, in the every-day affairs of ordinary life.

I had already, mainly through the teaching of Carlyle and Ruskin, had my faith in the saving efficacy of English methods of national organisation shattered. And on my return from abroad, set before me as Educational Ideal to combine the German talent for organisation with our English love of freedom and self-reliance—supposing such union to be possible.

We English, certainly, do not sufficiently understand corporate life. You Germans are not sufficiently accustomed to stand alone. If the virtues of both could be blended in each, a more capable generation would grow up on both sides of the German Ocean, and the two chief branches of the great Teutonic family—the one greatest on land—the other greatest on sea—could, if knit in friendly alliance, deliver Europe from the absurdity and crime of internecine war; and, leading her in the paths of peace towards larger and deeper living, furnish an example of virtue and wisdom to the whole Earth.

The present moment is propitious for such an alliance. His Majesty, the German Emperor, is half an Englishman. He has already shown this by his practical and energetic initiative, in the most varied walks of life. His present unpopularity arises from this fact, and from the circumstance that the unwholesome democratic unrest of the age prefers a vicious millionaire, who flatters its ignorant pretensions, to a virtuous sovereign who understands the necessity of leadership. This remarkable Prince affords us an example of true manliness.

Upon the throne of England is still seated—thank God—the venerable lady who is his grandmother. As example of the old English, and also old Germanic, womanly virtues, she is beloved by our whole race, and respected, nay venerated, by the entire world.

The Imperial Houses are thus intimately related, and the two Peoples should become, as of old, Brothers.

The movement towards this intimacy was begun as early as the middle of this century, chiefly by two men. One stood next the English throne itself. The other was son of a Craftsman—a Son of the People—but Prince in the Empire of the Spirit.

The departed husband of the Queen—Albert the Good—Prince Consort—whose gifts were only fully appreciated after his untimely death, was a German, and yet the father of all future Kings of England and future Emperors of the British World-Dominion.

Thomas Carlyle—the greatest Prophet of England in this century—drew no little of his inspiration from the history and literature of Germany. He was the immortal Historian of the great Frederick, England's quondam friend. Clad like an Elisha in the mantle of his Elijah, Göthe—one of Germany's greatest sons—he imparted to the English world the quintessence of the supreme epoch of Germany's spiritual evolution. He was the writer who led the English language back to its native strength in the creative fount of Teutonic idiom, and announced the glad tidings of the German Illumination in true German, but at the same time Old English, expression.

Let us follow their good examples. Every people, as every man, must go to pieces, if it remains alone and works in isolation.

Germany never could do this, for she has ever been the Heart of Europe. We English dare never more attempt it. We are no longer insulated inhabitants upon a few islands in the Atlantic; we have become citizens of an Empire which encircles the whole earth.

But an alliance between Germany and England alone, would not suffice. Both nations must attempt to combine, as far as may be, German deductive thought, depth of feeling and organising talent, and English inductive thought, self-control, strength of will, and power to observe and apply, with French imagination and power of lucid expression.

In Abbotsholme we are trying to realise this combination, in order that we may learn to understand the distinctive features of the three nations and thereby awake respect and high appreciation—and, if possible, friendship—between them.

As regards the School. If Germany, on the one hand, teaches us the best method of instruction, we on the other hand can, I think, furnish you with a picture of harmonious education. Let us combine the best German School-*instruction* with the best all-round English School-*life*. Then we shall have the perfect Educative School as it appeared to the imagination ot a Herbart and a Ruskin.

It is not by a hostile competition of shopkeepers, nor

by envy and jealousy, but by friendly intercourse and coöperation, that all nations of the earth will attain some day to the Ideal of Divine Humanity.

In this hope, at least, we English and Germans are working here together.

CECIL REDDIE, B.Sc. Edin., Ph.D. Gött.,
Founder and Headmaster of The New School Abbotsholme.

ABBOTSHOLME, DERBYSHIRE, ENGLAND.
End of Nov., 1896.

LIST OF REVIEWS AND CRITICISMS ON *EMLOHSTOBBA*.

No.	Name.	Place.	Date.
1.	Letter from L. R. (Pfarrer).	Chur, Switzerland.	June 12, 1897.
2.	Letter from Pedagogic Seminar of the University of Jena, signed by Prof. Rein and forty members.		June 15, 1897.
3.	Criticism by a German Professor of Pedagogics.		June 20, 1897.
4.	Criticisms upon *Emlohstobba* by the Director of a German Gymnasium.		June 28, 1897.
5.	Scotsman.	Edinburgh.	June 28, 1897.
6.	Rostocker Anzeiger.	Rostock.	July 1, 1897.
7.	Manchester Guardian.	Manchester.	July 6, 1897.
8.	Allgemeine Litterarische Rundschau.	Berlin.	August 1, 1897.
9.	Tägliche Rundschau.	Berlin.	August 4, 1897.
10.	Naturwissenschaftliche Wochenschrift.		August 22, 1897.
11.	Die Frau.	Berlin.	September 1, 1897.
12.	Versöhnung.	Berlin.	September 1, 1897.
13.	Letter from Dr. H. Stoy.	Jena.	September 13, 1897.

German Verdicts

No.	Name.	Place.	Date.
14.	Die Hilfe.	Berlin.	January 23, 1898.
15.	Jahresbericht der Erziehungs-Anstalt zu Keilhau.		April, 1898.
16.	Pädagogisches Monatsblatt.	Leipzig.	April, 1898.
17.	Die Wage.	Wien, Leipzig, Berlin.	August 20, 1898.

SOME ADDITIONAL CRITICISMS ON *EMLOHSTOBBA*.

No.	Paper.	Title.	Date.
1.	Königlich privilegirte Berliner Zeitung.	Warum sind uns die Angelsachsen überlegen.	July 1, 1897.
2.	Mässigkeits-Blätter.	Das letzte Fuder Heu.	August 1, 1897.
3.	Der Hausdoctor.	Emlohstobba.	August 1, 1897.
4.	Pester Lloyd.	Der Schulstaat Emlohstobba.	August 29, 1897.
5.	Deutsche Volksstimme.	Emlohstobba.	November 1, 1897.
6	Deutsche Zeitschrift für Ausländisches Unterrichtswesen.	Unter : Bücherschau.	January 1, 1898.
7.	Leipziger Lehrerzeitung.	Die Schule der Zukunft.	March 2, 1898.

FROM A CLERGYMAN AND PEDAGOGUE OF SWITZERLAND, THE LAND OF PESTALOZZI.

CHUR, *June* 12, 1897.

DEAR SIR AND FRIEND,—*Emlohstobba* (it requires some thought to spell the name right) was lent to me by Professor S—— before I was able to buy it for myself. It has given me some delightful hours. To you is given to speak out what has been working in the hearts of many, who have had neither the courage nor the ability to express it. Truly a great work ! Perhaps I am too enthusiastic, but I should like to say that, in any future history of pedagogics, this little book must be named along with the classic writings of Salzmann, Pestalozzi, Herbart, Zilla, and Spencer. You have had a glorious opportunity of combining the best that scientific pedagogics have yet given to the world, in the structure raised by Herbart and Ziller upon the foundations of Pestalozzi with the school life of England, to form an ideal system for the future.

There is, as your study of philosophy must long ago have taught you, a wide discrepancy between Herbart's intellectual philosophy and his pedagogics. The latter makes entirely for freedom. The error lies in this, that far too great an influence upon the formation of character is ascribed to the intellect. Instruction can hardly contribute much to the education of the will upon the plane of intellect, and scarcely anything to the education of the true ethical will. The strength and health of personality, which we desire and aim at above all things, can be developed only in a school life such as Abbotsholme offers, and such as I too can imagine to some extent.

The first part of your work reads like a romance, or perhaps I should say a fairy tale, but a fairy tale which refreshes one's soul. We live in an age of social Utopias. A pedagogic Utopia is, if possible, even more needful, and, as your Utopia already approaches so closely to existing facts, so much the better.

The criticisms in your second part are certainly not too sharp, at least my experience bears you out. My special gratitude is due to you for your support in the fight against alcohol. You have, in short, done a service for which old E. M. Arndt, in the Islands of the Blest, will give you such a handshake, that you would fare badly if you had not played, rowed, and boxed so valiantly in England.

And now I wonder what the loyal Germans will say about it; I am myself often angry with them in spite of, or rather in consequence of, the fact that I am German to the core. Still in any case it is you who will be right, even though you have to wait a little. Meanwhile we of the young cohort look to you as a bold and stout leader into the Promised Land of better times.

L. R. (Pfarrer), Chur, Switzerland.

The Pedagogic Seminary of the University of Jena sends hearty greetings to Dr. Lietz, and thanks for his interesting book *Emlohstobba*, coupled with the hope that the healthy principles he has there laid down for the education of a strong, independent, and vigorous race may be widely spread and find a speedy fulfilment.

Signed by Professor Rein, *Director of the Seminary*, and forty teachers from various lands.

CRITICISM OF "EMLOHSTOBBA" BY A GERMAN PROFESSOR OF PEDAGOGICS.

Your book is so refreshing and has such a healthy tone, that one will easily pardon any flights of imagination. Many in this country of course will not know how to make use of it, because they lack enthusiasm for real education, and are too bound up with the ideas of mere instruction or getting knowledge. They have refused to learn from Nature, and only care to consider the conventional ideas of man.

CRITICISM UPON "EMLOHSTOBBA," BY THE DIREKTOR OF A GERMAN GYMNASIUM.

Your book *Emlohstobba*, which has lately appeared, has given me great pleasure. I have for years fought for these same ideals, and have endeavoured to win the victory for them. For my own part I have no doubt that our school system is tending towards the physical and moral ruin of the nation.

Our one-sided brain work, our total disregard of Physiology and Psychology, our fatal mistake of subordinating everything to knowledge —knowledge which is not acquired by reasoning or logical processes, but simply learned by heart and crammed, these can result in no blessing to any race.

I quite agree with what you say of the connection between the instruction-school (*Unterrichtsschule*) and the tavern. If this tavern-loafing is not checked, we must surely fall. The man who can infuse into our boys a greater love of God's fresh air and wholesome nature, will do his country incalculable service.

You will surely remember the Educational Conference of 1890, and the words of H.M. the Emperor at the opening. His speech awoke in every German heart the hope that now at last the German nation was to have an educational system suited to its peculiar genius, and at the same time suited to the needs of the close of the nineteenth century.
am sorry to say that the result of the conference has been very different from what the Emperor's words led us to hope. The reason is not far to seek. Herr von Gossler, the Minister of Education, had picked men to carry out his own views. If the Pope, in the days of Luther, had assembled his cardinals to consult about the reform of the Church, you can imagine what sort of Reformation we should have had.

I have not, however, given up hope of reform in our schools, and comfort myself with Schiller's words : "Long years and centuries may the mummy last, till time and necessity tap at the empty shell." That the education shell is empty there is no doubt.

Had I the necessary means, and were everything in this country not dependent upon certain certificates, I would send my boys not to a German school but to Abbotsholme ; however, £100 a year is too much for my circumstances, though I consider that sort of education well worth the sum.

F. S.

Scotsman (Edinburgh), *June* 28, 1897.

From Berlin comes a book entitled *Emlohstobba*. It is further described by its author, in the vague German in which it is written throughout, as "Romance or Reality?" and, except that it is clearly the work of an educationist with aspirations towards the founding of an ideal school for the upbringing of the young, is rather a nebulous and misty production. It inculcates in a series of chapters half descriptive, half hortatory, the necessity of combining the English love of independence with the German thoroughness and disciplinarianism in matters educational ; and it draws its most highly-coloured pictures of the perfect school from an English institution. It has photographic pictures that show happy groups of young people engaged in various forms of agricultural and *technical labour* at a fine place in the country ; and *it discusses most known theories of education in the light of a capital plan of schooling.* The book should prove both useful and interesting to those who can read German and are concerned to let the Germans know what they can learn from this country as to the best way of keeping school.

Rostocker Anzeiger, *July* 1, 1897.

Emlohstobba is the fancy title of a book which Dr. Lietz has just published. At first we thought the book was a sequel of Bellamy's *Looking Backward,* and were inclined to turn away from it with disappointment ; but the pictures at the end, reproduced from photographs, were clearly not those of the future, so we began to read the book.

After looking through it casually we felt compelled to study the contents more closely. Is there in reality such a Model School existing as the book describes, where the Latin proverb, "Mens sana in corpore sano," is put into practice? Rouse up, you fossilised pedagogues, you who pretend to direct the race and cure social evils by your scientific phrases, religious dogmas, and needless accessories. Read this book, and get an insight into the fact that the time has come to break with the antiquated system, in order that a new day may dawn for education. Or, better still, go to Emlohstobba; it is not in the moon, but is Abbotsholme, in Derbyshire, England. There you can learn something. When you return thence you will carry back new ideas, and the German schools, too, will thrive and become a blessing to the Fatherland.

MANCHESTER GUARDIAN, *July* 6, 1897.

Under the title of *Emlohstobba: Roman oder Wirklichkeit?* Dr. Hermann Lietz has written an enthusiastic description of The New School, Abbotsholme, Derbyshire. It is illustrated by alluring photographs of the open-air life of the pupils. That an English educational experiment should awaken such admiration in Germany cannot but be gratifying to an Englishman's national pride. But from another point of view the book is somewhat disappointing. The contrast between the old system and the new as "Unterricht" and "Erziehung" is largely an unfair rhetorical antithesis; for every intelligent teacher has the ideal of "education" as opposed to "information" in view, and no system or theory will make the unintelligent teacher anything but mechanical. *The author does not grapple with the real problem—whether Dr. Reddie's "return to nature" is compatible with the demands of our complex civilisation. That it provides a pleasant and wholesome life for some boys who are not capable of deriving profit from the severer routine of the ordinary school would be conceded by many whose approval goes no further; but does it give adequate intellectual training and discipline for the city life of the present day? The experiment can only be properly tested when there has been sufficient time to observe the after-careers of boys trained under its auspices.*

ALLGEMEINE LITTERARISCHE RUNDSCHAU (BERLIN),
August 1, 1897.

If the name Emlohstobba is read backwards, the name Abbotsholme is produced, and an account of this English educational establishment, founded by Cecil Reddie, forms the first part of this little work, which is written with invigorating freshness.

A new kind of school is the object-lesson there presented to us, in which tricky Latin *extemporalia* and other ballast are banished ; and instead, the pupils are seen hay-making, wrestling, felling trees, digging potatoes, &c. In short, the beautiful dream of Pestalozzi, "the harmonious education of all the powers," has been realised, and the photographic pictures in the book leave us no doubt on the subject.

The second part of the work is of a more theoretical nature : it treats of the fight of the new Educative School against the old Instruction School, in which the author takes up the cause of the former with energy and warmth.

We Germans especially could learn many a grain of pedagogic wisdom from this brilliant book.

TÄGLICHE RUNDSCHAU (BERLIN), *August* 4, 1897.

Ein neues System der Jugenderziehung, das dem Ideal Pestalozzis von der "harmonischen Ausbildung aller Kraefte" schon erheblich nahe kommt, ist seit einigen Jahren in England begruendet worden. Dr. phil. Hermann Lietz, Lic. theol., unternimmt es, in einem Buch, das den sonderbar klingenden Titel *Emlohstobba* fuehrt, die neue Schule und deren Einrichtungen und Ziele zu schildern (Berlin, bei Ferd. Duemmler). Das Buch, dessen Untertitel "Roman oder Wirklichkeit" anfaenglich den Eindruck macht, als wollte es nach bekannten Mustern Schulzustaende aus dem Jahre 2000 schildern, ist im Ganzen doch eine ernsthafte Studie. Die Schule, wie sie dort beschrieben wird, besteht in der That, und zwar in *Abbotsholme,* auf einem groesseren Gut in der Naehe der Stadt Rocester (Derbyshire) in England (Emlohstobba ist die Umkehrung von Abbotsholme). Das ganze Gut mit allen seinen Wirthschaftsraeumen, mit seinen Wiesen und Aeckern, Waeldern und Seen bildet gewissermassen einen *Schulstaat,* in dem die Schueler mit ihren Lehrern und dem noethigen Gesinde ganz fuer sich leben. Der Leiter dieses neuen Schulstaates ist Dr. *Reddie,* der zwei Jahre lang in Goettingen studirt hat und dort auch promovirt ist. Seine Anstalt ist ein Privatunternehmen, das seine Zoeglinge ueberall hernimmt. Die Schueler muessen saemmtlich dort wohnen und haben an Verpflegungs- und Schulgeld jaehrlich 2000 M. zu zahlen.

Die Reddiesche Schule bricht voellig mit den. Ueberlieferungen der alten Unterrichtsschule, die *gar keine* koerperliche Bethaetigung der

Jugend verlangt und nur langsam und nach widerwillig ihre Schueler in das Turnen einfuehrt. Die "*Erziehungsschule*" will dagegen nicht bloss einseitig den Verstand, sondern den ganzen Menschen bilden ; auch der Koerper, Arm und Bein, Auge und Ohr, Muskeln und Sehnen sollen geuebt und gestaehlt werden. Deshalb zieht sie als Unterrichtsmittel Spiele, koerperliche Uebungen und Arbeiten mit heran, in denen sich die natuerliche geistige und koerperliche Gewandtheit, Muth und Kraft der Jugend bethaetigen koennen. Nach den Schilderungen Dr. Lietz', der aus persoenlicher Anschauung den Unterrichtsbetrieb in der Reddieschen Erziehungsschule kennen gelernt hat, verlaeuft der Tag dort etwa nach folgendem Stundenplan. . . .

Dieser kurze Abriss wird genuegen, um die paedagogische Methode der Schule von Abbotsholme erkennen zu lassen. Sie verlangt von ihren Schuelern nur etwa fuenf Stunden geistiger Arbeit, gewaehrt daneben 5 Stunden planmaessige koerperliche Arbeit und Uebung, zehn Stunden Schlaf, vier Stunden fuer Mahlzeiten, Baden, Ruhepausen u. s. w. Dass sich mit einem derartigen System Gutes erreichen laesst, kann nicht zweifelhaft sein. Sein Hauptvorzug liegt darin, dass das Schulleben den Trieben und Strebungen der kindlichen Seele entspricht, allen Organen, die im Kinde wach sind, allen seinen Gliedern die Moeglichkeit gesunder, der Kindesnatur entsprechender, freier Bethaetigung verschafft. Frische, Elastizitaet und Empfaenglichkeit des Geistes wird hier sicherer erreicht, als dort, wo wohl der Unterricht ausgiebiger ist, oder ohne jegliche Benutzung der Erziehungsmittel verlaeuft, die das Leben selbst gewaehrt. N.

NATURWISSENSCHAFTLICHE WOCHENSCHRIFT,
August 22, 1897.

Die Thatsache, dass Debatten ueber unser Schulwesen seit Langem auf der Tagesordnung stehen und nicht wieder von derselben verschwinden, giebt zu der Hoffnung Veranlassung, dass vielleicht doch noch in nicht gar zu ferner Zeit ein zeitgemaesser Unterricht sich anbahnen koennte, dass unser verfahrenes Schulwesen vielleicht doch noch einmal im Verlauf der naechsten 100 Jahre das der Zeit entsprechende Geleise finden koennte. Das vorliegende Buechelchen ist eins von denen, die Propaganda machen moechten fuer eine "harmonische Ausbildung aller Kraefte, fuer eine Schule, in der nicht bloss einseitig der Verstand ausgebildet wird, sondern die gesammte menschliche Natur: Koerper, Arm, Bein, Auge, Ohr, Muskeln und Sehnen so gut, wie aesthetische und sittliche Faehigkeiten." Verf. bietet zunaechst eine Schilderung eine Tages im neuen Schulstaat Abbotsholme, der ein von Cecil Reddie (dem Begruender der Schule, wie sie das Ideal des Verfassers bildet) verfasstes Nachwort beigegeben ist, in dem der Wunsch ausgesprochen wird, dass deutsche und englische Eigenthuemlichkeiten sich zur Schaffung und Begruendung der neuen Schule verbinden möchten. Im 2. Theil des Buches bespricht Verf. die Systeme der alten " Unterrichts " und der neuen " Erziehungs "-Schule.

DIE FRAU. MONATSSCHRIFT FUER DAS GESAMMTE FRAUEN-LEBEN UNSERER ZEIT. HERAUSGEGEBEN VON HELENE LANGE, *September*, 1897.

Emlohstobba . . . mit einer mystificierenden Einleitung, deren Wert zweifelhaft erscheint, wird hier ein Schul-system entwickelt und empfohlen, dessen Wert unzweifelhaft erscheint. Es soll eine Vereinigung geistiger und koerperlicher Ausbildung bieten, die gerade der Jetztzeit fehlt, und die sich in der ruhmlichst bekannten Anstalt, Abbotsholme bei Derby in England, in mustergiltiger Gestalt findet. Sie will das Beste der deutschen und Englischen Erziehungsmethoden verbinden. Die Lektuere kann jedem denkenden Paedagogen nur warm empfohlen werden.

" VERSÖHNUNG " (A MONTHLY MAGAZINE). BERLIN, *September*, 1897.

The Instructional School of the present day shows us what the Educative School ought *not* to be. From a recently published book we gather some notion of an ideal school of this kind which does actually exist.

The author, who was a teacher in The New School Abbotsholme, Derbyshire, England, unrolls before us such a vivid picture that we feel a keen desire to visit the place and start life again as children.

I enjoyed the book so much that I cannot help warmly recommending it. Any one who is not attracted by the title will be converted by the pictures. We find here joyous vigour and strength, like the first breath of morning, and at the same time much solemn earnestness. So we begin to read, or rather we learn, we work, we run, we enjoy it all with those who are living the life there, and we feel ourselves drawn into an atmosphere of brisk and living evolution.

Lietz boldly tells parents and educators the naked truth. Being myself, fortunately, *not* an orthodox pedagogue, I still love a whiff of fresh air, and to me the ideal has not become, as to so many professional schoolmasters, a chimæra. Thank heaven that I am no pedagogue at all, and so can love Nature, who will not allow herself to be tight-laced. Besides myself there are thousands more of such outsiders. The time has come for us to meet and coöperate. We only need a leader in order to conquer.

But this will never be, so long as the matter is merely discussed here and there in educational papers. The battlefield must be one on which the great questions of humanity are fought out in earnest in a Press which appeals to the educated, the energetic, and the progressive.

I cannot take the lead, but I am fired by a sacred enthusiasm to lay aside all pusillanimity and to give a helping shove—just one shove. *Where are the men in whom zeal is combined with power to organise, who could start a popular movement, which would bring into our schools life and joy?*

The question of education has already passed beyond the stage of criticism and mere talk. Dr. Lietz's book proves that there exist practical men, who are able to set a bright example. The matters with which he deals are too weighty to be discussed in a short space; I can only give indications here, you must read for yourselves the book.

A new type of teacher is wanted; men who realise that they are spiritual guides; teachers who prize knowledge only as it moulds life and steels character; men of maturity who, nevertheless, have not lost touch with childhood; men who can value and develop individual characters, who can build up souls, set hearts on fire; men who are alert, magnanimous, and devoted.

Away with the school from its prison—the overgrown town; give us space, playgrounds and halls for games, contests and all manner of exercise; let us have instruction and practice in handwork; let us have teaching and learning direct from Nature; let us have rambles through field and forest; let us have farm-work and bridge-building; let us develop their feeling of responsibility by entrusting to the young important duties. Let there be, moreover, choir and orchestra, for art and poetry are youths' best friends. The educator must be to the children a friendly counsellor, *not* one who intrudes, but one who stands by them through thick and thin. Such conditions as these will send into the fight real living men, sound and strong as old carved oak.

I cannot close without some short quotations.

* * * * * *

Through these few sentences you can judge of the spirit which animates the book. Let it not have been written in vain, let it raise for us in earnest the question, " Where are the men to prepare the way for us in Germany ? " The time calls aloud for them. Let them stand forth.
WILHELM SPOHR.

STOYS'CHE ERZIEHUNGS-ANSTALT (JENA), *September* 13, 1897.

GEEHRTER HERR DOKTOR,—Ich muss Ihnen bestens danken fuer Zusendung der Schrift des Herrn Dr. Lietz. Mit grossem Vergnuegen habe ich die Schilderungen Ihres Schul—und Anstaltslebens gelesen, die freilich nur haetten gewinnen koennen, wenn mehr Einzelnes, Thatsaechliches angefuehrt worden waere. Ich beglueckwuensche Sie zu Ihrer hingebenden wie gesegneten paedagogischen Arbeit. Nach meiner Auffassung, Sie werden ein offenes Wort eines warmen Freundes Ihrer Bestrebungen recht verstehen, ist die ganze Schrift des Herrn Dr. L. nicht geeignet die besondere Eigentuemlichkeit und die besondere Bedeutung Ihrer Arbeit deutlich hervortreten zu lassen.

Ich freue mich, Sie kennen gelernt zu haben, und, haette ich von Ihrer Anstalt etwas gewusst, wuerde ich bestrebt gewesen sein, mich mit Ihnen laenger zu unterhalten. Vielleicht kommen Sie spaeter einmal wieder nach Jena. Mit freundlichen Gruss.

Bin ich,
Ihr ergebener,
Dr. HEINRICH STOY.

DIE HILFE (BERLIN), *January* 23, 1898.
EMLOHSTOBBA.
ROMAN ODER WIRKLICHKEIT ?

Bilder aus dem Schulleben der Vergangenheit, Gegenwart oder Zukunft ? Von Dr. phil. Hermann Lietz, Lic. theol. Mit 22 Lafeln in Autotypie.

Ein wunderlicher Buchtitel ! wird mancher bei sich denken. Und doch sind in diesem Buche Darlegungen enthalten, die eine ganze Zukunft in ihrem Schosse tragen. Eingedenk des Satzes : Wer die Jugend hat, hat die Zukunft, kaempft der Verfasser von *Emlohstobba* fuer eine Umgestaltung unserer Unterrichtsschulen zu Erziehungsschulen. Das Buch erinnert in mancher Beziehung an Rousseaus Emil. Der gerade in unserer Zeit immer staerker sich erhebende Ruf Rousseaus : Zurueck zur Natur! geht auch durch dieses Buch in seiner Art hindurch. Es ist klar und gefaellig und dabei doch begeistert und begeisternd geschrieben, es ist voll von praktischem Idealismus, voll von warmer Liebe zur Jugend und zum Erzieherberuf. Der auf den ersten Blick etwas seltsam aussehende Titel des Buches *Emlohstobba* wird sofort klar, wenn man ihn umkehrt, d. h. von rechts nach links liest. Dann lautet das Wort Abbotsholme und bezeichnet den Ort, in welchem wirklich eine solche Schule vorhanden ist, wie sie der Verfasser von der Zukunft fordert. Lietz war selber Lehrer an der "New-School" Abbotsholme. bei Rocester (Derbyshire, England).

Im Buche wird uns "ein Tag im neuen Schulstaat Emlohstobba" geschildert. Die Schule liegt draussen, fern von der Stadt, in laendlicher Abgeschiedenheit. Sie ist zugleich ein groesseres Landgut. "Die Landschaft mit Thal und Ebene, mit Feld und Fluss, Bache und Berg, Wald und Wiese soll den Knaben ein stets geoeffnetes, erstes und letztes Lehrbuch sein." Die Art des Schulbetriebes koennte man kurz als die naturgemaesse bezeichnen. Geistige und koerperliche Arbeit stehen in rechter Wechselbeziehung zu einander, wie ein Blick auf den dem Buche beigefuegten "Tagewerkplan" lehrt. Fuenf Stunden sind der geistigen Arbeit gewidmet, 5 Stunden der koerperlichen Arbeit, der Koerperuebung und Kunstuebung, 10 Stunden dem Schlaf, 4 Stunden fuer Mahlzeiten, Baden, Ruhepaufen u. s. w. Woechentlich ist ein Freinachmittag fuer Ausfluege zu Fuss oder auf dem Zweirad, und ein Freiabend fuer Konzert, Gesellschaftsspiele, Auffuehrungen, Litteratur.

Was an Methodik, Didaktik u. s. w. durch die Arbeit der grossen Paedagogen der letzten Jahrhunderte errungen und klar gelegt ist, finden wir in Abbotsholme in praktischer Anwendung. Hier sucht man die so lange aufgespeicherten reichen Schaetze der gewaltigen paedagogischen Arbeit zu heben und fuer die Erziehung wirklich nutzbar zu machen, wie dies ja auch nur der Art der praktischen Englaender entspricht. Besonders erfreulich—und fuer die Lefer dieses Blattes sympathisch—ist die Heranbildung der Zoeglinge von Abbotsholme fuer praktische Arbeit. Solche giebt es genug auf dem mit der Schule verbundenen umfangreichen Landgut.

Wie der moderne Sprachunterricht in Abbotsholme "zu einem unvergleichlich festen, voelkerverknuepfenden Bande" benutzt wird, so ist man dort auch davon ueberzeugt, dass die Handarbeit jener vornehmsten Zoeglinge " eine starke Bruecke wird abgeben koennen ueber die klaffenden gesellschaftlichen Klassenunterschiede."

Es ist eine Lust, sich von dem Verfasser an der Hand seines Buches im neuen Schulstaat Emlohstobba herumfuehren zu lassen. Ueberall gewahren wir frisches, frohes, natuerliches Leben, ein Lernen mit Lust und eine Lust am Lernen, weil eben der Koerper hier auch zu seinem Rechte kommt. Das Ideal der Schule ist—wie der Leiter derselben Dr. phil. Cecil Reddie in dem Vorwort als Nachwort sagt—" deutsche Organisation mit englischer Unabhaengigkeits und Freiheitsliebe zu verbinden." In diesem Sinne arbeiten englische und deutsche Lehrer dort zusammen. Die Devise der Erziehungsschule lautet: *mens sana in corpore sano*. Ihr Ziel ist Vorbereitung aufs Leben durch Ausbildung eines charakterfesten Willens. Darum giebt es in der Erziehungsschule keinen anderen als erziehenden Unterricht. Wie einst beim Uebergang zum 16. und zum 19., so wird auch heute beim Uebergang zum 20. Jahrhundert gewaltiger denn je altes mit neuem ringen. "Viele kleine Scharmuetzel werden dabei stattfinden. Aber die Entscheidungsschlacht wird auf dem weiten Gebiet der Volkserziehung geschlagen werden. Hie Unterrichtsschule!—hie Erziehungsschule! ist die Parole. Welche wird siegen? Davon wird das Wohl der Nation abhaengen. Verhelft der Erziehungsschule zum Siege! Und die Nation ist gerettet. Wir sehen, es ist ein hohes Ziel, dem der Verfasser von Emlohstobba zustrebt: die Rettung der Nation. Sie kann nur durch eine sittliche Reugeburt unseres Volkes erfolgen. Wird diese nicht durch aehnliche Ereignisse wie im Anfang dieses Jahrhunderts herbeigefuehrt, so ist es unsere Pflicht, an der Neugestaltung unseres Volkslebens nach Kraeften mitzuarbeiten. Das kann nur durch rechte Jugenderziehung geschehen. Alte Schaelke sind—mit Luther zu reden—nicht mehr fromm zu machen. Aber die Jugend ist bildungs-und begeisterungsfaehig. Wer mit ihr recht umzugehen weiss, kann sie fuehren, wohin er will. Auf der rechten Erziehung der Jugend—und diese geht bis zum 20. bezw. 19. Jahre— ruht die Hoffnung der Nation. Darum gilt es, die Jugend in die rechte Schule zu schicken, und das kann nur die Erziehungsschule sein. Fuer sie kaempft der Verfasser von Emlohstobba. Fuer sie muesste jeder rechte Jugendlehrer begeistert sein, wie es der treffliche Verfasser von Emlohstobba ist. Wo aber folche Begeisterung fuer den Erzieherberuf nicht vorhanden ist, muesste ein Buch wie dieses imstande sein, sie zu wecken.

Wunstorf.   HEINR. KUEHNHOLD.

18. HELPING TO BUILD THE DINGLE-DAM. (*Summer, 1894*).

Copyright

JAHRESBERICHT DER ERZIEHUNGSANSTALT ZU KEILHAU, OSTERN, 1898.

Das Buch fuehrt den seltsamen Titel : *Emlohstobba*. Und ruehrt von einem jungen Paedagogen her, der hauptsaechlich in Jena vorgebildet, einige Zeit in England gewirkt hat. Er entwirft uns ein Bild von einem englischen Internat zu Abbotsholme, dies ist der richtige Name, den der Verfasser umgestellt hat, und schildert es uns in schwungvoller Sprache als das Ideal einer modernen " Erziehungsschule."

Mit einer etwas phantastischen Vision, in der jener Besucher von E. im Traume die ganze papierne Herrlichkeit der *alten Schule* in Flammem aufgehen sieht, schliesst der erste Teil des Buches, dem der Leiter der hier geschilderten Anstalt, Dr. C. Reddie noch ein feinsinniges Nachwort beigefuegt hat, worin er die Verschmelzung des deutschen, englischen und franzoesischen Geistes als Ziel der Erziehung hinstellt.

Das Erziehungsideal, das der Verfasser mit warmer, wohlthuender Begeisterung vertritt, ist kurz gesagt : harmonische Entwicklung der Kraefte, *mens sana in corpore sano*: ein gesunder Geist in einem gesunden Leibe. Im Grunde will er also nichts anderes, als was Rousseau, Pestalozzi, Herbart, Froebel[1] und ihre zahlreichen Anhaenger gewollt haben. Eigenartig aber bei Lietz ist seine gruendliche, entschiedene Absage an das Alte und die feste Ueberzeugung, dass in den englischen Alumnaten, vorzueglich in Abbotsholme das Ideal der Erziehung in hoeherem Grade verwirklicht sei als in den weitaus meisten deutschen Schulen.

Die jetzt thaetige Generation, die im Wettbewerb der Voelker so grosse Erfolge, auch dan Englaendern gegenueber, erringt, ist in der *Unterrichtsschule* gross geworden. So schlecht und verrottet, wie der Verf. sie hinstellt, kann diese also doch wohl nicht sein.

Ueberhaupt ist es bedenklich von einer *Unterrichtsschule* im Gegensatz zur *Erziehungsschule* zu sprechen. Denn "wehe den Schulen, die nicht zugleich Erziehungsschulen sind " (Strebel). Sie sollen es aber nach des Verfassers Meinung nicht nur in weit hoeherem Sinne als bisher sein, er geht noch weiter, wie Rousseau will er Rueckkehr zur Natur, aus dem verderblichen Boden der Grossstaedte will er die Jugend hinausverpflanzen auf das Land, dort sollen Alumnate wie jenes Emlohstobba errichtet werden. Der Staat kann solche Anstalten nicht gruenden, aber er soll

---

[1] Mit dem letztgenannten beruehrt sich Lietz vielfach, Froebels Wahlspruch : Kommt, lasst uns unsern Kindern leben, ist auch der seine, und die Schilderung von Emlohstobba gemahnt sehr an Chr. Langethals : Keilhau in seinen Anfaengen.

sie schützen und ihnen Freiheit zur Entwickelung gewaehren. Wie sie aber gegruendet werden sollen, das deutet der Verfasser nur an.

Wir koennen also nicht zugeben, dass die Notstaende in unserm Erziehungswesen so schreiend sind; wir müssen uns auch dagegen verwahren, dass wir einfach englische Vorbilder nachahmen sollen. Es ist ferner nachdruecklich darauf hinzuweisen, dafs vieles von dem, was L. mit Recht verlangt, von deutschen Paedagogen nicht nur laengst erkannt, sondern bereits durchgefuehrt oder doch in die Wege geleitet ist. Aber wir wollen es dem Verfasser danken, dass er laut und eindringlich auf gewisse Grundwahrheiten der Paedagogik hingewiesen und das Verlangen nach ihrer allgemeinen Durchfuehrung lebhaft wachgerufen hat, und wollen ihm zugeben: die Gefahr ist nicht gering, dass Deutschland im Erziehungswesen von anderen Nationen ueberfluegelt wird. Mit ihm sind wir ueberzeugt, dass die eingeleitete Reform nicht stocken und stehen bleiben darf, und dass dazu auch die Privaterziehungsanstalten ihr redliches Teil mitwirken koennen.

PÄDAGOGISCHES MONATSBLATT (LEIPZIG), *Heft* 4, 1898.
AUS DEM GEBIETE DER SCHULLEITUNG UND SCHULVERWALTUNG.

EIN DEUTSCHES LANDERZIEHUNGSHEIM.

VON H. WIGGE.

Es giebt Buecher, die unter aller Kritik sind; es giebt auch Buecher, die ueber jede Kritik erhaben sind.

Emlohstobba—Abbotsholme—von Dr. *H. Lietz*—ich las und las. Es verschwand gar bald die Unlust, die mir zuerst die Spielerei mit den Eigennamen erweckte. Ich wurde waermer und waermer und sog immer langsamer die Gedanken ein, um mir den Genuss zu verlaengern, und versank oft ins Traeumen und Gruebeln, nicht in ein Traeumen und Gruebeln, wie es sich einstellt, wenn die Seele beim Lesen ihre eigenen Wege wandelt, o nein, ich war bei der Sache, sehr bei der Sache. Ich sah das alles verwirklicht, was da geschrieben stand, sah verwirklicht, was Jahre hindurch mein Sinnen und Denken, mein Wuenschen und Hoffen gewesen war, eine neue Schule, ein neues Lehren und Lernen, und sah mich darin in froher, meine Kraefte bis zum Aeussersten anspannender Arbeit. Und sein ganzes Koennen und Wollen in Arbeit umsetzen, das ist ja die Quelle des Menschengluecks.

Ich las und las, und was sich in mir zum ewigen Schlummer niederlegen wollte, Thatkraft, Arbeitslust, das heisse Sehnen nach einem Wirken, das mich aufzehrt, es flammte noch einmal empor und machte mich wieder jung.

Es war mir, als arbeitete ich an der neuen Schule. Sie lag dort, wo der Kampf ums Dasein die Gotteswelt noch nicht entstellt, und die Gotteswelt in ihrer Urspruenglichkeit und Natuerlichkeit, sie war der Jugend erstes Lehrbuch, wie sie erstes Lehrbuch der Menschheit war und ewig ihr Lehrbuch sein wird.

Das Lehren war Leben und Leben das Lernen, Gottesdienst des Menschenherzens der Religionsunterricht, Kunstanschauung und Kunstuebung die kuenstlerische Erziehung, Gebrauch der Sprache der Sprachunterricht, Messen, Versuchen, Bauen die Geometrie, Arbeit in Garten und Feld, Erfahrung, Beobachtung der Natur die Naturwissenschaft, Nachleben und Nachstreben die Geschichte, Wandern und Reisen die Erdkunde, dienende Glieder das Zeichnen und die Handarbeit.

Die Jugend unterwarf sich dem Gesetz und Gebot und lernte befehlen ; sie uebte Selbstbeherrschung und lernte andere beherrschen ; sie badete sich in Licht, Luft und Wasser, in Wetter und Sturm, in Frost und Hitze und hielt sich gesund ; sie leistete Handreichung bei allem, was das Schulleben und das Leben einer Alumnatsfamilie mit eigener Wirtschaft an koerperlicher Arbeit mit sich bringt, beim Graben und Pflanzen, beim Heuen und Ernten, beim Anfertigen und Reparieren von Geräten und Anschauungsmitteln, gerade so, wie es in jedem erziehungstuechtigen Elternhause geschieht, und machte so den Knaben zum dereinstigen Arbeitgeber ; sie spielte die Spiele einer unverweichlichten Jugend und gab so dem Koerper und dem Geiste Jugendfrische mit auf den Lebensweg.

Unterricht, Kunstuebungen, koerperliche Uebungen, Spiel, Arbeit, Schulleben waren die Erziehungsmittel, Klassenzimmer, Betsaal, Konzerthalle, Feld, Garten, Wiese, Wald, Spielplatz die Erziehungsstaetten.

So war's in der *new school Abbotsholme* bei *Rocester* in *Derbyshire*, England, wohin uns der Verfasser im Geiste fuehst. Etwa ein Jahr wirkte er dort, und was er dort sah und hoerte, was sich als Jugenderziehung vor seinen Augen abspielte, das spannte seine Begeisterung und seinen Willen und liess in ihm den Entschluss reifen, seinem Vaterlande ein Reformator der Erziehung zu werden. In dem Herzen warme Liebe zur Jugend und zum Volke, im Kopfe tiefe Einsicht in die Schaeden und die Bedurfnisse der Zeit, in der Tasche den Plan einer neuen Schule fuer Deutschlands hoehere Jugend, so kehrte er in die Heimat zurueck.

Eine neue Schule fuer Deutschlands hoehere Jugend—der Plan war nicht neu. Schon im Jahre 1882 hatte Dr. *Goering* ganz denselben Gedanken gefasst. Genesen von dem Glauben an den Wert der antiken Bildung, abgestossen von einem Unterrichte, des nichts anderes sei als ein ermuedender Kreislauf von Buechern, zu Buechern, von Philologie zu Philologie, ueberzeugt von dem antinationalen Charakter des hoeheren Schulwesens, welches die Jugend im Daemmerlichte einer fremden Kultur und eines der Wirklichkeit abgewandten Gelehrtenlebens erziehe und der Kultur unserer Zeit entfremde, forderte er neue Grundsaetze fuer die hoeheren Schulen, forderte er fuer diese ein nationales, ein deutsches Fundament und als solches den vollen Bildungsinhalt der Gegenwart und Wirklichkeit.

Das geplante Privatinstitut, das Goerings Erziehungsideen verwirklichen sollte, blieb ein schoener Traum. Das Unternehmen scheiterte trotz der zaehen Energie, mit der es eingeleitet zu sein schien, und trotz der Sympathie, die hochstehende Maenner und Frauen ihm entgegenbrachten. Woran? Mir ist Naeheres nicht bekannt geworden. Offenbar war die Position des klassischen Philologismus, des alten Kirchen und Roemertums noch zu stark, um mit dem ersten Ansturm genommen zu werden, noch zu wenig gestaerkt das Selbstbewusstsein der germanischen Volksseele, um sich auf sich selber zu besinnen. Selbst der Mahnruf, der in dem *kaiserlichen Schulprogramm* vom 4. Dezember 1890 durch die Lande ging, er loeste den Bann nicht, in den ein antinationaler Geist das deutsche Schulwesen geschlagen. So stark blieb noch der Blick getruebt, dass der nationalsoziale Verein, der die nationale Idee zum Licht- und Leitstern fuer alle Lebensfragen des deutschen Volkes zu erheben sich zur Aufgabe gemacht hat, bei der Festlegung seines Schulprogramms im vergangenen Jahre ganz aus der Rolle fiel, als es sich um die hoeheren Schulen handelte. Finanzielle und soziale Gleichstellung der akademisch gebildeten Lehrer mit den Richtern—das war der einzige Zukunftsgedanke, den dieser Verein, der auf andern Gebieten so tief- und weitschauend sich bewiesen, jener Seite der Schulfrage abzugewinnen vermochte. Darin ein nationales Moment zu entdecken, duerfte mit einigen Schwierigkeiten verbunden sein. Als ich in der Debatte die Erziehungskraft der antiken Lateinschule verneinte und fuer unsere hoeheren Schulen eine nationale Basis wuenschte, da erregte ich den heiligen Zorn eines mir gegenuebersitzenden Gymnasialprofessors, der nach solchen Aeusserungen dem nationalsozialen Verein kaum noch angehoeren zu koennen meinte und seine Naehrmutter mit der kindlichen Pietaet vergangener Jahrhunderte verteidigte.

Ein kurzes Fruehlingsrauschen vom Kaiserthrone her, dann war's wieder still. Winterstarre, Geistesstarre. Doch unter dem unnatuerlichen klassischen Firniss, den die hoeheren Schulen wie einen Alp auf unser deutsches Geistesleben legten, schlummerte die nationale Lebenskraft, unter dem antinationalen Drucke immer von neuem sich reckend und dehnend, sich spannend und auf baeumend zum Gegendrucke.

Lietz nimmt Goerings Plan auf. Er nimmt ihn auf mit jener Klarheit ueber das Ziel, wie sie die direkte Anschauung eines Vor- und Musterbildes verleiht, und mit jener Klarheit ueber die Mittel und Wege zum Ziele, welche das Studium und die Praxis Herbart-Zillerscher Paedagogik zeitigt. *Jena und Abbotsholme gestalteten seine paedagogischen Ideale.* Dort erstand der Erneuerung des deutschen Schulwesens ein neuer Vorkaempfer. Ein Hoffen, das noch nicht enttaeuscht, ein Streben, das noch nicht gescheitert, junges Feuer, junge Begeisterung, junge Erkenntnis und junge Einsicht wirft er hinein in die grosse paedagogische Bewegung unserer Tage.

Aus seinem grundlegenden Werke spricht so viel Frische, so viel Kraft, so viel Jugend und Zukunft, dass man voellig verdorrt oder voellig verstockt sein muss, um nicht fortgerissen zu werden. Schlag auf Schlag wird gefuehrt gegen das System der alten Unterrichtsschule, und Zopf auf Zopf faellt unter den scharfen Schlaegen. Es bricht zusammen das Gebaeude, das einigermassen wohnlich war, als das Haus den Nachwuchs erzog, als das deutsche Volksleben noch keine eigenen Kulturschaetze gezeitigt hatte, als der nationale Geistesquell noch nicht sprang, als das Kind der Mutter Germania noch kein Vaterland und noch nichts Vaterlaendisches hatte. Es schwindet der Wahn, dass die, die im Staube der Antike wuehlen und die Truemmer von Hellas und Rom zu Erziehungsstaetten machen, dem deutschen Volke Leiter und Fuehrer erziehen koennen. Es schwindet der Wahn, dass Friedrich Wilhelm I., Ziethen und Bluecher Dummkoepfe waren, weil sie nicht Griechisch und Lateinisch verstanden. Waere einem Arndt, einem Stein, einem Scharnhorst, einem Cromwell, einem W. Pitt keine andere Weisheit und keine andere Kraft mitgegeben auf ihren steilen, gefahrvollen Lebensweg als die klassische der Schule, ihre Namen waeren nicht mit goldenen Lettern eingetragen in das Buch der Geschichte. Nicht klassische Bildung, nicht Wissen, nicht Gelehrsamkeit hat der Menschheit die grossen Entdecker, Erfinder, Kulturverpflanzer, Dichter und Propheten geliefert, das deutsche Elternhaus hat es gethan. Aber wo sind sie heute, die alten Elternhaeuser voll Saft und Kraft, voll deutscher Zucht und deutscher Sitte, voll Natuerlichkeit und Geistesfrische? Sie sind seltener geworden, viel seltener. Nur auf dem Lande duerfte man sie noch finden. Auf landlicher Scholle sind ja ueberhaupt fast alle Maenner aufgewachsen, welche altersschwache Kulturen vor dem Verderben, vor der Verweichlichung zu retten verstanden. Das aber, was heute das Land noch hervorbringt an nationaler Jugendkraft, das geht zum groessten Teile verloren in den hoeheren Schulen, den Schuelerpensionen und den Unterrichts-Alumnaten. Kernig, sehr kernig muss sein, was in ihnen an Leib und Seele gesund bleibt.

Jedes Ding hat seine Zeit, und die Zeit der Schulen, welche der Jugend Lesen, Schreiben, Rechnen, Katechismus, Griechisch, Lateinisch, Hebraeisch, Mathematik u. s. w. beibringen wollen, die Grammatik eindrillen, Extemporalien schreiben lassen, Censuren erteilen und Pruefungen abhalten, ist fuer immer dahin. Sie sind Anachronismen, Kulturanomalien, von der Zeit vergessene Reste einer laengst abgelaufenen Entwickelungsperiode. Sie haben sich selber ueberlebt. Die Schoepfungsthaten menschlicher Geistesarbeit sind nicht mehr auch ihr Verdienst, im Gegenteil, sie hemmen dieselben. Sie hemmen, sie laehmen, sie schaedigen, sie verderben und verdienen mit ihren falschen Zielen, ihren falschen Mitteln und ihrer unpsychologischer Methode eigentlich nicht einmal mehr den Namen *Unterrichts*schule. Zum Fluch ist heute geworden, was einst die Erziehung des Hauses zu ergaenzen geeignet war. Bekaempfung und Vernichtung verdient, was frueher Unterstuetzung und Pflege verdiente.

Ihre Zeit ist dahin. Die schiffbruechigen Vertreter der alten Unterrichtsschule, welchen die Schulfrage weiter nichts ist als eine Brot-, Titel- und Wuerdenfrage, sie klammern sich krampfhaft an die letzten Planken ihres ehemals vielleicht stolzen Fahrzeuges. Es hilft ihnen nichts. Auch die alten Bacchanten wollten von ihrem Leben und ihrer Art Schule nicht lassen, und der Entwickelungsstrom des Kulturlebens warf sie schliesslich doch zu dem Toten. Das alte Unterrichtssystem wird und muss zusammenbrechen, unter sich die klassischen Philologen, die klassischen Direktoren und Professoren, Extemporalienhefte, Grammatiken, Grundrisse, Censuren und Examina begrabend, und auf seinen Truemmern wird und muss die *Erziehungsschule* sich erheben, wenn das Vaterland gross und stark und maechtig bleiben, wenn das deutsche Volk eine Zukunft haben soll. Der Erziehungsschule wird erreichbar sein, was dem Elternhause von heute schwer und der Unterrichtsschule von heute gar nicht erreichbar ist; sie wird dem Vaterlande deutsche Frauen und deutsche Maenner und dem deutschen Volke Leiter und Fuehrer geben.

Ihr Ziel ist: Entwickelung aller Seiten, aller Kraefte, Sinne, Organe, Glieder und guten Triebe der kindlichen Natur zu einer moeglichst harmonischen Persoenlichkeit; nicht Lesen, Schreiben, Griechisch, sondern Leben lehren. Und wie im Ziel, so verfaehrt sie auch in den Mitteln entgegengesetzt wie die alte Unterrichtsschule. Diese holte sich den Zoegling nur auf wenige Stunden, die neue Erziehungsschule holt ihn moeglichst fuer den ganzen Tag. Jene holte sich ihn zur Beibringung theoretischer Kenntnisse und Fertigkeiten in die Schulstube, diese holt sich ihn zur Entwickelung aller seiner Kraefte nicht nur in die Menschen- und Stadtschulstube, sondern hinaus in Gottes Schulstube draussen, in Wald und Feld, auf Wiese und Flur, in Fluss und See, auf den Bauplatz und in die Werkstaette. Jene giebt ihn in die Hand von Leuten mit guten Zeugnissen ueber Griechisch, Lateinisch, Mathematik, Lesen, Schreiben und Katechismus, diese vertraut ihn Juenglingen und Maennern, Jungfrauen und Frauen mit jugendlich-ungebrochenen Koerpern an, Seelen, Geistern, welche sie durch Herz, That und Wort aufs Leben vorzubereiten wissen. Jene verfahren mit dem Zoegling als Drillmeister fuer Examina nach den Paragraphen veralteter Regulative, diese so, wie etwa der alte Arndt mit seinen Jungen und Pestalozzis Gertrud mit ihren Toechtern.

Ein neu Geschlecht durch eine neue Erziehung! Doch die Entwickelung geht im Kulturleben nicht so vor sich, dass ein Altes bis zu einem bestimmten Tage wirkt und vom naechsten Tage an ein Neues an seine Stelle tritt Die Uebergaenge sind allmaehliche—zum Glueck fuer die Menschheit. In stillen Thaelern oder auf der Hoehe der Berge waechst oft schon hier und dort die neue Lebensfrucht, waehrend auf weiter Ebene noch die alte kuemmerlich dahinsiecht.

Im tannenumrauschten und sagenumwobenen *Ilsenburg a. Harz* wird mit Beginn dieses Schuljahres unter Lietz' Leitung die erste Erziehungs- schule als "*deutsches Landerziehungsheim*" ins Leben treten. Es stellt sich in den Dienst der Eltern der Grossstadt, die nicht in der Lage sind, die einseitige Wirkung der Schule auf ihre Kinder wenigstens einiger- massen wieder aufzuheben und auszugleichen, sowie der Eltern vom Lande, die ihre Kinder nicht einer Staatspension und noch viel weniger einer "Presse" anvertrauen wollen. Deren Soehne will es aufnehmen und sie zu deutschen Juenglingen erziehen, die an Leib und Seele gesund und stark, die praktisch, wissenschaftlich und kuenstlerisch tuechtig sind, die klar und scharf denken, warm empfinden, stark wollen, erziehen

durch Zusammenleben, -spielen und -arbeiten von Zoeglingen und
Erziehern, durch streng hygienische Lebensweise, durch taegliche Koer-
peruebungen wie Wandern, Laufen, Spielen, Schwimmen, Rudern,
Turnen, durch taegliche koerperliche Beschaeftigungen, als da sind
Arbeiten im Garten und im Wald, auf dem Felde oder der Wiese, in der
Werkstaette oder auf dem Bauplatz, durch taegliche Kunstuebung,
Zeichnen nach der Natur, Singen, Instrumentalmusikuebung, planmaessige Anleitung zum Verstaendnis von Werken der Kunst, durch
besondere Veranstaltungen zur Pflege des sittlich-religioesen und vater-
laendischen Sinnes, wie taegliche Morgen- und Abendandachten,
religioese Einwirkung bei feierlichen Gelegenheiten, Feier von Gedenk-
tagen, Betonung des religioes-sittlichen Moments in allen Unter-
richtsfaechern und durch einen den Gesetzen der Erziehungskunst und
Erziehungswissenschaft entsprechenden Unterricht—just wie in Abbotsholme.

Damit hat die Schulreform, diese groesste aller Kulturaufgaben des
kommenden Jahrhunderts, auch bei uns praktische Gestalt gewonnen.
Ein Fuerstenkind der neuen Zeit mit nationalem Fuehlen und Denken,
ein thatkraeftiger, weitschauender Kaiser ergriff die Initiative. Mit dem
genialen Blick eines Staatspaedagogen zeichnete er den Weg ; hinter ihm
stand die Nation, standen die besten Kenner und Vertreter des Volks-
und Schullebens—die Berliner Schulkonferenz, die Direktoren und
Lehrerkollegien der hoeheren Schulen liessen ihn bis auf wenige ruehm-
liche Ausnahmen im Stich. Jetzt erobern sich im ersten deutschen
Landerziehungsheim die deutschen Gedanken vom Auslande her die
deutsche Heimat. Sie mussten auswandern, um hier Praxis werden zu
koennen. Ueber Abbotsholme fuehrte der Weg von der stillen
deutschen Studierstube nach Ilsenburg.

Der Prophet gilt nichts in seinem Vaterlande. Didaktische Ergeb-
nisse, wie sie die Pestalozzische und die Herbart-Zillersche Schule in
Deutschland gezeitigt haben, hat kein anderes Land aufzuweisen. Das
Vaterland ueberlaesst es dem Auslande, die Schaetze zu heben.
Theoretisch ist bei uns der Boden fuer eine Erziehungsschule besser
geebnet als irgendwo, im Abbruch des alten Systems spielt der Deutsche
seine Michelrolle weiter, laesst er sich von anderen Voelkern ueberfluegeln.
Er sieht ruhig zu, wie diese sich mit seinen Waffen tuechtig machen zum
friedlichen, vielleicht auch zum blutigen Kampf ums Dasein.

Es scheint, als staenden wir endlich an einer Wende der Dinge, als
wuerde das hoehere Schulwesen nunmehr eingelenkt in die Bahnen echt
deutscher Erziehung.

Und das *Volksschulwesen?* Es ist nicht in dem Masse zurueckgeblieben hinter den Idealen und den praktisch-erzieherischen Arbeiten der grossen Paedagogen vergangener Zeiten, eines Luther, Comenius, Salzmann, Gutsmuths, Pestalozzi, Herbart, Jahn, Arndt, Fichte, Froebel u. a.—aber zurueckgeblieben ist es auch. Die umfangreiche litterarische Reformbewegung der letzten Jahrzehnte hat auch die Praxis der Volksschulen wenig erreicht. Auch sie sind Unterrichtsanstalten mit Buecherweisheit und Wortkultus geblieben, und ihre Reformbeduerftigkeit gerade war es, welche zu der gegenwaertigen Reformbewegung den Anstoss gab.

Was in Abbotsholme verwirklicht wird und in Ilsenburg verwirklicht werden soll, das sind die Reformgedanken der deutschen Volksschulpaedagogen, uebertragen auf das hoehere Schulwesen, es sind im Wesen dieselben Prinzipien, auf welche auch Martin und ich theoretisch eine Volkserziehungsschule gruendeten. In unseren " Grundlagen " heisst es u. a. : " In der uns vorschwebenden Schule widmet sich der Lehrer den Kindern den ganzen Tag. Beobachtungen im Freien, Spaziergaenge und Ausfluege koennen sich ueber den ganzen Nachmittag ausdehnen, ja, selbst den Abend und die fruehen Morgenstunden in Anspruch nehmen. Zwei Nachmittage werden ganz besonders zum Baden, zum Spielen, zu koerperlichen Uebungen und koerperlichen Beschaeftigungen ausgenutzt. Und wenn des Lehrer einmal an einem Tage zehn Stunden im Kreise der Kinder verweilen muss, seine Arbeit ist nur scheinbar eine groessere, denn von den zehn hat er sicherlich die meisten in Gottes freier Natur zugebracht, und das reibt die Kraefte nicht auf, sondern haelt Geist und Koerper jung und frisch."

Eine solche Ausgestaltung der Volksschule hatte vor uns meines Wissens noch keiner gefordert, und wir forderten sie umsonst. Es ist zu verstehen, dass die Behoerden den Reformvorschlaegen gegenueber zurueckhaltend sind und nur mit grosser Vorsicht an Aenderungen herantreten. Aber gerade in der Erziehung und Bildung der Jugend kommt es doch weniger auf die behoerdlichen Bestimmungen, weniger auf den Buchstaben der Verordnungen an, als auf den Geist, der wirkt, weniger darauf, Verfuegungen lautgetreu auszufuehren, als darauf, sie mit Leben, mit Gegenwart und Zukunft zu fuellen, und darum muesste es bedenklicher sein, die Jugend der Schablone, der Lohnarbeit, dem Ruhenden und Toten anzuvertrauen, als der Begeisterung, dem Idealismus, der jungen Thatkraft.

Tausende stehen am Wege und betteln um beglueckende Arbeit ; sie bieten ihr Bestes an, ihre waermste Liebe, ihre hoechste Kraft, und das alles moechten sie einsetzen fuer die Heimat, fuer das Vaterland—will niemand sie dingen? Um Arbeit betteln sie, um beglueckende Arbeit an der Jugend des deutschen Volkes, wie sie Abbotsholme und Ilsenburg gewaehren, doch einfacher kann sie sein, bescheidener und ein wenig Armut dabei. Das waere wohl muehseliger, aber nicht weniger selig. Landerziehungsheime koennen wir den Kindern der Volksschule nicht bieten, die Doerfer, die kleinen und kleineren Staedte beduerfen ihrer ja auch nicht ; aber im Sinne des Landerziehungsheims koennen wir an den Kindern des Volkes wirken.

Der neuen Zeit ein neu Geschlecht durch eine neue Erziehung ! Soll auch die Idee der Volkserziehungsschule erst auswandern, um sich die Heimat erobern zu koennen? Soll auch hier das Ausland ernten, was das Vaterland gesaeet hat?

DIE WAGE (WIEN, LEIPZIG, BERLIN), *August* 20, 1898.

DR. ROBERT SCHEU. EIN SCHULSTAAT.

Waehrend wir noch darnach ringen, die leitenden Gedanken unserer idealen Schule zu gewinnen, waehrend wir noch Diejenigen zu ueberzeugen suchen, die Alles, was ihre Ohnmacht nicht begreift, Traeumerei nennen, waehrend wir noch zu beweisen haben, dass es ausser dem Bestehenden ueberhaupt noch Moeglichkeiten gibt—ist unter anderen Breitekreisen Erkenntnis schon lange zur That gereift. Waehrend wir noch bei den Worten sind, ist anderwaerts bereits gebaut und versucht worden ; und so viel ward an Erfolg errungen, dass wir in der angenehmen Lage waeren, die Fruechte fremder Erfahrung zu pfluecken, wenn wir nur genug Kraft zur—Nachahmung haetten !

Wenn man dieses Buch nur aufblaettert und die vielen reinen Photographien betrachtet, die ihm angeschlossen sind, fuehlt man sogleich das Wehen einer frischen, neuen Luft. "Das Einfangen eines Bienenschwarms," "Baumfaellen," "In der Werkstaette," "Beim Bau eines Taubenhauses," "Unsere Boote," "Bau einer Bachschleuse," "Die Kartoffelernte"—um was handelt es sich da ? Um eine Robinsonade ? Nein, um eine Schule ! Aber, Gott sei Dank, das spielt eben in— England ! . . .

Man ahnt bereits, was hier unter Schule verstanden wird. Der ganze erste Theil des Buches schildert diesen kleinen, edlen Staat. Zuerst wird das als Utopie vorgefuehrt. Dann wird zur grossen Freude verrathen, dass Emlohstobba wirklich ist. . . .

Die Erziehungsschule braucht natuerlich Lehrer, die in ungebrochener,

German Verdicts

freudiger Jugendlichkeit ihre Aufgaben erfuellen. Sie werden daher schon ganz anders vorbereitet ; nicht nach dem Universitaetssystem, welches sie der Jugend entfremdet, sondern nach einem eigens zu dieser idealen Absicht erfundenen System, wodurch Geist und Koerper der Lehrer elastisch erhalten werden. In Jena sind solche Anstalten schon verwirklicht. Mit Recht werden die Lehrer verworfen, vor denen die Schueler wie unerforschliche Geheimnisse liegen, Lehrer, die sich von ihren Schuelern wie von Feinden abschliessen und dann wieder mit vorschnellem Urtheil zur Hand sind, die mit 30 Jahren ausser Stande sind, mit den Buben zu laufen und zu spielen, dafuer aber das Beispiel des Kartenspielens und Trinkens geben, Erzieher, die selbst nicht erzogen sind.

Was an "Emlohstobba" so schoen ist, das ist die milde Guete, mit der hier die juengsten Menschensoehne als Selbstzweck und als volle Menschen betrachtet werden. Diese frueh Anerkannten werden dann frei, tapfer, froehlich, siegreich und selbst wieder geneigt, anzuerkennen, mild und stark zugleich. Man kann sich ueber die Siege dieser Rasse nicht wundern ! Der Einzelne wird nicht dem Zufall ueberlassen, in hundert Beschaeftigungen kann er sich frueh entdecken. Fern von Bosheit und Erniedrigung, hat er Zeit, ungleich wachsende Begabungen der Reihe nach zu entwickeln und niemals wird ihm aller Werth abgesprochen oder weggenommen. Er lernt fruehzeitig in einem Ganzen zu leben, ohne List und Krieg und Pariagefuehle. Und alles das ohne Herdenzwang und Moralphraseologie, durchaus wuerdig und frei.

Die Jugend scheint mir die eigentliche Zeit des Communismus. In der Jugend, wenn ueberhaupt ja, ist Gelegenheit und Moeglichkeit, grosse Ungerechtigkeiten auszugleichen und einige Vorbereitungen fuer den *gleichen Kampf* um's Dasein zu schaffen, der ja nur unter der Bedingung natuerlich und gerecht ist, dass keiner mit gebundenen Haenden auf den Kampfplatz tritt. Vor der Jugend moege der haessliche Classengeist schweigen. Hier mindestens sollten Privilegien fallen. Wie fern und wie schwierig auch die Neuordnung der Gesellschaft sein moege—in der Schule kann heute schon Vieles verwirklicht werden, was im Staatsleben noch ein nebelhaftes und vielleicht fragwuerdiges Ideal ist. Darum ist die Reform der Schule eine *Vorfrage* im eminenten Sinn, ein erstes und naechstes Problem, vielleicht der Schluesselpunkt der Lage. . . .

19. DIGGING UP POTATOES. (*Winter, 1893*).

Copyright

CHAPTER XIII.

An English Exposition of the System
in process of Development
at Abbotsholme.
1896.

CHAPTER XIII

AN ENGLISH EXPOSITION OF THE SYSTEM IN PROCESS OF DEVELOPMENT AT ABBOTSHOLME, DECEMBER, 1896.

FOUNDATIONS OF SUCCESS: A PLEA FOR A RATIONAL EDUCATION.

By STANLEY DE BRATH, Member of the Institute of Civil Engineers, a former Assistant Master at Abbotsholme. London, December, 1896.

THE historical part of the present work would hardly be complete without some mention of Mr. de Brath's book, which is, in its main features, an English exposition of the system in process of development at Abbotsholme.

We quote from some lengthy reviews which appeared in some of the leading papers of the country, in order to enable those who are unacquainted with the book to judge for themselves whether we are right in our opinion.

These reviews render any quotations from the book itself superfluous, and show sufficiently that—instead of "suggesting a system which is mostly original," as *The Spectator* writes—Mr. de Brath's ideas bear such a close resemblance, almost amounting to identity, to the principles laid down by us in 1889 and since put into practice and developed, that we may consider these criticisms virtually apply to the work and aims of Abbotsholme.

That we do not stand alone in this opinion is shown by a contribution below, from the Assistant Masters of the School, the majority of whom were acquainted with the place before Mr. de Brath, as an Assistant Master, was initiated into Abbotsholme methods.

PRESS NOTICES.

The Times, *December* 18, 1896.

Mr. S. de Brath, the author of this vigorous and stimulating little volume, is of the opinion, which is probably shared by most people who have given serious attention to the subject, that the system of secondary education at present in vogue in this country is very imperfectly adapted to the real conditions of modern civilisation and to the higher needs of modern culture. Measuring "success" by no sordid or material standard, but by the fitness of the citizen to discharge the duties, personal, industrial, and social, of citizenship, he starts from the assumption that the foundations of success of this kind are to be sought in a system of "rational education." As he says himself (in his Preface) :—

"A successful nation is made up of successful units, and I have had primarily in view the parents who, having to think first of their children's success in life, are dissatisfied with the existing state of things; under which, after an education costing at least a thousand pounds, large numbers, perhaps a majority, of boys leave school knowing nothing but a very moderate amount of Latin and Greek, quite insufficient to give them an interest in classical literature, and the rudiments of half a dozen other 'subjects,' in none of which they take any real interest or can stand any test. Many parents also desire for their children more practical and manual training, more development of the social and artistic side of human nature, and a better acquaintance with the treasures of our English tongue, as well as greater care to avoid the moral disasters which are,

An English Exposition

alas! not of rare occurrence. To these I have tried to indicate a way of realising their desires."

The method pursued by Mr. de Brath is to give a summary of the principles of rational education as expounded by recognised authorities on the subject, English and foreign, or, in his own language, " to present natural laws which have been slowly worked out by the labour of many minds " ; and on the basis of these principles to propound a definite scheme for their practical embodiment in a school to be established for the purpose. Of course it may be urged that education is a practical art, and that the principles or natural laws expounded by Mr. de Brath are mainly derived from the writings of men who had no practical experience of the art. But such a criticism would not apply to Froebel, the originator of the Kindergarten system, and, so far as it applies to any of the authorities cited by Mr. de Brath, he might very justly answer that the art of education as practised in this country is not very remarkable for its success as tested by results, and that he at any rate is for his part perfectly prepared to bring his principles to the test of practice. His own scheme (p. 185) is as follows :—

"The leading principles of such a school as it is proposed to organise may be summarised as follows :—

"That all instruction and occupation shall be interlocked and co-ordinated ; that the learners shall be as far as practicable brought into contact with the things about which they learn, rather than with descriptions of these things, and that the influence of the surroundings rather than mere instruction be looked to for mental and moral development.

" That relief from over-pressure shall be obtained by limiting brain work for juniors to a weekly average of four-and-a-half hours, and for seniors to five-and-a-half hours, per day.

"That economy of time be secured by employing only the very best educational methods, apparatus, and teachers.

"That the English language and literature be made a staple of instruction on the humanist side.

" That the practical and manual side of education be developed side by side with the intellectual and social, not with the view of turning out amateur mechanics, but to insure that all knowledge is put to use, and that skill and handiness be acquired.

"That at least one modern language be taught conversationally and thoroughly.

" That music be restored to a regular place in the school course,

"That personal attention be insured by reducing the size of the classes, so that all that is taught shall be taught thoroughly to all, up to the full measure of their capacity."

It is obvious that the principles here set forth are of two kinds—those which relate to the theory and method of education, and those which relate to its matter. The former would perhaps meet with more or less general assent; the latter, however, at once revive the old controversy between the Humanists and the Realists, and would probably give rise in practice to endless dispute. The Humanists would insist that, other things being equal—that is, the method of instruction being the same— the subjects which they propose to employ as the matter of instruction are better adapted for the purpose than those favoured by the Realists; and the latter would at once join issue on this fundamental point. Into this high and ancient controversy we cannot enter here. It is a more practical criticism, perhaps, that the system advocated by Mr. de Brath needs capital for its initiation and faith in its principles for its success. To this end Mr. de Brath desires "that an association be formed, not exceeding sixty participating members, who shall each subscribe not less than £200 towards a capital fund of £12,000, to be used for the purpose of founding a school for boys not exceeding 250 in number, and of subsidising one or more Kindergartens; this capital sum to be redeemable by sinking fund"; and he develops at some length the details of the scheme on which the proposed association is to work. It remains to be seen whether there exists among fairly well-to-do parents sufficient discontent with the existing system of secondary education and its results, and sufficient agreement with the principles expounded and the methods recommended by Mr. de Brath, to induce them to coöperate in establishing such an association as he proposes and in providing the capital required to start a school on "rational principles." If this should prove to be the case, we should watch the progress and results of the experiment with no little interest. Most people agree that the existing system of secondary education is by no means all that it should be. Inquiry and discussion have probably done all that could be expected of them, and so far it is not much. There remains the path of experiment to be tried, and though we should hesitate to endorse all Mr. de Brath's views, we wish him well in his enterprise.

20. THE HAY FIELD. (*Summer, 1891*).

Copyright

An English Exposition

THE ACADEMY, *January* 23, 1897.

Various reasons have of late led many thinking men to doubt whether the English system of secondary education is worthy of the name of system. Classical tradition still controls the public schools; and in many of them the " modern side " is found not to be a brilliant success, and is maintained more as a grudging concession to the utilitarian spirit of the age than as a proper method of education, using that word in its etymological sense. "Latin and Greek," as a headmaster once remarked to the present writer, "are the most effectual agents in keeping a boy's nose at the grindstone." The statement was probably true, from that teacher's point of view; but only because the teaching of the ancient languages has been methodised, and because it is easier to find persons capable of giving precisely that kind of drill than of giving really intelligent instruction in other branches.

The whole question of school education has been treated in a masterly manner by Mr. S. de Brath in a book of some 200 pages, entitled, "The Foundations of Success: a Plea for Rational Education." Mr. de Brath modestly disclaims originality in his treatment of the subject; but originality often consists as much in orderly arrangement and logical sequence of ideas as in novelty; and this is a subject on which it would be difficult to write anything new. The keynote of the work is that our present systems need reform; that " success in this workaday world (and success here means existence) has come to depend more and more on 'directive skill'—power to direct the forces of inanimate nature, and of less able men, whether in units, classes, or races "; that " instruction aiming at this 'directive power' is largely given in the State-aided technical and secondary schools for the masses, and must be still more widely given in the near future "; and that such instruction " is far superior both in planned order and method to that of the expensive class, schools usually called secondary." He complains that in our public schools, and in our secondary schools in general, far too little attention is paid to the co-ordination of the various branches of instruction, and points out that Germany and America have made great strides towards a consistent co-ordination; that—

"The one, by patient study of the mental operations, has discovered, and the other, with characteristic keenness, is applying, a new form of 'concentration' whereby, instead of science, mathematics, history literature, language, and manual training being treated as entirely different 'subjects,' they are linked together, by handling each so as to afford illustrations to the others."

These two nations, which are our two great rivals in trade, are precisely the nations which have revised their educational system; and they have done so in accordance with the fact that the wealth of a manufacturing State lies in the number of producers actively engaged, in their individual skill, and in the intelligence with which they are directed. Yet the two nations differ in mental aptitude. The present writer was much struck with a remark made by the American manager of a very large German electrical manufactory, that while German workmen were more conscientious and trustworthy, American sub-managers were preferable to Germans on account of their greater fertility of resource and energy.

Mr. de Brath draws special attention to the present time as England's opportunity.

"In the last years of the eighteenth century it was Continental war destroying commerce; in the last years of the nineteenth century it is Continental militarism sapping it. Hundreds of thousands of workmen are withdrawn from production, and heavy taxes oppress the trading classes. . . These facts will not continue indefinitely; the magnitude of the expenditure forbids it. While they last, they are England's opportunity."

Our public and secondary schools are "the schools for the officers of industrialism, and these are more imperatively needed by England than the technical schools we are now tardily endowing. Wise direction of industrialism is of the essence of the matter. Is it needful to insist that all skill comes first of taking thought? or that directive skill is even more useful than manual skill?"

These quotations show the ground on which Mr. de Brath builds. The superstructure is a careful treatise on physical and biological facts, on physical education, on mental education, on moral education, on method, on the stages of growth, and on the co-ordination of instruction, and a concluding chapter treats of some practical suggestions.

Mr. de Brath does not hesitate to begin at the beginning. Adopting the modern scientific definition of energy, he deals with the transformation of the chemical energy absorbed as food into heat, necessary to sustain the temperature of the body; into motion of its parts, necessary to all vital processes; and into that portion which is active in the brain, the manifestation of which is consciousness. With a short sketch of the nature of variation, transmitted to progeny, and of heredity he passes on to remark that while " we cannot change the facts which have made the degenerate, the neurotic, the hysterical, and the criminal," yet

An English Exposition

the future of young persons is greatly influenced by their environment, and that "we have only to make a suitable environment for growing organisms if we wish to mould them to our ideals; and this is the meaning of education." "It is environment that has produced variations in the past, as it is to it that the horticulturist and the stock-breeder look to produce those at which they aim; so to it, and not to mere didactics, must the educator look for his results also." And "education becomes the provision of such an environment as will favour the ethical process in the fullest application of that term; one which takes account of the physical and intellectual side of that process as well as of its moral side." The ethical process culminates in "renunciation as the gate of the higher life."

Physical education comes first in order. The use of the body in all its muscular development, so as to evolve skill, leads not only to greater acuteness in the senses, but also to the mental habit of using them. Therefore the child should be trained by example more than by precept to use his eyes in observing natural objects and recording the observations; his ear in musical exercises; his hands in drawing and in carpentry, for boys, in dress-cutting and cookery for girls. Such training makes capable men and women; "its lessons can never be learned by precepts alone, they are to be acquired by actual personal endeavour expended on real things." The *corpus sanum* is next considered, and a number of very practical maxims, gained in the school of experience, are laid down for combating and repressing the evils not uncommon in public schools.

But Mr. de Brath does not confine himself to general exposition; he gives a detailed table of divisions of the day, as in his opinion they should be spent in a school. Each week twenty-nine lessons of three-quarters of an hour each are interposed between intervals devoted to play, meals, and music. Work and violent exercise after meals are avoided, and not more than four lessons ever succeed one another. There can be no doubt that such conditions as these are favourable to the physical health and mental development of boys and girls.

Mr. de Brath defines the purpose of mental education as required to give—(1) habits of close observation; (2) discrimination of likenesses and differences; (3) power of correct inference; and (4) that command of language which is necessary for correct formulation, or for calling up a clear mental image. The "knowledge," which is sometimes spoken of as if it were the purpose of mental education, comes incidentally. As a matter of method, the formulation of a general truth should be reached only through repeated trials. It is interesting to contrast the old and the suggested way of learning that the square on the hypotenuse of a right-angled triangle is equal to the sum of the squares on the other two sides. As every one knows, the usual method is to give the boy the proposition to learn ; if he understands it, so much the better ; if he does not, he is a duffer. "The right way," according to Mr. de Brath, "because the natural path of discovery, is to show that a right-angled triangle, of which the sides enclosing the right angle are in the proportion of 3 to 4, has the third side equal to 5 of the same units of length, and that $3^2 + 4^2 = 5^2$; to go on to show that the same relation holds between the sides in other cases, both arithmetically and by actual mensuration (or weighing) of the constructed squares. The general rule can then be inferred ; and lastly, we can start with the rule and prove it deductively, as in Euclid I., 47. It must never be forgotten that "words come to a child as pure conventions till he sees the actual things," and the same is to some extent true with most adults. As things are at present, "almost all our teaching is from words, and the retention of words is alpha and omega." But our instruction should aim at teaching not what to think, but how to think ; and a program is laid down in which the two chief divisions are the life of man and the life of nature.

The subject of moral education is next considered. Morality is defined as "the wise direction of the daily stock of energy ; wise habits of expenditure of this stock preclude unwise habits ; " and character " is that nature of mind which practises wise thought and action." The cultivation of the sense of beauty, of the sense of right, and of the infinite, are obviously the goals to aim at in moral training. The last, which involves religion, is worthy of special care ; and it must never be forgotten that here, above all, example is of far more worth than precept —that our religion is our daily life as actually lived.

A chapter on "Method" follows, with details of application in actual teaching. And here we note the difficulties to be contended with. Our universities, instead of allowing the "Lehrfreiheit" of the Continent, impose restricted courses, and test the progress of the student by examinations. This evil is a great one ; and its harmful influence on the prosperity of the country is almost incalculable. For it is necessary for the schools to aim at preparation for the university, and this involves the compulsory acquisition by all boys of a number of subjects, in which many take little or no interest. Our universities also place a wrong goal before the eyes of students, the majority of whom read with the object of passing an examination, or of distancing their fellows, or of securing a scholarship, instead of with the intention of training their mental faculties for their life-work. Especially in science is this to be deplored ; for the originative faculty, and the power of management of fellow-men, is not to be tested by examination. The process leads to the selection of the unfit in a majority of cases, for a ready memory counts for more than ability to originate and to govern. The schoolmaster, however, has to take things as they are ; and Mr. de Brath does his best to adapt his curriculum to the existing state of university education. It is time that our authorities in higher education recognised that nine-tenths of the energy which is expended by teachers and pupils in examining and in preparing for examinations might be used with much more profit in exercising the faculty of origination, in which few men are wholly deficient.

The scheme, which Mr. de Brath propounds in his final chapter, for instituting a model school, has much to recommend it. Happy the boys who are under his system !

For comprehensive treatment of his subject, for thorough acquaintance with what has been previously written, and for lucid statement of common-sense principles, which are so obvious when clearly laid down as almost to appear to be truisms, this little work deserves the highest commendation. It is much to be hoped that its influence may be widespread, and that its teaching may be ere long translated into action. " Science is accuracy about common things," and with this definition, for which Mr. de Brath is responsible, his little treatise has good claim to be called scientific.

THE LITERARY WORLD, *April* 9, 1897.

Moreover, an examiner to some of the public schools informed Mr. de Brath that in the sciences, including mathematics, their lower forms were not nearly so well instructed as boys of the same age in the better of the Board Schools. We do not know which of the eight chapters in this excellent volume to praise the most. It is very plain that the author has studied his subject both absorbingly and long. The harvest of his labours is one of which to be proud. In his final section Mr. de Brath puts forward a scheme for the institution of a school such as would accord with the educational principles cherished by himself and others keen in the same important cause. We shall be anxious to learn whether he succeeds in obtaining the support necessary for the successful carrying out of his plan. We especially commend to parents the few pages under the heading, " The Wise Direction of Growth."

Athenæum, *May* 8, 1897.

Interesting specimen-schemes of the occupation of a typical school day and of the arrangement of subjects in a typical day's work are supplied, and much useful and suggestive matter is added concerning method and kindred topics. The volume closes with a practical proposal, which Mr. de Brath is willing " to take a share in carrying out." He proposes to form an association for starting and conducting a school in which boys shall be educated (at a reasonable cost) in accordance with the principles stated and explained in his work.

The Tablet, *July* 28, 1897.

The Foundations of Success, by Stanley de Brath (London : George Philip and Son), is a plea for a more rational education than is now given in England. It is a thoughtful and useful book, worthy of the attention of the instructors of youth, who will find in it many very sound and practical principles and recommendations. Even in the chapter on Moral Education—in which *Catholics* most expect deficiencies, and excessive reliance upon, for instance, mere information concerning the laws of life and growth—there is a great deal of common sense and sound religious principle. The book, then, on the whole is helpful. It looks to " success " in no extremely narrow sense ; and it points out the need of having our teachers in every class of school themselves first trained and taught to be teachers.

Leeds Mercury, *July* 29, 1897.

To general readers the most interesting portions of the work will be the twelve pages of practical suggestions at the close, and the nineteen pages of introduction on *national needs* at the commencement of the volume. In urging our national needs as a reason why education should be improved, the author reminds us of the continuous aggrandisement of Prussia.

The Spectator, *November* 6, 1897.

TRUE EDUCATION.

The author does not wish his countrymen to follow a foreign system blindfolded, but suggests a system himself, which is mostly original, but partly taken from other writers on the subject. If we are to keep our place as a manufacturing and commercial community, the sooner our secondary education is reformed the better. It is not so long ago that boys were being prepared for trade, manufacturing, farming, &c., by learning Latin verse composition, Greek, and ancient geography, instead of French or German, science, &c. The commercial travellers of Germany have been taught in the Real-Schulen, which are equivalent to the modern side of our public schools and grammar schools, and when they enter life they are provided with all the knowledge they require for commercial pursuits. Another very important point is the necessity that the teacher should learn how to teach, as he does in Germany, before he begins, and not, as sometimes in England, " learn his trade at the expense of the learners."

We will not enter into the details of this treatise, which are most interesting and instructive for those engaged in education, but merely give the names of the chapters and a few remarks on some of them Chap. 1, " Physical and Biologic Facts." Chap. 2, " Physical Education," of which " health and skill are the ends." " It involves training of the senses and of the Motor system," and the " wise direction of growth." In this section, notice the following remark : " Good digestion comes of plain food and regularity. Now boys are often told to retire at a regular hour. But children will not leave their play to attend to the calls of nature if they can help it. They will go constipated for days." Then follows how to deal with the matter. The tuck-shop and gluttony are not left out. " In one tuck-shop, managed by the school authorities, the net profits were £500." Impurity is not passed over, nor its baneful results in after-life, and the symptoms which ought to attract the attention of the master, and "platonic attachments" are most seriously dealt with too. At the end of it time-tables for winter and summer terms are given. Chap. 3, " Mental Education " :—

" Understanding is the pre-requisite of directive power and begins with observation. The purpose of mental education is to give (1) the habit of close observation, (2) discrimination of likenesses and differences, (3) correct inference, (4) command of language necessary to correct formulation, or the power to call up a clear mental image. The 'knowledge' often spoken of as if it were the purpose of mental education comes incidentally. . . . Teaching should be by things themselves, not descriptions of them, whereas our system of education is Words."

The rest of the chapter is taken up with "the subject-matter of instruction," "the value of Nature-Knowledge," as well as of "Humane Letters." Moral education, including religion, is treated of in Chapter 4, and is the best of all. "Moral education is not the preservation of innocence, but the gaining of wisdom; it is chiefly habit, and becomes 'character.'" "It depends much upon example, and a child, compelled for six hours a day to see the countenance and hear the voice of a fretful, unkind teacher, is placed in a school of vice." "A heroic character is built of little acts, as a great cathedral is of little stones." Inaccuracy and carelessness are included. "Unpunctuality, bad demeanour, and inaccurate replies (corrected by the master but not by the child) lead, in the long run, to indifference to truth." Self-denial is glorified in: "The Church has persistently kept before the eyes of men the lovely ideal of a life dead to the things of sense, and has found her ideal not in the life won, but in the life laid down." Then are treated fully the Sense of Beauty, punishments, matters of sex, and the sense of the Infinite. Of punishments is said: "Those who find constant resort to force necessary are not fit to teach; if the stick could reform, it would be their own shoulders that need it;" and of the Infinite: "Would it not give a keener sense of Infinity, if we were to verify more often that behind every physical phenomenon there is a force, unknown to the intellect, and thus to guard against the littleness of mind which deludes itself with the idea that to know a process is to understand its cause?" But space here commands us to bid "Goodbye" to the author, and thank him for what he has told us.

CRITICISM BY THE ASSISTANT MASTERS OF ABBOTSHOLME.

The Foundations of Success, published in December, 1896, was at once recognised by all those who had known the School even in its earliest years, as containing a very fairly full and methodical account of the general life, curriculum, and organisation of Abbotsholme.

The Ideals and Methods which had from the first been adopted there, or which had been assimilated from outside, or been developed from the experience gained there, were, in their entirety, little known to the public. This resulted from two circumstances: (i.) The secluded position of the School, and (ii.) The lack of leisure to describe completely, in a digestible form, the work which had been attempted and accomplished.

The Foundations of Success was written by a man who for a year was a member of the teaching staff of Abbotsholme, and who, being, when he came, quite new to the practice of teaching, was peculiarly receptive of what he found there.

While in no sense figuring as an official statement of the Abbotsholme system, the book had an interest and value to all connected with the School. For not only had it collected and tabulated their articles of faith, in a manner which they had failed to do completely through lack of time, but by publication it drew attention and criticism to many of the maxims which had shaped the practice of the School from its foundation. The public criticism of our work which followed the appearance of the book, was all the more valuable to us in that it could in no sense be recognised as intended for us personally. If adverse, it might point the road to improvement ; if favourable, it could not fail to give encouragement.

The extremely cordial reception of the book showed that many of the convictions to which, even in moments of difficulty and discouragement, we had given our unflinching adherence, were now recognised as sound by those whose position secured for their pronouncements universal attention.

The pith of the book, as found on p. 185, is quoted above in the review by *The Times*; but scattered up and down the text we find many of our guiding principles, of which we will cite the following :—

i. A reformed curriculum and school life, broad enough to leave no part of the boy's nature undeveloped.

ii. The dead languages relegated to a secondary position, instead of forming the staple of instruction.

iii. Instruction according to the ascertained psychological steps, resulting in a real mental training.

iv. Interlocking of all the studies in groups ; a simplification which transforms the wide range of subjects into practically only two connected wholes. The same truth approached from various sides (in various subjects) and thus indelibly impressed, and the underlying unity of Creation made apparent.

v. Things before words. The use of pictures and models. The School estate and community providing geographical features, types of plants and animals, illustrations of history and economics, problems for physics and mathematics.

vi. Manual work of various kinds compulsory for all; not merely as promoting handiness, physical growth, respect for labour, orderliness, &c.; but also as supplying opportunities for the application of indoor instruction, and as teaching the direction of labour and coöperation for the good of the community.

vii. The supreme importance of personal and social hygiene. Recognition of the stages of growth. Careful arrangement of clothing and food. No "grub" nor "grub-shop." Reduction of hours of book- and brain-work, and increase of hours of steady disciplined outdoor occupation and exercise. Periods of three-quarters of an hour for class, and intervals of a quarter of an hour between the periods, to clear the head and drive the blood over the body.

viii. General healthiness of character developed not alone by instruction and example, but by full occupation, many interests, and wholesome and beautiful conditions of life.

To have all these points brought together within the compass of a single book was most useful, and to find it received with such decided public approval was most gratifying to those who had supported for seven years a school where these maxims were being steadily applied.

THE ASSISTANT MASTERS OF ABBOTSHOLME.

December 11, 1899.

21. STACKING. (*Summer, 1893*).

Copyright

CHAPTER XIV.

A French Savant's Verdict.

CHAPTER XIV.

A FRENCH SAVANT'S VERDICT.

ÉCOLE D'ABBOTSHOLME : ET TRAVAUX MANUELS DES ÉLÈVES.[1]

[Reprinted from *La Science Sociale*, October, 1894.]

A quoi tient la Supériorité des Anglo-Saxons. Paris, Firmin Didot, March, 1897.
[For M. Demolins' article on the School see Chapter IX. ; for the rest of his interesting book we must refer the reader to the English translation, "Anglo-Saxon Superiority : to what it is due," London, Leadenhall Press, 1898.]

31, 12, '98.

LE mouvement en faveur du système d'éducation anglaise qui s'est produit depuis quelque temps en France donne un intérêt d'actualité à une des écoles anglaises qui sont des spécimens complets du genre, l'*Educational Laboratory* d'Abbotsholme (Derbyshire).

Cette école a été fondée en 1889 par M. Cecil Reddie, qui la dirige encore aujourd'hui. Située dans une verdoyante vallée, elle n'a rien de l'aspect froid de nos lycées-casernes, et plus d'un Parisien en ferait volontiers sa villa. Construite intentionnellement loin des villes, dans un pays de pâturages qui ressemble à un immense parc, entourée de jardins et de vergers, et flanquée de bâtiments de ferme, l'école est au centre d'un domaine assez vaste que traverse la rivière de Dove, et qui permet aux élèves de se livrer au canotage, à la pêche et à la natation. Le tennis, le cricket et le foot-ball ont leurs places réservées, et du haut d'une colline voisine on fait, en hiver, de superbes glissades.

Les bâtiments comprennent des salles de classe, un atelier, un réfectoire, des dortoirs, une bibliothèque et des salles de réunion. Ils sont disposés pour recevoir cinquante élèves de onze à dix-huit ans.

---

[1] *Revue encyclopédique Larousse.* December 31, 1898. Directeur : Georges Moreau.

Le régime alimentaire est confortable, quoique particulier et se rapprochant par certains côtés du régime végétarien. Il comprend, en effet, le poisson, les œufs, le pudding, le cacao, la bouillie, la marmelade et les fruits ; comme boissons : le thé, le lait et l'eau.

Les élèves font quatre repas par jour. Les tables sont de sept élèves environ. Les maîtres y prennent place, excepté au premier déjeuner.

Chaque élève a son lit, une armoire basse dont le dessus sert de lavabo, et un *tub* pour les ablutions du matin et du soir ; ils sont cinq ou six par dortoir. Leur coucher présente cette particularité qu'il n'y a pas de draps au lit, mais des couvertures de laine, grâce auxquelles en toute saison et par les froids rigoureux on dort fenêtres ouvertes.

Chaque dortoir est dirigé par un élève responsable de ses camarades et du matériel mis à leur disposition ; il a le titre de préfet et veille à tout. A huit heures du matin, après déjeuner, les élèves vont mettre leur dortoir en ordre ; tout est vigoureusement aéré ; les lits sont faits avec adresse, rapidité et précision.

Cette pension n'est pas accessible au commun des familles, car elle coûte, suivant l'âge des élèves, de 80 à 100 guinées (de 1,818 fr. 40 à 2,648 francs).

La journée se divise en trois parties à l'école d'Abbotsholme : le matin est consacré à l'enseignement dans la classe ; l'après-midi, au travail manuel et aux exercices physiques ; le soir, à des réunions et des lectures, mais les travaux des élèves ne sont point, pour ainsi dire, coupés en tranches distinctes et sans rapport l'une avec l'autre ; tout au contraire, le mélange intime du travail et de la vie ordinaire est une des bases de l'enseignement : plus le travail agit sur la personnalité de l'élève, plus son influence est durable, plus les résultats sont parfaits.

Le principe fondamental de l'éducation intellectuelle est l'observation des choses et des gens, et l'élève apprend d'abord à parler et à écrire sa propre langue en liant les mots aux choses qu'il a sous les yeux et sous la main. De l'étude de sa langue il passe à celle du français, de l'allemand et du latin ; mais pendant le temps respectivement attribué aux langues vivantes, "elles constituent le langage courant et usuel dans les classes et les travaux pratiques, à l'étude, à l'atelier et au salon ; elles s'incrustent ainsi dans la mémoire et dans les habitudes et ne s'en laissent plus détacher. L'analyse grammaticale suit l'usage des mots et ne le précède pas. En nous écartant dans nos lycées de cet ordre naturel et logique, *nous n'arrivons qu'à être muets en plusieurs langues.*" [1]

Quant au latin, ce court dialogue montrera les divergences qui séparent l'enseignement moderne et l'enseignement ancien :

---

[1] *La République française*, 6 novembre, 1894. (*Un nouveau type de collège.*)

Prima luce tintinnabulum sonat. E cubiculis eximus. . . Nonne currere amas ? Currere amo.—Quid tu censes ? Equidem dormire malo.—At hic cursus corpus sanum facit. Nonne corpus sanum habere vis ?—Hoc maxime volo.—Itaque quotidie curras, sic enim mentem sanam in corpore sano habebis.

A côté de l'étude des langues et en relation intime avec elles, on apprend l'histoire et la géographie, et notamment l'histoire romaine en latin. Pour les sciences naturelles, on commence par les faits courants de la vie ordinaire, de façon à conduire l'élève par une suite normale de faits aux lois générales de l'univers.

L'hygiène proprement dite, de même que l'hygiène intellectuelle et morale, destinées à donner et entretenir une santé parfaite, font l'objet d'un cours particulier.

Les mathématiques sont enseignées, autant que possible, à l'aide d'exemples concrets et en les liant aux sciences naturelles.[1]

La morale et la religion sont enseignées en les liant à l'histoire et en les rendant vivantes par des exemples tirés de la vie humaine.

Les leçons d'économie politique s'appuient sur les faits du jour, et les réponses des jeunes gens démontrent quel intérêt ils prennent à une démonstration qui, partie par exemple d'une scène de jardinage, arrive graduellement aux principes les plus subtils.

Détail caractéristique. Quelle que soit la branche de l'enseignement il n'est donné ni récompense ni prix : les élèves ne cherchent dans le travail bien fait que la satisfaction du devoir accompli.

En entrant à l'école, chacun apporte sa caisse d'outils. Une partie de l'après-midi est consacrée au travail dans l'atelier : les uns font de la menuiserie, ceux-ci tressent des paniers, ceux-là fabriquent de la poterie.

Au moment opportun, les abbotsholmiens travaillent au jardin, abattent des arbres, récoltent les pommes de terre, font la moisson, apprennent à élever les abeilles, à construire un bateau, une remise, une tribune, etc.

La gymnastique et les jeux en plein air occupent dans le programme une place importante, place légitime, puisque Wellington disait que les victoires remportées par les Anglais étaient dues à leurs champs de cricket. Tout cela, d'ailleurs, dans la mesure qui convient et de façon à éviter le surmenage physique, comme on évite le surmenage intellectuel.

De temps en temps des excursions assez longues permettent de se livrer

---

[1] " Des opérations d'arpentage rendent en quelque sorte tangibles les formules de la géométrie, et la comptabilité quotidienne de la ferme, de l'atelier, du jardin et du laboratoire forme un vivant commentaire de tous les calculs et de tous les chiffres qui se sont déroulés dans les leçons du matin." (*La République française*, loc. cit.)

à d'utiles observations et, grâce aux élèves photographes, chacun garde de sa promenade un souvenir durable.

Le soir est consacré au chant, à la musique, aux lectures, aux conférences ; les professeurs, les invités de passage, les dames, se réunissent dans la grande salle pour assister à ces divertissements.

Une fois par mois ont lieu des *debates*. Un sujet de discussion est donné, quatre orateurs sont désignés, deux dans un sens, deux dans l'autre, et la durée de chaque discours est limitée.

Parfois encore, les élèves sont initiés aux beautés dramatiques en jouant des scènes des différents chefs-d'œuvre. Un intérêt pratique s'attache à ces divers exercices, qui ont pour but de donner aux élèves l'habitude de parler en public, et l'aplomb nécessaire pour se présenter devant une grande assemblée. SANSAS.

PRESS NOTICES ON THE FRENCH, ENGLISH, AND AMERICAN EDITIONS.

ENGLISH.

No.	Name of Paper.	Place.	Date.
1.	Manchester Guardian.	Manchester.	May 11, 1897.
2.	Star.	London.	September 9, 1897.
3.	St. James's Gazette.	London.	September 14, 1897.
4.	Vectis.	Isle of Wight.	September 15, 1897.
5.	Spectator.	London.	September 18, 1897.
6.	Globe.	London.	October 13, 1897.
7.	Echo.	London.	October 15, 1897.
8.	Morning Post.	London.	October 21, 1897.
9.	Westminster Gazette.	London.	November 15, 1897.
10.	Bedford Times.	Bedford.	November 24, 1897.
11.	Journal of Education.	London.	November, 1897.
12.	Christian World.	London.	December 30, 1897.
13.	Ayr Advertiser.	Ayr.	January 8, 1898.
14.	Leeds Mercury.	Leeds.	January 22, 1898.
15.	Lancashire Daily Express.	Preston.	January 27, 1898.
16.	The Speaker.	London.	January 29, 1898.
17.	Tablet.	London.	January 29, 1898.
18.	Educational Times.	London.	February 1, 1898.
19.	Review of Reviews.	London.	February, 1898.
20.	British Medical Journal.	London.	February, 1898.
21.	Dundee Advertiser.	Dundee.	March 12, 1898.
22.	Sunday Times.	London.	April 24, 1898.
23.	Daily Mail.	London.	July 15, 1898.
24.	Ladies Field.	London.	July 23, 1898.
25.	Christian Age.	London.	August 3, 1898.
26.	Morning Advertiser.	London.	August 13, 1898.

A French Savant's Verdict

No.	Name of Paper.	Place.	Date.
27.	Westminster Gazette.	London.	September 17, 1898.
28.	Irish Times.	Dublin.	September 17, 1898.
29.	Globe.	London.	September 19, 1898.
30.	New Age.	London.	September 22, 1898.
31.	Belfast News Letter.	Belfast.	September 22, 1898.
32.	Academy.	London.	September 24, 1898.
33.	Weekly Sun.	London.	September 25, 1898.
34.	Manchester Evening Mail.	Manchester.	September 26, 1898.
35.	Aberdeen Free Press.	Aberdeen.	September 26, 1898.
36.	N. British Daily Mail.		September 26, 1898.
37.	World.	London.	September 28, 1898.
38.	Sheffield Telegraph.	Sheffield.	September 28, 1898.
39.	Liverpool Courier.	Liverpool.	September 29, 1898.
40.	Westminster Gazette.	London.	September 30, 1898.
41.	Newcastle Weekly Chron.	Newcastle.	October 1, 1898.
42.	Bookseller.	London.	November, 1898.
43.	Dublin Express.	Dublin.	October 1, 1898.
44.	Birmingham Gazette.	Birmingham.	October 3, 1898.
45.	Glasgow Evening Times.	Glasgow.	October 4, 1898.
46.	Glasgow Herald.	Glasgow.	October 6, 1898.
47.	Daily Chronicle.	London.	October 11, 1898.
48.	Liverpool Mercury.	Liverpool.	October 12, 1898.
49.	Daily Graphic.	London.	October 15, 1898.
50.	Umpire.	London.	October 16, 1898.
51.	St. James's Gazette.	London.	October 17, 1898.
52.	Manchester Gazette.	Manchester.	October 18, 1898.
53.	Literary World.	London	October 21, 1898.
54.	Birmingham Post.	Birmingham.	October 25, 1898.
55.	To-day.	London.	October 29, 1898.
56.	Literature.	London.	October 29, 1898.
57.	Critic.	London.	November 3, 1898.
58.	Bradford.	Bradford.	November 10, 1898.
59.	Pall Mall Gazette.	London.	November 23, 1898.
60.	Nottingham Guardian.	Nottingham.	November 28, 1898.
61.	University Correspondent.	London.	December 17, 1898.
62.	Church Bells.	London.	December 30, 1898.
63.	University Correspondent.	London.	January 17, 1899.
64.	East Anglian Daily Times.		January 9, 1899.
65.	Guardian.	London.	March 22, 1899.
66.	Sunday Sun.	London.	May 14, 1899.
67.	University Correspondent.	London.	September 23, 1899.
68.	Lady's Pictorial.	London.	November 4, 1899.

MANCHESTER GUARDIAN, *May* 11, 1897.

It is always interesting to see ourselves as others see us ; it is especially pleasing to see ourselves as we are seen by M. Edmond Demolins, for he gives us praise enough, and his good work as editor of *La Science Sociale* entitles his opinion to some weight. The facts of the case, and he has examined them carefully, force him to acknowledge the superiority of the Anglo-Saxon. But he is no mere empty Anglo-phile; it is his patriotism, as he frequently tells us, that has led him to examine the question, for the future is fraught with danger to France if the power of the Anglo-Saxon is allowed to grow unrivalled. He accounts for the inferiority of the French by their methods of education and the nature of their family life. *The French education, which gives a wide but superficial knowledge, is excellent for producing Government officials, but it does not fit the youth of the country for the struggle for life;* and the French family system, in teaching the children complete dependence on the parents, delays their recognition of the part that they have to play, whereas the English system inspires a greater self-confidence and gives a greater power of resource. This is the reason, according to M. Demolins, why the French are now so unsuccessful as colonists. *Last century in this respect they were quite on equal terms with the English, but then the life was different. The new and evil system began with Napoleon.* A centralised Government such as his was in need of a great number of officials, and he altered the school and college education in such a way as to provide them. Despite revolutions, despite the name of republics, his system has continued, and the tendency to centralisation has even increased. Now M. Demolins contends that the more centralised a Government is, and the more that a Government post is the aim of the youth of the country, the greater will be their lack of initiative and the more deeply rooted their habits of passive obedience, and consequently the weaker must the nation inevitably become. As a whole the book is exceedingly interesting. *Sometimes we may think that the author's knowledge of England is inadequate, and that he is too apt to draw general conclusions from stray circumstances, as when, neglecting the great public schools, he makes the experimental school of Abbotsholme, in Derbyshire, represent the educational system of England*, or as when he concludes that the Scottish working classes are refined, because when he took tea with an artisan in the village of Penicuik his cup was rinsed out each time before being refilled. And certainly the "Edinburgh Summer Meetings" seem accountable for much of his knowledge of English character and customs. But these faults do not materially detract from the real value of the book. The chapters on the education of children in France and England and on the different ideas of patriotism show at once thoroughness of investigation and power of judgment, and certainly no saner explanation has yet been given of the decrease of the French population than that of M Demolins. His book would make an interesting supplement to Taine's

Notes sur *Angleterre* and Hamerton's *French and English*. But while these two writers were men of letters who took the standpoint of the uninterested spectator, M. Demolins is rather a scientist, and his book aims at the practical result of reform. *It cannot claim to be considered as literary*, but the clear subdivisions, the interesting tables, and the sociological theories make it quite easy to read.

THE SPECTATOR, *September* 18, 1897.
THE SUPERIORITY OF THE ANGLO-SAXON.

Is it national modesty or national indifference to foreign opinion which has led us to take so little notice of the extraordinary compliment paid to our race by France? M. Demolins' book, *A quoi tient la Supériorité des Anglo-Saxons*, was published last April, went through five editions in two months, and became the subject of innumerable articles in the French papers, many of them signed by men of real celebrity (quotations from these make an interesting appendix to the volume). Yet the Anglo-Saxons went their way, careless of this tribute paid to them by jealousy not less than admiration. The book, of course, has no direct message for us; indeed, *it has almost a demoralising effect to see ourselves so persistently held up as the example*. Nevertheless, it is very well worth reading, not only for the light it throws upon the condition of France, but also, and chiefly, for its indirect lesson. The Anglo-Saxon civilisation succeeds because it is the most individualist, or, as M. Demolins calls it, the most particularist, in the world; because the Anglo-Saxon ideal of life and conduct is of all the most profoundly opposed to Socialism. *The Anglo-Saxon race wins not because it has the most coal or the best natural frontiers, but because it has the best men.* What makes the Englishman superior to the Frenchman, on M. Demolins' showing is, *first, his power of initiative; secondly, his willingness to take risks and responsibility; thirdly, his eagerness for work.* All these qualities are opposed to Socialism, which has two aspects. A man may be a Socialist because he desires to help others, or because he desires others to help him; and it is the Socialists of this latter class alone who are numerous and important. Socialism, says M. Demolins, is not the protest of the new against the old; it is the protest of the old against the new. In the old world, before steam-power and machinery, a man was born into a definite setting, with work mapped out for him, and little prospect of rising beyond that work. He was born into a rut, and found everything prepared for his passage along it. The world changed, society became organised on a different basis ; man is born merely as an individual, largely stripped of local opportunities and local hindrances ; the would-be worker has to go in search of work instead of stepping into his father's shoes. He acquires greater freedom of movement, greater prospects ; but also he has to meet keener competition and run greater risks. Socialism aims at limiting the individual's risks and opportunities ; it is, says M. Demolins, the last great struggle of the old guild system. But the modern world of enterprise sees in Socialism its natural enemy ; it demands freedom to work and freedom to acquire on the most unrestricted scale, and in the modern world of enterprise Anglo-Saxons are the masters.

The Frenchman is not a Socialist, so M. Demolins has to make a name for him. He is a Communitarian as the Anglo-Saxon is Particularist. *He relies, that is, not merely on himself, but upon his surroundings, his family, his connections, and so forth ; he does not believe in self-help.* Let us translate the summing-up of a Frenchman's views for his son :—

" MY DEAR CHILD,—First of all count on us ; you see how we economise so as to be able to give you the best possible portion at your marriage. We are too fond of you not to smooth away all the difficulties of life from your path, so far as in us lies. Secondly, count on our relations and friends, for support and introductions to help to find you a career. Then count on the Government, which has innumerable places to dispose of ; the life is easy, there is no risk, the pay is regular, the rise is automatic by the simple process of deaths and retirements ; so much so that you can know beforehand that at such an age you will be receiving so much, and so on ; and finally, that at such an age you will have a nice little pension ; so that, after having done nothing to speak of all your life, you will be able to do nothing at all at an age when a man is still fit for work. But, my dear child, since these places are not over well paid, for one cannot have everything, you must also count on what your wife will bring you. Therefore you must first of all look for a rich woman ; but don't worry, we will look for her, we will find her for you. There, my dear child, is the advice which our love for you suggests."

From this philosophy of life certain consequences follow. First, a man who has to provide so completely for each child cannot afford to have many children : hence, a diminishing population. This form of thrift gives France a good deal of spare money, which in this country would go to paying for boots, nurses, and perambulators, and the rest. But money in French hands does not fructify rapidly ; *the Frenchman knows how to save money, the Englishman how to make it.* The *bourgeois* or middle class in France has lost the taste for agriculture. Business and commerce are looked upon as inferior in social status to posts under Government or the liberal professions ; also, they are risky investments of capital, and the Frenchman's philosophy of life is essentially a penny-wise philosophy. Therefore both by social prejudice and by caution every young Frenchman is guided towards Government employ which can only be obtained by passing examinations, so that from an educational point of view France is one vast cram-shop. Where there is competition there must be failures ; and *the French young man, who has been brought up with the aspirations proper to a cram-shop, if he cannot attain the necessary standard, lacks the qualities which would enable him to find work in some other direction.*

For the gravamen of the whole indictment brought against the existing order in France is that it does not produce resourceful and energetic men. The pick of the country's intelligence goes into the bureaux to be tied up with red tape. Those who cannot find employment as functionaries see no disgrace in living on their parents and the dowry of their wife. Parents carry their excessive fondness so far, that they will even discourage their children from settling in a distant town. Colonisation is impossible for a class brought up to despise agriculture and trade, to say nothing of manual labour. In short, what France lacks is a spirit of enterprise in her young men ; and certainly if the young Frenchman is the flaccid creature which M. Demolins describes, there is no doubt about our superiority. It is not merely a question of our " self-made man," though any one would think from reading M. Demolins that the late Mr. Barnato must seem to him the supreme type of humanity. In any profession, in the navy or in the army, there are crowds of young men willing and eager to take up any responsibility. What makes the difference it is not easy to say. M. Demolins and a good many of his critics blame the French youth's incompetence on his training, and declaim the familiar commonplaces about the advantages of a practical " modern education." *The* lycee *is contrasted with glowing accounts of some agricultural college and of a Scotch establishment which we should describe as "faddy." Neither of these is in any way representative of English education.* If we were asked for the secret of the Englishman's success, we should reply that it is the nature of the beast. He is unpoetical, yet he writes the best poetry ; a shopkeeper, yet with no superior among soldiers ; lavish, even wasteful, yet he amasses money ; governed by a Monarchy, yet with more control over his governors than any citizen in the world. One can only explain this mass of contradictions by the extraordinary freedom of individual development with us. Our shopkeeper is a shopkeeper and not a soldier as well ; we realise that the fierceness of modern competition gives a man enough to do with one occupation. The individual chooses his career, and pursues it without let or hindrance from society. The result is a far greater equality among citizens than exists in France. Nothing in M. Demolins' account of his own country so much impresses one as the completeness of class separations ; there is very little passage from grade to grade. A peasant may grow rich, chiefly by petty economies, but he generally remains a peasant, denying himself comforts, even decencies. The blouse is the symbol of a real distinction ; whereas with us the working man dresses like any one else, except when the nature of his work necessitates a difference ; and Mr. Keir Hardie was almost constrained to invent a fancy costume when he wished to draw attention to himself in the House of Commons. The Irishman, who is also a " Communitarian," has a deal in common with the French ; like them, in the upper classes, he has a craving for "something under Government," which in Ireland is apt to mean a security against the need for over-exertion at any period of his life ; but out of Ireland, with his characteristic quickness of assimilation, he becomes General, Governor, Prime Minister, or what you will ; very seldom, however, does he create a great business. Like the French, also, in the peasant classes, he has household gods that "plant a terrible fixed foot " ; his parting from the paternal mud cabin is like the parting of soul and body ; but like the Breton peasant also, he bestows on this centre of his affections scarcely more elaboration than a gipsy on his camp. The Englishman, who is ready to be gone at a moment's notice wherever fate and fortune call him, nevertheless sets about laying down turf in the garden of a villa that he will be sub-letting next year. The superiority of the Anglo-Saxon, from M. Demolins' point of view, consists largely in his determination to have the best of what he can get for the present, and to trust in himself (and a life assurance) for the future.

GLOBE, *October* 13, 1897.

ANGLO-SAXON SUPERIORITY.

Considerable interest has been aroused in Paris by a book written by M. Edmond Demolins, in which the author asks himself and his readers in what the superiority of the Anglo-Saxon race consists. As might have been expected, the French critics of the book will not allow that any such superiority does exist, and have said so with much unnecessary violence. But M. Deschaumes publishes in the *Gaulois* an article which is honourably distinguished from the rest by being written with decent civility towards this country.

* * * * *

There is, however, another and a much more important statement to which we must take exception, and that is that the English Government is in the habit of taking the initiative and directing the energies and capital of the nation towards useful enterprises at home and abroad. If M. Deschaumes knew anything of England he would know that the exact opposite is the case; that nothing is ever due to Government initiative, and that this is the very reason why we enjoy that "material and practical prosperity" which M. Demolins so justly envies in us. Every great work has been started by private initiative, and it is in this absolute personal freedom and absence of Government coddling that the superiority of the Anglo-Saxon consists.

MORNING POST, *October* 21, 1897.

ANGLO-SAXON SUCCESS.

M. Demolins belongs to the class of Frenchmen who are open to conviction touching the merits of alien races and countries. He goes farther, and, obeying the dictates of an earnest patriotism, seems to recommend to his countrymen such a radical change of institutions, even of grooves of thought, as, admitting their possibility, could only be the outcome of many generations. Meanwhile he is haunted by the spectre which he calls—

"The superiority of the Anglo-Saxons. If it is not proclaimed, it is endured and dreaded. The fear, the suspicion, and sometimes the hate excited by the Englishman prove it sufficiently. We cannot move a step in the world without meeting him. When our eyes turn towards possessions that once were ours it is to see the English flag floating over them. The Anglo-Saxon has supplanted us in North America, which we formerly occupied from Canada to Louisiana, in India, in Mauritius, in Egypt."

Seeking the reasons of this decadence, the author divides his work into three principal heads, examining the differences which prevail in the system of education, the private and public lives of the two races. One can cordially endorse much that is brought forward by M. Demolins against various educational abuses in France. *It is evident that the almost universal desire of young Frenchmen to obtain positions under Government, of whatever nature they may be, is a source of weakness to the social system, since as a rule it is only the unsuccessful who think of adopting other careers.* On the other hand the book would lead the uninitiated to suppose that what the author calls " chauffage," which, he fittingly says, consists in giving in the shortest time *"possible a superficial knowledge sufficing for the moment for the requirements of an examination,"* is unknown among us. The author's fixed ideas on Anglo-Saxon superiority lead him to look with perhaps too great indifference on France's latest enemy—Germany.

"The great peril, the great danger, the great adversary is not, as we believe, on the other side of the Rhine : Militarism and Socialism will relieve us from that enemy, and before long. The great peril, the great danger, the great adversary, is on the other side of the Channel, on the other side of the Atlantic, in any spot where are to be found a pioneer, a settler, a squatter of the Anglo-Saxon race."

Much good sense marks the writer's appreciation of the class of men which furnishes the largest proportion of representatives of the people in France.

"A journalist is obliged by his occupation, to think, to judge, to write quickly. His thought is hardly conceived when it is printed, it has never the time to ripen. . . . To discuss great national interests are required, above all, wisdom, reflection, maturity of judgment, tolerance, good sense, and the practical knowledge of affairs."

L'esprit de famille, a phrase which has no equivalent in our tongue, and which leads French parents to sacrifice themselves to the future of their children, and these same children to rely too much on the efforts of their families and relations to advance them in life, tends, according to M. Demolins, to the destruction of individual initiative and to the formation of men incapable of understanding that prosperity should be due to individual effort. After, it must be confessed, employing very dark colours, the author perceives some reassuring symptoms in the social order of his country, and, seeing all that precedes, one is most surprised to find him putting in the front rank the encouragements given of late years to colonisation. As the stability of a country's political institutions is an absolute necessity of its progress, it is good to learn that the general public in France, which has hitherto been in this particular a disturbing element, is less disposed than formerly to turn its attention to political affairs. A striking example of this new tendency is to be found in the diminished popularity of the exclusively political newspapers. It is true that they are replaced by more frivolous organs, the influence of which is not to be approved, but the direct effect is less pernicious to political stability. One cannot but be impressed by the earnestness of M. Demolins' able work, while believing that he asks what is impossible of the genius of a race which can claim the distinction of having ever been a pioneer in the domains of art, science, and imaginative literature.

THE ECHO, *October* 15, 1897.

Continental critics are not in the habit of exalting the virtues of the Anglo-Saxon, but M. Edmond Demolins, a distinguished economist, in his book, *A quoi tient la Supériorité des Anglo-Saxons*, is frank in his admiration, and exhorts his countrymen to take pattern by us. He differentiates us as *particularistes* in contrast with Latins and Germans, who are *communautaires, sacrificing their precious liberties to the State for the sake of the help they expect from it. On the contrary, the Anglo-Saxons take care to defend their liberty against interference on the part of the State. They ask to be alone responsible for their own destiny, and count only on their labour, energy, perseverance, and determination. Initiative, which is lacking in the Frenchman, is the keynote of the life of the Englishman.* This is what French fathers and mothers say to their sons: "Count on us; we are saving for your future. Count on relatives and friends to make your way; they will push you on. Count above all on the Government which disposes of so many places. But the pay is slender, and your bread must be buttered, so you must marry a rich wife. That is our affair. Leave it to us, and be tranquil. She shall be found." That is the French ideal. Now, M. Demolins protests that it is a false ideal, and one that saps the energy of the nation. French parents are wrong, and their children are wrong. The whole system is wrong. Anglicise yourselves as much as possible, he tells his countrymen, and he paints vivid pictures of typical English careers. But, we fancy, he preaches to deaf ears. *National habits and character cannot be put on like a coat.*

WESTMINSTER GAZETTE, *November* 15, 1897.

FRENCH VIEWS OF ANGLO-SAXON SUPREMACY.

Everybody on the other side of the Manche is now reading this book, and no wonder. French papers of all opinions and shades of opinion have given it long notices. Alike the soberest and the most Anglophobe organs are loud in its praises. The scurrilous *Libre Parole* and (where John Bull is concerned) the equally scurrilous *Petit Parisien* here join issues with the *Temps* and the *Débats*. The Ultramontane *Croix*, chiefly read by country curés, and the *Intransigeant*, delicate morsel of Parisian flâneurs, pronounce the same verdict. *M. Demolins' book is the book of the day, and must be read.* Hard as are the home truths he tells his countrymen, they are timely, and should produce a deep and lasting impression. "*At the present time,*" he writes, "*the Anglo-Saxon race represents the most active, most progressive, and most rapidly increasing of any on the world's surface.* It suffices for the Anglo-Saxons to plant themselves no matter where, and straightway that especial spot is transformed, we see there civilisation in its latest development, a young society springing up promising to surpass the old. Look at New Caledonia and our own Oceanic possessions ; compare these with Australia and New Zealand. *See what Spain and Portugal have done with South America, and what the Anglo-Saxon has done with the North. Here we have day contrasted with night.* But instead of shaking our fists at the English like grandames in a rage, let us study the causes of their supremacy in a manly and emulating spirit. *Let us find out the reasons of this prodigious expansion, this extraordinary aptitude at civilisation and the means of attaining the same.*" It is strange, yet true, that in spite of Rousseau and the immense influence of his great work on education, French mothers, still entrusting their children to wetnurses, fool them to the top of their bent as they grow older, finally handing them over to the red-tapeism of pedagogy. M. Demolins is far from leading his readers on to a warpath. Calmly, and in a truly philosophic spirit *he traces French failures in colonisation to the vices of French bringing-up and education, to the evils inseparable from bureaucracy and centralisation, and to the deadening effects of thrift carried to miserliness.* Very interesting is the chapter on the home, considered as a moral or material force (le mode d'établissement au foyer). In his opinion—and we quite agree with M. Demolins here—the money spent by English artisans and working people in beautifying their homes, and on what may be called the æsthetic needs of existence, is a far better investment than the French peasant's in State loans. The former system, our author writes, " helps to form a gentleman " (rend apte à devenir un gentleman).

It must be admitted, however, that the parsimony of the peasant owner is hardly his fault. It is a heritage of the *ancien régime*, of that frightful period when not only was the peasant compelled to bury his poor silver piece, but to hide his best clothes and bit of bacon from exciseman and tax-gatherer. Many other passages equally suggestive might be pointed out. *The book is one to read and ponder over. Unfortunately it will be lost upon German readers.* M. Demolins' second preface, headed " *On the pretended superiority of the Germans* " (Sur la prétendue supériorité des Allemands), *and his chapter on education in Germany and the Emperor's views thereon, will more than suffice to cause its confiscation beyond the frontier.*

M. B.-E.

BEDFORD TIMES, *November* 11, 1897.
THE SUPERIORITY OF THE ANGLO-SAXONS.

Perhaps the last country from which we should expect to receive a book written to demonstrate the superiority of the Anglo-Saxons is France. Yet—as many of my readers are already aware—one of the most popular French books of the year bears the title, *A quoi tient la Supériorité des Anglo-Saxons.* And the author, M. Edmond Demolins, does not propose the question in any doubt as to the superiority; for *his object in writing his book is to discuss the grounds of the Anglo-Saxon superiority in order to show his countrymen how to escape national and industrial annihilation.* He finds the Englishman everywhere. "The Anglo-Saxon," he says, "has supplanted us in that North America which we once occupied from Canada to Louisiana, in India, in the Mauritius, in the former Isle of France, in Egypt. He dominates America by Canada and the United States; Africa by Egypt and the Cape; Asia by India and Burmah; Oceana by Australia and New Zealand; Europe and the whole world by his commerce, his industry, and his politics." Other nations have colonies, but they are colonies of officials, dominating territories which they neither people nor develop; *whereas the Anglo-Saxon, as soon as he puts his foot on any corner of the globe, at once introduces into it the latest developments of European civilisation.* " See," says he, " what we have made of New Caledonia and our other possessions in the South Seas, and see what the Anglo-Saxons have made of Australia and New Zealand. See what Spain and Portugal have made of South America, and see what the Anglo-Saxon has made of North America. It is the contrast of night and day ! " Even in Algiers, close at their gates, and which they have had for sixty years, the French are in danger of being swamped by Europeans of other nationalities. As the author recognises the futility of merely denouncing this superiority of the Anglo-Saxon and of " pointing the finger at the Englishman like old women in a rage," *he sets himself the task of finding out the secret of this "prodigious power of expansion, of this extraordinary faculty for colonising," and the means of acquiring it.*

The chapters of the book first appeared separately in *La Science Sociale*, a review of which the author is the editor, and which is not to be confounded with socialistic organs. M. Demolins was the favourite disciple and is now the most zealous successor of Le Play, who based social reform upon a careful and scientific study of existing conditions among the people. This *Science Sociale* of Le Play's school is severely individualistic, and consequently distinctly antagonistic to the communistic principle more or less active in what is generally called Socialism. M. Demolins distinguishes between social organisations based upon a communistic principle (*societés à formation communautaire*) and social organisations based upon a particularist or individualistic principle (*societés à formation particulariste*). *Anglo-Saxon social organisations are particularist, while those of France and Germany are communautaire*. This is the keynote to our author's book. *The Anglo-Saxon is persistently individualistic, even when acting corporately.* He possesses personal initiative, is the embodiment of the principle of self-help, can take care of himself, can readily adapt himself to new conditions of life, is not afraid of difficulties, indeed is never so much himself as when he is combatting obstacles which would paralyse others. M. Demolins traces this characteristic through all the private and public relations of life. The Anglo-Saxon's school-life makes a man of him, not—as in France and to an increasing extent in Germany—a mere pedant, or State functionary, or office-holder, or clerk. The Anglo-Saxon's home is not a mere *foyer*—that is, a determinate locality where he happens to be born and to which he is connected by ancestry, by living relations, and by political and social ties—but any place where he is his own master and from which he can exclude all intrusion from the outside. Hence, *the Anglo-Saxon home has a moral—using the word in a broad sense—rather than a material or a local character.* Hence, also, in the Anglo-Saxon home, the actual habitation is of minor importance, and can be changed more easily, than is the case with the homes of other races. Hence, again, the Anglo-Saxon's home, being distinctly personal to himself and not dependent upon local or hereditary conditions, more readily develops the sentiments of dignity and independence—or, as our author says, gives an aptitude "to become a gentleman" as distinguished from an hereditary nobleman or a serf, both of whom are members of close castes—and predisposes to personal effort. M. Demolins contrasts the political *personnel* in France and Britain. In France, the

Chamber of Deputies is three-fourths composed of members of the liberal professions and ex-functionaries of state, with only a small representation of agriculture and industry ; while in the British House of Commons all the several interests are largely represented. *The Anglo-Saxon conception of patriotism differs also materially from that of most other races.* There is a patriotism based upon the religious sentiment, as among the Arabs, Turks, &c.; a patriotism based upon commercial competition, as in former times among the Mediterranean states ; there is a State patriotism based upon political ambition, as in France, Germany, Russia, &c. ; but *the Anglo-Saxon patriotism is based upon the independence of the private life.* Hence springs what to a Frenchman is the extraordinary facility with which the Anglo-Saxon will expatriate himself without a hope of returning. Hence also the independence of the Colonies ; and *the tendency to arrange international difficulties by arbitration rather than by war.* The patriotism of religious sentiment is at present confined to the deserts ; the patriotism of commercial competition i obsolete ; the State patriotism of political ambition is moribund ; but the patriotism of the independence of the private life exhibits all the characteristics " of things that are growing and to which the future belongs." It operates naturally and spontaneously ; *it encourages the production of wealth ; and it develops moral greatness.* The chapter on the different conceptions of solidarity is mainly a refutation of M. Bourgeois's proposition that the individual is subordinate to the community. *The Anglo-Saxon conception is that the community exists for the individual.* The discussion as to what social conditions are most favourable to happiness, leads M. Demolins to the conclusion that happiness consists not in labour or effort, but in the aptitude for effort. And to secure this aptitude it is necessary that parents should realise that all they owe to their children is a manly and robust education ; that the young should be convinced that it is their duty to be self-dependent, and that in marrying each party to the contract should seek for a companion and not a dower ; that the Government should keep down its scope and its functionaries at a minimum, and thus compel the young to look for independent careers that involve effort, individual initiative, and personal labour ; and that the official, the politician, the idle should be less highly considered than the agriculturist, the industrial, and the man of business.

I intended to have dwelt longer upon our author's very interesting chapters on the scholastic *régimes* of Britain, France, and Germany. *It must suffice to say that he vigorously condemns those characteristics of the school régimes of Germany and France which tend to produce a race of mere func-*

tionaries and professional men. The almost universal ambition of the youth of France among all classes is to obtain a civil or military appointment. *All the effort of life is thus concentrated into the few years of college or school cram;* all power of initiative is suppressed in the official docility of the functionary; *there are a hundred applicants for every post; the rejected are unfit for independent life; and the really wealth-producing occupations are robbed of those who ought to be engaged in them.*

The book is as interesting to Anglo-Saxons as to Frenchmen. It ought to be used by us, not merely as a testimony to our excellences, but *as a warning to show what we ought to avoid in our educational and social systems.*

A. R.

JOURNAL OF EDUCATION, *November*, 1897.

This is a remarkable book—or pamphlet, we should rather call it—*an excellent instance of that power of rapid generalisation and epigrammatic style of which the French are past-masters,* and it strikes, moreover, a dominant note which is less commonly heard in France than with us. *Perhaps at bottom an Englishman has as profound a belief in himself and his nation as a Frenchman has, but he has not the Frenchman's* amour propre, *which prevents him from indulging in self-criticism, and if in any quarter of the world he finds, or thinks he finds, things better managed than at home, he fires off a letter to the* Times, *or writes a book to prove the superiority of a French to an English Eton, of Danish to English butter.* This is not the way with Frenchmen, and it is a novelty to find one of themselves telling them that French civilisation is proceeding on the wrong tack (*déraillée*); that, in the struggle of life, they are on the losing side; that, unless they change their ways and habits of thought, decadence in an accelerating ratio is inevitable. According to M. Demolins, *Anglo-Saxondom* (*i.e.*, the English and the Americans) *succeeds because it is particularist* (i.e., *individualist*); *Germany fails because it is socialistic; France fails because it is communitarian.* In other words, the German expects that everything shall be done for him by the State; the Frenchman relies partly on the State, still more on his family and connections; *the Englishman alone is* αὐτάρκης, *self-centred and self-reliant.*

It would be easy to pick holes in this sweeping generalisation—to show, for instance, that M. Demolins' contrast between the dreaming East and the wide-awake West breaks down completely in the case of Japan; that *when transplanted to Australia the Celt is as enterprising and go-ahead as*

22. THE LAST LOAD. (*Summer, 1892*).

Copyright.

the *Anglo-Saxon*; but such criticism does not fall within our province. *It is not so much to blood as to training that M. Demolins traces the difference between the two nations, and the first third of the book is devoted to an account of the opposed school systems.* France, according to him, is one vast cramming establishment, a sort of glorified University of London, where every appointment, from a tide-waitership to a secretaryship of state, is decided by examination, where the highest ambition of every *bourgeois* is that his son should obtain a snug Government post, with not a great deal to do, a modest but certain income automatically increasing, and a decent pension at the end of the vista. Such is the dark background on which M. Demolins throws his magic-lantern slides of English schools. *In an auspicious moment, M. Demolins met at Edinburgh, where he was a Summer Meeting* conférencier, *Dr. Cecil Reddie, and visited under his guidance his school at Abbotsholme; thence he was passed on to the offshoot of Abbotsholme at Bedale; afterwards he made the acquaintance of an establishment which is not named, but can be no other than the Colonial College, Hollesley Bay.* All these are depicted in glowing colours, and contrasted with the dreary treadmills that the French call *Lycées*. Far be it from us to doubt the truth of the pictures, or to insinuate that these three establishments do not deserve all the good that is said of them. *What does astound us is that it never seems to have dawned on M. Demolins that these schools, so far from being typical of English schools, are almost unique of their kind, and hat three schools (it would be difficult to name a fourth) are a narrow and unstable basis on which to rest a glorification of Anglo-Saxondom. The English, we read, have been before Frenchmen in realising the changed conditions of modern life, and have risen to the occasion. The essential need of the times is to turn out youths who are able to shift for themselves under any circumstances, to produce practical men of energy, not public functionaries or simple men of letters, who know of life only what they have learned from books, which, to tell the truth, is very little.*

Here, again, M. Demolins' theory of life seems to us *borné* and inadequate. To get on is not the whole duty of man. But our purpose is to chronicle, not to criticise. *It is well worth knowing what an intelligent Frenchman considers the ideal school of the future,* and, though his book is sure to be quoted as a warning against State interference and the importation of French methods, *there is little danger of English readers mistaking, as French readers have done, his partial sketches for a national portrait gallery.*

The Christian World, *December* 30, 1897.

In *La Foi et la Vie*, an able French Protestant journal just started, *a remarkable article appears on the reception in France of M. Demolins' book, " La Supériorité des Anglo-Saxons." It is the book of the hour.* Hundreds of articles have been written about it, representing every phase of French opinion. The general verdict is that M. Demolins' thesis as to Anglo-Saxon superiority is proved, and that France needs to enter upon a most searching investigation into its causes. Very striking are the utterances on the point of leading French writers. M. Demolins himself holds that this relative superiority comes from education. "In England they form men. In France one forms functionaries, people who depend upon others." Says M. Lemaître, "*This is an infinitely painful book, but it is one that must be read.*" "This book worries me," adds M. Françisque Sarcey. M. Bourget, in the *Figaro*, urges that "one must try to understand the political laws which the Anglo-Saxon has learned to observe in his development." M. Prevost tells his countrymen that "we must change our morals, but above all our institutions, especially our *régime* of succession and our old administrative organisation." *M. Sabatier holds that it is* "*religious faith, the Bible, Protestantism," that constitute the secret of English success.* Perhaps the most remarkable admission is that made by *l'Association Catholique:* "The prosperity of the Protestant peoples is explained by the fact that they have better kept the faith, and more consistently practised the Decalogue, than the decatholicised Catholic nations." *Altogether the verdict of history on Protestantism seems to be becoming plain to everybody, Catholics included, with the single exception of our own* "*Protestant Church as by law established.*"

Leeds Mercury, *January* 22, 1898.
ANGLO-SAXON SUCCESS.

Recent works by a Frenchman (M. Edmond Demolins) and an Italian (Signor G. Ferrero) supply the text for a brilliant paper on "*The Success of the Anglo-Saxons."* According to those writers, it depends upon qualities in which both Frenchmen and Italians are deficient—*conscientiousness in work and endurance of monotony. Stress is also laid upon the superior sexual morality of the English and the Germans as an important influence in their success.* The following extract will indicate the views of the writers named :—

"England succeeds," says Signor Ferrero, "because it is a country of

A French Savant's Verdict

hard work undistracted by a thirst for fresh sensations, and dominated by a sense of duty in the details of life. England succeeds, says M. Demolins, because it is a country of self-help. It is the country of self-help because the whole course of Anglo-Saxon education tends to make men self-reliant ; because Anglo-Saxon society is 'particularist,' not 'communitarian,' composed, that is, of individuals, not of families for units ; *because in these communities the individual takes rank in virtue of himself, not of his occupation;* lastly, because they are the least socialistic communities in the world, the states which interfere least with their citizens, whether to restrain or protect."

The different methods of education pursued in France, England, and Germany also affect greatly the character of the future citizen. Illustrations are given of the differences which characterise the Frenchman and the Englishman, and it is observed—

"*If the world is to be served by its best men, there must be free competition everywhere, and no handicaps; a ready passage from one class to another always open. Men must not be afraid either to go up or go down.*" Well, in France, if we may believe M. Demolins, caste still remains ; people are slow to attempt to go up, and are in mortal terror lest they should appear to be going down. In France you have the symbol of social differences in dress ; with us every one dresses alike. The French workman, with the blouse, gets the blouse into his very composition. He may amass money, for, although he is not a good man to make money, he is good at saving it, but he simply becomes a rich workman ; his tastes, his speech, his dress, and his dwelling are what they were before ; the only difference is that he has money in the bank. The same phenomenon presents itself in Ireland, where one may see the family of a farmer who rents a thousand acres of excellent land, living in a cabin with earthen floors, and dressed as no English workman on thirty shillings a week would care to be seen. That is, says M. Demolins, because Ireland is Celtic and belongs to the primitive communitarian type, where the home is a fixed and material centre with an extraordinarily strong hold upon the affections, but where the only conception of duty to the home is to keep a roof-tree over it, to keep the family centre unchanged. *The English workman*, on the other hand, does not value himself much on his savings or on his family, but a great deal on his personal respectability. He *desires, first of all, comfort; plenty to eat for himself and his wife and his children; a decent house for them to live in; decent clothes for them to wear. He prefers to raise the standard of comfort rather than to lay up for a rainy day, trusting to his own exertions if a pinch comes. Self-reliance rather than prudence is his virtue, and prudence is not a virtue that gets much work out of a man.* He has no attachment to any spot; he will go wherever his work takes him; and, if he sees his way clear to better himself by emigration, he will emigrate. The Irish workman emigrates under the pressure of dire necessity, and with pangs like the parting of soul and body; he is always looking homewards from his exile. The French workman is more prudent than the Irish, and is therefore seldom driven to expatriate himself. *The English work man, comparatively devoid of the sentiment for his country, emigrates for better wages;* and, if he emigrates, does not lay by money either to return home or to bring his kinsfolk after him, but spends it as he makes it in improving his social condition. *Consequently the passage from class to class in Anglo-Saxon communities is continuous and almost imperceptible; in America classes hardly seem to exist except as defined by the rate of expenditure.* The Englishman, as compared with the Frenchman, has a wide field of choice. In France, a man who follows one of the black-coated professions accounts himself disgraced if his sons have to live by trade in any form, and simply does not contemplate the possibility of their labouring in their shirtsleeves. *With us the sons of an Earl may run a steam laundry, may set up as wine or tea merchants, or, if they feel a taste for more elegant employments, may open a milliner's shop.* When capital is not forthcoming for their ventures, and brains are pronounced inadequate for such things as have to be done nowadays with brains, the younger sons emigrate to Texas, and set up a ranch; when they have dropped their money over that, they conduct tram-cars in New York, or open a lamp store in San Francisco. *No gentleman would like his sons to do these things at home, but few mind how the "lost legion," that Mr. Kipling writes of, makes its way abroad. In the United States this last remnant of the old prejudice has disappeared, and no occupation seems to be accounted degrading; all are honourable, and more or less so in proportion to the profits.*

THE LANCASHIRE DAILY EXPRESS AND STANDARD,
January 27, 1898.

THE SUCCESS OF THE ANGLO-SAXON.

Several Continental writers of considerable eminence and philosophic acumen *have lately set themselves to inquire why the Anglo-Saxon race, though it is pacific and not military in its national character, is able to acquire so large a share of the earth's surface*, why our Colonial Empire is greater than that of any of the military powers of Europe, *and why Britons promise to become the dominant race of the civilised world.* In the new number of the *Quarterly Review*, two of these books, one by an Italian writer, Signor Ferrero, and the other by the French author, M. Edmond Demolins, are reviewed. M. Demolins' work concerns us most, for it is confined to answering the question, "Wherein lies the superiority of the Anglo-Saxons?" *The Quarterly Reviewer's summary of M. Demolins' conclusions contains points both of much interest and practical value to the thoughtful Englishman.* M. Demolins admits that although as an industrial worker, the German excels, " it looks very much as if the whole direction of new civilisations would fall into Anglo-Saxon hands." *Now we cannot lay the flattering unction to our souls that Anglo-Saxon dominance is due to superiority of intellect.* Among the Latin races, now admittedly decaying, men are to be found of greater intellectual brilliancy and power than even the race of eminent Englishmen produces, saving in very exceptional cases, while, as Mr. Benjamin Kidd has pointed out in his " *Social Evolution*," *the average man among the Moderns does not attain anything like the intellectual development of the Ancient Greeks.* The qualities which tend to promote the supremacy of the Anglo-Saxons, are rather those qualities, very largely moral, which go to constitute what is called their "social efficiency." "Great Britain," says the Quarterly Reviewer, "spreads faster and farther than any other European nation." The French population is diminishing : it is only maintained at a stationary condition by large drafts from the nations around it. *The Germans* are more productive, and send out numbers of emigrants annually. But these *do not leave the Fatherland for the reason that Englishmen do, because the home population is pressing upon the means of subsistence, but in order to escape the military despotism which interferes materially with the social efficiency of the Teuton.* Moreover, *when the German goes abroad he becomes absorbed into the nationality of other peoples. The Anglo-Saxon retains his racial and national characteristics.* He carries the manners and customs of his country with him, and plants a New England wherever he settles. *The so-called German colonies of Africa are no colonies at all, but possessions only.* Their German population is confined to a few officials. The tide of German emigration flows to America, where the all-pervading Anglo-Saxon elements swallow it up, and the qualities in which the Teuton excels do but minister to the success of the dominant race. The Anglo-Saxon, says M. Demolins, " succeeds by reason of his greater enterprise, his independence of character, and his power of initiation, all of which are partly cause and partly effect of his social system." England succeeds, in short, because it is the country of self-help. The Anglo-Saxon's education tends to make him self-reliant: he is individualistic, not "communitarian." The French parent considers that it is his duty to provide a living for each of his children, so he cannot afford to have many. Hence the voluntary limitation of families in France, which accounts largely for the stationary population. The English parent gives his boy a good education, and then expects him to rely upon his own exertions for his livelihood. The son of the Frenchman looks to his father to provide him with a means of living which will not unduly tax his power of exertion. Hence the most common ambition among Frenchmen is to get their sons into the official class, so that they may have a comfortable income, and not be overworked. "All the best brains of the country seem to seek an employment which will deliver them from any undue demand upon their energy; they are drawn towards posts in the service of the State, which leave the holder no doubt as to the continuance of his income, and offer a comfortable pension for old age." *In England, the best brains are drawn towards fields of labour that give more scope for both enterprise and activity.* " *The ambition of the average Englishman is to be his own master*; the ambition of the average Frenchman is to be head of a department." *The Anglo-Saxon wants to make his own way for himself*; the Frenchman wants to have his way made for him. From this one inference, which M. Demolins draws, is clear: Anglo-Saxon communities succeed because they are the least Socialistic countries in the world of civilisation. Paradoxical as at first sight it may seem, it is nevertheless true that Anglo-Saxon communities display the greatest social efficiency because they are the least Socialistic. *Socialism is the protest of the laggards, according to M. Demolins. It is the " creed of those who are afraid of progress," one condition of progress being a rivalry of life under stress of necessity.* " The struggle for life," connotes the Reviewer, translating M. Demolins, " *is a hard fact nowadays, and the Anglo-Saxon welcomes it because he is backing himself to win, and because his notion of happiness consists as a rule in exertion.* The Latin seeks to avoid the struggle, and is anxious to call in Government—'the State, which is the new Providence of Socialism'—to ordain that the pace shall be slackened." But, says this philosophic French writer, " *social salvation is like religious salvation," every man must work out his own. That is a lesson we must not forget if we desire to maintain the supremacy of the Anglo-Saxon race.*

A French Savant's Verdict

THE SPEAKER, *January* 29, 1898.

The *Edinburgh Review* is very solid this month. . . . "The Success of the Anglo-Saxons" is based on the recent works of M. Demolins and Signor Ferrero, though the latter is rated rather higher than he deserves. The conclusion is that the Frenchman, with his preference for comfort over adventure, and the Italian, with his instability and excitableness, *are going under in the competition with the hard-working, pushing Northerner. And, as the German emigrant loses his nationality and the English emigrant does not, the victory will ultimately rest with our section of the Teutonic race.*

THE TABLET, *January* 29, 1898.

A FRENCH VIEW OF THE RACE ELEMENT IN IMPERIAL EXPANSION.

An exposition by a Frenchman of the causes which have carried the Anglo-Saxon to the van of modern progress, and left his Gallic neighbour lagging behind, cannot be very pleasant reading for the writer's fellow-countrymen, more especially as he finds them in qualities inherent in the two races, instead of in adventitious circumstances, conspiring in favour of the one, and against the other. A work in which such novel ideas are broached could not fail to excite a considerable amount of attention, and M. Demolins' *A quoi tient la Supériorité des Anglo-Saxons?* must have caused many anxious searchings of heart among the more thoughtful of his French readers. He goes straight to the root of the matter, and sees in the opposite ideals of life, which form in the two countries the basis of national character, the answer to his query. Self-help is the key to the one, as dependence, whether on parental aid in the early stages of life, or on official patronage later, forms the mainspring of the other. The very family devotion and self-sacrifice of French parents, who hold it a duty to lay by a provision for every child, are trammels on the expansion of the race, since, on the one hand, they render small families an economic necessity, and tend, on the other, to diminish the self-reliance of the rising generation. *The young Frenchman is consequently kept in leading strings to an age much later than that at which his English contemporary has usually struck out alone into the deep waters of life to sink or swim by himself.* The former may not legally marry before five-and-twenty, if even so remote a progenitor as a grandmother forbid the banns, and usually submits with equanimity to have a bride chosen for him by the family conclave. His future way of life is equally matter for decision by the same authority, a salaried post under Government, with its safe but narrow limitations, generally constituting the *ne plus ultra* of his own or his relatives' ambition. *A career safeguarded by the groove of mediocrity seems to them far preferable to one involving greater risks, but allowing freer play to individual energy and ambition.* While the domestic hearth is thus securely fenced round against disaster, the *higher qualities of the man are stunted by the absence of keen competition with his fellows. The very thrift so much lauded by English writers is made by M. Demolins a count in his indictment of his compatriots, and he awards the palm of national virtue to the opposite extreme of prodigality conspicuous in the Anglo-Saxon.*

We can, indeed, easily perceive for ourselves the radical difference in social tendencies which he points out, by turning in thought to the common story of an English household with the map of the world open before its younger members, and the migratory instinct strong in their blood. Official harness, welcome to the French youth, is intolerable to their more enterprising natures, and all chances of hazard and hardship are preferable to its constraints. The haven of a secure provision, the armchair comforts of a fireside existence are thrown up for pioneering at the ends of the earth, or for fighting the battle of empire on the restless frontier, where its buttresses are built up of the lives of its citizens. The history of the race is epitomised in Felicia Hemans's lyric, "The Graves of a Household," for it is not alone of the group clustered round a single hearth, but of all the children of the Island Mother, that it may be said that " Their graves are severed far and wide by mount and stream and sea." *Thus English colonisation outruns annexation, and the efforts of statesmen towards retrenchment of imperial responsibility have often been thwarted by the predestining force of racial impulse.* The tendency to minimise trouble and anxiety modifying the entire structure of French society reacts strongly on the national investments, rendering it, as M. Demolins says, the main ambition of every Frenchman to have his fortune in a portfolio. The *rentier*, living on dividends earned by South African mines or American railways, is spared all thought for the morrow, but contributes nothing, on the other hand, to the welfare of the community to which he belongs. A financial crisis threatening this fancied security shakes the foundations of the State, just because the securities then endangered are so widely held that their collapse becomes a national catastrophe. *The Frenchman's proclivities, in short, in favour of a tame and facile prosperity, render him, with all his effusive love of country, a much more inefficient citizen than his less ostentatiously patriotic*

Anglo-Saxon neighbour. A writer in the *Edinburgh Review,* commenting on M. Demolins' work, points out to his readers the significant fact that *France has thrice built up, and twice lost a great transmarine empire. The East and the West have successively seen her flag lead the van of European conquest, only to be displaced in both by that of her English rival.* Will the vast regions she has similarly acquired in Africa and Asia again drop from her grasp, because the instincts of her inhabitants are not such as to qualify her for being the brood-mother of nations? *This striking book is one among many indications of the passing away with the dying century of many of its earlier social ideals.* The phase of industrial development passed through by the nations of Europe during its middle period required the concentration at home of energies which, *now that that task has been completed, must increasingly tend to seek a new sphere for their exercise abroad.* The vast workshops of the world, having been wrought up to their full capabilities, demand the creation of new markets for products far in excess of home consumption, and the expansive forces set free by the relaxation of the internal strain are exerting that outward pressure which we see in *the universal craving for colonial extension.* The cry for peace, invoked as the sheltering deity of productive development, is exchanged for the spirit of militarism called out by the requirements of the new wants of the nations. Who now dares to advocate a Little England, or to limit empire by the yard-measure of Manchester industrialism? How completely the old order has changed is shown by the unanimity with which *the leaders of both parties in the State have recognised war itself as preferable to the abdication by England of her primacy in the markets of the East.*

Equally dead is the materialistic shibboleth proclaiming the highest aim of society to be "the greatest happiness of the greatest number." In the beatific animalism of the West Indian negro, the utilitarian counsels of this gospel of the trough find their most complete fulfilment. *But the later evangel takes character instead of enjoyment as the test of progress, and declares the production of the highest type of humanity to be the loftier function of society. Not repose but strife, not ease but effort, forms the school of the civic virtues, which wither in the lulling atmosphere of the* faitnéant's *paradise of content.* Indeed, the ideal of happiness proposed, is in itself the crucial test by which to classify communities or individuals. The Caliban who sees it in a bottle, is a savage, on a level with the Hottentot, and below the Zulu, whose fierce fighting rage is a less degrading passion. M. Demolins' *bourgeois* Frenchman, again, whose *summum bonum* consists in luxury or pleasure, stands many degrees lower in the scale of being than *the typical Englishman of his pages, whose enjoyment is found in the most strenuous exertion of his faculties of mind or body*. With such a man his life's work, whether it be the rule of an Indian district, the direction of Egyptian irrigation, or the disciplining of foreign levies under his country's flag, is his ruling passion, dearer than domestic ties, than health, wealth, leisure, or than the lower gratifications in which lower natures find contentment. *England is great because she produces such citizens in larger proportion than any other land, and has their service ever in reserve for any emergency*. They are, moreover, the product of her social system, of *an aristocracy sufficiently elastic to absorb the best element of the middle class, while still exclusive enough to maintain the tradition of duty and responsibility which is the highest prerogative of birth. Nor could they be raised up save from a class still upholding a higher standard of honour than that of the purely commercial morality of one which depends solely on wealth for prestige*. No country held such traditions higher or dearer than France, who made "*Noblesse oblige*" the motto of her hereditary aristocracy, and if she have now lost touch with whatever was best in her *ancien régime*, it is due to the advent to power under the Second Empire and Third Republic of a plutocracy of the Bank and the Bourse on whom no such axiom of conduct is incumbent. But among all the pernicious influences answerable for that deterioration of aim of which M. Demolins is so quick to detect the signs among his fellow-countrymen, *assuredly the displacement of religion as an elevating social and moral force is the first and greatest*. In demonstrating that national greatness is based upon national character, he has postulated a striking truth, and he has only to carry his inquiry a stage farther to show that *no lofty ideal of life can be permanently maintained, unless it have behind it that faith in the Unseen which alone gives a sanction to its prescriptions*.

EDUCATIONAL TIMES (LONDON), *February 1, 1898.*

AS ANOTHER SEES US.

This book is as interesting as the title is flattering. Its contents are nothing short of encyclopædic, embracing matters pertaining not only to the teacher's craft, but also to that of the social economist and the politician. *Thus it deals with school curricula, effects of cramming, the right aims of education, a comparison between North and South America, the Briton, Frenchman, and German as colonists, the low birth-rate in France,*

A French Savant's Verdict

the present low and falling rate of interest, the rearing of children, the statistics of trade in the Suez Canal, the effects of trade-unionism, the pretended superiority of the Germans, and the qualities of the Emperor William. But, since reviewers must be limited in space, *we prefer to deal only with the early part of the book, which treats on education.*

M. Demolins is disposed to criticise France and French methods, and for this purpose *England is highly appreciated, and the merits of the few are attributed to the many.* A map of the world, on Mercator's projection, appears on the outer cover, and the Anglo-Saxon is dressed in his favourite colour, red. Then the question is posed: Why is he there so plentifully, and why are Frenchmen and Germans mostly conspicuous by absence? The answer is, in brief, that the Anglo-Saxon educates men; the French and Germans educate functionaries. The difference is radical; it begins in the cradle, and ends with the grave. "The Anglo-Saxon is to-day at the head of the most active, progressive, and overflowing civilisation. . . . What is the secret of this prodigious power of expansion?" Considering the pretended superiority of the Germans, M. Demolins dismisses our Teutonic competitors in a few words—*rather fewer, perhaps, than our English manufacturers would bestow on them.* France's real rival is Britain. Wherever an Anglo-Saxon pioneer settles down, there is generally a man who will make a success of life, even though he have no army of functionaries to back him.

M. Demolins asks himself this question: "Does the French school system make men? Does the German? Does the English?" The answer to the first two questions is "No!" To the third "Yes." The reason of the French failure is given very succinctly. The young Frenchman places before himself as his highest ambition some comfortable Government appointment—army, magistracy, administration, consulate, roads and bridges, mines, or something of the sort. French parents do not like risky businesses, or removal to foreign lands or colonies. Their son will have a *dot* himself, and marry a wife with another. So he can rely on the family, on his wife's family, on the State, and on his social environment in general. Now, Government billets must be obtained by examination, since birth and protection are not so effectual for advancement as formerly. For this reason examination successes are the aim of a young Frenchman. This entails the entire organisation of the school for the obtaining of such successes; examinations are the sum and substance of school life. But *success in examination demands cramming; that is, " superficial, but for the moment sufficient, knowledge of the subjects of an examination."* No human being could know them thoroughly, for the programme is encyclopædic; one can but skim and use the memory to a prodigious extent. The typical *French boarding school follows military lines; obedience is the great thing—"passive obedience, uniformity of sentiments and ideas, in a word, all that deprives man of his personality."* All the differences which might arise from family influences tend to be obliterated; *all intelligences are melted into one mould; anything like free and spontaneous action must disappear.*

It is an admirable training for an official. The ground is beautifully prepared for your receiving instructions in this capacity and implicitly carrying them out with machine-like regularity, as all functionaries should. But, alas! everybody cannot be a functionary, though in France everybody wants to be one, and thus it happens that no young Frenchman receives a proper education in agriculture, manufactures, or commerce. None but the plucked would in any case take to such poor, mean occupations, and, by the exigencies of cram, no one has been prepared for them. *To fill any independent situation you need enterprise, initiative, self-reliance, and a strong will, the very qualities that officialdom has no need of, and which are well stamped on in French schools.*

Lastly, the system produces journalists, encyclopædic beings who can talk and write a little on everything, in cyclopædic fashion; nothing deep or thorough. "Our present school system forms functionaries; it cannot yield any other product. Above all, it is not adapted for forming men."

The *German school system is quickly dismissed by M. Demolins, who seems to do it less than justice.* The chapters devoted to it are mainly taken up by the dicta of the German Emperor, *who accuses professors not of lack of knowledge or method, but of neglecting to form character or take note of the necessities of the present time. German schools, says the Emperor, have failed both from the practical and from the political point of view. M. Demolins is more concerned to show us that Prussia,* last of the great European powers (what of Russia?) to enter the ring of civilised nations, *is busy playing at the part of Philippe II. or Louis XIV.* two centuries behind the time for such personages, than to show us exactly the cause of failure, if there be failure, in the Prussian school programme. Indeed, before he leaves his inquiry as to Germany, he breaks out into eleven solid pages of laudation of an English Colonial College, whilst Germany still heads his lines.

What charms our author in the Colonial College is chiefly its unlikeness to anything French or German. The struggle for life is put before the young Englishmen in brilliant colours; if any one sinks, let it rather be the neighbour than himself. There are farms in this college, dairy and poultry and other farms, workshops, boat-houses; the men are taught the use of tools, bee-keeping, forest culture, cattle breeding and rearing, repairing of agricultural machines, shoeing of horses, the construction of rafts, St. John ambulance work. All this is not taught to poor wretches without fortune, but to the sons of rich or well-to-do families in England. *Above all, M. Demolins is delighted with the idea that the College owes its inception to private initiative, and not to the State. And, truth to tell, English statesmen and teachers may do worse than listen to voices from the Continent which persistently warn us against the hand of the State in secondary education. It may be that in England we shall reach a solution of the secondary education problem which will yield us a maximum of benefit from the State organisation of secondary education, and a minimum of bad results;* but we are not likely to attain this end without a frank ack owledgment that State interference *may* be a very bad thing. M. Demolins is not the only man who warns us against the grinding down to one monotonous, rigid, uniform level which too often ensues as a result of State interference. M. Max Leclerc had *a few years ago a great deal to say on this question in a book on English secondary schools, which attracted much attention at the time of its publication.* Numerous as the faults of our system, or want of system, may be, our critics admit that *we can form character, and leave untouched the initiative and enterprise of our young people.*

Here, in conclusion, are nine *procédés* in respect of which M. Demolins sees the superiority of English over French parents. There is some truth in the picture he draws; we could wish there were more. His portraiture of us must be looked upon as idealistic rather than as a simple resemblance to the original.

1. Anglo-Saxon parents do not regard their children as belonging to them, as a mere continuation of their personality, a kind of survival of themselves. On the contrary, they are independent beings, and so considered.

2. From first to last parents treat their children as if grown-up, and thus make them real personalities with a well-marked individuality.

3. In matters educational, parents aim at the future, at the fresh necessities of life, and not at suiting past conditions.

4. The Anglo-Saxon parent has not only care of health, which we have, but of strength, and aims at the full development of physical energy.

5. Children are early placed in contact with real circumstances. They go and come alone, execute errands and commissions within their range.

6. Parents generally cause their children to learn some manual occupation. They do not despise manual labour, as we French do. [Alas! M. Demolins.]

7. Parents are ahead of their children in their knowledge of things useful and new. They want few theories, but go for facts.

8. Authority is little used towards children.

9. Children know that English parents do not take on themselves the duty of making their positions in life. The English father gives no portion.

On the whole this is a clever book, and one upon which the *thoughtful teacher, he who knows our defects and cannot be flattered into dropping the cheese at the decisive moment*, will do well to reflect.

REVIEW OF REVIEWS, *February*, 1898.

MORALITY AND SELF-HELP.

THE SECRET OF ANGLO-SAXON SUPREMACY.

Such is the question which is discussed in the *Edinburgh Review*, by a Reviewer who takes as his text the works of Signor Ferrero and M. Demolins. As the theory of the latter has already been described at some length in the columns of this *Review*, it will suffice to quote a sentence or two in which this Reviewer summarises the Frenchman's views.

SELF-HELP THE SECRET OF ENGLAND'S GREATNESS.

He says, for instance: "It sounds a paradoxical thing to say, but it is nevertheless profoundly true, that France is a nation in process of being ruined by the thrift and prudence of its citizens. To live poorly because it is so much easier to save money than to make it, to have no children for fear they should die of starvation, that is the summing-up of the Frenchman's penny-wise philosophy; and, if there is truth in logic, it is the individual Frenchman who is keeping France back in the race, just as it is the individual Anglo-Saxon who is winning the battle for his community. England succeeds, says M. Demolins, because it is the country of self-help. It is the country of self-help because the whole course of Anglo-Saxon education tends to make men self-reliant."

ADAPTABILITY THE GERMAN IDEAL.

There is more novelty, even if there be not so much truth, in the theory of the Italian. Signor Ferrero recognises frankly and without reserve the certainty of the domination of the Teutonic race. Germans and English appear to him to be destined to submerge the world. The Latin races will be but as little pleasure islands in the midst of the Teutonic ocean. According to him, it is the German rather than the Englishman who possesses the requisite qualities which carry with them the sceptre of the world. He says: "It is the Germans who are to be the great civilising agency of the future, the cement of new societies, because the German is of all men the most adaptable." The Reviewer upon this remarks that—" The workers in the new worlds may be Germans, so may the foremen of industry, but it looks very much as if the whole direction of new civilisations would fall into Anglo-Saxon hands."

MORALITY AS A CAUSE OF SUPREMACY.

The most interesting theory advanced by Signor Ferrero is that the Teutonic races are beating the Latin in the struggle for existence chiefly because of their greater regard for the seventh commandment. This is not exactly the way he puts it, but that is really what it comes to. The Reviewer says:—

"Both Signor Ferrero and M. Demolins are of opinion that the winners in the international struggle are winning because they are the people who have known how to adapt themselves to the changed conditions of life. But Signor Ferrero points you to a physiological difference. In the Latin the sexual impulse develops earlier and remains more powerful than in the Teuton; it wastes a worker's energy and it distracts his attention. Consequently the colder northern, though not superior in skill or intelligence to the southern—Signor Ferrero says he is inferior—works harder at all work and more steadily at mechanical work. M. Demolins assigns a moral cause. The Anglo-Saxon succeeds, he says, by reason of his greater enterprise, his independence of character and his power of initiation, all of which are partly cause and partly effect of his social system. Signor Ferrero may or may not be right in connecting this greater excitability and liveliness with a more strongly erotic temperament; but it is interesting to get from a Latin observer the admission that English standards of sexual morality do not rest upon an elaborate hypocrisy. Not only does he concede the greater chastity of our race and the more ideal character of attachments between men and women of Teuton stock; but he recognises on the most material grounds the value of this superiority. In the comparative chastity of Englishmen and German lies a very great cause of their success in the struggle for existence."

MONOGAMY AND MONOTONY.

It is true that the Italian is careful to deprive the English and Germans of any credit for their superior morality, which he thinks is due rather to their approximation to the type of the neuter bee than to any superiority of moral sense. The development of modern industrialism, with its excessive division of labour, is contrary to the genius of the artistic and excitable Latins, but—"It suits the character of English workmen because the Englishman is more patient and capable of methodic labour, thanks to his sexual coldness. The Englishman, says Signor Ferrero, is a monogamous animal, while at any given moment the Latin's horizon is apt to be occupied by a petticoat or a succession of petticoats. Allied to the superior sexual morality of the English and Germans is a more practical conception of duty."

Whatever may be the absolute truth or untruth of Signor Ferrero's theories, it is noteworthy indeed that this Italian disciple of Lombroso, after a scientific examination of the causes which have made for victory in the struggle of the nations, should ascribe so high a place to the influence of continence. Sex-passion uncontrolled handicaps races as fatally as it does individuals. It is like steam. It is the driving force of life if it is kept within bounds. In excess it bursts the boiler.

BRITISH MEDICAL JOURNAL, *February* 19, 1898.

WORK AND PLAY.

Two foreign writers have recently expressed their admiration for the Englishman's power of playing. We use the term "Englishman" for want of a better to express the nation or nations of mixed parentage who now inhabit these islands from Wick to the English Channel, some parts of the North of Ireland, and many parts of the British colonies in North America, Australia, and New Zealand. Mr. J. N. Ford, in a letter published some time ago in the *New York Tribune*, wrote: "I should like to know what it is that enables Englishmen to accomplish more in the way of work than Americans usually do. Two reasons suggest themselves to my mind—one, that Englishmen go about their work more methodically than Americans; the other, that their climate is better adapted to work in. They have no such enervating summers as fall to our lot. A man may live in London for twelve months of the year and feel no worse for it; but I defy a man to live in New York for twelve months straight through without feeling the worse for it."

Mr. Ford, however, concludes that the real secret of the Englishman's increased output is due to the fact "he never wastes time, and the consequence is that he never seems busy; while we waste so much that we seem always to be driven to death with work." M. Ed. Demolins also, who is a serious student of social science, is much struck by the Englishman's power of playing. In his work entitled *A quoi tient la supériorité des Anglo-Saxons ?* he gives much space to its consideration. He says that a lover of paradox might undertake to prove either that the English are the people who work the most or that the English are the people who work the least. He says that there is in fact nothing comparable to the Englishman's power of work except his power of resting. The Englishman, he says, gives in the least time possible the greatest quantity of work possible, in order to be able afterwards to give himself the greatest possible quantity of rest. By rest (*repos*) M. Demolins does not mean doing nothing, for he finds the true cause of the desire to do work rapidly in order to have the more leisure in the Englishman's love of the country, which again he puts down in large measure to the love of a home, a place apart, where a man may be independent and "comfortable"—a word which, together with "home," he finds it impossible to translate into French. He notices that if we swarm into towns in early manhood we stream out again in large numbers as soon as a competency is made. Further, he notices that even when in full work many city workers contrive to have their homes in the country, and many others to steal the Saturday to Monday with a great approach to regularity. It is rather comforting to find that a keen observer like M. Demolins is so strongly impressed by the Englishman's love of country life, for the enormous growth of our town populations might make one fear that this hereditary characteristic was dying out. His explanation of our habits of work may not be complete, for he hardly gives sufficient weight to the love of sport, but his explanation is sound as far as it goes, and is much to be preferred to doubtful speculations as to climatic influences on the power of working.

DUNDEE ADVERTISER, *March* 12, 1897.

Wherein lies the superiority of the Anglo-Saxon? This question, which by its form pays a compliment to the British race, is the title of a remarkable book by a Frenchman, M. Demolins, the well-known editor of *La Science Sociale*. It has produced a sensation in France, and that it is well worth notice in this country any one may see from an expository article in the current number of the *Edinburgh Review*. M. Demolins is a patriot who best shows his love for his native land by fearlessly exposing its weaknesses. He sees three European nations engaged in forming colonial empires, while only one of them succeeds, and he asks why that successful nation is Britain, not France. Germany is dismissed. Germany sends forth every year thousands of her industrious, well-trained sons to the New World, where they fall into an existing order of things, learn another language, and are lost to the Fatherland. Germany, then, is no menace to France; her power of producing cheap goods does not seriously affect the French manufacturer; and militarism and Socialism are delivering France from her enemy across the Rhine. "The grand peril, the grand menace, the grand adversary," says M. Demolins, "are on the other side of the Channel, on the other side of the Atlantic; they are wherever is found a pioneer, a settler, a squatter of Anglo-Saxon blood. People despise this man because he does not come, like the German, with big battalions and guns of the latest pattern. They despise him because he comes alone, and with a plough. That is because they do not know the worth of a plough and the worth of the man." In this epigrammatic fashion M. Demolins exposes the causes of French inferiority. Beginning with education, he has much censure to level which curiously resembles our own fault findings with British public schools. The French boy is crammed with information, with beliefs, with aspirations, with rules of conduct. He has a formula by which inconvenient questions are solved. As he grows to manhood he is led to understand that his parent will decide his future—starting him in a profession, or, better still, obtaining for him a Government post with a small fixed income, to be supplemented by his interest on investments. Parental forethought also arranges a suitable marriage with a girl adequately dowered. Thus he is settled in life without ever conceiving the notion that it is a duty to provide for himself, and having for his "bright ideal" the career of a Government official with a regular salary. M. Demolins contrasts this with the British way. Our boys, whatever may be their educational shortcomings, are not turned out pedants. As they advance in years they are made to realise that they must rely on themselves. They have no special affinity for Government offices, and no great liking for indoor routine work of any kind. They move off to South Africa, to British Columbia, to Texas, as to their natural element. In a sentence M. Demolins traces Britain's success to individual self-help; France's failure to the habit of leaning first on the parent and then on the State as the great dispenser of favour and employment; the result being that while the Briton goes out with a plough and forms himself into colonies of other men similarly equipped, the Frenchman is a home-keeping person, given to counting over his savings, and committing the work of empire-building to a class which is sustained only by political ambition and military energy. Many flags, but no ploughs —that is the ailment. M. Demolins, it will be seen, takes broad views, and we can conceive another criticism of France which better allowed for its undoubted commercial energy, its mechanical skill, its patient labouring of the land. But in the main contention he cannot be far wrong. Restless diplomats and enterprising soldiers alone cannot make an empire. The workers must follow them or go in front. As things are in France, colonial aggrandisement is a passion for which the nation as a whole will risk much, but for which the individual Frenchman is indisposed to face sacrifices. Hence the superiority of the Anglo-Saxon, who acquired an empire before he knew it—in a fit of absence of mind. A foreign observer of British character and institutions must almost of necessity use a large brush to make his pictorial contrasts. M. Demolins, by way of rousing France, credits us with a freedom from Socialism which goes beyond the truth, or, at any rate, involves a closer definition. It would be safer to say that in Britain Socialism is always practical; we do not theorise; we enlist the services of the municipality or of the State when these are obviously for the public advantage. They can never be regarded as for the public advantage when they destroy individual initiative. The problem which seems too much for France, and which in our rude way we contrive to solve, is how to employ the collective power of the nation without weakening the mainspring of individual energy. By self-help, by force of personal initiative—so M. Demolins interprets the case—we have made and kept a world-wide dominion, while France has made and lost three colonial empires, and may yet lose a fourth.

SUNDAY TIMES, *April* 4, 1898.

We have it on the word of John Murray, the publisher, that every man has a book in him. In the case of M. Edmond Demolins, it is a fortunate circumstance that the book has come out. It bears the pleasing title, "Anglo-Saxon Superiority," a title of itself, in these days of decreasing British exports, to raise the author to the front rank of popularity. The first edition was exhausted in a few days. One of its chapters, added as a second preface, deals with a criticism that the author thinks might be advanced, viz., that the Germans are infringing on Anglo-Saxon superiority, and, according to one or two critics, especially Mr. Williams, of "Made in Germany" fame, and Mr. Maurice Schwob, England's manufacturing supremacy is threatened.

M. Demolins examines the case. He admits that during the last fifteen years German products have come to the front in the most surprising manner, and that French commerce has recoiled all along the line, losing its former positions one by one. How stands the case with Britain? Must she follow the example of France? Our author thinks not, and proceeds to show why.

Germany is a very poor country; its people must limit their wants, and have done so from early times. The famous and much-vaunted German simplicity is a virtue of necessity. Thanks to low wages and small needs, German industry has from early times been confined to the manufacture of common and low-priced articles. Now these conditions, which in themselves constitute real inferiority, have for the moment become an advantage to Germany; why?

Because the development of the conditions of transport has allowed new and backward countries to become purchasers of cheap and common articles with which Germany floods the world's markets. Her purchasers are simple, uncivilised, or half-savage peoples. You can find such persons even in so-called civilised countries. Merry England contains not a few people who are ignorant of the fact that a penny screwdriver whose handle breaks at the first trial, is a most expensive tool; elegantly-dressed women seem not to know that German jackets, which will not last out one winter, are very dear compared with a good English cloth. Germany has at the present moment a great market for the cheap article of poor and even bad quality, but M. Demolins does not think this can last.

German merchants have joined in associations aiming at commercial expansion. These associations have constituted a capital fund, organised exhibitions of their products to make them known, and have worked to obtain information as to the needs of customers.

Now, association is to M. Demolins the proverbial red rag to the bull. Pronounced individualist though he be, he cannot conceal from himself that association has some advantages, such as those already enumerated. But where will Association, first cousin to Socialism, end? It can minimise, but not conceal, inferiority. It may, indeed, give German manufacturers and traders powers which they could not otherwise possess; but it does not give them the personal power to progress and expand which they lack. In a word, Germans don't stand on their own legs.

It appears that the French Ambassador at Berlin, the Marquis de Noialles, forwarded to the French Minister of Commerce a document [1] dealing with German trade in the Transvaal, and this document plainly shows where German inferiority comes in. Its author states that German merchants "require their Government to help them with information and protection," to avoid the disappointments they have suffered when attempting to struggle against English competition.

It appears that German capital is too small; that German traders are ignorant of the conditions of the market; that they export things the Transvaal does not want; do not pack them sufficiently, and do not leave sufficient initiative to local agents. Much of this, by the way, is not unlike the criticism passed by English merchants on themselves and their methods. M. Demolins rather scores a point when he points out that there is of necessity rivalry between German traders themselves, and that this divergence of interest will make association increasingly difficult as time goes on.

"Let us now," says our laudator, "look at the Anglo-Saxons; we shall see that their methods of industrial and commercial expansion are very different.

By themselves, solely by personal initiative, without any support from private association or from public association—to wit, the State—they have possessed themselves of the world's markets, and they have done so by virtue of certain social conditions. People who have accomplished alone, without any external help, what others have only been able to do —and to do much more imperfectly—by grouping themselves, give by that very fact the measure of their undeniable superiority.

"And they will maintain that superiority despite the efforts the Germans are now making to gain command of the world's markets. They will maintain it by virtue of that superiority which the personal action of a great manufacturer or merchant possesses over collective action by associated manufacturers or merchants."

Then M. Demolins proceeds to show that the very essence of successful manufacture and commerce is the quality of constant change, ready adaptation to manifold conditions. The inherent vice of all association, the constant sacrifice to accord and agreement, will not permit the conditions that lead to success to flourish.

[1] The article appeared in the *Moniteur Official du Commerce*, May 13, 1897.

The German has two characteristic inferiorities which will fatally compromise his future expansion. Demolins admits that Hanover and Westphalia have shown themselves to be individualists and able to colonise. But the rest of Germany is different; as colonists the Germans are simply absorbed. On arrival in the United States the children of the Fatherland read German papers and have beautiful German names. The next generation reads English papers and bears Anglicised names. The rapidity with which the German disappears must indeed be a grief to his august and most Christian master; and be it observed that it is an Anglo-Saxon community which devours him.

The second characteristic inferiority is a result of the proclamation of the empire in 1871. Old Germany—poor, manufacturing, and economical, with its modest but solid qualities—had the germ of expansion within it; but a new and Imperial Germany has arisen that is full of evil and has devoured old Germany. The evil fruits of imperial Germany are militarism, officialdom (" fonctionnarisme "), and Socialism; and these isms have never produced, and can never produce, economic and social prosperity.

France only suffered through Louis XIV. from the two first of these plagues, and look, where is she to-day !

At first a society seems greatly strengthened by militarism and an army of functionaries; the forces of the nation are centralised by this tremendous mechanism. Spain and France have passed through these eras; Prussia has arrived there to-day, and has now its Grand Monarch.

Just because this *régime* centralises all living forces, it ends by atrophising them, by annihilating, exhausting, and sterilising them, and then ensues profound, and sometimes irremediable, decadance. . . . Even the Emperor of Germany will not escape this fatal law. . . . As for decadence, we French do but precede the Germans. Let them cease to rally us."

LADIES' FIELD, *July* 23, 1898.

" A quoi tient la supériorité des Anglo-Saxons " is the title of a new book by M. Demolins, of Paris, which is making no small stir in the educational world of our neighbours over the Channel. The special point of admiration in M. Demolin's review of the national system of education, both in this country and America, is elicited by the fact that it engenders independence of action, and makes our great public schools, Eton to Oxford, schools of sterling manhood, not of barrack-educated youths and boys. The outdoor life, the comforts, the surroundings of our public schools, our games and athletics, make for manhood and confidence. Practical energetic men, not officials and functionaries, are placed at the head of Anglo-Saxon educational institutes. "Compare Spain and South America, England and North America, to see the difference." "Young men educated thus succeed in life." Elsewhere we are shown how independence has made the Anglo-Saxon race. "Tel l'enfant, tel le jeune homme, tel l'homme." The emphatic remarks of our French contemporary, *Revue Pédagogique*, are well worth reading.

MORNING ADVERTISER (LONDON), *August* 13, 1898.

THE SUPERIORITY OF THE ANGLO-SAXONS.

A prominent French author uses the question, "To what is due the superiority of the Anglo-Saxons?" as the title of a new book in which he frankly admits Anglo-Saxon superiority, and seeks to set forth the causes thereof. The author is M. Demolins, editor of *La Science Sociale*; and a prominent Parisian firm published his book. M. C. de Mann's instructive review of M. Demolins' work appeared in the *Literary Digest*, October 9, 1897, emphasis being placed on the author's thesis that French decadence is primarily due to dependence upon the community in contrast to Anglo-Saxon dependence upon individual enterprise. The author makes a mistake, says the same paper, according to M. de Mann, in ignoring completely the moral forces and trusting entirely to political and practical measures to bring about the needed reorganisation of French society. M. Demolins' views are given additional prominence by the endorsement they have just received from another prominent Frenchman, the late M. Jules Steeg, who for years was considered one of the leading educators of France. The endorsement of M. Steeg appears in *Revue Pédagogique* (Paris, May), where a minute analysis of the work is given. M. Demolins' book opens with a defence of the title in these words : "It is useless to deny the superiority of the Anglo-Saxons. We may be vexed by this superiority, but the fact remains despite our vexation. We cannot go anywhere about the world without meeting Englishmen. Over all our possessions of former times the English or the United States flag now floats. The Anglo-Saxon has supplanted us in North America, which we occupied from Canada to Louisiana ; in Mauritius, once called the Isle of France ; in Egypt. He dominates America, by Canada and the United States ; Africa, by

Egypt and the Cape; Asia, by India and Burma; Oceanica, by Australia and New Zealand; Europe and the entire world by his commerce, by his industry, and by his politics. The Anglo-Saxon world is to-day at the head of that civilisation which is most active, most progressive, most devouring. Let this race establish itself anywhere on the globe, and at once there is introduced with prodigious rapidity the latest progress of our Western societies, and often these young societies surpass us. Observe that we Frenchmen have done with New Caledonia and our other possessions in Oceanica, and what the Anglo-Saxons have done in Australia and New Zealand. Observe what Spain and Portugal have made of South Africa, and what the Anglo-Saxons have made of North America. There is as much difference as between night and day." Considering the superiority conclusively proved, the author proceeds to search for the cause of this superiority. He finds the secret of this irresistible power of the Anglo-Saxon world in the *education of its youth*, in the direction given to studies, to the spirit which reigns in the school. The English and the people of the United States have perceived that the needs of the time require that youth should be trained to become practical, energetic men, and not public functionaries or pure men of letters, who know life only from what they learn in books. M. Demolins has personally studied with care some prominent English schools. In these he found the school buildings, not as in France, immense structures with the aspect of a barrack or a prison, but the pupils were distributed among cottages, in which efforts were made to give the place the appearance of a home. They were not surrounded by high walls, but there was an abundance of air and light and space and verdure. In place of the odious refectories of the French colleges, the dining-room was like that of a family, and the professors and director of the school, with his wife and daughters, sat at table with the pupils. M. Demolins' study of schools in the United States was made from descriptions given by Frenchmen who have travelled or resided there. He finds that education among us is systematically organised in a manner quite unknown in France. He praises much institutions in which the pupils earn their living while pursuing their studies. He relates the history of a student who began his university studies owing some twenty-three dollars. During the four years he was at the university he earned enough to live on, paid his debt, and left the institution with a little sum on hand. What is especially praised is that the students who thus earn their living are none the less respected by their fellows. In institutions, however, where there are not pupils thus earning their living, the education received gives a spirit of decision, a habit of self-reliance, so important in a country where, with but few exceptions, a young man is expected to make his own way in the world, and where he must learn betimes that if he rises he must depend on his own energy and his own tenacity. In thus comparing education in England and the United States with education in France, it is suggested that after all there may be something in racial instincts which causes Anglo-Saxons to give their children an education which differs so much from that given in France. Boys are early accustomed to go about alone in these countries, and even girls are trusted in a manner unknown in France. Children grow up with the knowledge that in the struggle for life they must rely upon themselves. From this point of view, M. Steeg observes, in his review of the book, it would not be sufficient for the French to change their methods of education. They must change their ideas on certain subjects—a very difficult thing to do, for these ideas are, many of them, born with them, and may almost be said to be in their blood. These defects in French ideas are thus set forth by M. Steeg :—" A foolish prejudice which appears to increase with the progress of instruction leads the fathers of families in France, in the middle-class especially, to direct the ideas of their sons to the careers called 'Liberal' and to public office. The choicest of our youth have their minds trained in this direction, and the vital professions—agriculture, industry, commerce, those which produce wealth and the true force of a country—tempt in France, with a very few honourable exceptions, only youth of inferior mental force. To make of their son an officer, a lawyer, a public functionary, such is the dream in France of a great multitude of fathers and mothers. Thus, in place of passing through a practical apprenticeship to life, of being prepared in his youth for the material difficulties he will encounter later on, the young Frenchman, from sixteen to twenty-five, and even longer, has but one object, that of passing examinations which will enable to enter the careers so crowded. They are fortunate who get into them. How about the others who do not get in? At twenty-five they find themselves without any position, and what is worse, without any preparation for the professions and occupations which are not closed to them. The education they have received has given them no initiative, no spirit of decision, no habit of relying on themselves."

ACADEMY, *September* 24, 1898.
AS OTHERS SEE US.

The superiority of the Anglo-Saxon over his neighbours, of the British lion over the Gallic cock, is so gracefully, if sorrowfully, acknowledged by M. Demolins that we hasten to confess our inferiority in one respect at least. We generally turn out much uglier books. M. Demolins has written a special introduction for English readers, in which he expounds luminously and well the various elements which have gone to make up what we call "England," the Saxons and Celts, the Angles, the Normans, the Danes, and the rest. And as a perusal of the work will be as wholesome for English readers as it could be for French ones, we welcome it cordially even in its somewhat unattractive English dress.

That a Frenchman should have the courage to put forth a book declaring, by its very title, the superiority of the Anglo-Saxon over the Latin races is a very interesting fact. That his book should have been received not merely with respect but actually with favour by the Parisian world of letters, and that ten thousand copies of it should have been sold in six months, is certainly not less interesting. Anglomania—we use the word in no insulting sense—had always had its votaries in France and, indeed, on the Continent generally, but a year ago one might have supposed that Chauvinism and the Dual Alliance had left Paris no time to weigh Anglo-Saxon merits (such as they are) with either good sense or candour. M. Demolins seems to have judged his countrymen differently, and the success of his book proves him to have been right. The book is a curious one, and will both amuse and instruct its English readers. Its author (who is a zealous student of social questions and the editor of *La Science Sociale*, a monthly review devoted to their discussion) traces Anglo-Saxon superiority, in the first place, to our educational system. Wellington, we know, did *not* say that Waterloo was won on the Playing Fields at Eton, but M. Demolins does. Only, paradoxical as it may seem, it is not the Playing Fields of Eton, but the playgrounds of two obscure schools in Derbyshire and Sussex, in which the battles of our race are really won. Indeed, our great public schools, in which we all trust, and our Board schools, which are the pet and pride of the Radical party, are not even noticed by M. Demolins, who reserves his enthusiasm for the two educational establishments above mentioned, and the "University Extension" (!)—which "gives horribly to think," as our author would say.

A French Savant's Verdict

But though M. Demolins has apparently a somewhat mistaken view of the importance of Abbotsholme School and its kindred establishment, and even perhaps of the splendours of University Extension and the Edinburgh "Summer Meeting," he has none the less, as regards education, got successfully to the root of the matter. French schools, he says, are adapted solely for turning out Government officials and small functionaries. Their aim is to teach their pupils how to pass the examination which leads to a public appointment. The multiplying of officials in France causes all the best of the nation to look to an official career for maintenance and employment. English schools, on the contrary (according to M. Demolins), are adapted for turning out not officials but Men. This, in spite of the modern mania for competitive examinations in England, strikes us as an entirely sound criticism, and it is a proof of our author's sagacity that he should have realised it so clearly. What M. Demolins has not realised is that the tendency of modern England is to fall into precisely the same blunder which has told so heavily on the France of to-day. We, too, have been smitten with the mania (for it is nothing less) for competitive examinations. The Army, the Navy, the Indian and Home Civil Services, &c., &c., are all its victims. If our author had perceived this he would probably have seen reason to doubt whether the Anglo-Saxon was quite the clear-sighted creature in educational matters which he depicts him. Furthermore, had M. Demolins visited India he would have found his admired Anglo-Saxons, at vast expense, setting up an educational system which produces precisely the same defects which he notes in the France of to-day. He would have found in India the same multitude of young men being educated with only one career in view—namely, a small post in a Government office. He would have found the same contempt, fostered by a vicious system of education, for manual labour, agriculture, or commerce, the same dangerous number of *déclassés* recruited from those natives who have failed in the competition for official appointments. We greatly fear that the Anglo-Saxon of to-day is perilously near the time when he may cease to deserve the many kind things which M. Demolins has to say about him. *Chauffage* ("cram") is, alas! by no means confined to France, or why did Mr. Wren, during his lifetime, flourish so exceedingly?

We have not space here to treat of the many interesting points raised by M. Demolins in the course of his book, and can only indicate briefly what these are in order that our readers may be tempted thereby to study the book for themselves. Besides the account of French and English education mentioned above, we have a very interesting (and extremely amusing) survey of German education as conceived by the German Emperor and King of Prussia. The bitter irony with which M. Demolins demolishes that scheme is one of the most effective things in the book. Then we have a chapter on French education as it should be, and one on the French population question full of wisdom and statistics, a rare combination. The characteristics of the Anglo-Saxon and his life are suggestively discussed and illustrated, and then follows an extremely valuable chapter contrasting *Le Personnel Politique* of England and France. After this a series of aspects of public life in the two countries are examined, and an appendix gives a most interesting collection of criticisms of the work gathered from the French press. The book should be read and pondered by every one who has the true interests of " Panglosaxonism " (to coin a portmanteau word) at heart.

ABERDEEN FREE PRESS, *September* 26, 1898.

ANGLO-SAXON SUPERIORITY: TO WHAT IT IS DUE.

This work, dealing from a French point of view with " the causes of the superiority of the English-speaking peoples," has had great vogue in France, where it has passed through at least ten editions. The Anglo-Saxon is an object of much consideration to the lively people beyond the Channel. The knight of the pen who eats John Bull's bread and calls himself Max O'Rell has found in John Bull and his island a profitable subject of literary exploitation. M. Demolins with his ten editions holds up John Bull and Brother Jonathan as examples to be followed, at least in their educational and industrial methods. Jacques Bonhomme likes well to hear of John Bull, and to get before him into Mandalay and Fashoda, not to mention the Niger and sundry other places. As a unit of a polite nation M. Demolins explains in a preface to this English edition that he hopes the British public will not misunderstand the meaning and import of his book, and in particular that they will not take his opinions as applying to " all the inhabitants " and " all the institutions " of Great Britain. In this same introduction the reader immediately comes upon a few samples of the delightful art of generalisation so characteristic of the French. What M. Demolins does, he says, is to " carefully isolate and exclusively consider " the phenomena traceable to the Anglo-Saxon influence which gives England and America their " social originality and superiority." This method of isolation and ex-

A French Savant's Verdict

clusion has its conveniences. For one thing it simplifies authorship. Let us come to one or two of the generalisations. The Celts, who predominate in some parts of the United Kingdom, have "no liking for the absorbing pursuits of agriculture," and in the Anglo-Saxon world they "mostly fill the ranks of the lower proletariat, or higher in the social scale —the liberal and political professions." Or, as we might express it, the Celt is either a hodman or a spouter. Even for Norman influence M. Demolins has no great respect, for he says that "Whilst the Celtic element weakens, especially the lower classes, by dragging them into labouring pauperism, the Norman element weakens especially the upper classes, by promoting Lordolatry, Patronage, and Snobbery." It is among the Celtic and Norman elements, he goes on to say, that Socialistic doctrines have found any echo in the Anglo-Saxon. All this the English reader is told to forget ; it is the Anglo-Saxon element alone which he is invited to consider, and his history is briefly summarised from the first landing of the Saxons onward—the Saxon ever triumphing and demonstrating "the undeniable superiority of social over political power." In answering the question to what the Anglo-Saxon superiority is due, M. Demolins does not dwell on the race qualities so prominent in his prefaces. To these he applies his process of exclusion. Of a hundred French boys from school seventy-five wish to enter Government offices. That is a national misfortune to begin with. To this end the school system is directed. Its efforts are put forth to enable boys to pass entrance examinations, and the pupils are hurried forward, with superficial smatterings of knowledge, to be before the age limit. So the education system does not "form men"; on the contrary, it inspires young people with disgust for agricultural, industrial, or commercial life, and "teaches them the alleged superiority of public functions." The German school system is alleged to have failed also properly to prepare men for the battle of life, or even for being good citizens—a speech by the Emperor going into detail on this point is cited by M. Demolins, who remarks that "if the social question could be summed up in one formula we might fearlessly say that the question is specially one of education." And in Britain upon the whole the dominant idea, according to this French observer, is to impart an education that will really be of service in the conduct of life. Particulars are given, some of them derived from inquiry and observation in Edinburgh, where the author delivered a course of lectures and attended the Summer Meeting in four consecutive years. The future of the world, it is suggested, for the benefit of the French, and with a good deal of reason, lies with the Anglo-Saxon pioneer and settler. "The man is not much considered, because he does not come, like the German, along with big battalions and perfected weapons; he is despised because he arrives with his plough and by himself. This comes from our being ignorant of what that plough is worth, and what that man is worth." The French are told by their Mentor that "English education and the whole social atmosphere develop in the highest degree the capability of the race to rise and triumph over the contemporary difficulties of existence." The low birth-rate question is discussed, and found to turn ultimately upon the conditions imposed on the family by the French social state. French children have to get "portions," while British are, to the infinite advantage of the nation, left to provide for themselves.

In successive essays the Frenchman and the Anglo-Saxon at school, in private life, and in public life are compared and contrasted, with the view of pointing a moral useful to France. They are brilliant essays—too sweeping in their generalisations, it may be allowed, and not to be accepted without reserve, but focussing attention upon some good points in our Anglo-Saxon ways. Much stress is laid upon our individualism, or "particularism," as an element in the prosperity of our people—every man, according to the old formula of Adam Smith, doing the best for himself and thereby doing the best for the community. "Happiness," according to M. Demolins' putting of it, is not in work but in "fitness for work," and—

To obtain this rare product, we want—

Parents fully convinced that they owe their children nothing but education, though a manly education;

Next, young men fully convinced that they will have to shift for themselves in life;

Young men fully determined to seek in marriage a help-mate, not a dowry;

A Government that will reduce to a minimum its own prerogatives, and the number of its functionaries and officials—a measure the effect of which would be to attract young men to the independent callings, which demand exertion, private initiative, and personal labour;

In fine, and as a consequence, a social state in which the politician, and the idle man, shall reap less consideration than the agriculturist, the manufacturer, and the trader.

A French Savant's Verdict

NORTH BRITISH DAILY MAIL, *September* 26, 1898.

It is always instructive and almost invariably unpleasant to hear what other people think about us. In the present instance, however, the very title of this work gives a fillip to our national vanity that most Frenchmen would agree to be superfluous and unnecessary, and certainly the self-complacency to be derived from a perusal of its pages will be neither small nor superficial, for the author metaphorically pats the Anglo-Saxon on the back and tell him not to be in the least afraid of the "Made in Germany" bogey, it is a passing phase, a development arising from the conditions of labour obtaining in Germany which favour the production of cheap and common goods taken in connection with the contemporary increase in the means of transport to new and backward countries where such goods would be welcomed. The German manufacturers took this tide in commercial affairs at the flood, and by syndicating their resources they have gained a superiority in new markets over the less adaptable British houses. But—and the author insists strongly on this point—"the present expansion of the German race is the product of Old Germany, not of New"; new Imperial Germany will produce, and is producing, militarism, officialism, and Socialism. How comforting to the patriotic Briton to read that the much vaunted educational system of Germany, which is being held up like the brazen serpent in the wilderness for the inept British schoolmaster to look upon and be saved, has been condemned, and that in no measured terms, by the Emperor himself as a failure technically, practically, and politically. In equally vigorous language the author himself denounces the school system of his own country as being calculated to produce armies of administrative officials utterly incapable of initiative, will power, or constant effort, all factors so essential to industrial success. Our own system of bringing up our boys, while admittedly faulty in many respects, yet produces men able to give a good account of themselves in the struggle for existence, endowed with healthy bodies, not particularly averse to hard work, and so constituted as to experience the keenest pleasure in the facing and overcoming of difficulties. That our system does produce this kind of man our colonial and industrial records show, but it is a question if an imitation of Continental methods of education, as seems to be the tendency in some quarters at the present day, will keep up the quality as well as the quantity of the output. Naturally this matter of education reacts very strongly on public life, the result being generally the impress of what M. Demolins calls a "communistic formation" on France and a "particularistic formation" on Britain. The Frenchman and German have had their individuality dwarfed and stunted by their upbringing, while the Anglo-Saxon emerges from his chrysalis state individualistic and self-reliant. We cannot enter into the many questions discussed so ably and so temperately by the author, they all bear the marks of careful thought, and are deductions from exhaustive inquiries; nor can we endorse fully many of the author's opinions, our notion of patriotism for instance, but we give him credit for placing before us a great theme scientifically treated in the most liberal-minded spirit, shirking no difficulty, mercilessly candid. To us it ought to prove as valuable as it is interesting, for it proclaims from the mouth of one who is no great well-wisher to this country the features of our life which it behoves us to preserve if we wish to retain the superiority which is grudgingly but honourably admitted even by our enemies.

SHEFFIELD TELEGRAPH, *September* 28, 1898.

FRANCE AND ENGLAND.

M. Demolins is a pupil of Le Play and editor or "director" of *La Science Sociale*, the monthly organ of a movement which owes its origin to that reformer. With M. Demolins, as with Le Play, social science must be based upon a wider induction from social facts carefully observed. Nothing human comes amiss to him, and his appeal to facts is irresistibly convincing. This book, which was published in 1897, consists largely of essays first printed in *La Science Sociale*. It caused a similar sensation amongst French readers to that produced amongst ourselves by "Made in Germany." In two months it had run through five editions, and the French Publishers' Appendix to this translation, in which the Press notices, signed and unsigned, are given at considerable length, helps to explain its sudden popularity. The translation is made from the tenth French edition, and it has a special introduction by the author, addressed to English readers. We could wish that the book had a more pleasing cover, and that the title-page was less obtrusive, for these things prejudice the reader, and set him against the contents before he gets to them. Apart from this the volume is attractive—too attractive, as some may think, for a people not lacking in self-complacency. The author starts by describing—with a map to help him—what he means by "Anglo-Saxon superiority." "Although we do not all acknowledge it," he says, "we all have to bear it, and we all dread it; the apprehension, the suspicion, and sometimes the hatred provoked by L'Anglais proclaim the fact loudly enough. We cannot go one step in the world without coming across L'Anglais. We cannot glance at any of our late possessions without seeing there the Union Jack." In a year 160 French ships pass through the Suez Canal, of German ships 260, whilst of British ships there are 2,262! "It is not sufficient," says M. Demolins, "to point out this superiority, to 'denounce' it in Parliament or in the Press, or to shake our fists at L'Anglais, like angry old women." What is needed is an explanation, and for Frenchmen it is a matter of life and death. The essays which attempt this explanation are grouped under three heads, dealing with the Frenchman and the Anglo-Saxon, "At School," "In Private Life," and "In Public Life," respectively. The conclusion arrived at is that whilst Anglo-Saxons are taught from the first to be independent and self-helpful, Frenchmen are hemmed in by conventions and restrictions which suppress the impulses that promote progress. Their schools are not as ours; they are brought up with different aims and expectations; they prefer rather to reduce their numbers than to risk hardship from too strenuous competition. To a Frenchman the present position of his country may well seem critical. There are indications that the springs of life are failing. Year by year the number of deaths increases, whilst the number of marriages and of births declines. In 1890 the number of births was 100,000 less than in 1881; and lower by 38,446 than the number of deaths. It is demonstrable that this is due to social causes, and Anglo-Saxons will only be too glad if a study of their habits helps to find a remedy. But although M. Demolins knows England, his knowledge has been acquired under exceptional circumstances, which render it fragmentary, and, at times, misleading. It is curious, *e.g.*, in reading of the Anglo-Saxon at school, to have our attention confined to a school founded so lately as 1889 on novel and experimental lines. The system may be good and, perhaps, better adapted than others for transplantation; but it is not that which prevails at present, and it will probably remain exceptional. We think, too, that M. Demolins, throughout, is not sufficiently on his guard against hasty generalisations—the English are not so entirely individualistic as he thinks they are, and they value solidarity as much as M. Bourgeois does, and see no inconsistency in socialistic individualism. Why we are what we are, is a question which yet seeks solution. M. Demolins may, incidentally, throw light upon the answer, but we take it that the main value of his book will be to instigate his own countrymen, though it may help us to a better understanding of our neighbours, and should secure our sympathy in their manifold perplexities. The book is a store-house of facts, which need, however, to be supplemented by other facts, less flattering to our self-esteem. It is a book which deserves to be widely read, and, incidentally, it will allay the fears of those who dread the commercial rivalry of Germany.

LIVERPOOL COURIER, *September* 29, 1898.

Racial controversy, like disputation concerning religion, is apt to become acrimonious, and the narrower the dividing line, the more bitter the contention is likely to be. So much is exemplified at the present time by the polemics of Saxon and Celt in the correspondence columns of the *Courier*. It is of course natural that men when they feel strongly should express themselves in vigorous terms; and who shall condemn the sentiment which makes one's place of birth the dearest and sweetest, and one's "ain folk" the very best in all the earth? Yet it is regrettable that a theme of this sort could not be discussed temperately, for it undoubtedly has a scientific and practical side of the utmost importance. Is it possible for the races of the world to remain distinct and unmixed, given certain political and social conditions, and if so, is it desirable? So far as colour is concerned, it may be assumed that experience gives the answer. Eurasians, Creoles, and all colour-mixtures of the human species indicate that that is the way to extinction. As regards white races, the presumption is that they will mingle when the circumstances will allow. Even differences of language and religion, as we know, although very powerful barriers, are not insurmountable, and so far as the inhabitants of these islands are concerned we cannot help thinking that our correspondents, dogged Saxons and perfervid Scots alike, might turn the race question to much better account b trying to take note of the blending which has taken place, and the results. Some ten years ago the Duke of Argyll in the course of a correspondence, afterwards collected and published by Mr. Bernard Quaritch, declared: "We are all mongrels, and not only are we all equally mongrels, but we are the result of the intermixture of precisely the same breeds all over the United Kingdom." This, of course, is merely destructive as regards race claims. A very clever book, however, has lately been written in France, and run rapidly through ten editions, entitled *Anglo-Saxon Superiority: to what is it due?* This work is by M. Edmond Demolins, and as it has now been Englished by M. Louis Bert Lavigne, and published by the Leadenhall Press, controversialists should peruse it.

A French Savant's Verdict

It is something to have the superiority of the English-speaking peoples —for in reality that is what is meant by "Anglo-Saxon"—admitted from a French point of view. But M. Demolins shows that he has been studying what has happened in our midst, and very precisely formulates the process. The Saxons, in a word, are the base of our solidarity. Coming here in the fifth century, and driving away the Celts, who represented the "communistic clan formation," those "particularists" have ever since been the assimilating force in the country. They did not rise against the Angles when they came, but endured much before turning on the aggressor. They seemed to be meekness itself in presence of Danish invasion till the Danes compelled them to rise. When the Normans came they were received almost without resistance. History says that the Normans, who belonged to the "communistic state formation," were conquerors, but in reality the Saxons absorbed them even by a process of non-resistance. They were not politicians, those Saxons. They were not soldiers, and never fought till compelled. They were agriculturists, and there was genuine implantation into the soil in their case. They attached the utmost importance to the rights of the individual, the sanctity of the family, and their "common law," and their juries proved the basis of all that is best in our constitution. As a matter of course the Saxons cannot have done all this without themselves undergoing considerable modification. This is just the point. They have watered down much, including Norman snobbery, and although there still exists a "Celtic fringe," the ancient Celtic dislike of work has been greatly modified. M. Demolins points out that from the outset the Celts mostly filled the ranks of the lower proletariat, or, higher in the social scale, the liberal and political professions. The broad, individualistic middle class, which is the basis of all solid society, would have been lacking without the Saxons, whose family and scholastic ideas still prevail, and, according to this Frenchman, account for our wonderful expansion, and the all-pervading influence of our race.

The Frenchman may not be accurate in every respect. He has perhaps more faith in the assimilative capacity of the Saxon element in America than the Americans themselves, although he works it all out with the precision of a mathematical proposition. The Saxon works; is strong individually and in the family; and his system, all the really important features of which have been preserved, comes out on the right side as regards the population question, and in connection with commercial supremacy. Even though the Saxon may neglect the Forum and allow Celtic Tammanyism to flourish in his municipal affairs, there is no fear of the ultimate triumph. Whether this be right or wrong, it is certainly demonstrated that the Saxon is an integral part of the foundation and framework of a noble edifice, and as Mr. Mackenzie MacLeod frankly admits, he had a glorious career even before the Celt became his partner. And as the partnership exists, and is beneficial to both, why should there be any quarrelling or recrimination? We plead for good fellowship, and it might be promoted by a habit of accuracy on both sides. Who are the Celts? The usual answer is the Scots, the Irish, and the Welsh, but it is entirely misleading. Prior to the Scottish war of independence there were in that country no fewer than five well-marked nationalities. Mr. Steel speaks of Burns as a Celtic poet, but Burns was a Lowland Scot, who sang of his "Highland Mary," and of things Highland generally in varying strain. In truth he knew not, as he confessed, what blood ran in his veins. And the remark holds good of the people of the island of Britain as a whole. The most definite thing that can be said is that the east is mainly Teutonic, and the west preponderatingly Celtic, with considerable dashes of Scandinavian thrown in all round our coasts. To take the place names of the little peninsula between the Mersey and the Dee, for example, we find such names as Kirby, Irby, Frankby, Greasby, and Thingwall, with a name like Landican as neighbour to the last-named, which is as suggestive of the Norseman as Tynwald in the Isle of Man, or Dingwall and hundreds of other specimens of place nomenclature in the North of Scotland. It may be true that there is little evidence of permanent implantation so far as the Norsemen are concerned, other than yellow hair and a tolerably distinct type of feature among the people and graveyards which bear evidence of having been selected on the familiar Norse principle—within sight of their beloved sea; but that their sojourn made its mark there can be no doubt.

And if we glance at the sister isle, it will be found that the population of the east and north is mainly Saxon, while in the extreme south-west the basis is Iberian. Even in Munster and Connaught, many who imagine themselves Celts are the descendants of Saxon colonists, and it is as true of parts of Ireland as of great English and Scottish cities that clear facial traces of mixed origin may be discerned sometimes among different members of one family. This is no reason why local patriotism should not exist—far from it. All that is contended for is reasonableness and due regard to the highest considerations. The Saxon is none the worse for a little intermixture of Scottish ardour and Irish enthusiasm, while Cymric sentiment, with its warm glow and wonderful tenacity, has

A French Savant's Verdict

also its place and use. No sensible Saxon would desire that the Celt had gone out with King Arthur and the Knights of the Round Table legends, with the poems of Ossian, or the exploits of Owain Glyndwr. He knows that under the union the Celts have furnished great commanders, warriors, statesmen, and leaders in every sphere. On the other hand, the Saxons as a basic element in the partnership, and as the richer and numerically stronger partner, have not been unappreciative or wittingly unkind. There is room for all, and work to be done in which all are required to lend their aid with heart, hand, and brain. "Saxon and Norman and Dane are we," sang Tennyson in his "Welcome of Alexandra." He might have added a round dozen to the number of elements of origin; but let not the members of this mixed family get into the habit of throwing taunts and sneers at one another. The world should know that they are all Britons, and that they mean to work together for the fulfilment of the destiny mapped out by the French critic—who, by the way, hails from Southern France.

WESTMINSTER GAZETTE, *September* 30, 1898.

The work is not without its value on this side of the Channel. All the schools in England are not conducted on the excellent models which our author has described so accurately. *It is indeed rather amusing to the British reader to find our scholastic system represented in this distinguished foreigner's pages by such heterodox establishments as Abbotsholme and Bedales —for these, we presume, are the schools to which M. Demolins alludes.* We heartily commend *Anglo-Saxon Superiority*, even to readers fresh from the volumes of Mr. Bodley and Baron de Coubertin. There are many things in it concerning the condition of our neighbours which supplement very opportunely the information contained in *France* and *The Evolution of Modern France*. The chapter on the all-important question of the Birth Rate we have found specially interesting.

BOOKSELLER (LONDON), *November*, 1898.

We are glad to welcome an English translation of this book, which has deservedly aroused unusual attention in France. The author, M. Demolins, a disciple of Le Play, the French Economist, is the editor of the French *Social Science Review*, and recognised as a careful and observant student of social phenomena. The book consists of a series of

32

papers which first appeared in the pages of the *Review*, the arguments of which are drawn from a careful study of English History, and from a personal observation of some phases of our English life. It must have required some courage on the part of a foreigner to have reached the conclusions here formulated, and to have set them down in so definite and so unqualified a fashion. He points out the fact well recognised in this country, that the Anglo-Saxon has always struggled for his social independence. To put it in the author's own words, the Anglo-Saxons belong to the particularistic formation of society in which the tendency is to rely not on the community, but on self or the individual, while the French and Germans are rather examples of the communistic type of society, which relies more on the community, the group, the family, or the tribe. Hence it is that the Anglo-Saxon has an initiative, an individuality which is bound to succeed in the great struggle for existence all over the world. A large part of the book is occupied by a comparison of the educational systems of England, France, and Germany, altogether to the advantage of the former, which, we are told, alone produces men, while the others only produce officials. *Speaking generally, this description of English educational system is fairly correct, but it is somewhat to be regretted that the special examples quoted should have been exceptional experiments rather than typical examples of English public schools.* M. Demolins also draws several examples from the neighbourhood of Edinburgh, a part of the United Kingdom exceptionally advantageous for his argument. At the same time, even Frenchmen admit that the *main course of his argument is unassailable,* and that the conclusions to which he arrives, however unpalatable to French national pride, are well grounded. For English readers, the book will, of course, have a special interest, for it is seldom that our social conditions are examined by a foreigner so scientifically impartial, and so ready to appreciate the advantages which to the Anglo-Saxon are merely a part of his common national heritage.

Dublin Express, *October* 1, 1898.

THE SUPERIORITY OF THE ANGLO-SAXON.

Just at a time when the celebration of the Queen's Diamond Jubilee was displaying to the world the full force and vast resources of the British Empire, M. Edmond Demolins published a book which attracted in France an instant and widespread attention. The name of the author was scarcely known outside a circle of literary men interested in the science of sociology. He had been the most enthusiastic and the favourite pupil of the celebrated Le Play, and after the death of his master he succeeded to his place as editor of a monthly review called *La Science Sociale*. His book, immediately on publication, became the sensation of the hour, and in two months ran through five editions. Every literary man of standing devoted at least one article to its contents, and the peculiar thing about its success is that every writer, even M. Drumont, the blindest and most violent of Anglophobes, praised its purpose and agreed with its conclusions. Now, the book, while based on a profound and philosophical conception of social phenomena, is as wildly alarmist and as grossly exaggerated as anything ever written by Mr. Stead in his most violent convulsions of pessimistic denunciation. It exaggerates the merits of the Anglo-Saxon, and, to emphasise the contrast, still more strangely depreciates the qualities which strike us as most commendable in the character of the French. We cannot help suspecting that there is a subtle touch of ironical self-abasement in the tone adopted by M. Jules Lemaître and other writers when they contemplate the rapid and hopeless decadence of the nation to which they belong. It is one of the peculiar characteristics of the decadence of modern France—a characteristic which differentiates it from the decadence of all other people—that it is going on with the full cognisance, and perhaps also with the full acquiescence, of the French people themselves. It has become a fashion among literary men in Paris to analyse its nature, and to speculate deeply concerning its causes and even its most remote tendencies. This impartiality of introspection, this examining of oneself from the point of view of the whole of humanity, is possible only in minds endowed with the cosmopolitanism of the French intellect. The French people are singularly ignorant of facts—particularly of facts relating to the habits and modes of thought of the other nations of the world—but no nation has ever had sympathies so broad or so universal, or so clear a conception of abstract things, or a judgment so unbiassed or so unclouded. This explains the peculiar attitude they have adopted with regard to their own supposed inferiority—an attitude which presupposes a power of philosophic abstraction, of objective contemplation of their own personality, of which no other race has ever been capable. Let us add that they treat the question with an irony which is also exquisite and essentially French. It is necessary to know these facts before we can understand why it is so—that a people whose vanity and self-importance are almost as great as our own are, nevertheless, able to read with equanimity an account of their own moral and physical decadence.

M. Demolins explains that the chief superiority of the Anglo-Saxon lies in his system of education—in his peculiar views of public and private life. His system of education aims at producing practical men, full of self-reliance and independence. The Anglo-Saxon belongs to the particularistic, whereas the Frenchman belongs to the communistic formation. In the latter state every man leans for support on his neighbour, and looks for assistance and protection from the State. An English schoolboy may not know the difference between an amphimacer and an amphibrachys, but he has learnt how to rely on himself, and is fitted in a manner for the struggle of existence. " Ask a hundred young Frenchmen just out of school, to what career they are inclined," says M. Demolins, " three-quarters will answer that they are candidates for Government offices."

It is, therefore, the primary object of all French schools to prepare their pupils solely for examinations, and this, observe, is not the object of any school which pretends to educate. The methods used for the purposes of teaching are very different from those in use for the purposes of cramming. It is scarcely necessary to point out that this is precisely the fault at the present moment of nearly all our Irish schools. We are moving in a wrong direction. We are producing, perhaps, excellent examination machines, but we are not fitting the youth of Ireland " for the struggle of existence." Since the publication of M. Demolins' book the French system of education has been criticised with so much asperity, even by professors vitally interested in its continuance, that there is every reason to believe that in a short time radical changes will completely alter both its objects and its methods. The education which the Anglo-Saxon receives at home encourages his habits of independence and self-reliance quite as much as the education which he receives in an English public school. He is not taught to look to his parents to support or assist him, but knows that at a comparatively early age he must, to use a piece of forcible slang, shift for himself. " Now, how do we prepare our children? What do we teach them?" asks M. Demolins.

"We teach them that the ideal, the supreme wisdom in life, is to avoid as much as possible all its difficulties and uncertainties. We tell them, ' My dear child, first of all rely upon us. You see how we save money in order to be able, at the time of your marriage, to give you as large a portion as possible. We are too fond of you not to do our utmost to ease for you the difficulties of existence. Next, rely on our relations and friends, who will exert their influence to find you some cosy berth. You must rely on the Government, too, which dispose of an innumerable quantity of comfortable posts, perfectly safe—and salary paid regularly at the end of the month; advancement automatic, through the mechanism of retirements and deaths. So that you shall be able to know in advance what your emoluments are to be to such-and-such an age. At such another age, too, you will retire and be entitled to a pension—a good little pension. So, after doing very little work during your administrative career, you will be enabled to do nothing at all at a time of life when a man is still capable of activity. But, my dear child, as these situations imply but indifferent pay (for we cannot get everything), you must reckon on what your wife may bring you. A moneyed wife must therefore be found; but do not be uneasy about this, we'll find you one. Such is, my boy, the advice which our love dictates.'"

The young man who hears such language daily at home, in society, and in the street is very soon convinced that there is no other plan of life either reasonable or possible for him. He marries, gets a "dot" with his wife adjusted to his income and position, has a child, and finds that within the next twenty years he must retrench his income in order to save up a sum approximately equal to that which his wife brought him. He has another child, and the difficulty of his situation has doubled. He is unwilling, therefore, to have more children, and his economy compromises the credit, and his sterility the population, of France.

No one will be inclined to deny the force of M. Demolins' argument respecting the relative composition of the English and French Legislative Chambers. As land is the basis of all wealth, so agricultural interests are the most constant and the most important in a nation. No country is properly, or even safely, represented which does not give to land its due preponderance. In England the House of Lords is practically composed of landlords, while in the House of Commons the landed interest is represented by 132 members. Commerce, next in order, and industry together have in the House of Commons a combined total of 232 representatives, while the liberal professions are adequately represented by 107 members. Now, in the French Chamber of Deputies agriculture, commerce, and industry combined are represented by 135 members only, while the liberal professions have as many as 286 representatives. Of these 50 are physicians not over-troubled with patients, 65 journalists ever on the look-out for crisis or sensation, and 123 lawyers who live on the insecurity of property, the uncertainty of law, and the general confusion of the social and moral world. Here, at all events, the English

House of Commons is incontestably superior, though M. Demolins is wrong in attributing the cause to the Anglo-Saxon character without previously giving us an adequate reason for the existence of a state of affairs in the American Congress strikingly analogous to the composition of the Chamber of Deputies.

But M. Demolins still hopes in the regeneration of France. He thinks that contact and competition with the Anglo-Saxon (an admirable instance of which is the Fashoda question) is very salutary as an example. Among other symptoms he mentions the universally-recognised failure of the present system of education in France (a system of which we have a striking and unfortunate example in Ireland), the introduction of English games and exercises into schools and amongst the youth generally; the overcrowding of the administrative and liberal professions, which will bring into favour the more lucrative and independent pursuits of commerce and colonisation, and, above all, the growing discredit into which politics and politicians are falling. Finally, M. Demolins draws hope from the following thought which occurs in one of his letters to M. Jules Lemaître :—

"The French mind is clearer and more methodical than the Anglo-Saxon mind; and these qualities are essential in our work as leaders and pilots of the belated nations of the West. Our confidence ought to be increased by the fact that the French are, from all appearances, the people that most closely resemble the Anglo-Saxons—more, at any rate, than the Spaniards or Italians—and, notwithstanding appearances, more than the Germans, who are still blessed with their Louis XIV."

Such is the book which has created so much sensation in France. And yet its conclusions are neither very accurate nor very true. The impression it leaves on the mind, in spite of M. Demolins' enthusiastic optimism, is that France is irretrievably decaying. That impression is mainly produced by contrasting the merits of the Anglo-Saxon with the faults of the Frenchman, a method of argument which requires no great skill nor deep knowledge to support. It will not, we think, increase the Anglo-Saxon's pride in himself, for even the dullest of that race will suspect a book which talks rapturously of the culture, refinement, and elegance of the British workman's home.

BIRMINGHAM GAZETTE, *October* 3, 1898.

It is the unexpected that happens, and a book admitting Anglo-Saxon superiority from the pen of a distinguished Frenchman must surely be reckoned among the unforeseen. " Anglo-Saxon Superiority, to What it is Due," by Edmond Demolins, now translated (and admirably translated) by Louis B. Lavigne, and published by Simpkin, Marshall & Co., is in many respects a surprising book. The author directs the monthly review, *La Science Sociale*, and is a pupil of Le Play, who after twenty-five years' study in Europe and Asia established the foundations of social science. M. Demolins is no ordinary Frenchman, no shrieker, no mere sensationalist. He is earnest and sincerely patriotic, and has the courage of his opinions. To do his countrymen justice, they are taking him seriously. The book, which assumes the undeniable superiority of the Anglo-Saxons, but more especially of the English breed, has rapidly run through ten editions, and strange to relate, nearly all the best writers and thinkers of France have given in their adhesion. M. Demolins analyses, dissects with the stern, cold impartiality of a man of science who is determined to see things as they are, but who loves his country and is earnestly desirous of raising his countrymen to the Anglo-Saxon level. No wonder the book has caused a sensation. In literary and scientific circles the name of Dreyfus now hides its diminished head, and that of Demolins, as a potential saviour of his country, takes its place.

He begins by anticipating the natural repugnance of his countrymen to admit Anglo-Saxon superiority. But he insists that though all Frenchmen do not acknowledge it, all have to bear it, and all dread it ; the apprehension, the suspicion, and the hatred provoked by the English proclaim the fact unmistakably. The French traveller cannot go a step without coming on the English. He cannot glance at any of his country's late possessions without seeing there the Union Jack. The Anglo-Saxon has supplanted him in North America, which the French once occupied from Canada to Louisiana ; in India ; at Mauritius (the old Isle of France) ; and in Egypt. The Anglo-Saxon, pestilent fellow, rules America, by Canada and the United States ; Africa, by Egypt and the Cape ; Asia, by India and Burmah ; Austral Asia, by Australia and New Zealand ; Europe and the whole world, by his trade and by his policy. Having thus begun at the beginnings M. Demolins gives a map, a terrible map, of which the darkened shades represent the sphere of Anglo-Saxon influence, and truly there does not seem much of the world left for aspiring Frenchmen. That fact being established, she wants to know why it is ; why the brilliant Gaul is ousted everywhere, why he seems to be gradually passing away in a sort of painless extinction. Our scientist puts in the knife without mercy, but with the best intentions, asking his countrymen to see what they have made of New

Caledonia and other possessions in Austral Asia, and to compare it with what Englishmen have made of Australia and New Zealand. Incidentally he points to Southern America under the Spanish and Portuguese ; and to North America as transformed by the ubiquitous and irrepressible Anglo-Saxon. " It is like night and day ! " he exclaims. He mocks at Germany as a rival of England. In his judgment Frenchmen are not men, Germans are not men, and only the Englishman is a man. He admits no congenital inferiority. The French and German school systems are to blame ; they do not produce men. They cripple individuality, crush the power of initiative, teach reliance on the Clan, the State, the Corporation. The facts are undeniable, he says, and a remedy must be found. It is not sufficient to point out British superiority, to " denounce " it in Parliament or in the press, to shake fists at the English like angry old women. The situation must be examined as men who would be equal to it ; with exactness and most coolly, so as to become acquainted with its real properties. Why do Anglo-Saxons absorb the peoples with whom they come into contact ; and why do the French, after sixty years' occupation of Algeria, find themselves in danger of absorption by the European strangers among them ? What is the secret of the Britisher's infinite power of expansion, and that extraordinary aptitude to civilise ; and what are the means of doing it ? The question, says this great authority, is for France one of life and death. What is to be done ? How shall we compete with the terrible English, who threaten the submergence of all other peoples ? His answer is sufficiently clear.

The French educational system must go, root and branch. The present plan reduces the birth-rate, compromises the financial situation, and constitutes, therefore, a double inferiority. English education prepares children for the struggle for existence. The sons are not bolstered up as in France ; nor are they taught to look to the dowry of a wife for their maintenance. M. Demolins, who knows his England, expands with vigour, but with calculated system, on these themes, and also upon the manner in which his mode of home life contributes to the Anglo-Saxon's success. Then the Frenchman is of Communistic build, while the Anglo-Saxon is Particularistic, both terms having here an especial meaning, the one referring to the inborn instinct of the French to rely on others, the other describing the inborn instinct of the Anglo-Saxon to depend upon himself. The colonising power of a nation, says our author, is the test of its social power. It betokens the spirit of initiative and the exact force of expansion. France cannot colonise ; Germany cannot colonise. Both export soldiers and officials without stint, but not much more. Their colonies are mostly theoretical ; they do not take root ; and the reason is that in both cases their educational system produces excellent officials, but is especially unfitted to form men. Wherefore Frenchmen fill the air with their complaints, instead of finding out the course followed by those who rely on individual initiative. The French tradition of education and home training compromise the vitality and social power of the nation ; the English system and the whole social atmosphere develop in the highest degree the capability to triumph over contemporary difficulties of existence. Men reared in the English way—made strong in their bodies, accustomed to material facts, having been always treated as men, trained to rely on themselves, and looking on life as a battle—are fit to cope with the difficulties of life ; even enjoy them ; they expect them, and mean to triumph over them. And being fitted for the strife, they improve in it as in their element. Such emigrants do marvels : accomplish miracles with but a modicum of public power at their backs. " The great peril," says our author, warming to his work, " is not across the Rhine ; militarism and Socialism will spare us the trouble of getting rid of that enemy—and that before long. The great peril, the great rivalry . . . are wherever is to be found an Anglo-Saxon pioneer, an Anglo-Saxon settler or squatter. The man is not much considered because he did not come like the German with big battalions and perfected weapons ; he is depised because he arrives with his plough, and by himself. This comes from our being ignorant of what that plough is worth, and what that man is worth." Truly John Bull has nothing to complain of here. On the other hand, M. Demolins' estimate of his countrymen caused Jules Lemaître to write : " An infinitely painful book, but we must swallow the bitter cup to the dregs."

It is impossible to give here anything like a complete analysis of a book at once so fascinating and so replete with solid facts. Incidental passages are, however, expressive, and we quote one or two :—The French are more economical than the English, yet more ride first-class in France than in England. This is because the dignity of the lower-class French is inferior to that of the lower-class English. The French newspapers aim at amusement ; their politics are only amusements. The English journals rely on " facts, facts, facts." The French collegiate tutor is an awful personage, with a frock-coat and an unapproachable dignity, who only opens his mouth to drop moral precepts for the young.

M. Demolins has seen an English head dressed in tweed with a Tam o' Shanter cap and heavy boots, who, moreover, was not exhaling maxims and profundities. An excellent book, and one that deserves to be a classic. But it lacks completeness. We do not think that M. Domolins has in every case "touched the spot." Doubtless he thinks many things which, outspoken as he is, it was impossible for him, as a Frenchman, to say. One only we are tempted to suggest as an unmentioned source of English superiority. The French, though of communistic social formation, lack mutual confidence. The English, though individualistic in feeling, are confident that in a tight place they can always depend on their countrymen to the death. In reverse, the British soldier does not cry "Treason," nor can Englishmen conceive a British officer forging a letter to clinch a conviction against a brother officer, even under the pressure of military discipline.

GLASGOW EVENING TIMES, *October* 4, 1898.
A THOUGHTFUL BOOK.

"Anglo-Saxon Superiority — To What it is Due," by Edmond Demolins (London : The Leadenhall Press, Limited), is a translation from the tenth French edition of "A quoi tient la Supériorité des Anglo-Saxons," which treats the subject from the point of view of an enlightened and unbiassed Frenchman. In the case of this work, which has aroused much interest and criticism in France, the process of seeing ourselves as others see us is much more pleasant than it usually is. M. Demolins has a very hearty admiration, founded on thorough and first-hand information, for the Anglo-Saxon character and social system. He begins by contrasting the French, German, and English school systems, keeping in view the question which of them is best fitted to form men, and thereafter he shows how the French system of education reduces the birth-rate and compromises the financial situation of France, showing in strong contrast how Anglo-Saxon education prepares children for the struggle for existence, and how the Briton's home life contributes to his success. We cannot do better than quote the following passage which illustrates the young Frenchman's

OUTLOOK ON LIFE :—

"How do we prepare our children ? What do we teach them ? We teach them that the ideal, the supreme wisdom in life, is to avoid as much as possible all its difficulties and uncertainties. We tell them, 'My dear child, first of all rely upon us. You see how we save money in order to be able, at the time of your marriage, to give you as large a portion as possible. We are too fond of you not to do our utmost to ease for you the difficulties of existence. Next, rely on our relations and friends, who will exert their influence to find you some cosy berth. You must rely on the Government, too, which dispose of an innumerable quantity of comfortable posts, perfectly safe and salary paid regularly at the end of each month; advancement automatic, through the mechanism of retirements and deaths. So that you shall be able to know in advance what your emoluments are to be at such and such an age. At such another age, too, you will retire and be entitled to a pension—a good little pension. So, after doing very little work during your administrative career you will be enabled to do nothing at all at a time of life when a man is still capable of activity, but, my dear child, as these situations imply but indifferent pay (for we cannot get everything), you must reckon on what your wife may bring you. A moneyed wife must therefore be found; but do not be uneasy about this, we'll find you one. Such is, my boy, the advice which our love dictates.' The young man who hears such language daily at home, in society, in the very street, not unnaturally gets accustomed to the idea of relying on others more than on self; he is consequently disposed to shun all careers requiring continuous exertion and mental activity. He would never dream of braving the uncertainties of agriculture, industry, or commerce, and simply prepares for a tranquil existence. Such a conception of life results in paralysing a man's energy and will power; it makes him a very coward who deliberately turns his back on the difficulties which he ought to overcome; he only seeks pleasure, is thoroughly incapable of dealing with the serious side of life, and becomes, in fine, the very worst instrument for that moral action of which the power of exertion and triumph over self are the principal points."

The cure for this morbid condition M. Demolins sets forth thus :—

FRANCE WANTS

"Parents fully convinced that they owe their children nothing but education, though a manly education. Next, young men fully convinced that they will have to shift for themselves in life. Young men fully determined to seek in marriage a help-mate, not a dowry. A Government that will reduce to a minimum its own prerogatives, and the number of its functionaries and officials—a measure the effect of which would be to attract young men to the independent callings which demand exertion, private initiative and personal labour; in fine, and as a consequence, a social state in which the politician and the idle man shall reap less consideration than the agriculturist, the manufacturer, and the trader. All this, you see, is no easy performance. But such a combination of reforms alone can ensure for humanity the greatest possible sum of happiness in this world of ours; this alone can instil into our sons first the taste and then the love of work and exertion. And there is no other fundamental solution to the social question."

A WRONG CONCLUSION.

Occasionally the author is apt to generalise wrongly from facts whose significance he has over-estimated, as in the following remarks about the Briton's tendency towards travelling third-class:—

"You know that many railway trains in England have no second-class carriages attached to them, because the public have fallen into a habit of leaving them untenanted. On the other hand, the number of first-class passengers, according to statistics which I have before me, is, in proportion to the traffic, considerably less than on the Continent. Moreover, even as I am writing this, I hear that one of the principal British railway companies is considering the advisability of suppressing first-class carriages all over their system, and that the appointed committee of inquiry has approved the measure, on account of the small number of passengers that avail themselves of the first-class accommodation. *Apropos* of this, people mention the case of the Duke of Cumberland, a relative of the Queen, who always goes third-class. Economy is not the reason of this, for the English and Americans are generally given to liberal expenditure. On the other hand, the French, who are not so rich and of an essentially saving temperament, furnish a proportionately larger percentage of first-class passengers. We must, therefore, look for another reason. The only one I can see is the difference in the bearing and manners of the Anglo-Saxon lower classes, as compared with the same classes on the Continent. We object to travel in the company of people whose dress is poor and manners vulgar or offensive; whereas the greater dignity displayed by men of the lower class belonging to the Anglo-Saxon race makes this contact unobjectionable."

The third section of the book, a contrast between the Frenchman and the Anglo-Saxon in public life, is well reasoned and acute. Altogether, this is a thoughtful and admirable contribution on a subject of first importance to France, and the interest it has aroused there is thoroughly justified. It is one also which Anglo-Saxons will read with pride in as well as with profit to themselves.

A French Savant's Verdict

DAILY CHRONICLE, *October* 11, 1898.
BUREAUCRACY AND LIBERTY.
(BY AN INDIVIDUALIST.)

At the present time a remarkable movement of opinion is in progress on the Continent with reference to the relations between the individual and the State. Except among anarchists of the communistic type this movement has not as yet taken a pronounced political form. But it is busily manifesting itself in literature, and in works of a more or less scientific character, dealing with social and political philosophy. The emergence of this movement in a political shape is merely a question of time. Among the principal nations of the Continent it is felt by an ever increasing circle of people, drawn from almost all ranks and sections of the community, that the existing relations between the individual and the State are of an extremely unsatisfactory character. These relations, so far from improving, are daily getting more and more strained. On the one hand the individual is steadily losing faith in the military and bureaucratic classes, who are the State in its concrete form. On the other hand these classes are constantly engaged in dragging the private citizen limb by limb into their net, weaving coil upon coil of artificial regulations around him, until anything like free and unfettered movement becomes impossible. Some years ago it was believed that the State Socialists would be able to construct a *via media*, where the interests of the individual and the State would be reconciled and harmonised. But neither in Germany nor England, nor anywhere else, have the State Socialist school been able to formulate a systematic exposition of the faith that is in them. And yet they have had the field almost entirely to themselves for the last five-and-twenty years. As a result of this failure State Socialism in Germany at least is visibly on the wane. The Social Democrats are also allowing the principles on which their party was founded to drop quietly out of sight. At the Stuttgart Congress two of the ablest leaders of the party, Auer and von Vollmar, openly describe these principles as Utopian, and urge their followers to adopt a policy of practical reform. A short time ago utterances of this character would have led to expulsion from the party; to-day they are greeted by the Social Democratic delegates with tumultuous applause. The most important and pressing of these practical reforms is the destruction of German bureaucracy, and the determination to uphold and extend individual liberty. "Their fight," says Mr. Gaullieur, "is a bitter fight, a life and death struggle between official bureaucratic Germany with its ludicrous standards of honour and culture, its absolute tyranny and its growing corruption on one side, and the people on the other." On these and other points relating to the Continental system of government, Mr. Gaullieur is well qualified to speak. He is a Continental by birth. He was educated in French-speaking Switzerland, and at the German Universities. But he has now become a citizen of the United States. Perhaps his hatred of bureaucratic methods and the appalling injustice and corruption inseparably connected with them at times obscure his judgment. But it is difficult to resist a violent feeling of indignation at the shameless and unprincipled manner in which officialdom stifles and circumvents the simplest demands of justice. The Dreyfus affair has shown us that some Continental officials do not scruple to use forgery and perhaps assassination to uphold the prestige of their caste. This is not an isolated case. Mr. Gaullieur gives instance after instance of a similar character to show that these abominations are a recognised part of the bureaucratic machine as it is run in France and Germany. From this point of view Mr. Gaullieur's book is a work of considerable value.

In Grave's volume on the Individual and Society the reaction against Contintental "autoritairism" is exhibited in the most uncompromising fashion. Grave has had an eventful career. He began life as a shoemaker, then he became a printer; at present he is the editor of a Parisian journal called the *Revolt*. He is a man of considerable originality and power of exposition. His pictures of the actual condition of the Continental workman are very vivid and realistic. Extremes beget extremes. Grave meets the doctrine of the omnipotence of the State with the counter doctrine of the complete autonomy of the individual. This is Anarchism. It is difficult to avoid the impression that the fantastic idea of complete individual autonomy has been forced upon Grave and many of his compatriots by the abuses of bureaucracy. His dream is of a social existence in which every human being, without distinction of sex, age, or race, will be able to develop and give free play to all their capacities. He looks around upon French society and sees the individual hemmed in on every side, and forced into unnatural moulds which have been prepared for him by the State. He perceives how individual life and character are crushed, stunted, and destroyed by such a system. With characteristic French logic he demands the abolition of all external authority and the establishment of the exclusive supremacy of the individual over his own life.

A French Savant's Verdict

M. Demolins deals with the evils of the bureaucratic system on national life and character. M. Grave points out the effects of these evils on the individual; M. Demolins points out their disastrous effects on the nation. His book on Anglo-Saxon Superiority is a skilfully drawn indictment of bureaucratic methods, and its immense success in France is a proof that the public mind is ceasing to believe in social salvation through officialism. It is difficult to believe that the Anglo-Saxons possess as many virtues as M. Demolins credits them with, but it was a happy idea of his to contrast the expansion of Anglo-Saxondom all over the globe with the comparative failure of France as a world Power. He ascribes the failure of France to the communal structure of French society, and the success of England to the individualistic structure of society over here. In this country he tells us that the individual prevails over the community, private life over public life, and the useful professions over the liberal and administrative professions. On the whole, his main contentions contain a considerable amount of truth, but his generalisations are often too sweeping, and his statements on matters of fact are not always to be accepted without reserve. It is a mistake to assume that the Scotch and the Irish are Celts, and that the English are Anglo-Saxons. Professor Huxley was of opinion that there was probably as much Celtic blood in England as in Ireland. M. Demolins makes too much of racial characteristics. Climate and geographical position have had a great deal to do with making this country what it is. Nevertheless, M. Demolins' volume will be of immense service to his fellow-countrymen if it teaches them to lean less on constituted authority and more upon themselves.

DAILY GRAPHIC, *October* 15, 1898.

"ANGLO-SAXON SUPERIORITY."

The title sounds presumptuous, but it is a Frenchman who gives it. M. Edmond Demolins is a French student of social science, trained in the rigidly scientific school of the economist Le Play. Chance seems to have induced M. Demolins to study English social and industrial life, but having begun the study he was so impressed with what he saw that he set himself to try and discover the causes of the brilliant success of the Anglo-Saxon race. The results of his study were published in France about the middle of last year, and his book, *A quoi tient la Supériorité des Anglo-Saxons*, rapidly ran through a large number of editions. It is the tenth edition which has just been translated—and extremely well translated—into English.

M. Demolins deals with his investigations and comparisons under three main heads—school life, domestic life, and public life. Under the first head it will be gratifying to Englishmen to learn that this painstaking French observer has a higher opinion of English education than of the German systems, which have been so much held up for admiration in this country. The German schools, like the French, he contends, destroy individuality instead of developing it, and his whole thesis is that the strength of a nation depends on the strength of the individuals in it. On this ground also M. Demolins attaches little importance to the recent commercial and industrial progress of Germany. State aid or State enterprise, he argues, can drive a nation forward for a time at a very rapid pace, just as France advanced under the autocracy of Louis XIV. and of Napoleon I., but this rapid advance is at the cost of the mental vigour of the nation. People who are drilled and disciplined in every sphere of life, as are the Germans under the Emperor William, lose the power of initiative and have ultimately to give way before the more powerful individuals of other nations. Man for man, he says, the German merchant or settler is inferior to the Englishman, and therefore in the long run it is the Englishman, or the Anglo-Saxon, who absorbs the German—not the German the Englishman.

The superiority which M. Demolins discovers in English schools, owing to this greater freedom from State control and to the manner in which they develop individual character, he finds also in English family life. The primary blight on the French family in his eyes is the smallness of it, and that smallness he traces to the Frenchman's notion that it is his duty to provide for his children, instead of teaching them that they must provide for themselves, as an English child is taught. As a consequence, each additional child involves the necessity of the accumulation of an additional fortune for its endowment. As this is obviously a serious matter where there are many children, French parents take care to have few.

But where does this difference in the Englishman's and the Frenchman's conception of parental duty come from? Why is it that the Englishman thinks that he has done his duty when he has given his sons the best education he can afford and then chucked them on the world, while the Frenchman feels that he must watch over his son until death severs the tie between them? M. Demolins finds the answer to these questions in what may be called the differences of racial organisation.

A French Savant's Verdict

The Anglo-Saxon race is frankly individualistic or particularistic in its formation; the French race, like most of the other races of the world, is still largely communistic. A French family, like an ancient Roman family or a modern Hindoo family, is to a large extent an indivisible unit. Parents, children, and grandparents constantly live together in the same house, and the family property remains intact. The head of the household cannot, even if he would, leave his money or his land outside his family, except with regard to a small proportion of the whole. Any attempt to break up this tiny communistic group is looked upon as an act approaching to sacrilege. Hence the difficulties in the way of French emigration, difficulties so fully recognised in France that a French statesman of mature years recently, without creating a smile, declined the offer of the Governor-Generalship of Algeria on the ground that he could not leave his father.

It is not easy to see how a tendency of this character having its origin deep down in the roots of the race can be removed. But M. Demolins suggests various reforms in the French social system which it is within the power of the Legislature or of public opinion to remove. He specially attacks the over-centralisation of the Government, complaining that the bureaucratic system that results destroys individual initiative, while it encourages young Frenchmen to devote all their energies to obtaining an ill-paid post in a Government office. This portion of M. Demolins' teaching is not without importance to ourselves. Within the last few years there has been a great growth in the size of nearly all the Government departments in London, and the country is shortly to spend nearly two millions sterling in building new Government offices, to be inhabited by clerks who will probably spend a large part of each day in writing unnecessary letters and receiving and docketing others. The spirit of bureaucracy is happily altogether alien to the English mind, but in all countries it is found that bureaucracies contain within themselves a power of expansion which needs to be incessantly curbed by the watchfulness of the taxpayers.

In this notice it has only been possible to touch upon the more salient points in M. Demolins' book, but the reader will find a number of extremely interesting minor issues very brightly dealt with. Not unnaturally, with such an object in view as the title of the book discloses, M. Demolins has painted everything he saw in England the brightest pink. Probably he would have found that some of the rose colour vanished upon closer inspection. Happily our national vanity is not so great that we are likely to accept without cautious reserve all M. Demolins' praise of English institutions.

Abbotsholme

UMPIRE, *October* 16, 1898.
THE ANGLO-SAXON RULES THE WORLD.
SOME STARTLING CONCLUSIONS BY A FRENCHMAN.
THE BOOK OF THE YEAR.

The most important and significant book of the year is written by a Frenchman. In English it is entitled "Anglo-Saxon Superiority: To What it is Due." The author is Edmond Demolins.

The theme of the writer is the extraordinary expansion of the Anglo-Saxon race over the whole earth. By contrast he points out the decadence of the French, who are losing wealth and population and fail to colonise. Anglo-Saxon expansion menaces the future of the French race. The Germans are not to be counted as rivals. Almost as much as Frenchmen they are choked by militarism and Socialism.

In a few words M. Demolins thus points out the immense colonising power of the Anglo-Saxons and the comparative failure of the French:—

ANGLO-SAXONS PEOPLING THE WHOLE EARTH.

See what we have made of New Caledonia and our other possessions of Australasia, and see what they have made of Australia and New Zealand.

See what has become of Southern America under Spanish and Portuguese rule, and behold the transformation of Northern America in the hands of the Anglo-Saxon. It is like night and day.

The following simple figures may form another illustration of that undeniable superiority.

From official statistics we find that the following ships have passed through the Suez Canal in the course of one year:—

French ships	160
German ships	260
British ships	2,262

Even in Algeria, which is quite close to us, and which we have occupied for the last sixty years, there are as yet but 300,000 French people, as against 250,000 Europeans of different nationalities, who threaten to submerge us.

As for the Germans, he has this to say:—

They are town-dwellers, who more willingly emigrate as clerks than as farmers. They therefore do not establish their race upon the soil in the fashion of the Anglo-Saxon. So, whenever they find themselves in contact with him, they are absorbed by him.

Thus, while the English body of consumers—that which always and everywhere looks for English goods—is constantly increasing through the settling of fresh colonists all over the globe, and the ceaseless extension of the Anglo-Saxon world, the body of German consumers tends to diminish in number through the absence of agricultural colonisation and the rapid absorption of the German element by the more resisting and more absorbing Anglo-Saxon race.

He gives much attention to the French system of education, which is a prolific source of national decadence.

If you ask young Frenchmen just out of school to what career they are inclined, three-quarters of them will answer you they are candidates for Government offices. . . . Independent callings, as a rule, only find their recruits among young men who have been unsuccessful in entering other careers.

PERVERTED FRENCH FAMILY LIFE.

As causes of French decadence, M. Demolins includes the habits of over-saving, of restricting the size of families, of giving large dowries to daughters, and of leaving to sons fortunes sufficient to support them in idleness :—

You fire with indignation at the idea of leaving your children no hereditary fortune. Your fatherly love revolts at the thought. You are forgetting that the Anglo-Saxon father who gives no money to his children gives them in reality what is infinitely more than money; he gives them precisely what we are anxious to give, but cannot succeed in giving to ours—that devouring spirit of initiative, that capacity to take care of themselves which we would fain purchase with gold, and which all the gold we actually put by so painfully, so meanly, only smothers.

As a matter of fact, we go on saving, living as beggars, and practising systematic sterility so as to allow our children to live without working, or by working as little as possible. We fancy we are thus assuring their future. However, look around you, and see what men rise in the world, are most successful in all careers, and everywhere get the best places. Nine times out of ten such men are parvenus—self-made men —men who originally had to rough it, and who only succeeded through their dogged perseverance and personal initiative.

And now look at the others, *fils de famille*, thus named rightly because they rely more on their families than on themselves, more on their parents' fortune and prospective wives' dowry than on their own work. Well, these *fils de famille* are sinking daily to the very bottom; they are, as a rule, inferior to all in everything, in spite of having received a "first-class" education; they have lost in this country all influence, all authority; they have made a monarch an improbability. Incapable as they are of improving themselves by their work, they only succeed in maintaining themselves if their case is that of an only son or through the instrumentality of a *mariage d'argent*.

Young men brought up in the Anglo-Saxon way—that is, made strong in their bodies, accustomed to material facts, having always been treated as men, trained to rely on themselves alone and looking upon life as a battle, *the Christian view of life*—bring a superabundance of youthful strength to cope with the difficulties of existence; they enjoy these difficulties, expect them, triumph over them; fitted as they are for the strife, they improve in the midst of it as in their element.

And now judge, compare, and come to a decision. I have tried to show what are the hidden springs which move that race to threaten and invade the older and more decrepit societies. The miracle which is being accomplished by that race is that they are on the point of ousting others with but a modicum of public power their at backs. Where, then, lies their power? They can boast the strongest social power—and social force is bound to prevail over all the armies and public powers in the world.

The great power, the great rivalry, are not, as we think, on the other side of the Rhine; militarism and Socialism will spare us the trouble of getting rid of that enemy—and that before long.

The great peril, the great rivalry, are on the other side of the Channel, and on the other side of the Atlantic; they are wherever is to be found an Anglo-Saxon pioneer, an Anglo-Saxon settler or squatter. The man is not much considered, because he does not come, like the Germans, along with big battalions and perfected weapons; he is despised because he arrives with a plough and by himself. This comes from our being ignorant of what that plough is worth, and what that man is worth.

When once we know that, we shall know where the danger is, and at the same time where the remedy lies.

A CONTRAST IN FARM LIFE.

M. Demolins contrasts the dwellings of English and Scotch farmers and workmen with those of Frenchmen of corresponding classes :—

I visited a farm not far from Edinburgh, and found among the agricultural classes the same tendency to rise.

As we alighted at the R—— station we found the farmer, who had come to meet us. I assure you, you might have taken him for a banker a diplomatist, or a rich bourgeois; in one word, he looked a perfect gentleman. His jacket was of excellent cut; from head to foot he was dressed like a man who goes to a good tailor. These small details—and the following—are not useless; you will by and by appreciate their importance.

The farm is within a mile of the station, and the farmer's dwelling-house is close to the farm buildings. A well-kept avenue, with flowers on either side, leads to it. I noticed also a flower-bed opposite the door. The dwelling presents the exterior aspect of a comfortable English house. We enter. There is a carpet in the hall; the stairs, too, are carpeted, and so is the landing. We are now in the drawing-room, where we are welcomed by the mistress of the house. She does so without the least embarrassment, as a lady will do. The conversation does not flag, and embraces the most varied subjects. The lady speaks very tolerable French, which denotes a good education. Tea is brought in and very nicely served. The servant is not a heavy, awkward, country wench, dressed as a peasant girl promoted straight from the stable to the parlour; there is a certain style about her; she wears a pretty, white, well-starched apron, and on her head is the smart little cap worn by maid-servants in all respectable English households. These details point to a good middle-class way of living, for all this has evidently not been improvised on our account.

I am trying all along to analyse my impressions and compare everything I see here with the things of the same kind which I have observed elsewhere. I can thus best give each thing its relative value. Consequently, as I behold this British farmer, his home and mode of living, my mind naturally reverts to the types of farmers which I have had opportunities of observing in different parts of France.

I select the farmer of Normandy—a rich country. I have in mind a Norman farmer whom I have visited several times. He works an estate of three or four hundred acres—precisely the size of my Scotchman's estate. He is a rich man, for he gives his only son a portion of one hundred thousand francs (£4,000). He might therefore live in comfort. However, he has not the least idea, the least wish, of doing so. He dresses like our peasants, in a blue blouse, save on market days, when he goes to the town and wears clothes patched and dirty enough to please the most fastidious. In style his wife matches him, washes her own linen at a public fountain, and in costume, manner, and conversation does not differ from the maid in the farmyard. The inside of the dwelling is in harmony with the inmates. The whole of the family life is spent in a large room, whose floor is on a level with the farmyard and overlooks it. The walls, badly whitewashed, are bare.

The only furniture consists of a long straight table, in appearance like a plank placed on a couple of trestles. Masters and servants eat at this table, without a tablecloth. Round the table are a few benches in keeping with the table. There are three or four odd, badly-stuffed chairs. The kitchen range is in this room, and so is the sink. That is all. I do not give this description as a isolated one; it is, on the contrary, that of the most common French farmer type, and every one of my readers has been able to observe it a hundred times. Yet this sort of thing does not shock our feelings, because we consider this mode of life quite natural. It seems to us that a tiller of the ground cannot, and ought not to live differently, and that agriculture implies for the agriculturist lack of comfort and no lack of dirt.

It should be added that the English workman, unlike the French, saves but little; he spends about all he earns. To better his position, he counts less on his saving power than on an increase in his returns through promotion to a higher grade of his calling. He is, indeed, most keen in seizing hold of any opportunity to improve his position. To this effect he has no hesitation in expatriating himself, as is proved by the multitude of Anglo-Saxon emigrants. In the matter of providing for the future, the English do not do much besides insuring their lives, so as to leave some resources—in case of death—to the widows. This accounts for the development and wealth of insurance companies in Great Britain and America.

M. Demolins thus sums up the difference between

FRENCH AND ENGLISH HOME LIFE:

Our bourgeois live meanly, either to satisfy their taste for society and dress, or to be able to save for their children. Our workmen live miserably, in order to satisfy many useless, illusory, or sinful desires.

It is not so much that they lack money as the want of knowledge how to use it.

The most judicious use of money—all this tends to prove it—is to form for one's self first of all as pleasant and comfortable a home as is consistent with our means. Money thus spent is money safely invested.

Such a use of money does not only obviate other and much heavier expense, but develops man's dignity in the highest degree, a feeling of independence, the habit of exertion, and a progressive tendency.

When a man possesses these fundamental qualities he has resolved the social question on his own account and becomes his own master and independent of others.

THE SYSTEMS OF GOVERNMENT.

A very significant chapter is devoted to the different composition o. the French and English Parliaments. It is very clearly explained by two diagrams. In the French Chamber of Deputies an insignificant majority of the members derive their income from agriculture or industry, which together form the basis of national wealth. The law and the liberal professions furnish the vast majority of members. Thus in France the State is an inverted pyramid, precariously balanced on its apex. In England agriculture and industry furnish the vast majority of Parliamentary representatives.

In the French Chamber of Deputies there are fifty physicians. Why are they deputies? Because they have no practice. It is a result of the French system of education. France is overrun by a proletariat of idle, useless, starving, learned men.

"Why the Anglo-Saxons are more hostile to Socialism than Germans and French" is a chapter of profound interest. The author believes that Socialism is almost inevitable in Germany. The reason he gives is because the Government has been overpaternal, interfering in an arbitrary manner with the rights or the independence of the family.

There has been less of individualism, and the desire expressed of having something or somebody to take entire charge of men's lives and property. The English workman wants a higher standard of life for himself and for his brethren, and in trying to get that much shows self-reliance and increased energy. In conclusion, he says :—

While on both sides of the Rhine and of the Alps we are trying, by all possible means, to warm up a weakening patriotism; whilst we are passing reviews of our troops and celebrating military anniversaries, one adversary, whom we do not see or whom we despise because he is not, like us, armed to the teeth, is tranquilly furrowing the seas with his innumerable ships, and gradually filling the world with his innumerable colonists.

Here is one of M. Demolins' final warnings to his countrymen :—

It is written : "In the sweat of thy face shalt thou eat bread." This sentence is not only the foundation of social power, but also that of moral power. Nations which, by all sorts of convenient combinations, manage to escape that law of intense personal labour are bound to moral depression and inferiority. Thus the redskin compared with the European ; thus the Oriental compared with the same European ; thus the Latin and German races compared with the Anglo-Saxon.

MANCHESTER GUARDIAN, *October* 18, 1898.

We noticed the interesting work of M. Edmond Demolins called *A quoi tient la Supériorité des Anglo-Saxons* when it first appeared nearly eighteen months ago. Here, therefore, we need not do more than chronicle the appearance of a readable English version. . . . M. Demolins, however, should have left his new preface unwritten. As a sketch of early English history, designed to show that the Saxons absorbed Angles, Danes, and Normans in turn, it is painfully unscientific as well as inaccurate. The accounts of the struggle between Mercia and Wessex and of the later Danish invasions are utterly misleading. This sketch seems to be based on Augustin Thierry's worthless history of the Conquest, from which no serious historian would quote nowadays, as M. Demolins has done. The point is of some importance, because the author's wild theories about our racial history are the most unsatisfactory feature of his book.

LITERARY WORLD, *October* 21, 1898.

ANGLO-SAXONS EULOGISED.

It is extraordinary that this book, written by a Frenchman, setting forth the superiority of English-speaking peoples over other races, should have reached a tenth edition in France, and should have been favourably noticed by French newspapers and reviews. Its author, M. Demolins, makes a careful and intelligent comparison between Anglo-Saxons on the one hand, and Frenchmen and Germans on the other. The conclusion he arrives at is that the Anglo-Saxons of Great Britain and America are so educated and brought up as to be better equipped for the battle of life than Frenchmen and Germans. The secret of Anglo-Saxon superiority is the fact that Anglo-Saxon peoples belong not to the Communistic formation, but to the Particularistic formation. In other words, Anglo-Saxon institutions develop the individual and train him to work for himself without looking to the State or the community at large for aid. Of Anglo-Saxons as individuals, it may be said that God helps them because they help themselves. And Anglo-Saxon communities, made up of individuals, every one of whom is doing his level best to achieve prosperity for himself, are prosperous in the aggregate. France is decadent because Frenchmen as individuals are too prone to look to the State to help them. Germany is in danger of decadence because Germans as individuals are subject to too much interference by the State. Their present ruler " does not realise that the only way for a sovereign to promote individual energy is to withdraw his own personal action ; private initiative begins where State intervention ends."

M. Demolins' book is well worth reading, not merely because it is a pleasure to find a Frenchman of ability showering praises on the Anglo-Saxon race, but because it contains a lesson and conveys a warning. If M. Demolins is right in thinking that the cardinal cause of the success of the Anglo-Saxon race in fighting the battle of life, the secret of their " prodigious power of expansion," their " extraordinary aptitude to civilise," consists in the fact that they belong to the Particularistic formation, the conclusion seems to follow that Anglo-Saxons should continue to be Particularists, and that they should repel the intrusion of the Communistic and Socialistic ideas which, from time to time in recent years, have left their traces on enactments passed by the Parliament of our country. But this is a matter we must leave to be debated by those who swear by the opposing tenets of Individualism and Socialism.

BIRMINGHAM POST, *October* 25, 1898.

The title of this book is soothing to our *amour propre*, but contains no revelation for us. " Anglo-Saxon superiority ! " It has been the modest foundation of our faith for generations. We have affirmed it of ourselves of our own proper knowledge :—

> " There are no men like English men,
> Where'er the light o' day be,
> There are no hearts like English hearts
> So stout and bold as they be."

But it is not to minister to our national vanity that M. Demolins has written this book, which has attained great popularity in France, rapidly passing through ten editions. His theme is not so much Anglo-Saxon superiority as French decadence and how it may be arrested. As to our superiority we will give God thanks, and make no boast of it ; and if there be in us, in our methods and habits that from which our friends across the Channel may learn a lesson that shall conduce to the prosperity and happiness of France, there is no Englishman worthy of the name who will not welcome honest emulation in all that makes for the golden year of our hopes, the amelioration and progress of the human race. The world is wide, its resources practically infinite, there is room and scope for all without grudging or envy. The superiority of the Anglo-Saxon is assumed. "He rules America by Canada and the United States; Africa by Egypt and the Cape; Asia by India and Burma; Australasia by Australia and New Zealand; Europe and the whole world by his trade and industries and by his policy," says our author. "Although we do not all acknowledge it, we all have to bear it, and all dread it; the apprehension, the suspicion, and sometimes the hatred provoked by *l'Anglais* proclaim the fact loudly enough. We cannot go one step in the world without coming across *l'Anglais*." What, then, is the cause of this superiority? Primarily, M. Demolins attributes it to our training of our young folk. The French school system "forms chiefly good officials; it is hardly capable of producing anything else. It is especially unfitted to form men." The failure of the German school system is described as complete; it does not form men, and the scheme of the German Emperor is ridiculed as preposterous. The author contrasts it with English ideals towards the attainment of which we have made some progress, and adds: "When we think that not only the pupils of one college, but really a whole nation, are brought up under such methods, and launch out into the world armed *cap-à-pie* with such practical power, then we can understand a good many things. Then we can see who are the men who have a right to call themselves the masters of the future, and who are bound to become the masters of the world; then we can feel that our sons ought not to be brought up under German, but under Anglo-Saxon methods, unless we wish them to be ousted and crushed as completely as mere Red Indians. Figure to yourselves, indeed, one of the unfortunate young man trained in a German school, to the mere contemplation of the Prussian monarchy and of Prussian militarism—having as grounds of his education Prussian geography, Prussian history (or, rather, that of the Prussian dynasty), foreign to every practice of an independent life—figure this young man suddenly brought face to face, on any point of the globe, in competition with one of the fine fellows whose practical training we have just described. Which of the two is really prepared for that future which the new continents offer and make necessary for the men of the Old World?" In reading the chapter entitled "Does the English

School System Form Men?" *giving detailed particulars of the methods of certain selected schools, we are tempted to say, O si sic omnes!* But it is, no doubt, true that in English schools the individual has to rely principally on his own energy and resources, and thus learns life—learns to become a man; and true that this is largely the secret of whatever success we have attained. But we have generations of hard work before us ere such a picture can be accepted as that of typical English schools. What is said of the method in which we—Frenchmen and Englishmen—ought to bring up our children holds up a high standard: we dare accept no more of M. Demolins' praise than that, of the two, we have come a little nearer to it. "Young men," he says, "brought up in the Anglo-Saxon way—that is, made strong in their bodies, accustomed to material facts, having always been treated as men, trained to rely on themselves alone, and looking upon life as a battle (the Christian view of life)—bring a superabundance of youthful strength to cope with the difficulties of existence; they enjoy these difficulties, expect them, triumph over them; fitted as they are they improve in the midst of it as in their element." In dealing with the Fernchmen and the Anglo-Saxon in private life and in public life the contrast is again made rather too favourable for us, but we accept without reservation the definition of patriotism which the author evolves: "That State patriotism, founded of political ambition, is but an artificial, spurious patriotism, which leads people to ruin. Real patriotism, on the contrary, consists in energetically maintaining private independence against the developments and encroachments of the State, because such is the only way of ensuring social power and prosperity for the fatherland." Those who adopt the tone of Mr. Jeafferson Brick that "we air a great people and we must be cracked up" may purr content over M. Demolins' pages; the wiser will find much matter for thought, which will often be far from self-complacent. Anyway, it is a remarkable book.

LITERATURE, *October* 29, 1898.

For the comfort of Anglo-Saxons M. Edmond Demolins' *A quoi tient la Supériorité des Anglo-Saxons* has been translated into English, and published by the Leadenhall Press, under the title of "Anglo-Saxon Superiority: to What it is Due" (3s. 6d.). Principally to an excellent system of education is the answer given by M. Demolins to his own question; he is of the opinion that, while the French school dwarfs the intelligence of the boys, and robs them of their energy and initiative the English school is a most potent instrument in the formation of character. Other reasons given are the prevalence of officialism in France, the dislike of the landed proprietors for the country, the partition and subdivision of the land, the habit of leaning on the strong arm of the State; but it is impossible to avoid the conclusion that the real cause, the *causa causans*, is to be sought in the very different composition of the two races. The mixture of Saxon, Angle, and Scandinavian, with the slightest dash of Celt, has proved, on the whole, more successful than the formula of Celt, Frank, and Latin which constitutes the French nation.

BRADFORD OBSERVER, *November* 10, 1898.

It has often been said that the drawing of an indictment against a nation ought to be scheduled as "a dangerous occupation." The author of this book, however, proceeds with a very light heart to do something even more perilous. He pronounces judgment on whole races, and, untroubled by facts, sweeps into his generalisations all those which figure most conspicuously in modern history. Concerning these M. Demolins has a theory, or rather, to do him justice, several theories. His root-theory is that individualism is essentially Anglo-Saxon. He believes, too, that individualism is the one principle which saves and enriches society. He thus arrives at the conclusion, not a little refreshing in a Frenchman, that the Anglo-Saxon is the saviour of society, and will ultimately dominate the world. To English readers this is fairly comforting, till we reflect that in this tight little island-home of ours it is extremely difficult at this time of day to say who is who. For M. Demolins has another theory. He believes that Socialism grows out of the original depravity of the Celtic race, that it is a principle which spells ruin to societies, and that therefore the Celtic race is doomed to disappear. He finds proofs of the ascendency of the Anglo-Saxon everywhere, and complacently believes that wherever the Saxon is, there individualism, pure and undefiled, prevails. It is a pity to disturb such serene complacency, but the fact remains that, Mr. John Morley himself being witness, *there is more practical Socialism in this Anglo-Saxon England than in any other country on the face of the earth. This is awkward for M. Demolins.* Equally troublesome is the fact that in America the Irish are Republicans, and the American Republican party is the great stronghold of individualism. There are Celts who are Socialists and there are Anglo-Saxons who are individualists, always granting that you can find

A French Savant's Verdict

pure samples of the species. But the contrary can also be maintained with equal force and truth, and *the upshot of the matter is that to indulge the passion for racial theorisings of this kind is a mere ploughing of the sand.* Those who wish to see how cheerfully, and with what an "air," this exercise can be engaged in may read this book.

PALL MALL GAZETTE, *November 28*, 1898.

To thoughtful and educated Spaniards the situation of their beloved country at the close of the century must be mortifying well nigh to the bounds of endurance, even by a people among whom the deluding word "Patience!" is still supposed to be one of the keys to contentment. It is so brutally plain that the national decadence which began with Philip II. has not yet touched its lowest point. Other nations in the meantime had their ups and downs. Spain's movement has been uniformly downhill. The king, with the longest title of any European sovereign, bids fair to start the twentieth century with little really to his name except the Iberian Peninsula minus Portugal. The inflated mendacious title will no doubt still be retained, but every time the instructed foreigner hears it uttered or sees it in print he will smile, and the thoughtful Spaniard in the like case will shrug his shoulders and feel sorry for himself and his country.

Why, one wonders, cannot a people with so strong an inheritance of character and innate ability uprise and shake off the cobwebs of delusion and fatuity which cloud them? Climate explains something. The enthusiast who in England devotes his leisure moments to tennis and golf and ardent criticism of the Government would not be so energetic in Spain. One perspires less in a state of resignation or apathy than in a passion of discontent, and the main thing with individuals, after all, is to live the life that is most convenient. *But habit explains even more than climate.* The average Spaniard is *not anxious to think for himself, except about matters that are necessarily quite personal.* He is taught, like his fathers before him, that he must submit to functionaries, whether these are of the Church or the State, and his education is not of a kind to enable him to see readily the defects in his superiors, still less to devise remedies for the misdeeds that come from these defects. The lack of homogeneity in the country even now is another cause that must not be overlooked. One sees that fine word "patriotism" in the leading articles of the provincial press, but, however much it may move the writer, its effect upon the reader is dubious. Spain is a bundle of provinces, officially linked and labelled a kingdom, but it has never properly welded into a nation with sympathies and aspirations alike in the North, the South, the East, and the West. Amid this rampant mere provincialism the political wire-puller works easily for his own ends and those of his party. The scandal of one province, even though really of national importance, does not deeply interest the people of another province. Even Madrid responds to this spirit of prevailing parochialism. True, there are the Senate House and the Cortes in its midst, but the gossip of the cafés is more to it than the stately periods of Spain's statesmen in her Houses of Parliament, as reported in the journals. Add to these causes (no exhaustive list, by the way) that singular national trait which persuades Spain that she who was once so great cannot, while Providence rules, become insignificant, no matter what Spaniards do or fail to do, and one may perhaps see something of poor Spain's extraordinary weakness. *She is the ostrich among the nations; with her head in the sand she is blind to the ruin that is stealing upon her.*

BRITISH SUPERIORITY.

Without wishing to exult in the flattering deductions that all Anglo-Saxons will draw from the book, one may earnestly invite Spain to read M. Demolins' sober and enlightening volume—*A quoi tient la Supériorité des Anglo-Saxons*. We, of course, knew it all before. Dr. Smiles, in "Self-Help," made the knowledge popular; the youth who starts in life with the chilly yet bracing realisation that he has only himself to depend upon may die a millionaire and a lord, comforted on his deathbed by the reflection that he has set a useful example to others and been one more proof of the vigour and profit of the individualistic spirit. The rest of Europe, according to M. Demolins, is mainly gliding to destruction (by Anglo-Saxon absorption) in the easy and fatal barque of *la formation communautaire*. *Education in Spain is still, of course, chiefly in the hands of the clergy, who are not likely to teach their pupils, at all costs of comfort, to foster the qualities that lead to robust independence.* Moreover, Spanish parents have not the Spartan courage of English parents. They do not care so much that their sons shall become great and wealthy by striking out into the world; as in France, so here, it seems to them best that their boys be promptly provided with dowried wives who shall at once relieve them from all anxiety about the future. If to to this blessing be added a small official appointment, their joy is complete. And the worst of it is that Young Spain accepts the situation with avidity, quite indifferent to the fact that its latent energies and aptitudes are all murdered in this ready sacrifice of its nobler ambitions. Once in a safe corner Young Spain considers its education ended. *It tries to rejoice in its good blood and gentlemanly manners and in the tradition of past national greatness.* And it hopes, against private conviction, that there may still be something in special prayers from the lips of the Church and in the porterage of saintly effigies through its streets in times of grave national peril. Poor Spain! Even as, in the words of M. Jules Lemaître, the superiority of her vaudeville writers and cooks shall not save France from being trodden underfoot in the irresistible march of Anglo-Saxon power, so Spain will not be protected by her courteous manners, her blue blood, and her comfortable traditions.

EDUCATION AND GOOD GOVERNMENT.

It is always a thankless task to advise others unasked, and the doctor who intrudes upon a man who is no patient of his (and, moreover, believes himself in perfect health) and tells the man that he is in a dying state, must not be surprised if he is kicked downstairs. *We will, however, take all risks, and remind Spain that with education and good government she still has an excellent chance of reformation.* Europe, as a whole, would be delighted to see a stable and prosperous people in its south-western extremity. Even Anglo-Saxons have not at present any desire to add the peninsula to their long list of possessions, and, though they may doubt us in Madrid, our sympathies are with Spain in her trouble to a degree that might almost be termed unreasonable, *viewed by that cold light of practicality which is supposed to be the chief illuminant of the Anglo-Saxon mind.*

Education and good government! Put thus in four words, it seems so simple a programme. But we all know that in Spain, at any rate, it is not a simple prescription. The clergy will resent the imputation that their educational methods are not only obsolete but pernicious, and those who are in office will be properly indignant at the charge that they are not doing the best possible for Spain's administration and development. To be sure, there are the journalists; and all praise to those few of them who are endeavouring to create an honourable and effective public opinion in a country which has not yet learned that the Press ought to be the mouthpiece rather than the inspirer of the public. The Cortes seems hopeless. In no country is the parliamentary rhetoric of a higher order, and in no country perhaps, except Portugal, are the people more dishonestly represented by their representatives. These worthies understand something of the virtue of the magic phrase "Self-Help!" But they go farther even than Dr. Smiles would approve in their application of it. They help themselves to all the good things that are in their reach, and devote themselves to the consolidation of their own interests with supreme contempt for the people and supreme neglect of conscience.

Who then shall interfere in this household of Spain when its mother the Church and its father the Government (no matter what this calls itself) are not yet persuaded that they do not know how to manage their own children? It is a baffling question. The Pope might do much, to be sure. But his Holiness is in the position of a bachelor uncle of extremely old-fashioned views. With the best intentions he might only increase the disorder and infelicity of the household. It has to be remembered, moreover, that for centuries Spain has respected advice from Rome, more by word than by action showing conformity to it.

The time may yet come when Europe will have to shock Spanish pride by sending a commission of experienced "matrons" into its household. Even as things are, intelligent Spaniards do not mind openly wishing that English experts could be put at the head of Spain's financial affairs. What we have done for Egypt, they say, we could surely do for Spain.

NOTTINGHAM GUARDIAN, *November* 28, 1898.

A FRENCH VIEW OF ENGLISH SUPREMACY.

M. Demolins, the author of "Anglo-Saxon Superiority," has himself prepared for the English public a translation of this work, which, published last year, created a sensation and made him famous. It might have been thought, as one of his French critics remarks, that "the definite affirmation of Anglo-Saxon superiority contained in the very title might rouse the wrath of Chauvinists." But it was exceedingly well received. M. Jules Lemaître, in *Le Figaro*, devoted repeated articles to emphasising the lessons which M. Demolins strove to teach his fellow-countrymen ; and nearly every French journal of importance gave it attention. Fortunate, perhaps, was M. Demolins in bringing out his book just when he did. A year ago Marchand's mission to Fashoda was not dreamt of by one man in a million. The delay of a year would have found the French public, probably even the best of the Parisian journals, in no mood for calmly appraising the merits of a work which sang the virtues of the Anglo-Saxon race, and whose author bade his countrymen look to the character of Englishmen and the social system of England as models for imitation. M. Demolins is right in supposing that such a book would be welcomed on this side the Channel. *We like to see ourselves as others see us, even when the view is not in all respects a flattering one.* Still more agreeable is it to be presented with a portrait of the national character by the hand of one *who recognises our good points, and who can tell us not only that they are admirable, but why they are.* M. Demolins, however, is not indiscriminate in his praise. In a preface specially addressed to his English audience, he begs that he may not be misunderstood. His admiration for Englishmen and English institutions does not embrace everybody and everything. " By the application of the methods of social analysis devised by F. Le Play, and completed by H. de Tourville, I seek (he says) to carefully isolate and exclusively consider the phenomena which appear to be derived from *Anglo-Saxon influence, because these phenomena alone ensure for England and the United States their social originality and superiority.* Above all, I endeavour to make a clear distinction between these phenomena and the customs and institutions peculiar to the Celts and Normans." His theory as to the root difference between the Anglo-Saxon element on the one hand and the Celtic and Norman elements on the other, rests upon the individualism of the one as contrasted with the Socialism of the other. To use his own terms—which are employed with a special meaning of their own—the Celts and the Normans belong to the "Communistic formation," the Anglo-Saxons to the "Particularistic formation"—thus named "because instead of causing the community to predominate over the individual, the individual is made to prevail over the community, private life over public life, and in consequence the useful professions over the liberal and administrative professions." The Celtic race belongs to the communistic clan formation. It has more taste for public than private life, and prefers politics to agriculture, commerce, and industry. The Norman race, M. Demolins thinks, has left profound traces in the English system. These are seen in enormous domains, in the law of primogeniture, in hereditary nobility, and the House of Lords ; also in *the organisation of the English universities, and in* " *the spirit of snobbery.*" The " Celtic element weakens especially the lower classes, by dragging them into labouring pauperism ; the *Norman element weakens especially the upper classes by promoting lordolatry, patronage, and snobbery.*" It is among these two elements, Celtic and Norman, that Socialistic doctrines have found any echo in the Anglo-Saxon world, as in Australia and New Zealand, where Scotch and Irish abound among politicians " *The whole history of England,*" says M. Demolins, " *is affected and explained by the slow but constant evolution of the Saxon through the dense*

34

Celtic and Norman shell"; and he proceeds to sketch out the principal scenes in the "great stirring drama." In his preface to the French edition the author emphasises the Anglo-Saxon superiority over the Latin races in epigrammatic and striking phrases. " See," he exclaims, " what we have made of New Caledonia and our other possessions of Austral Asia, and see what they have made of Australia and New Zealand. See what has become of Southern America under Spanish and Portuguese rule, and behold the transformation of Northern America in the hands of the Anglo-Saxon. It is like night and day." And he points out, as another illustration, that while France and Germany between them sent in one year 420 ships through the Suez Canal, no less than 2,262 British ships passed in the same period. It is no use, he says, to shake fists at the English, " like angry old women." The question is to find out the secret of their prodigious power of expansion, of their extraordinary aptitude to civilise—" for our sons and ourselves," he adds, it is a " question of life or death."

In order to discover the secret M. Demolins submits the typical Englishman and Frenchman to a comparative analysis in the school, in the home, in private life, and in public affairs. He finds, in short, that the whole system of French education and social life tends to unfit his countrymen for and to divorce them from the active enterprises of trade, agriculture, and commerce ; and hence, for example, their failure as colonists. School life in France is not only inferior to the English mode in its effects on physique ; but, owing to the universal desire to obtain official employment, either in the army or in the civil service—which means passing examinations of encyclopædic scope—the practice of " cramming" is more general and carried further than here. The French system is eminently suited to produce functionaries ; the English system produces men. To adopt a few sentences from M. Lemaître's article, the author proves that the birth-rate is reduced and kept down by the necessity of providing for the establishment of each son, and portioning each daughter. He shows how systematic sterility places temporarily on the market a great deal of money which is withdrawn from commerce and industry to be transformed into Stock Exchange property. *He shows that the Anglo-Saxons educate their young men for the struggle of existence, cultivate in them a taste for work, and that they are consequently free from apprehension on the score of long families ;* added to which the English nome life—liberal and comfortable even among the country people and workmen—promotes individual dignity and moral worth. He shows how the propensity for officialism and the estrangement from agriculture, industry, and commerce, fills the Chamber of Deputies mainly with ex-officials, journalists, and professional men, whereas in the English House of Commons there is a large majority of representatives of agriculture and trade. He shows, finally, that the English are fortunate in being almost wholly inimical to Socialism, which (remarks M. Lemaître) "is the very oldest of exploded doctrines, and the most disastrous for individual activity and dignity." What are the remedies which M. Demolins recommends to his fellow-countrymen? It is useless, he contends, to seek social regeneration through moral action, pure and simple. The young men of France must be educated and trained so as to develop in them more strongly the quality of individual initiative, taught to rely less on the provision made for them by parents, and on the prospects of official careers, and more on their own energy and enterprise. They must be able to "take life more earnestly." This is a long order. But M. Demolins thinks he detects a movement along the path, and he finds several symptoms of it. First, the increasing contact and competition with the Anglo-Saxon race (which, he points out in an earlier chapter, have done so much for the French Canadian). Second, the recognised failure of the French system of education. Third, the development of physical exercises in youth, one manifestation of which is seen in the adoption of sporting words of English origin, and the popularity of sporting papers—though, possibly, many Englishmen may not feel disposed to felicitate their neighbours upon these things. Other symptoms are the overcrowding of the administrative and liberal professions, producing, in its turn, a tendency to return to rural life, and the independent professions, the encouragement of colonisation, the growing discredit of politics and politicians, and the reaction against militarism as the great obstacle to social reform. We who have just gone through the excitement of the Dreyfus "affaire" and the Fashoda scare may be disposed to doubt the accuracy of M. Demolins' judgment in reference to the popularity of the army in France. But he rests upon bedrock facts, which will remain facts when the excitement has subsided. One of these facts is that even ardent "militarists" themselves try to prevent their own sons from spending the full term in barracks, knowing well that a young man's career is broken, or at least made difficult, by a prolonged sojourn there. Since the passing of the last military law the schools which save for their pupils two years out of the three are besieged with candidates—the crush at the door is fearful. "Surely," says M. Demolins, "there could not be a more eloquent nor a more spontaneous protest." In the upper classes all fathers and mothers scheme for this end—*how their boys may escape military service;* the lower classes submit to it reluctantly, and with not unfounded jealousy at their more fortunate betters. "An institution thus deserted by its most eloquent defenders is in a very bad way indeed. Can this militarism *à outrance* last even as long as ourselves? I do not think so. The financial situation and public interest will settle the matter, if common sense does not. Militarism is not necessary to enable a great country to play her *rôle* in the world. Great Britain demonstrates the fact by its example." M. Demolins also recognises in the activity of Socialism another favourable symptom, but we have not space to follow the rather involved train of reasoning by which he explains how this is to be regarded as merely the flashing up of an expiring flame. Concluding his remarkable work, the author presses home the moral that nations and individuals must submit to the decree—"In the sweat of thy face shalt thou eat bread." And in this only will they find salvation, socially and morally. "Nations which, by all sorts of convenient combinations, manage to escape that law of intense personal labour are bound to moral depression, and inferiority." The details of the author's argument, based on his own observations of education and social life in England and Scotland, are extremely interesting. But in his anxiety to make out a strong contrast he creates an impression that is hardly to be justified ; *for he takes a model school, intended to train young men for colonial life, and holds it up as a type of the English system.* No doubt such a school does illustrate in a very marked degree the directions in which the English system of education differs from the French. Still, the impression likely to be produced upon the mind of the French reader, that it is an average sample, is scarcely fair to him. Similarly, the neat and well-furnished cottage of a Scotch workman is hardly a fair specimen of the home of the average British labourer. Nor is it in many parts of Great Britain that farm-hands are paid 95s. a month in addition to cottage rent free. Other examples of the tendency to exaggerate the case in support of his theory might be mentioned ; but even when this is said, M. Demolins' work is one that will repay study. It throws a great deal of light upon the peculiarities of the French character and social system, and helps us to understand some things that are puzzling and mysterious without such a key.

A French Savant's Verdict

UNIVERSITY CORRESPONDENT, *December* 17, 1898.
THE SUPERIORITY OF THE ANGLO-SAXON.

Last year M. Edmond Demolins, one of the leaders of the Social Science movement in France, published a book under the title of "A quoi tient la Supériorité des Anglo-Saxons?" which created a great sensation in Paris. Five editions were exhausted within two months—others followed in quick succession—and the work was, two or three months since, issued in English form by the Leadenhall Press. In the preface which the author has written for the English edition he expresses the hope that the English public will not misunderstand the meaning and import of his book, nor take his opinions as applying to all the inhabitants and institutions of Great Britain. His object has been to carefully isolate and exclusively consider the phenomena which appear to be derived from Anglo-Saxon influence, because to these alone he believes that England and the United States owe their social originality and superiority.

In the preface to the French edition—not written for Englishmen—the author opens with an admission of Anglo-Saxon superiority. . . .

Book I. of the work proper is headed "The Frenchman and the Anglo-Saxon at School," for we read in the opening lines "Every nation organises Education in its own image, in view of its customs and habits; Education in its turn reacting on the social state." To find the key to this sentence (and the whole work) we must turn back to p. xiii. of the Preface to the English edition. "The Anglo-Saxon state," we read here, "belongs no longer to the communistic but to the particularistic formation, thus named because instead of causing the community to prevail over the individual, the individual is made to prevail over the community, private life over public life, and in consequence the useful professions over the liberal and administrative professions." So in the first chapter "Does the French school system form Men?" M. Demolins remarks that the aim of seventy-five out of every hundred young Frenchmen just leaving school is to get into Government offices—of which France has so many. For this every nerve is strained, in school, and out of school. *The Government service and the liberal professions stand first and second,*—commerce, agriculture, and industry nowhere in middle-class estimation. The first evil result of this system comes out in school. Examinations are the gate to government employment, hence *le chauffage* (otherwise "cram") and overwork. Unquestioning obedience, complete abdication of his own will, characterise the perfect official—he is essentially an instrument in the hands of some other man—hence the barrack discipline of the *grand internat* (the big boarding-school), the embryo official's training-ground. "Such bringing-up," we quote M. Demolins, "suppresses in young men the habit of free and spontaneous action and originality."

"Does the German School System form men?" is the next question. It does not, is the conclusion, fortified by the not-yet-forgotten diatribes of the Emperor himself against the shortcomings of the Prussian system and his suggested heroic remedies. Does the English School System form men? Well, it is patent (to foreigners) that the young Englishman is generally full of initiative, of self-reliance, of ability to make his own way. Let us examine the English educational system, says M. Demolins, to see if there is anything in it to account for this. *We are inclined to think that this is the weakest part of the whole work. The author has taken one of the "new" schools for examination—one where gardening and building, and singing, and land surveying, and farming enter into the curriculum—he approves of it highly, but if he has made his compatriots think it a typical English School he has led them into a great error.* The final chapter of this first book is, however, very good. *M. Demolins has got at the leading principles underlying the best English education, and expounds them enthusiastically for the foreigner's behoof.*

Book II. carries on the comparison into the private life of the Frenchman and the Anglo-Saxon, to show that the results of differences in education are reflected here. . . . The two chapters dealing with these points are packed with interest. *Among the English on the other hand his education prepares the young man for the struggle for existence; and his home-life contributes greatly to his success.*

The differences between the French and Anglo-Saxon types persist into the public life of the nations. To expound them is the motive of M. Demolins' Third Book—in which he also points out what the French ought to do to hold their own against the threatening expansion of the other race. . . . *The second chapter demonstrates how and why the Anglo-Saxons are of all people most hostile to Socialism; the third and fourth draw equally favourable comparisons with respect to Anglo-Saxon notions of solidarity and patriotism;* the fifth enquires "What Social state is most conducive to Happiness?" and decides "*not* the French." The final chapter discusses in more hopeful strain various symptoms of social regeneration the author discovered (last year) in French society. Altogether the book is a truly remarkable one, and well deserves careful reading by all thoughtful Englishmen, who at the same time cannot fail to find many defects in it.

A French Savant's Verdict

UNIVERSITY CORRESPONDENT, *January* 7, 1899.

A correspondent regrets that in reviewing M. Demolins' book on Anglo-Saxon superiority we omitted to notice the interesting question raised in the preface to the second French edition. Pointing out that for fifteen years French commerce has been gradually receding before the advance of German commerce, the author discusses the question whether Anglo-Saxon trade is similarly threatened. He admits that German industry has recently been at some advantage as compared with Anglo-Saxon so far as the cheaper and commoner articles are concerned, but after a learned discussion *arrives at the conclusion that this advantage has been due to temporary causes.*

GUARDIAN, *March* 22, 1899.

M. Demolins' essay on the causes of Anglo-Saxon superiority excited considerable interest in France on its first appearance. It called attention to certain undeniable faults in French education and society, and held up as an example of better things a people of whom Frenchmen are not very fond. Nevertheless, it was, on the whole, well received. *It is not a very profound or exhaustive production.* The introductory historical sketch is full of crudities. The sharply drawn distinction between the Anglo-Saxon, the Norman, and the Celtic types of character in the British Isles *implies a far more absolute separation of race from race than can be proved from history or is probable from the nature of things.* The author has framed an abstract Anglo-Saxon out of certain prominent characteristics of Englishmen—the attachment to home, the passion for private enterprise, the love of country life, and so forth. It will surprise most Englishmen to hear that they care little for politics, which they abandon to the Celt, or that they are patriotic simply because national power ensures the absolute freedom of the home. M. Demolins is not always accurate even as regards the facts of the day. For example, it is not true that English parents of the better class generally take care to have their sons instructed in some manual trade. Nor is he always circumspect in his deductions from admitted fact. When he infers from the smallness of the English army the absence of militarism in English society, he forgets that it is only our happy insular situation which enables us to do with so few troops. When he concludes that his countrymen lack enterprise because they put their savings into Stock Exchange securities, whilst the Americans put their savings each into his own undertaking, he forgets the inevitable difference between a country of limited extent and old civilisation and a new country of enormous size and half-untouched resources. In a word, *the French love of clearness, simplicity, rounded argument, and precise conclusions occasionally leads M. Demolins to neglect the complexity of social phenomena and their causes.*

We hasten to add that there is much liberality and common sense in M. Demolins' essay. Starting from the fact that the Anglo-Saxon race has actually occupied many of the finest regions outside Europe, and has acquired a sort of economic sovereignty in many more, whilst the domain of the Latin nations, and especially of France, shows no similar expansion, he asks what the causes of Anglo-Saxon superiority are. *He finds them in a better education, a better home life, and a healthier political condition.* In regard to education, *he emphasises the merits of the English system*, the care taken to make schools comfortable and school life pleasant, the attention given to physical culture, the endeavour to develop a manly and independent character. In French schools, he says, the confined and unwholesome mode of life, the half-monastic, half-military discipline, and the excessive demands upon the mental powers tend to produce youths without originality, without the spirit of enterprise, without the knowledge of their kind, or the capacity of helping themselves. *He is mistaken, by the way, in thinking that the "crammer" is a peculiarly French institution.* With regard to domestic life, M. Demolins dwells upon the high standard of comfort prevailing even among the lower classes of English society, and its good effects in promoting the vigour and self-respect of the people. He thinks, and doubtless is right in thinking, that thrift may be pushed too far ; that life may be impoverished and energy cramped by incessant parsimony ; and that saving a fortune for a child is not the highest duty of the parent. M. Demolins considers the French parent's ambition to leave his son independent as the prime cause of the restriction in the size of families. In this restriction he sees the root of many evils. An only child loses the excellent discipline which is afforded by the intercourse of brothers and sisters in a large family. He counts on having a comfortable provision made for him without exertion on his own part. He never really reaches his emancipation. And after all what most fathers can bequeath to an only son, now that the rate of interest has fallen so low, is just that pittance which dwarfs the mind whilst it supports the body.

Turning to the comparison of public life in the Anglo-Saxon, and in the Latin world respectively, M. Demolins notes that the composition of Parliament in England is altogether different from the composition of Parliament in France. In England agriculture, manufacture, and commerce are fully, though not exclusively, represented in the Houses. In France professional men far from eminent in their professions, journalists, and officials form the great bulk of the members. *Here we may observe that M. Demolins contradicts his own theory about Anglo-Saxon indifference to politics and absorption in private industry.* He also forgets that the difference is not one of race. In no English-speaking community save the United Kingdom can it be said that the Parliament adequately represents the wealth, the enterprise, or the practical ability of the people. The peculiarity which M. Demolins notes in our Parliament is the result of aristocratic traditions which induce the public to choose their representatives by preference from those classes which formerly governed the country. It is above all the result of the fact that members are not paid for their services. The other counts of M. Demolins' indictment against French politics—the needless multiplication of officials, the enormity of taxation, and the excesses of State interference—are too familiar to need commentary. But we may remark that *he over-rates the exemption of the Anglo-Saxon communities from Socialist influences. Although the English dislike for abstractions prevents all but a small minority of Englishmen from calling themselves Socialists, Socialist measures are popular and are patronised even by Conservatives. The United Kingdom is moving in the same direction as the Latin countries. Officials are multiplying, taxes are increasing, and legislation is always encroaching upon individual initiative.*

M. Demolins is too apt to mistake for inherent differences of race differences due chiefly to historical circumstances. At the same time, *he is too sanguine in his expectations of what can be done by changes in education and in social life. Mature nations, like mature men, do not easily change their characteristic qualities.* Besides, circumstances are usually too strong to leave a nation much choice as to what it will do. *The Anglo-Saxon did not go abroad until Columbus and Da Gama had opened out new worlds.* The Frenchman, if he now resolved to go abroad, would not find vacant a single land where Europeans can live without degenerating. The scarcity of coal and iron condemns France to a secondary place in industrial enterprise and mechanical ingenuity. *It might be questioned how far the Anglicising of mankind is desirable,* and *how far the " struggle for life " is the ideal state.* Although the English race has spread over half the globe, *the glory of the English name rests principally on the achievements of men who lived and died within these little islands, most of them before the present phase of Anglo-Saxon civilisation had begun.* But M. Demolins will have done unquestionable good if he can induce some of his countrymen to understand and to appropriate what is really excellent in English ways, or even if he can convince them that our practical success is not simply the result of a pre-eminence in bad faith, covetousness, and cruelty, and every species of moral depravity.

UNIVERSITY CORRESPONDENT, *September* 23, 1899.

M. Demolins is about to start a school at Vernueil, but as it is apparently intended to break with all existing French institutions it can only have a limited success.

A late Harrow master, M. Duhamel, is going to work on sounder lines. In the school he is about to open he does not propose to cut himself adrift from the University, but to graft English methods on to the existing system; and lastly, that liberal-minded ecclesiastic, Père Didon, who has already achieved such remarkable results at his schools of Arcueil and Lacordaire, is proposing to found yet another in which the English methods of teaching self-reliance and self-government are to be still further developed. It is with these men that the future of French education lies. The others, with all their making and re-making of "programmes," may render the brains of the race a little sharper or cleverer; they will never affect its heart and will.

AMERICAN.

No.	Name of Paper.	Place.	Date.
1.	Bulletin.	Pittsburgh.	July 10, 1897.
2.	Amer. Review of Reviews.		August, 1897.
3.	Commercial Advertiser.		September 10, 1898.
4.	The Journal.	New York.	October 2, 1898.
5.	New York Evening Post.	New York.	October 15, 1898.
6.	Times Herald.	Chicago.	January 22, 1899.
7.	Chicago Record.	Chicago.	January 28, 1899.
8.	Daily Interocean.	Chicago.	January 30, 1899.
9.	Indianapolis News.	Indianapolis.	February 1, 1899.
10.	Home Journal.	New York.	February 1, 1899.
11.	Argonaut.	San Francisco.	June 26, 1899.

New York Evening Post, *October* 15, 1898.
ANGLO-SAXON SUPERIORITY.

Few books have so quickly got the public ear as did this of M. Demolins. Appearing in April of last year, it ran through five editions in two months, and as many more have since been called for. One would suppose the audacity of the title would have provoked a storm of angry denunciation from the mercurial writers for the French press ; but it did nothing of the kind. With singular unanimity they recognised the book as the faithful chastisement of a friend, and did full justice to the grave and severe patriotism of the author. Indeed, this reception of a work truly merciless in its plain speaking is one of the most hopeful signs of progress, in true comprehension of herself and of the conditions of national health and solid recuperation, which France has given. The people cannot be wholly unsound at heart which can listen to such a lesson with quiet and attentive teachableness. Jules Lemaître spoke for them all when he called it " an infinitely painful book," but added, " We must swallow the bitter cup to the dregs."

M. Demolins treats his subject like a physician making a calm and scientific diagnosis of his patient's case, and prescribes his remedies and the regimen to be followed with so masterful a tone that the sick man is disposed to put himself unreservedly into the hands of his doctor. As a professional economist, the author makes very evident his scientific zeal in investigation, and his earnestness in wishing to understand his country's problem and find a cure for her ills. His theme is the maintenance of national eminence in the world, especially in the enlargement of national influence, the preservation of the vigour of the stock, the growth of its colonial offshoots, the filling of the world with its swarming numbers, and the growing dominance of its ideas, its traits, and its language. He has to account for the confessed fact that France and the Latin races have dropped behind in this race, while England and America have increased the pace and are foremost in the struggle.

M. Demolins' method is to analyse the life and habits of the contrasted races at school, in private life, and in public activity. This is the largest triple division of his work. Under the first he inquires which system best forms Men. Under the second, he compares the birth-rate, the family thrift, and the preparation of children for the struggle for existence. Lastly, he deals with the political trend of the races, and their relative dependence on the State or upon individual initiative for securing private happiness and the common weal.

The comparison between English and French schools will not be satisfactory to Englishmen and Americans. When the author speaks of the faults of French methods of education, we listen to an expert whose statements are authoritative ; but *when he contrasts these with the assumed excellences of English schools, we have to disclaim, in great measure, the superiority which he concedes to the latter. The example which he chooses as an illustration is not of a prevalent type, but a quite recent, and in some respects a new, experiment. Neither England nor America is free from " cramming," from superficial glibness of recitation, from the hot race for marks and honours, or from the tricks which give success in examinations to shallow work.* We find comfort in believing that we are making progress, but it would not be honest to accept the praise which M. Demolins bestows. *Then it is hardly a generation since parliamentary commissions started the reform of the English universities, and began their emancipation from the narrow and stereotyped classicism which had lasted for centuries. It will not do to find the secret of English power and American progress in the local methods of school education for youth, because the world-encircling system of English colonies and the American transformation of a continent long preceded the current ideas of broad and practical education, and were astonishing the world when, as yet, there was little that was characteristic in our schools, and we were, in fact, looking to France and Germany for our models.*

In dealing with family life and the home education and habits of the French, *our author comes closer to the causes of national characteristics, though it may still be a question whether the education produces the characteristics, or is itself the natural expression of hereditary traits long since evolved in the history of the nation.* M. Demolins is, however, conclusive authority for the fact that French youth are lacking in independence, in self-reliance, in enterprise. They are habituated to look to their parents for a settlement in life ; for the selection of a career ; for the choice of a husband or wife ; for the portion or dower which shall insure a livelihood. They look implicitly to their parents thus to place them, and accept the place as the decree of Providence. For one of the French bourgeoisie to break out of these trammels would seem to require almost as great a wrench as for the heir of an English landed estate to tear up the family settlement, break the entail, and work for his own living till the death of his father shall make him owner in fee. A habit of thought and action may become so nearly universal among a people that the violation of the artificial code may seem worse than breaking all the commandments of the decalogue. We might think that the result of this in France would be that the poor, who have nothing, would profit by their poverty to gain the vigour and initiative which their betters have lost ; but it would seem that the poor ape the rich, and that the father of a brood of sans-culottes has the same dominion as the head of a great family.

There are occasional examples which show what might come of the rude training of necessity. Audubon naïvely tells how his father, one of twenty sons of the poor fisherman his grandfather, was put to the door of the hut at the age of twelve, clad in a tow shirt and trousers, and bade in heaven's name to find a way to get his own bread. In that case the heroic treatment succeeded, and the outcast made his way through fishing-boats and smacks to the quarter-deck of a man-of-war, and reached both rank and wealth. If there had been more Frenchmen of that breed, Demolins would not have to lament the lack of self-reliance or the dwindling of the birth-rate. But the exception seems to prove the rule, and we have to accept the author's conclusion that dependence on parents has produced timidity in the struggle for life, has been followed by penny-wise thrift which is content with petty employments and small official places that are permanent, has led to a fear of family burdens and to the birth of few children or none, until the native population of France is sensibly diminishing, and an immigration of Swiss and Italians is filling the vacuum and changing the elements of the nation.

Turning to the phenomena of public life, the working of the same causes is seen. *A paternal government has long treated the people as children, ruling their local life in even the smallest matters, discouraging all initiative, whether in the repair of a bridge or the tiling of a schoolhouse roof, and referring nearly everything to the decision of the central authority.* There has thus grown up what M. Demolins calls the communistic form of society, marked by personal dependency and weakness of character, as distinguished from the particularistic form, in which there is self-reliance and private initiative. The author answers the question of his title-page by saying that France is a nation having the first of these forms of society, with all the weakness and danger of decadence that come from it, while the English-speaking peoples are striking examples of the second, with all the enterprise, energy, and growth which belong to it.

Socialism he finds to be the logical outcome of dependence upon central authority, the abdication of personal initiative becoming more and more complete till the State absorbs all direction and responsibility for the conduct of life, and, of course, absorbs also the capital and property from which the livelihood is to be produced. He sagaciously shows how natural it is that Socialism should be antipathetic to self-reliance, and that the slight hold it has taken in Anglo-Saxon communities is strictly harmonious with the prediction to be drawn from the scientific analysis of the forms of society and their tendencies.

He argues, too, that Socialism must be self-destructive ; for *as the great examples in the world's history show that individual self-reliance and personal initiative give success in the inexorable struggle for existence*, the lack of them brings decadence of the whole community, destruction of the capital which was to support the industries of the people, and the sure and hopeless impoverishment of the individual along with the State. With general poverty must come decay of art, of science, of intelligence.

The remedy is the resolute change of habits of thought and activity. God helps those who help themselves. The next generation must be taught to stand on their own legs, not to expect to be carried by their parents or their community, large or small. They must be ready to strive and sweat in the race under the open sun, and not to saunter through Arcadia leaning on each other and wreathed with flowers. The laurels must come after the struggle. They must fully accept the creed that the nation is only the organisation of the individuals, and that it can be strong, energetic, self-reliant, and prosperous only as the individual shows the same characters and does his part towards impressing them on the whole.

The lesson M. Demolins reads his countrymen is not for Frenchmen alone. Every candid Englishman and American needs to take it to heart and note how he can profit by it, putting on the cap that will fit many of us quite as well as our neighbours.

Times Herald (Chicago), *January 22*, 1899.

Not often is an author given either the opportunity or the ability to write a book that will produce a social cataclysm. Yet M. Demolins seems to have done something of the sort in France. His work, entitled "Anglo-Saxon Superiority : to What it is Due," is the talk of the day in that country. It has been translated into English, and is published in this country by R. F. Fenno & Co., New York. Needless to say that it is also attracting its share of attention on this side of the water. The title alone is sufficient to secure this end. The author is a Frenchman, and the title is a confession. The fact that one Frenchman exists ready and willing to admit the inferiority of his race to anybody or anything is a sufficient advertisement. One expects to be treated to a fine repast of humour or irony, such a treatise as Max O'Rell would have given us under this title. But not so. M. Demolins is a patriot, and he has the welfare of his native land very much at heart. He believes that the Anglo-Saxon is a superior type, and he wishes to bring his fellow-countrymen to his own humble way of thinking, that they may profit thereby. *It is not our purpose to express any opinion as to the validity of M. Demolins' argument. His claim is certainly very flattering to all Anglo-Saxons, and is more appropriately made by a foreigner.* Suffice to say that the book, coming on the heels of the Dreyfus case, which had set many Frenchmen to thinking, has given rise to a perfect furore of self-examination in the land of the excitable Gaul. The French press unanimously admit the ability of the author, and several leading writers have gone so far as to agree with his conclusions.

What, in short, does M. Demolins say? That the Anglo-Saxons are "particularistic" in their form of government, the French "communistic"; that is to say, the former develop individual reliance, the latter lean upon each other. This is exemplified even in the school. The Englishman or American trains his sons for useful careers, the Frenchman for positions under the Government. Agriculture and the productive callings are greatly neglected in France, as every parent wishes his son to become a "fonctionaire," a lawyer, a doctor, or a journalist. The Anglo-Saxon idea of home promotes individual and personal worth. Again, the French dowry system occasions such a drain on parents that children are avoided. Hence the low birth-rate and the preponderating death-rate. The room thus made in the country is filled in by the overflow of other races—a menace, in time, to the very existence of the French people. Again, Socialism, which has its headquarters in Germany, is rife in France, but does not flourish among Anglo-Saxons.

No wonder that this bold book has stirred up a tempest among the countrymen of M. Demolins. Before opening it at all we feel that the author must have studied deeply, and prepared his facts and arguments with care before daring to launch such a thunderbolt. He would be a rash man else. Careful perusal convinces the reader that the author has studied the Anglo-Saxon history and institutions with more breadth of comprehension and less of prejudice than is ordinarily possible to the Latin mind. An introduction to the English edition consists of a succinct history of Anglo-Saxon predominance and growth from the fifth century to the present time. A map, of which the parts occupied by the Anglo-Saxons are marked by shading, is a striking feature. One who is familiar with the facts cannot avoid being impressed on first looking at this map. We observe that the Philippine Islands, Cuba, and Porto Rico are still left white—a striking testimony to the timeliness of the author's note of warning. The print has scarce had time to dry upon his pages before these terrible Anglo-Saxons seize other large portions of the globe. The seriousness of his purpose is revealed in the closing sentences of the preface to the French edition :—

"The question, indeed, is to find out the secret of that prodigious power of expansion, of that extraordinary aptitude to civilise—and the means of doing it.

"Such an investigation is the object of this series of studies—for our sons and for ourselves, a question of life and death."

He takes up the school systems in detail and separately of France, England and Germany, asking of each, "Does it form men ? "

"Ask a hundred young Frenchmen just out of school to what careers they are inclined ; three-quarters of them will answer you that they are candidates for Government offices. Independent callings, as a rule, only find their recruits among young men who have been unsuccessful in entering those careers. Of course the State cannot accept all these candidates for public functions ; a certain number only must be picked and a selection organised. Examination is the great entrance door to these careers. To be successful at the examination is therefore the young Frenchman's chief pre-occupation, since all his future hangs on this success. Now, the surest way of preparing successfully for examinations is *le chauffage*—cramming—since we must call it by its name. What is *chauffage ?* It consists in imparting, in as little time as possible, a superficial but temporarily sufficient knowledge of the programme of an examination."

This sort of thing, the author claims, does not conduce to the formation and preparation of useful and self-reliant citizens. Those who fall are not fitted for any independent career. *The cramming process, moreover, tends toward general superficiality and an inability to go to the bottom of things.* These remarks are interesting to Americans, for, despite the fact that the author sees so much that is worthy imitation in our educational system, *we know very well what cramming is in this country. But he has studied educational processes in England more carefully than those of this country.*

Does the German school system form men ? The French attributed their defeat by Germany partially to the difference in school systems. Imitation became the order of the day.

"As we borrowed their military institutions, so we borrowed their scholastic methods, their pedagogy, their philology—that famous German philology, so subtle, so keen. Let the brats of the second form have good Latin texts, and you'll see how the country will rise again, the doctors of the university would say. And admiring France would repeat those magic words. How is it that what yesterday was an incontestable truth has become to-day a mistake? For no one doubts that it is a mistake; every one is agreed to that on both sides of the Rhine."

It is the German Emperor himself who has protested against the present system of education. Briefly, the Emperor's idea is to educate young men with reference to their usefulness to the State, and not with reference to their taking an independent position in the world.

"Figure to yourselves, indeed, one of the unfortunate young men trained in a German school to the mere contemplation of the Prussian monarchy, and of Prussian militarism—having as grounds of his education Prussian geography. Prussian history—or, rather, that of the Prussian dynasty, foreign to every practice of an independent life—figure this young man suddenly brought face to face on any point of the globe in competition with one of the fine fellows whose practical training we have just described."

The "fine fellows" above referred to are, of course, Englishmen. In a chapter on the English school system a description is given of a boys' school in which he distinguishes an endeavour to avoid every kind of forcing, while at the same time every natural aptitude is developed simultaneously, scholastic, manual, and artistic instruction are given equal attention. The reader will notice that this describes what would certainly be an ideal institution for America. Here there is too great a tendency on the part of teachers to push their own specialties or to curb natural aptitudes, and to force pupils along distasteful lines. However that may be, the author praises the English system in that its main object is the fitting of young men to take care of themselves.

We can hardly comprehend, here in America, how serious a national evil the dowry system is, as described by M. Demolins. A Frenchman's first thought, on becoming the father of a child, is to provide for it a suitable portion, and then it becomes his ambition to link that child in marriage with some one having a similar portion. Hence, the smaller the number of children the less amount of money must the parents lay by for this purpose.

"You have just married. One year later you have one child. Is your vision that of a fair little head, a sweet smile? No; the vision is the surging ghost of a dowry, a portion which you will have to find. Eighteen months or two years later another child—that is another portion. Two portions in twenty-five years! You feel unequal to doing more, and in presence of material impossibility you make up your mind to stop the expense. And that is why the French have few children."

In 1890 there were 100,000 less births in France than in 1881. Marriages also diminish year by year, and this is a factor working against national morality. In 1890 there were 20,223 less marriages than in 1884, and the decrease has been constant. Norway doubles her population in fifty-one years; Austria, in sixty-two; England in sixty-three; Denmark, in seventy-three; Sweden, in eighty-nine; Germany, in ninety-eight; and France in 334!

The dowry system is partly responsible for the French tendency to convert all resources into ready money. Thus, though France is a great money market, her resources are not engaged in foreign enterprises. Although most financial issues have their birth in Paris, yet great and advantageous enterprises are in the hands of Anglo-Saxon capital. Suez is already in English hands, says the author; Panama is very likely to pass into the hands of American citizens. Always the Anglo-Saxon! The French pay their money, but they do not reap the fruit. They run the chances, and somebody else gathers the profits.

Another feature of Anglo-Saxon life which conduces to dignity, self-respect and force of character is that race's idea of the home. The author visited numerous dwellings of English miners and found them clean, neat, and tidy, even when the wages were small. The French peasant keeps the same house in his family through many generations, but the interior is often that of a hovel, without cleanliness and without comfort. The Anglo-Saxon has no such love of locality, but wherever he goes takes his home with him. He spends his money as he goes and aims rather to better his condition than to save any petty sum. Hence a spirit of ambition and enterprise is fostered.

We have not time to go more fully into M. Demolins' argument. We must notice, however, that Socialism does not flourish among the Anglo-Saxons because their motto is, "Help Thyself," a motto which is at variance with the doctrines of Socialism. The author advises Frenchmen to study the Anglo-Saxons and to profit by their example. Will they do so? If they do, if this stirring appeal of M. Demolins shall succeed in setting them thinking and in establishing a new order of things, then his book will be regarded hereafter as epochal, and it will rank with such works as Don Quixote in point of influence. But this reflection is in the domain of prophecy and does not pertain to the reviewer. Suffice to say, that it is at present creating little less than a social earthquake in France.

INDIANAPOLIS NEWS, *February* 1, 1899.
ANGLO-SAXON SUPERIORITY.

It has been a favourite task with some writers to visit a foreign country, remain there a long or a short while, and, returning to their native land, set about writing a book which shall show how much better off the native land is than the country visited. It is unusual for a man to sit down deliberately and study out what is wrong with his own fatherland and make a book from the results of his study. This is what Edmond Demolins has done in his book, *Anglo-Saxon Superiority: To What it is Due*, and as a consequence he has stirred France to the depths, and the best men of that country, such as Georges Rodenbach, MM. Drumont, Jules Delahaye, Jules Lemaître, Françisque Sarcey, L. Descaves, Paul Bourget, Marcel Prevost, François Coppee, and others, unite in praising M. Demolins for his bravery in setting the truth before France and the world. As might be expected from a book with this title, the sale has been immense. France and Germany have read it now for about a year, and the edition before us, translated by L. B. Lavigne, is from the tenth French edition. If one expects to find in this book whose title glorifies the Anglo-Saxon a mass of humorous protest such as Bourget or Max O'Rell would have written, he will be disappointed ; M. Demolins is very much in earnest. He is an ardent Frenchman and longs for the well-being of his native land, but he has come to believe that the Anglo-Saxon is a superior type, and he believes that his fellow-countrymen and his country will profit by copying the methods of the Anglo-Saxon. . . .

He finds much fault also with the German system of education, and reserves all his praise for the English plan, taking for his example a typical boy's school, in which he finds that an effort is made to avoid anything like forcing, while at the same time every natural aptitude is taken advantage of, and scholastic, manual and artistic instruction receive equal attention. He finds, in short, that the English system achieves the excellent result of turning out young men who are fitted to act and to think for themselves.

He discusses also patriotism, and he shows that the French and the Anglo-Saxon ideas of the fatherland are radically different. He thinks that the Englishman takes his country with him wherever he goes; the Englishman's country is wherever he may live in freedom. This, thinks M. Demolins, helps the Anglo-Saxon to repudiate militarism, and in this connection he gives us some gratifying figures:—

Since 1816 seventy-two arbitration treaties have been signed between different countries in the world. Out of this number, twenty-three concerned England and thirty-six the United States. All the other countries together have had recourse to arbitration only thirteen times.

We have not space to mention even a tithe of the good points in this book; it should be read by every thinking Anglo-Saxon. The author is nowhere dogmatic; he argues with documents and statistics. The book is intended to awake the French people to the necessity of changing a mode of life which has continued for 200 years, without at all keeping up with the world; it has stirred up the best men and the best part of the Press in France, and that it will work some part of reform no one can doubt. Anglo-Saxons who read this book will not be deceived by M. Demolins' fine picture of the race to which they have the honour to belong, but they will read between the lines and be thankful that at any rate we have not such a long road to travel toward the zenith of civilisation.

HOME JOURNAL (NEW YORK), *February* 1, 1899.
THE ANGLO-SAXON MODEL.

It is easy to see why this book should be deemed epochal in France, receiving the plaudits of such critics as Jules Lemaître, Françisque Sarcey, M. de Kerohant, and almost countless others of the French press, Parisian and provincial, and independent literary and sociological critics; but that they should applaud and endorse it speaks volumes for the liberality of the modern French mind—its comparative freedom from that fatal national *chauvinism* which demands words of peace when there is no peace—indiscriminate praise when faults should be scourged.

To describe the book in detail would be almost like transcribing it, its range of subjects is so varied. M. Demolins lays especial stress upon what I might term the Malthusian view of the French people in regard to the size of families—the inevitable *dot* appearing to control all such questions as the bringing of human souls into the French world. This, of course, is more notable in the *bourgeoisie* and social aristocracy, the peasants rather continuing in the good old way their fathers trod, and surrounding their tables with "olive-plants," regardless of the insistent demands of the said plants for continuous watering with hats, caps, shoes, clothing, food, and the general *et ceteras*. The obstinacy, indeed, with which the Frenchman clings to the idea of a marriage settlement for his bairns is among the curiosities—I might say, the anachronisms—of the age. I doubt whether M. Demolins' book will improve matters in this regard; but there is no doubt that it has produced a marked sensation.

We of the United States and England have no cause to find fault with M. Demolins, if we love indiscriminate praise; and the English will doubtless smile at the gentle vinegar-infusion of his hit at hypocrisy in politics. The point, however, which I would make in this connection, not exactly as combating M. Demolins' view, but as suggesting that he may be carried away with an idea, is this: he views us rather from the outside. He sees the model, snug English home, minus the wretchedness of the hovel. He sees success, and that seems to be enough for him. He does not, I think, give sufficient emphasis to the far greater capacity of the French nature for throwing off its troubles and getting, so to say, into the sunshine. It can never be sufficiently emphasised that of all present nations the Anglo-Saxon knows most crucifixion of the soul. Its ambition frequently turns to a curse; its strict, stern passion for business a very Moloch, in which the weaker elements are caged and consumed. Men go to the guillotine in France with a smile, who would, as Anglo-Saxons, commit *felo de se* in their cells. Christ, the greatest of moralists, said: "A man's life consisteth not in the abundance of the things which he possesseth." Our owr youth learn early to call no man rich who is not well up into the millions. Americans abroad make a lavish display of money, for the sake of showing their ability to do so. We lack the typical content of the French *foyer*; though still retaining that sweetest of words, which M. Demolins so greatly admires: "Home."

I am considering this volume from its sentimental and ideal, rather than its strictly ethnological, standpoint—with the question of what constitutes the highest happiness of the greatest number as the foremost one. It is not my business to determine the relative merits of the ascetic principle or that of the *dolce far niente*, and, even if it were, the word ascetic would be strangely misapplied with reference to the average

Anglo-Saxon way of living ; nor could one possibly accuse the average Frenchman of being an illustration of the *dolce far niente*. As I understand M. Demolins, however, he is mortified at the physical and economical inferiority of the Gallic race, and wishes to see France arise from her apathy in some matters. He wants to see her strong as compared with England and the United States, for instance. He half dreads the march of the all-conquering Anglo-Saxon idea ; and, if this had been written within the past few months, he would doubtless have used poor Spain also as "a horrible example." To my mind M. Demolins is seeking to change race characteristics, while disclaiming any intention of mere national imitation. How he proposes to effect this is to the political student the most pregnant part of the book. Briefly, he would discourage the craze for office-holding, and encourage the individualism in business which he considers so characteristic of the Anglo-Saxon. It is always a question whether it is best to make a man discontented with himself merely because discontent has an ascetic quality in it. I should agree, of course, that it is better for France to grow stronger, if she has any idea of *la revanche*, any lingering design upon Alsace-Lorraine. But I am not sure that M. Demolins does not expect more of France than she can accomplish. Certainly she cannot Saxonise herself ; would she be any happier if she could ?

These few hints may serve in lieu of a more extended analysis of a most fascinating and significant book. No wonder it has passed through ten editions in France ; it might well pass through as many in this country. While it is mortifying to Frenchmen as a revelation, it is accepted by many of the truest sons of France as a good, though bitter, medicine. Whether Demolins has held the mirror up to nature as regards our national and race virtues, so as to do full justice to France, may be considered another question. The tone, indeed, is intensely patriotic ; it is not in any sense fulsome as regards our race ; yet somehow it does not seem to me as if M. Demolins has probed our faults and perils as a race as deeply as he might have done.

CANADIAN.

No.	Name of Paper.	Place.	Date.
1.	Montreal Star.	Montreal.	May 27, 1899.

23. VIEW FROM THE BIG CHIMNEY, LOOKING NORTH. (*Summer, 1899.*)

Copyright.

A French Savant's Verdict

FRENCH.

No.	Name of Paper.	Place.	Date.
1.	Etudes Religieuses.		September 20, 1897.
2.	Figaro.	Paris.	September 29, 1897.
3.	Revue des deux Mondes.		October 1, 1897.
4.	Gaulois.		October 6, 1897.
5.	L'Express Lyon.	Lyons.	October 8, 1897.
6.	République Française.		October 8, 1897.
7.	Impartial de l'Est.		November 24, 1897.
8.	Revue Municip.		December 11, 1897.
9.	l'Irlande libre.	Paris.	January 1, 1898.
10.	Verité.		January 8, 1898.
11.	Courrier de Havre.	Havre.	March 30, 1898.

LA RÉPUBLIQUE FRANÇAISE, *October* 8, 1897.

L'EDUCATION ANGLAISE JUGEE PAR UN ANGLAIS.

Taine et, plus récemment, M. Demolins ont attribué à l'éducation scolaire une influence décisive dans la formation du caractère et de la volonté, qui caractérisent la race anglaise. Ce jugement, fondé dans une certaine mesure, est empreint d'une certaine exagération et pèche par un excès d'optimisme, s'il faut en croire un rédacteur de la *Revue de Westminster*, M. Hill, qui, peut-être, tombe dans l'excès contraire. M. Hill, qui paraît être un observateur très attentif, insiste exclusivement sur les défauts qu'il veut corriger et néglige absolument les qualités que l'orgueil de ses compatriotes fait suffisamment valoir. Il reproche à l'éducation britannique contemporaine de manquer totalement son but si bien déterminé par Auguste Comte, dans une maxime fameuse : *savoir, pour prévoir, afin de pouvoir* ; elle *bourre* l'esprit sans le développer, et livre à la société des jeunes gens qui, pour la plupart, après cinq ou six ans de soi-disant culture intellectuelle, sont incapables de traduire une page d'Homère, un paragraphe de Tacite et même quatre ou cinq phrases de français et d'allemand. Qu'ils sortent des grands collèges classiques ou des externats urbains, les jeunes Anglais sont dépourvus d'idées générales et de connaissances précises, et ne possèdent que très imparfaitement l'intelligence du présent, du passé et de l'avenir. Chose plus grave encore, ils seraient incapables de tout raisonnement suivi et n'arriveraient que par exception à rattacher les effets aux causes.

Un point de ce réquisitoire me paraît être au-dessus de toute contestation, c'est, en thèse générale, la faiblesse des études de l'autre côté de la

Manche et l'ignorance qui en est l'accompagnement obligé. M. Hill a recherché les auteurs responsables de ce qu'il appelle la faillite (*failure*) de l'èducation moderne dans la Grande Bretagne : il croit les avoir trouvés et il les dénonce sans pitié à l'opinion publique. Si les fils et les filles d'Albion sont mal instruits et mal élevés, la faute en retombe tout entière, d'après lui, sur les parents, qui se déchargent trop aisément, sur des tiers, de leurs devoirs les plus évidents et les plus essentiels.

M. Hill pose en principe que les parents doivent être les auxiliaires et même les collaborateurs des maîtres, que leur concours est indispensable pour donner a l'instruction toute son utilité et à l'éducation toute son efficacité, et il démontre, par des arguments tranchants comme l'acier, que l'abdication complète de l'autorité paternelle ou maternelle entre les mains d'un pédagogue quelconque est grosse de conséquences désastreuses. Les déductions sont très serrées et, malgré la forme paradoxale qu'elles revêtent, elles renferment des indications qui peuvent intéresser tout le monde.

Absorbés par les affaires, distraits par des occupations multiples, la plupart des pères de famille, en Angleterre, comme dans tous les pays, confient à des professionnels le soin d'instruire et d'élever leurs enfants. Cette délégation de leurs pouvoirs et de leurs obligations est parfaitement naturelle, puisqu'elle est imposée par des nécessités impérieuses, et aurait sans doute échappé au réquisitoire de M. Hill, si elle n'avait pas dépassé toute mesure. Les Anglo-Saxons, trop vantés parfois, ne se bornent pas à se décharger sur autrui des devoirs qu'ils sont matériellement hors d'état de remplir ; ils entendent, en général, rester aussi complètement étrangers à la culture de leurs rejetons qu'à l'élevage des lapins dans les plaines de l'Australie. Lorsqu'ils sortent par hasard de cette indifference coupable, c'est pour se permettre des propositions saugrenues sur les programmes ou des marchandages éhontés sur le prix de la pension.

Quelques extraits de correspondances paternelles, cités par la *Revue de Westminster*, ne témoignent pas, en effet, de ce robuste bon sens, dont on se plaît à faire l'apanage des sujets de la reine Victoria. Un père de famille pressé insiste pour qu'on enseigne à sa progéniture, qui sait à peine lire, "les mathématiques, la mécanique, la chimie et la physique." Un autre, très ferré sur l'économie domestique, rappelle que son fils n'a fait son apparition au collège ou à l'externat que onze jours après la rentrée, et revendique énergiquement un rabais proportionnel à ces onze jours. *Time is money*.

Tout en reconnaissant que le temps c'est de l'argent, le rédacteur de la *Revue de Westminster* morigène les parents trop pressés et les parents trop avares, et il engage les autres à se tenir en relations très fréquentes avec les professeurs et les maîtres dont il leur importe de connaître et de mesurer la valeur intellectuelle et morale. On n'escompte pas un effet de commerce sans se renseigner sur le crédit du souscripteur ; pourquoi les Anglo-Saxons montrent-ils moins de sollicitude pour leurs enfants que pour leurs écus ? En un sens, et pour employer le langage des affaires avec des hommes d'affaires, comme le sont nos voisins, l'éducation de la jeunesse est la plus importante des *affaires*, qui, bien ou mal conduite, se traduira un jour par des bénéfices ou par des pertes.

L'échec de l'éducation doit être attribué, en grande partie, selon M. Hill, aux habitudes de paresse et d'indiscipline que l'intervention familiale pourrait et devrait prévenir ou réprimer. "Lorsque les élèves, dit M. Hill, s'apercevront que leurs parents sont en rapports fréquents avec les maîtres, lorsqu'ils se rendront compte que leur application et leurs progrès sont identiquement jugés par ces deux sortes d'autorités, ils seront poussés, dans la plupart des cas, à redoubler de diligence et d'efforts, pour mériter les éloges de leurs parents et de leurs amis." Le temps, que les parents prélèveront sur leurs plaisirs ou leurs affaires pour prêter main forte aux maîtres ne serait certainement pas du temps perdu.

M. Hill va plus loin encore ; il va même si loin que ma timidité de continental hésiterait peut-être à le suivre, s'il s'agissait de mes compatriotes ; il prescrit aux parents d'assister de temps en temps aux classes, d'écouter les leçons et les cours, et de se former une opinion personnelle sur la valeur de l'enseignement au double point de vue de la formation de l'intelligence et du caractère. Si la compétence leur manque, ils peuvent l'acquérir, en consultant les bons écrits pédagogiques, ou en recourant aux lumières des professionnels. L'accomplissement de cette tâche exigera, il ne faut pas se le dissimuler, autant de discernement que de discrétion et de mesure.

Les pères de famille, en Angleterre, ont, à mes yeux, le mérite incomparable de n'être pas hypnotisés par les professions libérales ou bureaucratiques ; ils deviendront des éducateurs presque parfaits s'ils aident les maîtres à fortifier la discipline et les études dans les collèges et dans les externats, et ils ne risqueront plus d'être accusés d'avoir engendré des écoliers qui ont toujours l'air de n'avoir ni père ni mère.

A. B.

Revue des Deux Mondes, *October* 1, 1897.

LA SUPERIORITE DES ANGLO-SAXONS ET LE LIVRE
DE M. DEMOLINS.

Il n'est pas nécessaire d'être un grand philosophe pour savoir que toutes les races humaines ont leurs qualités et leurs défauts, que leurs défauts sont étroitement liés à leurs qualités, qu'il y a partout du bien et du mal, que la perfection n'est pas de ce monde. Il n'est pas besoin non plus d'avoir profondément étudié l'histoire pour se convaincre qu'en ce qui concerne la prospérité des républiques et des empires, certains défauts sont plus nuisibles que d'autres, qu'il en est de très pernicieux, que quelques-uns sont vraiment utiles, qu'à cet égard, les peuples sont fort inégalement partagés. Les défauts des Grecs les ont perdus, les défauts des Romains ont contribué autant que leurs vertus à leur assurer la domination universelle. Telle imperfection morale est une force, telle autre est une faiblesse : " Otez à l'Anglais, a-t-on dit, un peu de sa morgue, de son intraitable orgueil ; donnez-lui la sensibilité sympathique qui lui manque, la faculté d'entrer facilement dans l'âme et les sentiments d'autrui ; vous aurez peut-être affaibli cette puissance de conviction, cette confiance en lui-même et en son droit, cette fermeté du vouloir qu'on a souvent admirées, vous l'aurez rendu moins propre à remplir sa mission dans le monde."

L'ingénieux et éloquent auteur d'un livre qui a fait du bruit M. Edmond Demolins, frappé de l'étonnante puissance d'expansion des Anglo-Saxons, s'est appliqué à nous démontrer qu'ils nous sonte de tout point fort supérieurs.[1] M. Demolins est un économiste distingué de l'école de M. Le Play, et en sa qualité d'économiste, c'est le rendement qu'il considère en fixant le prix, en réglant le tarif des vertus et des défauts des peuples. A quiconque se vante d'avoir reçu de la nature tel ou tel avantage, il demandera toujours : "Quelle utilité t'en revient-il ? " Or il a constaté que si nos voisins d'outre-Manche réussissent dans toutes leurs affaires et ont créé un immense empire, qui est assurément un des prodiges de l'histoire, ils en sont redevables moins encore à leurs aptitudes naturelles qu'aux leçons qu'on leur donne dans la famille et dans l'école, et il a constaté aussi que nos défauts innés, originels, qui nous font beaucoup de tort, nous en feraient moins s'ils n'étaient fortifiés, aggravés par un déplorable système d'education. . . .

Si M. Demolins s'était borné à se plaindre que trop de parens

[1] *A quoi tient la Supériorité des Anglo-Saxons,* par Edmond Demolins.

24. VIEW FROM TOBOGGAN HILL, LOOKING NORTH-WEST. (*Summer, 1893.*)

Copyright.

A French Savant's Verdict

n'aient pour leurs fils que de médiocres ambitions, que trop de jeunes Français aient un goût prononcé pour la vie facile et une répugnance marquée pour les entreprises laborieuses ; s'il lui avait suffi de combattre nos préjugés, nos préventions, les abus de notre bureaucratie, le prestige qu'ont pour nous les fonctions publiques et notre respect superstitieux pour les professions libérales ; si, en un mot, il s'était contenté de nous dire notre fait et ne s'était soucié que d'avoir raison, son livre, si excellent qu'il fût, aurait produit peu d'effet, n'aurait ému personne. Il a pensé fort justement que, pour faire pénétrer la vérité dans les cœurs, il faut les émouvoir, et que de toutes les figures de rhétorique, la plus émouvante est l'exagération. . . .

M. Demolins s'est amusé à nous faire croire que nos orgueilleux voisins avaient inventé le travail, la vertu et le bonheur. Il a pris plaisir à représenter l'Angleterre comme un radieux soleil, où l'on chercherait vainement une tache, et notre pauvre France comme un trou noir. Il a voulu secouer nos nerfs en nous persuadant que d'un côté de la Manche, tout est pour le mieux, que de l'autre, tout va de mal en pis.

La Grande-Bretagne que nous dépeint M. Demolins est vraiment une terre bénie de Dieu, où tout le monde se fait une joie de remplir les devoirs de son état, où le grand souci de tous les pères est de préparer leurs fils à la vie sérieuse, où tous les enfans sucent les vertus viriles avec le lait. Dans ce pays où il n'y a point d'oisifs, on ne compte que sur soi, on entend se suffire à soi-même, on rougirait d'avoir des obligations à autrui, de se faire aider, recommander, et les jeunes filles qui ont le plus de chances de se marier sonte celles qui n'apportent rien en dot. Tout Anglais est un homme complet ; grâce à l'éducation qu'il reçoit, toutes ses facultés sont en harmonie, et en sortant du collège, où il n'a acquis que des notions utiles et saines, il est apte à tous les métiers.

Personne ne pousse aussi loin que lui l'indépendance du caractère et de l'esprit ; il se fait à lui-même ses principes, ses opinions, ses jugemens ; il méprise les maximes reçues, le langage de convention et le servile troupeau des imitateurs. Il a sur les Celtes, sur les peuples latins, sur les Allemands, un autre avantage plus précieux encore : c'est l'intensité de son attention et sa puissance de travail, qu'égale sa puissance de repos. Mettant moins de tempts à abattre sa besogne, il lui en reste plus pour se reposer. Est-il rien de comparable au repos des dimanches anglais? On n'en a jamais mesuré la hauteur, la profondeur et la longueur.

La laborieuse et vertueuse Angleterre a atteint un degré de prospérité que notre imagination celto-latine a peine à concevoir. Tous les ouvriers anglais vivent largement et rien ne manque au confort de leur intérieur. Ils ont tous un piano. Ils prennent le thé sur une grande table carrée, que recouvre une nappe d'un tissu fin ; on voit sur cette table un joli service de porcelaine, cinq ou six assiettes de gâteaux variés, et ce qui est admirable, avant de reprendre du thé, ils ont soin de rincer leur tasse, "raffinement, dit M. Demolins, qui constituerait un progrès dan la plupart de nos maisons." Aussi ces ouvriers soucieux d'orner leur logis et leur vie ont-ils une tenue, un respect d'eux-mêmes, une dignité que nous ne connaissons pas. Ils sont tous des *gentlemen* commencés. Est-il nécessaire d'ajouter qu'ils sont parfaitement heureux ? Les autres peuples travaillent à contre-cœur, à leur corps défendant ; c'est une peine, un châtiment qu'ils s'infligent par nécessité ; ils pensent comme les Turcs qu'il vaut mieux être assis que debout, couché qu'assis. Les Anglais ne sont heureux que debout, et le travail est pour eux une source inépuisable de bonheur. Apprenez à lire dans leurs yeux, et vous reconnaîtrez "qu'ils ont tous au fond de l'âme une does formidable de contentement, que la vie leur apparaît sous des couleurs gaies que nous ne pouvons même pas soupçonner."

Hélas ! qu'est-ce que la France ? Un pays d'oisifs, de paresseux, où le travail, l'effort sont des supplices auxquels on cherche à se dérober en exploitant son prochain ou en invoquant l'aide et le secours de la communauté. Ainsi en use le frelon à l'égard de l'abeille. C'est un frelon que cet adolescent vigoureux et robuste, qui se fait entretenir par sa famille. C'est un frelon que ce jeune homme qui rêve d'épouser une héritière et de se faire entretenir par sa femme. C'est un frelon que ce jeune bureaucrate qui, dédaignant les professions indépendantes, est entré dans l'administration pour avoir la joie et la gloire d'être entretenu par le budget. Nous sommes un peuple de frelons, et le travail étant la seule source de vrai bonheur, nous sommes une nation triste, chagrine, morose, et la mélancolie qui nous ronge fait un cruel contraste avec la belle humeur, l'allégresse britannique. Qui de nous peut se vanter d'avoir au fond de l'âme " une dose formidable de contentement ? "

Comme je l'ai dit, si M. Demolins tenait à convaincre ses lecteurs, il tenait encore plus à les émouvoir, et il y a bien réussi. Quelques uns ont été consternés, navrés, atterrés. J'ai un voisin de campagne que ce terrible livre a plongé dans un sombre chagrin, dans un profond abattement ; il rougissait de n'être pas né Anglo-Saxon. . . . Je lui accordai que

M. Demolins avait eu raison de vanter la puissance de travail des Anglais, qu'ils se donnent tout entiers à ce qu'ils font, que rien ne les distrait de leur affaire ou de leur idée, qu'ils peuvent rester de longues heures sans prononcer une parole inutile, qu'ils n'en disent qu'à Dieu dans leurs interminables litanies, parce que cela ne tire pas à conséquence ; qu'ils n'en disent jamais aux hommes avec qui ils concluent un marché. Mais je lui représentai que s'il nous échappe beaucoup de propos inutiles ou indiscrets, cela tient à ce que nous sommes un peuple sociable, que la sociabilité a ses avantages, que si le travail intense est une source de bonheur, les distractions ont leur douceur, que les étourdis qui ont le don de s'oublier sont peut-être plus heureux que les gens âprement intéressés, qui ne se perdent jamais de vue.

Il eut peine à m'écouter jusqu'au bout.—"Eh ! oui, reprit-il, et pendant que nous bavardons, ils prennent aux quatre coins du monde tout ce qui est bon à prendre, et nous avons leurs restes, s'ils nous font la grâce de nous les laisser. Ce n'est pas nous qui aurions inventé de donner à la jeunesse une éducation pratique et harmonieuse ! Mettons le feu à nos collèges ; ce sera un bon commencement." Je lui fis remarquer que le collège anglais, harmonieux et pratique, qu'a visité M. Demolins, est de fondation très récente et n'a encore que cinquante élèves, qu'il a été spécialement créé pour préparer les jeunes gens qui se proposent de s'établir aux colonies, qu'on s'applique à les mettre en état de se tirer d'affaire dans toutes les difficultés et dans toutes les situations de la vie d'aventure ; que le fondateur de ce collège, le très habile docteur Cecil Reddie, homme de haute taille, solidement musclé, toujours vêtu en touriste, portant une blouse en drap gris, des culottes courtes, de gros bas de laine repliés au-dessus des genoux, une solide paire de chaussures et, sur la tête, un béret, ressemble beaucoup à un pionnier, à un *squatter*, et qu'il juge très sévèrement les écoles anglaises, qu'il accuse de ne plus répondre aux conditions de la vie moderne.

"L'enseignement actuel, disait-il à M. Demolins, forme des hommes pour le passé, et non pour le présent. La majorité de notre jeunesse gaspille une grande partie de son temps à étudier les langues mortes, dont très peu ont l'occasion de se servir dans la vie. On effleure les langues modernes et les sciences naturelles, et on reste ignorant de tout ce qui concerne la vie réelle, la pratique des choses et leurs rapports avec la société. Ce qui rend la réforme difficile, c'est que nos écoles subissent l'influence des Universités, pour lesquelles elles préparent un certain nombre de leurs élèves. Or ces Universités, comme toutes les vieilles corporations, ne sont pas maîtresses d'elles-mêmes ;

un spectre invisible et intangible plane au-dessus du directeur et des maîtres ; c'est l'esprit de tradition et de routine." Je fis observer à mon voisin que depuis trois siècles l'Angleterre est une pépinière de hardis pionniers, d'intrépides défricheurs de terres lointaines, que ceux qui ont colonisé le nouveau monde et l'Australie n'avaient point été élevés par le docteur Reddie, que lorsqu'ils s'embarquèrent, l'éducation harmonieuse n'avait point été encore inventée, qu'il est permis d'en conclure que l'esprit de tradition et les vieilles méthodes ont du bon et que les inutilités ne sont pas toujours inutiles.

Il se calma et ne parla plus de brûler nos collèges. Je l'assurai que, d'après les renseignemens que j'avais pu recueillir, les ouvriers anglais n'ont pas tous des pianos, qu'au fait M. Demolins n'en a vu qu'un dans le salon de cet ouvrier mécanicien, qui mange à son goûter de cinq espèces de gâteaux et se croirait perdu d'honneur s'il reprenait du thé sans avoir rincé sa tasse, que ses camarades ne vivent pas tous dans l'abondance, que quelquesuns sont assez misérables et habitent des bouges, qu'éprouvant le besoin d'étourdir leurs chagrins, ils se livrent à la boisson, que, s'il en faut croire les bruits qui courent, il y a un certain nombre d'ivrognes en Angleterre, que M. Demolins le sait et qu'il sait aussi que ces ivrognes ne sont pas tous des gentlemen. "Vous avez tort, ajoutai-je, de vous laisser aller au découragement ; M. Demolins ne nous promet-il pas que si nous combattons résolument nos vices naturels, si nous réformons nos goûts, si nous nous défasions de nos habitudes, nous pourrons, Dieu aidant, devenir des Anglo-Saxons de deuxième classe ?—Bah ! M. Demolins a voulu nous ménager répliqua t-il." Le fond de sa pensée est que, pour avoir l'esprit d'entreprise et d'initiative, il faut habiter une île et que, la France n'étant pas une île, nous se serons jamais qu'un peuple de frelons. Je lui repartis qu'effectivement il est assez difficile de convertir la France en île, mais qu'il n'est pas rigoureusement démontré qu'il faille être un peuple insularie pour posséder certaines vertus qui font prospérer tes Etats.

Afin de l'en convaincre, comme il lit facilement d'anglais, je lui prêtai un ouvrage en deux volumes, intitulé : *France of To-day*, —*la France d'aujourd'hui*. L'auteur de ce livre aussi agréable qu'instructif est une Anglaise née dans le comté de Suffolk, qui, savante en agriculture, très versée dans l'economie politique, a parcouru à plusieurs reprises nos provinces du Nord et du Midi, de l'Est et de l'Ouest, pour savoir comment on y vit. Elle a procédé à une enquête en règle et causé avec tout le monde. Elle connaît nos défauts et nous les reproche, elle connaît nos qualités et nous en loue.

Elle a un faible pour nos paysans propriétaires, dont elle admire l'industrie et les patiens labeurs. Elle pose en principe qu'en tout temps, le Français fut de tous les peuples celui qui aimait le plus passionnément la terre, que de cette passion dérivent et ses défauts etses vertus. . . .

Miss Betham a l'âme trop britannique pour ne pas regretter que la chambre à coucher de nos cultivateurs soit trop souvent un sombre taudis, elle pense que leur inquiète prévoyance des accidens possibles est une vertu, qu'ils supporteront mieux le malheur que ces fermiers anglais "qui veulent singer les *squires* et vivre comme des capitalistes," qu'en sacrifiant leurs aises à leur passion pour la terre, ils sont devenus une classe politique, que par leurs épargnes et leur travail, ils ont réparé des désastres qui semblaient irréparables, que, par leur sagesse d'électeurs, ils ont préservé leur pays d'inutiles révolutions. "Nous autres Anglais, conclut miss Betham, nous sommes un peuple de locataires, la France est un pays de propriétaires." Elle estime que chacune de ces deux conditions a ses avantages et ses inconvéniens, et elle cite un journal de Londres qui publiait naguère de remarquables études sur la vie dans les villages anglais : "Vous n'avez aucune idée, écrivait l'auteur de ces études, de l'état de servilité anquel sont réduits les cultivateurs dans quelques-unes des grandes terres où ils ont trouvé à s'établir. Le *squire* possède la chaumière, il peut à son gré concéder ou retirer les lots de terrain. Sa femme et ses filles donnent du charbon, prêtent des draps, visitent les malades. Ces pauvres gens se soumettent passivement à leur destinée, qui est de faire tout ce qu'on leur dit de faire, de prendre tout ce qu'on leur donne et de se montrer reconnaissants. C'est le royaume des bonnes intentions et de la bienfaisance ; mais pour y être heureux. il faut renoncer à toute virilité d'âme et à la dignité d'un citoyen."

Cette citation rasséréna un peu mon voisin. Il fut charmé d'apprendre que, quoi qu'en dise M. Demolins, les Anglais n'ont pas tous l'âme virile, qu'ils ne sont pas tous des héros, que si l'Angleterre produit des hommes de forte volonté et des pionniers incomparables, elle est aussi le pays des assistés. Il remercia miss Betham d'avoir mis du baume sur sa blessure ; il était moins honteux d'avoir dans ses veines un sang celto-latin, il osait redresser un peu sa tête de velche. . . .

Il avait encore d'autres étonnemens. M. Demolins distingue les nations communautaires et les nations particularistes. Chez les peuples communautaires, dans lesquels il comprend les races latines et les Allemands, l'Etat est une providence chargée de veiller au sort des particuliers, qui lui sacrifient de grand cœur leurs plus précieuses libertés, en échange des secours qu'ils attendent de lui. Dans les sociétés particularistes, le principal souci des individus est de défendre leur liberté contre toute immixtion de l'Etat ; ils entendent répondre seuls de leur destinée, ils ne comptent que sur leur travail, leur énergie, leur persévérance, leur volonté. Or s'il est vrai que l'Anglo-Saxon, disait mon voisin, soit de tous les peuples le plus particulariste, comment se fait-il que les Américains soient protectionnistes à outrance ? Pourquoi ont-ils voulu que l'Etat prît sous son patronage la prospérité de leur commerce et de toutes leurs industries ? Pourquoi y a-t-il chez eux tant de gens qui aiment à vivre sur le commun, que les pensions qu'ils leur servent grèvent le budget d'une dépense de 800 millions de francs ? S'il est vrai que la principale préoccupation de l'Anglo-Saxon soit de faire lui-même ses affaires et de s'affranchir de toute tutelle, d'où vient que le parlement et le gouvernement anglais reculent sans cesse les limities de leur compétence et se mêlent de beaucoup de questions, qui autrefois n'étaient point de leur ressort ? Pourquoi l'Etat a-t-il déclaré que toute école primaire qui accepterait ses subventions serait tenue d'admettre les inspecteurs de Sa Majesté, et de se conformer aux prescriptions d'un code approuvé par le parlement ? Pourquoi tout le monde a-t-il voulu être subventionné et inspecté ? Pourquoi, au cours des vingt dernières années, les dépenses de l'instruction publique sont-elles devenues une des lourdes charges du budget ?

Autres questions. Si les Anglais font passer avant tout les libertés individuelles, dont nous faisons si bon marché, pourquoi sommes-nous libres à notre choix de travailler le dimanche, si cela nous plaît, ou de tirer la perdrix, ou d'aller au concert, et pourquoi ne le sont-ils pas ? S'il est vrai, comme l'affirme M. Demolins, qu'ils considèrent le travail intense comme une source de bonheur, pourquoi leurs ouvriers mécaniciens, qu'ils aient ou non des pianos, se sont-ils mis en grève pour contraindre leurs patrons à ne les faire travailler que huit heures par jour ? Pourquoi. . . . Ses pourquoi ne finissaient pas.

Il faut des centaines de mots pour expliquer cette chose confuse, incertaine et flottante, cette combinaison instable qu'on appelle le caractère d'un homme ; il en faut plus encore pour définir tant bien que mal le caractère d'une nation. Volontairement, à dessein, M. Demolins, qui n'avait en vue que l'intérêt de notre éducation, a pris le parti de tout simplifier et d'oublier que toute question a plusieurs faces. Il demanda un iour à un jeune Anglais qui exploite un *run* de moutons dans la

Nouvelle-Zélande ce qui le séduisait dans cette existence. "C'est la vraie vie, c'est l'indépendance," lui répondit le jeune *squatter*. "Vous le voyez, ajoute M. Demolins, le besoin d'indépendance est bien ce qui domine et actionne toute la vie de l'Anglais ; on peut tourner et retourner le problème, on arrive toujours à cette solution."

Il a raison : à certains égards l'Anglais est le plus indépendant des hommes, et lorsqu'il n'a pas chez lui ses coudées fronches, il a bientôt fait de s'embarquer pour la Nouvelle-Zélande. Il a l'imagination hardie et le pied léger. Il est fier de sa patrie, mais il n'a garde de s'y enraciner. La véritable Angleterre n'est pas pour lui une île de 23 millions d'hectares ; c'est une certaine manière de vivre, de sentir, de penser, et cette patrie mobilisée et transportable l'accompagnera au bout du monde. Où qu'il s'établisse, il s'arrangera pour jouir de la liberté civile, individuelle et domestique. Ennemi juré de tout ce qui le met à la gêne, il a réduit la famille à sa plus simple expression : toi et moi, ou, selon les cas, moi et toi ; le reste, ce sont les autres ou le prochain, et les autres commencecent à l'enfant, et comme l'enfant est un prochain tapageur, encombrant, incommode, qui fourre souvent ses doigts dans son nez et son nez où il n'a que faire, on le tient à distance et, autant que faire se peut, on l'élève par procuration. . . .

Et cependant, cet insulaire si jaloux de son indépendance a ses assujettissemens, ses servitudes ; ne lui demandez pas de secouer son joug, son joug lui plaît. Plus que personne, il est esclave de ses habitudes, de ses préjugés nationaux. Il lui est plus facile de courir le monde, de traverser les mers que de sortir un instant de sa peau pour entrer dans celle des autres. En ceci bien différent des Romains, auxquels il aime à se comparer, impénétrable et imperméable, il vit côte à côte avec les races étrangères sans leur rien emprunter et sans leur ried donner, et l'éloignement qu'il a pour elles et qu'elles ont pour lui sera toujours le même.

Autant qu'à ses préjugés, il est assujetti à ses besoins factices, à l'étiquette, aux minuties du confort. Il n'a jamais dit comme Socrate : "De combien de superéuités je puis me passer !" Aucun autre peuple ne se fait une idée aussi compliquée du bonheur, et comme ils ont l'esprit de détail et qu'ils attachent une grande importance aux petites choses, il suffit d'une bagatelle qui leur manque pour appauvrir et gâter leur vie. Leurs statisticiens se plaignent que les jeunes gens se marient de moins en moins, que c'est une des raisons qui contribuent au succès de la propagande féministe. "Que voulez-vous ? me disait un jeune Londonien ; au prix que coûte aujourd'hui le bonheur en Angleterre, je ne suis pas assez riche pour faire celui d'une Anglaise." Et notez qu'il ne suffit pas d'être heureux, qu'il faut être considéré, et que le code de la respectabilité est encore une affaire très compliquée. Ce code prescrit tout ce que doit faire un Anglais, ce qu'il doit dire, ce qu'il doit penser, ce qu'il doit boire et manger, les opinions littéraires et autres qu'il doit professer, les usages, les conventions qu'il est tenu d'observer pour mériter le respect. Cet homme qui se flatte d'être indépendant est si dépendant de l'opinion d'autrui, qu'il aime mieux pâtir que de faire quoi que ce soit qui puisse nuire à la considération qu'on a pour lui. Telle famille anglaise, qu'un revers de fortune oblige à se retrancher, recourra à tous les expédiens plutôt que de diminuer son train de maison. Que deviendrait-on si on n'avait plus le nombre réglementaire de domestiques, que le code déclare obligatoire pour quiconque veut être respectable !

Le fond de l'affaire est que, pour mériter le respect d'autrui et sa propre estime, il faut être riche, que les pays anglo-saxons sont ceux où la pauvreté fait la plus triste figure et où le veau d'or a les plus chauds adorateurs. Encore l'Angleterre a-t-elle sur les Etats-Unis l'avantage de posséder une aristocratie héréditaire. Quoique M. Demolins semble avoir plus d'admiration pour les milliardaires américains que pour les grands hommes de Plutarque, il est permis de penser avec un célèbre publiciste anglais, M. Bagehot, que le fétichisme du rang social sert de correctif au fétichisme des grandes fortunes, qu'il est utile à une société d'avoir deux idoles, que quand deux idolâtries sont en lutte, il y a quelque chance de succès pour la vraie religion, qu'au surplus le culte des grandeurs héréditaires est moins dégradant que la plate vénération pour l'argent.

Un anglophobe reprochait à M. Demolins de n'avoir pas dit que le caractère distinctif du bonheur anglais est d'être un bonheur qui ne rend pas heureux, que si nos voisins ont le pied léger, c'est qu'ils ne se trouvent pas bien chez eux, qu'on ne s'en va guère des endroits où l'on a le cœur à l'aise, qu'au surplus la création de l'immense empire britannique est due avant toutes choses à l'habileté, aux savans calculs, à la prévoyance d'un gouvernement aussi avisé que bien informé, à une politique traditionnelle, à la fois audacieuse et prudente, et qui, toujours à l'affût des occasions, n'est jamais embarrassée par ses scrupules. M. Demolins a dit ce qu'il voulait et devait dire. Il avait à cœur de frapper un grand coup sur les frelons, de les contrister, de les mortifier, de les étonner, de les irriter. Il pensait avec raison que la contrition prépare l'amendement, que les surprises font naître les curiosités, que la colère, le dépit fouettent le sang, que tout vaut mieux qu'une apathique indifférence et un idiot contentement de soi-même.

Les plus intelligens de ses lecteurs ont deviné ses intentions, approuvé ses artifices. Il voulait nous contraindre à faire notre examen de conscience ; il en a usé comme les prédicateurs qui ne convertiraient personne, s'ils n'exagéraient les choses en mal comme en bien.

"Malheur, s'écrient-ils, à vous qui ne remarquez pas la poutre qui est dans votre œil, et ne voyez que la paille qui est dans l'œil de votre prochain !" Ils affaibliraient l'effet de leur discours s'ils confessaient à leur auditoire que la paille du prochain est le plus souvent une poutre, et que cette poutre est quelquefois aussi grosse que la nôtre.

G. Valbert.

EGYPTIAN.

No.	Name of Paper.	Date.
1.	Egyptian Gazette.	September 22, 1897.

25. VIEW FROM THE BIG CHIMNEY, LOOKING SOUTH. (*Summer, 1899.*)

Copyright.

CHAPTER XV.

Some Weightie Criticisms upon the
Three Books.

CHAPTER XV

SOME WEIGHTY CRITICISMS UPON THE THREE BOOKS ON THE ABBOTSHOLME TYPE OF SCHOOL.

WE have selected from the mass of Press Notices and private criticisms in our possession for a place in a separate chapter the following extracts, because they are of a more magisterial character.

It has been a matter of some surprise to ourselves to observe how readily the British public swallowed the gospel of Anglo-Saxon selfishness, as propounded by the eloquence of M. Demolins. One would think that he had held up for public adoration the ordinary English school. Instead of this he selected a school which owes its very origin entirely to a revolt against the insufficiency of the English Public Schools.

The greater part of his diatribes applies with as much force to England as to France. The yearly sacrifice of innocents on the altar of competitive cram; the absurd rush after Government appointments; the lack of real individuality in the youth; all this is as much the product of English scholastic folly as of French. It is true we have encouraged games and given on the whole more attention to physique. But this was not always so, and most people are aware it is now not only overdone but badly done.

There is nearly as little pedagogic wisdom in our athletic training as in the class instruction. On the other hand the Frenchman is taught French, while the Englishman is not taught English.

Would we had the pen of M. Demolins and we would write a book, as eloquent as his, to prove that, if England produces beef, France produces brains. And yet England could do with more brains: more in her Army, more even in her Navy, not to mention her National Administration, probably the most extravagant in Europe.

If France is really so decadent, how is it she is so dangerous? If she has not overrun the globe with colonists, she has managed somehow to dominate mankind with her ideas.

The fact is M. Demolins has raised a great question, but not answered it. He has made the sleepy English open their eyes to behold their Empire. He has shown that the Anglo-Saxon motto, "Every man for himself," suits the conquest of an empire. He has not touched the question whether Anglo-Saxon individualism can consolidate it—or even organise decently a single town.

As regards the basis of his criticisms—his theory of the Saxon—we are quite certain that he is mistaken. That there is room in the world for Saxon torpor we readily allow. But to ascribe to it all the glory of Britannia is to ignore the evidence of history. If we might venture on an anatomical analogy, the Saxon is the fat, where the Angle is the muscle, the Celt the nerves, and the Norseman the blood.

Some Weighty Criticisms

While therefore we join issue with M. Demolins as to the causes of our material prosperity, we acknowledge that his book may do France much good. For undoubtedly she has great faults.

The greatest, if we may venture to express an opinion in so delicate a matter, is this : her habit of too rapid generalisation and tendency to run each latest theory to death. This is the cause of nearly all her calamities. In her schools, therefore, the boys should be more carefully taught the dangers springing from this well-known intellectual fault.

On the other hand, we English would find that what in France is poison would in England be excellent medicine. We need precisely the gifts which the Frenchman possesses in too eminent a degree. We need discipline, method, clearness, polish, affection, and ideas.

But we did not intend to write a criticism ourselves on M. Demolins and must no longer detain our readers from the weighty criticisms to which we referred above.

In doing so, however, we must offer our most cordial personal thanks to M. Demolins, not only for his appreciation of our work, but because, as a matter of fact, his French brain did for our English brain exactly what France has done for the world, namely, enabled us to see more clearly the real significance of our efforts.

St. James's Budget, *December* 24, 1897.
TWO VIEWS OF THE ENGLISH PUBLIC SCHOOL.[1]

Any time in Paris this summer one saw in all the booksellers' windows displayed conspicuously a book in buff paper covers that looked

[1] By the writer of the article on The New School Abbotsholme, in the *St. James's Budget*, December 20, 1895.

at first sight like a new novel. But this book, about which all Paris was talking, was no new romance by Zola or Daudet. It was a book by Edmond Demolins, a professor of sociology. Its title was "A quoi tient la Supériorité des Anglo-Saxons?" which might be freely translated, "Why have the English a greater Colonial Empire than the French or the Germans?" Monsieur Demolins begins his book by saying: "It is in the school that is found the most obvious contrast between England and the nations of Western Europe. This contrast is extremely well marked, and permits the observer to discover at their birth the deep-seated causes of the superiority of the Anglo-Saxon. Each people organises education in its own image; in the image of its manners and customs. Education, in its turn, reacts upon the social state." Monsieur Demolins then goes on to point out what he conceives to be the main principle, the fundamental idea underlying the educational system (particularly the system of secondary education) of Germany, of France, and of England. What the secondary schools do in France and Germany is, above all, to produce and manufacture functionaries. They train young men to be very apt and able at passing those examinations which open the portals of State employment. Now, to be a successful State functionary certain qualifications are necessary. The duties of the State functionaries are, above all, routine duties. How the civil servant becomes the slave of formality—the devotee of red-tape—we all know. That is, says Monsieur Demolins, one of the proximate causes why the French and Germans do not make good colonists—*i.e.*, why in agricultural colonisation German and French emigrants tend in the long run to be ousted by English emigrants, with their greater powers of initiative and self-reliance. The mainspring of these particular qualities in the English M. Demolins sees in the social and political system of England, with its traditional minimising of State activity and maximising of individual activity.

From all the secondary schools of England and Scotland M. Demolins selects one for portrayal to his French readers as the ideal institution for training the successful man of business, organiser of labour, colonist, or statesman. Well, where and what is this ideal secondary school which M. Demolins puts on a pinnacle for the admiration and envy of the French nation? It is Abbotsholme, in Derbyshire. But poor praise this would be, in the eyes of those who have an intimate knowledge of the inner life and working of the public and private secondary schools of England, if it were true that M. Demolins depicts Abbotsholme as a representative specimen of existing scholastic bodies. This is not at all the case. To M. Demolins's discriminating eye, Abbotsholme is not so much the type of the secondary school of the present, as of the future—but linked on to the present by the very force of that continuity of development which is characteristic alike of all real and true organic growth, and of English institutions in general. M. Demolins devotes nearly forty pages of his book to a minute account of the principles and practices in operation at Abbotsholme, and winds up with the affirmation that it is from this type of school that we must look for the very highest and most perfected development of those qualities of individuality which have given England her industrial and commercial supremacy. Thus he represents Abbotsholme, not at all as an average English secondary school, but as the cutting edge of that progressive movement that slowly and imperceptibly readapts vital institutions to changing surroundings. He represents Abbotsholme, in fact, as the practical forecast of the "public school" of the future—the near future, let us hope.

How are we to reconcile this extremely appreciative estimate of our English public schools with the severe indictment recently levelled against them at home? Among recent indictments, none expresses a criticism more generally admitted than Mr. Stanley de Brath's book. "The Foundations of Success." In a word, it may be said that M. Demolins puts his fingers on the virtues of the public school, and Mr. de Brath on its defects. The good qualities of our public schools are, for the most part, associated with their open-air life, their games, and the free organisation of these by the boys themselves, their tradition of good manners and "good form." The defects of our public schools are particularly associated with their indoor life, their method and matter of instruction.

Mr. de Brath's book is an attempt to bring together and focus into one survey, to co-ordinate into a unified system the teaching of these modern educational pioneers. The attempt is for the most part lucidly and comprehensively made. But Mr. de Brath does not rest satisfied with a merely theoretic survey. He formulates a practical program of scholastic studies based on the scientific principles enunciated. Now this program bears a resemblance, almost amounting to identity, with the program actually in operation at Abbotsholme. The coincidence may be partly explained by the fact that Mr. de Brath's program and the Abbotsholme program are both professedly based on a conscious endeavour to incorporate the principles laid down by the great educational reformers of modern times. But there is another fact which makes the coincidence less striking. Mr. de Brath published his book, fresh from a year's work and study at Abbotsholme as an assistant master. He has been ill-advised to conceal this fact from his readers.

JORNAL DO COMMERCIO (RIO DE JANEIRO),
August 9, 1897.

HOW THE ENGLISHMEN EDUCATE THEIR SONS.

A great sensation is being created in France by the book of a man whose name is perhaps only known to those who take a special interest in social science, M. Edmond Demolins. The title of the book is, " Wherein Lies the Superiority of the Anglo-Saxon ? " and it shows on its cover a planisphere, where red spots mark the parts of the globe in which men of this race, subjects of Her Gracious Majesty, or compatriots of Mr. McKinley, hold a real and effective supremacy.

A mere look at the map is sufficient to awake in any Latin mind thoughts tinged with a certain melancholy. M. Edmond Demolins studies in all its aspects the problem of the superiority of the Anglo-Saxon race, or, if one objects to the word superiority, the problem of its expansive force, of its prosperity, of its vitality, of its energy.

Although compact, for it does not exceed 400 pages, M. Demolins' book does not leave unexplained any of the many factors producing this indisputable result, which is shown by the map to which I have alluded. He does not hesitate to attribute the greater part of this result to the English system of education, which makes men, while that of nearly all Latin countries produces mere functionaries.

Although the English education is, on the whole, better adapted than that of any other nation to modern conditions of life, they are themselves in England still trying to remove any of the defects which it may perchance contain, and to improve it still more. With this end in view a school was founded a few years ago in that country whose programme of instruction and education eliminates all the items which arise from old prejudices and routine, and breaks with all the scholastic traditions which are not justified by practical experience. For instance, the worship of athletics, which in the usual English schools is excessive, as compared with the general neglect of physical culture in Continental schools—this physical culture the school of which I am going to speak attempts to organise scientifically.

This is how Dr. Cecil Reddie, the director of this school, sets forth his plan of education.

[Here follow long quotations.]

The school founded by Dr. Reddie began its work in October, 1889, at Abbotsholme, a country estate situated in Derbyshire. An important point in this new scheme of education is that the school be in the country. Although of recent origin, this school has already given birth to another of the same type, founded by one of the Abbotsholme teachers, Mr. Badley.

Neither school has any resemblance with ours. With us school buildings are cold and bare; theirs are English country houses, giving the feeling of actual life, and reproducing the aspect of a home, not that of a barrack or prison. Everywhere there is air, light, space, foliage, instead of a yard between high walls. This impression increases still more as one goes inside.

[Here follow more quotations.]

There is a widely approved feeling in England and the United States that the method which exacts work by competition is very defective; it bases progress on a feeling of envy, not on the sentiment of duty, and thus develops one of the worst tendencies of human nature. To train boys to be men, it is necessary to treat them largely as men, appealing as much as possible to their conscience. Very much the same thing is felt in the United States. Here is an extract from a letter of the Director of the High School of St. Paul, Minnesota :—

"We never give prizes to our students and never make them compete. It frequently happens that they write compositions on the same subject. When criticising and correcting their work, I take the greatest care not to let my pupils detect who did best. I tell every one 'Your work is superior, or inferior, to that of last time, or of the other day,' but never 'to that of any other student.' I take it that it is bad for the child to say to himself, 'I am superior to this or that one.' He should say, 'I am superior to what I was a week ago!'"

These words, so true, so well weighed, are a formal condemnation of the method employed in nearly all the schools of the whole world.

. . . . . .

The results achieved by the Abbotsholme boys are already so satisfactory, that Dr. Reddie proposes to increase the building, so as to be able to hold a hundred boys instead of the fifty now there.

. . . .

Abbotsholme

Such is the school which represents a distinct advance in the education of complete men, with all the faculties and all the power of energy and initiative developed, so as to make self-reliant men, who will not want to be tied to the apron-strings of the State.

To-day, when the question of the education and preparation of youth for the battle of life—constantly becoming more acute—preoccupies all thoughtful minds in Europe, it is impossible that such questions should be treated with indifference in a country like Brazil, new, full of vigour, with unexplored wealth, and capable of a brilliant future.

Brazil, perhaps more than any other country, needs a new generation, robust in body and mind, which would find in its own country, without having to emigrate, the most convenient field for employing its faculties, energy and enterprise. It seems to me, therefore, that the extract which I have just made from one of the most important chapters of M. Demolins' masterly book should be read with interest. With this in view, I have sacrificed other parts of the book, perhaps more attractive but less weighty.

If the reading of this chronicle inspired in any Brazilian pedagogue the idea of founding an institution analogous to Abbotsholme, I think he would not regret the step.

ALTER EGO.

TIJDSCHRIFT VOOR ONDERWIJS EN OPVOEDING. (REVIEW OF INSTRUCTION AND EDUCATION.) By Dr. J. H. GUNNING, Wzn., Oudrector van het Gymnasium te Zwolle, Privat docent in Paedagogie, Universiteit Utrecht.
Amsterdam : W. Versluys, October, 1898.

A QUOI TIENT LE SUPÉRIORITÉ DES ANGLO-SAXONS ? par DEMOLINS.
Paris : Maison Didot (1897), onzième Mille Fl. 1, 90.

EMLOHSTOBBA, ROMAN ODER WIRKLICHKEIT, von Dr. H. LIETZ.
Berlin : Dümmlers Verlagsbuchhandlung. M. 3.0.

THESE are two books, which have made, in the country of their birth, a justifiable sensation and raised a great deal of talk.

They can be discussed very conveniently together, because both of them treat practically of the same subject, viz., the excellence of English education.

The subject of the first work is of course wider ; only the first of the three parts into which the book is divided up treats of *le Français et l'Anglo-Saxon dans l'Ecole*. But I should advise every educationist not to leave unread the other two, entitled : *le Français et l'Anglo-Saxon dans la vie privée*, and *le Français et l'Anglo-Saxon dans la république*.

These chapters not only contain many beautiful and important hints, but practically, as regards their tendency, belong to the first part. The whole book, which is remarkable for its clearness and perspicuity even for a Frenchman, is nothing else than this answer to the question put upon the cover : To their educational system.

The author is one of the best disciples of the sociologist le Play, and belongs to a class of men which is seldom found in France, viz., to such men as do not publish the ripe fruits of their investigations and thought until they have for years quietly, industriously, and independently collected data. He is a sociologist, that is to say, he studies all the phenomena of human society at home and abroad, of the present and the past, according to the strictest physiological method, and tries to show their connection. Supported by a small number of partisans, who, like himself, are devoted solely to increasing their scientific material, he has published, during several years past, a monthly review, *La Science Sociale*, which is little known in France, probably on account of its sober and solid contents.

These studies have brought him necessarily to the question chosen for the title of his book.

The answer he has given has made such an immense sensation, because every reader saw at once on what a solid basis of observations and reflections it was founded, and the work of a man, who was hardly known till now, has become within a few weeks a "Livre sensationnel."

As I said, the argument is simplicity itself. The author asserts that all forms of human society can be reduced to two large groups, viz. : *les sociétés à formation communautaire* and *les sociétés à formation particulariste*. The first group can be subdivided into these : one where the man leans upon the family (tribe or class), and the other where he leans on the State. The former are found in the East, and the latter in France and Imperial Germany. Of the second group, the author knows of only one representative, viz., where the individual leans only on himself, and where the number of Government officials and the functions of the State are reduced to a minimum. That is the Anglo-Saxon race.

With inexorable logic, though not without partiality, he explains that the future belongs exclusively to societies of the second kind, and that societies of the former kind are condemned to go to sleep, to stand still and to decay, and therefore inevitably must go to ruin.

He describes, with many details, the advantages of the "formation particulariste," and he becomes rather eloquent when he explains that these advantages are not only of a material, but even more of a moral, character.

On the question, "How did the English get their 'formation particulariste'?" the author gives the answer: "Through the system by which they educate their children." He has explained before, in a historic summary, how far race and descent have played a part in this question.

The French educational system forms mainly officials, lawyers, and journalists; the Anglo-Saxon one forms MEN. The aim of a French father is to provide his son with (1) a situation and (2) with a wife with means (the contrary arrangement is also useful). The son knows this and counts on it. The son of Anglo-Saxon parents, on the contrary, knows that he must rely only on himself.

The whole social question, the author says somewhere, is not a question of salary, but of conduct of life; therefore it is a question of education.

For that reason the whole book practically speaks about education, but of education in the largest sense of the word, comprising everything which has the tendency, both in public and private life, to develop in the individual such qualities as give to the nation its peculiar character. Most of the critics, whose articles are mentioned in an appendix, show that they understand this. It is most remarkable to see with how much sympathy and shame this work—which is such a blow to French self-satisfaction—has been received.

Can it now mend matters?

If one considers that there are few nations which are so conservative and "routinier" as the French (notwithstanding deceptive appearances to the contrary), and if one considers the success which Laboulaye achieved years ago with his work, "Paris en Amérique," and when one then looks, for instance, at the proceedings of the Dreyfus affair, one is not inclined to give to this question an optimistic answer.

But this does not concern us, and one might ask if this work, which is written for the French and deals with the English, is of any value to us Dutch. But such a question would betray little sagacity. For, though the foundation of our national character has undoubtedly a greater resemblance to that of the English, and though we still preserve in our institutions, customs, and views many traits of that kinship, the French influence has made itself so strongly felt, and so much has been modelled here after the French pattern, especially since the day when Napoleon held us under his iron yoke, that only too much of what M. Demolins blames in France is equally applicable to Holland.

In reading this work, we are struck every moment by the thought that in reality no nation exists which is more like the English than ourselves ; that all their brilliant qualities have also adorned our nation in the seventeenth century ; and that it was through these that we became powerful, just as they now make the English people so mighty. But, at the same time, it shows that we have become degenerate, and have been led by well-meaning, but doctrinaire, statesman on a track which dooms to death the Anglo-Saxon element in us and encourages all the qualities which cause decay in the Latin races.

Just as in France, our whole education is calculated to deprive the boy of his independence ; to teach him to lean on others and, for the same reason and with the same fatal necessity, to cause a dislike for agriculture, commerce, and industry—in a word, for all the callings which requires initiative and pluck—and nourishes a craving for official situations with fixed salaries.

Those who do not from their own reflections grasp how deadening this is to a nation, can learn it from M. Demolins.

The vital importance of this matter justifies an extensive criticism in a Review of Instruction and Education.

It is certainly a most difficult, but also a most important, question : how to organise education in such a way that the child shall be trained to independent action, to personal initiative, to self-help.

For that reason, we have suggested the introduction of manual labour n the Primary School, because we think that the teacher who occupies himself in the school with such work inevitably must see the defects and the pernicious consequences of all abstract instruction, as it has been imparted up to the present time, when the master expounds and the disciple merely repeats.

Subsequently, Mr. den Hollander pointed out to us, that we were beginning the matter at the wrong end, and that a thorough reorganisation of our Primary Education ought to precede the introduction of manual work. It makes no difference to me, provided people will only wake up. Time certainly will not stand still.

Meanwhile, I recommend all teachers to study the lives of great men from this point of view : asking if the great majority of them did not receive a school education characterised by incompleteness and irregularity; an education which made them enter life with the conviction: If I don't find the right road myself, certainly no one will find it for me.

The reader will already perceive that M. Demolins' work is, in the highest degree, suggestive. When one has once started discussing it, one can hardly stop, and there is no doubt that it will give rise to fruitful discussions in educational circles. It is full of animated descriptions, as, for instance, that of the life of a French and English gentleman farmer. There is also plenty of insight. He remarks, for instance, that attachment to a home in the *material* sense, as a rule, is coupled with little sense of comfort and with a low standard of life; while, on the contrary, nations which understand home in the ethical sense easily emigrate, but know how to make themselves comfortable everywhere, and consequently have a higher standard of life. These are remarks which one can extend on reflection to several other classes of phenomena; and this is very instructive.

It appears to me that Monsieur Demolins has overlooked one point, viz., that the greatest stumbling-block for his reforms are the mothers.[1]

Notwithstanding all the idealising of "The Mother" in the whole modern literature, the hard word must be spoken. It is the selfishness of the mothers, very wrongly called "motherly love," which surrounds their children with every kind of precaution; which tries to eliminate all chances of evil from them; which wishes to keep them always under their wings, and, moreover, likes to display the success of their darlings in school: it is this hardly disguised selfishness which breeds a race that is void of all enterprising spirit. Every one who has observed a large English family must have been surprised by the appearance of coldness and indifference with which the English mother bids farewell to her children, and says "goodbye" in the same simple manner to one son who leaves for Australia as to another who is only going to Eton. Therefore, if the English have such a success with their education, a great deal is due to the English mother.

I am very sorry to state that the weakest, and most superficial, point in Monsieur Demolins' book is the chapter which treats of school education. Not so much because he makes untrue observations, or draws wrong conclusions, but because, speaking about German schools, he confines himself to an analysis of the notorious speech, which the German Emperor delivered at the Congress of 1890, a speech which, even in Ger-

[1] A point which has not escaped the attention of the author of "Emlohstobba," *vide* pp. 31, 41-42, 174.

many, is no longer considered a serious one by any expert schoolmaster, at least so far as its positive part is concerned; and because he does not do them justice when he treats, in the preface to the second edition, of the *apparent* superiority of the Germans.

There is nothing to say against his thesis that Imperialism—that is the principle of the all-powerful, paternally supervising State authority—necessarily must become, in the long run, for the Germans a cause of decline and decay. But the author overlooks the fact, that the German learns in his school two valuable things, (1) to work, resolutely, steadily and systematically, and in a quick *tempo* without loafing, and (2) to have respect for exact knowledge in every direction, even the theoretical. This last quality accounts for the fact that nowhere more than in Germany is the scholar the right-hand man of the manufacturer, and it is owing to this fact (as I have been told by able experts) that German industry has raised itself to its present superiority, which makes even England so uneasy.

And how does Monsieur Demolins proceed when he speaks about the English schools? Does he follow his own principles and methods, and does he give an objective and complete account of these schools? Nothing of the kind. Probably because he would have been obliged, in that case, to state that there is nothing so conservative and mediæval as the two English Universities with their "annex colleges." He only speaks about two boarding schools, one Dr. Reddie's, of whose exterior appearance we have an attractive description, the other his disciple Badley's, both products of quite recent date, and therefore not proper types of the average or usual English education, but on the contrary most interesting attempts at reform in England itself.

One sees that this is both one-sided and partial. However, the damage is not great, because it must be acknowledged that Monsieur Demolins admires in these schools exactly what is generally praiseworthy in English education. In these schools, however, these principles are brought into practice more systematically and more judiciously.

*　　　*　　　*　　　*　　　*

The above-mentioned Dr. Reddie is also the hero of the second work. "Emlohstobba" is nothing else than Abbotsholme reversed, and is the name of the country place in Derbyshire where Dr. Reddie founded his school.

Dr. Lietz, a talented disciple of Rein of Jena, who has been working in Abbotsholme for some time, draws a most enthusiastic picture of it. Whoever may be anxious to know more details about it can consult his work, which completes, in a most successful manner, the work of Monsieur Demolins.

After having spoken so extensively about the latter, I cannot permit myself to speak in detail about Dr. Lietz's work. I only want to state that the description which he gives of Abbotsholme and also the various beautiful autotypes,[1] are sufficient to make one's mouth water.

Abbotsholme is a perfected Noorthey, which, as the reader may know, was founded by the illustrious de Raadt, on English principles, and is continued in the same spirit by the present director, Dr. Lely. Abbotsholme, like Noorthey, is only approachable by boys of well-to-do parents on account of the high fee, and this reduces a little the social importance of these experiments.[2] But Abbotsholme is not a refuge for the spoiled children of rich people, who could not succeed elsewhere, which Noorthey certainly was, at least for some time; neither does it cram for any University or other examination as Noorthey, compelled by circumstances, still does. (Which means, in this case, compelled by Dutch mothers and Dutch customs.)

The description of Abbotsholme fills, after all, only one-third of the book. The two other parts contain (1) A very severe criticism of the school system now existing in Germany, called by the author Unterrichtsschule, and (2) an explanation of the wished-for school of the future, which he characterises as Erziehungs-schule.

The first of these parts gives us the impression that we ought not to imitate the Germans. It is not all gold that glitters there either. Especially what Dr. Lietz says about the pernicious influences which the German youth is exposed to outside the school, and against which the school does nothing (except make absolutely impractical police regulations), has been confirmed to me from several sources.[3]

When one reads what the author writes (on pp. 125–127) about the Leaving Examination in Germany, that the candidates have to be rompted and dragged through by the examiners, and that so many are in a deadly fright the while, one is inclined to ask if our Dutch examinations, notwithstanding all the defects, so masterfully pointed out by Dr.

---

[1] Which, though entirely independent of those of Monsieur Demolins, confirms them in every point. But it is interesting to notice how different the Frenchman is from the German in his descriptions. The latter cannot leave off theorising and demonstrating, especially when he mounts his hobby horse: compare "Emlohstobba," pp. 51, 60 with an article by the same author in Rein: *Aus dem pädagogischen Universitäts seminar*, Heft vii. pp. 86-152.

[2] *Vide* "Emlohstobba," pp. 39-40.

[3] *En passant* I may quote here that for these reasons Dr. Lietz is a vehement antagonist of beer. He addresses many hard words to his colleagues on account of their devotion to their national drink.

van Berkum in this Review, are not practically better, or rather, I should say, less unsatisfactory than the German.

Taken all in all, the accusations of Dr. Lietz confirm the verdict of Monsieur Demolins. Germany must decay if it does not alter its system of education betimes. But, at the same time, we Dutchmen must learn from this—if, at least, we choose to open our eyes—that we run exactly the same risk.

In the last part the author sketches what he hopes for the future, and mentions the ways and means to attain his aim. This chapter is of especial interest to teachers.

The author emphasises very rightly that the reason why the new Erziehungs-schule must take the place of the old Unterrichts-schule is that it has become an impossibility in modern life to divide instruction and education between the school and the family in such a way that the school undertakes to instruct and the family to educate. The family cannot do it any longer, and therefore the school must both instruct and educate. This is a reality, and sentimental exclamations are of no use against inexorable facts.

Reader, we have chatted together a little about these two books, but I did not want to write a criticism which would exonerate you from reading them. Therefore set to work, teachers in higher and lower schools, club together, if necessary, and buy these two books; read them diligently and discuss them amongst yourselves. But beware of one danger, to which I must draw your attention. Do not try to find in these books arguments for pet ideas which, in reality, have nothing to do with educational questions. That would be the best means to render abortive a salutary movement. There is nothing that impresses us more favourably in Abbotsholme than the absence of all doctrinaire and sectarian views.

That this danger is not an imaginary one, Dr. Lietz himself proves. Abbotsholme is not a school for boys and girls nor, like Cempuis,[1] a nursery of fads and wild experiments, *Sapienti sat.* Hear what the Director himself writes: " Every nation, as every individual, must go to pieces if it isolates itself, and works only for itself. Germany never could do this, for she has ever been the Heart of Europe. We English dare never more attempt it. We are no more insulated inhabitants upon a few islands in the Atlantic. We have become citizens of an Empire which encircles the whole earth. But an alliance between Germany and England alone would not suffice. Both nations must attempt to combine as

[1] This was a school in the neighbourhood of Paris which had to be closed —TRANS.

far as possible, French imagination and power of lucid expression and German deductive thought, organising power, and heartiness, with English inductive thought, self-control, strength of will, and power to observe and apply."

What do you say to this, my Nationalist friends? Yet Dr. Lietz, who has lived in this school, still dreams of a *national education*, of a Pan-Germanism, &c.; he wishes to follow his Emperor, this *jugendlicher Held*, this Pedagogue on the Throne, who, for instance, expects from the school that it shall furnish *soldiers for him* to combat the social Democracy. "*Um nichts in der Welt möchten wir darum unsere militärische Erziehung missen*," p. 184.

Is not this typical?

But neither has Mr. Jules Lemaître grasped this feature. In his critique upon Demolins' book he began his famous attack upon the ancient languages, yet the latter did not afford any pretext for his attack, for Latin is taught even in the ultra-modern Abbotsholme, which educates for all careers and accordingly does not train (cram) for any special one. If it was the intention of Mr. Lemaître to distract attention from the main point, then he has attained his end; the discussions about Monsieur Demolins' work, which were at first so lively, are now silenced, while those about the dead languages are still increasing.

I hope that we shall follow another course in Holland, because the question of the dead languages, however important it may be, is not the vital question, and it is a mistake to believe that when the dead languages (or, at least, Greek,) are removed, "tout sera pour le meiux dans la meilleure des éducations."

When one discusses, in a lofty spirit, only the principal question—how to re-organise our national education so as to produce once more a strong, enterprising nation, sparkling with life—then mere questions of "classical" education will be reduced to their right proportions and will settle themselves.

Dr. J. H. GUNNING, Wzn.
Ex-Rector of the Gymnasium at Zwolle, Holland.
Privat docent in Pedagogics, Utrecht.

Jena, *September*, 1898.

Some Weighty Criticisms

NOVA SKOLA.

By K. P. POBYODONOSTSEFF, author of *The Reflections of a Russian Statesman.*

Moscow, 1898.

A Russian sympathiser, Mr. V. V. Sokoloff, has kindly sent us the following translation of the Preface to the above book, which is, he says, creating a great sensation in Russia. This is both on account of its contents and on account of the exalted position of the author as Procurator of the Holy Synod of Russia, and tutor of the late Emperor Alexander III.

THE PREFACE.

Last year (1897) there was pubished in Paris a book by M. Demolins : *À quoi tient la supériorité des Anglo-Saxons ?* As this book dealt with the most important questions of social order, all civilised peoples in Europe turned their attention to it, and the book ran through many editions.

The greater part of this book was devoted to the consideration of the instruction and education given in French and English schools. But, even after the publication of this book, the author went on to discuss the school question in the periodical *La Science Sociale,* of which he is the Director.

The increasing importance of the school-question in all countries, and particularly in Russia, urges us to furnish some account of the writings of M. Demolins for the benefit of Russian readers. These we have taken from the above-mentioned book and the above-mentioned periodical, *La Science Sociale.*

There is no doubt that the organisation of schools after the model of the English schools described may not suit all classes of society, every social grade or every purse.

Russia, in particular, possesses, less than any other country, the conditions under which could be put into practice the principles of these English schools.

But the author's critical examination of the French system of school education, and of the methods adopted by The New School Abbotsholme, ought, of course, to be taken into consideration by professional teachers and by all friends of popular education in Russia.

It is difficult not to agree with the author when he complains that our school system takes but little notice of the needs of the child's soul, while organising the school in accordance with abstract principles and from the point of view of teachers, professors, and officials ; and also when he tells us of the teacher's lack of moral influence when he deals with his pupils as a mere mass, mechanically hearing their lessons.

From his observations in a country which has a much better system of education, the author brings forward the old maxims which we have either forgotten or think no more about. (1) No instruction can be successful, but must be dead, if it does not, all the time, arouse in the pupils a lively interest in the subject-matter, and train the will to do honest work. (2) Knowledge is useless unless it is accompanied by practical skill; it can only become real and produce good results when it is based upon practical experience and proved by practical application.

THE MOVEMENT TOWARDS THE REFORMATION OF THE SCHOOLS OF EUROPE.

By the REV. P. A. SMIRNOFF, M.A., *President of the Education Department in Petersburg.*

The New School urges masters to awake in their boys a friendly feeling towards foreign nations, so that the different peoples may develop an interest in each other. It urges them to awake and strengthen in the boys a frank and open character.

It gives the teachers valuable hints how to prevent the growth in the young of an inclination to double-dealing and telling lies.

It tells them how to act so as to accustom the boys to use their own brains to solve the problems set, without having recourse to copying answers from their schoolfellows, a practice often carried on in our schools to the great injury of the work.

It tells them how to proceed so as to develop, alongside with the mental culture, the growth of a high character and of a will firmly directed towards the good.

Most valuable are the methodical directions, given in The New School, which relate to the instruction in the native tongue as well as the ancient and modern languages, and other subjects. By means of these methods we could avoid the extremes which our schools have reached, where the instruction has become highly complicated, and trusts solely to the pupils' memory.

The New School gives most useful advice regarding the preservation of the boys' health, and the harmonious development of all their powers, spiritual as well as bodily; so that they may enter life sufficiently developed in mind and heart, possessing the knowledge how to attack any work assigned them, and possessing bodily powers which have been strengthened but not overstrained, so that they remember with affection the school which gave them their education.

LA VÉRITÉ SUR "L'ÉDUCATION NOUVELLE."[1]

Le volume que M. Ed. Demolins intitulé "l'Éducation nouvelle"[2] continue à avoir un grand succès de lecture et ce qu'on est convenu d'appeler une bonne presse. Cependant cet ouvrage n'a d'autre mérite que de vulgariser certaines notions pédagogiques qui ne présentent en elles-mêmes aucune nouveauté, et d'être le prospectus étendu de la future école des Roches, près de Verneuil, France. M. Demolins traite très habilement un sujet tout d'actualité, et, grâce à la forme engageante et franche de son livre, le public passe sur les confusions de fond sans les soupçonner, disons même en partageant les inconséquences de l'auteur. En effet, dans un ouvrage antérieur, intitulé "A quoi tient la supériorité des Anglo-Saxons," M. Demolins avait déjà soutenu avec bonheur une thèse très prenante par la forme, mais sujette à caution quant au fond.

Si c'est un art méritoire que de présenter en un tout harmonieux des matériaux disparates, nous devons féliciter M. Demolins d'y avoir réussi. Ces félicitations, nous n'hésitons pas à les lui accorder. Non pas que sa méthode soit bonne, mais il s'en est servi pour faire de bonne propagande. On ne saurait répandre trop d'idées fécondes dans ce qu'on appelle le "grand" public.

En prenant la plume, M. Demolins a présupposé chez lui-même une connaissance exacte et complète de l'éducation que reçoivent en Angleterre les jeunes garçons des classes dirigeantes. A condition de n'y pas regarder de trop près, nous accédons volontiers à cette prétention. Mais M. Demolins mérite moins de confiance lorsqu'il invite ses lecteurs d'abord à admettre d'emblée la supériorité des Anglo-Saxons, et ensuite à l'attribuer à l'éducation que reçoivent les classes dirigeantes. Il tombe même tout à fait dans le sophisme lorsque, poussé par son désir d'acclimater en France l'éducation anglaise, il se saisit avidement d'une éducation dite "nouvelle" qu'il a découverte en Angleterre, et présente cette éducation "nouvelle" comme l'essence de l'éducation anglaise. M. Demolins ne

[1] *La Suisse Universitaire*, Revue Mensuelle de l'enseignement secondaire et supérieur. Rédaction : Chemin Malombré, 14. Genève. IVe Année, No. 7, Avril, 1899.
[2] *L'Éducation nouvelle ; l'école des Roches*, par Edmond Demolins.

s'est pas aperçu qu'une éducation baptisée en Angleterre du nom de nouvelle, peu de temps avant ses voyages d'étude dans ce pays, ne pouvait que différer de l'éducation anglaise courante, à moins que cette épithète ne fût qu'un leurre.

Aussi, tout en louant chez M. Demolins l'excellence des intentions, et l'excellence de la cause dont il s'est fait l'avocat, tout en nous rangeant parmi les partisans les plus convaincus de l'éducation "nouvelle," que nous avons été l'un des premiers à recommander aux pères de famille anglais, nous devons aux lecteurs de la *Suisse universitaire* de remettre, dans la mesure où nous le pouvons, les choses au point.

D'après ce qui précède, on voit que, dans l'ouvrage de M. Demolins, le titre et le livre ne font pas un. Il faut distinguer le livre d'avec son titre si l'on ne veut par procéder, comme l'auteur, par voie de confusion.

Par la publication de son ouvrage antérieur sur la supériorité des Anglo-Saxons, M. Demolins avait suscité chez certains de ses compatriotes un état d'esprit auquel on peut attribuer la popularité de son second volume. M. Demolins a tiré parti de cet état d'esprit pour appliquer à l'éducation sa thèse favorite. Aussi, autant l'idée qu'il se fait de la supériorité des Anglo-Saxons est exagérée, autant les conséquences qu'il en tire pour la pédagogie sont-elles entachées d'erreur.

Entendons-nous. M. Demolins n'est pas dans une erreur absolue. Il ne se trompe que relativement.

En effet, attribuer la supériorité des Anglo-Saxons, laquelle, sans être entière, est incontestable sur certains points, au système d'éducation de leurs classes dirigeantes, c'est intervertir l'ordre des choses. Car leur supériorité s'est manifestée avant qu'ils possédassent une éducation nationale : celle-là a commencé à s'affirmer nettement sous le règne d'Elisabeth ; celle-ci n'a reçu qu'au siècle dernier la forme qu'admire M. Demolins. Les jeux qui en sont le trait distinctif ne sont pas autochtones, le livre qui l'a inspirée—autant qu'un livre peut inspirer des faits—est l'*Emile* de Rousseau. L'éducation dite anglaise a été indigène en France jusqu'au temps de la Réformation. C'est la St-Barthélemey, c'est l'exode des protestants, c'est la monarchie absolue, c'est la Révolution, c'est l'Empire qui, par autant de degrés, ont amené l'extinction complète de cette éducation. La France la retrouvera facilement si elle a la sagesse de le vouloir.

Bref, M. Demolins est dans le vrai quand il signale la supériorité *acquise* des Anglo-Saxons. Il est dans le faux lorsqu'il attribue cette supériorité, vis-à-vis des Français, à une éducation spécifiquement anglaise, et, dans la mesure où son livre procède de prémisses mal posées, les conclusions en sont boiteuses.

M. Demolins—nous l'avons indiqué plus haut—pèche surtout par l'exagération.

Il porte aux nues la valeur morale du système anglais. Admettons avec lui—puisqu'il le veut—que le système français conduise l'élève au mensonge. En bonne logique il ne s'ensuivra pas que le système anglais abolisse le mensonge, ou déracine mieux qu'un autre le penchant au mensonge. A la pratique, on découvre que le principe d'autorité qui est à la base du système anglais est un principe infiniment moins formel qu'en France. Les occasions de mensonge explicite sont donc infiniment moins fréquentes. D'ailleurs nous n'avons pas trouvé, au cours d'une longue expérience pédagogique, que les jeunes Anglais respectent la vérité mieux ou autrement que les jeunes Suisses ou les jeunes Allemands. Il est même dans le caractère anglais de ne pas crainde les accommodements avec la vérité. Maîtres et élèves, en ceci, sont les uns et les autres ce qu'en termes de convention on appelle " un peu jésuite." Ces accommodements ne sont pas nécessairement chez eux un signe de bassesse, témoin l'adage *it takes a gentleman to know when to tell a lie* (un galant homme seul sait mentir à propos).

Cependant, malgré ces tempéraments, il y a en Angleterre autant d'indiscipline parmi la jeunesse qu'ailleurs, une tendance passionnelle pour le moins aussi forte (qu'on réfléchisse un instant aux suites d'une alimentation très échauffante et d'une culture physique intense) ; une disposition au pari certainement plus prononcée qu'ailleurs (conséquence du développement excessif et *voulu* des instincts sportifs) ; un penchant à la boisson qu'un professeur d'université n'a que trop souvent l'occasion de déplorer.

Et si, au point de vue de l'instruction, on a pu appeler le bachelier ès-lettres moyen de France un " prodige de néant," on ne fera aucun tort à l'Anglais de grade correspondant en l'englobant dans la même condamnation.

M. Demolins s'exagère aussi les avantages d'une culture physique *intense* pour la jeunesse des écoles. Elle produit beaucoup de jeunes gens au corps trop long et à l'ossature grêle. Ces jeunes gens, en Suisse, seraient pour la plupart déclarés inaptes au service militaire. Ils ne seront que par exception des hommes forts et endurants. Dans l'alpinisme, où nous avons fréquemment pu nous livrer à des comparaisons intéressantes, nous n'avons constaté en faveur des Anglais aucune supériorité sensible. En général les Anglais n'aiment pas et supportent mal la marche. D'ailleurs la taille du soldat est chez eux en décroissance marquée, et leurs journaux se sont occupés sérieusement, ces derniers temps, des résultats plutôt alarmants des statistiques scolaires concernant la santé et le développement physique des enfants de la bourgeoisie. Enfin l'esprit d'initiative, le goût de l'indépendance qu'inculquent les sports scolaires n'a pas toute la portée morale qu'on croirait. Nous lisions l'autre jour dans les colonnes du *Spectator* que sur cinq Anglais il y en a un dans l'administration, et nous savons d'ailleurs que si le socialisme d'Etat n'est pas né en Angleterre, le peuple anglais a en somme l'esprit machinal, routinier et apathique.

Sous ces réserves, nous ne faisons pas mystère de notre admiration pour l'éducation anglaise. Elle a réussi à tirer de l'*internat* tout le parti qu'on en peut tirer. C'est un très beau et très incontestable titre que les pédagogues anglais se sont acquis à l'estime publique.

D'autre part, n'oublions pas que pour dépasser, et de beaucoup, les Anglais, il suffirait, sur la base de l'*externat*, qui est la nôtre en Suisse, de faire trois choses : 1° Attacher à chaque collège une campagne ou terrain accidenté avec eau courante où les écoliers se donneraient libre carrière toutes les aprèsmidi de trois heures à la tombée de la nuit. 2° Faciliter à notre jeunesse, sur ce terrain, toutes les occupations manuelles, sportives, agricoles, industrielles pour lesquelles les enfants ont un goût naturel. 3° Implanter chez eux le sens de la hiérarchie, les amener à se donner républicainement des chefs responsables envers les autorités de tout ce qui se passerait dans ces " domaines scolaires " où les maîtres proprement dits n'auraient accès qu'à titre d'amis et de conseillers.

Les propriétaires de biens-fonds qui lègueraient à l'Etat, dans le voisinage de chaque ville, un domaine destiné à la jeunesse des écoles, seraient les bienfaiteurs de leur pays, des philanthropes selon le cœur de Pestalozzi. Ils auraient fait, pour l'intronisation parmi nous de l'éducation "nouvelle," la seule chose que le corps enseignant, avec l'appui de l'Etat, ne puisse pas accomplir par lui-même.

En effet, l'éducation "nouvelle," que M. Demolins confond si volontiers avec l'éducation anglaise, serait réalisée dans ses traits essentiels par l'institution des "domaines scolaires," complétée par certains changements à apporter dans l'organisation de nos collèges et gymnases.

Ce que M. Demolins ne sait pas, ou feint de ne pas savoir—car, vis-à-vis des Français, la distinction pourrait nuire à l'efficacité de son plaidoyer—c'est que l'éducation " nouvelle " a été conçue pour corriger certains défauts criants inhérents au système anglais.

Elle a pour but : 1° d'appliquer en Angleterre les principes pédagogiques élaborés en Allemagne et en Suisse ; 2° de modifier la vie de l'internat anglais dans le sens de la vie de famille, telle que les collégiens d'Allemagne et de Suisse la connaissent sous le toit paternel ; 3°

d'affranchir, si possible, les jeunes internes des désordres sexuels dont l'internat est la cause ; 4° de ramplacer en une certaine mesure le sport proprement dit, qui tend à avilir, à énerver et à corrompre certaines natures, par des occupations plus intelligentes telles que les travaux manuels, agricoles, industriels, la connaissance de la nature acquise en plein air, etc. ; 5° d'enseigner les choses avant les mots, les sciences avant les langues, les langues avant la grammaire, les langues modernes avant les langues anciennes ; 6° de pratiquer, en tout enseignement, les méthodes intuitives et directes ; 7° de donner pour pierre d'angle à l'éducation morale l'action *libre, volontaire* et *naturelle* de l'élève.

On voit que cette éducation " nouvelle " est tout simplement une synthèse pratique des meilleurs principes éducatifs connus. La pédagogie de Rousseau et de Pestalozzi y verse ce qu'elle a de meilleur et l'anglaise y fait apport de son principe fondamental : la communauté scolaire autonome. . . .

Pour terminer, expliquons brièvement où " l'Education nouvelle " prit naissance. Il y a environ quinze ans, le hasard des relations sociales entre célibataires groupait, à Edimbourg, quelques jeunes novateurs et sociologues sous l'influence du professeur Patrick Geddes, dont l'esprit tout à fait original s'était fortement imprégné des idées sociologiques sorties de l'idée-mère du transformisme, en Angleterre, en France et en Allemagne. Le groupe ainsi formé n'a cessé depuis lors de se recruter dans le milieu ambiant et s'est affirmé par des œuvres et des institutions d'une valeur positive. De ce groupe est sorti M. Cecil Reddie, docteures-sciences d'Allemagne, versé dans la science pédagogique telle qu'on l'intend en Suisse et en Prusse, mécontent de la pédagogie anglaise, telle qu'au collège il l'avait d'abord subie et ensuite pratiquée lui-même.

Des méditations du Dr. Reddie et de ses consultations avec d'autres, sortit ensuite, armé de pied en cap, le programme de la " Nouvelle Ecole " à Abbotsholme, dans la vallée de la Dove, sur les confins des comtés de Derby et de Stafford. Ce programme était à la fois le plan d'études, le manifeste et le prospectus d'un institut fort bien conçu, correspondant exactement aux idées mûries par son auteur et présentant des garanties tout à fait sérieuses de succès financier. L'institut pédagogique d'Abbotsholme fut bientôt suivi de celui de Bedales dans le Surrey, puis de celui du Dr. Lietz à Pulvermuhle près d'Ilsenbourg en Allemagne, et enfin de l'école des Roches en France. Mais comme ces instituts pédagogiques—qui se prêtent admirablement aux explosions d'enthousiasme des publicistes—ne sont après tout que des produits d'exception d'une application générale difficile, nous avons de la peine à comprendre que M.

Demolins attende de leur introduction en France la régénération des Français.

Néanmoins, la variété des types d'institutions scolaires étant une force précieuse pour un pays, et le type en question s'accordant très bien avec les prédispositions naturelles des jeunes Suisses, nous serions heureux que le Dr. Reddie trouvât des imitateurs parmi nous.

F.-F. Roget.

26. GARDENING AND GEOMETRY. (*Spring, 1896.*)

Copyright.

CHAPTER XVI.

"Educational Ideals and Methods."

1897.

CHAPTER XVI.

CONTRIBUTIONS TO THE ORGANISATION OF A NORMAL TERTIARY (HIGHER SECONDARY) SCHOOL.

IN January, 1898, we commenced the publication of our Experimental Results in a Series, to which the present volume belongs.

No. 1 was "A Short Sketch of the Educational Ideals and Methods to be followed in a Normal Tertiary School, together with a Work-Plan and Report Form, constituting a Normal Program of Work for English Boys of 11 to 18 years of age, belonging to the Directing Classes, a Synopsis of Educational Science, and a form for recording the worth of each boy."[1]

Originally this was intended merely for a better Report Form. It was, in fact, the fifth we elaborated, the first having been printed in 1889. But, in the execution, we enlarged our aim and attempted to make, at one and the same time, a short epitome of Educational Science, in order to secure the sympathy and coöperation of the Parents and Homes in the School life and work. We expanded this still further to embrace a minute Analysis of the whole School Life and Curriculum, showing what

[1] George Allen, London. 1s. net.

in our view was the entire Field of Study which boys of the Directing Classes should traverse in their school career. We further developed the sheet to include a careful analysis of the various physical, mental, artistic, and moral powers, which such a curriculum would be able to develop ; and this we arranged in such a way, that, with a minimum of labour, the masters could estimate easily what standard the boys had reached. We will not attempt to enter into further details here, as the sheet itself is sufficiently clear. But having had it in practical use for nearly three years in its present form, we are able to say that it has been of enormous assistance in training the masters *what* to teach and *how* to teach, in training the boys to comprehend what the School life is intended to create, and in securing that parental coöperation, without which School and Home must remain antagonistic influences, with the unfortunate result that the unity of the boy's life is destroyed. As this harmony is the supreme aim education should have in view, we consider that from this point of view alone the sheet in question is worthy of public consideration.

We are quite aware that this form is capable of further improvement ; and we are constantly at work upon its development. Its main value is perhaps that it is the first attempt, we believe, ever made to present at one glance the whole system of forces acting on a schoolboy.

We print below the only two notices we have seen in the public Press. The first, taken from an English Educational Journal, exhibits a blank ignorance of its significance, whereas the second, written by an educational expert in Switzerland, pays us the high compliment of translating its main doctrines verbatim.

THE SCHOOLMASTER, *June* 4, 1898.

Form of Report for a Normal Tertiary School. By C. REDDIE, B.Sc. (George Allen. 1s.)

Prodigious ! This word escaped us. Wonderful ! followed. A sheet twenty-five inches by nineteen inches closely printed on both sides, the obverse containing a normal program of work for English boys of eleven to eighteen years of age belonging to the directing classes (of The New School Abbotsholme) ; a synopsis of educational science, and a form for recording the work of each boy, and the reverse a short sketch of the educational ideals and methods of the normal tertiary school. The parents are requested to study carefully the explanation of their boy's report, which explanation, we may observe, is a complete analysis of the means and purposes of a whole-sided education, and incapable of being understood by very few but professed educationists, and are informed that "from the analysis of practical life, education leads us to the synthesis of a theory, armed with which we return to practical life on a higher plane of existence." The very perfection of this report form is appalling. If all parents were schoolmasters it might be gratefully received. The instructions to H.M. Inspector suggest a yearly report to parents. Perhaps the educational authorities would like to see this perfect model ! We must give the compiler credit for a most painstaking production.

LES APHORISMES D'ABBOTSHOLME.[1]

[Reprinted by permission from *La Suisse Universitaire*, December, 1899.]

I.—La raison d'être de l'éducation est d'aider la jeunesse à se servir de ses yeux pour voir, de ses oreilles pour entendre et de son cœur pour comprendre. Enseignons donc aux enfants à tout apercevoir autour d'eux, non pas au hasard, comme lorsqu'ils sont laissés à aux-mêmes, mais d'après un ordre constant qui ne perdra jamais de vue le but suprême—l'élèvation du type humain par l'évolution harmonieuse de la personnalité toute entiére.

L'élève peut ne pas être conscient des influences qui façonnent son corps, son intelligence et son cœur. Mais on peut lui inspirer un vif

[1] "Voir : A short sketch of the Educational Ideals and Methods to be followed in a Normal Tertiary (Higher Secondary) School." By Cecil Reddie, headmaster of The New School Abbotsholme, with the coöperation of H. Lietz and G. H. Hooper.—London : George Allen, 1898. One shilling net.

sentiment de ce que sa vie devrait être et le rendre capable de vivre comme il le doit ; l'éducation se meut dans ses propres fins en entourant l'enfant de doctrines, en développant chez lui des aptitudes dont l'effet sera de le faire travailler avec elle à l'évolution qu'elle poursuit.

L'éducateur a pour première tâche de réunir autour de l'élève de bons matériaux, de lui préparer un milieu riche en bons éléments de vie. Ceux-ci nourriront la nature durant son épanouissement graduel. Ce milieu c'est l'*Ecole*. Tout dépend des matériaux dont elle est construite. L'Ecole se compose d'un Etat et d'une Vie ; que tous deux soient excellents, sinon tout est perdu.

L'éducateur a pour seconde tâche d'exercer les facultés de perception, d'enseigner à l'enfant à'observer la nature qui lui est extérieure et la nature qui est en lui, de lui donner la clef et du monde qu'est l'Homme et du monde des choses.

Mais l'enfant ne fera que peu de progrès s'il ne peut emmagasiner des empreintes de ses perceptions pour les reprendre à loisir, et y réfléchir. Aussi apprendra-t-il à se représenter sous une figure d'abord matérielle, ce qu'il aura vu ou éprouvé. Il se le représentera au moyen de tableaux, d'images, de sons, de dessins ; au moyen de l'écriture, de la langue, de la musique.

Mais cela est encore insuffisant. Les symboles extérieurs sont destinés à lui faciliter l'acquisition de symboles mentaux. Ceux-ci se transportent sans valise. Ils n'occupent pas de place. Ils sont indéfiniment multipliables, la volonté les appelle ou les écarte. En comparant, en rapprochant ses souvenirs, la jeunesse se fait des principes, des lois, des idées, un idéal, autant de forces qui grandissent, agissent, vivent de la vie de la jeunesse et en déterminent en retour la couleur, la saveur, la valeur sourtout. Si toutes ces opérations forment par leur succession une ligne ascendante vers la lumière et le bien, l'éducation de l'enfant est chose faite.

Au jeune homme que le hasard heureux de la naissance ou les institutions sociales appellent, s'il n'y forfait, à prendre place parmi les membres des classes dominantes, l'éducateur proposera un plan d'études qui le prépare à sa tâche. Pour un tel adolescent, l'histoire et la géographie sont les deux études maîtresses. La connaissance de l'Homme et de sa Maison, voilà le pavillon central auquel viendront s'adjoindre les autres sujets. Le langage est le premier des instruments utiles à l'étude de l'Homme et de la Nature. Mais la connaissance des langues pour les langues ne rentre pas dans le giron de la pédagogie. Celle-ci vise d'autres fins.

"Educational Ideals and Methods"

II.—L'Education soumet à une analyse la pratique courante de la vie, elle en concentre par voie de synthèse le meilleur, elle établit la théorie de ce meilleur et, sous le nom de pédagogie, en fait l'application à la jeunesse. Elle rend ensuite cette jeunesse à la pratique courante de la vie, après l'avoir *élevée* d'un ou de plusieurs degrés au-dessus de cette pratique.

L'écolier reçoit son éducation à la fois du milieu, de l'entourage préparé pour agir sur lui, et de forces dont l'action est intérieure.

Les influences du milieu sont celles qu'entretient le gouvernement de l'école. Elles découlent de l'autorité des maîtres, des règles et coutumes de l'école, du travail quotidien, de l'esprit de la communauté scolaire. De toutes les forces éducatrices extérieures à l'élève, les traditions de son collège sont les plus puissantes. Elles sont aussi les dernières à se former dans toute école, comme dans toute autre communauté humaine. C'est à les créer, à les diriger et à en assurer l'efficacité que le fondateur d'une communauté scolaire mettra tous ses soins. C'est à la qualité, à la nature de cet esprit particulier à son école que se mesurera l'aptitude pédagogique, l'originalité du chef, et que ses élèves se feront reconnaître dans la vie. Moins l'autorité du maître s'exerce par les voies directes, plus elle est pénétrante, forte et durable. Elever par l'influence subtile et presque inaperçue du milieu, agir sur le cœur par des affections que le cœur est à peine conscient de subir, c'est faire œuvre d'éducateur. C'est aussi toucher au point où l'action de l'entourage ne peut plus être distinguée du travail des forces intérieures.

Celles-ci n'ont pas leur source dans une tendance voulue imprimée aux écoliers par le gouvernement de l'école. Elles sont, par leur origine, humaines, personnelles, sociales. C'est d'abord la vie et l'exemple du maître, et l'exemple des camarades plus âgés. C'est l'attachement réciproque, les relations bonnes et franches entre instituteur et disciple. Ce sont les fêtes de l'école, ses réjouissances et solennités. Ce sont les cultes en commun.

L'*Education*, nous le répétons, *élève* l'homme. Elle envisage en lui l'être agissant et même l'artiste, car l'art est un acte. L'Instruction, par contre, *instruit* l'homme ; elle ne l'elève pas, elle l'équipe. On peut avoir reçu une bonne éducation sans avoir la moindre instruction.

III.—L'Instruction a trait aux facultés de penser et de connaître. Elle a pour but de faire naître et d'entretenir chez la jeunesse le ressort unique de tout savoir et de tout pouvoir : l'intérêt. L'Instruction nourrira la curiosité dont les enfants sont d'eux-mêmes portés vers la nature et la vie humaine, elle généralisera la curiosité, elle en assurera la santé, elle la dotera de puissance en présentant à la jeunesse un ensemble bien relié de sciences soigneusement triées. Et le choix de ces sciences sera fait de telle manière qu'elles ceignent les jeunes esprits d'un faisceau d'idées où le caractère trouvera force et rectitude. Car l'Instruction, en guidant l'intérêt de l'enfant dans les directions les plus diverses, arrache la jeunesse à l'oisiveté et lui apporte les moyens de formuler des jugements vrais et de bien agir, comme l'Education, en lui donnant de bonnes habitudes, en lui offrant de bons exemples, en lui procurant une bonne compagnie, le tout sous la forme d'une communauté bien ordonnée, d'une vie bien reglée, fomente en elle un vif désir de former ces jugements droits et vrais, de vivre cette vie juste et saine.

Ce développement de l'esprit par l'instruction, ce renforcement du caractère par l'education déterminent ensemble l'évolution de la volonté. Le jeune être sort de cette école fort, sûr de soi, même discipliné et moralisé.

IV.—L'Ecole combine l'éducation et l'instruction. Nous l'appellerons école secondaire, en nous rappelant que dans cette école se recrutent et se forment les classes dominantes de l'avenir. L'Ecole prend l'enfant pour en développer entièrement et harmonieusement toutes les facultés—corps, esprit et cœur—soit l'être physique, intelligent, moral et spirituel. Elle fait de luli l'être " vivant " par excellence, elle le façonne en un membre sain, raisonnable et utile de la société humaine.

Les écoles françaises et allemandes font porter leur effort sur le cerveau au détriment du corps et du cœur. Les écoles anglaises négligent la tête et le cœur dans leur zèle pour l'athlétisme. L'Ecole doit réunir en elle les mérites de ces tendances en les équilibrant. Rien n'est porté à son programme qui n'ait son but précis. Rien ne se passe chez elle qui ne soit employé au résultat suprême. Rien ne s'y fait qui soit inutile, et rien d'utile n'en est omis. Les méthodes particulières y concourent à la méthode générale.

On n'y perd pas une heure de temps. L'enfant s'y occupe toute la journée à des travaux variés ou à des récréations variées. Il échappe ainsi au vagabondage.

On y exerce toutes les facultés à tour de rôle. L'enfant n'y souffre jamais d'un excès d'effort—la fatigue—ni d'une insuffisance d'occupation—l'ennui.

La surveillance y est bonne. Elle enraie tout exercice excessif du corps (l'athlétisme), du cerveau (le surmenage), de la volonté (l'appétence), combattant ainsi dans ses causes l'épuisement physique, mental et moral. Elle supprime l'oisiveté, laquelle a sa source dans un manque d'occasions de travailler ou de jouer, et la mollesse, provenant d'un manque d'entrain pour le travail ou la récréation. Enfin, avec le secours de la méthode, la surveillance scolaire assure le morcellement des études en degrés adaptés à l'âge des enfants, imprimant au développement juvénile une marche plus régulière et éliminant du progrès toute fatigue.

V.—Les Etudes sont réparties en deux groupes, et dans chaque groupe les sujets forment un ensemble et sont réunis par l'enseignement.

Les sujets du premier groupe se rapportent à l'homme ; ce sont l'histoire, la musique, la langue, la morale, la religion. Ces sujets forment les humanités et l'enseignement n'en rompt point le faisceau.

Les sujets du deuxième groupe se rapportent à la nature ; ce sont la géographie, la physiographie, les sciences naturelles et expérimentales, la géométrie et les mathématiques. Celles-ci sout enseignées d'après leurs applications concrètes. Les sujets sont traités comme formant un tout.

Ces deux groupes, dont les parties sont disposées comme autant de rayons partant de l'idée centrale et y revenant, ont én point de contact par où ils se pénètrent mutuellement : la liason se fera entre eux par les affinités que la géographie et l'histoire ont l'une pour l'autre.

L'enseignement s'appuie sur les applications pratiques, sans rejeter les moyens théoriques. Il se donne hors de l'école aussi bien qu'en classe. Il fait usage, il est vrai, des livres et de la parole, mais avant tout il met l'élève en relations avec les objets réels.

Les études sont dominées par la pédagogie.

VI.—La Pédagogie scolaire, qui est dérivée de l'expérience et de la science, remplace la tradition, la routine et le zèle arbitraire. Grâce à elle, l'instituteur prend son bien dans tous les pays qui ont contribue à la créer. A elle nous devons le mobilier scolaire, le matériel d'instruction, les images et modèles, et surtout les méthodes. L'instruction, ainsi ménagée, coûte moins et rapporte davantage. A résultants égaux, il y a économie de forces, et un bénéfice est rendu disponible. C'est tout profit pour l'élève. Non seulement on lui évite de se fatiguer en pure perte, mais encore les forces ainsi épargnées contribuent à l'énrichissement de la vie.

La pédagogie ne s'en tient pas à présenter sous leurs symboles écrits ou parlés l'Homme, la Nature, les actes et les choses. Elle fait précéder ces symboles des objets eux-mêmes, ou au moins de leurs images et modéles, elle fait faire les actes que l'instruction décrit. Elle donne un enseignement méthodique, qu'elle dispense en "parts," dispose en " degrés," selon les règles physiologiques et psychologiques énoncées par Herbart et Rein. Elle enseigne les langues selon les lois de l'esprit. Elle fait enseigner la géographie d'un pays par un enfant de ce pays, l'histoire d'un peuple dans la langue de ce peuple, par un de ses représentants. Ainsi compris, ainsi pratiqué, l'enseignement devient une culture, les études sont un voyage sans fin, l'instruction est une porte ouverte sur la vie, l'éducation se fait en esprit et en vérité. En un mot l'Ecole se substitue aux écoles.

F. F. R.

27. THE NEW BUILDINGS, FROM THE NORTH. (*Winter, 1899.*)

Copyright.

CHAPTER XVII.

Schools and Projected Schools on Abbotsholme Lines.

CHAPTER XVII.

SCHOOLS AND PROJECTED SCHOOLS ON ABBOTSHOLME LINES IN ENGLAND, GERMANY, FRANCE, RUSSIA, SWITZERLAND, ETC.

As early as 1891 we had begun to plan a scheme whereby we hoped our New Type of School would in due course reproduce itself, as all healthy organisms tend to do, according to natural law. That is to say, when the parent School had reached maturity it would, we hoped, found other Schools.

Our first need was the founding of a Fore-School, where boys could be trained between seven and eleven, so as to be fit to enter Abbotsholme, or similar schools, on the completion of their eleventh year.

For this is the period of life for which there is at present in England no proper provision. Children between these two ages require to be taught largely by women and in company with girls. They ought to be well grounded in English, and have a simple, all-round education, connected with their own language and their daily life and surroundings. And if any other language be admitted, it should be French, but only at the completion of their ninth, or better, their tenth, year. We emphasise the need of a proper training in English, for as a matter of fact, the English do not know their own language, and this is one chief reason for the national inarticulateness and poverty of thought. It hampers the teaching of every subject, that English children do not know accurately the meaning of the commonest words. And I suppose even our so-called educated classes rejoice in the possession of a vocabulary of about four hundred words.

The early introduction of Latin is the main cause of this, and therefore Latin must be absolutely abjured. And for the same reason French should not come too early. To learn French sounds like going to a higher social sphere, and therefore some parents will always run after it. Let them understand, however, that in a regenerated England the command of English will be the chief path to success, when we have abolished the snobbish worship of scholastic veneer.

Up to the present time this project of a Fore-school has come to nothing. But at an early date we hope to see the first one in England opened by two of our former colleagues, who did excellent work at Abbotsholme, and have since made a special study of children of the ages in question,—Mr. W. Clifford Pilsbury and Miss Baker.

Our scheme for planting colonies, to which we referred also in Chapter X., had to be postponed, mainly because of the English dislike of method and system, and preference for competition.

It is always easier for ambitious assistant-masters, even when they pooh-pooh the School, to which they have attached themselves, and from which they are drawing livelihood and ideas, to set up a faithful copy as a rival institution, than to create a really new scheme. When this occurs, the School, which trained them, comes in for more sneers than gratitude. For it is at once easy to point out defects, and more politic if the object is purely selfish. But if our aim is national we cannot but deplore the weakening of the parent by a policy such as this. Such offshoots should not be premature, but should await the full maturity of the parent School.

This is a feature in the Woodard Schools which we cannot too heartily commend.

Although, then, this hope of ours has not been realised, we have, nevertheless, cause for satisfaction at finding that so many schools have been started, which owe their inception to our work.

Not only have some English schools adopted entirely, or partially, our general scheme, but several foreign schools have been established in frank and cordial imitation of our own. The first of these, and that most like Abbotsholme, is Dr. Lietz's school at Ilsenburg, with which we are in close alliance.

In France is the School of M. Demolins, who has had the rare courage to be willing to learn from France's so-called natural enemy, "Perfidious Albion." (We wish England would take the hint.) There are other schools projected in Russia, Switzerland, and elsewhere, of which no doubt more will be heard in a few years. We shall watch with interest their development, and hope they will be magnanimous enough, while improving on our imperfections, to remember that our faults have perhaps helped them as much as our merits; and that they will be generous enough to permit us *en revanche* to learn some day by actual observation how much better our work here may be done.

MODERN (*i.e.* RECENT) EDUCATIONAL EXPERIMENTS IN EUROPE.

Schools of the Abbotsholme Type.

(A Paper read at the International Congress of Women held in Westminster Town Hall, London, June 29, 1899.)

By Cecil Reddie, B.Sc., Ph.D.,
Headmaster of The New School Abbotsholme, England.

[Printed exactly as delivered.]

I HAVE been asked by the Committee of Arrangements of the International Council of Women to give you, in the space of fifteen minutes, some account of Recent Educational Experiments in Europe. More particularly I am to speak about Dr. Lietz's school at Ilsenburg in the Harz, opened in April last year, and about my own work during the past ten years at Abbotsholme. The whole subject is, I understand, to be dealt with from as broad and philosophical a standpoint as possible.

I must confess that I was rather appalled at the task thus set me, particularly as I received your kind invitation somewhat recently. I felt, however, that I ought to try and assist, in however humble a way, this important and significant Parliament of Women, and I was especially anxious to speak about the school of my friend Dr. Lietz, for in all my experience as an educator I never met a more attractive character,

Schools on Abbotsholme Lines

and never spent a more delightful year than the year he assisted me at Abbotsholme.

Fortunately my subject is less wide than might at first appear. Dr. Lietz's school and my own are in aims, methods, and organisation so similar that they can, for our purpose to-day, be, most usefully, considered as the same.

This identity is not surprising. Both schools abandon, and this in no half-hearted manner, the criminal absurdities perpetuated by prejudiced ignorance and stereotyped custom, which in all countries masquerades as the epitome of human wisdom, successfully manufacturing mental and moral imbecility. Both schools aim at combining all that is best in German and English education: German school-instruction with English school-life, German discipline with English spontaneity, German method with English initiative, German sense of duty to the State with English self-reliance. To aid this marriage of ideas, the two schools are intimately allied. We do not, of course, exchange our boys. As children have one home, so boys should have one school— their second home—and ought to remain in it from eleven to eighteen, not be sent from place to place, from teacher to teacher. School programs may be identical; schools never: for living beings can never be the same, and, in education, personal influence is supreme. Our boys, then, remain with us seven years in order to pass through the whole curriculum and live the whole life. To go elsewhere before the end would mean to interrupt their harmonious growth, dislocate their circle of thought, and render our whole scheme abortive.

But, in place of exchanging boys, we exchange masters. Only thus can we get foreign teachers who can enter into our life, and only thus can Englishmen learn at present the fundamental principles underlying the educator's art.

By mutual visits in vacation our two schools get nearly all they need of foreign influence. They realise the value of a foreign tongue when it unlocks the treasures of a new world, and reveals the wealth of another nation's culture. Especially is this true of the sister countries, Germany and England.

Thus, without losing our identity as members of a definite school community, we widen our horizon through happy intercourse with a similar miniature world abroad, physically, mentally, and morally a fit place of sojourn for the young and inexperienced.

I need not detain you long over projected schools in France, Russia, and elsewhere, upon the same lines, for, although conceived, they are not yet born. The best known of these, that planned by M. Demolins in France, naturally interests me much, because he has written about my own efforts with so much appreciation and eloquence, although, as he has never visited Abbotsholme, not always with entire correctness. It I do not altogether share his belief in "Anglo-Saxon superiority," or in Latin and Keltic degeneracy, and if I do not believe that the intellectual fogginess, frigid manners, and calculating selfishness of England are altogether preferable to the luminous thought, polished courtesy, and unpremeditated generosity of France, I none the less believe that France needs more of English free initiative, as I believe that England needs more of German social discipline and French intellectual clearness.

It is natural to suppose that by mixing French and English boys at school, each might imbibe the virtues, and none of the vices, of the other nationality. But this is not a plan which commends itself to me. I am not in favour of International Schools. They involve the fatal plan of moving boys, singly, or in batches, from one environment of men and things to another, during the most critical period of youth.

If you have followed my argument thus far, you will have guessed that I am equally opposed to our modern system of Preparatory Schools, which has quite upset the original English "Public" School system. A Fore-school, educating boys and girls together till eleven, violates no law of nature. But a scheme of education which moves boys, in the crisis of youth, at fourteen, from one school to another, can never be sanctioned by physiology. To go to a foreign school then would, of course, be worse.

French culture can, moreover, be brought into English schools through individual French teachers and through vacation visits to France. Indeed the day will come when no English master will be considered educated at all, unless able to speak and write English, French, and German; whether he know Latin or Greek or Hebrew, will not be even asked.

A school-staff thus able to absorb the culture of three civilisations, would soon infuse into English boys some of that world culture, the absence of which, at present, renders us unfit to govern adequately the vast Dominion which accident, rather than deliberate plan, has given us. All school-life should, however, rest fundamentally on the national life. Prolonged study abroad should come later, and should be recognised and encouraged by the University. But British universities are, at present, little more than provincial colleges, instead of being international seats of universal culture.

Meanwhile, M. Demolins' efforts to propagate on French soil foreign educational improvements ought to arouse sympathy among all who remember what we owe to the matchless intellectual services of France. England might with advantage follow his example and introduce at home the method and clearness that make France one of the most formidable powers of the world. When M. Demolins' school is actually alive, I hope to find practicable some measure of that coöperation with him, to which he has so cordially invited me; but it must be in the direction I have indicated above.

That our Abbotsholme type of school promises to become the type of the future seems plain if we may judge from the universal interest it has aroused,

Schools on Abbotsholme Lines

Personally I have been embarrassed by the mass of correspondence from all parts of the world—Siberia and Patagonia, New Zealand and the United States, not to speak of Europe—which has almost overwhelmed me. Even in old-fashioned England are to be found imitators. Some are so cordially and avowedly. Others have adopted detached bits of our program in silence and somewhat timidly, with one eye nervously watching Mother Grundy. Even the so-called "public" schools begin to doubt if their stereotyped arrangements are the epitome of educational perfection.

As you are to have a paper, I understand, on these developments in England, I need add no more, but will merely sum up what precedes by saying: This important movement proves that the old education and the old type of school are doomed.

What, then, is, in brief, the NEW?

For details I have no time to-day. For them I must ask you to read M. Demolins' *Anglo-Saxon Superiority*, first published in *La Science Sociale*, October, 1894; Dr. Lietz's *Emlohstobba*, 1896; and Mr. Stanley de Brath's *Foundations of Success*, also 1896. In these three books you will find much of our Abbotsholme life, presented from three different points of view, which are in the main those of France, Germany, and England.

It is very pleasant, especially after ten long years of toil, to find one's work appreciated. But there is a risk that critics may misapprehend the real ends in view, and unintentionally misrepresent the nature of the work described. I am, therefore, glad of this opportunity to make clear what, from my own standpoint, are the main ideas underlying our work at Abbotsholme, and I am glad in this to be able to associate myself completely with my friend, Dr. Lietz.

Having, however, no gift of eloquence, I trust this formidable and critical audience will pardon all shortcomings. Words, moreover, call up, after all, only the ghosts of things; and no life worth describing can ever be described adequately. In order to be understood, it must be lived.

It is impossible, in the time allotted me, to give you even an outline of our aims and methods. This I have, however, already published on a single sheet, showing at a glance the whole school life. May I venture to direct your attention to it? The name is "Educational Ideals and Methods for a Tertiary School," published by George Allen. As Dr. Lietz was associated with me in the work, it shows the close accord between his views and mine, and between his school at Ilsenberg and Abbotsholme.

For my purpose now I will select a few of the most important points, and try briefly to make them intelligible.

There are in the population three classes—the millions, the thousands, the hundreds. For them three kinds of schools are needed. Our school is intended for the highest class—the class, namely, which teaches, organises and inspires—the social brain and heart. (See *An Educational Atlas*, London, Allen.)

For all classes the education must be divided clearly into two stages :—

1. We have to form the *man or woman*.
2. We have to form the *citizen*.

To form men and women the education must be general.

To form the citizen it must be special.

General education is the work of schools.

Special education is the work of universities.

The length of the education differs for each class.

For the directing class the general education should last till 18.

This education up to 18 has three stages—from 3 to 7, kindergarten ; from 7 to 11, fore-school ; and from 11 to 18, school.

It is the last stage—the education of the directing class between 11 and 18 in the so-called tertiary school that we have chosen. Up to 11 boys and girls should be educated together, and mainly by women. After 11 boys should be trained by men, girls by women. Co-education during this period is unnatural and dangerous. After 18 boys and girls should mix at the university precisely as they would in ordinary life and under similar limitations. As the type improves the limitations will slowly widen.

The education between 11 and 18 should be *one* school only. Boys should not go, during the crisis of adolescence, from one school to another.

The preparatory school system is of recent and haphazard origin, and is pedagogically unsound, and to have lads, all of nearly the same age, massed together to the exclusion of younger and weaker boys, which is now so customary in England, reminds one of the French *lycée*. The effect is to accentuate competition and to produce roughness. To have juniors to protect refines the seniors; to have seniors to respect and imitate stimulates the juniors. Worship of the male type is the natural hero-worship of adolescence, and comradeship is the natural outlet for the affections among normal boys during this period. Like everything else, it needs careful direction or it may become morbid.

The tertiary school must not be so large as has lately become usual. It should hold about 100. This number one man can really direct. If it is larger, the school is divided into sets and cliques, or, at least, the unity is lost. Most English schools to-day of this class are overgrown, because they try to give special and general education together. If they are organised, the program and discipline is apt to be too rigid and mechanical, and the personal element disappears. If not organised thus, they remain a chaos. At the present time English boys require much more discipline —physically, mentally, and morally. In class and out of class this is of supreme importance. Germans are so disciplined in the street that they need perhaps less elsewhere.

A school of about 100 allows seven classes of about

fifteen each. Such classes can be properly taught without the neglect of any. The boy remains in each for one year, and in each, his studies, games, and occupations are arranged to suit his physiological and psychological development. The whole school and curriculum thus becomes a Living Educational Model.

Boys and girls all contain the active powers of one sex and the latent powers of the other. In boys must be developed the male powers of course chiefly, but also, in proper proportion, the female powers. In particular, we must develop in our boys not only will but love, not only memory but imagination, not only intellect but intuition, not only strength but grace. All the studies and the whole life of the school should aim at developing a harmonious unity. For instance, Nature should be studied, not merely as it was by Tyndall, but as it was by Ruskin. A boy should not merely gaze on men and things with the cold analytic eye of the scientist, but also with the glowing imagination of the poet. In this way he will always see the body and soul of things together. He will never feel any opposition between philosophy and religion. He will understand that philosophy arises from the analytic studies of the scientist, and that religion is the necessary creation of the poet. He will not muddle up the beautiful symbols of religion with the dry facts of history, but will draw life and inspiration from earth below and heaven above, from nature outside him and from his soul within.

Our curriculum observes the two fundamental

principles of instruction :—(1) There is a proper sequence or *Nach*einander, the work for one year resting on the work of the year before, and becoming the foundation for the work of the following year; and (2) all the work of the year in each class is interlocked in accordance with the principle of *Neben*einander, so that all the work forms really part of one subject, and the circle of thought grows harmoniously. All disconnected, scrappy information is avoided. In this *Neben*einander, or interlocking, we recognise that the studies connected with Nature—or Naturalistics—form one, and studies connected with Man—or Humanistics—form another minor circle, the two being associated respectively with mathematics and morals, and meeting where geography touches history.

As regards the way in which both Nature and Man should be studied :—The whole school serves as our living, working model ; the estate, or school kingdom, our book of geography, nature-knowledge, and mathematics ; the school life, our manual of history, art and morals ; the whole as our text-book of religion.

The passage of the boy through the seven classes represents the evolution of humanity.

The prefects in organising the juniors are learning to be fathers as well as directors of the national life.

The rewards and punishments employed are, as far as possible, the natural, inevitable outcome of the boy's own actions, accentuated only when it is necessary to overcome youthful obtuseness or obstinacy.

The whole place and life depict a happy, wholesome,

harmonious existence, in fact, shows what the world would be if under sane and rational government. When the boy leaves he has attained to a conception of the universe outside him and within him as a harmonious unity; and with that in his mind, and the love for harmonious life in his heart, he will be able to begin those special studies which are to fit him for a place in the community.

At the present day, above all, he is to be taught that social regeneration is only possible through education, and in particular that of the directing class. That they must aim not at climbing on to a snug perch above the weltering chaos of our modern life, but at battling with it until we have again social order. If boys are taught to work for the work's sake, their eyes will be not on the prize, but on the goal.

We do not wish them to aim at over-refinement, fastidious delicacy, affected culture, or even at the highest good, if this is to be basely purchased at the cost of others. We wish them simple, faithful, honest. We wish them to love sincerely without hypocrisy, to labour honestly without self-seeking. We wish them to be lords of their lives and givers of their lives, but particularly givers. The chief object we have in view is not success, as usually understood, but a new and higher type of men.

I have to thank you for your indulgence while I have essayed this impossible task of putting into fifteen minutes what could easily fill a large book.

The Outlook, *November* 26, 1898.

AN EDUCATIONAL EXPERIMENT IN FRANCE.

L'Education Nouvelle. By Edmond Demolins. Paris : Firmin-Didot.

M. Demolins is about to try an experiment to which we most heartily wish success. It appears that there is a widespread dissatisfaction in France with the results of the French system of education : it is too much centralised, too one-sided, aims at cramming the brain without training the intelligence, reduces all to a dead-level, neglects the moral and physical side of our nature. M. Demolins has been struck with the effect of English education in training character, and particularly with The New School Abbotsholme, and Bedales ; and he has conceived the idea of starting a French school on the same lines. The book before us sets forth his plan in detail, and gives an account of the English schools just mentioned. These schools claim to save, by a new method, fully half the time usually spent in learning Latin and Greek, and include in their curriculum not only the usual school subjects (together with a good many sciences), but also such things as gardening, building, wood-cutting, haymaking, farming and dairy-farming, carpentry, carving, and modelling.

A good portion of this book has little interest for us in England, except in so far as it shows the dissatisfaction of the French in a system which injudicious persons have urged us to adopt. But the methods of teaching recommended well deserve the attention of all interested in education. The author is not a deep thinker, it is true, and he falls into some of the usual fallacies. When he complains of the short period allowed in a school curriculum for French, he forgets that boys are learning French all the time they are learning Latin and Greek. It is well known that boys on a Modern Side in an English school, as a rule, know far less English than Classical boys, and can neither write nor speak correctly, even though they may give more time to English proper. The author also believes that Greek and Latin can be learnt by reading, without learning paradigms of grammar by heart. In this we are confident he is wrong, having tried the system in our own person with more than one language. But it is quite possible that the method he commends for beginners is right. This is to furnish them with translations in the earlier stages, and not make them learn declensions and conjugations at first ; these are to be hung on the wall in their sight for reference. By this means progress is more interesting and rapid ; pupils are able to read whole books at a time instead of scraps and snippets. The author also advocates, though less boldly, the use of conversation; and here we are confident he is right. We recommend this portion of the book to the attention of headmasters, though in the present lamentable dearth of able headmasters we doubt whether one will have the courage to try it.

We wish M. Demolins had studied the English public school proper. Those schools he describes seem to us to be admirably well adapted for small classes of boys, and for those who look forward to life in the colonies; the average boy would probably be very happy there, and would learn a great deal, though we doubt if the system will produce scholars or men of letters such as the public schools occasionally do produce. But, after all, the main end of education is to produce brave and honourable men; and this is achieved by almost all English schools.

PAEDAGOGISCHE BLAETTER, *im November*, 1898.
PREUSSISCHES ODER SAECHSISCHES SYSTEM?
VON PROFESSOR W. REIN IN JENA.

Je kleiner der Schulorganismus, desto paedagogisch wirkungsvoller wird er sein; je groesser, um so mehr Schwierigkeiten entstehen fuer die erziehliche Einwirkung auf die einzelnen. Vor allem wird es der Seminardirektor bedauern muessen, wenn er Massen regieren soll, wo seine Aufgabe in der Erziehung von Lehrern liegen soll. Dass diese in kleinerem Kreise, nicht abgezogen von der Verwaltung eines grossen Schulorganismus mit seinem unvermeidlichen Schreibwerk u. s. w., intensiver gestaltet werden kann, wird jeder mir ohne weiteres zugeben, wenn es auch vorkommen mag, dass besonders hervorragende Direktoren alles umspannen koennen, ohne dass die besondere Aufgabe darunter leidet.

Auch hinsichtlich der Behandlung der Schueler bietet das saechsische System gewisse Schwierigkeiten. Herr Oberschulrat Israel will das nicht gelten lassen, und ich kann es ihm wohl glauben, dass er die Schwierigkeiten zu ueberwinden in der Lage war, aber auch hier wird er mir zugeben, dass das getrennte System eine Erleichterung bietet, die willkommen geheissen werden muss, da der Charakter der Behandlung und die Fuehrung der Zoeglinge dort und hier eine einheitlichere und damit wohl auch gleichmaessigere sein kann. Ebenso duerfte die leidige Internatsfrage damit einer Loesung entgegengefuehrt werden, wenn die

Abbotsholme

Fachschule als Externat, bei der Vorbereitungsanstalt das Internat zugelassen wird.[1] Denn ein gut eingerichtetes und in freiem Geiste geleitetes Internat ist von groesstem Segen fuer unsre Jugend. Den Veraechtern desselben wuenschte ich, dass sie eine Zeit lang Gelegenheit haetten, die Internatsanstalten zu *Abbotsholme* in Derbyshire, zu *Eton*, *Rugby* oder die zu *Ilsenburg* a. Harz (Dr. Lietz) kennen zu lernen. Ich glaube, sie wuerden von ihren Vorurteilen kuriert und wuerden sich nicht mehr gegen das Internat an sich, sondern gegen die falsche Form desselben wenden, die allerdings einem die ganze Einrichtung verleiden kann.

[1] Im Koenigreich Bayern ist es bekanntlich umgekehrt. Eine thoerichtere Einrichtung laesst sich allerdings kaum denken. Sie mag sich historisch entwickelt haben; aber gerade an diesem Beispiel sieht man recht deutlich, wie das, was ist, keineswegs immer das Vernuenftige ist, und dass die paedagogische Theorie recht hat, auf so verfehlte Entwickelung hinzuweisen.

28. THE SCHOOL BUILDINGS FROM THE SOUTH. (*Winter, 1899.*)

Copyright.

CHAPTER XVIII.

The New Buildings.

1899.

CHAPTER XVIII.

THE NEW BUILDINGS, 1899.

WITH the building of the new wing we arrive at what is practically the third foundation of the School. A full description of these buildings will be impossible here, and we will content ourselves by quoting an article from the School Magazine of Midsummer, 1899, which gives a brief outline of the present situation and policy of the School.

NEW DEVELOPMENTS.
[Reprinted from *The Abbotsholmian*.]

Now that the School Year 1898–9 is nearing its close, without, I am glad to say, our having had any illness to remind us that we were full to overflowing and had no sickroom, I take this opportunity to offer my very cordial thanks to the Abbotsholme Parents and Guardians for the great kindness and sympathy manifested to us during the whole of the very difficult crisis through which the School has unavoidably been passing.

I am, moreover, now able to give rather more precise information as to the time when the present Extensions may be expected to be ready for use.

Of course, as every one knows, nothing is more difficult

to control than building operations, and for that reason I have hitherto said little on the subject. But the marvellously favourable weather, which has hitherto attended the work, has enabled us to make such substantial progress, that the close of this Summer Term will witness the roofing in of the New Wing, notwithstanding the fact that, during the progress of the work, several large additions have had to be made to our building program, in order to insure a really first-rate result. For instance, the entire northeast wall of the Old Building was pulled down and rebuilt during the Christmas Vacation, which was the reason why I had to recommend, as a precaution, the postponement, for a week, of the boys' return at the beginning of the Spring Term.

If the good fortune, which has hitherto accompanied us, does not forsake us now, the building will come into partial use, I am assured, at the beginning of *September*, and will be entirely completed before Christmas.

I am anxious to celebrate an event, so important in the history of the School as this, in a becoming manner, which would not be possible unless all those interested in Abbotsholme were able to attend the Inauguration Ceremony. I should, therefore, feel obliged if the parents would kindly give me their opinion as to whether Midsummer Day, 1900, appears to them a satisfactory time for the Formal Opening.

We have a particular desire to have our festival upon that day, because we have, during the last few years, chosen the 24th of June as "Empire Day"—and upon this, our National Fête-Day, the School joyfully and solemnly recounts, "Lest we forget," the past glories of our Fatherland and Race, and the present duties and brilliant possibilities of our vast Empire, which already dominates one-third the Land and all the Sea.

We believe that our quiet work here is a Patriotic work; that in our humble corner, we too are helping build up an Empire fit to endure. We wish, then, the opening of this first portion of our carefully designed workshop for training Rulers to take place upon a day of such good omen.

It only remains for me to remark how fortunate we are in having the School at such a conjuncture, in so excellent a state, and under such exceptionally able and admirable Prefects, as has been the case throughout the last two years. It speaks well, moreover, for the spirit which has animated not only the Masters and Boys, but also the Servants of the School, that everything, during two rather trying and difficult years, has gone on with almost absolutely the customary quiet regularity. It is a proof that the discipline of the School is no mere fine-weather behaviour, but can be depended upon when the ship is shifting cargoes in mid-ocean. But for this admirable discipline, and the constant and willing help rendered by the boys themselves in maintaining it, the present revolution in our domestic concerns might have seriously impeded the ordinary work of the place.

But, in addition to our usual program, the boys have carried out some important works upon the Estate, such as constructing the Skating Pond, and completing the new Lower Garden. It must not, however, be imagined that the class-work has been neglected. There are many persons, little acquainted, I am afraid, with the trend of Modern Education, who suppose that Abbotsholme is a refuge for physical, mental, and moral imbeciles, a hot-bed of "fads" and "cranks." Nothing can possibly be more wide of the real facts. Abbotsholme is an Educational Laboratory for training men. The physique, the intelligence, and particularly the morals of the boys here will stand comparison with the products of even the very best schools in England. And as soon as the country abandons the discredited system of examinations, which test little else than the ephemeral memory of phrases, I have no doubt our boys will be estimated intellectually also at their real value. Even as matters stand, one of our number, who is by no means the ablest boy here, has recently passed into one of the Cambridge Colleges in the first class, and third on the list, after little more than a year's specialisation in the subjects required for that examination. This would not, of course, be a remarkable feat for a boy educated at the ordinary type of school which is organised nearly solely for this special purpose; but in our case, it is necessary to devote one year only to this specialisation, and it is satisfactory to find by experiment that under these conditions our boys can pass the ordinary tests.

I need not, however, emphasise this point, for everything in England and abroad is moving in the direction of the Educational aims and methods which we have earnestly striven to realise during our brief existence.

But, *ars longa, vita brevis*. We ought, then, I trust without absurd diffidence, as also without unbecoming self-congratulation, to look back upon our ten years here with modest pride and thankfulness at what we have been able to accomplish, and look forward to the New Chapter in our history, which will shortly open, with confidence, and with, if possible, a greater determination to perfect a school which has, we are told, "already inaugurated a new epoch in the history of Education."

The New Buildings

What, then, have we accomplished? We have gathered here a body of close on eighty persons, Ladies, Masters, Boys, and Servants, animated, I believe all, with a spirit of honest work and affectionate sincerity—virtues not, I fear, too prevalent in this luxurious, worldly and materialistic age. We have organised a small kingdom which, for our Educational purposes, it would be indeed difficult to match.

The one drawback which has hitherto trebled our difficulties and cramped all our usefulness—the lack of proper Buildings—this drawback, after five years of careful planning, we shall soon see removed, if not entirely, yet to a very large extent.

All this, then, we have accomplished in ten years. What may we not hope, therefore, to accomplish in the future, when at length so many obstacles will have been removed from our path?

With more space, our first need will be more boys. And for more boys I confidently look to the Abbotsholme Parents and Guardians. When I see coming here from single homes, not merely one boy, or even two, but three, four, five, and even seven of the same family, I cannot doubt the confidence of our Parents in our Curriculum, our Methods, and our Life.

But it is not enough to send us brother after brother, highly as we appreciate that. To enable all the boys now to do their best, we need, at a reasonably early date, a school of that definite size—ultimately about a hundred—for which our plans have been laid, and our Curriculum organised, for ten years past.

We neither need, nor desire, a too sudden rush of new boys. We would rather increase slowly and steadily, as has been our good fortune hitherto. Thus only can the new material get into proper touch with the old, and the old leaven the new thoroughly.

The New Wing will easily accommodate about another twenty-five or thirty. Is it too much to hope that the opening in January will bring us an increase of at least twenty? I am anxious that we should be able to reject all that are not up to our present excellent standard. But it is, of course, imperative that we should not have our new rooms empty long.

There is another reason for thus inviting assistance. As every one knows, the School has been written about (or "boomed" as the phrase is) in Germany, Russia, Holland, and particularly in France and French-reading countries, during the past few years, almost entirely, I may add, without our previous knowledge. The result has been countless foreign Press notices, and an avalanche of letters to me, from all parts of the world, asking for information and applying for the admission of boys.

I see no objection to admitting a few boys from foreign countries, especially when they are of exceptional ability, manners, and character. It awakens an English boy's ambition to have to emulate the exploits of outlanders. Moreover, I have found that the brighter brain of the German, Swedish, and French boy acts in a very salutary manner upon the somewhat dull Anglo-Saxon. The presence of foreigners promotes, moreover, international friendship and universal peace.

While, therefore, we shall willingly admit a few foreign boys of merit, we have not the slightest intention of letting Abbotsholme become a so-called "Cosmopolitan School," and of exchanging our carefully-trained elder boys for the elder boys of those foreign schools which have been, or

The New Buildings

are now being, established in Germany, France, and Russia, upon Abbotsholme lines. I have myself developed a scheme that will enable us to coöperate with that excellent school in Germany, which is under my friend and former colleague Dr. Lietz. But it is quite out of the question that our elder boys should spend abroad one of their last years at school, in exchange for similarly expatriated foreign boys of seventeen to eighteen. Such a scheme might possibly be of some value to foreign schools where our English school life is little known. They would thus get well-trained English seniors from good schools to become "Guides, Philosophers and Friends" to the juniors in the foreign schools. But I must say—though this may savour of British prejudice—that I am not prepared to exchange any Prefects of mine (save in rare and very exceptional cases) for boys of seventeen to eighteen taught in a foreign school but not trained for leadership. Their masters, trained as they are to teach admirably, can indeed help us to improve our pitiable English class-instruction, but their boys cannot take the place of English boys as Prefects.

Moreover, no English boy of the Directing Classes ought to leave school before eighteen. He cannot be properly educated if he does. If he afterwards goes abroad, it should be, not to a School at all, but to a University, Technical College, or whatever else their Specialistic Seats of Learning may be designated. Some of our boys have done this, and with success. But for boys to go at seventeen, for their last year, to a French or German school—this would be (as all schoolmasters, and even elder schoolboys know) for them to lose the most precious year of school life—the year of responsibility, the year of honourable influence as Prefect, the year in which all the teaching and living of their school days is brought to a final climax and the whole rounded off into completeness. I have already urged, for other reasons, reducing the school period by one year, to let boys leave at eighteen, instead of nineteen; but the period cannot be further curtailed without grave loss, both to the individual and to the school. For if the boys who have longest breathed the atmosphere of the place, and have most assimilated the best of its influence —if they are to be removed prematurely to inspire tone into some foreign school, who is to take their vacant place and look after their juniors and young brothers left behind, and keep up the tone of their English school? Surely not a body of foreign boys, however able and virtuous, who are strange to the local ways, strange to the boys, and strange to the national idiom and national ideals. It is obvious to any parent who understands English School Life, that such a scheme of exchanging boys is utterly impracticable, however charming in theory. I need not go into the question whether the exchange could take place at any earlier period of the school life, because English parents are never likely, save in exceptional cases, to entertain such a project. A boy cannot, moreover, in my view, belong to more than one school; and one of the most vital needs of English youths at the present time is *to remain in the same school for the whole period from eleven to eighteen*, instead of being transferred at the highly critical period of puberty into new surroundings among new people.

But it by no means follows that boys should never go abroad, or, if so, should go abroad, as is often the case at present, at odd times, without such journeys having any connection whatever with their school Curriculum. I

The New Buildings

have already suggested on our Term's Report Sheet [1] the advisability of our boys going abroad at certain periods, chosen to fit in with our French and German courses, because such visits stimulate interest in the Geography, History, Life, and Manners, as well as the Language, of the two chief cultural nations of Modern Europe : and I can conceive no better way of carrying out that proposal than to do what some thirty of us did last August. We visited the German Abbotsholme in the Harz, and all who went would, I am sure, be glad if they could go again. This summer, however, Dr. Lietz and his boys will visit Abbotsholme. Other parties might, of course, visit similar schools in France, when they are in actual existence, such as the school which is being planned by M. Demolins. But as said above, this is quite a different thing from exchanging boys for part of their school life. After all, valuable as are modern languages, especially when studied as we study them here, in connection with the Geography and History, the Life and Ideals of the respective nations, and not merely as Language apart from Life :—valuable, I say, as all this is, foreign languages, whether modern or ancient, are not to be preferred to an adequate study of our own much neglected English Tongue. Neglect is degrading English. The Englishman who can speak and write English really well is a *rara avis*, and is getting rarer. Yet even foreign tongues are learnt, largely or mainly, to help us learn our own. Similarly a boy who is in a "Cosmopolitan School" in England this year, France next, and Germany the year after—such a cosmopolitan youth will be "neither fish, flesh,

---

[1] "Ideals and Methods of a Normal Tertiary School" (George Allen, Ruskin House, Charing Cross Road, London. 1s. net).

fowl, nor good red herring"; he may learn the vices of all, he is unlikely to retain the virtues of any.

It will be seen, then, that we do not intend to admit foreign boys wholesale. But as they are knocking at our doors wholesale, it is difficult to resist filling with them our vacant Halls in the New Wing, and I therefore very earnestly beg all our good friends to lend us their help at this conjuncture. A few Outlanders we will gladly have, especially Teutons and Americans, our own blood, and, as heretofore, they may rely on being treated absolutely as we treat our own English youth; but the vast majority of the school must be English boys, or else there would be, indeed, no point in foreigners coming here; for they would learn nothing of English Life, nor of English Speech unless the school remained, as hitherto it has been and is, essentially English. Our *maximum* of foreigners so far has been four per cent., our *average* one-half per cent.

Another, and much more valuable, use that we can make of the aforesaid foreign Abbotsholmes, is to exchange masters with them. This, again, we have actually done, beginning, as we always should, with experience before proceeding to theorise. One of my colleagues went as Assistant-master to Dr. Lietz in April, 1898, to help him start his school, and was afterwards succeeded there by one of our most brilliant old boys, Dr. Drugman, who had just taken his doctorate with honours at the University of Bonn. Through such exchange of our masters, then, particularly, and through such holiday visits of our boys, we can look for great help from these foreign Abbotsholmes, but not through any exchange of pupils during term: which would only upset the unity of their life, the unity of their curriculum, and destroy the harmony of their growth. I will not say that the exchange can in no case take place, but it should not take place unless it appears good to all concerned, not only the boy himself or his parents, but the school which he will temporarily leave and the school which he will temporarily join. Moreover, the success of the experiment, when made, will in most, if not all, cases be in direct proportion to its rarity. If several English boys are at the same school abroad, whatever happens they will learn not a word of the foreign tongue that they do not know already.

In my view, then, it is essential for the right organisation of a Tertiary School like Abbotsholme, that the boys remain there from eleven to eighteen, and that no exchange of boys with foreign Abbotsholmes occurs unless in a few very exceptional cases. I have insisted upon this point, because I see, in some quarters, a notion springing up that learning modern languages should be the chief aim of Modern Education. To learn merely French and German is vastly better than to learn merely Latin and Greek, especially if we mean to study the actual countries and living peoples, and not the printed language only; but *the main end of education must ever be to enable a man to think in his own tongue and live in the real present.*

As regards the question of Co-education I wish to say a word, as some people seem to suppose that we are about to introduce it here. Nothing can be more opposed to our plans or our convictions. I have long maintained that from seven up to eleven boys ought to be educated in a Fore-school with girls, in proper, that is about equal, proportion, and mainly under women teachers; and I am glad to be able to announce that my old colleagues—Mr. W. Clifford Pilsbury and Miss Baker—are about to organise a Fore-school on these lines.

After eleven, boys require to be under men, and, in my view, need a life and curriculum so different from that required by girls, that co-education would be simply a costly, unnecessary, and probably useless experiment. I have myself taught girls of ages running from eleven to eighteen. I have discussed the question of co-education with men and women, and with boys and girls. The conclusion I have reached is that the results anticipated from co-education will not be realised. On the contrary, the difficulties of school organisation will be multiplied, and the physiological troubles of youth will be accentuated. I believe that boys can be refined and girls made less fragile, in a very perfect manner without co-education at all. Those, too, that can teach boys cannot always teach girls, and *vice-versâ*. Two types are needed, or else a new type, able to teach both, will have to be discovered. It is surely hard enough already to find masters and mistresses who can teach and guide at all. Should we, unless obliged, increase our difficulties? Some years ago I believed that boys might be improved if between eleven and eighteen they were partly under women teachers. (I am quite sure that women, if they are really women, can always help men and boys by their power of sympathy with all that is inspiring and refined.) But after some years' experience with a mixed staff of men and women, I reached the conclusion that women are not in their right place as teachers in the class-room of a boys' school. They cannot be treated as men; yet they often vaguely expect to be treated at once as men and as women. They may become, moreover, a very disturbing influence in a school staff. Accordingly, women's influence should be introduced, not by substituting women for men as officers of a boys' school, but by providing opportunities for boys to meet women and girls frequently and easily at social functions of all kinds, mainly in the holidays, but also, as far as possible, during term. The School Festivals, which should be far more numerous and less formal than they have usually been in the past, provide such opportunities. Above all, the mothers and sisters of the boys should have opportunities of visiting the school and of seeing the boys without constraint to a larger extent than has hitherto been deemed possible. Finally, the ladies attached to the school will exercise their refining influence precisely in proportion as they are not brought into competition with the masters.

This co-education notion is entirely of feminine origin and comes from the United States, where various well-known causes have brought the education of all classes into female hands. In a few years, at this rate, America will not possess a single male teacher. To women in Europe this promises a brilliant future for their sex. England alone has an overplus of a million women, hunting for a living. Dominating boys at school is a consoling substitute for ruling husbands at home, a pleasure economic forces are, alas, making daily more impossible. Finding the occupation suits themselves, women have rather rashly concluded it necessarily suits the boy. The practice appears, however, less monstrous if the boys are mixed with girls. Besides, the company of boys will—it is argued—be good also for the girls as well as for the mistresses. The question, however, arises, Is all this equally beneficial to the boy? American example seems to show that a Mixed Staff of men and women is difficult to maintain, and that sooner or later the men retire in favour of the women. Perhaps this excessive female influence accounts for certain peculiarities in American men reminding one of France. Anyhow, it is difficult to grant that if exclusive male influence is bad, excessive female influence will be better.

Suppose we reverse the situation (for what is sauce for the gander may be sauce for the goose). Will women allow girls to be trained mainly, or entirely, by men? The question needs no answer. It is clear that both male and female influence have their right place, but for boys the chief influence should be masculine, as for girls it should be feminine, if at least we want the best results. I do not think English fathers will abdicate their right to help form the character of their boys : I do not believe English Boys will prefer, in the schoolroom or cricket field, female persuasion to virile command. Bismarck dated his life as a boy from the day he left petticoat government for the rule of men. It becomes, then, purely a question how feminine influence can be best introduced. This I have endeavoured to answer above.

As regards the supposed influence of girls on the morals of boys, I am absolutely sure that no need exists for such heroic salvation, if boys of normal nature are allowed to live a sane and rational life such as they live here. I doubt if any school in existence excels Abbotsholme in this respect. Vice is, indeed, manufactured by ridiculous modern civilisation, and not least by the absurd nineteenth-century school system, which never teaches a boy anything about his bodily nature save through mysterious, vague hints in sermons, hints which are nearly absolutely thrown away ; a system which gives him no adequate ethical and æsthetic instruction, but which forces his brain during the crisis of puberty to exert itself unnaturally in cramming for competitive examinations and scholarships. The vice is thus mainly manufactured by the system. Change the system and the vice will mainly vanish with it. Give a boy a life worth living and he will not waste his life. Give him a life void of all affection, a weary round of competitive rivalry from morning to night, and Nature will avenge the outrage of her Laws. Co-education, therefore, in my view, is no cure for what is caused by wrong feeding, by over-stimulation of the nervous system through alternately games and cram, by general ignorance of hygiene, and by lack of refinement and of outlets for affection. If, however, the influence of women is, as I believe, essential in the life of man and boy (though better kept outside workshop, office, and classroom), surely we should export some of our over-population of women to our brothers and sons in the colonies, where the English are brutalised by the absence of all refining influences. While boys and men there are becoming animals for want of sisters, mothers, and wives, boys at home are being made into toys and invalids amid an admiring circle of female relatives, with no other outlet for their natures. At a lecture, a year or two ago, I made this obvious and rational proposal to export some of our girls, but the suggestion was greeted with shrieks of horror by the audience, which of course was, as usual, almost entirely made up of women—trying to kill time.

It might be expected that before concluding I should say something about our New Buildings. It has been our practice, however, hitherto to say as little as possible about plans not yet carried out. A better opportunity will occur when the buildings are quite finished and we assemble next summer for the formal Inauguration. I will only, therefore, say here that we have aimed at simple beauty and solid strength, at light, warmth, air, and space, at securing indestructible materials and noble proportions, believing that one of the greatest influences in education is furnished by the house we live in. We trust that all Abbotsholmians will feel, that now they have not only a School-State to be proud of, but have a School-House not unworthy of our little kingdom and its short, but eventful history. To them we look to shed lustre upon their School by showing to what Deeds it has inspired them.

C. R.

"Empire Day," *June* 24, 1899.

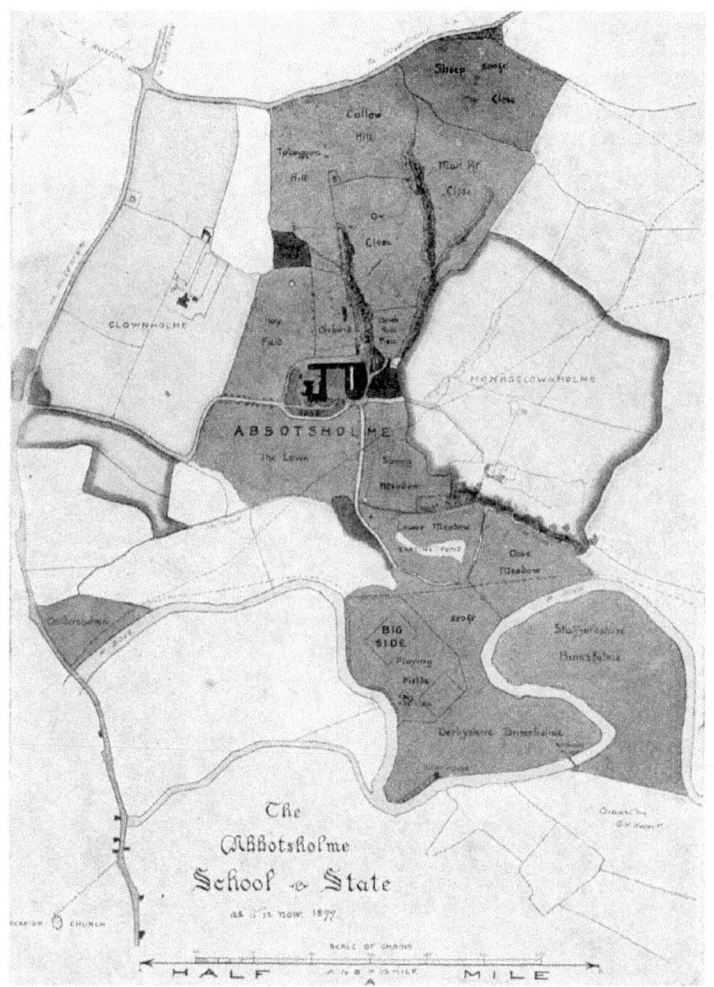

29. THE ABBOTSHOLME SCHOOL-e-STATE, IN 1899.

Copyright.

APPENDICES.

APPENDIX A.

LETTER OF APPLICATION TO THE GOVERNORS OF THE CHARITIES OF ST. DUNSTAN'S-IN-THE-EAST, FOR THE HEADMASTERSHIP OF ST. DUNSTAN'S COLLEGE, FROM CECIL REDDIE.

GENTLEMEN,

I beg respectfully to present myself as an applicant for the Headmastership of St. Dunstan's College, and to submit the following statement of my qualifications for the appointment.

I was born in October, 1858, at Fulham. On the death of my father, the late James Reddie, of the Admiralty and Victoria Institute, I obtained a Foundation Scholarship at Fettes College, Edinburgh, where I remained six years. At the end of this time, in 1878, I obtained an Exhibition at the University of Edinburgh, where I commenced the study of Medicine.

After having studied Anatomy under Professor Sir William Turner, Botany under the late Professor Dickson, and Zoology under the late Professor Sir Wyville Thompson, I decided to pursue a more distinctly scientific career, and entered the Chemical Laboratory of the University under Professor Crum Brown, F.R.S.

I studied Chemistry there three years, and at the same time went through a course of Physics and Practical Physics under Professor Tait, and of Mathematics under Professor Crystal.

After having obtained the Hope Prize Scholarship, I graduated in 1882 Bachelor of Science.

The same spring I was, after competitive examination, elected by the Senatus Academicus Vans Dunlop Scholar in Chemistry and Chemical

Pharmacy, which required me to study Chemical Science for the three following years in some European University.

I decided on Göttingen, and entered the Laboratory of the late Professor Hübner, under whose immediate supervision I worked two years until his sudden death.

At the same time I studied Mineralogy and Crystallography under Professor Klein, Geology under Professor von Könen, the Chemistry of Sugar under Professor Tollens, and the General History of Philosophy under Professor Baumann.

Meanwhile I was in private pursuing diligently the study of the German language, and after two years presented a Thesis (a copy of which is enclosed), and was thereafter admitted to examination in Chemistry and Mineralogy.

After examination before the Philosophical Faculty I received the degree of Master of Arts and Doctor of Philosophy *magno cum laude*, which is the highest degree but one given by the German Universities, and the highest usually conferred on a foreigner.

I enclose a copy of my Doctor's diploma.

I had while in Germany decided on embracing the scholastic rather than the academical career, and with this object was studying the educational methods pursued in the German Gymnasien (Public Schools), one of which had just been rebuilt on a magnificent scale in Göttingen. I also made the acquaintance of a large number of the masters and boys of this Institution, and by this means got considerable insight into the working and the effects of the German system.

On my return to Edinburgh I organised a small Laboratory and delivered courses of lectures on Chemistry, suited to students preparing for the medical degree at the University, and was engaged for one session in giving demonstrations in Biological Chemistry in the Botanical Laboratory of the University, at the request of Mr. Geddes, the Senior Demonstrator.

I was then appointed Lecturer on Chemistry at Fettes College.

In the summer of 1886 I made a tour in Germany and Switzerland, during which I accepted the invitation of Subrektor Raydt of Ratzeburg to visit him at the Gymnasium of that town.

In the previous year Herr Raydt had, on a mission from Prince Bismarck, visited the principal Public Schools of England, with the object of reporting to the German Government upon our athletic exercises and school system, which that Government wish to imitate in some particulars. From him I was able to collect much valuable information about the conduct of German Schools, especially as to the teaching of Science. I also became further acquainted with the books used in their professional and commercial education.

On my return to Edinburgh I was selected by the Committee on University Extension to deliver a course of lectures on Chemistry.

In the following February came the appointment to a Science Mastership in Clifton College, and I commenced my duties here in April.

I have, during this last year, been occupied in teaching Mathematics, Physics, and Chemistry, to boys taken from both the upper and lower forms, and from both the classical and modern sides of the School. This has given me considerable experience in teaching boys of different calibre.

I have further taken my share, twice a term, in the ordinary examination work of this School, and have got some acquaintance with the methods used to test boys of different age and different faculty.

I have further gained some experience of the powers of younger boys, having examined each term the boys of the Junior School department of Clifton College in their Science work—Geology and Physiology.

I have also had private pupils in German, advanced Chemistry, and Dynamics.

My ordinary work being in three of the departments of the School, I have obtained considerable insight into the way in which the general work is arranged and carried out.

Although my work has in recent years been largely confined to Science, I am yet from my German studies and from my early classical education neither wholly ignorant of linguistic studies nor blind to their importance both as a humanising influence and as giving a mastery over speech, which, although the main instrument of thought, is too often neglected by scientists.

I think that from the range of the subjects I have studied, and from my experience in various departments of scholastic work, as well as the thoroughness with which I have pursued one subject—Chemistry, that I may claim to consider myself in some measure fit to direct the work of a large School, as well as to teach certain subjects personally. The Headmaster of such a school as St. Dunstan's ought to be, it seems to me, in a position to examine into the work of every department. Without pretending to be an expert in every one, I think my classical studies at School and my scientific and German studies later would enable me to undertake adequately this general direction of the intellectual work of the School.

As regards the physical, social, and moral activities of School-life I should wish to say a few words.

It would be my object, should I receive this appointment, to keep in touch with the progress of educational methods of all kinds, whether in America, Europe, or at home.

My observations of German boys, who are, intellectually, probably the best drilled in the world, but who have no physical training at School except a little gymnastics (and who have often in conversation deplored this want), as well as the remarks let fall from their Masters, have intensified my original opinion of the value of sports not only as a physical and even intellectual, but also as a moral factor in education.

It would therefore be my object to organise very completely the physical exercises of the School.

I should endeavour, further, to develop the social life of the School in such a way that the day-boys might very really share in and get the benefit of this corporate life, without in any degree losing the advantages of parental supervision.

I may add that, although a member of the Church of England, I have from long residence in Scotland become accustomed to work with people of other creeds, and it certainly is my desire to refuse coöperation with no one on account of any religious views whatsoever.

In conclusion I have to lay before you testimonials from some who have had experience of my work.

Owing to the sudden death, during my work in Göttingen, of my Master, Professor Hübner, with whom I worked more intimately than with any other of my teachers, I was unable to get from him any testimonial; I forward, however, one given me in 1884 by Professor Klein, under whom I was studying Mineralogy, and who, as one of the board which examined me for the Degree of Doctor, is well qualified to certify my scientific attainments, and one from Professor Crum Brown, under whom I studied in Edinburgh.

I had intended to forward you a testimonial which I have received from some old pupils of mine, now at various Universities, who have stated their opinion of my qualities as a master, from the point of view of the taught. But as you limit the number of testimonials I have considered it best to send, together with a letter from the Headmaster of Clifton College, who suggested this application to me, a testimonial from the Headmaster of Fettes College, Edinburgh, under whom I worked as a boy and afterwards as a master, and who has known me many years.

Appendices

I have further obtained permission to mention to you several persons who have known me long and from whom you can obtain any further particulars. Lord Inglis, in particular, as Head of the University of Edinburgh, can speak of my career there.

I have the honour to be,
GENTLEMEN,
Your obedient servant,
CECIL REDDIE.

Clifton College, Bristol,
10th *March*, 1888.

TESTIMONIALS.

1. From ALEX. W. POTTS, M.A., LL.D., late Fellow of St. John's College, Cambridge, Head Master of Fettes College, Edinburgh.
2. From the REV. JAMES M. WILSON, M.A., late Fellow of St. John's College, Cambridge, Head Master of Clifton College, Bristol.
3. From CARL KLEIN, Ph.D., Professor of Mineralogy and Petrography, and Director of the Mineralogical Institute in the University of Göttingen.
4. From ALEX. CRUM BROWN, D.Sc. Lond., M.D., F.R.S., Professor of Chemistry in the University of Edinburgh.

REFERENCES.

1. The RIGHT HON. JOHN INGLIS, D.C.L., LLD., Lord Justice General of Scotland, and President of the Court of Session. Chancellor of the University of Edinburgh.
2. HIS HONOUR J. W. DE LONGUEVILLE GIFFARD, M.A., Her Majesty's Judge of the County Court, Exeter.

TESTIMONIALS.

I.

From ALEX. W. POTTS, M.A., LL.D.
Late Fellow of St. John's College, Cambridge.
Headmaster of Fettes College, Edinburgh.

THE LODGE, FETTES COLLEGE,
March 7, 1888.

Dr. CECIL REDDIE was at Fettes College for about six years, leaving in 1878. He distinguished himself in the classical and mathematical studies of the School, and left high in the Sixth Form.

He bore an admirable character in all respects, and, though entering fully into the life of the School, was marked by a greater thoughtfulness and spirit of enquiry than is usual with boys at School.

On his return from Germany, where he obtained great distinction in Science, Dr. REDDIE assisted me for two years in the Science teaching here, did good work in the Laboratory, and left it in a much improved condition.

His studies and attainments would seem to fit him eminently for directing a Modern and Scientific School, to which, in addition to special qualifications, he would carry with him the wider culture and general discipline of a Public School.

A. W. POTTS, M.A., LL.D.

II.

From the REV. JAMES M. WILSON, M.A.
Late Fellow of St. John's College, Cambridge.
Headmaster of Clifton College.

CLIFTON COLLEGE, BRISTOL,
March 5, 1888.

GENTLEMEN,

Dr. REDDIE has been at Clifton College for one year. I selected him for the post which he now holds, as a teacher of Chemistry and Physics and Mathematics, out of a large number of able candidates, because I was so well satisfied as to his knowledge, and general ability, and above all of his high character and unflinching industry and conscientiousness in work. And I have not been disappointed in these respects.

He is moreover a most pleasant colleague, with strong social interests, and with a personality and character that impresses those who are brought in contact with him.

You would be perfectly certain, if you appoint him, that you would have to deal with an absolutely straightforward man, who would put the interests of the school first, and his own nowhere.

He has an unusual degree of originality in educational views, and has to some extent tested them here and elsewhere.

It is by my advice that he is seeking some post where he may have greater freedom for developing his methods than he can have here, where he is not senior in any department, and has to work on fixed lines.

You would have in him a man who would accept loyally the general aims and design laid down by yourselves, but who would require considerable freedom in the management of detail.

It should be added that he is a thoroughly good German scholar, and could take the highest work in this department.

Perhaps it may be thought that he has not had enough experience as a master; but a man of 28, with a good deal of experience already gained, makes much more out of a year of school work than a man of 23 or 24 fresh from the University. I do not think you would find him inexperienced.

He is very sympathetic and gentle with boys, personally interested in them, and attractive to them. I have no doubt that he would be both just and popular.

I very heartily commend him to the consideration of the Council.

Yours faithfully,
JAMES M. WILSON.

To the Governors of St. Dunstan's College.

III.

From Dr. CARL KLEIN.

GÖTTINGEN, 14th August, 1884.

Ich bescheinige hiermit, dass Herr Cecil Reddie waehrend seiner hiesigen Aufenthalts mit gutem Erfolge die Vorlesungen ueber Mineralogie und Krystallographie gehoert und sich auch an den mineralogisch-crystallographischen Uebungen mit Eifer betheiligt hat.

Die demgemaess erborbenen mineralogischen Kentnisse befähigen

Herrn Reddie in die Reihe der Forcher auf jenen gebieten einzutreten und setzen ihn in die Lage gleichfalls als Lehrer thätig zu sein.

Er ist zu hoffen, dass ihm bei seinen Anlagen und seinem ernsten wissenschaftlichen Streben auch in genannter Hinsicht der Erfolg spaeter nicht fehlen werde.

Dr. C. KLEIN,
Ord. Prof. der Mineralogie
und Petrographie an der
Universitaet Goettingen,
Direktor des Mineral.-petrogr. Instituts dortselbst.

[Translation.]

Göttingen, 14th *August*, 1884.

I hereby attest that Mr. Cecil Reddie during his residence here has attended the lectures on Mineralogy and Crystallography with good results, and that he has taken part in the practical mineralogical and crystallographic exercises with ardour.

The knowledge thus obtained fits Mr. Reddie to enter the ranks of original investigators in these departments, and places him at the same time in the position to be a teacher of the subject.

It is to be hoped that, in consideration of his talents and his earnest scientific aspirations, he will not fail to obtain recognition and reward later on.

Dr. C. KLEIN,
Prof. of Mineralogy and Petrography
at the University of Göttingen,
and Director of the
Mineralogical Petrographical Institute.

IV.

From ALEX. CRUM BROWN, D.Sc. Lond., M.D., F.R.S.
Professor of Chemistry in the University of Edinburgh.

I have much pleasure in stating that I have known Dr. Cecil Reddie since he began his studies in this University.

He went through a very complete course of Science, including Mathematics, Physics, Chemistry, Botany, and Zoology. He graduated as

Bachelor of Science in the Department of the Physical Experimental Sciences, and he obtained, after a rigorous examination, conducted by written papers and also practically in the Laboratory, the Vans Dunlop Scholarship in Chemistry.

He then went to Göttingen, where he studied under the late Professor Hübner, and graduated as Doctor of Philosophy, presenting as his Thesis the record of an interesting research carried out by him under Professor Hübner's oversight.

Dr. REDDIE has had the means of acquiring a sound scientific education, and, in my opinion, he has profited by these means. He has a sound knowledge of General Physics, and a really good and extensive as well as sound practical knowledge of Chemistry.

I believe that he is able to teach well and effectively all the scientific subjects which belong to a school curriculum.

ALEX. CRUM BROWN.

University of Edinburgh,
March 14, 1888.

APPENDIX B.

"An Educational Atlas," London : G. Allen, 1900, 5s.

The Atlas is intended as a companion book to *Educational Ideals and Methods* (Allen, 1898, 1s.), and *Abbotsholme* (Allen, 1900, 10s. 6d.).

It aims at presenting to the eye, upon successive single sheets, so as to be seen at a glance, some of the possible ways of organising portions of school work.

To make the matter real and concrete, actual experiments are here tabulated, which have been found not altogether lacking in value, although not regarded as in any sense final.

In particular *A Classification of Schools* (page 1) will be found important as illustrating Chapter VIII. in *Abbotsholme*.

Some other plates of interest may be named :—

An Examination Report.
A General Work-Plan for a Tertiary School.
Time Tables for Spring, Summer, and Winter Terms.
Examination Time Tables.
A School Order as it should be, &c.

APPENDIX C.

ENGLISH EDUCATION EXHIBITION,
IMPERIAL INSTITUTE, *January* 5 *to* 27, 1900.

BRIEF CATALOGUE
OF THE ABBOTSHOLME EXHIBIT.

[Reprinted from pages 61, 62, 63, and 64, of the OFFICIAL CATALOGUE.]

N.B.—This Exhibition was planned in June, 1898; but we heard nothing of it till November 2, 1899, when we were asked if we cared to exhibit. We had therefore only from November 2nd till December 25th to get our exhibit ready.

The New School Abbotsholme, Derbyshire.

(A Tertiary (Higher Secondary) School for Boys between 11 and 18.)

On the Wall.

A SHORT SKETCH OF THE EDUCATIONAL IDEALS AND METHODS OF THE SCHOOL. Published by Mr. George Allen, Ruskin House, 156, Charing Cross Road, London, W.C.

[This is printed on the back of the Term Report Form (No. 2) hanging below.]

Its purpose is to secure coöperation between Home and School.

THE WORK-PLAN AND REPORT-FORM.
This serves the following purposes:—

(*a.*) It gives, at one glance, a synopsis of educational science, showing how the School environment and school-life mould the boy.

(*b.*) On the left is an analysis of the educational influences at work in the School. The whole School serves as our living working model; the estate, or school kingdom, our book of geography, nature knowledge, and mathematics; the school life the manual of history, art, and morals; the two together our text-book of religion.

(*c.*) The central portion indicates the manner in which the school life and surroundings are made the basis of instruction.

(*d.*) The work plan or curriculum is given in the central vertical column.

(*e.*) On the right comes an analysis of the results aimed at, namely, the production of an all-round harmoniously developed man.

This column, when filled in, serves as the boy's term-report.

A CLASSIFICATION OF SCHOOLS.

This is an attempt to show how a Tertiary (higher secondary) School like Abbotsholme may be expected to fit some day into a reorganised English educational system.

This classification is based on the following thoughts :—

(*a.*) Society should be hierarchic (not aristocratic, nor plutocratic, nor democratic), and should be governed by the capable.

(*b*). An educational system should express the organisation of human society in the simplest possible form, so as to be readily understood by the young and ignorant.

(*c.*) While the Schools express the necessary separation into classes, the University should express the unity which underlies the universe, and the communion reached by the proper coöperation and interdependence of all classes.

(*d.*) An educational system should recognise that the physiological and psychological forces operating in different classes are not identical at the same age. Each type requires its special chart of development, its attainable ideal, and its proper field of work.

(*e.*) Briefly, to sum up, an educational system should be a working model of the nation it is intended to create.

MAP OF THE SCHOOL ESTATE OR KINGDOM.

The School Estate is at once a laboratory, lecture hall, workshop, museum, and art studio, containing all the chief geographical types ; it is a class-room of geography, and furnishes the starting point in the study of naturalistics.

(The three photographs show the outlook north and east and south from the highest pinnacle of the new wing.)

THE PLAN OF THE SCHOOL BUILDINGS (now being erected, or to be erected shortly).

Ultimately these will be very extensive and complete, though intended only for a strictly limited number of boys, it being impossible to get satisfactory results otherwise.

On the west of the Botanic Garden come the earth cabinets, which serve as an object lesson both in hygiene and biology, being constructed after an original design which has been employed at Abbotsholme

Appendices 637

during the last ten years with excellent results, and which has been imitated in Germany and elsewhere.

THE SCHOOL ORDER.

This shows how the boys are divided into sets. The basis of the classification is, as far as possible, age ; the object being to keep every one in his natural position, and to maintain and not destroy harmonious growth by preventing and not encouraging premature specialisation.

(N.B.—The photograph in the corner shows the School Group of Summer, 1899.)

THE TIME TABLE (Summer).

Briefly the day is divided, in the main, thus :—
In the morning : book or indoor work, $4\frac{1}{2}$ hours.
In the afternoon : hand or outdoor work, 4 hours.
In the evening : social recreation, 2 hours.

THE EXAMINATION REPORT FOR SUMMER 1893.

This shows how we mark and combine the marks given for all subjects a boy learns, or all things he can do.

PHOTOGRAPHS. FIVE VIEWS OF THE SCHOOL BUILDINGS.

On the Table.

The things placed on the table are intended to exhibit in some detail how the work of the School is carried out.

THE MASTERS' RED BOOKS, IN WHICH THEY RECORD EACH DAY THE WEATHER, THEIR DAILY WORK, THEIR OWN MOOD, AND THE MOOD OF THE BOYS :—

Hour.	Set.	Subject.	Short Summary of Work done.	How Set as a whole coöperated.
10·0	The 16's.	Geography.		

Criticisms on individual boys, which, having no value after the year is over, may then be destroyed, are written in pencil on the blotting paper. This can be torn out, leaving behind the more permanent records of the standard of work reached, the object in view being to ascertain what under definite conditions boys can produce.

THE MASTERS' PINK BOOKS.

One of these is devoted to each subject each Master teaches, and in it he writes a detailed analysis of each lesson given.

PILE OF BOYS' GREY NOTE BOOKS.

Each boy notes down towards the close of each period a brief summary of the lesson as developed on the blackboard (or otherwise) by the Teacher.

BOX CONTAINING THE PHOTOGRAPHIC CATALOGUE OF THE PICTURES AND DIAGRAMS USED IN THE CLASS INSTRUCTION. (ALL PHOTOGRAPHS ARE BY THE BOYS.)

FOUR PACKETS OF EXAMINATION PAPERS OF 1893.

These papers show exactly how the examinations were conducted.

THE CHART OF WEIGHTS (1890–1894).

This shows how we record the physical growth of the boys, and so contrast :

(*a*.) The boy's growth at School and at home.
(*b*.) His growth in the different seasons of the year.
(*c*.) His growth at various ages.
(*d*.) The effect of country life after town life.
(*e*.) The effect of systematic School occupation after unsystematic occupation at home.

THE HEALTH BOOK AND HEALTH REPORT.

Records exactly every occasion on which a boy receives medical or surgical help, however slight. Whatever ailments occur are made, if possible, object lessons in hygiene. One boy is medical officer. He keeps the Health Book, and, under proper supervision, dispenses minor remedies.

MENU BOOK AND CLOTHES LIST.

For ten years a record has been kept of every meal given in the School.

FOLIO OF DRAWINGS.

This exhibits work done in the School, showing how important a part drawing plays in the curriculum, bringing together natural science, carpentry, surveying, decoration, &c., &c., &c.

THE PHOTOGRAPHIC HISTORY OF ABBOTSHOLME.

Every photograph has been produced in the School by Masters or Boys.

BOOKS, PAPERS, &c., ABOUT ABBOTSHOLME.

A Full Catalogue of this Exhibit and a List of Books, and other Publications about Abbotsholme, can be had of Mr. George Allen, London.

30. PLAN OF THE NEW BUILDINGS.

Copyright,

LESSON:

Taken from the Anthology used in Abbotsholme School Chapel.

Man is not changed by WhiteWashing or gilding his habitation; a people cannot be regenerated by teaching them the Worship of enjoyment; they cannot be taught a spirit of sacrifice by speaking to them of material rewards. It is the soul Which creates to itself a body; the idea Which makes for itself a habitation. The Utopist may see afar from the lofty hill the distant land Which Will give society a Virgin soil, and a purer air; his duty is to point it out With a gesture and a Word to his brothers; but he cannot take humanity in his arms, and carry it there With a single bound; even if this Were in his poWer, humanity Would not therefore have progressed.

Progress is the consciousness of progress. Man must attain it step by step, by the sWeat of his broW. The transformation of the medium in Which he lives only takes place in proportion as he merits it; and he can only merit it by struggle; by devoting himself and purifying himself by good Works and holy sorroW. He must not be taught to enjoy, but rather to suffer for others; to combat for the salvation of the World. It must not be said to him, "Enjoy; life is the right to happiness"; but rather, "Work; life is a duty, do good Without thinking of the consequences to yourself." He must not be taught, "To each according to his wants," or "To each according to his passions." But rather, "To each according to his love."

To invent formulae and organisations, and neglect the internal man, is to desire to substitute the frame for the picture.

Say to men: "Arise, come and enjoy; the banquet of life awaits you; overthrow those who would prevent you from entering"—and you will make egotists who would desert you at the first temptation.

But say to them: "Come, suffer; you will hunger and thirst; you will, perhaps, be deceived, be betrayed, be cursed; but you have a great duty to accomplish": they will be deaf, perhaps, for a long time, to the severe voice of virtue; but on the day that they do come to you, they will come as heroes, and will be invincible.

Mazzini's "Europe: its condition."
1852.

THE END.

[N.B.—A Sequel to "Abbotsholme" is in the Press, and will appear shortly, giving a criticism on the present educational outlook in relation to the Future of the Anglo-Keltic World Dominion.]

UNWIN BROTHERS, THE GRESHAM PRESS, WOKING AND LONDON.

For Product Safety Concerns and Information please contact our EU
representative GPSR@taylorandfrancis.com
Taylor & Francis Verlag GmbH, Kaufingerstraße 24, 80331 München, Germany